D1706320

Dictionary of Literary Biography

1 *The American Renaissance in New England,* edited by Joel Myerson (1978)

2 *American Novelists Since World War II,* edited by Jeffrey Helterman and Richard Layman (1978)

3 *Antebellum Writers in New York and the South,* edited by Joel Myerson (1979)

4 *American Writers in Paris, 1920-1939,* edited by Karen Lane Rood (1980)

5 *American Poets Since World War II,* 2 parts, edited by Donald J. Greiner (1980)

6 *American Novelists Since World War II, Second Series,* edited by James E. Kibler Jr. (1980)

7 *Twentieth-Century American Dramatists,* 2 parts, edited by John MacNicholas (1981)

8 *Twentieth-Century American Science-Fiction Writers,* 2 parts, edited by David Cowart and Thomas L. Wymer (1981)

9 *American Novelists, 1910-1945,* 3 parts, edited by James J. Martine (1981)

10 *Modern British Dramatists, 1900-1945,* 2 parts, edited by Stanley Weintraub (1982)

11 *American Humorists, 1800-1950,* 2 parts, edited by Stanley Trachtenberg (1982)

12 *American Realists and Naturalists,* edited by Donald Pizer and Earl N. Harbert (1982)

13 *British Dramatists Since World War II,* 2 parts, edited by Stanley Weintraub (1982)

14 *British Novelists Since 1960,* 2 parts, edited by Jay L. Halio (1983)

15 *British Novelists, 1930-1959,* 2 parts, edited by Bernard Oldsey (1983)

16 *The Beats: Literary Bohemians in Postwar America,* 2 parts, edited by Ann Charters (1983)

17 *Twentieth-Century American Historians,* edited by Clyde N. Wilson (1983)

18 *Victorian Novelists After 1885,* edited by Ira B. Nadel and William E. Fredeman (1983)

19 *British Poets, 1880-1914,* edited by Donald E. Stanford (1983)

20 *British Poets, 1914-1945,* edited by Donald E. Stanford (1983)

21 *Victorian Novelists Before 1885,* edited by Ira B. Nadel and William E. Fredeman (1983)

22 *American Writers for Children, 1900-1960,* edited by John Cech (1983)

23 *American Newspaper Journalists, 1873-1900,* edited by Perry J. Ashley (1983)

24 *American Colonial Writers, 1606-1734,* edited by Emory Elliott (1984)

25 *American Newspaper Journalists, 1901-1925,* edited by Perry J. Ashley (1984)

26 *American Screenwriters,* edited by Robert E. Morsberger, Stephen O. Lesser, and Randall Clark (1984)

27 *Poets of Great Britain and Ireland, 1945-1960,* edited by Vincent B. Sherry Jr. (1984)

28 *Twentieth-Century American-Jewish Fiction Writers,* edited by Daniel Walden (1984)

29 *American Newspaper Journalists, 1926-1950,* edited by Perry J. Ashley (1984)

30 *American Historians, 1607-1865,* edited by Clyde N. Wilson (1984)

31 *American Colonial Writers, 1735-1781,* edited by Emory Elliott (1984)

32 *Victorian Poets Before 1850,* edited by William E. Fredeman and Ira B. Nadel (1984)

33 *Afro-American Fiction Writers After 1955,* edited by Thadious M. Davis and Trudier Harris (1984)

34 *British Novelists, 1890-1929: Traditionalists,* edited by Thomas F. Staley (1985)

35 *Victorian Poets After 1850,* edited by William E. Fredeman and Ira B. Nadel (1985)

36 *British Novelists, 1890-1929: Modernists,* edited by Thomas F. Staley (1985)

37 *American Writers of the Early Republic,* edited by Emory Elliott (1985)

38 *Afro-American Writers After 1955: Dramatists and Prose Writers,* edited by Thadious M. Davis and Trudier Harris (1985)

39 *British Novelists, 1660-1800,* 2 parts, edited by Martin C. Battestin (1985)

40 *Poets of Great Britain and Ireland Since 1960,* 2 parts, edited by Vincent B. Sherry Jr. (1985)

41 *Afro-American Poets Since 1955,* edited by Trudier Harris and Thadious M. Davis (1985)

42 *American Writers for Children Before 1900,* edited by Glenn E. Estes (1985)

43 *American Newspaper Journalists, 1690-1872,* edited by Perry J. Ashley (1986)

44 *American Screenwriters, Second Series,* edited by Randall Clark, Robert E. Morsberger, and Stephen O. Lesser (1986)

45 *American Poets, 1880-1945, First Series,* edited by Peter Quartermain (1986)

46 *American Literary Publishing Houses, 1900-1980: Trade and Paperback,* edited by Peter Dzwonkoski (1986)

47 *American Historians, 1866-1912,* edited by Clyde N. Wilson (1986)

48 *American Poets, 1880-1945, Second Series,* edited by Peter Quartermain (1986)

49 *American Literary Publishing Houses, 1638-1899,* 2 parts, edited by Peter Dzwonkoski (1986)

50 *Afro-American Writers Before the Harlem Renaissance,* edited by Trudier Harris (1986)

51 *Afro-American Writers from the Harlem Renaissance to 1940,* edited by Trudier Harris (1987)

52 *American Writers for Children Since 1960: Fiction,* edited by Glenn E. Estes (1986)

53 *Canadian Writers Since 1960, First Series,* edited by W. H. New (1986)

54 *American Poets, 1880-1945, Third Series,* 2 parts, edited by Peter Quartermain (1987)

55 *Victorian Prose Writers Before 1867,* edited by William B. Thesing (1987)

56 *German Fiction Writers, 1914-1945,* edited by James Hardin (1987)

57 *Victorian Prose Writers After 1867,* edited by William B. Thesing (1987)

58 *Jacobean and Caroline Dramatists,* edited by Fredson Bowers (1987)

59 *American Literary Critics and Scholars, 1800-1850,* edited by John W. Rathbun and Monica M. Grecu (1987)

60 *Canadian Writers Since 1960, Second Series,* edited by W. H. New (1987)

61 *American Writers for Children Since 1960: Poets, Illustrators, and Nonfiction Authors,* edited by Glenn E. Estes (1987)

62 *Elizabethan Dramatists,* edited by Fredson Bowers (1987)

63 *Modern American Critics, 1920-1955,* edited by Gregory S. Jay (1988)

64 *American Literary Critics and Scholars, 1850-1880,* edited by John W. Rathbun and Monica M. Grecu (1988)

65 *French Novelists, 1900-1930,* edited by Catharine Savage Brosman (1988)

66 *German Fiction Writers, 1885-1913,* 2 parts, edited by James Hardin (1988)

67 *Modern American Critics Since 1955,* edited by Gregory S. Jay (1988)

68 *Canadian Writers, 1920-1959, First Series,* edited by W. H. New (1988)

69 *Contemporary German Fiction Writers, First Series,* edited by Wolfgang D. Elfe and James Hardin (1988)

70 *British Mystery Writers, 1860-1919,* edited by Bernard Benstock and Thomas F. Staley (1988)

71 *American Literary Critics and Scholars, 1880-1900,* edited by John W. Rathbun and Monica M. Grecu (1988)

72 *French Novelists, 1930-1960,* edited by Catharine Savage Brosman (1988)

73 *American Magazine Journalists, 1741-1850,* edited by Sam G. Riley (1988)

74 *American Short-Story Writers Before 1880,* edited by Bobby Ellen Kimbel, with the assistance of William E. Grant (1988)

75 *Contemporary German Fiction Writers, Second Series,* edited by Wolfgang D. Elfe and James Hardin (1988)

76 *Afro-American Writers, 1940-1955,* edited by Trudier Harris (1988)

77 *British Mystery Writers, 1920-1939,* edited by Bernard Benstock and Thomas F. Staley (1988)

78 *American Short-Story Writers, 1880-1910,* edited by Bobby Ellen Kimbel, with the assistance of William E. Grant (1988)

79 *American Magazine Journalists, 1850-1900,* edited by Sam G. Riley (1988)

80 *Restoration and Eighteenth-Century Dramatists, First Series,* edited by Paula R. Backscheider (1989)

81 *Austrian Fiction Writers, 1875-1913,* edited by James Hardin and Donald G. Daviau (1989)

82 *Chicano Writers, First Series,* edited by Francisco A. Lomelí and Carl R. Shirley (1989)

83 *French Novelists Since 1960,* edited by Catharine Savage Brosman (1989)

84 *Restoration and Eighteenth-Century Dramatists, Second Series,* edited by Paula R. Backscheider (1989)

85 *Austrian Fiction Writers After 1914,* edited by James Hardin and Donald G. Daviau (1989)

86 *American Short-Story Writers, 1910-1945, First Series,* edited by Bobby Ellen Kimbel (1989)

87 *British Mystery and Thriller Writers Since 1940, First Series,* edited by Bernard Benstock and Thomas F. Staley (1989)

88 *Canadian Writers, 1920-1959, Second Series,* edited by W. H. New (1989)

89 *Restoration and Eighteenth-Century Dramatists, Third Series,* edited by Paula R. Backscheider (1989)

90 *German Writers in the Age of Goethe, 1789-1832,* edited by James Hardin and Christoph E. Schweitzer (1989)

91 *American Magazine Journalists, 1900-1960, First Series,* edited by Sam G. Riley (1990)

92 *Canadian Writers, 1890-1920,* edited by W. H. New (1990)

93 *British Romantic Poets, 1789-1832, First Series,* edited by John R. Greenfield (1990)

94 *German Writers in the Age of Goethe: Sturm und Drang to Classicism,* edited by James Hardin and Christoph E. Schweitzer (1990)

95 *Eighteenth-Century British Poets, First Series,* edited by John Sitter (1990)

96 *British Romantic Poets, 1789-1832, Second Series,* edited by John R. Greenfield (1990)

97 *German Writers from the Enlightenment to Sturm und Drang, 1720-1764,* edited by James Hardin and Christoph E. Schweitzer (1990)

98 *Modern British Essayists, First Series,* edited by Robert Beum (1990)

99 *Canadian Writers Before 1890,* edited by W. H. New (1990)

100 *Modern British Essayists, Second Series,* edited by Robert Beum (1990)

101 *British Prose Writers, 1660-1800, First Series,* edited by Donald T. Siebert (1991)

102 *American Short-Story Writers, 1910-1945, Second Series,* edited by Bobby Ellen Kimbel (1991)

103 *American Literary Biographers, First Series,* edited by Steven Serafin (1991)

104 *British Prose Writers, 1660-1800, Second Series,* edited by Donald T. Siebert (1991)

105 *American Poets Since World War II, Second Series,* edited by R. S. Gwynn (1991)

106 *British Literary Publishing Houses, 1820-1880,* edited by Patricia J. Anderson and Jonathan Rose (1991)

107 *British Romantic Prose Writers, 1789-1832, First Series,* edited by John R. Greenfield (1991)

108 *Twentieth-Century Spanish Poets, First Series,* edited by Michael L. Perna (1991)

109 *Eighteenth-Century British Poets, Second Series,* edited by John Sitter (1991)

110 *British Romantic Prose Writers, 1789-1832, Second Series,* edited by John R. Greenfield (1991)

111 *American Literary Biographers, Second Series,* edited by Steven Serafin (1991)

112 *British Literary Publishing Houses, 1881-1965,* edited by Jonathan Rose and Patricia J. Anderson (1991)

113 *Modern Latin-American Fiction Writers, First Series,* edited by William Luis (1992)

114 *Twentieth-Century Italian Poets, First Series,* edited by Giovanna Wedel De Stasio, Glauco Cambon, and Antonio Illiano (1992)

115 *Medieval Philosophers,* edited by Jeremiah Hackett (1992)

116 *British Romantic Novelists, 1789-1832,* edited by Bradford K. Mudge (1992)

117 *Twentieth-Century Caribbean and Black African Writers, First Series,* edited by Bernth Lindfors and Reinhard Sander (1992)

118 *Twentieth-Century German Dramatists, 1889-1918,* edited by Wolfgang D. Elfe and James Hardin (1992)

119 *Nineteenth-Century French Fiction Writers: Romanticism and Realism, 1800-1860,* edited by Catharine Savage Brosman (1992)

120 *American Poets Since World War II, Third Series,* edited by R. S. Gwynn (1992)

121 *Seventeenth-Century British Nondramatic Poets, First Series,* edited by M. Thomas Hester (1992)

122 *Chicano Writers, Second Series,* edited by Francisco A. Lomelí and Carl R. Shirley (1992)

123 *Nineteenth-Century French Fiction Writers: Naturalism and Beyond, 1860-1900,* edited by Catharine Savage Brosman (1992)

124 *Twentieth-Century German Dramatists, 1919-1992,* edited by Wolfgang D. Elfe and James Hardin (1992)

125 *Twentieth-Century Caribbean and Black African Writers, Second Series,* edited by Bernth Lindfors and Reinhard Sander (1993)

126 *Seventeenth-Century British Nondramatic Poets, Second Series,* edited by M. Thomas Hester (1993)

127 *American Newspaper Publishers, 1950-1990,* edited by Perry J. Ashley (1993)

128 *Twentieth-Century Italian Poets, Second Series,* edited by Giovanna Wedel De Stasio, Glauco Cambon, and Antonio Illiano (1993)

129 *Nineteenth-Century German Writers, 1841-1900,* edited by James Hardin and Siegfried Mews (1993)

130 *American Short-Story Writers Since World War II,* edited by Patrick Meanor (1993)

131 *Seventeenth-Century British Nondramatic Poets, Third Series,* edited by M. Thomas Hester (1993)

132 *Sixteenth-Century British Nondramatic Writers, First Series,* edited by David A. Richardson (1993)

133 *Nineteenth-Century German Writers to 1840,* edited by James Hardin and Siegfried Mews (1993)

134 *Twentieth-Century Spanish Poets, Second Series,* edited by Jerry Phillips Winfield (1994)

135 *British Short-Fiction Writers, 1880-1914: The Realist Tradition,* edited by William B. Thesing (1994)

136 *Sixteenth-Century British Nondramatic Writers, Second Series,* edited by David A. Richardson (1994)

137 *American Magazine Journalists, 1900-1960, Second Series,* edited by Sam G. Riley (1994)

138 *German Writers and Works of the High Middle Ages: 1170-1280,* edited by James Hardin and Will Hasty (1994)

139 *British Short-Fiction Writers, 1945-1980,* edited by Dean Baldwin (1994)

140 *American Book-Collectors and Bibliographers, First Series,* edited by Joseph Rosenblum (1994)

141 *British Children's Writers, 1880-1914,* edited by Laura M. Zaidman (1994)

142 *Eighteenth-Century British Literary Biographers,* edited by Steven Serafin (1994)

143 *American Novelists Since World War II, Third Series,* edited by James R. Giles and Wanda H. Giles (1994)

144 *Nineteenth-Century British Literary Biographers,* edited by Steven Serafin (1994)

145 *Modern Latin-American Fiction Writers, Second Series,* edited by William Luis and Ann González (1994)

146 *Old and Middle English Literature,* edited by Jeffrey Helterman and Jerome Mitchell (1994)

147 *South Slavic Writers Before World War II,* edited by Vasa D. Mihailovich (1994)

148 *German Writers and Works of the Early Middle Ages: 800-1170,* edited by Will Hasty and James Hardin (1994)

149 *Late Nineteenth- and Early Twentieth-Century British Literary Biographers,* edited by Steven Serafin (1995)

150 *Early Modern Russian Writers, Late Seventeenth and Eighteenth Centuries,* edited by Marcus C. Levitt (1995)

151 *British Prose Writers of the Early Seventeenth Century,* edited by Clayton D. Lein (1995)

152 *American Novelists Since World War II, Fourth Series,* edited by James R. Giles and Wanda H. Giles (1995)

153 *Late-Victorian and Edwardian British Novelists, First Series,* edited by George M. Johnson (1995)

154 *The British Literary Book Trade, 1700-1820,* edited by James K. Bracken and Joel Silver (1995)

155 *Twentieth-Century British Literary Biographers,* edited by Steven Serafin (1995)

156 *British Short-Fiction Writers, 1880-1914: The Romantic Tradition,* edited by William F. Naufftus (1995)

157 *Twentieth-Century Caribbean and Black African Writers, Third Series,* edited by Bernth Lindfors and Reinhard Sander (1995)

158 *British Reform Writers, 1789-1832,* edited by Gary Kelly and Edd Applegate (1995)

159 *British Short-Fiction Writers, 1800-1880,* edited by John R. Greenfield (1996)

160 *British Children's Writers, 1914-1960,* edited by Donald R. Hettinga and Gary D. Schmidt (1996)

161 *British Children's Writers Since 1960, First Series,* edited by Caroline Hunt (1996)

162 *British Short-Fiction Writers, 1915-1945,* edited by John H. Rogers (1996)

163 *British Children's Writers, 1800-1880,* edited by Meena Khorana (1996)

164 *German Baroque Writers, 1580-1660,* edited by James Hardin (1996)

165 *American Poets Since World War II, Fourth Series,* edited by Joseph Conte (1996)

166 *British Travel Writers, 1837-1875,* edited by Barbara Brothers and Julia Gergits (1996)

167 *Sixteenth-Century British Nondramatic Writers, Third Series,* edited by David A. Richardson (1996)

168 *German Baroque Writers, 1661-1730,* edited by James Hardin (1996)

169 *American Poets Since World War II, Fifth Series,* edited by Joseph Conte (1996)

170 *The British Literary Book Trade, 1475-1700,* edited by James K. Bracken and Joel Silver (1996)

171 *Twentieth-Century American Sportswriters,* edited by Richard Orodenker (1996)

172 *Sixteenth-Century British Nondramatic Writers, Fourth Series,* edited by David A. Richardson (1996)

173 *American Novelists Since World War II, Fifth Series,* edited by James R. Giles and Wanda H. Giles (1996)

174 *British Travel Writers, 1876-1909,* edited by Barbara Brothers and Julia Gergits (1997)

175 *Native American Writers of the United States,* edited by Kenneth M. Roemer (1997)

176 *Ancient Greek Authors,* edited by Ward W. Briggs (1997)

177 *Italian Novelists Since World War II, 1945-1965,* edited by Augustus Pallotta (1997)

178 *British Fantasy and Science-Fiction Writers Before World War I,* edited by Darren Harris-Fain (1997)

179 *German Writers of the Renaissance and Reformation, 1280-1580,* edited by James Hardin and Max Reinhart (1997)

180 *Japanese Fiction Writers, 1868-1945,* edited by Van C. Gessel (1997)

181 *South Slavic Writers Since World War II,* edited by Vasa D. Mihailovich (1997)

182 *Japanese Fiction Writers Since World War II,* edited by Van C. Gessel (1997)

183 *American Travel Writers, 1776-1864,* edited by James J. Schramer and Donald Ross (1997)

184 *Nineteenth-Century British Book-Collectors and Bibliographers,* edited by William Baker and Kenneth Womack (1997)

185 *American Literary Journalists, 1945-1995, First Series,* edited by Arthur J. Kaul (1998)

186 *Nineteenth-Century American Western Writers,* edited by Robert L. Gale (1998)

187 *American Book Collectors and Bibliographers, Second Series,* edited by Joseph Rosenblum (1998)

188 *American Book and Magazine Illustrators to 1920,* edited by Steven E. Smith, Catherine A. Hastedt, and Donald H. Dyal (1998)

189 *American Travel Writers, 1850-1915,* edited by Donald Ross and James J. Schramer (1998)

190 *British Reform Writers, 1832-1914,* edited by Gary Kelly and Edd Applegate (1998)

191 *British Novelists Between the Wars,* edited by George M. Johnson (1998)

192 *French Dramatists, 1789-1914,* edited by Barbara T. Cooper (1998)

193 *American Poets Since World War II, Sixth Series,* edited by Joseph Conte (1998)

194 *British Novelists Since 1960, Second Series,* edited by Merritt Moseley (1998)

195 *British Travel Writers, 1910-1939,* edited by Barbara Brothers and Julia Gergits (1998)

196 *Italian Novelists Since World War II, 1965-1995,* edited by Augustus Pallotta (1999)

197 *Late-Victorian and Edwardian British Novelists, Second Series,* edited by George M. Johnson (1999)

198 *Russian Literature in the Age of Pushkin and Gogol: Prose,* edited by Christine A. Rydel (1999)

199 *Victorian Women Poets,* edited by William B. Thesing (1999)

200 *American Women Prose Writers to 1820,* edited by Carla J. Mulford, with Angela Vietto and Amy E. Winans (1999)

201 *Twentieth-Century British Book Collectors and Bibliographers,* edited by William Baker and Kenneth Womack (1999)

202 *Nineteenth-Century American Fiction Writers,* edited by Kent P. Ljungquist (1999)

203 *Medieval Japanese Writers,* edited by Steven D. Carter (1999)

204 *British Travel Writers, 1940-1997,* edited by Barbara Brothers and Julia M. Gergits (1999)

205 *Russian Literature in the Age of Pushkin and Gogol: Poetry and Drama,* edited by Christine A. Rydel (1999)

206 *Twentieth-Century American Western Writers, First Series,* edited by Richard H. Cracroft (1999)

207 *British Novelists Since 1960, Third Series,* edited by Merritt Moseley (1999)

208 *Literature of the French and Occitan Middle Ages: Eleventh to Fifteenth Centuries,* edited by Deborah Sinnreich-Levi and Ian S. Laurie (1999)

209 *Chicano Writers, Third Series,* edited by Francisco A. Lomelí and Carl R. Shirley (1999)

210 *Ernest Hemingway: A Documentary Volume,* edited by Robert W. Trogdon (1999)

211 *Ancient Roman Writers,* edited by Ward W. Briggs (1999)

212 *Twentieth-Century American Western Writers, Second Series,* edited by Richard H. Cracroft (1999)

213 *Pre-Nineteenth-Century British Book Collectors and Bibliographers,* edited by William Baker and Kenneth Womack (1999)

214 *Twentieth-Century Danish Writers,* edited by Marianne Stecher-Hansen (1999)

215 *Twentieth-Century Eastern European Writers, First Series,* edited by Steven Serafin (1999)

216 *British Poets of the Great War: Brooke, Rosenberg, Thomas. A Documentary Volume,* edited by Patrick Quinn (2000)

217 *Nineteenth-Century French Poets,* edited by Robert Beum (2000)

218 *American Short-Story Writers Since World War II, Second Series,* edited by Patrick Meanor and Gwen Crane (2000)

219 *F. Scott Fitzgerald's* The Great Gatsby: *A Documentary Volume,* edited by Matthew J. Bruccoli (2000)

220 *Twentieth-Century Eastern European Writers, Second Series,* edited by Steven Serafin (2000)

221 *American Women Prose Writers, 1870-1920,* edited by Sharon M. Harris, with the assistance of Heidi L. M. Jacobs and Jennifer Putzi (2000)

222 *H. L. Mencken: A Documentary Volume,* edited by Richard J. Schrader (2000)

223 *The American Renaissance in New England, Second Series,* edited by Wesley T. Mott (2000)

224 *Walt Whitman: A Documentary Volume,* edited by Joel Myerson (2000)

225 *South African Writers,* edited by Paul A. Scanlon (2000)

226 *American Hard-Boiled Crime Writers,* edited by George Parker Anderson and Julie B. Anderson (2000)

227 *American Novelists Since World War II, Sixth Series,* edited by James R. Giles and Wanda H. Giles (2000)

228 *Twentieth-Century American Dramatists, Second Series,* edited by Christopher J. Wheatley (2000)

229 *Thomas Wolfe: A Documentary Volume,* edited by Ted Mitchell (2001)

Documentary Series

1 *Sherwood Anderson, Willa Cather, John Dos Passos, Theodore Dreiser, F. Scott Fitzgerald, Ernest Hemingway, Sinclair Lewis,* edited by Margaret A. Van Antwerp (1982)

2 *James Gould Cozzens, James T. Farrell, William Faulkner, John O'Hara, John Steinbeck, Thomas Wolfe, Richard Wright,* edited by Margaret A. Van Antwerp (1982)

3 *Saul Bellow, Jack Kerouac, Norman Mailer, Vladimir Nabokov, John Updike, Kurt Vonnegut,* edited by Mary Bruccoli (1983)

4 *Tennessee Williams,* edited by Margaret A. Van Antwerp and Sally Johns (1984)

5 *American Transcendentalists,* edited by Joel Myerson (1988)

6 *Hardboiled Mystery Writers: Raymond Chandler, Dashiell Hammett, Ross Macdonald,* edited by Matthew J. Bruccoli and Richard Layman (1989)

7 *Modern American Poets: James Dickey, Robert Frost, Marianne Moore,* edited by Karen L. Rood (1989)

8 *The Black Aesthetic Movement,* edited by Jeffrey Louis Decker (1991)

9 *American Writers of the Vietnam War: W. D. Ehrhart, Larry Heinemann, Tim O'Brien, Walter McDonald, John M. Del Vecchio,* edited by Ronald Baughman (1991)

10 *The Bloomsbury Group,* edited by Edward L. Bishop (1992)

11 *American Proletarian Culture: The Twenties and The Thirties,* edited by Jon Christian Suggs (1993)

12 *Southern Women Writers: Flannery O'Connor, Katherine Anne Porter, Eudora Welty,* edited by Mary Ann Wimsatt and Karen L. Rood (1994)

13 *The House of Scribner, 1846-1904,* edited by John Delaney (1996)

14 *Four Women Writers for Children, 1868-1918,* edited by Caroline C. Hunt (1996)

15 *American Expatriate Writers: Paris in the Twenties,* edited by Matthew J. Bruccoli and Robert W. Trogdon (1997)

16 *The House of Scribner, 1905-1930,* edited by John Delaney (1997)

17 *The House of Scribner, 1931-1984,* edited by John Delaney (1998)

18 *British Poets of The Great War: Sassoon, Graves, Owen,* edited by Patrick Quinn (1999)

19 *James Dickey,* edited by Judith S. Baughman (1999)

See also DLB 210, 216, 219, 222, 224, 229

Yearbooks

1980 edited by Karen L. Rood, Jean W. Ross, and Richard Ziegfeld (1981)

1981 edited by Karen L. Rood, Jean W. Ross, and Richard Ziegfeld (1982)

1982 edited by Richard Ziegfeld; associate editors: Jean W. Ross and Lynne C. Zeigler (1983)

1983 edited by Mary Bruccoli and Jean W. Ross; associate editor Richard Ziegfeld (1984)

1984 edited by Jean W. Ross (1985)

1985 edited by Jean W. Ross (1986)

1986 edited by J. M. Brook (1987)

1987 edited by J. M. Brook (1988)

1988 edited by J. M. Brook (1989)

1989 edited by J. M. Brook (1990)

1990 edited by James W. Hipp (1991)

1991 edited by James W. Hipp (1992)

1992 edited by James W. Hipp (1993)

1993 edited by James W. Hipp, contributing editor George Garrett (1994)

1994 edited by James W. Hipp, contributing editor George Garrett (1995)

1995 edited by James W. Hipp, contributing editor George Garrett (1996)

1996 edited by Samuel W. Bruce and L. Kay Webster, contributing editor George Garrett (1997)

1997 edited by Matthew J. Bruccoli and George Garrett, with the assistance of L. Kay Webster (1998)

1998 edited by Matthew J. Bruccoli, contributing editor George Garrett, with the assistance of D. W. Thomas (1999)

1999 edited by Matthew J. Bruccoli, contributing editor George Garrett, with the assistance of D. W. Thomas (2000)

Concise Series

Concise Dictionary of American Literary Biography, 7 volumes (1988-1999): *The New Consciousness, 1941-1968; Colonization to the American Renaissance, 1640-1865; Realism, Naturalism, and Local Color, 1865-1917; The Twenties, 1917-1929; The Age of Maturity, 1929-1941; Broadening Views, 1968-1988; Supplement: Modern Writers, 1900-1998.*

Concise Dictionary of British Literary Biography, 8 volumes (1991-1992): *Writers of the Middle Ages and Renaissance Before 1660; Writers of the Restoration and Eighteenth Century, 1660-1789; Writers of the Romantic Period, 1789-1832; Victorian Writers, 1832-1890; Late-Victorian and Edwardian Writers, 1890-1914; Modern Writers, 1914-1945; Writers After World War II, 1945-1960; Contemporary Writers, 1960 to Present.*

Concise Dictionary of World Literary Biography, 20 volumes projected (1999-): *Ancient Greek and Roman Writers; German Writers; African, Carribbean, and Latin-American Writers.*

Dictionary of Literary Biography® • Volume Two Hundred Twenty-Nine

Thomas Wolfe

A Documentary Volume

Dictionary of Literary Biography® • Volume Two Hundred Twenty-Nine

Thomas Wolfe
A Documentary Volume

Edited by
Ted Mitchell

A Bruccoli Clark Layman Book
The Gale Group
Detroit • San Francisco • London • Boston • Woodbridge, Conn.

Printed in the United States of America

The paper used in this publication meets the minimum requirements of American National Standard for Information Sciences–Permanence Paper for Printed Library Materials, ANSI Z39.48-1984.∞™

Library of Congress Cataloging-in-Publication Data

Thomas Wolfe: a documentary volume / edited by Ted Mitchell.
p. cm.–(Dictionary of literary biography: v. 229)
"A Bruccoli Clark Layman book."
Includes bibliographical references and index.
ISBN 0-7876-3138-8 (alk. paper)
1. Wolfe, Thomas, 1900–1938. 2. Wolfe, Thomas, 1900–1938–Criticism and interpretation–History.
3. Novelists, American–20th century–Biography. I. Mitchell, Ted. II. Series.

PS3545.0337 Z86276 2000
813'.52–dc21 00–042952
[B] CIP

10 9 8 7 6 5 4 3 2 1

In memory of Edna Adeline Mitchell, 1930–1998

Contents

Plan of the Series

. . . Almost the most prodigious asset of a country, and perhaps its most precious possession, is its native literary product–when that product is fine and noble and enduring.

Mark Twain*

The advisory board, the editors, and the publisher of the *Dictionary of Literary Biography* are joined in endorsing Mark Twain's declaration. The literature of a nation provides an inexhaustible resource of permanent worth. We intend to make literature and its creators better understood and more accessible to students and the reading public, while satisfying the standards of teachers and scholars.

To meet these requirements, *literary biography* has been construed in terms of the author's achievement. The most important thing about a writer is his writing. Accordingly, the entries in *DLB* are career biographies, tracing the development of the author's canon and the evolution of his reputation.

The purpose of *DLB* is not only to provide reliable information in a convenient format but also to place the figures in the larger perspective of literary history and to offer appraisals of their accomplishments by qualified scholars.

The publication plan for *DLB* resulted from two years of preparation. The project was proposed to Bruccoli Clark by Frederick G. Ruffner, president of the Gale Research Company, in November 1975. After specimen entries were prepared and typeset, an advisory board was formed to refine the entry format and develop the series rationale. In meetings held during 1976, the publisher, series editors, and advisory board approved the scheme for a comprehensive biographical dictionary of persons who contributed to North American literature. Editorial work on the first volume began in January 1977, and it was published in 1978. In order to make *DLB* more than a reference tool and to compile volumes that individually have claim to status as literary history, it was decided to organize volumes by topic, period, or genre. Each of these freestanding volumes provides a biographical-bibliographical guide and overview for a particular area of literature. We are convinced that this organization–as opposed to a single alphabet method–constitutes a valuable innovation in the presentation of reference material. The volume plan necessarily requires many decisions for the placement and treatment of authors who might properly be included in two or three volumes. In some instances a major figure will be included in separate volumes, but with different entries emphasizing the aspect of his career appropriate to each volume. Ernest Hemingway, for example, is represented in *American Writers in Paris, 1920–1939* by an entry focusing on his expatriate apprenticeship; he is also in *American Novelists, 1910–1945* with an entry surveying his entire career, as well as in *American Short-Story Writers, 1910–1945, Second Series* with an entry concentrating on his short stories. Each volume includes a cumulative index of the subject authors and articles. Comprehensive indexes to the entire series are planned.

Since 1981 the series has been further augmented by the *DLB Yearbooks,* which update published entries and add new entries to keep the *DLB* current with contemporary activity. There have also been *DLB Documentary Series* volumes which provide biographical and critical source materials for figures whose work is judged to have particular interest for students. One of these companion volumes is devoted entirely to Tennessee Williams.

We define literature as the *intellectual commerce of a nation:* not merely as belles lettres but as that ample and complex process by which ideas are generated, shaped, and transmitted. *DLB* entries are not limited to "creative writers" but extend to other figures who in their time and in their way influenced the mind of a people. Thus the series encompasses historians, journalists, publishers, book collectors, and screenwriters. By this means readers of *DLB* may be aided to perceive literature not as cult scripture in the keeping of intellectual high priests but firmly positioned at the center of a nation's life.

DLB includes the major writers appropriate to each volume and those standing in the ranks behind

**From an unpublished section of Mark Twain's autobiography, copyright by the Mark Twain Company*

them. Scholarly and critical counsel has been sought in deciding which minor figures to include and how full their entries should be. Wherever possible, useful references are made to figures who do not warrant separate entries.

Each *DLB* volume has an expert volume editor responsible for planning the volume, selecting the figures for inclusion, and assigning the entries. Volume editors are also responsible for preparing, where appropriate, appendices surveying the major periodicals and literary and intellectual movements for their volumes, as well as lists of further readings. Work on the series as a whole is coordinated at the Bruccoli Clark Layman editorial center in Columbia, South Carolina, where the editorial staff is responsible for accuracy and utility of the published volumes.

One feature that distinguishes *DLB* is the illustration policy–its concern with the iconography of literature. Just as an author is influenced by his surroundings, so is the reader's understanding of the author enhanced by a knowledge of his environment. Therefore *DLB* volumes include not only drawings, paintings, and photographs of authors, often depicting them at various stages in their careers, but also illustrations of their families and places where they lived. Title pages are regularly reproduced in facsimile along with dust jackets for modern authors. The dust jackets are a special feature of *DLB* because they often document better than anything else the way in which an author's work was perceived in its own time. Specimens of the writers' manuscripts and letters are included when feasible.

Samuel Johnson rightly decreed that "The chief glory of every people arises from its authors." The purpose of the *Dictionary of Literary Biography* is to compile literary history in the surest way available to us–by accurate and comprehensive treatment of the lives and work of those who contributed to it.

The *DLB* Advisory Board

Introduction

Thomas Wolfe, a true child of the twentieth century, was born in Asheville in the Blue Ridge Mountains of North Carolina on 3 October 1900, and died on 15 September 1938, eighteen days short of his thirty-eighth birthday. During his eighteen-year literary career, Wolfe published four books: two acclaimed novels, *Look Homeward, Angel* (1929) and *Of Time and the River* (1935); a collection of stories, *From Death to Morning* (1935); and a nonfiction work, *The Story of a Novel* (1936), in which he describes how he wrote his second novel. After Wolfe's death his editor at Harper and Brothers, Edward C. Aswell, working with an enormous manuscript Wolfe had left in his care, produced two more novels, *The Web and the Rock* (1939) and *You Can't Go Home Again* (1940), as well as a collection, *The Hills Beyond* (1941), that included a fragment of a novel and short works. In the decades since Wolfe's death, more of his writing has been published, most recently *O Lost* (2000), an edited text of the original manuscript for his first novel that restores some sixty thousand words that were cut in the editing process of *Look Homeward, Angel.*

During his lifetime and at his death Wolfe was regarded as a writer of unquestioned genius. Malcolm Cowley proclaimed that Wolfe was "the only contemporary writer who can be mentioned in the same breath as Dickens and Dostoevsky." Other critics and admirers placed Wolfe firmly within the American tradition. V. F. Calverton called Wolfe "the prose Walt Whitman of the twentieth century." Stephen Vincent Benet wrote, "When all is said and done, he will stand with Melville." William Faulkner ranked Wolfe as one of the greatest American writers of the twentieth century because of his ambition "to reduce all human experience to literature." Wolfe was also recognized as a writer of the first rank abroad, especially in Germany where he was called "the American Homer."

In the more than sixty years that have passed since Wolfe's death, his reputation as a major American writer has suffered a decline. His novels–for a variety of reasons, not the least of which is their length–have often been omitted from American literature courses. Yet Wolfe's books, especially *Look Homeward, Angel,* continue to be printed and read. Published in the centennial year of Wolfe's birth, *Dictionary of Literary Biography 229: Thomas Wolfe, A Documentary Volume* details Wolfe's life and career and presents an implicit argument for a reassessment of Wolfe and a restoration of his proper position in the American canon.

From his undergraduate years to his death, Thomas Wolfe lived to write and wrote prodigiously. Early in his career he pursued a career as a playwright. As a teenager he could dash off a one-act play in an afternoon. As he became a more serious craftsman, he began turning out alternate versions of each play he wrote, and the repositories at Harvard University and the University of North Carolina at Chapel Hill are laden with his apprenticeship efforts. (Harvard's catalogue of his manuscripts lists 142 drafts and fragments of plays.) Wolfe always wrote about what he knew best. From his earthy antihero Buck Gavin in *The Return of Buck Gavin* (1919) to the greedy real estate sharks of *Welcome to Our City* (1923), the characters of his plays were the colorful men and women of the mountains of his youth. In the mid 1920s Wolfe turned from writing for the stage and discovered his true métier–the novel.

Wolfe's reputation as a writer was profoundly influenced by the publication of *Look Homeward, Angel.* Although critics recognized his genius, the autobiographical nature of the novel and the help Wolfe received from Maxwell Perkins, his editor at Charles Scribner's Sons, in bringing it to publishable form stamped him for some as a writer who was too tied to his own experience and who did not have complete control of his material. This charge was exacerbated later by Wolfe's generous praise of Perkins in *The Story of a Novel* for his aid in shaping *Of Time and the River.*

In *Look Homeward, Angel* Wolfe relentlessly unearthed minute details from his childhood and early manhood. In many cases, Wolfe used real names and modified others only slightly. When the novel was published, the citizens of Asheville annotated their copies with real names of local characters. "The book is about Asheville people," Wolfe's mentor, Margaret Roberts, wrote after reading *Look Homeward, Angel* in 1929, "some of it true, and some fiction, but all convincingly written, and so localized that any inhabitant of Asheville can identify every spot and person."

Wolfe's transmutation of his own experience into his novels, which continued throughout his career, drew fire from critics who charged that he was incapable of producing fiction that was not overtly autobiographical. In a 1 February 1932 letter to Julian Meade, who was writing an article on Wolfe for *The Bookman,* Wolfe provided a typically impassioned defense of his practice:

> I think the roots of all creation in writing are fastened in autobiography and that it is in no way possible to escape or deny this fact. I think that a writer must use what is his own, I know of no means by which he can use what is not his own–do you?–nor would I think it desirable that he should. I made once before what seemed to me a very clear and simple statement of this obvious fact–namely, in a short preface to the reader which I wrote at the beginning of "Look Homeward, Angel"–and I was accused by several critics, including one or two on the Asheville newspapers, of "evading the issue" and of trying to avoid a direct answer whether my book was about Asheville and its citizens by a clever twist of words. . . . I will say here and now that it is not about Asheville, North Carolina, and that it is not a faithful picture of the inhabitants of Asheville, North Carolina, or of any other place on earth that I have ever known; and finally, that I do not believe any book ever got written in this way. Certainly I could never write anything in this way: that is not the way a writer works and feels and creates a thing–he does not write by calling Greenville Jonesville or by changing the name of Brown and Smith to Black and White: if it's that easy let's all start out for the nearest town with a trunk full of notebooks and pencils and start taking down the words and movements of the inhabitants from the most convenient corner.

Wolfe's use of actual people in his writing is, of course, ultimately not important to the modern reader. What matters is that he succeeded in bringing his characters to life.

From the publication of *Look Homeward, Angel* to the end of his life, Wolfe was also attacked by critics for an alleged lack of structure in his novels. Since his own life provided the form of his fiction, Wolfe's writing is exuberantly inclusive. In life there are no outlines to follow, and the myriad discoveries that Wolfe included in his writing lacked the harmonious symmetry that some critics preferred. His sometimes repetitive, inspired prose did not conform to the congruities of the traditional novel built upon an arch of a defined beginning, middle, and end. As Wolfe re-created in fiction the world he had known, he relinquished the contrived plots that some critics required. The art of creation, not convention, formed the organic structure of his work. His pages were comprised of the daily occurrences of sleeping, waking, eating, wrangling, loving, dying–the rhythms and beat of life itself.

Maxwell Perkins intuitively understood Wolfe's qualities as well as his limitations. In a remembrance of Wolfe that Perkins was writing at the time of his own death, Perkins maintained that Wolfe "needed a continent to range over, actually and in imagination. And his place was all America. It was with America that he was most deeply concerned, and I believe that he opened it up as no other author ever did for the people of his time and for the writers and artists and poets of tomorrow. Surely he had a thing to tell us."

–*Ted Mitchell*

Acknowledgments

This book was produced by Bruccoli Clark Layman, Inc. Karen L. Rood is senior editor. George Parker Anderson was the in-house editor.

Production manager is Philip B. Dematteis.

Administrative support was provided by Ann M. Cheschi, Dawnca T. Williams, and Mary A. Womble.

Accountant is Kathy Weston. Accounting assistant is Amber L. Coker.

Copyediting supervisor is Phyllis A. Avant. Senior copyeditor is Thom Harman. The copyediting staff includes Brenda Carol Blanton, Melissa D. Hinton, William Tobias Mathes, Jennifer S. Reid, Nancy E. Smith, and Elizabeth Jo Ann Sumner. Freelance copyeditor is Rebecca Mayo.

Editorial associates are Michael S. Allen, Margo Dowling, Richard K. Galloway, and Michael S. Martin.

Layout and graphics supervisor is Janet E. Hill. The graphics staff includes Karla Corley Brown and Zoe R. Cook.

Office manager is Kathy Lawler Merlette.

Photography editors are Charles Mims, Scott Nemzek, and Paul Talbot.

Digital photography supervisor is Joseph M. Bruccoli. Digital photographic copy work was performed by Abraham R. Layman.

SGML supervisor is Cory McNair. The SGML staff includes Linda Dalton Mullinax, Frank Graham, Jason Paddock, and Alex Snead.

Systems manager is Marie L. Parker.

Typesetting supervisor is Kathleen M. Flanagan. The typesetting staff includes Kimberly Kelly Brantley, Sarah Mathes, Mark J. McEwan, Patricia Flanagan Salisbury, and Alison Smith. Freelance typesetters are Wanda Adams and Vicki Grivetti.

Walter W. Ross did library research. He was assisted by Steven Gross and the following librarians at the Thomas Cooper Library of the University of South Carolina: circulation department head Tucker Taylor; reference department head Virginia W. Weathers; Brette Barclay, Marilee Birchfield, Paul Cammarata, Gary Geer, Michael Macan, Tom Marcil, Rose Marshall, and Sharon Verba; interlibrary loan department head John Brunswick; and Robert Arndt, Jo Cottingham, Hayden Battle, Barry Bull, Marna Hostetler, Nelson Rivera, Marieum McClary, and Erika Peake, interlibrary loan staff.

The editor would also like to recognize and thank the following people and organizations: Eugene H. Winick; The Estate of Thomas Wolfe; Houghton Library, Harvard University; Leslie A. Morris and Tom Ford; Pack Memorial Public Library, Asheville, North Carolina; Philip Banks, Laura Gaskins, Zoe Rhine and Ann Wright; Firestone Library, Princeton University; Margaret M. Sherry and the late Alexander D. Wainwright; Wilson Library, The University of North Carolina at Chapel Hill; Alice Cotten and Jerry Cotton; J. Todd Bailey; Tim Barnwell; Deborah A. Borland; Adelaide Wisdom Benjamin; Arlyn and Matthew J. Bruccoli; James W. Clark Jr.; Adele and James Cleary; Carole Conrad; Mary Aswell Doll; Joan Hellman; Jan G. Hensley; John L. Idol Jr.; Stanley L. Johnson; Richard S. Kennedy; Richard Knapp; David Latham; Aldo P. Magi; Joanne Marshall Mauldin; Chris Morton; the late Margaret Rose Roberts; Clara Stites; David Strange; and Denis W. Thomas.

Permissions

American Review for Robert Penn Warren, "A Note on the Hamlet of Thomas Wolfe" (May 1935).

The Asheville Citizen for Thomas C. Wolfe, "In Devising Torture Cruelties Nordic Race has Demonstrated the Superiority it Boasts of" (19 July 1925); Irene Wright, "Altamont Of Novel Is Not Asheville, Tom Wolfe Insists" (31 January 1937); unsigned articles, "Foreign Land Is Scene Of Story Being Prepared" (9 August 1931), "Tom Wolfe Completes His Second Novel And Has Started On Third" (15 March 1932), "Tom Wolfe's New Story Describes Asheville In Real-Estate Boom Days" (26 April 1934), "Thos. Wolfe Comes Home For First Time Since Writing Novel" (4 May 1937), "Tom Wolfe To Spend The Summer Writing At Cabin Near Here" (4 July 1937), "Wolfe Leaves After Summer Visit Here; Finishes New Story" (3 September 1937), "Tom Wolfe's Story Recalls Murderous Rampage of Negro" (10 September 1937), "Tom Wolfe Improving At Seattle Hospital" (1 September 1938), "Thomas Wolfe Enters Johns Hopkins Hospital" (9 September 1938), "Undergoes Operation" (14 September 1938), "Condition of Tom Wolfe Is 'Very Grave'" (15 September 1938), "Thomas Wolfe Is Dead At 37 After Lengthy Illness" (16 September 1938).

Asheville Citizen-Times for Paul Clark, "Preview of new Thomas Wolfe stamp available" (19 October 1999).

The Asheville Times for Walter S. Adams, "Amazing New Novel is Realistic Story of Asheville People" (29 October 1929); Lee E. Cooper, "Wolfe Denies 'Betraying' Asheville" (4 May 1930); unsigned articles, "Statue Made Famous In 'Look Homeward Angel' Stands Vigil Over Grave" (4 May 1930), "Thomas Wolfe Welcomed By Friends Here" (4 May 1937), "Thomas Wolfe, Noted Novelist, Seriously Ill at Seattle, Wash." (15 July 1938).

Atlantic Monthly for excerpts from Malcolm Cowley, "Thomas Wolfe" (November 1957).

The Carolina Magazine for Maxwell Perkins, "Scribner's and Tom Wolfe" (October 1938).

The Charlotte Observer for May Johnston Avery, "Tom Wolfe Paints Picture Relentless For Truthfulness With Homefolks Characters" (30 March 1930); Gertrude S. Carraway, "Thomas Wolfe, 37 Today, Plans Early Return to Native Mountains To Live" (3 October 1937).

The Estate of Thomas Wolfe (Copyright © 1999), reprinted by permission of McIntosh & Otis, Inc., for Thomas Wolfe documents and photographs from the Wolfe collections at the University of North Carolina at Chapel Hill and Houghton Library, Harvard University; for excerpts from *The Autobiographical Outline for Look Homeward, Angel*, edited by Lucy Conniff and Richard S. Kennedy (N.p.: Thomas Wolfe Society, 1991); excerpts from *The Autobiography of an American Novelist,* edited by Leslie Field (Cambridge, Mass.: Harvard University Press, 1983); excerpts from *Beyond Love and Loyalty: The Letters of Thomas Wolfe and Elizabeth Nowell,* edited by Richard S. Kennedy (Chapel Hill & London: University of North Carolina Press); excerpts from *To Loot My Life Clean: The Thomas Wolfe–Maxwell Perkins Correspondence,* edited by Matthew J. Bruccoli and Park Bucker (Copyright © 2000 by the University of South Carolina); excerpts from *My Other Loneliness: Letters of Thomas Wolfe and Aline Bernstein,* edited by Suzanne Stutman (Copyright © 1983 by the University of North Carolina Press); excerpts from *The Notebooks of Thomas Wolfe,* edited by Richard S. Kennedy and Paschal Reeves (Copyright © 1970 by the University of North Carolina Press); and excerpts from *Thomas Wolfe Interviewed, 1929–1938,* edited by Aldo P. Magi and Richard Walser (Baton Rouge & London: Louisiana State University Press, 1985).

Hamish Hamilton for excerpts from Cyril Connolly, "Thomas Wolfe," in his *Previous Convictions* (London, 1963).

HarperCollins Publishers, Inc., for excerpts from *The Web and the Rock* (1939), *You Can't Go Home Again* (Copyright © 1934, 1937, 1938, 1939, 1940 by Maxwell Perkins as Executor of the Estate of Thomas Wolfe; Copyright renewed © 1968 by Paul Gitlin, Administrator C.T.A.); *Harper's Magazine* for excerpts from William Styron, "The Shade of Thomas Wolfe" (April 1968).

Harvard Library Bulletin for Maxwell Perkins, "Thomas Wolfe" (Autumn 1947).

The Hills Beyond (1941); excerpts from Edward C. Aswell, "A Note on Thomas Wolfe," in *The Hills Beyond* (1941).

Kenyon Review for John Peale Bishop, "The Sorrows of Thomas Wolfe" (Winter 1939).

Nation for unsigned, untitled article (24 September 1938).

The New Republic for Hamilton Basso, "Thomas Wolfe: A Summing Up" (23 September 1940); for Malcolm Cowley, "Thomas Wolfe's Legacy" (19 July 1939); for unsigned article, "Tom Wolfe" (28 September 1938).

The New Yorker for Clifton Fadiman, review of *The Web and the Rock* (24 June 1939).

New York Evening Post for Kenneth Fearing, "A First Novel of Vast Scope" (16 November 1929).

New York Post for Hershel Brickell, review of *Of Time and the River;* for May Cameron, "Thomas Wolfe's Superb Farewell" (22 June 1939); for unsigned editorial (16 September 1938).

The New York Times for John Chamberlain, review of *Of Time and the River* (8 March 1935); for unsigned article, "M. E. Perkins, 62, Scribner's Editor" (18 June 1947).

The New York Times Book Review for J. Donald Adams, "Thomas Wolfe's Last Book" (26 October 1941) and Margaret Wallace, "A Novel of Provincial American Life" (27 October 1929).

The Raleigh (N.C.) *News and Observer* for Jonathan Daniels, "Wolfe's First Is Novel of Revolt" (20 October 1929).

Publishers' Weekly for Thurston Macauley, "Thomas Wolfe: A Writer's Problems" (24 December 1938).

The Saturday Evening Post for illustration by F. R. Gruger for Wolfe's "Child by Tiger" (11 September 1937).

Scribner, a Division of Simon & Schuster, Inc., for excerpts from *Look Homeward, Angel* (Copyright © 1929 by Charles Scribner's Sons; Copyright renewed © 1957 by Edward C. Aswell, as Administrator, C.T.A. of the Estate of Thomas Wolfe and/or Fred Wolfe); excerpts from *Of Time and the River* (Copyright © 1935 by Charles Scribner's Sons; Copyright renewed © 1963 by Paul Gitlin, Administrator C.T.A.); excerpts from *From Death to Morning* (Copyright © 1932, 1933, 1934, 1935 by Charles Scribner's Sons; Copyright renewed © 1960, 1961); excerpts from *The Letters of Thomas Wolfe,* edited by Elizabeth Nowell (Copyright © 1956 by Edward C. Aswell, Administrator C.T.A. of the Estate of Thomas Wolfe; Copyright renewed © 1984 by Paul Gitlin, Administrator C.T.A. of the Estate of Thomas Wolfe); excerpts from *The Letters of Thomas Wolfe to His Mother,* edited by C. Hugh Holman and Sue Fields Ross (University of North Carolina Press, 1968); for first page of "Angel on the Porch" from *Scribner's Magazine* (August 1929); for 9 July 1937 letter to Wolfe from *F. Scott Fitzgerald: A Life in Letters,* edited by Matthew J. Bruccoli (Copyright © 1994 by the Trustees under Agreement dated July 3, 1975 created by Frances Scott Fitzgerald Smith); *The Short Novels of Thomas Wolfe,* edited by C. Hugh Holman (Copyright © 1961 by Charles Scribner's Sons), and *The Complete Stories of Thomas Wolfe,* edited by Francis E. Skipp (Copyright © 1987 by Francis E. Skipp).

Seattle Times for unsigned article, "Thomas Wolfe, Ailing Novelist, En Route East" (7 September 1938).

Southern Review for excerpts from C. Hugh Holman, "The Dwarf on Wolfe's Shoulder" (April 1977).

Times Literary Supplement for review of *Look Homeward, Angel* (24 July 1930); review of *Of Time and the River* (22 August 1935); and review of *From Death to Morning* (21 March 1936).

Thomas Wolfe Review for James D. Boyer, "Nowell and Wolfe: the Working Relationship" (Spring 1981).

University of Oklahoma Press for Floyd C. Watkins, "Thomas Wolfe's Characters: Portraits from Life," in his *Thomas Wolfe's Characters: Portraits from Life* (Norman, Okla., 1957).

University of Pittsburgh Press for the map of Wolfe's western journey.

Yale Review for excerpts from John Halberstadt, "The Making of Thomas Wolfe's Posthumous Novels" (Autumn 1980).

Dictionary of Literary Biography® • Volume Two Hundred Twenty-Nine

Thomas Wolfe

A Documentary Volume

Dictionary of Literary Biography: A Documentary Volume

A Thomas Wolfe Chronology

1900

3 October — Thomas Clayton Wolfe is born at 92 Woodfin Street, Asheville, North Carolina, the last of William Oliver Wolfe and Julia Westall Wolfe's eight children.

1904

April — Wolfe travels with his mother, sister Mabel and brothers Fred, Ben, and Grover to St. Louis, where his mother operates a boardinghouse, "The North Carolina," at 5095 Fairmount Avenue, during the World's Fair.

16 November — Wolfe's brother Grover contracts typhoid fever and dies. Julia Wolfe and her children return to Asheville.

1906

30 August — Julia Wolfe buys the Old Kentucky Home at 48 Spruce Street in Asheville to operate as a boardinghouse.

September — Wolfe enters Orange Street School.

October — Julia Wolfe moves into her boardinghouse with Tom, leaving her husband and other children at 92 Woodfin Street.

1912

September — Wolfe enters the North State Fitting School (later called the North State School), a private school for boys operated by John Munsey Roberts and his wife, Margaret Roberts, who becomes a major influence upon Wolfe's life.

1916

13 May — Wolfe appears as Prince Hal in *Henry IV* in the North State Fitting School's pageant commemorating the tercentenary of William Shakespeare's death. He is embarassed by his costume.

May — Wolfe's essay, "Shakespeare: the Man," wins the bronze medal in a citywide contest sponsored by *The Independent Magazine*.

1 June	Wolfe graduates from the North Fitting State School.
12 September	Wolfe enters the University of North Carolina at Chapel Hill.

1917

June	Wolfe returns to Asheville for summer vacation and falls in love with twenty-one-year-old Clara Paul, one of his mother's boarders.
November	Wolfe's first publication, the patriotic poem "A Field in Flanders," appears in *The University of North Carolina Magazine.*

1918

March	Wolfe's first work of fiction, the short story "A Cullenden of Virginia," is published in *The University of North Carolina Magazine.*
Summer	Wolfe works at Langley Field, Newport News, Virginia, as a time checker and loader of cargo.
September	Wolfe enrolls in Professor Frederick H. Koch's course in playwriting, the newly organized Carolina Playmakers.
19 October	Wolfe's brother Ben dies of influenza in Asheville.

1919

14–15 March	Wolfe's first play, *The Return of Buck Gavin,* is performed by the Carolina Playmakers with Wolfe in the title role.
Spring	Wolfe wins the Worth Prize in Philosophy for his essay *The Crisis in Industry.* It is published as a pamphlet by the University of North Carolina.
Fall	Wolfe is named editor-in-chief of *The Tar Heel,* the University of North Carolina student newspaper.
12–13 December	Wolfe performs with the Carolina Playmakers in his *The Third Night: A Mountain Play of the Supernatural.*

1920

16 June	Wolfe receives the bachelor of arts degree from the University of North Carolina.
13 September	Wolfe is accepted to the Graduate School of Arts and Sciences, Harvard University, to pursue a master of arts degree in English. While traveling by train to Boston, he experiences "a rattling, tearing, sort of cough, full of phlegm" and soreness in his right lung, possibly the first symptom of the tuberculosis that ultimately leads to his death.
Fall	Wolfe studies playwriting as a member of George Pierce Baker's 47 Workshop. He becomes close friends with Baker's assistant Kenneth Raisbeck, later the model for "Francis Starwick" in *Of Time and the River.*

1921

25 January	Wolfe's *The Mountains,* a one-act play, is given a trial performance in the 47 Workshop's rehearsal hall.

March	Wolfe works on a play that eventually becomes *Mannerhouse.*
21–22 October	*The Mountains* is staged by the 47 Workshop at the Agassiz Theatre, Radcliffe College.

1922

19 June	Wolfe receives news his father is dying and returns to Asheville.
20 June	William Oliver Wolfe dies of prostate cancer. His son receives his M.A. degree from Harvard University while he is still in Asheville.
September	Wolfe returns to Harvard to study with Baker for another year and works on a full-length play that later becomes *Welcome to Our City.*

1923

11–12 May	*Welcome To Our City* is staged by the 47 Workshop at the Agassiz Theatre.
August	Wolfe revises *Welcome To Our City* and submits it to the Theatre Guild, an influential New York organization of stage producers, directors, and actors.
Fall	Wolfe returns to Asheville while awaiting the Theatre Guild's decision on his play.
November	Wolfe travels to New York and takes a temporary job soliciting contributions from University of North Carolina alumni.
December	The Theatre Guild declines *Welcome to Our City.*

1924

6 February	Wolfe begins teaching English as an instructor in the Washington Square College of New York University, a position he holds for nearly six years.
25 October	Wolfe leaves on his first trip to Europe aboard the *Lancastria.* He begins writing a satiric treatment of his voyage, which he later titles "Passage to England."
5 November	Wolfe lands in England.
December	Wolfe visits Paris, where the manuscript of his play *Mannerhouse* is stolen.

1925

January	Wolfe completely rewrites *Mannerhouse.* He tours Paris with Kenneth Raisbeck, Marjorie Fairbanks, and Helen Harding.
March–June	Wolfe travels in France, Italy, and Switzerland.
19 July	*The Asheville Citizen* publishes "London Tower," an excerpt from "Passage to England."
August	Wolfe leaves for New York aboard the *Olympic.* On 25 August, the day before the ship lands, he meets and begins an affair with Aline Bernstein, a set designer for New York theatres.
September	Wolfe resumes teaching at Washington Square College.
Fall–Winter	Wolfe's relationship with Bernstein deepens. He moves into a loft at 13 East Eighth Street that Bernstein rents as a studio while maintaining her Park Avenue residence with her family.

1926

23 June — Wolfe leaves on his second trip to Europe aboard the *Berengaria.* He travels in France and England with Aline Bernstein.

July — In Paris Wolfe begins an autobiographical outline for the novel that becomes *Look Homeward, Angel.*

August — Wolfe settles in London and begins working on the first version of his book. In the fall he visits Brussels for ten days and makes his first trip to Germany.

22 December — Wolfe leaves for New York aboard the *Majestic,* arriving in the city on 28 December. Settled back into the Eighth Street studio, he works for six months on the manuscript he now calls "O Lost."

1927

12 July — Wolfe leaves on his third trip to Europe aboard the *George Washington.* For two months he travels with Bernstein in France, Germany, Austria, Czechoslovakia, and Switzerland.

18 September — Wolfe arrives in New York aboard the *Belgenland.* He resumes teaching at Washington Square College and continues to work on "O Lost."

1928

March — Wolfe moves into a more spacious apartment at 263 West Eleventh Street where he completes the manuscript of "O Lost."

May — Wolfe begins work on a new novel, "The River People," which he later abandons.

20 May — Wolfe engages Madeleine Boyd as his literary agent for "O Lost" after it has been requested by several publishers.

30 June — Wolfe leaves on his fourth trip to Europe aboard the *Rotterdam.*

9 July — Wolfe lands at Boulogne and travels in France, Belgium, and Germany. He continues working on "The River People."

30 September — Wolfe is injured in a brawl at the Oktoberfest in Munich and is hospitalized.

4 October — Wolfe is released from the hospital. He continues to travel, visiting Oberammergau in Germany to see its Passion Play. He also visits Vienna and Budapest.

16 November — Upon his return to Vienna, Wolfe finds a letter from Maxwell E. Perkins of Charles Scribner's Sons expressing interest in publishing "O Lost."

December — Wolfe travels in Italy and leaves for New York from Naples aboard the *Vulcania* on 21 December. He arrives in New York on the last day of the year.

1929

2 January — Wolfe has his first meeting with editor Maxwell Perkins.

7 January — Perkins orally agrees to publish Wolfe's novel. Two days later, Charles Scribner's Sons formally accepts "O Lost." Over the next four months, Wolfe works closely with Perkins editing and cutting the manuscript.

5 February — Wolfe resumes teaching part-time at Washington Square College.

April — Wolfe changes the title from "O Lost" to *Look Homeward, Angel* at the request of Scribners editorial staff.

June	Manuscript of novel is sent to typesetter. Wolfe corrects proof of the novel while vacationing in Maine and Canada during the summer.
August	*Scribner's Magazine* publishes "An Angel on the Porch," a revised chapter from *Look Homeward, Angel.*
7 September	Wolfe makes a short visit to Asheville, his last trip to his hometown until 1937.
24 September	Wolfe resumes teaching full-time at Washington Square College.
18 October	*Look Homeward, Angel* is published. The novel causes an uproar in Asheville but generally receives favorable reviews.
December	Wolfe applies for a Guggenheim Fellowship to enable him to write in Europe with financial security.

1930

17 January	Wolfe resigns from Washington Square College, effective 6 February. He never works as a teacher again.
March	Wolfe is awarded the John Simon Guggenheim Memorial Fellowship.
9 May	Wolfe leaves on his fifth trip to Europe aboard the *Volendam.* He arrives in Paris ten days later.
6 June	Wolfe begins writing "The October Fair."
Summer	Wolfe travels in Switzerland, France, and Germany.
October	Wolfe settles in a flat at 75 Ebury Street, London. He maintains a steady writing regime.
12 December	Sinclair Lewis praises Wolfe in his Nobel Prize acceptance speech.

1931

February	Wolfe meets Sinclair Lewis in London. Wolfe's characterization of Lewis as Alexander McHarg later appears in *You Can't Go Home Again.* Wolfe visits Holland.
26 February	Wolfe leaves for New York aboard the *Europa,* arriving on 4 March.
11 March	Wolfe rents 40 Verandah Place, the first of four apartments he occupies in Brooklyn during the next four years. He works on a variety of material, including works posthumously published as *The Good Child's River* (1991) and *K-19* (1983).
Fall	Wolfe learns that Madeleine Boyd embezzled the $250 advanced by a German publisher for a translation of *Look Homeward, Angel.* Although Wolfe considers his relationship with his agent severed, Boyd is not formally dismissed.
November	Wolfe moves to 111 Columbia Heights in Brooklyn.
December	Wolfe works on the novella "A Portrait of Bascom Hawke."

1932

January	Wolfe's mother visits him in Brooklyn. He severs his relationship with Aline Bernstein.

April	"A Portrait of Bascom Hawke" is published in *Scribner's Magazine* and ties for the $5,000 short novel prize.
Summer	Maxwell Perkins rejects Wolfe's novel "K-19."
August	Wolfe moves to 101 Columbia Heights in Brooklyn.
October	Wolfe visits his father's relatives in York Springs, Pennsylvania. He takes a brief trip to Bermuda.
Fall–Winter	Wolfe works on material that eventually goes into "The Party at Jack's."

1933

February	Wolfe finishes the novella "No Door," published as "No Door: A Story of Time and the Wanderer" in *Scribner's Magazine* (July 1933).
April	Wolfe delivers a large portion of the manuscript he began as "The October Fair" to Perkins. He changes the title to "Time and the River".
May	Wolfe writes a discourse on loneliness, later published as "God's Lonely Man" in *The Hills Beyond.* He signs a contract for "Time and the River" that calls for delivering the complete manuscript on 1 August 1933.
Fall	Wolfe works past the deadline for "Time and the River," filling gaps in his manuscript and enlarging various episodes.
October	Wolfe moves to 5 Montague Terrace in Brooklyn.
November	At Perkins's suggestion, Wolfe gives several pieces from his manuscript to Elizabeth Nowell to sell to periodicals other than *Scribner's Magazine.*
14 December	Wolfe delivers a rough draft of "Time and the River" to Perkins. Following his editor's advice, Wolfe has not included material about his relationship with Aline Bernstein.

1934

January	Wolfe works with Perkins on the revisions of "Time and the River." He engages Elizabeth Nowell to be his agent for marketing his fiction to periodicals.
September	Wolfe visits the World's Fair in Chicago. Perkins sends the manuscript of his novel to the printer in his absence.

1935

February	Wolfe meets Muredach Dooher, whom he later allows to explore the sale of his manuscripts to collectors.
2 March	Wolfe leaves on his sixth trip to Europe aboard the *Ile de France.*
8 March	*Of Time and the River* is published by Charles Scribner's Sons. Arriving in Paris, Wolfe worries about the reception of the novel.
14 March	Wolfe receives a reassuring cablegram from Perkins about reviews.
24 March	Wolfe arrives in London and takes a flat at 26 Hanover Square.
23 April	Wolfe leaves London and tours Norfolk and Suffolk.
7 May	Wolfe arrives in Berlin, where he is lionized as a great new American writer.

26 May	Wolfe learns that Madeleine Boyd is planning to sue him for her commission of royalties from *Of Time and the River.*
27 June	Wolfe leaves for New York aboard the *Bremen.* He arrives on 4 July to find reporters waiting at the dock to interview him. The success of *Of Time and the River* is assured.
22 July–7 August	Wolfe participates in the Sixth Annual Writers' Conference at Boulder, Colorado. He delivers a speech, "The Making of a Book," that he later revises into *The Story of a Novel.*
August–September	Wolfe tours the West Coast, visiting Hollywood and San Francisco. He returns east by way of St. Louis, stopping to see the house where his brother Grover died in 1904.
1 October	Wolfe moves into apartment at 865 First Avenue in Manhattan.
14 November	*From Death to Morning,* a short-story collection, is published by Charles Scribner's Sons.
December	"The Story of a Novel" is serialized in three issues of *The Saturday Review of Literature.*

1936

10 February	Wolfe decides not to sell any manuscripts to collectors and refuses to pay Muredach Dooher an agent's fee. When Dooher refuses to return Wolfe's manuscripts, Wolfe sues him and Dooher brings a countersuit for breach of contract.
March	Wolfe begins work on "The Vision of Spangler's Paul," which is incorporated into the posthumously published *The Web and the Rock* and *You Can't Go Home Again.*
25 April	"Genius Is Not Enough," Bernard DeVoto's attack on Wolfe as an undisciplined writer who is too dependent on Maxwell Perkins, is published in *The Saturday Review of Literature.*
Summer	Wolfe begins to consider changing publishers.
23 July	Wolfe leaves on his seventh and last trip to Europe aboard the *Europa.* He goes straight to Berlin.
August	Wolfe attends the Olympic Games in Berlin. He visits Austria with Thea Voelcker, a woman with whom he has a brief affair.
8 September	Wolfe leaves Berlin by train for Paris. He witnesses the arrest of a fellow passenger at Aachen, which inspires him to write "I Have a Thing to Tell You."
17 September	Wolfe leaves for New York aboard the *Paris,* arriving a week later.
Fall	Wolfe works on "I Have a Thing to Tell You" and "The Child by Tiger."
November	The Dorman family brings a libel suit against Wolfe and Scribner's over their alleged depiction in "No Door."
26 December	Wolfe leaves New York for a trip to New Orleans.

1937

Early January	In New Orleans Wolfe meets William B. Wisdom, who later purchases Wolfe's personal papers and manuscripts and donates them to Harvard University. Wolfe mails the letters severing his relations with Scribners.
11 January	Wolfe leaves New Orleans by train. He makes stops in Biloxi, Atlanta, Raleigh, and Chapel Hill before arriving in New York on 25 January.
April	Wolfe sets out for his long-anticipated return trip to Asheville. He visits York Springs, Pennsylvania, and Roanoke, Virginia.
30 April	Wolfe stops in Yancey County, North Carolina, for a few days to look up Westall relatives. On 1 May he witnesses a shooting that is later fictionalized in his short story "The Return of the Prodigal." He also visits his half uncle, John Baird Westall, and listens to his account of the battle of Chickamauga, which he fictionalizes in "Chickamauga."
3–15 May	Wolfe stays in Asheville with his mother; it is his first return to his hometown since the publication of *Look Homeward, Angel.*
May–June	Back in New York, Wolfe prepares material for Nowell to submit for periodical publication. He writes "Chickamauga."
2 July	Wolfe returns to North Carolina and moves into a rented cabin at Oteen, near Asheville.
Summer	Wolfe finishes "The Party at Jack's," which is published in *Scribner's Magazine* (May 1939).
16–18 August	Wolfe appears at trial in Burnsville as a state witness to the shooting he witnessed in May.
2 September	Wolfe leaves Asheville and returns to New York, eventually moving into the Hotel Chelsea.
Fall	Wolfe's break with Charles Scribner's Sons becomes public knowledge. He searches for a new publisher and chooses Edward C. Aswell at Harper and Brothers as his editor.
31 December	Wolfe signs a contract with Harper for a novel titled "The Life and Adventures of the Bondsman Doaks."

1938

January	Wolfe launches into extensive work on his new novel, which involves the 1930 failure of the Central Bank and Trust Company in Asheville.
8 February	Wolfe wins his lawsuit against Muredach Dooher to recover manuscripts. He sees Perkins for the last time.
14 February	Wolfe writes a long synopsis of the "Doaks" book for his new editor, Edward Aswell.
March	Wolfe changes his mind about his new book and decides on a biographical chronicle, titled "The Web and the Rock," with George Webber as the protagonist.
17 May	Wolfe delivers first draft manuscript to Edward Aswell.
19 May	Wolfe lectures at Purdue University, "Writing and Living."

20 June	Wolfe takes a two-week tour of the western National Parks.
5 July	On a ferry from Seattle to British Columbia, Wolfe contracts a respiratory infection that activates dormant tuberculosis in his right lung.
July	Wolfe enters Firlawns, a private sanitorium, twelve miles from Seattle at Kenmore.
August	Wolfe is hospitalized at Providence Hospital in Seattle.
12 August	Wolfe writes his last letter to Maxwell Perkins.
10 September	Wolfe arrives in Baltimore and is admitted to Johns Hopkins Hospital.
12 September	Dr. Walter E. Dandy operates on Wolfe, a cerebellar exploration.
15 September	Wolfe dies of tuberculosis meningitis at 5:30 a.m.
18 September	Wolfe is buried in a family plot in Asheville.

1939

22 June	*The Web and the Rock,* a novel assembled from Wolfe's manuscript by Edward Aswell, is published by Harper and Brothers.

1940

18 September	*You Can't Go Home Again,* a continuation of *The Web and the Rock* manuscript, is published by Harper and Brothers.

1941

15 October	*The Hills Beyond,* which includes a fragment of Wolfe's final novel as well as short stories and sketches assembled by Edward Aswell, is published by Harper and Brothers.

Books by Thomas Wolfe

BOOKS: *The Crisis in Industry* (Chapel Hill: University of North Carolina, 1919);

Look Homeward, Angel (New York: Scribners, 1929; London: Heinemann, 1930);

Of Time and the River (New York: Scribners, 1935; London: Heinemann, 1935);

From Death to Morning (New York: Scribners, 1935; London: Heinemann, 1936);

The Story of a Novel (New York & London: Scribners, 1936);

A Note on Experts: Dexter Vespasian Joyner (New York: House of Books, 1939);

The Web and the Rock (New York & London: Harper, 1939; London: Heinemann, 1947);

You Can't Go Home Again (New York & London: Harper, 1940; London: Heinemann, 1947);

The Hills Beyond (New York & London: Harper, 1941);

Gentlemen of the Press: A Play (Chicago: Black Archer Press, 1942);

Mannerhouse: A Play in a Prologue and Three Acts (New York: Harper, 1948; London: Heinemann, 1950); newly edited as *Mannerhouse: A Play in a Prologue and Four Acts,* edited by Louis D. Rubin Jr. and John L. Idol Jr. (Baton Rouge & London: Louisiana State University Press, 1985);

. . . *"The Years of Wandering in many lands and cities"* (New York: Charles S. Boesen, 1949);

A Western Journal: A Daily Log of The Great Parks Trip (Pittsburgh: University of Pittsburgh Press, 1951);

The Short Novels of Thomas Wolfe (New York: Scribners, 1961);

Thomas Wolfe's Purdue Speech: "Writing and Living," edited by William Braswell and Leslie A. Field (Indianapolis, Ind.: Purdue University Studies, 1964);

The Mountains (Chapel Hill: University of North Carolina Press, 1970);

The Notebooks of Thomas Wolfe, 2 volumes, edited by Richard S. Kennedy and Paschal Reeves (Chapel Hill: University of North Carolina Press, 1970);

A Prologue to America, edited by Aldo P. Magi (Athens, Ohio: Croissant, 1978);

Welcome to Our City, edited by Kennedy (Baton Rouge & London: Louisiana State University Press, 1983);

K-19: Salvaged Pieces, edited by Idol (N.p.: The Thomas Wolfe Society, 1983);

The Hound of Darkness, edited by Idol (N.p.: The Thomas Wolfe Society, 1986);

The Complete Short Stories of Thomas Wolfe, edited by Francis E. Skipp (New York: Scribners, 1987);

The Starwick Episodes, edited by Kennedy (N.p.: The Thomas Wolfe Society, 1989);

Thomas Wolfe's Composition Books: The North State Fitting School 1912–1915, edited by Alice R. Cotten (N.p.: The Thomas Wolfe Society, 1990);

The Autobiographical Outline for Look Homeward, Angel, edited by Lucy Conniff and Kennedy (N.p.: The Thomas Wolfe Society, 1991);

The Good Child's River, edited by Suzanne Stutman (Chapel Hill: University of North Carolina Press, 1991);

Thomas Wolfe's Notes on Macbeth, edited by William Grimes Cherry III (N.p.: The Thomas Wolfe Society, 1992);

[George Webber, Writer]: An Introduction by a Friend, edited by Idol (N.p.: The Thomas Wolfe Society, 1994);

Antaeus, or A Memory of Earth, edited by Ted Mitchell (N.p.: The Thomas Wolfe Society, 1996);

Passage to England: A Selection, edited by Stutman and Idol (N.p.: The Thomas Wolfe Society, 1998);

O Lost, edited by Arlyn Bruccoli and Matthew J. Bruccoli (Columbia: University of South Carolina Press, 2000).

Editions & Collections: *The Face of a Nation: Poetical Passages From the Writings of Thomas Wolfe* (New York: Scribners, 1939);

A Stone, A Leaf, A Door: Poems by Thomas Wolfe, selected and arranged in verse by John S. Barnes (New York: Scribners, 1945);

The Lost Boy, edited by James W. Clark (Chapel Hill: University of North Carolina Press, 1992);

The Party at Jack's, edited by Suzanne Stutman and John L. Idol Jr. (Chapel Hill: University of North Carolina Press, 1995).

LETTERS: *Thomas Wolfe's Letters to His Mother, Julia Elizabeth Wolfe,* edited by John Skally Terry (New York: Scribners, 1943); revised as *The Letters of*

Thomas Wolfe to His Mother, edited by C. Hugh Holman and Sue Fields Ross (New York: Scribners, 1968);

The Correspondence of Thomas Wolfe and Homer Andrew Watt, edited by Oscar Cargill and Thomas Clark Pollock (New York: New York University Press, 1954);

The Letters of Thomas Wolfe, edited by Elizabeth Nowell (New York: Scribners, 1956); revised as *Selected Letters of Thomas Wolfe,* edited by Nowell, selected by Daniel George (London: Heinemann, 1958);

Beyond Love and Loyalty: The Letters of Thomas Wolfe and Elizabeth Nowell, edited by Richard S. Kennedy (Chapel Hill & London: University of North Carolina Press, 1983);

My Other Loneliness: Letters of Thomas Wolfe and Aline Bernstein, edited by Suzanne Stutman (Chapel Hill & London: University of North Carolina Press, 1983);

Holding on for Heaven: The Cables and Postcards of Thomas Wolfe and Aline Bernstein, edited by Stutman (N.p.: The Thomas Wolfe Society, 1985);

To Loot My Life Clean: The Thomas Wolfe–Maxwell Perkins Correspondence, edited by Matthew J. Bruccoli and Park Bucker (Columbia: University of South Carolina Press, 2000).

Papers:

The major collections of Thomas Wolfe's papers are the William B. Wisdom Collection in the Houghton Library at Harvard University, the University of North Carolina Library at Chapel Hill, and the Pack Memorial Library, Asheville, North Carolina.

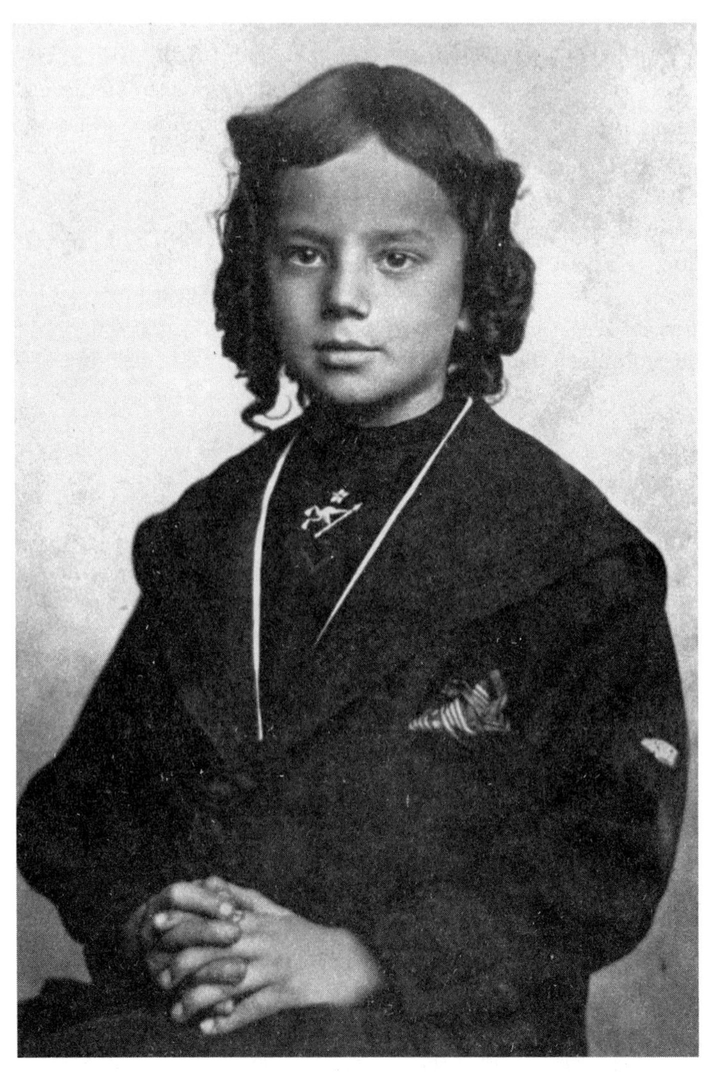

Thomas Wolfe in 1908. Wanting him to be her baby as long as possible, his mother, Julia, kept her son in Little Lord Fauntleroy curls until he was nine (The Thomas Wolfe Collection, Pack Memorial Public Library, Asheville, North Carolina).

Chapter 1

Asheville, 1900–1916

Born on 3 October 1900 at 92 Woodfin Street, Thomas Wolfe spent almost all of his first sixteen years in Asheville, North Carolina. The influence of the city and its surrounding mountains is unmistakably stamped on his life and literary achievements. He was the youngest of eight children born to tombstone-cutter William Oliver Wolfe and Julia Elizabeth Westall Wolfe.

In 1906 his mother purchased a boardinghouse, the Old Kentucky Home, and took six-year-old Tom to live with her, leaving her other children with their father. The disintegration of the family's unity had a profound psychological effect on young Wolfe, but despite the misery and disorder he described in Look Homeward, Angel, *his childhood was not altogether traumatic. He turned inward, but he was far from being a melancholy introvert, as his readers and critics have so often imagined him. He frequently escaped to the family home, which reverberated with noise and laughter and was dominated, for the most part, by his father's earthy humor and rhetoric. Wolfe affectionately remembered the roaring fires that his father built in the parlor and the occasions at the dinner table when W. O. heaped food on his son's plate. The boy loved reading, curling up on the lounge in the parlor, or sequestering himself in the playhouse that his father had built in the backyard. Taking trips in the South with his mother, he also acquired a love for traveling that lasted all his life.*

By the time Wolfe was twelve years old, his beloved teacher at the North State Fitting School, Margaret Roberts, pronounced him a genius and nurtured his talent as a writer. She became the mentor he recalled as "the mother of my spirit." By the time Wolfe was fifteen years old, his father decided that his son had completed enough local schooling and was ready for college. Although Wolfe was attracted to both the University of Virginia and Princeton, his father forced him to go to the state university at Chapel Hill, where W. O. believed that contacts for the law career envisaged for his son would prove valuable.

Birth, Home, and Family

Because no birth certificate exists, this news clipping from The Asheville Daily Citizen *the day after the event marks the first documentation of Thomas Wolfe's life. Neither W. O. nor Julia Wolfe registered the births of any of their eight children. (Birth registration in Buncombe County was not mandatory until 1915.) Not mentioned in the report, the son's name was Thomas Clayton Wolfe; he was named Thomas after his maternal grandfather, Thomas Casey Westall, and great-great grandfather, Thomas Westall. Wolfe received his middle name, Clayton, from a spiritualist clergyman, William Clayton Bowman, whom his mother admired.*

Around Town.

FORECAST till 8 p. m. Friday:—Rain tonight and Friday.

Born to Mr. and Mrs. W. O. Wolfe, a son.

W. L. Shope's condition is reported this afternoon as some better.

J. B. Goodson has accepted a position as salesman with H. S. Courtney.

There will be a meeting of St. Mary's Guild at Mrs. Dunn's studio on Friday at 3:30.

Mrs. T. D. Johnston will entertain the Gudger-Cocke bridal party at dinner Friday evening.

(The Thomas Wolfe Collection, Pack Memorial Public Library, Asheville, North Carolina)

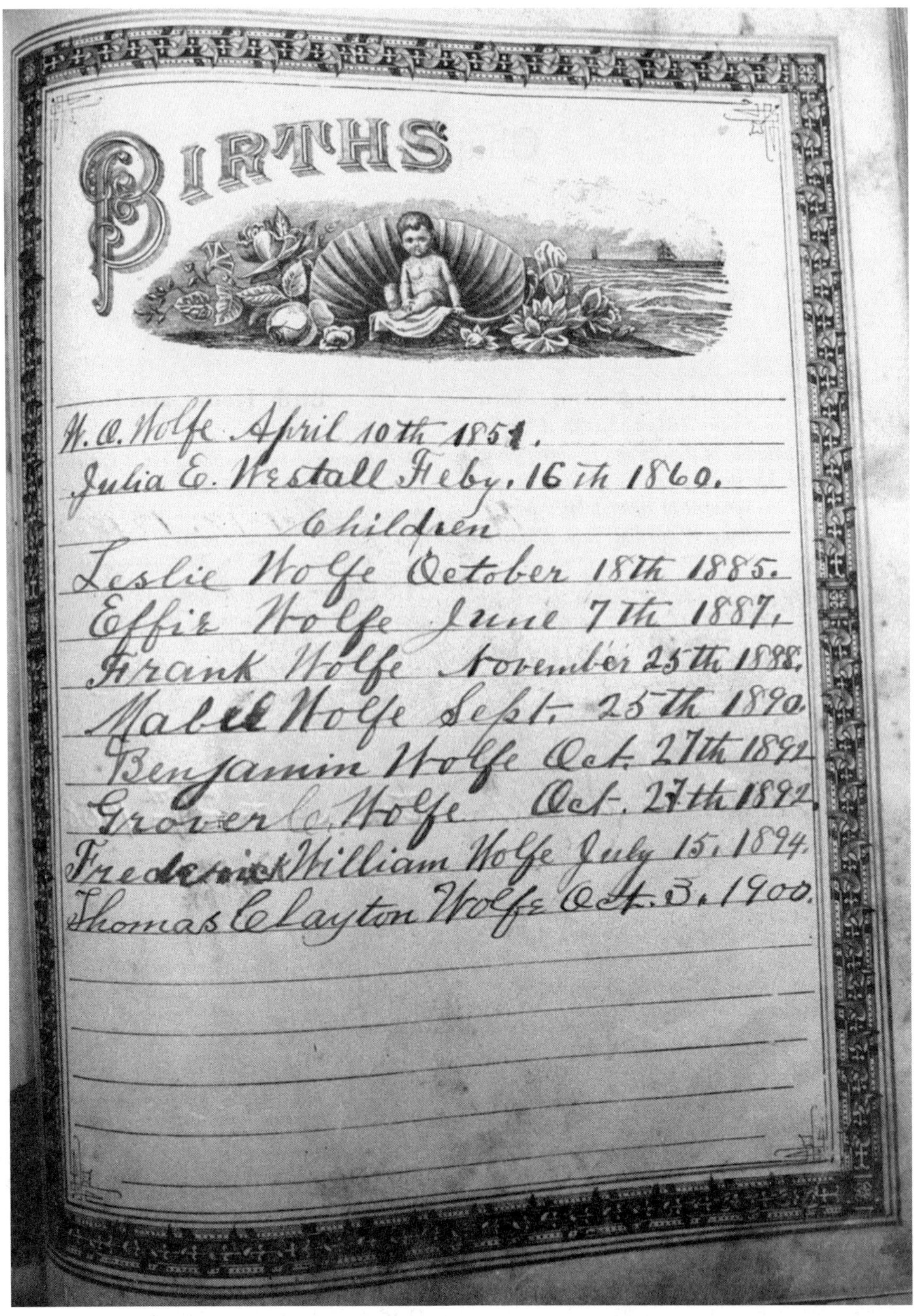

BIRTHS

W. O. Wolfe April 10th 1851.
Julia E. Westall Feby. 16th 1860.
Children
Leslie Wolfe October 18th 1885.
Effie Wolfe June 7th 1887.
Frank Wolfe November 25th 1888.
Mabel Wolfe Sept. 25th 1890.
Benjamin Wolfe Oct. 27th 1892
Grover C. Wolfe Oct. 27th 1892
Frederick William Wolfe July 15. 1894.
Thomas Clayton Wolfe Oct. 3. 1900.

The Wolfe family Bible listing the birth dates of Thomas Wolfe, his parents, and brothers and sisters (The North Carolina Department of Cultural Resources)

To me the characters in my book were real people, full-blooded, rich and interesting; they were pioneers of the sort which has built this country, and I love them.

–*Thomas Wolfe Interviewed*, p. 7

Major Thomas Casey Westall, Thomas Wolfe's maternal grandfather (The North Carolina Department of Cultural Resources)

Julia Westall Wolfe flanked by her two brothers, William H. Westall and James M. Westall, circa 1942 (The Thomas Wolfe Collection, Pack Memorial Public Library, Asheville, North Carolina)

William Oliver and Julia E. Wolfe, 1900, the year of Thomas Wolfe's birth (The Thomas Wolfe Collection, Pack Memorial Public Library, Asheville, North Carolina)

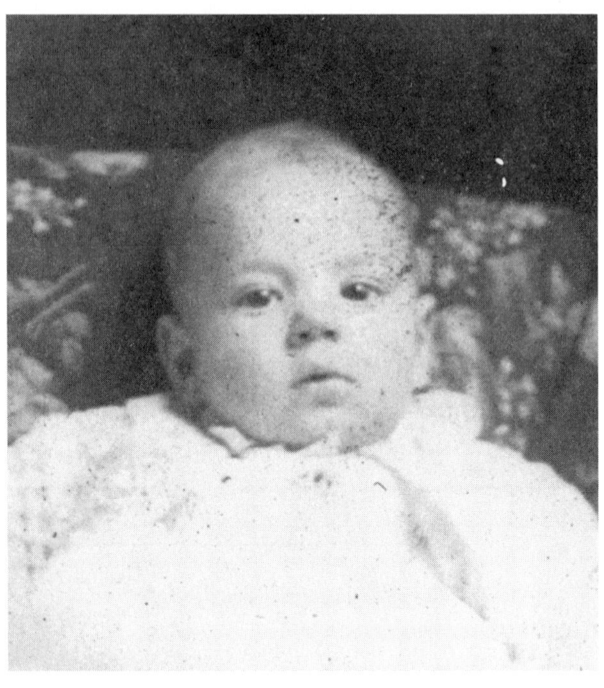

The earliest existing image of Thomas Clayton Wolfe, four months old (The North Carolina Collection, University of North Carolina Library at Chapel Hill)

The Wolfe family at 92 Woodfin Street, 4 July 1899; left to right: Effie, W. O., Mabel, Fred, Grover, Ben, Julia, and Frank (The Thomas Wolfe Collection, Pack Memorial Public Library, Asheville, North Carolina)

Never a writer to sentimentalize his past or suppress the harsh truths of his turbulent family history, Wolfe chronicled his conception, birth, and infancy, in the autobiographical notes (1926) he prepared for Look Homeward, Angel.

January 1–10, 1900–I was conceived.

April 4–May 22, 1900–Father at Greensboro, North Carolina, taking the Keeley cure for alcoholism.

June–Sept. 1900–Father drunk.

September 28–Oct. 2–Father maniacally drunk.

Oct. 2, 1900–Eight o'clock at night. Father returns home, enters my mother's room and attacks her. She escapes, wearing only her nightdress, runs downstairs and out-of-doors, calling for help. Mr. Colvin and Mr. Perkinson, our neighbors, come over and protect her from my father. My brother Frank, aged 14, has been sent for my uncle Will Westall. My sister Effie (15) hides herself at Josephine Britt's; Mabel (10-1/2) stays; Fred (6) is in bed. Ben and Grover (8), twins, are on the roof. Uncle Will arrives. My father is put to bed, and falls off into a heavy sleep.

Oct. 3, 1900–Ten o'clock in the morning. I am born.
Early July 1901–Before dinner on Sunday morning, father takes me out into the garden holding me in his arms. Goes deep back through the cool glade of the orchard–black wet spongy earth, to the open sunshine space. Over the fence, near Britt's is a cow. I imitate its sound. "Moo" First articulate speech. Father delighted. Tells story over and over getting me to repeat the sound all afternoon for guests and neighbors. The smell, the sound, the day I remember accurately–it was Sunday (the hot smell of dock weed in the rank rich South)

Spring 1902–They kept me in a great wicker laundry basket–I remember climbing to the edge and seeing vast squares of carpet below me: the sitting room was shuttered–the drowsy intermittent crowing of hens outside–a sleepy forenoon. Beyond in the parlor Effie practicing at the Piano–Paderewski's Minuet–Later this spring, I saw Effie go back to school. It was the recess hour–she was at Miss Ford's school in the brick house at the top of the hill–I was in the basket at the top of the steps–I watched her go up the hill–The Hazzards and the great house–at two o'clock each afternoon the negro drove up the drive for them.

That summer Fred had typhoid fever. Playing in the Hazzard drive, I was crushed by the grocery horse.

–*The Autobiographical Outline,* pp. 3–4

Families are strange and wonderful things and one never sees the mystery and the beauty in them until one is absent from them. When one is present, the larger values are obscured sometimes by the little friction of daily events.

–*The Letters of Thomas Wolfe,* p. 41

Wolfe at nine months. Julia Wolfe had all of her children photographed at this age (The Thomas Wolfe Collection, Pack Memorial Public Library, Asheville, North Carolina).

In the old parlour of the house on Woodfin Street–that musty old frame of the golden days, with its sweet cool narrow glade of orchard reaching far behind–I heard the sea for the first time. Below the marble-topped table, covered with the bible, the album, the stereoscope, and a glass-caged platter of waxen fruit, surrounded at every quarter by the horse-hair varnished sofas and chairs, enclosed by the four walls of sober brown, hung with the benign countenances of my whiskered ancestry–the first time, let me say, any of them had been hung–there were four great conch shells.

–and faint and far heard breakers pounding on the ends of earth.

–*The Notebooks of Thomas Wolfe,* pp. 48–49

Wolfe's recording of sensory details (especially food) pervades a large portion of Look Homeward, Angel. *In this notebook excerpt, Wolfe describes the early awareness of his protagonist, Eugene Gant.*

He saw that almost everything depended on communication, that communication was founded primarily in speech. But, even so, granted that children were thus imprisoned before they could talk, why had none of them described the horror, the futility, the revolting waste of the whole process, as soon as he had become articulate? The explanation came with electric horror. Eugene found that thought which was not built upon the sensuous images of speech was a house built on sand; he found, for example, on waking from a sound sleep, that what had been clear and sharp in his brain before he slept was now blurred, confused, inchoate, mixed with other thought and other time. For, without language, he saw that even the sense of time became confused.

Thus he was faced with the terror of watching the erasure, day by day, of all his mind had patiently and speechlessly elaborated. The stabbing truth came to him then at once that when his mind had learned to construct itself in speech images, it would be almost impossible to reconstruct its activity during the period when it had no speech.

All the feelers, the tender opening buds of taste and odor, were opening up in him, the cellular kernels of his powerful sensory organization, destined later to become almost incomparably hearty and exquisite, were expanding. He had the rare gift of enjoying the excellence of the common thing–of tasting to its final goodness the quality of a liberal slice of savory roast beef with creamed potatoes. He scented his food like an animal before tasting it: peaches and cream he gloated over sensually. He ate, when he could, on a bare table in the pantry: it was filled with musty spicy odors–the ghost of cinnamon, clove, new bread, vanilla flavoring. There one day, he met first the delights of toasted corn flakes. They came in a huge carton labelled *Force;* there was a picture of a comical, merry old man on the cover–as he remembered, an old man, with a hooked nose and chin, a Punchian and appetite-giving old man. For weeks he lived in hungry anticipation of toasted corn flakes, rich cream and sugar: the savory glutinous compound was the highest pleasure he had tasted.

–*The Notebooks of Thomas Wolfe,* p. 69

Julia Wolfe with the first of her eight children, Leslie. In Look Homeward, Angel *Wolfe described his mother's "grim and casual littering." Leslie died when she was only nine months old. She retained her name in* Look Homeward, Angel; *the author did not change the first names of those family members who died before the 1929 publication date of the novel (The North Carolina Collection, University of North Carolina Library at Chapel Hill).*

Frank Cecil Wolfe in 1906, the model for Steve Gant, who "had a piece of tough suet where his heart should have been. Of them all, he had had very much the worst of it. Since his childhood he had been witness to his father's wildest debauches. He had not forgotten" (The Thomas Wolfe Collection, Pack Memorial Public Library, Asheville, North Carolina).

Effie Nelson Wolfe Gambrell, eighteen years old, the model for Daisy Gant Gambell, who is described as "a timid, sensitive girl, looking like her name–Daisy-ish . . . She had very little fire, or denial in her; she responded dutifully to instructions. . . ." (The Thomas Wolfe Collection, Pack Memorial Public Library, Asheville, North Carolina)

Benjamin Harrison Wolfe, 1905, the model for Benjamin Harrison Gant. "Below his perpetual scowl, his face was small, converging to a point: his extraordinarily sensitive mouth smiled briefly, flickeringly, inwardly–like a flash of light along a blade" (The North Carolina Collection, University of North Carolina Library at Chapel Hill).

Mabel Elizabeth Wolfe Wheaton, circa 1915, the model for Helen Gant Barton. "Her face was full of heartiness and devotion, sensitive, whole-souled, hurt, bitter, hysterical, but at times transparently radiant and handsome" (The North Carolina Collection, University of North Carolina Library at Chapel Hill).

Frederick William Wolfe, circa 1914, the model for Luke Gant. "[H]e was Luke, the unique, Luke, the incomparable: he was, in spite of his garrulous and fidgeting nervousness, an intensely likeable person. . . ." (The North Carolina Collection, University of North Carolina Library at Chapel Hill).

The twins Grover and Ben in sailor suits; detail from Orange Street School class photo, 1898 (The Thomas Wolfe Collection, Pack Memorial Public Library, Asheville, North Carolina)

One morning in early summer, after Helen had returned, Eugene was wakened by scuffling feet and excited cries along the small board-walk that skirted the house on its upper side and led to the playhouse, a musty little structure of pine with a single big room, which he could almost touch from the sloping roof that flowed about his gabled backroom window. The playhouse was another of the strange extravagancies of Gantian fancy: it had been built for the children when they were young. It had been for many years closed, it was a retreat of delight; its imprisoned air, stale and cool, was scented permanently with old pine boards, and dusty magazines.

–*Look Homeward, Angel,* p. 287

W. O. Wolfe built this playhouse in the yard at the Woodfin Street house (The Thomas Wolfe Collection, Pack Memorial Public Library, Asheville, North Carolina).

Mabel Wolfe and Pearl Shope, The Dixie Melody Twins in Look Homeward, Angel, *circa 1914 (The Thomas Wolfe Collection, Pack Memorial Public Library, Asheville, North Carolina)*

The Mabel Wolfe-Ralph Wheaton wedding party, 28 June 1916, in the dining room of the boardinghouse at 48 Spruce Street; left to right: Miss Eugenia Brown; Thomas Wolfe; Miss Thelma Osborne; Mrs. C. A. Wheaton, mother of the groom; Miss Miriam Gambrell, flower girl; Mrs. Geraldine Norton, sister of the groom; Fred Wolfe; Miss Pearl Shope; Mr. Ralph Wheaton; Miss Mabel Wolfe; Mrs. Fred Gambrell; Benjamin Wolfe; Miss Sarah Lee Brown, flower girl; Mrs. W. O. Wolfe; Mr. W. O. Wolfe; Miss Claudia Osborne; and Mr. Fred Gambrell (The North Carolina Collection, University of North Carolina Library at Chapel Hill)

Thomas Wolfe's uncle Nobel Bachus Westall repeatedly calculated the end of the world (The Thomas Wolfe Collection, Pack Memorial Public Library, Asheville, North Carolina).

Around 1924–1925, Wolfe began writing notes about his childhood. These jottings constitute sensory impressions that later became a part of Look Homeward, Angel.

Things For Which I Have Cared, Being Young:
Sounds (a train far off in Southern hills; a horse at night on a deserted street, particularly cobbles)
Odors
Tastes (Food; drink)
Sights (Places; Pictures)
Touch
Books and Music and Women
(Smell-of Horses and of Leather on a Summer's day. Of melons, bedded in straw in a farmer's wagon-particularly watermelons.)
The Smell of old books.
And the rain that falls from lean tall trees, and wets their bark; particularly from pines, which is the tiger and the king of trees. Thick dripping rain from heavy leaves I can't abide.
The smell of cool markets, caverned under ground; and the smell of earth and cobwebs in a cellar.
The smell of tar when it comes spongy in hot streets; and the smell of boiling tar.
The smell of wet black earth and of trees, and of the air, in summer after rain.
My father's hands: the sound of them on his face and neck when he washed in the morning.
The wind and the snow; the beauty and loneliness of Autumn in the Southern hills.
The York imperials stored in the cellar.
(Despise: Sunday cake and ice cream, of mid-afternoon, at a visit.
"Jew bread."
Scrambled Brains and Eggs with Fried Green Apples.)

The year was early: the young tender grass came out, and erased the frozen brown of the meadows; the cherry trees were blooming, and the scent of a prime April was upon the land. The mornings carried yet a bite; but it grew warm sooner, and young boys, for whom the Spring is fashioned, now came nimbly from their beds, and strained at the leash to be on their way to school. Tar grew spongy on the streets at noon, and gave forth a pleasant, pungent odor; children plucked it

"Tom," circa 1907 (The North Carolina Collection, University of North Carolina at Chapel Hill)

from the pavement and rolled it in balls; the boys put it in their mouths and chewed it. Among the tender grasses the dandelions were springing; they gave forth an unforgettable odor stored with memories of a million Spring-times; an odor fraught, impalpably and inarticulately, to young boys, with unspeakable magic, and with romance, and youth. Each gleaming morning kissed them in their beds, quickening their hearts with nameless anticipations, bringing with it inchoate promises of high adventure and of mighty deeds.

The lettuce, in the cool dark beds of earth, beneath the trees, came cleanly from the ground, still dotted here and there along its crisp white roots with clumps of wet, black loam. It was a joy to pull it in the morning, when the dew was on its leaves; it was a wonder and a happiness to pull the radishes from the earth; to cleave their acrid crispness with the teeth and to eat them with the earth still clinging to them.

There was adventure in the finding of the red, wet plums buried in the long grass below the trees:–some grew large and ripe and cracked with their own sweetness. The hearts of boys beat faster because of all these things; but they were transformed, they passed into disembodied and ecstatic contemplation when, at mid-day, or in the afternoon, a wind sported through the orchards and rained fragrant blossoms on them in blinding, dizzying [end of page].

–*The Notebooks of Thomas Wolfe,* pp. 54–55

I don't know how I became a writer, but I think it was because of a certain force in me that had to write and that finally, like some kind of energy or torrent or pent power, burst through and found a channel. My people, as I have told you, were of the working class of people. My father, a stonecutter, was a man with a great respect and veneration for literature. He had a tremendous memory, and he loved poetry, and the poetry that he loved best was naturally poetry of the sound and rhetorical kind that such a man would like. Nevertheless it was good poetry, Hamlet's soliloquy, *Macbeth,* Mark Antony's funeral oration, Grey's "Elegy," and all the rest of it. I heard it all as a child; I memorized and learned it all.

–*The Autobiography of an American Novelist,* p. 6

The Monument Shop

Wolfe's father, William Oliver Wolfe, was born on 10 April 1851, in Adams County, Pennsylvania, seventeen miles northeast of Gettysburg. A tombstone-cutter by trade, his daily association with death contributed to his preoccupation with the melancholic and his alcoholism, traits he likely passed on to his son. But he also passed on the importance of work. In Look Homeward, Angel, *Wolfe described his father's appearance, "He was only past thirty, but he looked much older. He had long brown mustaches that hung straight down mournfully."*

Wolfe's father was a skilled artisan, as several existing examples of marble carvings he made for family members attest, but he never carved the angels he sold from his tombstone shop in Asheville's city square. In Look Homeward, Angel, *Wolfe used the simpering marble angel from Carrara to symbolize his father's frustrated dreams and ambitions.*

W. O. Wolfe (The North Carolina Collection, University of North Carolina Library at Chapel Hill)

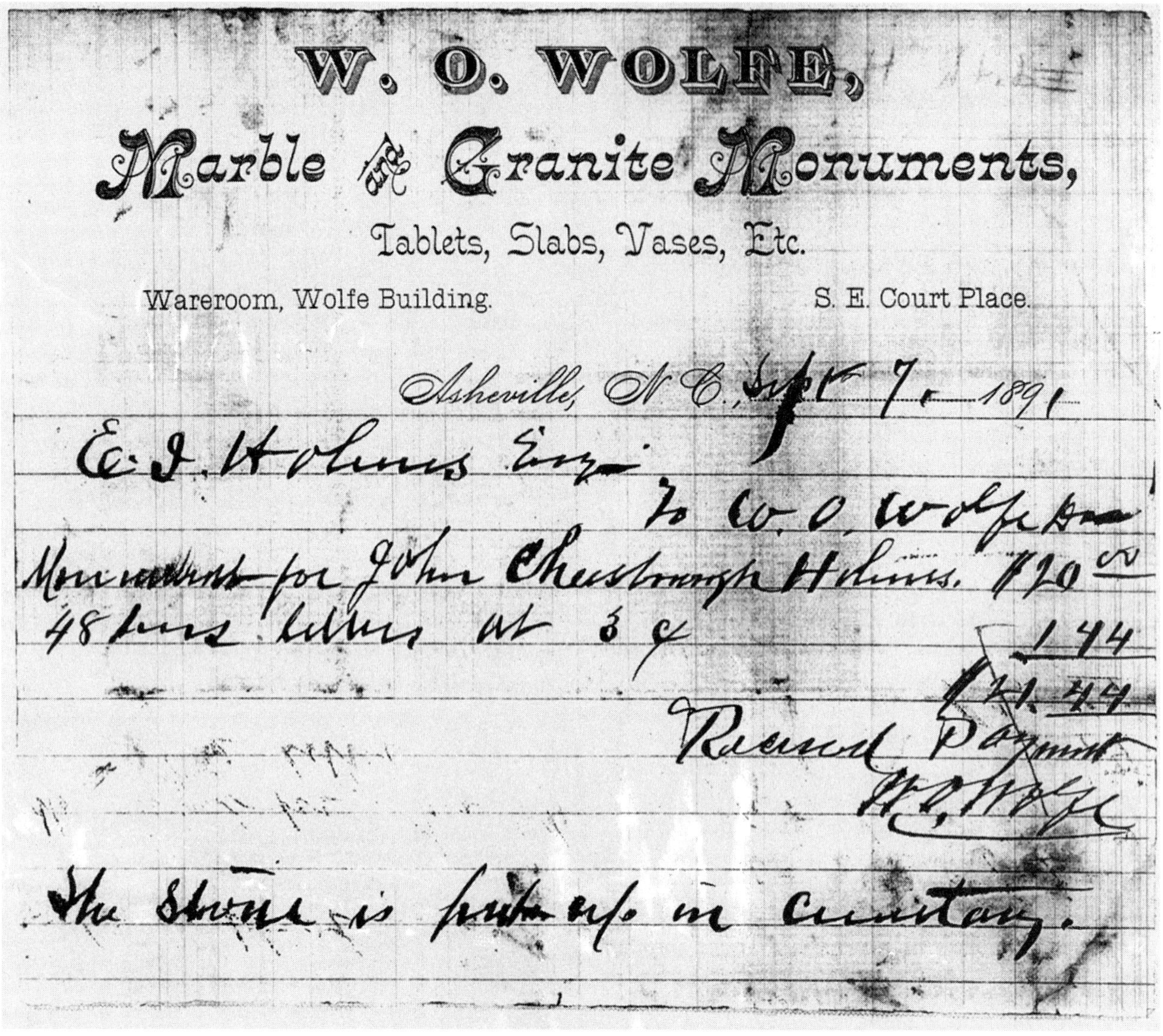

W. O. WOLFE,

Marble and Granite Monuments,

Tablets, Slabs, Vases, Etc.

Wareroom, Wolfe Building. S. E. Court Place.

Asheville, N. C., Sept 7. 1891

E. J. Holmes Esq.

To W. O. Wolfe Dr.

Monument for John Cheesborough Holmes. $120.00

48 [illegible] letters at 3 ¢ 1.44

$121.44

Received Payment

W. O. Wolfe

The stone is [illegible] in Cemetary.

Receipt in W. O. Wolfe's handwriting (The Thomas Wolfe Collection, Pack Memorial Public Library, Asheville, North Carolina)

> Writing is a business just the same as any other vocation. You have to use what you've got; you can't use what you haven't got. My father got calluses on his hands from his occupation of stone cutting, and I get calluses on my hand from writing with a pencil.
>
> –*Thomas Wolfe Interviewed,* p. 101

W. O. Wolfe's monument shop at 22 South Pack Square, described in Look Homeward, Angel *as "a two-story shack of brick, with wide wooden steps, leading down to the square from a marble porch." The man in the middle is believed to be W. O. Wolfe (The Thomas Wolfe Collection, Pack Memorial Public Library, Asheville, North Carolina).*

Marble angels from the tombstone shop of W. O. Wolfe. No angel in the vicinity of Asheville has been discovered to fit precisely the description in Look Homeward, Angel, *but the Hendersonville angel appears to be the most likely candidate. Another angel in Bryson City, North Carolina, also bears a close resemblance to the Carrara statue Wolfe described.*

Angel at the grave of Margaret Bates Johnson, one of W. O. Wolfe's imported Carrara angels, Oakdale Cemetery, Hendersonville, North Carolina (photograph by Ted Mitchell)

Poet Carl Sandburg visits the Johnson angel, July 1960 (photograph by Ball; The Thomas Wolfe Collection, Pack Memorial Public Library, Asheville, North Carolina).

The stones which he put up were still white and new, and in the lower right hand corner of each stone, he had carved his own name: W. O. Gant.

–*Of Time and the River,* p. 258

Otelia Davies statue, Green Hill Cemetery, Waynesville, North Carolina (photograph by Ted Mitchell)

They went down along the aisle by all the gravestones, marble porch, the fly-specked angels waiting among the gravestones . . .

–*The Lost Boy,* p. 29

Fannie Everett angel, Bryson City, North Carolina (photograph by Ted Mitchell)

Hattie McCanless angel, Old Fort, North Carolina (photograph by Ted Mitchell)

He never learned to carve an angel's head. The dove, the lamb, the smooth joined marble hands of death, and letters fair and fine–but not the angel.

–*Look Homeward, Angel,* p. 4–5

The Lost Boy

In April 1904 Thomas Wolfe traveled with his mother, sister Mabel, and brothers Fred, Ben, and Grover to St. Louis. Planning to mix business with pleasure, Julia rented a large house at 5095 Fairmount Avenue to operate as a boardinghouse for visitors from Asheville to the World's Fair, calling it "The North Carolina." Julia's profitable venture was cut short on 16 November when Grover died of typhoid fever contracted while working at the fairgrounds. It was Wolfe's first immediate contact with death.

Wolfe chronicled his brother Grover's death in Look Homeward, Angel, *utilizing details he had remembered or gathered from his family. In 1937 he gave Grover's death a fuller treatment in the novella* The Lost Boy.

So I waited for a moment for a word, for a door to open, for the child to come. I waited, but no words were spoken; no one came.

Yet all of it was just as it had always been except the steps were lower and the porch less high, the strip of grass less wide than I had thought. A graystone front, St. Louis style, three-storied, with a slant slate roof, the side red

The North Carolina, the boardinghouse Julia Wolfe operated at the St. Louis World's Fair, 1904 (The Thomas Wolfe Collection, Pack Memorial Public Library, Asheville, North Carolina)

Wolfe visited his mother's old St. Louis boardinghouse in 1935 on a return trip from the Annual Writers' Conference in Boulder, Colorado (The Thomas Wolfe Collection, Pack Memorial Public Library, Asheville, North Carolina).

As Wolfe developed episodes in "O Lost," the uncut version of Look Homeward, Angel, *he crossed out the notes he had made in his autobiographical outline (William B. Wisdom Collection, Houghton Library, Harvard University).*

brick and windowed, still with the old arched entrance in the center for the doctor's use.

There was a tree in front, a lamp-post, and behind and to the side more trees than I had known there would be. And all the slaty turret gables, all the slaty window gables going into points, the two arched windows, in strong stone, in the front room.

It was all so strong, so solid and so ugly–and so enduring and good, the way I had remembered it, except I did not smell the tar, the hot and caulky dryness of the old cracked ties, the boards of backyard fences and the coarse and sultry grass, and absence in the afternoon when the street-car had gone, and the feel of the hot afternoon, and that everyone was absent at the Fair.

It was a hot day. Darkness had come; the heat hung and sweltered like a sodden blanket in St. Louis. The heat soaked down, and the people sweltered in it; the faces of the people were pale and greasy with the heat. And in their faces was a kind of patient wretchedness, and one felt the kind of desolation that one feels at the end of a hot day in a great city in America–when one's home is far away across the continent, and he thinks of all that distance, all that heat, and feels: "Oh, God, but it's a big country!"

Then he hears the engine and the wheel again, the wailing whistle and the bell, the sound of shifting in the sweltering yard, and walks the street, and walks the street, beneath the clusters of hard lights, and by the people with sagged faces, and is drowned in desolation and no belief.

He feels the way one feels when one comes back, and knows that he should not have come, and when he sees that, after all, King's Highway is–a street; and St. Louis–the enchanted name–a big hot common town upon the river, sweltering wet dreary heat, and not quite South, and nothing else enough to make it better.

It had not been like this before. I could remember how it got hot in the afternoons, and how I would feel a sense of absence and vague sadness when everyone had gone away. The house would seem so lonely, and sometimes I would sit inside, on the second step of the hall stairs, and listen to the sound of silence and absence in the afternoon. I could smell the oil upon the floor and on the stairs, and see the sliding doors with their brown varnish and the beady chains across the door, and thrust my hand among the beady chains, and gather them together in my arms, and let them clash, and swish with light beady swishings all round me. I could feel darkness, absence, and stained light, within the house, through the stained glass of the window on the stairs, through the small stained glasses by the door, stained light and absence, and vague sadness in the house in a hot mid-afternoon. And all these things themselves would have a kind of life: would seem to wait attentively, to be most living and most still.

Then I would long for evening and return, the slant of light, and feet along the street, the sharp-faced twins in sailor suits upon their tricycles, the smell of supper and the sound of voices in the house again, and Robert coming from the Fair.

And again, again, I turned into the street, finding the place where two corners meet, turning at last to see if Time was there. I passed the house; some lights were burning in the house; the door was open, and a woman sat upon the porch. And presently I turned and stopped before the house again. I stood looking at it for a moment, and I put my foot upon the step.

The Boardinghouse

Thomas Wolfe's mother, Julia Elizabeth Westall Wolfe (1860–1945), was born in Swannanoa, nine miles east of Asheville. A shrewd, tough woman, her impoverished youth provided her with determination and fierce independence. Julia became obsessed with dealing in the real estate market of Asheville, a growing resort town. By the time of Thomas Wolfe's birth, she was almost never at home. Julia's marriage was plagued by her husband's physical violence and alcoholism.

By 1906 the Wolfes' marriage had reached a deadlock, but divorce was not considered respectable. As Mrs. Wolfe once explained to an interviewer, "When people were married they

Julia Elizabeth Wolfe, the model for Eliza Gant in Look Homeward, Angel *(The Aldo P. Magi Collection)*

The Old Kentucky Home (Dixieland in Look Homeward, Angel*), Julia Wolfe's boardinghouse. The seated figure at the lower right corner is believed to be Tom Wolfe (The Thomas Wolfe Collection, Pack Memorial Public Library, Asheville, North Carolina).*

stuck. Took them for better or worse, and if it was worse, just stuck to their bargain. Like I stuck to Mr. Wolfe."

On 30 August 1906, Julia Wolfe purchased a boardinghouse called the Old Kentucky Home from retired minister T. M. Myers, who gave the house its name in honor of his home state. In Look Homeward, Angel, *the house is called "Dixieland." Located at 48 Spruce Street, the boardinghouse stood around the corner from the family home on Woodfin Street. Julia took only six-year-old Tom with her when she moved into the boardinghouse. Her other children remained with their father at the family home. "When she bought this boardinghouse in 1906, she more or less left us," Tom's sister Mabel later explained. "She was busy with her boarders."*

Tom Wolfe rarely had a room of his own at the Old Kentucky Home, as he often was expected to surrender his privacy to his mother's boarders when business was good. In his autobiographical first novel, Look Homeward, Angel *(1929), he wrote of the strains that such conditions imposed on the lives of family members: "There was no place sacred unto themselves, no fixed place for their habitation, no place proof against the invasion of the boarders." Wolfe developed deep insecurities that lasted throughout his life.*

> For from the first, deeper than love, deeper than hate, as deep as the unfleshed bones of life, an obscure and final warfare was being waged between them.
>
> –*Look Homeward, Angel,* p. 18

BLOCK FROM SQUARE OR POSTOFFICE

NEWLY FURNISHED THROUGHOUT

Old Kentucky Home

48 Spruce Street **Asheville, N. C.**

JUST OFF THE CAR LINE

LARGE LAWNS NO SICK PEOPLE

RATES REASONABLE

MRS. JULIA E. WOLFE

PHONE 769 PROPRIETRESS

Our Auto Rides You from the Station to the House Free

Julia Wolfe's business card for her boardinghouse (The Thomas Wolfe Collection, Pack Memorial Public Library, Asheville, North Carolina)

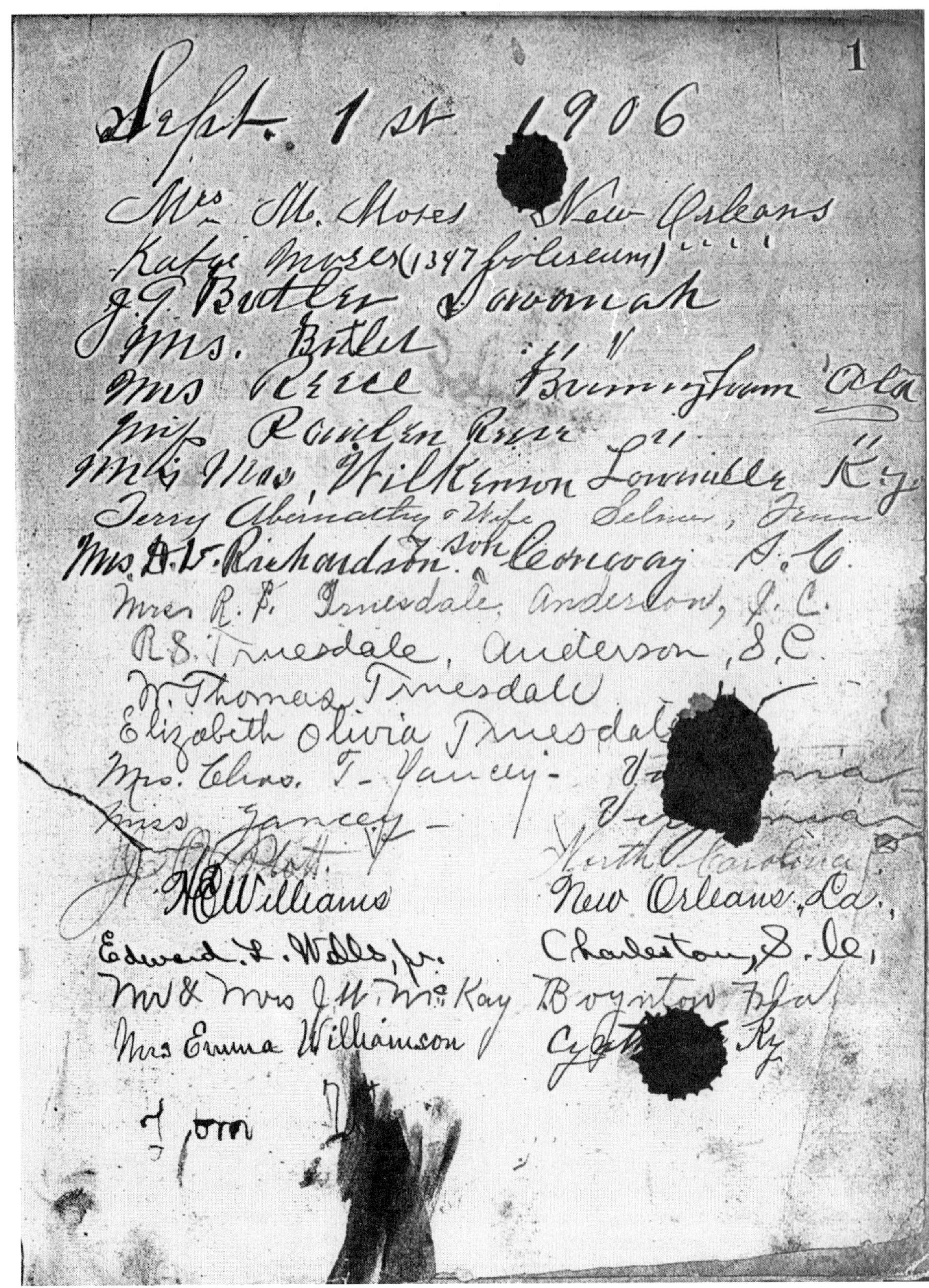

1

Sept. 1st 1906

Mrs. M. Moses New Orleans
Katye Moses (1347 Coliseum) " "
J. G. Butler Savannah
Mrs. Butler " "
Mrs Reese Birmingham Ala
Miss [illegible] Reese "
Mr & Mrs Wilkerson Louisville Ky.
Terry Abernathy & Wife Selma, [illegible]
Mrs. D. W. Richardson & son Conway S.C.
Mrs R. F. Truesdale, Anderson, S.C.
R. S. Truesdale, Anderson, S.C.
W. Thomas Truesdale
Elizabeth Olivia Truesdale
Mrs. Chas. T. Yancey – Virginia
Miss Yancey – Virginia
J. [illegible] Platt North Carolina
H. C. Williams New Orleans, La.
Edward L. Wells, Jr. Charleston, S.C.
Mr & Mrs J. H. McKay Boynton Fla
Mrs Emma Williamson [illegible] Ky

Tom

Opening page of Julia Wolfe's first ledger for her boardinghouse, signed "Tom W" at bottom (The North Carolina Department of Cultural Resources)

> This way, sir, for Dixieland. Mrs. Eliza E. Gant, proprietor. Just A Whisper Off The Square, Captain. All the comforts of the Modern Jail. Biscuits and home-made pies just like mother should have made but didn't.
>
> –*Look Homeward, Angel,* p. 225

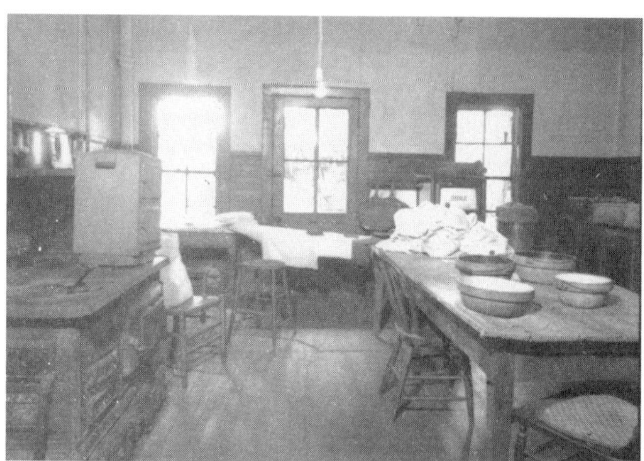

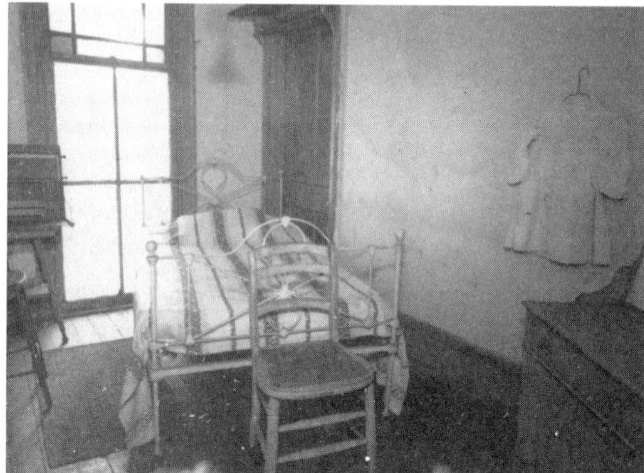

Kitchen, dining room, parlor, and bedrooms in the Old Kentucky Home as they appeared in 1949 when the house was first opened to the public as a museum (The North Carolina Department of Cultural Resources)

TRAVELING WITH MOTHER

Tom often journeyed throughout the South with his mother. Julia usually leased her boardinghouse during the winter months and made several trips out of state for her health, real estate speculation, or for Tom to see the country. In the winters from 1907 to 1916, they traveled to Florida, visiting St. Petersburg, Jacksonville, St. Augustine, Daytona Beach, and Palm Beach, as well as New Orleans, Louisiana. In 1913 they journeyed to Washington, D.C., to attend the first inauguration of Woodrow Wilson.

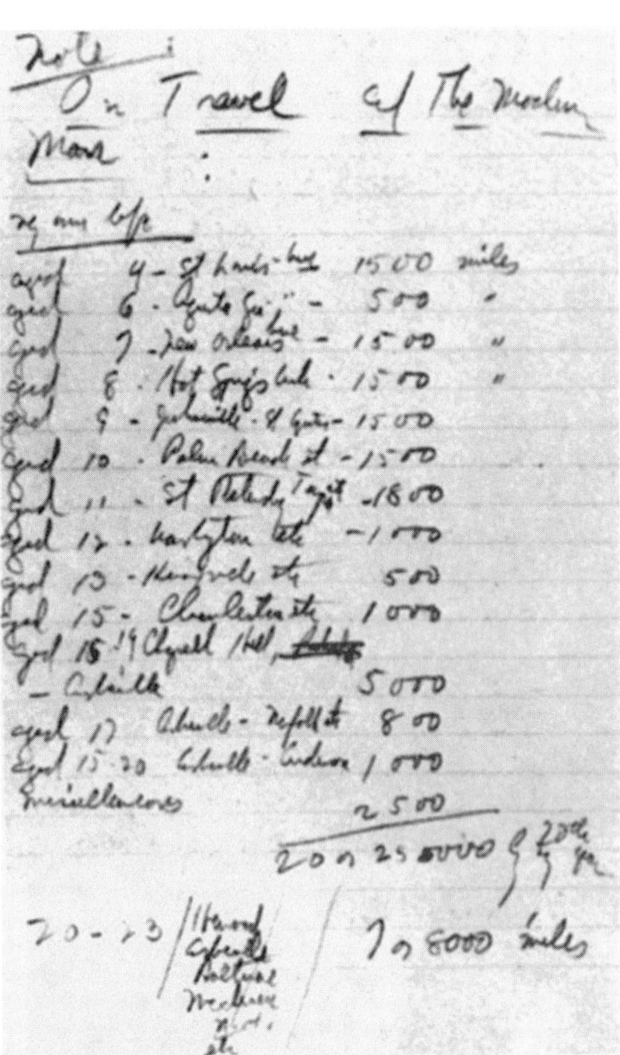

Notebook page in which Wolfe lists his travel record from the age of four (William B. Wisdom Collection, Houghton Library, Harvard University)

Wolfe and his mother at Hot Springs, Arkansas, 1910 (The Thomas Wolfe Collection, Pack Memorial Public Library, Asheville, North Carolina)

During their trips together, Tom shared a room with his mother and witnessed her constant parsimony. Meals were often leftovers Julia had taken from restaurants.

Did the trip to Florida (1909) follow on Papa's return from Hot Springs–or was it year before (or year later). My trip to Augusta with Papa–that early autumn–The trip with Mama during this period–Humiliation over her stinginess–the incessant wrangling–and the rolls and bread in the bedroom.

–*Autobiographical Outline*, pp. 7–8

Two views of Asheville–Wolfe's "Altamont"–as it appeared when he was a child (The North Carolina Collection, Pack Memorial Public Library, Asheville, North Carolina)

Pack Square, circa 1900. For Thomas Wolfe, the square was the center of the universe. His father's shop stood to the immediate right of the building with the tower near the center of the photo (The North Carolina Collection, Pack Memorial Public Library, Asheville, North Carolina).

An Asheville Life

"I think no one could understand Thomas Wolfe who had not seen or properly imagined the place in which he was born and grew up," Wolfe's editor, Maxwell Perkins, wrote in the Harvard Library Bulletin *(Autumn 1947). "Asheville, North Carolina, is encircled by mountains. The trains wind in and out through labyrinths of passes. A boy of Wolfe's imagination imprisoned there could think that what was beyond was all wonderful–different from what it was where there was not for him enough of anything."*

In the excerpt below from The Lost Boy, *Wolfe describes the importance of the town square to Grover.*

. . . . Light came and went and came again, the booming strokes of three o'clock beat out across the town in thronging bronze, light winds of April blew the fountain out in rainbow sheets, until the plume returned and pulsed, as Grover turned into the Square. He was a child dark-eyed and grave, birthmarked upon his neck–a berry of warm brown–and with a gentle face, too quiet, and too listening for his years. The scuffed boys' shoes, the thick-ribbed stockings gartered at the knees, the short knee pants cut straight with three small useless buttons at the side, the sailor blouse, the old cap battered out of shape, perched sideways up on top the raven head, the old soiled canvas bag slung from the shoulder, empty now, but waiting for the crisp sheets of the afternoon–these friendly

Pack Memorial Public Library as it appeared before it was demolished in 1926. Wolfe buried himself in the library after school, reading more books, the librarian claimed, than any other boy in North Carolina (The Thomas Wolfe Collection, Pack Memorial Public Library, Asheville, North Carolina).

The corner of the Square with W. O. Wolfe's monument shop

shabby garments, shaped by Grover, uttered him. He turned and passed along the north side of the square and in that moment saw the union of forever and of now.

Light came and went and came again, the great plume of the fountain pulsed and winds of April sheeted it across the square, in rainbow gossamer of spray. The fire department horses drummed on the floors with wooden stomp, most casually, and with dry whiskings of their clean coarse tails. The street cars ground into the square from every portion of the compass and halted briefly like wound toys in their old familiar quarter-hourly formula of assembled Eight. And a dray, hauled by a boneyard nag, rattled across the cobbles on the other side before his father's shop. The court house bell boomed out its solemn warning of immediate three, and everything was just the same as it had always been.

He saw that haggis of vexed shapes with quiet eyes–that shabby ancient of brick and stone, that hodgepodge of ill-sorted architectures that made up the square and he did not feel lost. For "Here," Grover thought, "here is the square as it has always been–and papa's shop, the fire department and the city hall, the fountain, pulsing with its plume, the light that comes and goes and comes again, the old dray rattling past, the boneyard nag, the street cars coming in and halting at the quarter hour, the hardware store on the corner there, and next to it, the library with a tower and battlements along the roof, as if it were an ancient castle, the row of old brick buildings on this side of the street, the people passing and the cars that come and go, the light that comes and changes and that always will come back again, and everything that comes and goes and changes in the square, and yet will be the same again–here," Grover thought, "here is the square that never changes, that will always be the same. Here is the month of April 1904. Here is the court house bell and three o'clock. And here is Grover with his paper bag. Here is old Grover, almost twelve years old–here is the square that never changes, here is Grover, here his father's shop, and here is time."

For so it seemed to him, small center of his little universe, itself the accidental masonry of twenty years, the chance agglomerate of time and of disrupted strivings. It was for him in his soul's picture the earth's pivot, the granite core of changelessness, the eternal place where all things came and passed and which abode forever and would never change.

The Square lay under blazing moonlight. The fountain pulsed with a steady breezeless jet: the water fell upon the pool with a punctual slap. No one came into the Square.

The chimes of the bank's clock struck the quarter after three as Eugene entered from the northern edge, by Academy Street.

He came slowly over past the fire department and the City Hall. On Gant's corner, the Square dipped sharply down toward Niggertown, as if it has been bent at the edge.

Eugene saw his father's name, faded, on the old brick in moonlight. On the stone porch of the shop, the angels held their marble posture. They seemed to have frozen, in the moonlight.

–*Look Homeward, Angel,* p. 617

The so-called "Niggertown" section of Asheville

The Grove Park Inn, the Asheville resort hotel built by patent-medicine manufacturer E. W. Grove in 1913

South Main Street (later Biltmore Avenue)

Biltmore, the largest private residence in the United States, constructed by George Vanderbilt near Asheville in 1895 (The North Carolina Collection, Pack Memorial Public Library, Asheville, North Carolina)

Parade of elephants on Pack Square, circa 1909. Wolfe incorporated his memories of the circuses that came to Asheville in his 1935 short story "Circus at Dawn" (The North Carolina Collection, Pack Memorial Public Library, Asheville, North Carolina).

A murder spree, reported in the 14 November 1906 issue of The Asheville Gazette News, *later provided Wolfe with key material for his fiction.*

Negro Desperado Kills Two Officers and Two Negroes

Officers Blackstock and Bailey Die in the Performance of Duty, and Captain Page is Wounded–Horrible Tragedies of a Night.

BLOOD-MADMAN HAD POWERFUL SAVAGE RIFLE

At Midnight He Roams Street Like a Pestilence, Firing With Devilish Skill at Every Human Form in Sight.

With four fresh murders to his credit, a price upon his head and armed to the teeth, a negro believed to be the noted desperado, Will Harris of Mecklenburg country, is being hunted today by armed posses and bloodhounds in the sections surrounding Asheville.

While many citizens with rifles and shotguns are scouring the mountains and valleys for the desperado, other citizens of Asheville mourn the untimely death of two brave police officers who, in the full discharge of their duty, fell at the midnight hour at the hands of this desperate negro. The scene enacted on the public streets of Asheville last night was verily one of horror, bloodshed and murder.

It was almost midnight when Police Captain Page and Patrolman Charles R. Blackstock were summoned to a place near the corner of Valley and Eagle streets in that section of Asheville once known as "Hell's Half-Acre." The police were told by a negro named Toney Johnson that another negro who claimed to be Will Harris was in the basement of a house in that section with a woman named Pearl, and that Harris had attempted to use a rifle which he carried.

Toney said that he and Harris had disputed and Harris had attempted to shoot him. The woman, Pearle, urged Toney to call the police and this Toney did. Mr. Page and Mr. Blackstock responded to the call, accompanied by Toney.

The First Victim

They found the room where Harris and the woman were located in a basement and very dark. The officers went to the rear of the place and tried the door.

Mr. Blackstock was in the lead and as the door swung open he threw his flash light into the room.

Almost instantly the negro Harris fired and the officer fell dead in the doorway. The negro continued advancing and shooting. Mr. Page, as he drew his revolver to return the fire, was shot in the fleshy part of the right arm. The arm was numbed, but he managed to retain his weapon. He backed off into the darkness, while Harris kept up a continuous fire.

Harris started up Eagle street and Mr. Page, realizing that he was up against a desperate character, hurried toward the square, where he met Patrolman J. W. Bailey, whom he informed that the man was headed toward town. He instructed Mr. Bailey to summon the other boys and told him that Mr. Blackstock had been killed. Mr. Bailey hurried across the square to Patton avenue, while Mr. Page took his course down South Main to meet the negro.

Shoots Three Negroes

Harris in the meantime had found his way up Eagle street toward South main, shooting at everybody and everything. After leaving the place where Patrolman Blackstock was killed, it is supposed that Harris shot to death a negro named "Jacko" Corpening. Corpening's body was found this morning near where the fight started.

Up Eagle street Harris shot and killed another negro named Ben Addison. Harris also shot and fatally injured Tom Neal. Neal staggered toward Dr. Bryant's office on Eagle street, shot through the groin.

Battle With Mr. Page

Harris turned into South Main still pumping lead. As he turned into the street he fired at another negro, George Jackson. The bullet cut a hole through Jackson's clothes but did not break the skin. Entering South Main street Harris crossed to the west side. By this time Capt. Page, although wounded and unable to use his right arm, heard Harris' random shots and went down the east side of South Main Street. At only a comparatively few yards' distance Mr. Page and the negro fought a duel across the street, the negro using his Savage rifle while Mr. Page faced this deadly gun with only a police pistol, and that in his left hand. During the fight Mr. Page continued down the street, while the negro went on up toward the square.

When Mr. Page had exhausted his pistol he hurried around the corner of Eagle street and up Market to City Hall for more cartridges and more men. The desperado continued up the street and Mr. Bailey, who had gone down Patton avenue to Shirriff's cafe, and who heard the exchange of shots between the negro and Mr. Page, hurried to the square. He darted across the square toward the Asheville Hardware company's establishment to face the oncoming negro. On his way Mr. Bailey called to several persons drawn to the square by the shooting: "I deputize you to help me in this." These were the last words that the brave officer spoke.

Murder of Mr. Bailey

After slipping across the square he took up a position behind a telephone pole in front of the hardware establishment. From this stand he fought it out with the desperado until one of the bullets from the Savage rifle pierced the 12-inch pole and entered Mr. Bailey's left breast, and the officer sank to the ground dead.

After killing Mr. Bailey the negro turned and started on the run down South Main street. He continued to fire at random and several persons who poked their heads out of windows in an effort to ascertain what the trouble was received shots from Harris' rifle. In front of the British-American club on South Main street Harris stopped long enough to fire at G. Spears Reynolds and two other gentlemen who, hearing the noise, had rushed down the steps, Mr. Reynolds being armed with a pistol. The bullet from Harris' gun went close to Mr. Reynolds' head.

Last Seen of Him

Harris continued his flight down South Main toward Biltmore. In front of Pelham's pharmacy Harris fired through a plate glass window. Further on and almost in front of the Southern Express company's office a man named Kelsey Bell, who roomed on the third floor, raised the window and looked out. He saw no one coming down the street, but turning saw Harris almost directly beneath him. At the same instant Harris saw Mr. Bell and throwing the gun to his shoulder fired. The bullet crashed through a pane of glass just over Mr. Bell's head. Harris then ran on down the street and this was the last seen of him.

After Mr. Page had secured a supply of ammunition from the police department he hurried again to the Square and found that Mr. Bailey had been killed. Chief of Police Bernard, who had just reached his home on Chestnut street, was notified over the telephone of the fight and he hastened to the city and took charge. At once realizing that quick action must be had if the negro was caught the chief sounded the riot alarm with the fire bell. Men hurriedly responded to the call, but delay was caused by lack of arms and ammunition. After a wait in an effort to secure arms the doors of the Asheville Hardware company were broken in and rifles and shotguns were secured. Claybrook James arrived on the scene shortly after this and gave his hearty approval of the course. Already a posse had been formed and men were on the track of the negro.

Posses Formed

Shortly afterwards posses were formed and lead by Patrolman Williams and Police Captain Taylor and also Patrolmen Adams, Lyda, Williams and Lominac. The officers were sent to the mountains east of the city and all night searched the regions round about. Chief of Police Bernard endeavored to get into communication with Mayor Barnard over the telephone but the wires were crossed and no service could be had.

Railroad Men Prompt

Fearing that the negro would take to the railroad Chief Bernard called the dispatcher's office of the Asheville division. B. O. Chapman, a dispatcher, was on duty there. He was quickly acquainted with the night's horrible tragedy and asked to render assistance. And he did. Taking the matter into his own hands Mr. Chapman notified every station on the Asheville division requesting that all trains be searched. The railroad men–always foremost in times of need–responded manfully and every conductor and every trainman went through the trains, freight boxes and passenger coaches, on the lookout for the murderer. So thorough and so prompt were searches conducted that it is certain Harris has not departed by railroad. In addition to notifying all telegraph stations and all trainmen Mr. Chapman called a special train from Spartanburg to bring bloodhounds to Asheville. The special train composed of an engine and one car, from Spartanburg to Asheville, including a wait at Tryon, was made in quick time. The train pulled out of Spartanburg at 3 o'clock this morning and arriving at Tryon was forced to wait there until the bloodhound could be brought in from the country. The special pulled into the Biltmore yard at 6 o'clock this morning and the bloodhound was soon set to work.

Scenes on Streets

At an early hour this morning the main streets of the city and Pack square were thronged with people. Men armed with rifles and shotguns found their way to police headquarters, ready and eager to go on a hunt for the desperate negro. For an hour or more Asheville resembled an armed city. It was about 8 o'clock that Deputy Sheriff Williams headed a posse. Some time before that hour, however, another posse went out. Men began gathering on horseback and at 10 o'clock Chief Bernard said that the several posses out numbered perhaps 200 men. The remains of Patrolman Bailey and Patrolman Blackstock and also the victim, Addison, had been removed to the undertaking establishment of Hare, Bard & Co., on South Main street.

Henry Clay Blackstock, father of the dead police officer, and a resident of Flat Creek township, was notified of the tragic death of his son. He came to request that he be given charge of the body. He had hurried from his home, 10 miles in the country, with a plea from the dead officer's mother that the remains of her boy be brought to her. The body of the dead officer was taken to Flat Creek this afternoon accompanied by an escort from the Odd Fellows lodge and members of the board of aldermen.

The Place of Death

At the undertaking establishment–a veritable place of death–hundreds of people found their way for a sorrowful view of the heroic dead. The dead officers had been placed on cots, one in front of the other. They still wore their uniform of blue, and pinned to their breasts were their badges of rank. Their helmets were placed on the cots just behind them. Across from the cots on which lay the dead officers was the body of Ben Addison. He was shot in the eye. Patrolman Bailey was shot through the heart and also in the mouth. Patrolman Blackstock was shot through the heart.

Saloons Closed

When Mayor Barnard reached the city this morning after learning of the battle he immediately took precautionary measures and ordered all saloons closed. The saloon dealers promptly complied with the mayor's order and have kept their places closed all day. Mayor Barnard then called a special meeting of the board of aldermen for 10 o'clock. At that hour the alderman met in the city clerk's office.

$500 Reward

The first thing that the aldermen did when the meeting was called to order was to offer a reward of $500 for the capture of the negro. Alderman Stikeleather moved that $250 reward be offered. Alderman Randolph amended this motion to make the amount $500. This prevailed. It was decided to hold a public memorial meeting in memory of the dead officers. On motion a committee of five and the mayor was ordered appointed to arrange for this memorial. The mayor appointed Aldermen Randolph, Burnett, Francis, Lipinsky and Stikeleather. The aldermen also passed a resolution requesting that Judge Allen outlaw the negro. Chief Bernard, who was present, stated that his officers were worn and tired but still eager for the hunt; that they had not taken time to eat or sleep but that all were constantly on duty. Mayor Barnard was authorized to swear in as many extra police as Chief Bernard might need. The chief said that for the present his force was sufficient. Alderman Lipinsky's motion that the board of county commissioners be requested to aid the city in the capture of the negro desperado was adopted.

On motion the mayor was instructed to appoint two members of the board to accompany the remains of Patrolman Blackstock to Flat Creek. Alderman Randolph and Burnette were appointed. Alderman Allen moved that the city bear all expenses incident to the funeral of the dead patrolman. The motion prevailed. The body of Patrolman Bailey was taken in charge by Pisgah lodge, Knights of Pythias, of which the dead officer was a member.

Mayor Barnard this morning sent Governor Glenn the following message:

"November 14.

"Hon. R. B. Glenn, Governor,

"Raleigh, N. C.,

"Asheville offers $500 reward for the negro supposed to be Will Harris, who killed four persons, including two policemen here last night. Want state to assist. What reward will you offer?

" ALFRED S. BARNARD.

"Mayor."

Solicitor Brown this morning sent to the grand jury two bills of indictment against Will Harris, charging him with the murder of Patrolman Bailey and Patrolman Blackstock. The grand jury returned the bills as true and the negro, whatever his name be, stands indicted for murder.

* * *

Wolfe fictionalized the murder spree in his novella The Child By Tiger, *which was later incorporated into his posthumously published novel* The Web and the Rock.

Dick moved on steadily, always in the middle of the street, reached the end of Valley Street and turned into South Main–turned right, uphill, the middle of the car tracks, and started towards the Square. As he passed the lunchroom on the left he took a swift shot through the window at the counter man. The fellow ducked behind the counter. The bullet crashed into the wall above his head.

Meanwhile, the news that Dick was coming was crackling through the town. At the City Club on Sondley Street, three blocks away, a group of the town's leading gamblers and sporting men was intent in a haze of smoke above a green baize table and some stacks of poker chips. The phone rang. The call was for Wilson Redmond, the police court magistrate.

Wilson listened for a moment, then hung the phone up casually. "Come on, Jim," he said in casual tones to a crony, Jim McIntyre, "there's a crazy nigger loose. He's shooting up the town. Let's go get him." And with the same nonchalance he thrust his arms into the overcoat which the white-jacketed negro held for him, put on his tall silk hat, took up his cane, pulled out his gloves, and started to depart. Wilson, like his comrade, had been drinking.

As if they were going to a wedding party, the two men went out into the deserted, snow-white streets, turned at the corner by the post office, and started up the street towards the Square. As they reached the Square and turned into it they heard Dick's shot into the launchroom and the crash of glass.

"There he is, Jim!" said Wilson Redmond happily. "Now I'll have some fun. Let's go get him." The two gentlemen moved rapidly across the Square and into South Main Street.

Dick kept coming on, steadily, at his tireless, easy stride, straight up the middle of the street. Wilson Redmond started down the street to get him. He lifted his gold-headed cane and waved it at Dick Prosser.

"You're under arrest!" Wilson Redmond said.

Dick shot again, and also from the hip, but something faltered this time by the fraction of an inch. They always thought it was Wilson Redmond's tall silk hat that fooled him. The bullet drilled a hole right through the top of Judge Redmond's tall silk hat, and it went flying away. Wilson Redmond faded into the doorway of a building and fervently wished that his too, too solid flesh would melt.

Jim McIntyre was not so lucky. He started for the doorway but Wilson got there first. Dick shot cleanly from the hip again and blew Jim's side in with a fast shot. Poor Jim fell sprawling to the ground, to rise and walk again, it's true, but ever thereafter with a cane. Meanwhile, on the other side of the Square, at police headquarters, the sergeant had sent John Chapman out to head Dick off. Mr. Chapman was perhaps the the best-liked man on the force. He was a pleasant, florid-faced man of forty-five, with curling brown mustaches, congenial and good-humored, devoted to his family, courageous, but perhaps too kindly and too gentle for a good policeman.

John Chapman heard the shots and ran forward. He came up to the corner by Joyner's hardware store just as Dick's shot sent poor Jim McIntyre sprawling to the ground. Mr. Chapman took up his position there at the corner behind the telephone pole. From this vantage point he took out his revolver and shot directly at Dick Prosser as he came up the street.

By this time Dick was not over thirty yards away. He dropped quietly upon one knee and aimed. Mr. Chapman shot again and missed. Dick fired. The high-velocity bullet bored through the post a little to one side. It grazed the shoulder of John Chapman's uniform and knocked a chip out of the monument sixty yards or more behind him in the center of the Square.

Wolfe as a Schoolboy

Wolfe attended this elementary school from 1906 to 1912, the first to sixth grades. Despite his being younger than the required age six to begin school, teacher Elizabeth Bernard allowed him to stay when he tagged along one day with his neighbor, Max Israel. Orange Street was called "Plum Street" in Look Homeward, Angel.

Orange Street School, Asheville, 1904 (The Thomas Wolfe Collection, Pack Memorial Public Library, Asheville, North Carolina)

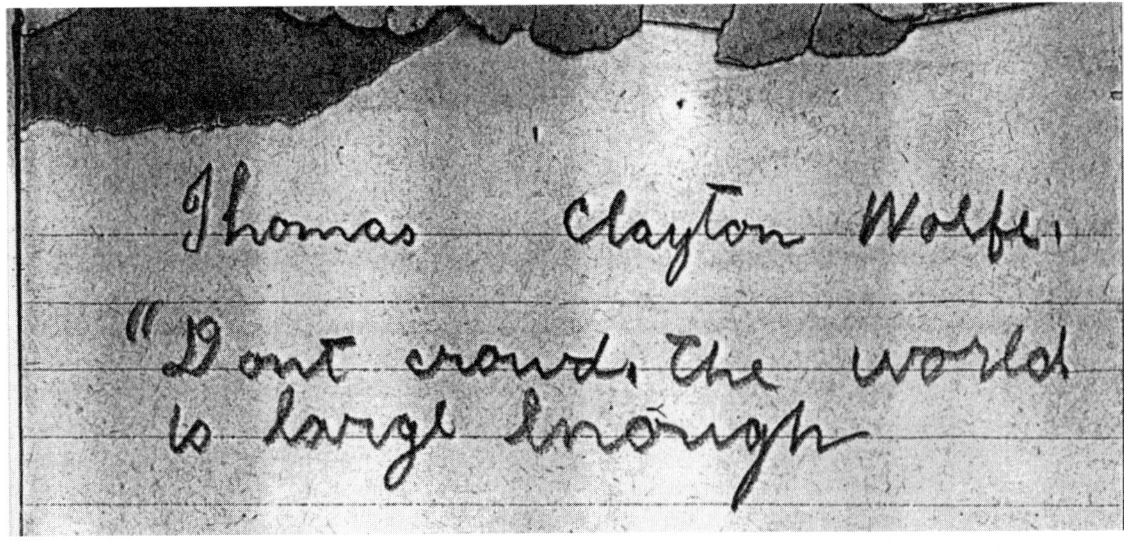

Thomas Clayton Wolfe.
"Dont crowd. The world
is large enough

Early signature, circa 1908, in Orange Street School notebook (The North Carolina Department of Cultural Resources)

Wolfe's fifth grade class, 1910. Wolfe is seated at the left end of the front row. His teacher, Bessie Moody, is standing at the left end of the third row (The Thomas Wolfe Collection, Pack Memorial Public Library, Asheville, North Carolina).

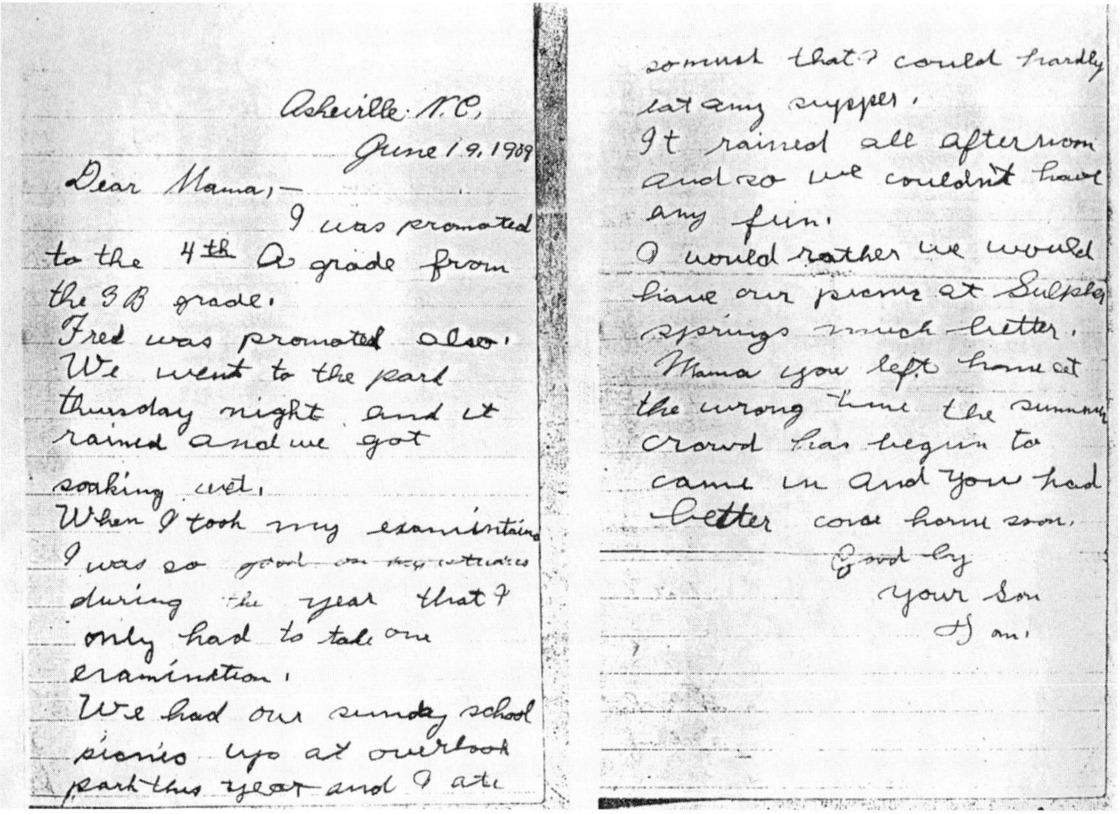

Asheville N.C,
June 19, 1909
Dear Mama,—
I was promoted
to the 4th A grade from
the 3 B grade.
Fred was promoted also.
We went to the park
thursday night and it
rained and we got
soaking wet.
When I took my examintain
I was so good [illegible]
during the year that I
only had to take one
examintion.
We had our sunday school
picnic up at overlook
park this year and I ate
so much that I could hardly
eat any supper.
It rained all afternoon
and so we couldn't have
any fun.
I would rather we would
have our picnic at Sulphur
springs much better.
Mama you left home at
the wrong time the summer
crowd has begun to
came in and you had
better come home soon.
Good by
your Son
Tom.

One of Wolfe's earliest surviving letters to his mother, who dominated his life and figured prominently in his writing (The North Carolina Collection, University of North Carolina Library at Chapel Hill)

North State Fitting School

In 1911 John Munsey Roberts became principal of Orange Street School. To compare progress of pupils as well as recruit students for a private school for boys he and his wife, Margaret, were planning to establish, Roberts held a writing competition. Roberts took the papers home and asked his wife to help select the best one, knowing her judgment would be unprejudiced. After reading some sixty papers, Mrs. Roberts came to Wolfe's. Looking up, she declared to her husband, "This boy, Tom Wolfe, is a genius! And I want him for our school next year."

A major influence upon Wolfe's life, Margaret Roberts nurtured his talent as a writer and awakened in him a love for fine literature. "It was through her that I first developed a taste for good literature which opened up a shining El Dorado for me." Wolfe alienated the Robertses with his portrait of Mr. Roberts as the brutal, dull-witted schoolmaster in Look Homeward, Angel.

John Munsey Roberts, circa 1908 (Collection of Ted Mitchell)

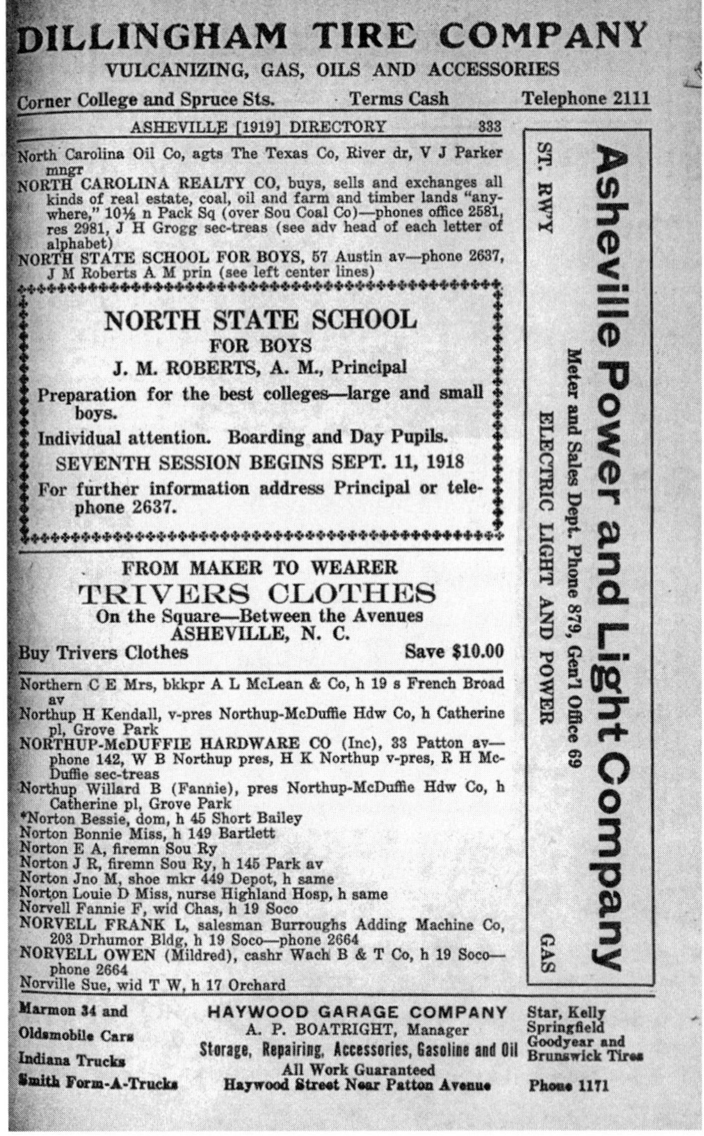

DILLINGHAM TIRE COMPANY
VULCANIZING, GAS, OILS AND ACCESSORIES
Corner College and Spruce Sts. Terms Cash Telephone 2111

ASHEVILLE [1919] DIRECTORY 333

North Carolina Oil Co, agts The Texas Co, River dr, V J Parker mngr
NORTH CAROLINA REALTY CO, buys, sells and exchanges all kinds of real estate, coal, oil and farm and timber lands "anywhere," 10½ n Pack Sq (over Sou Coal Co)—phones office 2581, res 2981, J H Grogg sec-treas (see adv head of each letter of alphabet)
NORTH STATE SCHOOL FOR BOYS, 57 Austin av—phone 2637, J M Roberts A M prin (see left center lines)

NORTH STATE SCHOOL
FOR BOYS
J. M. ROBERTS, A. M., Principal
Preparation for the best colleges—large and small boys.
Individual attention. Boarding and Day Pupils.
SEVENTH SESSION BEGINS SEPT. 11, 1918
For further information address Principal or telephone 2637.

FROM MAKER TO WEARER
TRIVERS CLOTHES
On the Square—Between the Avenues
ASHEVILLE, N. C.
Buy Trivers Clothes Save $10.00

Northern C E Mrs, bkkpr A L McLean & Co, h 19 s French Broad av
Northup H Kendall, v-pres Northup-McDuffie Hdw Co, h Catherine pl, Grove Park
NORTHUP-McDUFFIE HARDWARE CO (Inc), 33 Patton av—phone 142, W B Northup pres, H K Northup v-pres, R H McDuffie sec-treas
Northup Willard B (Fannie), pres Northup-McDuffie Hdw Co, h Catherine pl, Grove Park
*Norton Bessie, dom, h 45 Short Bailey
Norton Bonnie Miss, h 149 Bartlett
Norton E A, firemn Sou Ry
Norton J R, firemn Sou Ry, h 145 Park av
Norton Jno M, shoe mkr 449 Depot, h same
Norton Louie D Miss, nurse Highland Hosp, h same
Norvell Fannie F, wid Chas, h 19 Soco
NORVELL FRANK L, salesman Burroughs Adding Machine Co, 203 Drhumor Bldg, h 19 Soco—phone 2664
NORVELL OWEN (Mildred), cashr Wach B & T Co, h 19 Soco—phone 2664
Norville Sue, wid T W, h 17 Orchard

Asheville Power and Light Company
ST. RWY
Meter and Sales Dept. Phone 879, Gen'l Office 69
ELECTRIC LIGHT AND POWER
GAS

Marmon 34 and Oldsmobile Cars
Indiana Trucks
Smith Form-A-Trucks
HAYWOOD GARAGE COMPANY
A. P. BOATRIGHT, Manager
Storage, Repairing, Accessories, Gasoline and Oil
All Work Guaranteed
Haywood Street Near Patton Avenue
Star, Kelly Springfield Goodyear and Brunswick Tires
Phone 1171

Asheville directory listing for the Robertses' school, which Wolfe attended 1912–1916 (The North Carolina Collection, Pack Memorial Public Library, Asheville, North Carolina)

Margaret Hines Roberts in 1901, at the age of twenty-five. Wolfe biographer Andrew Turnbull described her as "the fairy godmother of Tom's youth" (Collection of Ted Mitchell).

I was born October 3rd. 1900 and there
begins the story of my existence. In
1904 I went to the World's Fair and
stayed there seven months. At the
age of five I was sent to school and
in in month or so learned the
Rudiments of reading and writing.
At eleven I started to school with
a gentlemen by the name of Roberts
and for the past two years have
been going to the school of same. Here
my brief existence and manuscript
must close as I am not a futurist
and therefore cannot continue. You might
we been a "pasterite," and told more of
your early life A short Cut:
A band of boys on the top of the hill.
A fire at the bottom.
The pellmell rush to the bottom
The trip and tumble of all.
An Amusing scene.

A 1914 excerpt from Wolfe's "# 3 English" composition book. In Margaret Roberts's hand is the comment, "You might have been a 'Pasterite,' and told more of your early life" (The North Carolina Collection, University of North Carolina at Chapel Hill).

The North State Fitting School at 157 Church Street, Asheville, founded by the Robertses. Wolfe became the first student enrolled in the school. He later described his four years (1912–1916) with the Robertses as "the happiest and most valuable years of my life" (The Thomas Wolfe Collection, Pack Memorial Public Library, Asheville, North Carolina).

Wolfe (second from left) with other students of North State Fitting School, 1915; left to right: Henry Harris, the model for George Graves in Look Homeward, Angel; *Joe Taylor; Julius Martin, the model for Julius Arthur; Junius Horner, the model for Justin Raper; Reid Russell; and Fred Thomas (The Thomas Wolfe Collection, Pack Memorial Public Library, Asheville, North Carolina)*

1.

Shakespeare: the Man

William Shakespeare was the greatest genius that ever lived, and loved, and wrought. He left to us the richest legacy of the dead, the rarest treasure ever bequeathed to mortal men.

Shakespeare is the most magnificent theme that may be considered. In writing of him it is as if I were endeavoring to grasp a globe so large that the hand can obtain no hold on it. To describe adequately his glory one must needs have "a muse of fire that would ascend the highest heaven of invention, a kingdom for a stage, princes to act, and monarchs to behold the swelling scene." Shakespeare truly was "the noblest man who ever lived in the tide of times." He belonged to all lands: Not all the poetry written before his time would make his sum. Not all that has been written since, added to that which was written before

First page of Wolfe's prize-winning essay. A month before the end of Wolfe's four years at the Robertses' school, he won the bronze medal for his essay "Shakespeare: the Man" in a citywide contest sponsored by The Independent Magazine *in honor of the tercentenary of Shakespeare's death. Margaret Roberts persuaded Wolfe to recast the essay in oratorical form for the student declamation contest, which he won (William B. Wisdom Collection, Houghton Library, Harvard University).*

Wolfe before he entered the University of North Carolina (The Thomas Wolfe Collection, Pack Memorial Public Library, Asheville, North Carolina)

Chapter 2

College and Apprenticeship as Playwright, 1916–1924

Thomas Wolfe entered the University of North Carolina at Chapel Hill in September 1916, shortly before his sixteenth birthday. Although his father was paying the bills and planning a career in law for him, Wolfe decided to continue the literary studies he had begun at the North State Fitting School.

Outside the classroom Wolfe pursued his interest in public speaking and formal debate and joined the staff of the college newspaper, The Tar Heel, *becoming its editor in his senior year. He wrote stories, plays, and poems for* The University of North Carolina Magazine *and became an associate editor of the college annual,* Yackety Yack, *in 1918. He entered into the social life of a university man and joined social fraternities. And with older classmen, he patronized the brothels in nearby Durham.*

In his junior year Wolfe focused his literary ambitions when he joined Frederick H. Koch's workshop in folk drama, The Carolina Playmakers. In 1919 Wolfe's one-act mountaineer play, The Return of Buck Gavin, *was given its premiere, with the author appearing as the mountain outlaw of the title.*

Teachers and Classes

Wolfe's imagination was fired by professors W. S. "Bully" Bernard, a classicist, as well as by Edwin Greenlaw and Henry Horace Williams, heads of the English and Philosophy Departments, respectively. His favorite freshman course was Greek, taught by Bernard, a demanding instructor who led Wolfe through Homer, Plato, and Euripides and instilled in him a love for Greek culture. In his first two novels Wolfe made extensive use of Greek philosophy and myth. He wrote of classical Greek in 1927: "There's not much cant and twaddle to the Greeks; they are really the living, aren't they? The dead are all about us."

Wolfe wrote Margaret Roberts in 1921 that she was one of "only three great teachers in my short but eventful life." The other two teachers were Williams and Greenlaw. Williams, well known for his contentious nature and eccentricity, described Wolfe as "one of six remarkable students in my thirty years experience." During each of Wolfe's final three years at Chapel Hill, he enrolled in one of Greenlaw's classes. In his junior year Wolfe took Greenlaw's English 21, a course in composition based on daily events and current affairs. Greenlaw's students experimented with writing about the world around them, a training that Wolfe utilized as a novelist.

Freshman Year

Eugene's first year at the university was filled for him with loneliness, pain, and failure. Within three weeks of his matriculation, he had been made the dupe of a half-dozen classic jokes, his ignorance of all campus tradition had been exploited, his gullibility was a byword. He was the greenest of all green freshmen, past and present: he had listened attentively to a sermon in chapel by a sophomore with false whiskers; he had prepared studiously for an examination on the contents of the college catalogue; and he had been guilty of the inexcusable blunder of making a speech of acceptance on his election, with fifty others, to the literary society.

And these buffooneries–a little cruel, but only with the cruelty of vacant laughter, and a part of the schedule of rough humor in an American college–salty, extravagant, and national–opened deep wounds in him, which his companions hardly suspected. He was conspicuous at once not only because of his blunders, but also because of his young wild child's face, and his great raw length of body, with the bounding scissor legs. The undergraduates passed him in grinning clusters: he saluted them obediently, but with a sick heart. And the smug smiling faces of his own classmen, the wiser Freshmen, complacently guiltless of his own mistakes, touched him at moments with insane fury.

–*Look Homeward, Angel,* pp. 394–395

Dressed neatly in a Biltmore homespun suit, Wolfe boarded the early morning train for Durham and then traveled by auto to Chapel Hill. He was three weeks short of his sixteenth birthday and already 6'3" when he arrived at the University of North Carolina on 12 September 1916, the first day of registration (The North Carolina Collection, University of North Carolina Library at Chapel Hill).

Fred Wolfe, Julia Wolfe, and Thomas Wolfe at Chapel Hill (The Thomas Wolfe Collection, Pack Memorial Public Library, Asheville, North Carolina)

William Stanly Bernard. Through Professor Bernard, Wolfe encountered the Platonic dialogues that provided many of the ideas that pervade Look Homeward, Angel *(1929), particularly the theme of preexistence. His Greek studies with Bernard also animated the background mythology of both* Look Homeward, Angel *and* Of Time and the River *(1935) (The North Carolina Collection, University of North Carolina Library at Chapel Hill).*

Prof. Edwin Greenlaw, whom Wolfe called "the Grim Ironist–one of the great creative forces in my life" (The North Carolina Collection, University of North Carolina Library at Chapel Hill)

Prof. Henry Horace Williams. His Philosophy 15, a study of ideas from Socrates to contemporary ethics, inspired Wolfe's interest in H. G. Wells and George Bernard Shaw (The North Carolina Collection, University of North Carolina Library at Chapel Hill).

THE UNIVERSITY OF NORTH CAROLINA

NAME Wolfe - Thomas Clayton ENTERED Sep. 1916 COURSE A. B. 1

NAME OF FATHER W. O. Wolfe P. O. Asheville (Woodfin St.) STATE N. C.

BORN 3 Oct. 1900 PREPARATORY SCHOOL OR COLLEGE North State School.

ENTRANCE CREDITS		1st Year 16-17	GRADES Fall	GRADES Spring	Credit Half Hours	3d Year 18/19	GRADES Fall	GRADES Spring	Credit Half Hours
E 3	C	½ ENGLISH	2	2	6	Mil. Tr.	P		2
H 1	P	½ MATHEMATICS	3	4	8	37/38 Eng	2	2 2	6
Cl	B	½ LATIN	3	2	8	31/32 Eng.	2	2 1	6
Gk 2	Z	½ GREEK	3	3	8	21/22 Eng		1 1	6⅔
L 3	D	½ HISTORY				15/16 Philos		2 1	4
G 3	P	GERMAN							
F	ph	FRENCH							
S	sc								
M 2½		½ BOTANY				120 96			
ENTRANCE CONDITIONS		½ ZOOLOGY				24			
Verg. 1-4		½ CHEMISTRY							
		CHEMISTRY							
		½ DRAWING							
		1½ ENGLISH	✓	✓	✓				

CONDITIONS REMOVED	2d Year 17-18	GRADES Fall	GRADES Spring	Credit Half Hours	4th Year 19-20	GRADES Fall	GRADES Spring	Credit Half Hours
Verg. 1,2,3,4 OK	¾ ENGLISH	1	1	6	23 English	2	1 1	
	¾ MATHEMATICS				41/42 "	2	2	
	¾ LATIN	2	2	6	34 " 34-35-36	2	2 2	
	¾ GREEK	2	a	3	10 Philosophy	2	2 1	
	GERMAN				History 14		2	
	FRENCH				English Seminar		2	
REMARKS	½ PHYSICS 1.9	3	2	8				
	½ CHEMISTRY	3	4	6	A.B. 1920			
	CHEMISTRY							
	½ Psychol.	3	3	6				
	Mil. Sci.	P	F	10				

LAW MED. GRAD. PHAR.

to the Lancet 6-18-45.

Wolfe's undergraduate transcript. Grades at the University of North Carolina were based on the following scale: Grade 1, 95–100 percent; Grade 2, 90–95 percent; Grade 3, 80–90 percent; Grade 4, 70–80 percent; Grade 5, 60–70 percent; Grade 6, below 60 percent. Grade 4 was considered a passing grade. (The North Carolina Collection, University of North Carolina Library at Chapel Hill)

An Early Romance

At the end of his freshman year, Wolfe returned home for the summer and fell in love with one of his mother's boarders, Clara Elizabeth Paul, from Little Washington, N.C., the model for Laura James in Look Homeward, Angel. *The twenty-one-year-old Clara was five years older than Wolfe, and his desperate love for her was one-sided.*

"A nice young boy, here, the son of my landlady, has a crush on me," Paul wrote from Julia Wolfe's boardinghouse in 1917. "Of course, I told him right away that I was engaged. I explained that I could never return his feeling. I was real sorry for him. But he seemed to understand. He'll get over it, I feel sure." Two weeks after Clara Paul left the Old Kentucky Home, she married Wallace M. Martin; she became the mother of two sons, and died two or three years later. Wolfe wrote the elegiac Look Homeward, Angel *passage "Come up into the hills, O my young love" in memory of Clara.*

He seized her fiercely, unable to speak. Then he buried his face in her neck.

"Laura! My dear! My sweet! Don't leave me alone! I've been alone! I've always been alone!"

"It's what you want, dear. It's what you'll always want. You couldn't stand anything else. You'd get so tired of me. You'll forget this ever happened. You'll forget me. You'll forget–forget."

"Forget! I'll never forget! I won't live long enough."

"And I'll never love any one else! I'll never leave you! I'll wait for you forever! Oh, my child, my child!"

They clung together in that bright moment of wonder, there on the magic island, where the world was quiet, believing all they said. And who shall say–whatever disenchantment follows–that we ever forget magic, or that we can ever betray, on this leaden earth, the apple-tree, the singing, and the gold? Far out beyond that timeless valley, a train, on the rails for the East, wailed back its ghostly cry: life, like a fume of painted smoke, a broken wrack of cloud, drifted away. Their world was a singing voice again: they were young and they could never die. This would endure.

He kissed her on her splendid eyes; he grew into her young Mænad's body, his heart numbed deliciously against the pressure of her narrow breasts. She was as lithe and yielding to his sustaining hand as a willow rod–she was bird-swift, more elusive in repose than the dancing water-motes upon her face. He held her tightly lest she grow into the tree again, or be gone amid the wood like smoke.

Come up into the hills, O my young love. Return! O lost, and by the wind grieved, ghost, come back again, as first I knew you in the timeless valley, where we shall feel ourselves anew, bedded on magic in the month of June. There was a place where all the sun went glistering in your hair, and from the hill we could have put a finger on a star. Where is the day that melted into one rich noise? Where the music of your flesh, the rhyme of your teeth, the dainty languor of your legs, your small firm arms, your slender fingers, to be bitten like an apple, and the little cherry-teats of your white breasts? And where are all the tiny wires of finespun maidenhair? Quick are the mouths of earth, and quick the teeth that fed upon this loveliness. You who were made for music, will hear music no more: in your dark house the winds are silent. Ghost, ghost, come back from that marriage that we did not foresee, return not into life, but into magic, where we have never died, into the enchanted wood, where we still lie, strewn on the grass. Come up into the hills, O my young love: return. O lost, and by the wind grieved, ghost, come back again.

–*Look Homeward, Angel,* pp. 455–456

Clara Elizabeth Paul, circa 1913, four years before she met Wolfe (The Thomas Wolfe Collection, Pack Memorial Public Library, Asheville, North Carolina)

Wolfe remembered Clara Elizabeth Paul in a 5 May 1924 letter to Margaret Roberts.

Did you know I fell in love when I was sixteen with a girl who was twenty-one? Yes, honestly–desperately in love. And I've never quite got over it. The girl married, you know: she died of influenza a year or two later. I've forgotten what she looked like, except that her hair was corn-colored.

–*The Letters of Thomas Wolfe,* p. 66

Postcard Wolfe sent to Margaret Roberts, 8 November 1917. Pictured here is South Building and the well–landmarks at the Universi ty of North Carolina. Wolfe wrote on the face of the card: "Do you remember what I said about Carolina? This scene is typical" (William B. Wisdom Collection, Houghton Library, Harvard University).

A Field in Flanders

THOMAS WOLFE

The low, grey clouds are drifting 'cross the sky,
While here and there the little smoke puffs break,
And now and then the shrapnel bursts on high,
And growling guns their mighty thunder make.

A war-ripped field,—with what a tale to tell!
A tale to cause the souls of kings to quake,
For here, within a smoking, bloody Hell,
Ten million risk their lives for Freedom's sake.

And to the right a ruined village burns,
And to the left a wood its secrets hold,
But in the gutted field the plowshare turns
A grinning skull which sneers its message bold.

"A Field in Flanders," a patriotic poem, was Wolfe's first published work, appearing in the November 1917 issue of The University of North Carolina Magazine. *In addition to the byline "Thomas Wolfe," he used "Thomas Clayton" and "T. C. Wolfe" for his other college publications.*

First Publications

By the onset of World War I, Wolfe was beginning to see his writing in print. In 1935 he recalled: "About this time, I began to write. I was editor of the college paper. . . . I wrote some stories and some poems for the magazine of which I was also a member of the editorial staff. The War was going on then; I was too young to be in service, and I suppose my first attempts creatively may be traced to the direct and patriotic inspiration of the War."

Wolfe's first story was published in The University of North Carolina Magazine *in March 1918.*

A Cullenden of Virginia

Thomas Wolfe

Four o'clock was 'zero hour.' It was now three-thirty and out across the bleak, level laud, gutted with shell pits and craters, the sky was becoming a pale, cold grey. All was silent, the guns had hushed their angry growling and were still. Both armies lay gripped in the ominous silence that precedes the attack.

To Roger Cullenden, waiting in his trench, it seemed that anything was preferable to this terrible, oppressive silence. It pounded on his ears with a thunder louder than that of the cannon. He felt that he must scream. His mind seemed unable to focus on any detail and, curiously enough, little absurd occurrences of his boyhood kept flashing back to him. These trivialities came flooding in and, rather helplessly, he wondered why. At intervals he would think of the impending attack, and then, it seemed his bones turned to water and his blood froze with the horror of the thought. He wondered desperately if he were a coward. He kept repeating over and over again to himself: "Good God! A Cullenden of Virginia a coward!"

Cullenden's father had fought in the Civil War, his grandfather in the Mexican War, and his great-grandfather in the War of 1812, and so on back as far as people could remember the name of the Cullendens of Virginia had come to be synonymous not only with the flower of aristocracy, but even more so with personal bravery. It had been but the natural, traditional thing for the present Cullenden Senior, when America entered the World War in 1917, to grasp his son by the hand, look straight into his eyes and tell him to go. Roger Cullenden went gayly, heedlessly, thoughtlessly,–going to war as he had gone about everything else in his care-free life.

All these things came crowding back as he crouched there in his trench, gazing unseeingly at his wrist watch with mechanical regularity. He was overwhelmed with a kind of weak self-pity and he suddenly felt a hot splash in his hand and realized that he was snuffling audibly. He cursed himself as a weak fool. Perhaps you can excuse Cullenden. He had been in the trenches only two weeks. It was his first experience of modern warfare. And then, too, he was only a boy.

Cullenden was cursed with an almost too vivid imagination. The day before a sentry had been careless enough to give the Boche snipers a fair shot at his head. And now, as Cullenden thought of the dead man and the gob of gore and brains where his head had been, he became very sick. He muttered: "God! Suppose I should get it like that!" And again he leaned against the walls of the trench overcome with the horror of it.

Once more he glanced at his wrist watch. Ten minutes to four. He looked around curiously to see how his companions were taking it. Some talked jerkingly to each other in a shaking voice. Others tried to give the impression of extreme calmness. One man was seated on a keg, apparently absorbed in a newspaper and puffing away vigorously on a pipe. Cullenden thought it rather strange that the newspaper was upside down and that the pipe had no tobacco in it. The young lieutenant walked among his men trying vainly to impart a cheerfulness that he himself was far from feeling. With a hand that shook, he consulted his wrist watch every half minute. The minutes seemed as hours to Cullenden waiting, waiting, waiting.

One minute to four. Cullenden thought he was stifling. He tried desperately to regain some part of his accustomed calm but it was no use. A whistle blew. A lieutenant in a cheery but rather falsetto voice quavered: "All up, men, let's go over, all together." At the same time, with a titanic crash, the barrage started and the ground trembled to the mighty roar of the big guns. By a supreme effort Cullenden dragged himself over the top of the trench and started out at a walk. The enemy machine guns were raking all along the line, doing their nasty work. The man beside him gave a funny little cough and crumpled up. Cullenden felt sick. The lieutenant was walking about thirty feet in front of him when a shrapnel shell burst squarely over his head. Cullenden felt himself drenched with the warm dew. His strained nerves could stand no more, and he yielded to the devil that tormented him. He flung himself, with a moan of terror, into a slight depression caused by a shell and pillowed his face in his hands. Then the sickening realization of what he had done swept over him. He,–a Cullenden of Virginia,–was a coward! Good God! What would people say?

Beyond him he heard faintly the sound of cheering. They had beaten Fritz out of his section of the first line trenches. His company would miss him soon, no doubt. They would think him wounded, while he lay here untouched! What would they say when they found him here! He would be disgraced. Think of the pain to his father, the disappointment of his friends. Cullenden thought most of his friends.

His mind flashed back to his college years. The dim, gray wraiths of the past began to come forth and remind him of his shame. One by one he recalled them–his friends–all in the service now–he knew not where–save only one of them–Johnny Millard. He had been his "alter ego" all during their four years of college. When Cullenden had enlisted, Johnny had enlisted with him, in order that they might fight the Hun together. And then some perverse fate had separated them. Dear old Johnny–where was he now! . . .

As Cullenden thought of these a new fear seized him, more potent than any he had yet known. It was a different fear. He was afraid of being thought afraid and, compared to this fear, mere physical fear could be easily borne. He thought of his father and uttered a groan. The disgrace would, he knew, well nigh kill the proud, sensitive old man.

Frantically he cudgelled his brain for some loophole. Then, suddenly, the evil impulse flashed upon him. They thought him dead or wounded. Well, then, why not be wounded! Slowly his hand moved along the ground and gripped the stock of his gun.

* * * * * * * * * * * *

For thirty minutes now the attack had raged. The great guns still roared their mighty thunder. The spitting fire of machine guns could be heard between explosions, shrieks, yells–everything in fact, that went to make up a red inferno. The second wave of the attack had just gone by, their figures looming darkly in the mist of early morning.

It was time for the third wave. A hazy line of figures advanced at a steady dog trot and passed over the place where Cullenden lay watching. But the Fritzies were doing wicked work with their machine guns. The line thinned perceptibly. A stocky figure came trotting up, stopped, whirled, as if meeting with some sudden impact and fell near the spot where Cullenden lay. Cullenden cursed, for he had been on the verge of pulling the trigger.

The wounded man heard him. He raised himself painfully on his elbow and said in cheerful tone: "What's the matter, friend! Did they get you too!" He looked at Cullenden's face a moment with dawning recognition, then burst forth: "Well, I'll be damned, Roger Cullenden!"

The man in the shell hole turned ashen. There could be only one voice in the world like that. He looked at the injured man closely. Beneath the accumulation of trench dirt, beneath a three weeks growth of beard, were the smiling features of Johnny Millard. The unbelievable had happened.

Johnny was saying with forced cheerfulness: "Nothing much wrong with me, old top. I got it through the leg. About six weeks in hospital will do for me, I guess. But tell me," anxiously, "where did they get you?"

Cullenden stuttered through white lips: "I–I–I," then dropped his head and was silent. Millard looked for a moment with a puzzled expression. "What's the matter, Roger? Why don't you answer? Why–" Then, all at once, the truth burst on his astounded senses. Disbelief, pain, anger were all mingled on his countenance. He clinched his hands convulsively and then he thought of how over there American boys–Americans with good red blood in their veins are giving it, while here lay his friend, a sneaking coward, lying faking. His friend, a Cullenden,–a descendent of fighting men. He wanted to say something. He tried, but his voice trailed off and ended in a sob.

With a terrible effort Cullenden raised his head. His face was chalk white and his eyes were terrible. They looked as if they had seen death.

However, he merely said in an unemotional voice: "Johnny," then his voice broke. "Johnny, everything you think is true and even that doesn't half express the whole truth. Do you know what I was about to do when you came up? Well, I was about to wound myself to save my face. Yes, I am everything you think and more. Good God!" His voice was high-pitched, hysterical.

But Johnny didn't hear the last. He had fainted from shock and loss of blood. Cullenden roused himself, went to where his friend lay and examined the wound. A nasty flesh stab, he saw, that required immediate attention. He never hesitated, but lifted the wounded man up in his arms and started back towards his trench. He had not gone far when a bursting shell reminded him that this ground, no longer covered by the barrage, was open to enemy fire. To go on meant almost certain death. Cullenden knew further that the field would be peppered by the enemy machine guns. But he never faltered, although by now the steel jackets were whining around him.

Cullenden was not afraid now. He had gone beyond fear–despair was now the only state his mind could know. Far away he heard the sound of cheering in the trenches. He knew it was for him–that down there men were hoping, praying for his safety–that men were watching with bated breath. He swallowed the lump in his throat. If they only knew the truth–the truth! He stumbled upon a machine gun emplacement, then pushed onward. Just three yards more and he had made it! As he reached the parapet of the trench, a white hot pain seared his lungs. He collapsed with his load. He knew, then, that he had gotten "it." Eager hands below dragged the two men into the trench.

Roger Cullenden slowly opened his eyes. A great red stain was slowly dying his shirt. He looked around at the little group that had formed about him. There was not one on whose face respect and admiration was not depicted. Thank God! They would never know the truth. What a fool–a cowardly fool–he had been! With a mighty effort he raised himself and looked at the sad faces around him. "Well, boys," he smiled, "They got me–got me good. But"–almost inaudible– "I am going out a Cullenden–of–Virginia." Slowly, flickeringly, his eyelids closed. Thirty seconds later he was dead.

Wolfe's successes at the university were reported in the local Asheville newspapers. The following is a 5 April 1918 story in The Asheville Citizen *about his third published poem.*

ASHEVILLIAN'S POEM FAVORABLY RECEIVED

"The Challenge," by Thomas Wolf, Wins Warm Approval From Durham Papers.

"The Challenge," a poem written by Thomas Wolf, an Asheville man who is now a student at the University of North Carolina, has received much favorable criticism, following its appearance in the pages of "The University Magazine" for March 1918. A Durham, N.C., newspaper, in writing of this poem says:

"Mr. Wolf's poem, 'The Challenge,' perhaps sets the high water mark for this number. It is full of fire, and its rythm [*sic*] is well sustained. It suggests Lowell's 'Present Crisis,' and is written in the same meter. The poem has many excellent lines, and the dignity of true poetry."

Thomas Wolfe is the son of W. O. Wolfe, of 48 Spruce street, this city. In addition to the verses, there is a story in the same number of the magazine, by Wolfe.

THE CHALLENGE

(Thomas Wolfe, in University Magazine.)

You have given us your mandates,–
 we have made our purpose clear.
We will buy the prize with red blood
 and no price will be too dear,
We will pay the price with manhood,
 –with the smoke from cannons
curled,
Until Freedom stands unchallenged
 with her banners to the world.

We have spoken,–you have heard us,
 –there can be no middle way,
The despot hurls his challenge. He
 extends his iron sway.
Now the time has come to reckon,–
 we protect with sword and lance,
The stars and bars of Freedom, the
 tri-color of brave France.

Look, ye tyrant, look and tremble
 your heart with fear he filled,
At the principle of nations which a
 dormant world has thrilled.
See,–our legions come to meet you.
 and their cause is pure and right,
With one purpose, all united, mighty
 armies come to fight.

History, the great Exemplar, shows
 us well those nations' path.
Those, who leave their altars holy
 cannot feel a righteous wrath,
By this token shall we profit,–we
 who know, shall different be,
Nation answers unto nation,–Mighty
 hands grip o'er the sea.

You, proud ruler, made the challenge,
 we have answered all in all,
Aye, we answered with all gladness,
 for we heard a great creed's call
To a war that is our cleanser–one
 that keeps us from decay,
One that makes for future freedom,
 –we are in our own to-day.

We have taken up the gauntlet,–we
 will answer blow for blow,
You have sent your blood and iron,
 pay thou then the cost, and go,
All our hearts are filled with glory at
 the wonder that well be,
We have taken up the gauntlet and,
 thank God, man shall be free.

* * *

Wolfe's fourth published poem, to World War I poet Rupert Brooke, appeared in the May 1918 issue of The University of North Carolina Magazine.

To Rupert Brooke

I know of one whose name shall never die,–
Who has hurled forth his soul's immensity
In one fire blazoned passage that will live
"As long as we have wit to read and praise to give,"
And by this burning sentence from his hand:
"There is a spot that is forever England."

By just this thought, I say, he's made a name so dear
That closer it shall grow each passing year
To English hearts; it was a blazing thought.
He had the spark,–he lived and loved and wrought
And poured in one short verse his whole heart's treasure,
Then, daring all, dared give the "last full measure."

When all which is has faded from men's thought,–
When we're forgotten,–our labors set at naught,–
When all to-day is gone,–then men will feel with joy
The written sprit of an English boy
Who died as he lived,–unpraised, unknown,
Unconscious of the mighty seed he'd sown.

When that is gone which men call everything,–
Our wretched aims,–the plots of marshal and of king,
His name will live. I would I could express

His beauty, truth and loveliness.
But I (and you) can only wonder when we read
The mighty love that's written here; for this his people
  bleed.

An age may silent be but for one Voice
That speaks its might travail. O rejoice
That even one to every age can be
Who has the latent spark, the eye to see,
The kindling heart by deep emotion fired,
The will to write that by the mind inspired.

If all were gone which the immortals gave,
How wretched would we live,–how like the slave!
They're sent to us at scattered times,–they speak Eternity
We madly trample under foot the flower we never see,–
The flower that blooms amongst us, buds and blooms, and
  then
Bursts forth in glorious sweetness for all the race of men.

Ben's Death

Wolfe's brother Ben died on 19 October 1918 of pneumonia after contracting the Spanish influenza in the pandemic that reached the United States in August of that year. Wolfe later stated that "the Asheville I knew died for me when Ben died. I have never forgotten him and I never shall. I think that his death affected me more than any other event in my life."

Benjamin Harrison Wolfe, circa 1915 (The North Carolina Collection, University of North Carolina Library at Chapel Hill)

BENJAMIN H. WOLFE PNEUMONIA VICTIM

SUCCESSFUL NEWSPAPER MAN IS DEAD.

Ashe.-Citz. 10-20-18

Coming Here to Prepare Himself to Serve His Country, He Contracts Influenza—Funeral Today.

Benjamin Harrison Wolfe, twenty-six years of age, an Asheville boy who made good in North Carolina newspaper circles, died yesterday morning at 4 o'clock at the home of his parents, Mr. and Mrs. W. O. Wolfe. He was a victim of pneumonia, that disease, attacking him after an illness of several days of influenza had predisposed him to the more serious malady. The funeral will be conducted this afternoon with representatives of the business department of The Citizen and others serving as pallbearers. Only open-air services at the grave will be conducted, in compliance with the regulations of the health department.

Soon after his graduation from the Asheville High school, Mr. Wolfe entered the business department of The Citizen where he showed a marked aptitude for this work. He left Asheville about two years ago to enter newspaper work at Winston Salem and while in that city, he achieved signal success in the business departments of both The Sentinel and The Journal. Except for a few months spent at Charlotte, the entire time that he was absent from this city was devoted to his favorite profession in Winston-Salem.

When the United States entered the war, Mr. Wolfe evinced an early desire to serve in behalf of his country. He was unable to enter the army or navy, however, because of physical disability. Believing that he might be able to prepare himself for duty, he returned here with the idea of overcoming the impairment which had made his enlistment impossible. He had been here but a few weeks when he was stricken with influenza and for the past several days he had been in a critical condition. His illness was borne with a patience that was characteristic of him and with a grim determination to overcome his affliction that rendered his failure to conquer the malady all the more tragic.

The deceased was personally popular with wide circles of friends in the cities of his birth and his adoption. He possessed many traits of character that contributed to his popularity. Close friends and business associates do not recall that Ben Wolfe spoke evil of any man. Cheerful and even tempered, friends and acquaintances found him the same at all times. His success was attended by fair dealing and a keen sense of justice. The thought of taking advantage of any one was foreign to his nature.

Surviving are a father and mother Mr. and Mrs. W. O. Wolfe; two sisters Mrs. F. W. Gambrill, of Anderson, S C., and Mrs. R. H. Wheaton, of Asheville; and three brothers, Frank Wolfe of Louisville; Fred Wolfe, of the United States navy, now at home; and Thomas Wolfe, a student of the University of North Carolina.

The services at Riverside cemetery will be conducted at 5:30 o'clock this afternoon by Dr. R. F. Campbell. The pall bearers will be William O. Boger Carlin McIntire, Randall Harris Luther L. Higgason, James Colvin Roy Swartzberg.

The Asheville Citizen, *20 October 1918*

nothingness of life; we can believe in the nothingness of death, and of life after death—but who can believe in the nothingness of Ben? Like Apollo, who did his penance to the high god in the sad house of King Admetus, he came, a god with broken feet, into the grey hovel of this world. And he lived here a stranger, trying to recapture the music of the lost world, trying to recall the great forgotten language, the lost faces, the stone, the leaf, the door. O Artemidorus, farewell.

X X X X X

Page from the manuscript of Look Homeward, Angel *in which Wolfe registered his grief over Ben's death (William B. Wisdom Collection, Houghton Library, Harvard University)*

Ben's death is movingly rendered in Wolfe's first novel.

They came quickly into the room. Eliza sat unmoving, oblivious of them. As they entered the room, they heard, like a faint expiring sigh, the final movement of breath.

The rattling in the wasted body, which seemed for hours to have given over to death all of life that is worth saving, had now ceased. The body appeared to grow rigid before them. Slowly, after a moment, Eliza withdrew her hands. But suddenly, marvellously, as if his resurrection and rebirth had come upon him, Ben drew upon the air in a long and powerful respiration; his gray eyes opened. Filled with a terrible vision of all life in the one moment, he seemed to rise forward bodilessly from his pillows without support–a flame, a light, a glory–joined at length in death to the dark spirit who had brooded upon each footstep of his lonely adventure on earth; and, casting the fierce sword of his glance with utter and final comprehension upon the room haunted with its gray pageantry of cheap loves and dull consciences and on all those uncertain mummers of waste and confusion fading now from the bright window of his eyes, he passed instantly, scornful and unafraid, as he had lived, into the shades of death.

We can believe in the nothingness of life, we can believe in the nothingness of death and of life after death–but who can believe in the nothingness of Ben? Like Apollo, who did his penance to the high god in the sad house of King Admetus, he came, a god with broken feet, into the gray hovel of this world. And he lived here a stranger, trying to recapture the music of the lost world, trying to recall the great forgotten language, the lost faces, the stone, the leaf, the door. O Artemidorus, farewell!

–*Look Homeward, Angel,* p. 557

Social Life

Wolfe was active in all phases of college life except organized athletics. He tried out for the track team but eventually gave up.

He Carried On. He Held High the Torch. He Did His Bit. He was editor, reporter, censor, factotum of the paper. He wrote the news. He wrote the editorials. He seared them with flaming words. He extolled the crusade. He was possessed of the inspiration for murder.

–*Look Homeward, Angel,* p. 535

He began to join. He joined everything. He had never "belonged" to any group before, but now all groups were beckoning him. He had without much trouble won a place for himself on the staff of the college paper and the magazine. The small beginning trickle of distinctions widened into a gushet. It began to sprinkle, then it rained. He was initiated into literary fraternities, dramatic fraternities, theatrical fraternities, speaking fraternities, journalistic fraternities, and in the Spring into a social fraternity. He joined enthusiastically, submitted with fanatical glee to the hard mauling of the initiations, and went about lame and sore, more pleased than a child or a savage, with colored ribbons in his coat lapel, and a waistcoat plastered with pins, badges, symbols, and Greek letterings.

–*Look Homeward, Angel,* p. 488

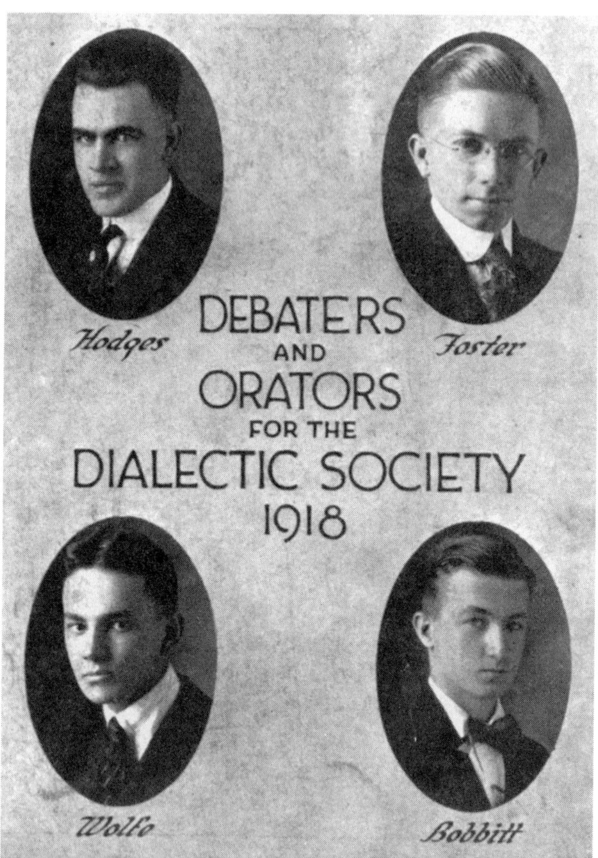

Wolfe with other debaters (The North Carolina Collection, University of North Carolina Library at Chapel Hill)

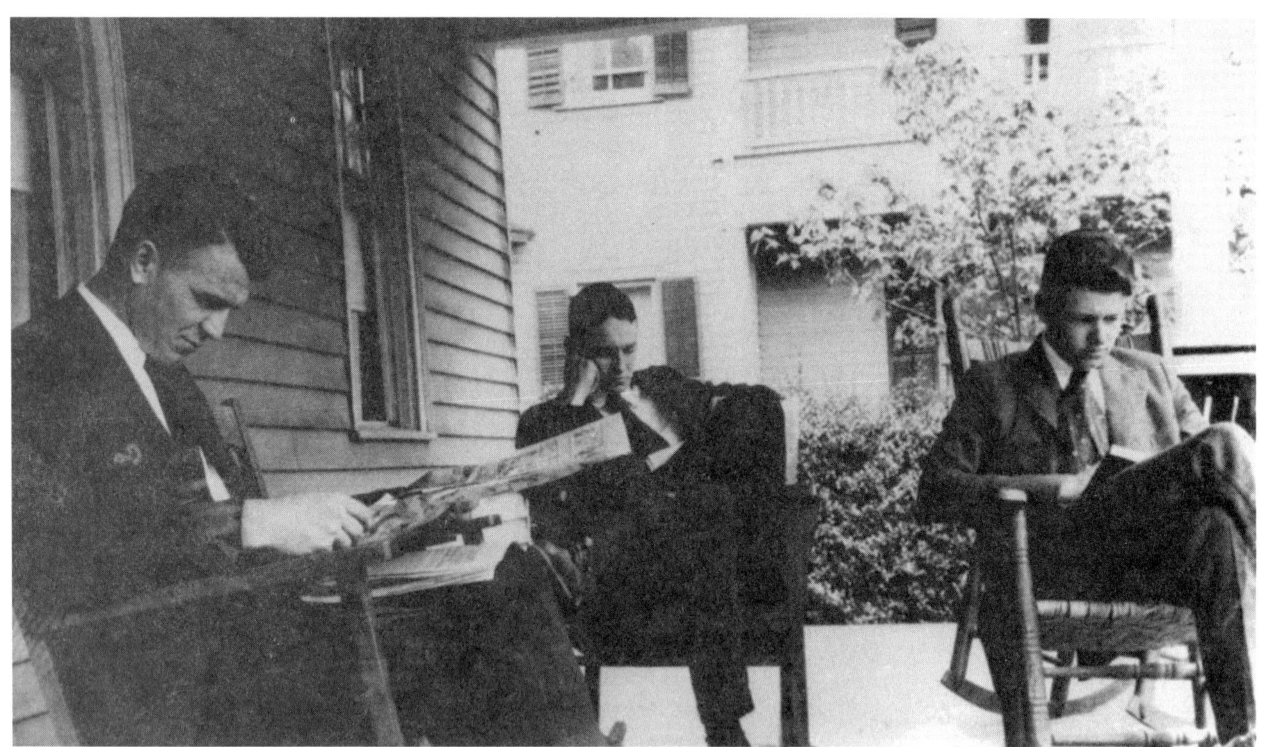

Wolfe, flanked by Beemer Clifford Harrell (left) and James Neveland Brand (right), on the porch of Pi Kappa Phi fraternity house at the University of North Carolina, between 1918 and 1920 (The Thomas Wolfe Collection, Pack Memorial Public Library, Asheville, North Carolina)

Wolfe (standing, center) with other members of Golden Fleece, one of the oldest honor societies at the university, 1919–1920 (The Thomas Wolfe Collection, Pack Memorial Public Library, Asheville, North Carolina)

Frederick H. Koch, founder of the Carolina Playmakers, and Wolfe as "Buck Gavin," the title role of his first play (The North Carolina Collection, University of North Carolina Library at Chapel Hill)

Beginning as a Playwright

Wolfe joined the newly organized Carolina Playmakers and Frederick H. Koch's course in playwriting in September 1918. The purpose of the Playmakers was to produce and promote original plays depicting North Carolina life and people. Wolfe played the title role in his first play, The Return of Buck Gavin, *which he wrote in one three-hour session. The play was produced on 14 and 15 March 1919.*

"I shall never forget his first performance," Koch wrote of Wolfe's portrayal of Buck Gavin. "With free mountain stride, his dark eyes blazing, he became the hunted outlaw of the Great Smokies. There was something uncanny in his acting of the part–something of the pent-up fury of his highland forbears." The students were delighted by Wolfe's performance, and for a time, "Buck" became Wolfe's nickname at Chapel Hill.

> If you want to write, start writing now in your own home town and write every day as hard as you can; do not think you have to go to Paris and wait for inspiration to strike.
>
> –*Thomas Wolfe Interviewed,* p. 34

GAVIN

(*With quiet determination*)

Yeah, I mean to tell you jes' that. That's what kep' pullin' me home; that's all I hanker to do an' after that's done let 'em come an' git me . . . an' to hell with 'em.

MARY

All right, Buck, I reckon you know. I'll git 'em.

GAVIN

(*To himself*)

With his boots off, hey? (*He sits down at the table.*) By cripes, that was like him, jes' like ol' Jim. Allus was a joker. (*He chuckles.*) I reckon that tickled him. Oh, Lord, that was a man fer you!

(*He rises and strides across the room.*)

MARY

(*Returning with a large bunch of arbutus*)

Reckon these'll do, Buck?

GAVIN

Guess so—too many, though. Here, le' me have 'em, I'll fix 'em. Say, how 'bout some vi'lets, got any? Jim was plumb daffy over 'em—the big blue uns. You know the kind, Mary?

From The Return of Buck Gavin. *The outlaw Gavin has returned to certain death to place violets over his fallen comrade's grave.*

Jonathan Daniels, Frederick J. Cohn, and Wolfe (right) in his second one-act play, The Third Night, *produced by the Playmakers on 12 and 13 December 1919 (The North Carolina Collection, University of North Carolina Library at Chapel Hill)*

In the 14 June 1919 issue of The Tar Heel, *the student newspaper, Wolfe wrote this editorial about the vitality of creative writing on the campus. He served as editor in chief of the publication from 11 October 1919 to 5 June 1920.*

The Creative Movement in Writing

Men are doing better writing on this campus than ever before in our university history. It is not the writer's purpose to analyze this movement,–to find and state its causes.

The reason, we think, is fairly obvious. Ten, or even five year's ago, the general criticism against college writers and their writing, was not so much against its technique and style as against the content. The college men, as a rule, simply had nothing to write about.

But the college men of Carolina have passed through a great adventure and it is inconceivable that, after what they have seen and felt, they should still have nothing to write about. This is manifestly the reason for the new standard.

The literary work of the students on this campus this year has not been sporadic–it has assumed well-defined proportions as a definite creative movement. Creative! That expresses it! Our men here are writing about that which they have experienced, and they are creating real stuff. The success of this new movement is more than gratifying.

Perhaps the most distinctive work that has been done in this line, is the work done under the auspices of the newly-formed Carolina Playmakers Association,–that most unique, but democratic organization which had the inception and is being directed by Prof. F. H. Koch, late of the University of North Dakota, where he directed a similar organization.

The purpose of the Playmakers Association is, briefly put, the production of original folk-dramas, dealing with the lives of Carolina folk. These plays are written by members of the new Dramatic Literature course, taught by Professor Koch; this course is a part of the Playmakers Organization.

Let us consider the tremendous possibilities of this dramatic movement. These plays depend on the folk lore and life traditions of North Carolina. Upon its richness depends much of the success of this movement. There is, obviously, no part of the country more widely endowed with diversified character types or with varied folk traditions than our own North State. A drama that draws its production from such a source must be real stuff; it comes directly from the hearts and lives of the people. When we consider that the folk-drama has been one of the most important influences in humanizing the world; when we see the tremendous influence it had over Greek civilizations, we may get some idea of the importance of this new movement.

Perhaps that explains the almost amazing success of the playmakers Association this year. Given its birth at a time when the normal activity of our college life was wholly deranged by the S. A. T. C., it has produced in two short semesters, five separate one-act productions, and is preparing to repeat two of these productions this Commencement week. It is not the writer's purpose to comment upon the success of these plays. Suffice it to say that critical but favorable comments have appeared in two New York dailies, in the Baltimore Sun, which also carried cuts of the productions along with a feature article, and, finally, that a comment and cuts of all the plays produced will be printed in the next current issue of the American Review of Reviews. In addition, practically all the leading state journals carried editorial comment.

The Playmakers Association is already more than a mere campus organization; it is already an organization of the community and, it is hoped its influence will shortly be felt and recognized throughout our state, and beyond.

It seems only fair to say that the Playmakers Association promises to be one of our most distinctive campus organizations. Plans have been made and are even now being favorably considered whereby a student will be given a gold "N.C." for excellent work done in dramatics, as he is now given the pin for making an intercollege debate. In any event, the Playmakers work is

UNIVERSITY OF NORTH CAROLINA
DEPARTMENT OF PHILOSOPHY

THE CRISIS IN INDUSTRY

(CROWNED WITH THE WORTH PRIZE)

THOMAS WOLFE

CHAPEL HILL
PUBLISHED BY THE UNIVERSITY
1919

THE CRISIS IN INDUSTRY

"Wars," the philosopher says, "are the birth pangs of truths." "Great wars," he continues, "are the birth pangs of master truths." We have just seen a great war come to its close.

If any truth has come from that war, it is the truth of modern labor becoming conscious of itself as a vital, breathing, compelling force. The industrial problem looms before us in an almost menacing aspect. We know today that the issue demands immediate settlement. Victorious in our war with the common foe we are today appalled by the mutterings of something far more dreadful,—industrial civil strife. Let us consider, for a minute, the viewpoint of the detached observer. One of Japan's most distinguished statesmen, Count Okuma, looking across the world at the great war just closed, declared it to be nothing less than the death of modern civilization. Just as the civilizations of Babylon, Egypt, Greece, Carthage, and the Roman Empire have crumbled in succession, so, in his opinion, our modern civilization is even now going the same way. Whether this be true or not, it is certain that from the world struggle we may see the destruction of an industrial civilization which the workers will not want to build back. And the danger now is that at this period of crisis, it may be easier to pass into ruin than to move onward. There is the problem.

In the midst of all these volcanic outbreaks of industrial trouble in the different parts of our country, thinking people are asking each other, "What does labor want?" It is a puzzling question. The wages for which labor works are higher than ever before, the living and working conditions of the workers are almost ideal compared with those of even a generation ago,—the whole industrial scheme seems regulated on a more humane scale.

Title page and first page for Wolfe's first separately published work. Although Wolfe was mainly interested in playwriting, his greatest literary distinction at the University of North Carolina was winning the esteemed Worth Prize in philosophy at the end of his junior year. In his essay The Crisis in Industry *Wolfe examines the labor problems that followed the Armistice.*

here to stay. Dramatics on an intensely organized scale have come to the Hill.

In other branches the work goes on. The class in English 21, which last quarter organized into a Peace Conference, and published their own Peace Treaty and Constitution of the League of Nations,–a document that received editorial comment of a favorable nature in the New York papers the Nation, the New Republic, the Survey, and many others, have this past quarter devoted their efforts to the production of a novel dealing with the labor problem in a typical American community. Excellent work has been done in completing two books of this three-book novel. The course has a most unique play mapped out for the next quarter; the writing will concern the development of our Carolina state.

Writing such as this has had an appreciable effect on the student literary publications; the magazine hastily organized after Christmas is declared to be equal, if not superior, to any that has ever been produced here. The movement is progressing; the encouraging fact is that greater things shall be done.

To you who read this, whether ye be Carolina students or prospects, let it have this significance: It may not be our lot, in our lives here at Carolina, to take part in the more spectacular activities of our college life, in athletics. But if we are not naturally endowed with athletic requirements, if we may not go out on the football field and cover ourselves with mud and glory,–remember: They also serve who only sit and write.

This movement is, I think, but one part of our University's swift, new progress–let us, all of us, attach ourselves to some activity and aid in that progress. "The old order changeth"–we are being carried forward in the deep, strong currents of our university's progress,–our new university which will add to the glory of the past the greater glory of the future.

Let us swim with the current.

–Thomas Wolfe.

THOMAS CLAYTON WOLFE
ASHEVILLE, N. C.
Age, 19; Weight, 178; Height, 6 feet 3 inches

Di Society; Buncombe County Club; Freshman-Sophomore Debate (2); Dramatic Association; Carolina Playmakers (3, 4), Author two One-Act Plays, Executive Committee (4); Associate Editor YACKETY YACK (3); Associate Editor *Magazine* (3), Assistant Editor-in-Chief (4); Managing Editor *Tar Heel* (3), Editor-in-Chief (4); Advisory Board *Tar Baby* (4); Worth Prize in Philosophy (3); Y. M. C. A. Cabinet (3, 4); Student Council (4); Athletic Council (4); Class Poet (3, 4); Chairman Junior Stunt Committee; German Club; Amphoterothen; Satyrs; Golden Fleece.

Σ Υ; Ω Δ; Π Κ Φ.

EDITING the *Tar Heel*, winning Horace's philosophy prize when only a Junior, writing plays and then showing the world how they should be acted—they are all alike to this young Shakespeare. Last year he played the leading role in the "Midnight Frolic" at "Gooch's Winter Palace", but this year it's the leading role on the "Carolina Shipping Board". But, seriously speaking, "Buck" is a great, big fellow. He can do more between 8:25 and 8:30 than the rest of us can do all day, and it is no wonder that he is classed as a genius.

One Hundred Three

Yearbook entry from Yackety Yack, *which indicates that Wolfe's classmates were convinced of his genius*

Wolfe in the spring of 1920, his senior year at the University of North Carolina; noted on back of photo: Age 19, Weight 178 lbs., Height 6'3" (photograph by C. P. Spruill; the North Carolina Collection, University of North Carolina Library at Chapel Hill)

One month before his graduation from the University of North Carolina, Wolfe on 17 May 1920 wrote to Lora French, a young woman he had romanced in Asheville.

I hate to leave this place. It's mighty hard. It's the oldest of the state universities and there's an atmosphere here that's fine and good. Other universities have larger student bodies and bigger and finer buildings, but in Spring there are none, I know, so wonderful by half. I saw old Carolina men home Christmas who are doing graduate work at Yale, Harvard and Columbia. It would seem that they would forget the old brown buildings in more splendid surroundings, but it was always the same reply: "There's no place on earth can equal Carolina." That's why I hate to leave this big, fine place.

–*The Letters of Thomas Wolfe*, p. 8

Wolfe, standing in the back row just above the "1920," with members of his graduating class at the University of North Carolina (The North Carolina Collection, University of North Carolina Library at Chapel Hill)

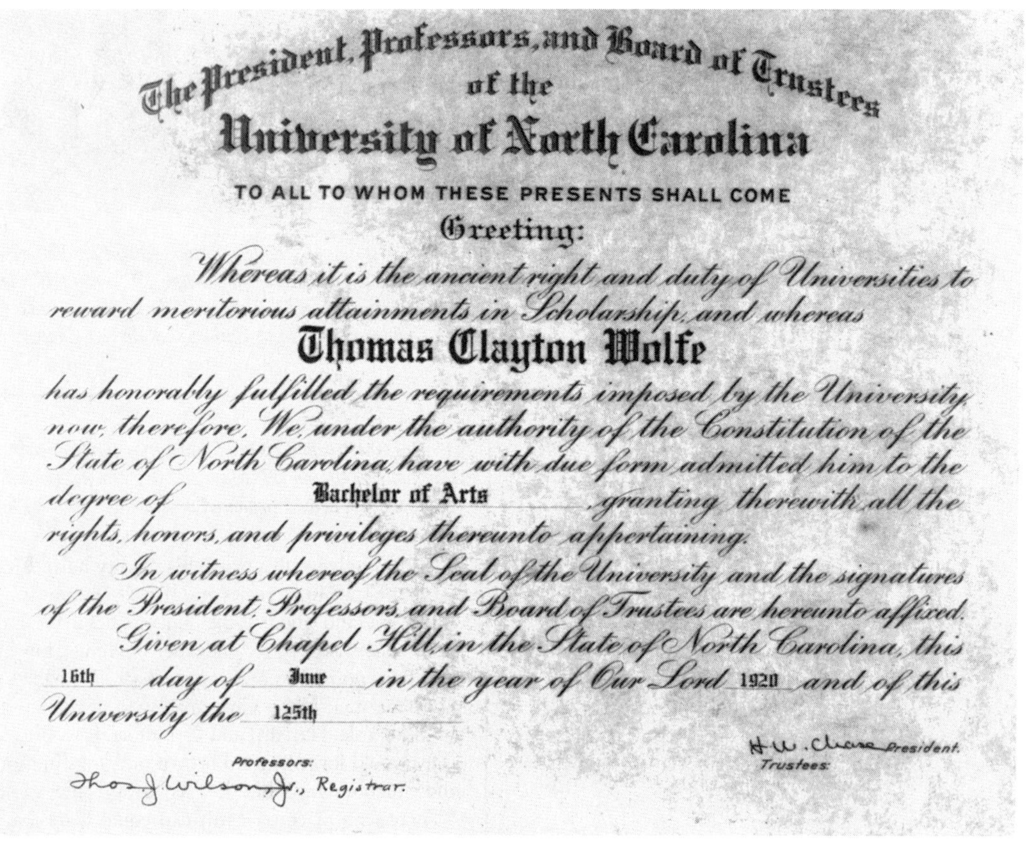

The President, Professors, and Board of Trustees of the University of North Carolina

TO ALL TO WHOM THESE PRESENTS SHALL COME

Greeting:

Whereas it is the ancient right and duty of Universities to reward meritorious attainments in Scholarship, and whereas

Thomas Clayton Wolfe

has honorably fulfilled the requirements imposed by the University, now, therefore, We, under the authority of the Constitution of the State of North Carolina, have with due form admitted him to the degree of Bachelor of Arts granting therewith all the rights, honors, and privileges thereunto appertaining.

In witness whereof the Seal of the University and the signatures of the President, Professors, and Board of Trustees are hereunto affixed. Given at Chapel Hill, in the State of North Carolina, this 16th day of June in the year of Our Lord 1920 and of this University the 125th

H. W. Chase President.

Professors: Trustees:

Thos. J. Wilson, Jr., Registrar.

Wolfe's undergraduate diploma (The North Carolina Collection, University of North Carolina Library at Chapel Hill)

In The Autobiographical Outline *Wolfe recalled the months before his departure for Harvard University.*

The summer of 1920 at home–Decide to go to Harvard for year–Departure home–That hot day–Horace at his window–Ringing of the great bell–Pendergraft's car–Papa's illness during commencement–Complaint against the heat–On his last legs but with two more years to live–The room I found for them–The awarding of diplomas–the suit I bought in Durham–Chase's whispered word to papa–Our class–The summer's passage–Maud–from South Carolina–at the end of the Normal season–Her married visitor–Down among the grapes–Mama's peering eyes through the kitchen window–Below the house–I lift her up–What's in here?–An old room–On the porch–leaning slightly against me–Vision of flowing pots beneath the bed–The departure–Chesterfield S.C.–"And across the sad years I shall know and be glad"–The summer before the girl from Orlando–"Eloise"–the little Swede–Her sister–The mountain walk–The porch on lower Spruce Street–The West Asheville house–The burnt mountain landscape–The clay gulleys like ugly scars–the raw red clay banks–the sunburnt patches of grass–The far sun haze toward the Pisgah mountains–The station section–The tannery buildings–The Ice House–The freights in the long cindered yard–The wretched houses of the Poor Whites above–The Westalls were probably never Poor Whites–Always had energy and intelligence to save themselves from this bilious idiotic sitting around. . . . Protests at the Harvard trip–Papa too feeble to care, "Don't bother me with it." Mama promises to give it–

–*The Autobiographical Outline,* pp. 57–58

Harvard

After graduating from the University of North Carolina, Wolfe declined a teaching job at the Bingham Military School, a private preparatory school in Asheville, worrying that he would risk sacrificing a writing career to become a "small-town pedant." Wolfe had set his sights on Harvard and was accepted for fall 1920.

Wolfe traveled first to Baltimore, where his father was receiving radium treatments at Johns Hopkins Hospital. Wolfe noted that his father's life seemed to be "hanging on by one rusty hinge, but hanging–As all the doctors: 'He will not live through the night' but generally he lives through the week–the doctors say it's extraordinary." After saying good-bye, Tom boarded the train for New York City, where he visited for several days, and then went on to Boston and Cambridge. He later fictionalized his transition from the South to the North in Of Time and the River.

"Good-bye, son," Gant said quietly again, giving the boy the pressure of his great right hand. "Be a good boy, now."

Wolfe at Harvard, circa 1920–1921 (The North Carolina Collection, University of North Carolina Library at Chapel Hill)

But already all the fires of life, so briefly kindled by this memory of the past, had died away: he was an old sick man again, and he had turned his dead eyes away from his son and was staring dully out across the city.

"Good-bye, Papa," the boy said, and then paused uncertainly, not knowing further what to say. From the old man there had come suddenly the loathesome stench of rotting death, corrupt mortality, and he turned swiftly away with a feeling of horror in his heart, remembering the good male smell of childhood and his father's prime–the smell of the old worn sofa, the chairs, the sitting room, the roaring fires, the plug tobacco on the mantelpiece.

At the screen door he paused again and looked back down the porch. His father was sitting there as he had left him, among the other old dying men, his long chin loose, mouth half open, his dead dull eye fixed vacantly across the sun-hazed city of his youth, his great hand of power quietly dropped upon his cane.

Down in the city's central web, the boy could distinguish faintly the line of the rails, and see the engine smoke above the railroad yards, and as he looked, he heard far off that haunting sound and prophecy of youth and of his life–the bell, the wheel, the wailing whistle–and the train.

Then he turned swiftly and went to meet it–and all the new lands, morning, and the shining city. Upon the porch his father had not moved or stirred. He knew that he should never see him again.

–*Of Time and the River,* p. 86

Premonition

The following fragment of a letter was written to his mother in mid September 1920, after arriving in Cambridge. It contains the first indication of the tuberculosis that eventually led to his death.

Now, foolish or headstrong, as you will, I must make or ruin myself from this time on, by my own pattern. You may think me very foolish, very unwise, if I do not accept the Bingham offer and come home–to teach. But let me paint you a picture of the probable future. "You can write and teach, too," you will say. Yes, yes, how fine, how hopeful that all is. In ten, fifteen years, I will be a sour, dyspeptic, small-town pedant, the powers of my youth forgotten or repressed,–bitter, morose, blaming Everybody but myself for what might have been. The awful thing about most people is their caution–the crawling, abject bird-in-a-hand theory.

The security of the present job–with its safe wage–is ever so much better than the uncertain promise of future glory. What matter if you kill your soul–your fire–your talent–you can play the game safe and manage to live. Live! Two or three months ago, I think, I was still a boy. Life has a certain golden colour. It was desirable and glorious. In a certain sense that has changed. I will tell you what has happened, and I do not tell you this to appeal to your emotions or your sympathies. I am past that. On the train coming up I developed a heavy cold, which hung on most persistently after I got here. The thing got down into my chest and a week or two ago, I began to cough,–a [at] first a dry cough–then a rattling, tearing, sort of cough, full of phlegm. I became worried. My right lung was sore. Of course I had to be out in all kinds of weather, and this didn't help. One night I started coughing here, in my room, and I put my handkerchief to my mouth. When I drew it away there was a tiny spot of blood on it. I was half sick with horror and I tried not to think of it. Thereafter when I coughed I kept my mouth closed and coughed in my throat. I swallowed pneumonia salve at night in huge balls, and rubbed my chest with the stuff. I ate cough drops. The cold got better, the cough subsided, it has gone now–and the soreness has disappeared from my lung. But that is not the important thing; when this thing happened–which, I think, meant little–I thought the worst, and saw the slow but certain advance of the old Skeleton with the Scythe–I saw the sure destruction–the erasure and blotting out of my dreams and my poetry–and myself–and I couldn't face it. And then, almost in a miraculous fashion, I steadied, my mind cleared and the old fear left me. I kept thinking of the words of Socrates just before they put him to death "For I hoped that I should be guilty of nothing common or mean in the hour of danger"–and these words gave me courage, and a measure of hope. And now, I feel, I can go on with a firmer step, and a more resolute heart. There is a new fatalism in my beliefs and I feel steady from whatever may come, but, whatever it be, I mean to express myself to the last ounce, meanwhile. I feel strong–I believe I look healthy–I have a good appetite–and since the work ended I have slept long. I weighed yesterday and with my overcoat my weight was over 200 pounds.

So if there is a sore or a corrupt place in me I feel that the rest of me–which is strong and healthy–should be able to put it down. And if that is true of my life–why not there as well. If there is a sore or a corrupt place in my life–why should not the rest of me–that part of me which has fed on poetry, and the eternal tragedy and beauty–wipe out old stains and ragged scars. I shall not call on you for more help; I doubt if anyone but myself can help me now. Be assured that I have you all ever in my mind but I have chosen–or God has chosen–a lonely road for my travel–a road, at least, that is pretty far removed from the highway and even the best of you–those who love me and, I believe there are a few, may have sympathy but little understanding. For all that you have done, I am ever mindful. How can you doubt that I ever forgot it–but don't remind me of it too much at this time. The world has come heavily upon me and Life has had me on the rack and has all but broken me–I need all my strength and it will yet be well. Good-bye for the present, and may God bless and prosper you all and bring you fortune and health.

All of which I thought myself an indistinguishable part grows dim and faint upon the shores of a receding world–I am alone on a perilous sea–and yet, God knows, I do not cease to love and think of you all one whit the less. For the present you may forward my mail to this address and as soon as I have another I will write and let you know. Please take care of your health, and keep warm, and eat food that is sufficient to sustain you. My love to Mabel and Fred, and tell them I will write as soon as possible

Faithfully your son–Tom

–*The Letters of Thomas Wolfe to His Mother,* pp. 7–9

Dear Mama: I had
about lost all touch
with the world I
knew about when I
wrote this card. I am
well located with a
North Carolina professor
doing graduate work
here at 48 Buckingham
St. I am writing
you ~~and~~ tonight!
This is a great place
with a lot of freaks
a lot of snobs and
a lot of good fellows.
Over 6000 enrolled.
No one knows you and
you don't care Tom

Postcard to Julia Wolfe, 29 September 1920, describing Wolfe's first impressions of Harvard. The North Carolina professor referred to here is N. W. Walker (The North Carolina Collection, University of North Carolina Library at Chapel Hill).

(3)

As Curtain Rises

~~the~~ Travers seated in rocker before fire, smoking short corn-cob pipe, reading newspaper. Glances impatiently at clock on mantel, then pulls heavy gold watch from pocket. The sound of scurrying feet on veranda without. Then a girl's laughing voice

Clara (Breathlessly) Father — look — see who's here! (She enters the room in a delightful flurry of excitement pulling the arm of a laughing young fellow behind her. Enter Richard Travers the son, just returned from college. A fine, slim, clean cut boy. P.T.Over

Page from the manuscript for The Mountains. *Professor George Pierce Baker was proud of Wolfe's first submission and told the class that Wolfe had accomplished in one act what he had seen three-act plays fail to do (William B. Wisdom Collection, Houghton Library, Harvard University).*

47 Workshop

During his first year at Harvard, Wolfe completed three of four courses required for his Master of Arts degree: English 33 (American Literature), English 47, and elementary French. Away from North Carolina and his family, Wolfe began devoting more time to his writing, jotting down ideas and reflections upon loose sheets of paper as well as in academic exercise books. He flung himself into his work as a playwright.

For three years he enrolled in Professor George Pierce Baker's playwriting course, familiarly known as the 47 Workshop. Baker had instructed playwrights and directors who then embarked upon successful careers on Broadway. (Eugene O'Neill was a 47 Workshop alumnus.)

In the following letter, written to Baker on or about 23 October 1921, Wolfe reacts to the criticisms of his first play produced at the 47 Workshop, the one-act The Mountains. *According to Workshop custom, the criticisms were written by the audience.*

Dear Professor Baker:

After reading the numerous *remarks,* euphemistically called criticism, on my play, and some few criticisms which I consider worthy the dignity of that title, I feel compelled to make some rejoinder in defense of my play. It is useless, of course, to try to argue my play into popular favor; if the people didn't like it I shall play the man and swallow the pill, bitter as it may be.

Many of the audience seem to be of the opinion that I conspired to make them as uncomfortable as possible for thirty-five minutes. One of the catchwords which these people are continually using is that a play is "depressing." My play has been called "depressing" so many times in the criticisms, and with so small a store of illuminating evidence that I am even now in doubt as to just what has depressed these gentle souls.

My play is wordy, I admit [but I] take it they didn't mean exactly this. The play itself, the theme, more than the manner and the execution, depressed them.

Now let us analyze the cause of this depression. Is it due to some monstrous distortion of character? I think not. Richard, as he now is, may be a little the prig but he is not unworthy of sympathy. Dr. Weaver, a tired, worn, kindly man, is surely deserving of a warmer feeling. Can we feel nothing but repugnance and dislike for a poor ignorant devil like Tom Weaver, who feeds on hate because he's never known anything else? Do Laura and Mag and Roberts turn us to loathing? No, I think not. The thing that shocks these good people is the ending. It is such a pity that Richard must go the way of his fathers. One can understand it of his Uncle Tom, but Tom hasn't got the fine understanding about these matters that a Harvard man would have. But to see Richard, whom they continually dub "the idealist" (because, I suppose, he preferred to practice his

George Pierce Baker in 1920. In a letter to his mother Wolfe wrote that Baker "is the greatest authority on the drama in America and in the last six years he has developed in this class some of the best dramatists in the country, several of whom have plays on Broadway now." Baker was the model for Professor George Graves Hatcher in Of Time and the River *(The Thomas Wolfe Collection, Pack Memorial Public Library, Asheville, North Carolina).*

profession rather than go out and shoot his neighbors–surely a normal desire)–to see him crack after all his fine talk, is more than they can bear. Dear me!

All I have to do to please these people is to change the ending slightly. Richard can go out with Roberts instead of with his father. Tom Weaver can slink off with a beaten look on his face, and the curtain speech can be given to Dr. Weaver, who might look upward and say: "Thank God! He wins where I have failed." The cause of depression having been thus removed by these slight changes, the curtain can descend leaving an audience to go home in a happy frame of mind, knowing that virtue and the higher education has triumphed, and myself–to go out and jump in the Charles River. This can never be! My show is over, they will not have to suffer again, but, even now, they can't egg me into changing the ending.

If the audience is depressed over my play, I am depressed over my audience. Good God! What do they want? What would they have me do? Are these people so wrapped in cotton-wool that they are unwilling to face the inevitable fact of defeat in a struggle like this? Let me write a contemptible little epic to small-town mean-ness (a favorite theme nowadays) in which the principal goes down to defeat from the parlor-and-gate slander of spinsters, and they will applaud me to the echo: "This is life! This is reality! This is a play of great and vital forces!" But let a man go down in a monster struggle with such epic things as mountains, and it is merely depressing and sordidly realistic. They can see no poetry to such a fight.

Why should I bother myself about all this any-way? I would like to be lofty and above such criticism, to feel like a statue attacked by a swarm of wasps, but these things [____?] and goad me. I sweated decent honest blood on what I thought was a decent, honest play. If my motive was that, I at least deserved a decent, honest criticism. I'm no pachyderm.

There was also considerable talk about my "psychology" and my "philosophy" in this play. If I've got to deal with this jargon, let me make my peace with all the "subtle-souled psychologists" straightway. Must I be accused of expressing my own personal philosophy in every play I write? Must an opinion uttered by one of my characters be taken from his mouth and put into mine, as an official credo? One critic found fault with a statement of Richard's to the effect that "a man may leave the sea or the town or the country, but it isn't often he leaves the mountains." Why blame me for such a statement? I didn't say it. Richard said it. Yet the critic would debate with me regarding the truth of an opinion uttered by a person with an antipathy toward his environment occasioned by what he believes to be the very holding power of that environment. Richard said he hated the mountains. I've never said any such thing. Weaver saw no beauty there. I see great beauty. Tom Weaver expressed faith in the curative quality of gun-shot to heal inter-family disorders. I hope I may be accused of no such "philosophy" for it seems that every stray observation is sure to be dignified as philosophy.

Others don't understand what they call the "psychology" of Richard. They can't understand how he could express the opinions and convictions he had, and yet give in at the end. If we must fool with "psychology" here, let me say that Richard's giving in has not to do with the psychology of an individual. It has to do with the psychology of a circumstance and a situation. To listen to such criticism, one would think that Richard was free to do as he chose, yet the whole struggle of the play is the struggle between his inner conviction and the other pressure. And the outer pressure wins.

If even this is lost on them–this, the one vital thing in the play–then indeed I am the most wretched and miserable of bungling pen-pushers and should know enough to quit now before I get to the point where people will say: "You had better have died when you were a little boy."

I don't know whether it be ungracious and unbecoming to fly my colors in the faces of my critics, but if they expect me to sit quietly by and chew the cud in the face of such nincompoop criticism, they are far wide of the mark. The crowning insult of all came when my play was put in the same category with "Time Will Tell." I thank God that the far-reaching wisdom of the founders saw fit to remove the names from the criticisms, for if I knew who wrote that, I would no longer be responsible for my actions.

–*The Letters of Thomas Wolfe,* pp. 19–21

Wolfe and Kenneth Raisbeck, circa 1921. Wolfe's closest friend in the 47 Workshop, Raisbeck failed to live up to his early promise as a playwright. "He had no poetry in him, but he was one of those who write poetry," Wolfe wrote in his notebook. He had "no sinew of creation, but he was one of those who go piously through the ritual of creating."

Oh, will you ever return to me,
my wild first power, will you return
When the old madness comes to
flicker in me and to burn
Slow in my brain like a slow fire
in a blackened brazier — dull like a
smear of blood,
Humid and hot and evil, slow-sweltering
up in a flood!
Oh, will you not come back
Oh, will you not come back,
again — will you not
my fierce song?

An untitled poem Wolfe wrote while at Harvard (William B. Wisdom Collection, Houghton Library, Harvard University)

Wolfe found the Widener Library at Harvard a source of surcease. He rewrote these pages from his notebook to describe Eugene Gant's ingurgitating the volumes of the Widener Library in Of Time and the River.

The interior of a great library–the shelves are lost in darkness above, and to either side they run off to infinity. They bend over, over, over as if they will whelm and crush the figure of Eugene who sits at a small table in the center with a white wedge of light which falls upon him. Books are piled high upon the table before him. Many lie open around him, and the one which he holds in his hand, he reads with savage voracity, with inconceivable rapidity, with terrific intensity. He throws it aside and plunges into another.

EUGENE. Of Shakespeare's plays alone in this library there are hundreds of editions, over five thousand separate copies. If I read one edition, I have read them all. Now there are here one million books in all–5000 into a million goes but 200 times. But I am reading 10 a day. In 20 days I would have finished. That won't do it.

Other men read books–I read libraries. Other men read books–I invade them. Other men taste–I swallow the whole.

I shall make one globe, not of my learning but of all learning. I shall make one globe, not of my life but of all life. I shall seize and possess the whole.

On the street today I must have passed a full hundred thousand of people. How {able?} were all the things they said! In a year's time that would be 36,000,000. In three years I would have touched the country.

My brain is giddy, my senses numbed, but my heart is filled with exulting joy. O God, O God, let me taste and know all life; make me the reed through which all winds must blow, the silver horn which plays both high and low.

As swift as a swallow,
As light as a flame,
What melodious sweetness,
What harmonious joy
Strange symphonies of *[breaks off]*

–*The Notebooks of Thomas Wolfe,* p. 23

The merciless dissection of books–probing the bowels of a man's writing–The table, paper, writing materials–all as good as theirs–The constant quest in bad books for good things–The book shops–Religious tracts–With a watch in one hand–to scan a page–The Farnsworth Room in The Widener Library–The laying waste of the shelves–The old lady who acted as Librarian–Her companion–On living abroad–

–*The Autobiographical Outline,* pp. 64–65

Universitas Harvardiana
Cantabrigiae in Civitate Massachusettensi,
Omnibus ad quos hae Litterae pervenerint Salutem in Domino sempiternam.
Nos Praeses et Socii Collegii Harvardiani, consentientibus honorandis ac reverendis Universitatis Inspectoribus in Comitiis sollemnibus
Thomam Clayton Wolfe
ad gradum Magistri in Artibus admisimus, eique dedimus et concessimus omnia insignia et iura ad hunc honorem spectantia.
In cuius rei testimonium litteris hisce Universitatis sigillo munitis die Iunii XXII anno Salutis Humanae MDCCCCXXII Reique publicae Americanae
Nos Praeses et Decanus Ordinis Academici, auctoritate nobis commissa nomina subscripsimus.
L. B. R. Briggs Decanus. A. L. Lowell. Praeses.

Wolfe's Master of Arts diploma, Harvard University, 1922 (The North Carolina Collection, University of North Carolina Library at Chapel Hill)

Wolfe received his M.A. degree in June 1922, but he wanted to continue to work with Professor Baker. After his father's death on 20 June 1922, Wolfe managed to secure his mother's support to enroll in the 47 Workshop for a third year. He began writing "Niggertown," which became Welcome to Our City. *In his excerpt from his 4 January 1923 letter to his mother, Wolfe discusses the impact of the deaths of his father and brother Ben.*

There is something sad and terrifying about big families. I think often of my childhood lately; of those warm hours in bed of winter mornings; of the first ringing of the Orange St. bell; of papa's big voice shouting from the foot of the stair "Get up, boy," then of the rush down stair like a cold rabbit with all my clothes and underwear in my arms. As I go through the cold dining room I can hear the cheerful roar of the big fire he always had kindled in the sitting room. And we dressed by the warmth of that fire. Then breakfast–oatmeal, and sausages, eggs, hot coffee, and you putting away a couple of thick meat sandwiches in a paper bag. Then the final rush for school with Ben or Fred, and the long run up the Central Avenue hill, with one of them pulling or pushing me along.

There is great sadness in knowing you can never recall the scene except the memory; even if all were here you could not bring it back.

Sometimes Ben and Papa seem so far away, one wonders if it were a dream. Again, they come back as vividly as if I had seen them yesterday. Each tone of their voice, each peculiarity of their expression is engraved upon my mind–yet it seems strange that it all could have happened to me, that I was a part of it. Some day I expect to wake up and find my whole life has been a dream. I think we all feel this;

"We are such stuff as dreams are made of and our life
Is rounded with a sleep"

We soak our bread in tears and swallow it in bitterness. It seems incredible to think that flesh that once I touched, that held me on its knees, that gave me gifts, and spoke to me in tones different from those of anyone else, is now unrecognizably corrupted in the earth.

These things may happen to others and we believe them; they happen to us and we believe them–never!

Yet somehow, in spite of all the stern persuadings of my reason, in spite of the inexorable and undeniable spectacle of universal death, I will fear no evil. Almost, I am tempted to say, I will believe in God, yes, in spite of the church and the ministers.

Please let me hear from you at once and take all kinds of care of yourself. I am well and working steadily on my play[.]

–*The Letters of Thomas Wolfe to His Mother,* pp. 35–36

W. O. Wolfe, shortly before his death (The North Carolina Collection, University of North Carolina Library at Chapel Hill)

While a student at Harvard, Wolfe began writing about the Broodys, a family much like his own. Wolfe drafted fragments in dramatic form depicting variously the Breens, Whitbys, and Batesons that prefigure material Wolfe later developed in Look Homeward, Angel.

The Broody's were a strange family. They never saw each other's good points till one of their number died. Then they were lavish in their affection. In their cooperative maudlinism they became almost affectionate in their regard for one another, differences were forgotten in their common intoxication of tears, the dear departed went through a gradual process of canonization, little inhumorous details of his life and habits were sloughed off until finally he stood forth in all the crackling starchiness of brand-new sainthood.

They were a passionate, tempestuous, erratic, irascible family and yet it is doubtful if they were capable of any real profundity of thought or feeling. They were always quarreling and cursing one another with varying degrees of intensity, and what is worse, in large unhappy families of this sort, they were continually splitting up into parties among themselves. Factionalism reigned supreme. This was the rotten spot, this destroyed them. For all large fami-

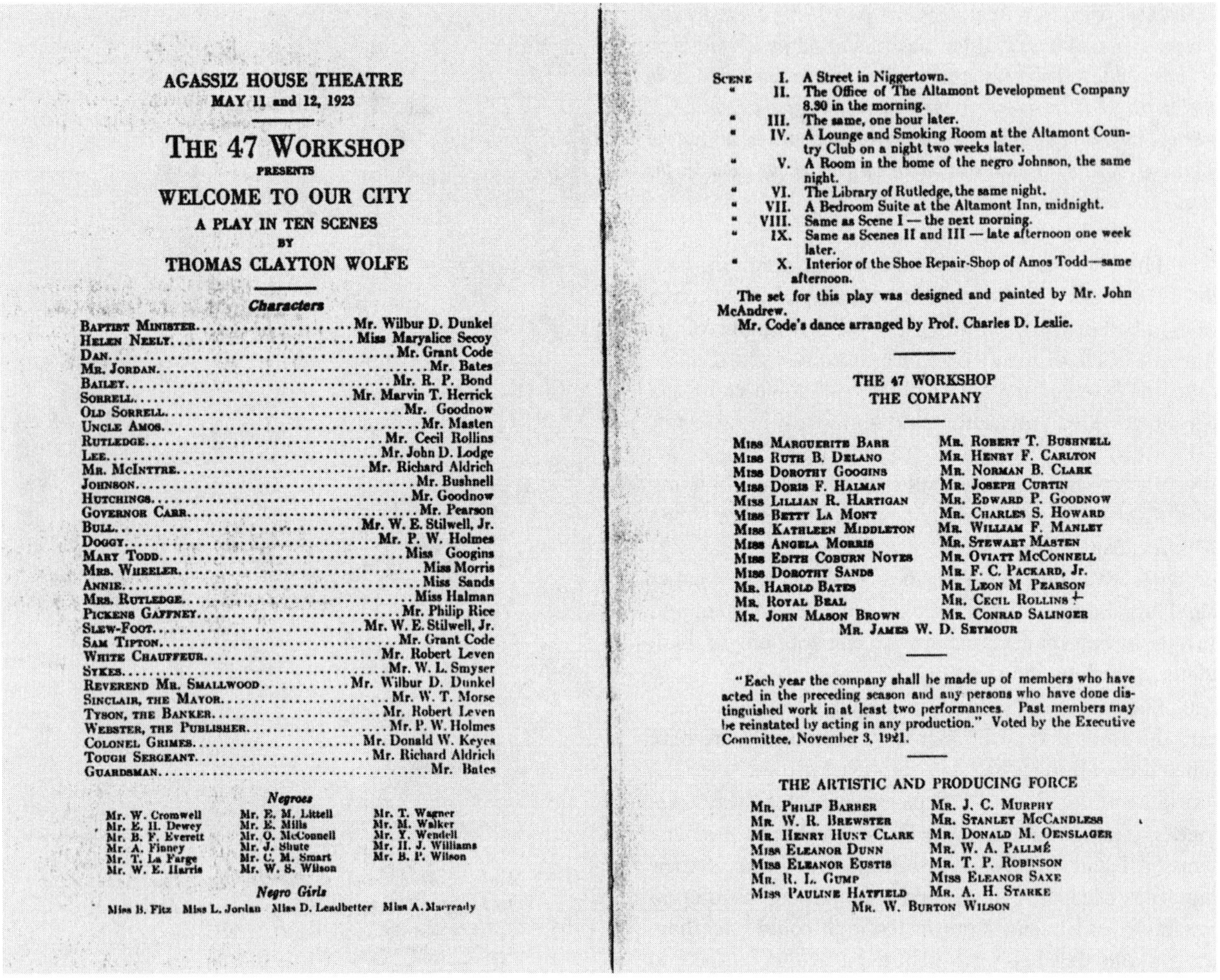

AGASSIZ HOUSE THEATRE
MAY 11 and 12, 1923

THE 47 WORKSHOP
PRESENTS
WELCOME TO OUR CITY
A PLAY IN TEN SCENES
BY
THOMAS CLAYTON WOLFE

Characters

Baptist Minister....Mr. Wilbur D. Dunkel
Helen Neely....Miss Maryalice Secoy
Dan....Mr. Grant Code
Mr. Jordan....Mr. Bates
Bailey....Mr. R. P. Bond
Sorrell....Mr. Marvin T. Herrick
Old Sorrell....Mr. Goodnow
Uncle Amos....Mr. Masten
Rutledge....Mr. Cecil Rollins
Lee....Mr. John D. Lodge
Mr. McIntyre....Mr. Richard Aldrich
Johnson....Mr. Bushnell
Hutchings....Mr. Goodnow
Governor Carr....Mr. Pearson
Bull....Mr. W. E. Stilwell, Jr.
Doggy....Mr. P. W. Holmes
Mary Todd....Miss Googins
Mrs. Wheeler....Miss Morris
Annie....Miss Sands
Mrs. Rutledge....Miss Halman
Pickens Gaffney....Mr. Philip Rice
Slew-Foot....Mr. W. E. Stilwell, Jr.
Sam Tipton....Mr. Grant Code
White Chauffeur....Mr. Robert Leven
Sykes....Mr. W. L. Smyser
Reverend Mr. Smallwood....Mr. Wilbur D. Dunkel
Sinclair, the Mayor....Mr. W. T. Morse
Tyson, the Banker....Mr. Robert Leven
Webster, the Publisher....Mr. P. W. Holmes
Colonel Grimes....Mr. Donald W. Keyes
Tough Sergeant....Mr. Richard Aldrich
Guardsman....Mr. Bates

Negroes

Mr. W. Cromwell, Mr. E. H. Dewey, Mr. B. F. Everett, Mr. A. Finney, Mr. T. La Farge, Mr. W. E. Harris, Mr. E. M. Littell, Mr. E. Mills, Mr. O. McConnell, Mr. J. Shute, Mr. C. M. Smart, Mr. W. S. Wilson, Mr. T. Wagner, Mr. M. Walker, Mr. Y. Wendell, Mr. H. J. Williams, Mr. B. P. Wilson

Negro Girls

Miss B. Fitz, Miss L. Jordan, Miss D. Leadbetter, Miss A. Macready

Scene I. A Street in Niggertown.
" II. The Office of The Altamont Development Company 8.30 in the morning.
" III. The same, one hour later.
" IV. A Lounge and Smoking Room at the Altamont Country Club on a night two weeks later.
" V. A Room in the home of the negro Johnson, the same night.
" VI. The Library of Rutledge, the same night.
" VII. A Bedroom Suite at the Altamont Inn, midnight.
" VIII. Same as Scene I — the next morning.
" IX. Same as Scenes II and III — late afternoon one week later.
" X. Interior of the Shoe Repair-Shop of Amos Todd—same afternoon.

The set for this play was designed and painted by Mr. John McAndrew.
Mr. Code's dance arranged by Prof. Charles D. Leslie.

THE 47 WORKSHOP
THE COMPANY

Miss Marguerite Barr, Miss Ruth B. Delano, Miss Dorothy Googins, Miss Doris F. Halman, Miss Lillian R. Hartigan, Miss Betty La Mont, Miss Kathleen Middleton, Miss Angela Morris, Miss Edith Coburn Noyes, Miss Dorothy Sands, Mr. Harold Bates, Mr. Royal Beal, Mr. John Mason Brown, Mr. Robert T. Bushnell, Mr. Henry F. Carlton, Mr. Norman B. Clark, Mr. Joseph Curtin, Mr. Edward P. Goodnow, Mr. Charles S. Howard, Mr. William F. Manley, Mr. Stewart Masten, Mr. Oviatt McConnell, Mr. F. C. Packard, Jr., Mr. Leon M Pearson, Mr. Cecil Rollins, Mr. Conrad Salinger, Mr. James W. D. Seymour

"Each year the company shall be made up of members who have acted in the preceding season and any persons who have done distinguished work in at least two performances. Past members may be reinstated by acting in any production." Voted by the Executive Committee, November 3, 1921.

THE ARTISTIC AND PRODUCING FORCE

Mr. Philip Barber, Mr. W. R. Brewster, Mr. Henry Hunt Clark, Miss Eleanor Dunn, Miss Eleanor Eustis, Mr. R. L. Gump, Miss Pauline Hatfield, Mr. J. C. Murphy, Mr. Stanley McCandless, Mr. Donald M. Oenslager, Mr. W. A. Pallmé, Mr. T. P. Robinson, Miss Eleanor Saxe, Mr. A. H. Starke, Mr. W. Burton Wilson

Playbill for Welcome to Our City *(The North Carolina Collection, University of North Carolina Library at Chapel Hill)*

lies quarrel. But when the quarreling and the cursing and the fighting is impartially distributed, while there is leaven of sympathy or condolence or mutual understanding between all there is hope.

But when a family divides itself against itself it can't stand. This happened in the Broody family. Slowly, imperceptibly, just like the slow poisonous growth of a rotten spot within the body the factional spirit grew within the family. It grew rotten ripe, then passed into dry decay and hardened. Joe and Sarah had aligned themselves against Seth and Eugene. They cursed each other privately now–party to party. Their talk was all of each other, bitter, acrimonious speech which poisoned speaker and listener alike and a deadly little snake uncoiled himself in the heart of each.

–*The Notebooks of Thomas Wolfe,* p. 24

Welcome to Our City

On 11 and 12 May 1923, the 47 Workshop staged Welcome to Our City. *The curtain went up at 8 P.M. and did not go down until midnight. The play was "the most ambitious thing–in size, at any rate–the Workshop has ever attempted," Wolfe wrote his mother, "there are ten scenes, over thirty people, and seven changes of setting." That spring, in a letter to George Pierce Baker, Wolfe stated his lofty theatrical ambitions: "I have written this play with thirty-odd named characters because it required it, not because I didn't know how to save paint. Some day I'm going to write a play with fifty, eighty, a hundred people–a whole town, a whole race, a whole epoch–for my soul's ease and comfort." Although disappointed by the reception to* Welcome to Our City, *Wolfe began a new play,* Mannerhouse.

> We have few poets in the South who write about the Spring, or of her coming, but she undoubtedly comes heralded by pomp, magnificence, and glory. After two years residence in New England I am painfully aware of many poets who write about the Spring; who sing her praises metrically or polyphonically, dilate on her quickening influences on poetic imagination, since she is their own sweet chuck and mistress; but who, living in New England, have never seen, felt, or experienced her presence in any way whatsoever. The truth, stated with brutal frankness, is that Spring abides in the South, where there are no poets and, with the utmost scrupulosity, avoids letting even the hem of her white robe touch New England, where there are many poets.
>
> –*The Notebooks of Thomas Wolfe,* p. 4

In this fragment of a late May 1923 letter to his mother, Wolfe recounts memories of North Carolina and writes of his determination to be an artist.

Dear Mama: I am sorry I have been so remiss in writing you but my time has been packed for three months now with my play and its aftermath. I went to New Hampshire with Prof Baker last week after my play. We had a good time up at his Silver Lake Home and I got a days rest. He wants me to go up there June 15 and finish writing my new play but I think I'll be here until June 15. Since I need the library. Prof Baker wants me to send my play to the New York Theatre Guild[.]

He said he thought it had a much better chance of success than "The Adding Machine"–a play, like mine, written in scenes which went off in New York last week after 3 months run Of course if I could only get a 3 mos. run I would make from eight to ten thousand dollars and be on my feet. If I could do this I would go to Germany in the Fall where I could live for one-quarter what it costs here.

I met a man the other day who lived last year in Munich and bought a house there for $50. He was living on the fat of the land, had a two room apartment for which he paid $1.00 a month and 'though living in princely fashion spent only $7.50 a week.

Of course the German mark is shot to pieces–you get now over 50,000 for a dollar. It is terrible for the Germans–poor people–but fortunate for us. I was talking this morning to Prof. Langfeld of the psychology department who is going to be in Berlin this summer and who lived there for 7 years. He is a great admirer of the Germans, thinks them far superior in every way to the French, and a race which can't be crushed. The terrible things of the war he called Prussianism–the work of a few autocrats–but the people are kind, intelligent, artistic and friendly–a great race.

Of course, some of the most interesting things in the theatre are being done in Germany–Where our laboring people and middle-class are going to see Bill Hart shoot 17 bad men, or C. Chaplin throw a custard pie, or Norma Talmadge in "Passion's Plaything", Germans with not enough to keep food in their mouths are saving their pennies to see Faust performed or hear Wagner's opera. If I sell one of my plays, I say, I shall do this. Prof Baker is in New York to-day. He is going to see the Theatre Guild in my behalf. He is a wonderful friend and he believes in me. I know this now: I am inevitable, I sincerely believe The only thing that can stop me now is insanity, disease, or death. The plays I am going to write may not be suited to the tender bellies of old maids, sweet young girls, or Baptist Ministers but they will be true and honest and courageous, and the rest doesn't matter. If my play goes on I want you to be prepared for execrations upon my head. I have stepped on toes right and left–I spared Boston with its nigger-sentimentalists no more than the South, which I love, but which I am nevertheless pounding. I am not interested in writing what our pot-bellied members of the Rotary and Kiwanis call a "good show"–I want to know life and understand it and interpret it without fear or favor. This, I feel is a man's work and worthy of a man's dignity. For life is not made up of sugary, sticky, sickening Edgar A Guest sentimentality, it is not made up of dishonest optimism, God is *not* Always in His Heaven, All is *not* always right with the world. It is not all bad, but it is not all good, it is not all ugly, but it is not all beautiful, it is life, life, life–the only thing that matters. It is savage, cruel, kind, noble, passionate, selfish, generous, stupid, ugly, beautiful, painful, joyous,–it is all these, and more, and its all these I want to know and, By God, I shall, though they crucify me for it. I will go to the ends of the earth to find it, to understand it, I will know this country when I am through as I know the palm of my hand, and I will put it on paper, and make it true and beautiful.

I will step on toes, I will not hesitate to say what I think of those people who shout "Progress, Progress, Progress"–when what they mean is more Ford automobiles, more Rotary Clubs, more Baptist Ladies Social Unions. I will say that "Greater Asheville" does not necessarily mean "100000 by 1930," that we are not necessarily 4 times as civilized as our grandfathers because we go four times as fast in automobiles, because our buildings are four times as tall. What I shall try to get into their dusty little pint-measure minds is that a full belly, a good automobile, paved streets, and so on, does not make them one whit better or finer,–that there is beauty in this world,–beauty even in this wilderness of ugliness and provincialism that is at present our country, beauty and spirit which will make us men instead of cheap Board of Trade Boosters, and blatant pamphleteers. I shall try to impress upon their little craniums that one does not have to be a "high-brow" or "queer" or "impractical" to know these things, to love them, and to realize they are our common heritage there for us all to possess and make a part of us. In the name of God, let us learn to be men, not monkies.

When I speak of beauty I do not mean a movie-close-up where Susie and Johnnie meet at the end and clinch and all the gum-chewing ladies go home thinking husband is not so good a lover as Valentino. That's cheap and vulgar. I mean everything which is lovely, and noble, and true It does not have to be sweet, it may be bitter, it does not have to be joyous, it may be sad.

When Spring comes I think of a cool, narrow back yard in North Carolina with green, damp earth, and cherry trees in blossom. I think of a skinny little boy at the top of one of those trees, with the fragrant blooms about him, with the tang of the sap in his nose, looking out on a world of back yards, and building his Castles in Spain. That's beauty. That's romance. I think of an old man in the grip of a terrible disease, who thought he was afraid to die, but who died like a warrior in an epic poem. That's beauty. I think of a boy of twenty-six years heaving his life away, and gasping to regain it, I think of the frightened glare in his eyes and the way he seizes my hands, and cries "What have you come home for". I think of the lie that trembles in my throat, I think of a woman who sits with a face as white and set as if cut from marble, and whose fingers can not be unclasped from his hand. And the boy of eighteen sees and knows for the first time that more than a son is dying, that part of a mother is being buried before her,–life in death, that something which she nursed and bore, something out of her blood, out of her life, is taken away. It's terrible but it's beautiful. I think of the devotion of a woman of frail physique to a father, I think of the daisy meadows on the way to Craggy Mountain, of the birch forests of New Hampshire, of the Mississippi River at Memphis–of all of which I have been a part and I know there is nothing so commonplace, so dull, that is not touched with nobility and dignity. And I intend to wreak out my soul on paper and express it all. This is what my life means to me: I am at the mercy of this thing and I will do it or die. I never forget; I have never forgotten. I have tried to make myself conscious of the whole of my life since first the baby in the basket became conscious of the warm sunlight on the porch, and saw his sister go up the hill to the girl's school on the corner (the first thing I remember) Slowly out of the world of infant darkness things take shape, the big terrifying faces become familiar,–I recognize my father by his bristly moustache. Then the animal books and the Mother Goose poetry which I memorize before I can read, and recite for the benefit of admiring neighbors every night, holding my book upside down. I become conscious of Santa Claus and send scrawls up the chimney. Then St. Louis. A flight of stairs at the Cincinnati rail road station which must be gone up,–the World's Fair, the Ferriss Wheel, Grover at the Inside Inn, the Delmar Gardens where you let me taste beer which I spit out, a ride on a bus-automobile–over the Fair Grounds with Effie–it is raining, raining–the Cascades in the rain–a ride in the scenic railway–scared at the darkness and the hideous faces–eating a peach in the back yard (St Louis)–I swallow a fly and am sick–and one of my brothers laughs at me. Two little boys who ride tricycle up and down the street–they dress in white and look alike–their father injured or killed in elevator accident (wasn't he)–I "commit a nuisance on the narrow strip of side yard and the policeman sees me and reports me–the smell of tea at the East India House–I'll never forget it–Grover's sickness and death–I am wakened at midnight by Mabel and she says "Grover's on the cooling board" I don't know what a cooling board is but am curious to see. I don't know what death is but have a vague, terrified sensation that something awful has happened–Then she takes me in her arms and up the hall–Disappointed at the cooling board–its only a table–The brown mole on his neck–The trip home–visitors in the parlor with condolences–Norah Israel was there–Then it gets fairly plain thereafter, and I can trace it step by step.

This is why I think I'm going to be an artist. The things that really mattered sunk in and left their mark–Sometimes only a word–sometimes a peculiar smile–sometimes death–sometimes the smell of dandelions in Spring–once Love Most people have little more mind than brutes: they live from day to day. I will go everywhere and see everything. I will meet all the people I can. I will think all the thoughts, feel all the emotions I am able, and I will write, write, write.

I won't say whether my play was good or bad. Some people in the staid Workshop Audience were shocked, most were enthusiastic, and a great many said it was the best play ever written here. Good or bad, win or lose, *[End of fragment.]*

–*The Letters of Thomas Wolfe to His Mother,* pp. 41–44

There's a play in everything that lives if we only had the power to extract it. . . .

–*The Letters of Thomas Wolfe,* p. 14

Washington Square College, which Wolfe called the School of Utility Culture in his fiction (The North Carolina Collection, University of North Carolina Library at Chapel Hill)

A College Instructor

While hoping for his work to be produced on Broadway, Wolfe realized he would have to support himself. Through the Harvard appointment office, he learned of a teaching job at Washington Square College of New York University and wrote Homer A. Watt, chairman of the English Department.

10 Trowbridge Street
Cambridge, Mass.
January 10, 1924

Dear Professor Watt:

I am informed that there will be several vacancies in the English department at New York University on the opening of the new term, in February. I have requested the Harvard Appointment Bureau to forward my papers, including letters and scholastic grades, to you. Mr. Dow, formerly of Harvard, and now an instructor at the uptown branch of the university, may also be consulted.

I was graduated, as you will note, from the University of North Carolina, in 1920, and received my master's degree in English from Harvard in 1922. The appointment office secured me an offer from Northwestern University in 1922, which I ultimately refused, in order to return for another year under Professor Baker at the 47 Workshop. Thus, I have been a student in the Graduate School for three years.

I have had no experience as a teacher. It is only fair to tell you that my interests are centred in the drama, and that someday I hope to write successfully for the theatre and to do nothing but that. My play is at present in the hands of a producer in New York but, even in the fortunate event of its acceptance, I feel the necessity of finding immediate employment.

I am twenty-three years old and a native of Asheville, North Carolina. I do not know what impression of maturity my appearance may convey but it is hardly in excess of my age. In addition, my height is four or five inches over six feet, producing an effect on a stranger that is sometimes startling. I think you should know so much in advance, as the consideration may justly enter into any estimate of my qualifications.

If New York University feels justified in offering me employment as an instructor in English, and if I am satisfied with the offer, I promise to give the most faithful and efficient service of which I am capable.

I hope you will find it convenient to reply to this letter at some early date.

–*The Letters of Thomas Wolfe,* pp. 56–57

Wolfe began teaching at Washington Square College on 6 February 1924 and taught there intermittently until 17 January 1930. Assigned three courses in English composition, he was promised 90 students (although 104 were accepted), eight to ten hours of classroom work, and twenty-six hours a week of theme reading; but he found the work took up nearly all of his time. In his 4 April 1924 letter to his mother he describes his life as a teacher and mentions his determination to go abroad at the end of the summer.

Hotel Albert
Eleventh Street & University Place
New York

Dear Mama: Just a few lines are all my time allows. I must go back to the interminable work of correcting papers:–like the brook, *that* goes on forever. On three days a week–or four–I can sleep late, and generally do, because, on my teaching days, I am so worn by nightfall that I sleep as though drugged. I don't know how to conserve nervous energy; I burn it extravagantly. However, I am not unhappy. I believe I am learning much although I am doing no writing. What time I have is usually spent at the theatre, or at the library, or in the open. When I am through grading papers, and writing my comments on the back, I don't feel in the mood for composition of my own. You can't serve two masters; I have elected to serve one, and I must see it through. Hereafter, I believe, I shall be able to do my work more quickly,–I yet retain my Presbyterian conscience; and I believe I do too much.

The shirts and socks have not come; I hope to get them soon–I am ragged. I must get a suit of clothes, too. This one is beginning to flap in the wind.

I got Mabel's telegram. I am sorry she can't come now; I had hoped to see her. However, a little later the weather will be milder. My late predictions of Spring were false; there was a heavy snow fall here on the first of April. Now, I believe Spring is here to stay. It is a fine, blue, sunny day–no wind.

I am off ten or fifteen pounds since coming here; but, then, I was growing fat and lazy in Cambridge. I shall try to hold on to what is left.

I live for September when I shall try to collect the remainder of my salary and go to England. I should have six months pay, dating from September first. Perhaps I can get away with seven or eight hundred dollars. I shall sail third class–steerage–a fast boat does it in five days, and I can hold my breath that long. I shall go down to the South of England, where, I am told, it is beautiful, and bury myself in a little village there; at one of the old inns where you can get good English ale, and beer. It will be cheap; perhaps forty or fifty dollars a month. I can write there for two months–away from the world I know. Anywhere, anywhere–out of *this* world.

How large, how golden seems that little sum of money. Yet how pitifully small it is. And how much wealth there is which has been got by dishonesty, trickery, and blind luck. They tell us in Sunday school to be industrious, and saving and steady:–we will be rich. It is not true. The world is filled with book keepers who have all these qualities; who work twice as hard as their employers. They shall die in a book-keepers bed, and go to a book keeper's heaven or hell where there are no interesting people.

The golden years of my life are slipping by on stealthy feet at night fall; there is a foot-print in the dark, a bell strikes twelve, and the flying year has gone. My life is like water which has passed the mill; it turns no wheels. And all of which I thought myself a part drifts by like painted smoke The great play is yet unwritten; the great novel beats with futile hands against the portals of my brain. Proud fool! I have eaten of the lotus and dreamed too deeply: the world is at me with its long fingers, and must have its payment. There is not time! If I but had a hundred years there might be some realization of my dreams. But I shall not live so long; and shall my dust taste better than a peddler's, when the worms are at me?

I had to draw on you at the end of the month–This month I shall do better Please watch your health; don't overwork. I send my love to you all

Tom.

–*The Letters of Thomas Wolfe to His Mother,* pp. 61–62

Hotel Albert, Eleventh Street and University Place, where Wolfe lived during his first year in New York. In Of Time and the River *he calls it the Hotel Leopold, "situated on a short and grimy street about two blocks from the university, northward, in the direction of Union Square" (The New York Historical Society).*

In another letter to his mother, Wolfe mentions the possible publication of The Return of Buck Gavin *and discusses his attitude toward his native state.*

Hotel Albert
Eleventh Street & University Place
New York
Monday–April 21, 1924

Dear Mama:–Written in haste and therefore short. Thanks for news of Koch. Called him yesterday: had breakfast with him this morning. He wants to put one of my old Carolina one act plays in new book–*Return of Buck Gavin.* It was hastily written in three hours at one sitting when I was 18. Honestly, I don't think I can afford to let my name go out with it. But we shall see

Pained at the implication in your letter that I was ashamed of North Carolina–only what is N.C. willing to do for me? I don't think there is a place there now for anyone who cares for anything besides Rotary and Lions and Boosters Clubs, real-estate speculation, "heap much" money, social fawning, good roads, new mills,–what, in a word, they choose to call "Progress, Progress, Progress" The only Progress is spiritual; the only lasting thing is Beauty–created by an artist. And N.C. has forgotten such as I.

N.C. needs honest criticism–rather than the false, shallow "we-are-the-finest-state-and-greatest-people-in-the-country"–kind of thing. An *artist* who refuses to accept fair criticism of his work will never go far. What of a *state?*

–*The Letters of Thomas Wolfe to His Mother,* p. 63

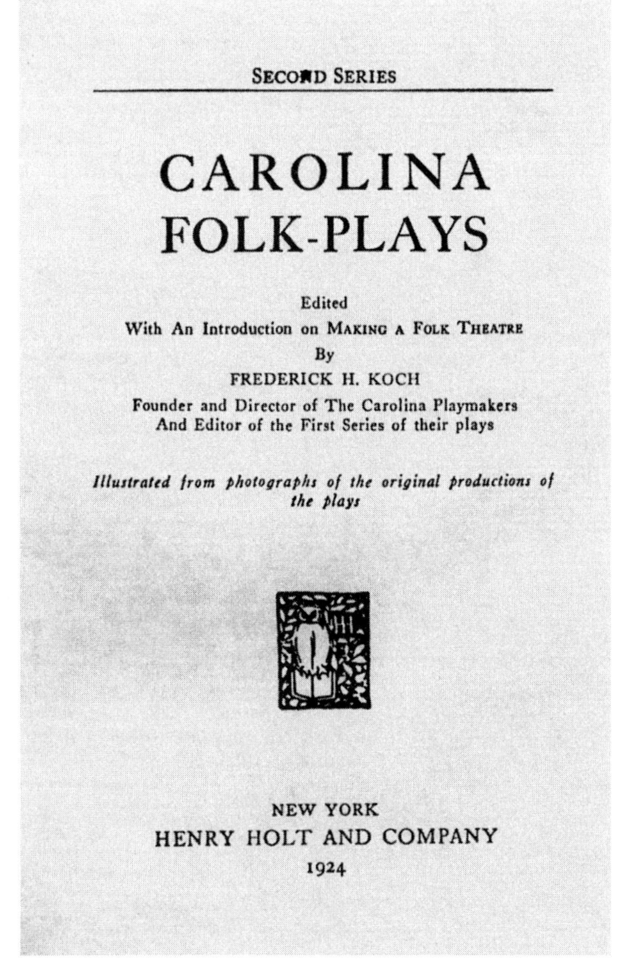
SECOND SERIES

CAROLINA FOLK-PLAYS

Edited
With An Introduction on MAKING A FOLK THEATRE
By
FREDERICK H. KOCH
Founder and Director of The Carolina Playmakers
And Editor of the First Series of their plays

Illustrated from photographs of the original productions of the plays

NEW YORK
HENRY HOLT AND COMPANY
1924

Title page for the collection that includes Wolfe's The Return of Buck Gavin, *his first appearance in a hardcover book*

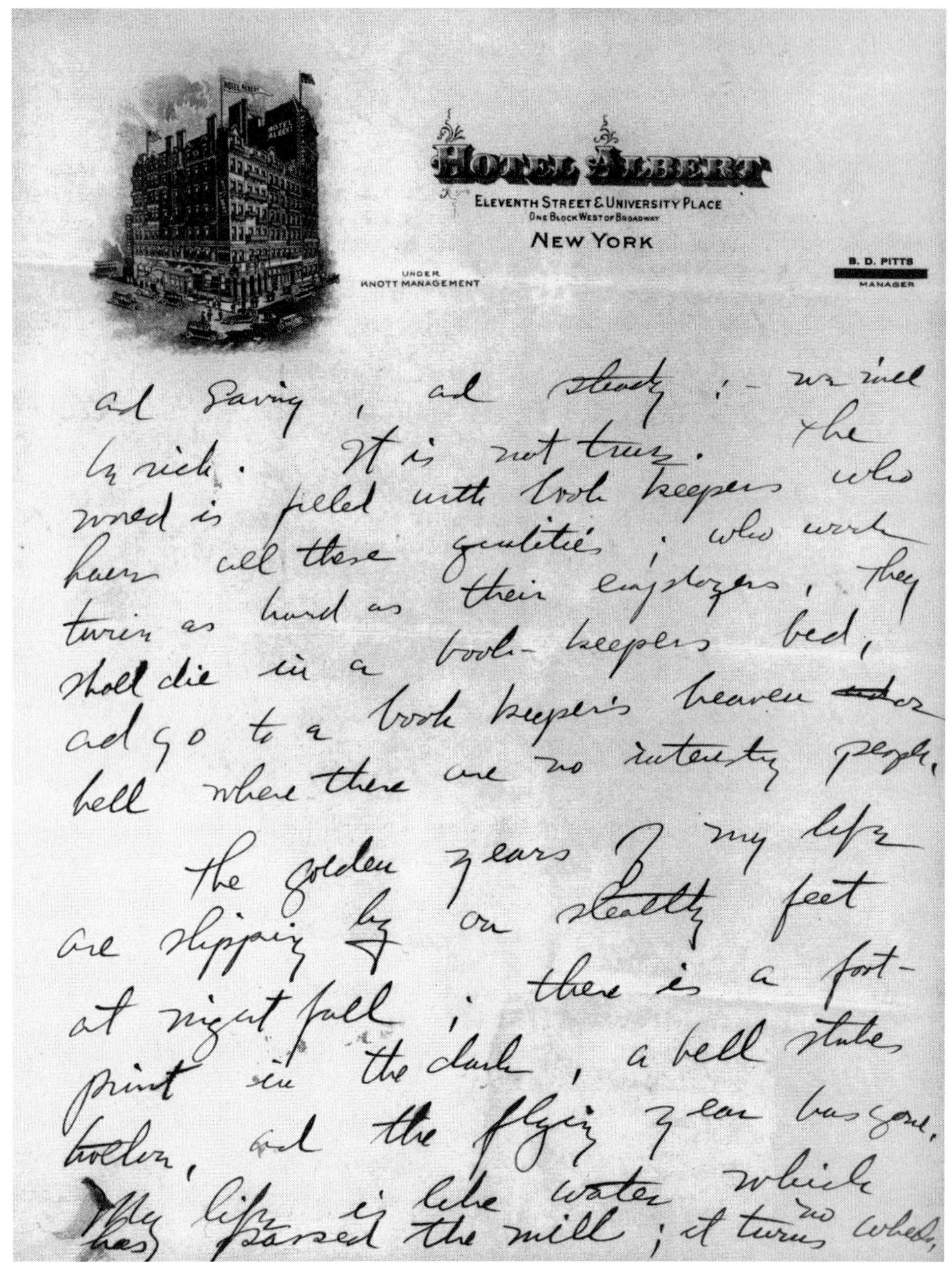

HOTEL ALBERT
ELEVENTH STREET & UNIVERSITY PLACE
ONE BLOCK WEST OF BROADWAY
NEW YORK

UNDER KNOTT MANAGEMENT

B. D. PITTS
MANAGER

and saving, and steady; — we will
be rich. It is not true. The
world is filled with book keepers who
have all these qualities; who work
twice as hard as their employers; they
shall die in a book-keepers bed,
and go to a book keeper's heaven or
hell where there are no interesting people.

The golden years of my life
are slipping by on stealthy feet
at night fall; there is a foot-
print in the dark, a bell strikes
twelve, and the flying year has gone.
My life is like water which
has passed the mill; it turns no wheels,

Last two pages from Wolfe's 4 April 1924 letter to his mother (The North Carolina Collection, University of North Carolina Library at Chapel Hill)

And all of which I thought myself a great craftsman is like painted smoke: the great play is yet unwritten; the great novel beats with futile hands against the portals of my brain: Proud fool! I have eaten of ~~the~~ lotus and dreamed too deeply; the world is at me with its long fingers, and must have its payment. There is not time! If I but had a hundred years there might be some realization of my dreams. But I shall not live so long; and shall my dust taste better than a peddler's, when the worms are at me?

I had to draw on you at the end of the month – this month I shall do better. Please watch your health; don't overwork. I send my love to you all

Tom.

25 September 1924 (The North Carolina Collection, University of North Carolina Library at Chapel Hill)

23 June 1926 (William B. Wisdom Collection, Houghton Library, Harvard University)

Passport photographs for Wolfe's first two trips abroad. Between the fall of 1924 and the end of 1928 Wolfe traveled to Europe four times, spending a total of two years in England and on the Continent.

Chapter 3

Look Homeward, Angel, 1925–1929

Finding it difficult to write while teaching at Washington Square College, Wolfe took a ten-month leave of absence abroad, beginning in the fall of 1924. On his return voyage, he met New York stage designer Aline Bernstein, who became the great love of Wolfe's life and provided the emotional and financial support that enabled Wolfe to write his first novel, Look Homeward, Angel *(1929).*

First European Sojourn

Wolfe planned to take a two-month leave of absence from teaching and write while traveling through Europe. He resolved to write 1,500 words a day while abroad. He maintained his resolve, but his sojourn stretched from October 1924 to August 1925. He did not return to teach until the fall of 1925.

Wolfe made use of the ocean journey by recording his thoughts, observations, and memories. He continued to work on this manuscript, which he titled "Passage to England" and submitted to The Asheville Citizen, *over the next five months as he extended his stay in Europe. The piece was a profane blend of fact and fiction including many unsavory details about Asheville. The following excerpts record his initial observations of his trip as well as his fictional self-projection, particularly his self-consciousness of his height.*

Sunday, Oct. 26 [1924]:

Today, for the first time in my life, I am beginning a more or less methodical record of the events which impinge on my own experience. I do this, I believe, because for the first time in my life I feel an utter isolation from such reality as I have known;

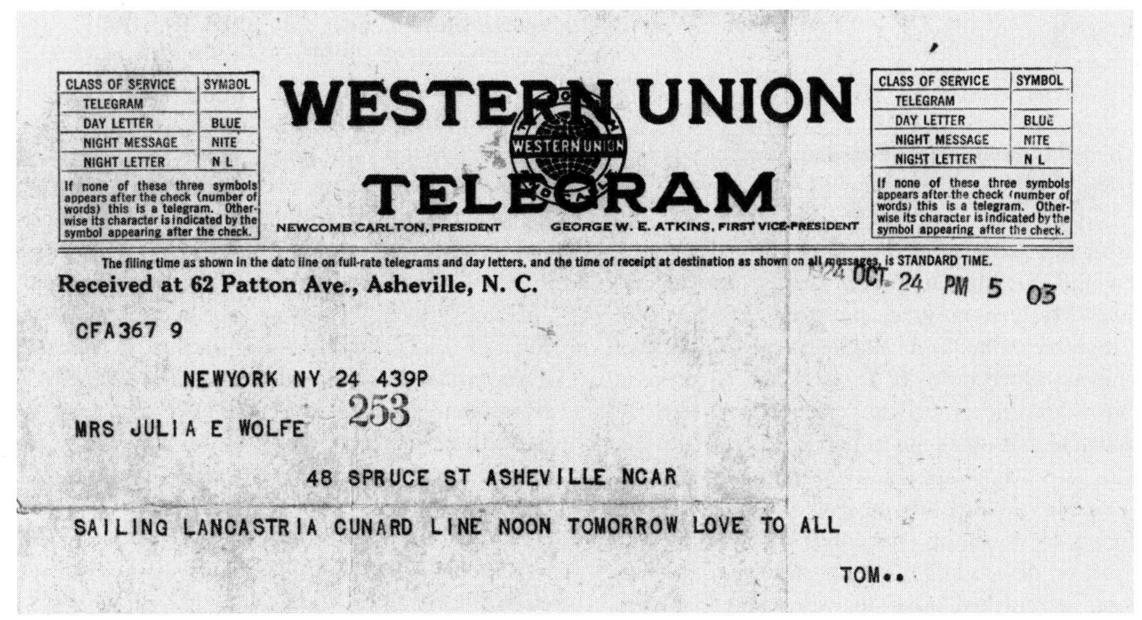

CLASS OF SERVICE	SYMBOL
TELEGRAM	
DAY LETTER	BLUE
NIGHT MESSAGE	NITE
NIGHT LETTER	N L

If none of these three symbols appears after the check (number of words) this is a telegram. Otherwise its character is indicated by the symbol appearing after the check.

WESTERN UNION TELEGRAM

NEWCOMB CARLTON, PRESIDENT GEORGE W. E. ATKINS, FIRST VICE-PRESIDENT

The filing time as shown in the date line on full-rate telegrams and day letters, and the time of receipt at destination as shown on all messages, is STANDARD TIME.

Received at 62 Patton Ave., Asheville, N. C. 1924 OCT 24 PM 5 03

CFA367 9

NEWYORK NY 24 439P

MRS JULIA E WOLFE 253

48 SPRUCE ST ASHEVILLE NCAR

SAILING LANCASTRIA CUNARD LINE NOON TOMORROW LOVE TO ALL

TOM..

Wolfe's 24 October 1924 telegram to his mother. Harvard professor George Pierce Baker had convinced Wolfe that traveling in Europe and absorbing its culture was necessary for his training as a writer (The North Carolina Collection, University of North Carolina Library at Chapel Hill).

because I know that I must live a good week longer with the people on this ship and that try as we may, we cannot get away from one another. The opportunities for observation are humorously unique.

The weather is magnificent–warm, bright, clear–there is no sea; the boat is perfectly steady.

There are less than one hundred of us on the cabin list. Let us see how thoroughly we can dislike one another before the voyage is over. Nine days with your companions is a long time, when the laws of accident govern their selection. I tried to leave New York yesterday as casually as if I had been taking a ferry ride to Hoboken; I was, nevertheless, in a tremendous state of excitement.

At eight o'clock I arose, had breakfast, sweated over my three bulging cases, and at eleven o'clock rode over to the Cunard piers at the foot of West 14th St. in a taxicab.

That was an hour before the *Lancastria* sailed. I went into the ship's writing room and scribbled four rather frantic letters to members of my family. Then I went on deck.

The space around the gang plank was thronged with people–passengers and their friends. I had avoided having anyone come on board to see me off; at the last minute two Jewish boys, students in my classes of Freshman composition at New York University, appeared. I gave one of them my letters to mail.

They were fascinated with the ship. They came on board and made a thorough inspection. In the writing room they appropriated sheets of the ship's stationery: in the smoking lounge they took huge boxes of the ship's safety matches.

. . . .

I had forgotten to mention that there is a young man on this ship who is too tall.

I had seen him making the promenade of the decks with three-foot strides; occasionally elderly gentlemen would stop him, and in the kindest tone imaginable, say: "My boy, how tall are you?", to which he would mumble some unintelligible reply, and rush angrily away. Once or twice I found him engaged in brief and rather impersonal conversation with some of the passengers, but for the most part he kept to himself.

My active sympathy and interest was aroused only when I saw this young man fall victim to a series of appalling accidents, all attendant on his height. On two occasions, descending the main stairway to the dining saloon, he cracked his head with painful violence against the woodwork of the upper landing. How often this had happened to him I cannot say, but I saw it happen twice. At another time, after a belated appearance for dinner, in the course of his extraordinary contortions to place his legs comfortably under the table, he upset the water bottle, two glasses, and a bottle of Nuits St. Georges which belonged to his angry neighbor. Two days later he passed me limping painfully, and in answer to my friendly inquiry, he answered rather bitterly that he had barked his shin in the most barbarous fashion against the sideboard of his bunk.

There was in his manner a kind of brooding and subdued excitement; his eyes gleamed madly and, from time to time, darted sidelong glances; and though he spoke little at first, he was liberal in passionate and half arrested gestures, as if he were already making preparations for an eloquence yet to come.

I thought the time was ripe for conversation; and extending my legs to their last capacity, I managed to keep abreast of him. Presently he began to speak:

"It is to be wondered at," he said, "if no one has ever written a book of a man for whom most of the contrivances of the earth are just uncomfortably a little too small; the beds a trifle too short, the tables a bit too low, the food and the drink a mite too scanty. It is in this poignant submission to things that are not quite large enough that the shocking differences of life are felt; one comes to realize the black curse of the three inches too much, to appreciate the awful distances that lie between the fractional separations–the only real distances.

"To be Gulliver, to be a giant in a world of tiny creatures–that is quite a different matter, for to a giant there are no giants, but only dwarfs and brothers.

"And even those poor stunted giants of our own times, who find their way ultimately into circuses and travelling carnivals, those two-by-two eight and nine feet titans, generally, I believe, the children of rather middling-sized parents, who doubtless look on them with much the same terror with which a hen might regard an ostrich egg, are inexorably separated from participation in a world of five feet eight, and cheerfully resigned to that separation.

"They dream, perhaps, of the heroic ages of their ancestors when giants grew to ample stature and pelted ships of mariners with stones the size of mountains, of times when the hills trembled at their approach, and rivers were bridged in a step. And dreaming so, perhaps, these starveling titans of our times erect a world behind the canvas–a mad and merry world in which all the laws of symmetry are broken; they marry the doll lady, or the fat woman, and sit at table with Jo-Jo-What-Is-It?, with the living skeleton, and with the clown. And that, too, is quite a different matter.

"For they have been touched by the lights of carnival, and all beyond the lights are phantom. They see the world vaguely as audience, which makes a stir and a noise beyond, and which pays its fee to look upon them.

"And to be a dwarf–that too is another thing, for it is to sit in a giant chair as a child of ten, to live delightedly in a world in which there is too much of everything. And a dwarf may sleep quite comfortably in a grown man's bed.

"But from these shapes of things, these patterns which pinch like a tight shoe, into which I would willingly mould my life, if I only could–how terribly am I removed!–not by a league or a world or the distance of a star, but Tantalus-like, by the tragic fraction that keeps the bending fruit and the flowing spring just from my lips. "

–*The Notebooks of Thomas Wolfe,* pp. 33, 37–38

Wolfe wrote from shipboard to his mother of his work on "Passage to England."

Cunard R M S "Lancastria"

one oclock P.M.

Tuesday, November 4.

Dear Mama: I am writing you this in the middle of the English channel, about two or three hours away from Cherbourg, France, where this letter will be mailed from the boat. After an hour or two at Cherbourg where the ship lands passengers bound for France, we cut back across the channel to the mouth of the Thames, where we proceed up the river to London and the end of my journey, which we should reach by noon to-morrow if we are quick enough to make the early voyage.

Last night at ten o'clock it was announced that the beacon lights of England were on our left, and I rushed on deck in the face of a howling wind to look on the lights of England–old England–on the Scilly Isles and on Land's End. This morning at six o'clock we slid in to the beautiful little harbor of Plymouth England, and I caught my first glimpse of English soil. A beautiful little town of 30000 people lay off in the distance, and round smooth green hills with little vegetation sloped down to the water. The tender came out to the boat to take off passengers in a hurry to reach London 200 miles away. I shall stay on the boat, for my fare is paid, and they must feed me, and the train fare from Plymouth is $10.00. No one who ever made a voyage has got as much from it as I have. The passenger list was small, only 96, and I got to know them all; and they included knaves, fools, aristocrats–Englishmen who have beaten up and down all the coasts of the world, and who think not as much of a two week's trip to America as you do of one to Miami. I have put it all on paper, day by day, all the drama, the tragedy and the comedy, the beauty and the mystery of the sea; and the courage and courtesy of these Englishmen who have made the sea their slave.

I shall send it back from London to morrow to The Citizen, if they care to publish a real piece of creation, and you may read at length what I have seen.

All my dreams are coming through. I am assured that I may secure very comfortably in London board and room for £2–10 sh a week–a little over $11.00; and that I may live comfortably in London on £5 or £6 a week–less than $30.00. The South of France is far cheaper; already I have recommendations to pensions at rates of 16 or 18 francs a day–80 or 90 cents.

I shall stay in London two or three weeks–then I may go on a walking trip through the beautiful country villages in Southern England. An old Englishman named Adams, and his wife, have invited me to visit them at their home in Rye, England Adams is mayor of the town–a very beautiful and famous village–and is returning from the States where the Rotary Club has feasted him. He is a Rotarian.

At my table is young Hugh Tennant, aged 32, who is of one of the greatest families in England; he is cousin to Lady Asquith. He is returning to England after five years at the British embassy in Washington. He knows Asheville very well: when he got on the boat he told me he had just come from a visit to the Vanderbilt's–the Cecil's. He was Cecil's best man. He has offered to write letters securing admission for me to the Houses of Parliament, and other places.

The weather is lovely–a terrific wind across the channel, but blue skies and a flashing sun. I an see the coast of France before me now–from the writing room.

We came across with an injury to the starboard engine, and we are two days late. The weather was lovely most of the time, good most of the rest, and rough only two or three days. I made the trip very well, although I felt sorry for myself once or twice when the boat began to pitch and roll. Seasickness is a kind of head giddiness accompanied by a vast indifference to everything in the world. I feel very well this glorious day, but am glad the sod of England will soon be beneath my feet.

I must finish this, having said not one tenth as much as I wished. I shall conquer the world on this journey; this voyage and this new world has changed my life. I know I will be lonely and disheartened often, but a wonderful experience is before me. We are fools to live in a narrow cage!

For God's sake, all of you must watch your health, and send me news. Always tell me the truth, but no worse than that. I may cable you my address and my safe arrival from London. But rush mail by *fastest boat* to American Express Co, London–Love to you all,

---

In Devising Torture Cruelties Nordic Race Has Demonstrated The Superiority It Boasts of

The article given below was written by Thomas C Wolfe, of Asheville, who is now studying in Europe. Mr. Wolfe is a graduate of the University of North Carolina and of Harvard University. He taught English during 1923-1924 at the University of the City of New York and this fall will return to his duties there.

LONDON TOWER

It will no doubt be pleasing to all of us who are quite sure of the Nordic supremacy in all matters requiring character and courage and honesty, and who believe that only by the continued domination of the Nordic may civilization be saved, to know that in the matter of devising abominable and revolting cruelties for the torture of the unconvinced we Nordics have shown the same superiority.

If there are any bold enough to deny us our right to this distinction we need only conduct them on an inspection of the Tower of London. The inventive genius (in which, as is well known, we Nordics excel) of a cunning little instrument known as "The Scavenger's Daughter", whereby the head and hands and feet of a malfactor may be simultaneously united, would excite; I am confident, the admiration of Edison.

The there is the rack, a pleasant instrument used for the purpose of making short gentlemen long and long gentlemen attenuated. This mighty instrument could be operated, we are told, "by a school-boy".

There is, by the way, a vast lewd irony in the implications of that phrase. The pivoting of the great coastal guns at Sandy Hook was balanced on machinery so delicately hinged that it could be operated "by a school boy"; the great hills the enemy must cross are sown with mines, and the power by which the earth shall take flight, is meshed two leagues below a button, which may be sounded "by a school boy". And I remember that as a child, I heard the phrase time and again from the honored lips of John the Sheriff, that remarkable man who seemed always just to have killed someone, or to be just on the verge of killing someone. I have never known a more complete devotion to art. Shortly after he killed the bad nigger Reece, an execution which occurred at the beginning of his career, and was marked by all the bold draughtsmanship of his earlier manner, he obtained his subject's skull, and kept it for the edification of his friends in a conspicuous position on the parlor mantel.

For a fuller account of this extraordinary work, I refer my readers to my latest Critique, which bears the title, "Since DePuincey: The Development of Murder as One of the Fine Arts During the Later Nineteenth and Early Twentieth Centuries". The example in question will be found in chapter VI: "Murder as an Abstract Opposed to Murder as a Representational Art; Together with Certain Speculations on Three Dimensional Murder and the Experiments of the Paulo-Post-Futurist School."

For a purely narrative and merited account, the uninformed will do well to read my commemorative ballad, beginning:

"I know that John the Sheriff,
Who shot the Nigger Reece,
And kept his skull for company
Upon his Mantelpiece...".

The expression "by a school boy" was a favorite one with John the Sheriff; I shall not soon forget, although I was scarcely ten years old at the time, the deep emotion with which he described the operation of his latest gallows; its trap, so beautifully poised that it might be sprung "by a school boy", coming in especially for generous praise.

Indeed, his enthusiasm for this instrument was so great that he constructed a tiny but thoroughly effective model, in which, according to the exigencies of the domestic cuisine, he accustomed to hang his poultry.

In his later years, embittered by the mean and restrictive conventionality of a society which gave no scope to free artistic expression, he encysted himself in solitude and seclusion, remarking bitterly that the time had now come "for the younger men to do the work". This utterance concealed, I have always believed a more sublime irony—what he really meant was "the school boy". No sadder spectacle of the old, age of a great artist, forgotten and alone, has been afforded, I believe, than that of John the Sheriff. Deserted by all save a few of his most devoted disciples, the old man stayed in his house for months at a time, deriving, perhaps, of nights, a debased and melancholy satisfaction

The only excerpt from "Passage to England" that was published during Wolfe's lifetime appeared in the 19 July 1925 issue of The Asheville Citizen. *The Thomas Wolfe Society published* Passage to England: A Selection *in 1998.*

Aline Bernstein, circa 1930s, whose belief in Wolfe's talent and financial assistance encouraged him during the writing of Look Homeward, Angel *(The Aldo P. Magi Collection, University of North Carolina at Chapel Hill)*

Wolfe spent November 1924 in England and then traveled to Paris. On his third day in Paris, a valise containing the manuscript of his work-in-progress, Mannerhouse, *was stolen. He had been working on the play intermittently for more than a year. He had no alternative but to rewrite it in its entirety. On New Year's Eve, Wolfe ushered in 1925 with his friend from Harvard, Kenneth Raisbeck, and Raisbeck's friends from Boston, Marjorie Fairbanks and Helen Harding. He and the trio took a motor tour of southern France, and their adventure furnished the material for several episodes in* Of Time and the River. *He also traveled in Italy and Switzerland before returning to England.*

> If you sit around thinking inspiration will come the 13th of every February or so, you'll never get any writing done. You are a literary workman, and ought to work every day.
>
> –*Thomas Wolfe Interviewed,* p. 35

Aline Bernstein

Wolfe left London in late August aboard the Olympic. *On 25 August, the day before he arrived in New York, he met Aline Bernstein, a married woman twenty years his senior. In* Of Time and the River *Wolfe recorded his first impressions of the woman who became Esther Jack in his fiction.*

He turned, and saw her then, and so finding her, was lost, and so losing self, was found, and so seeing her, saw for a fading moment only the pleasant image of the woman that perhaps she was, and that life saw. He never knew: he only knew that from that moment his spirit was impaled upon the knife of love. From that moment on he never was again to lose her utterly, never to wholly re-possess unto himself the lonely, wild integrity of youth which had been his. At that instant of their meeting, that proud inviolability of youth was broken, not to be restored. At that moment of their meeting she got into his life by some dark magic, and before he knew it, he had her beating in the pulses of his blood–somehow thereafter–how he never knew–to steal into the conduits of his heart, and to inhabit the lone, inviolable tenement of his one life; so, like love's great thief, to steal through all the adyts of his soul, and to become a part of all he did and said and was–through this invasion so to touch all loveliness that he might touch, through this strange and subtle stealth of love henceforth to share all that he might feel or make or dream, until there was for him no beauty that she did not share, no music that did not have her being in it, no horror, madness, hatred, sickness of the soul, or grief unutterable, that was not somehow consonant to her single image and her million forms–and no final freedom and release, bought through the incalculable expenditure of blood and anguish and despair, that would not bear upon its brow forever the deep scar, upon its sinews the old mangling chains, of love.

After all the blind, tormented wanderings of youth, that woman would become his heart's centre and the target of his life, the image of immortal one-ness that again collected him to one, and hurled the whole collected passion, power and might of his one life into the blazing certitude, the immortal governance and unity, of love.

"Set me as a seal upon thine heart, as a seal upon thine arm: for love is strong as death; jealousy is cruel as the grave: the coals thereof are coals of fire, which hath a most vehement flame."

And now all the faces pass in through the ship's great side (the tender flower face among them). Proud, potent faces of rich Jews, alive with wealth and luxury, glow in rich, lighted cabins; the doors are closed, and the ship is given to the darkness and the sea.

–*Of Time and the River,* pp. 911–912

Writing a Novel

Wolfe resumed teaching at Washington Square College in September 1925, and during the winter of 1925–1926 moved into a loft at 13 East Eighth Street that Aline Bernstein also rented as a studio while maintaining her Park Avenue residence with her husband and children. During their talks, Wolfe and Bernstein shared their childhood reminiscences. Encouraged by her, Wolfe decided to abandon playwriting and instead to write an autobiographical novel. He began jotting down ideas for his novel in a tablet and later a large hardcover book. After completing these notes, he commenced writing in accounting ledgers. He eventually filled seventeen ledgers.

Looking back on his career in a 30 April 1937 interview for the Bristol News, *Wolfe stated that he believed that in reality all books were autobiographical.*

All we have is the experience of our own life and the power to use it. This is especially true in the case of writers.

–*Thomas Wolfe Interviewed,* p. 81

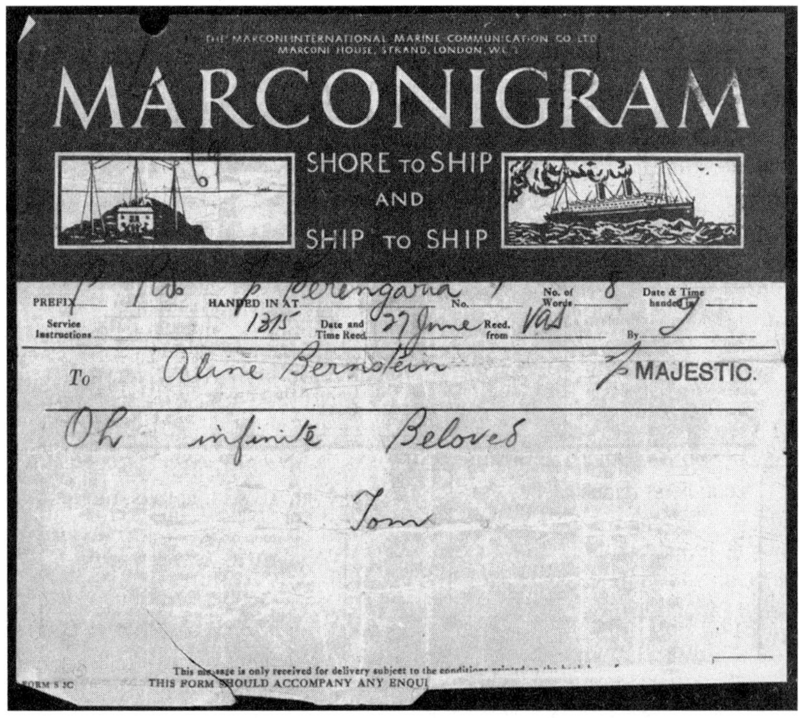
THE MARCONI INTERNATIONAL MARINE COMMUNICATION CO LTD
MARCONI HOUSE, STRAND, LONDON, W.C.

MARCONIGRAM

SHORE TO SHIP AND SHIP TO SHIP

PREFIX ... HANDED IN AT Berengaria No. ... No. of Words 8 Date & Time handed in ...

Service Instructions 1315 Date and Time Recd. 27 June Recd. from VAS By ...

To Aline Bernstein ⁄ MAJESTIC.

Oh infinite Beloved

Tom

This message is only received for delivery subject to the conditions ...

THIS FORM SHOULD ACCOMPANY ANY ENQUI...

Wolfe's wire of 27 June 1926 to Bernstein from the Berengaria *(William B. Wisdom Collection, Houghton Library, Harvard University)*

On 23 June 1926 Wolfe boarded the Berengaria *for his second trip to Europe. In a letter to Margaret Roberts, Wolfe describes his preliminary work on the manuscript that eventually became* Look Homeward, Angel.

Bath, England
July 19, 1926

Dear Mrs. Roberts:

Here are just a few lines–a short record of my doings since I left you. I was in Paris ten days, in Chartres two days, in London a week, and here two days. I am on my way to the North of England–to Lincoln and York for a few days, and finally to the Lake District, where I settle down to work. My trip has been fuller, richer, more fruitful than I had dared hope. I looked, and looked so fiercely the first time that I return now to something which seems to be opening itself for me.

I have begun work on a book, a novel, to which I may give the title of "The Building of a Wall"–perhaps not; but because I am a tall man, you know perhaps my fidelity to walls and to secret places. All the passion of my heart and of my life I am pouring into this book–it will swarm with life, be peopled by a city, and if ever read, may seem in places terrible, brutal, Rabelaisian, bawdy. Its unity is simply this: I am telling the story of a powerful creative element trying to work its way toward an essential isolation; a creative solitude; a secret life–its fierce struggles to wall this part of its life away from birth, first against the public and savage glare of an unbalanced, nervous brawling family group; later against school, society, all the barbarous invasions of the world. In a way, the book marks a progression toward freedom; in a way toward bondage–but this does not matter: to me one is as beautiful as the other. Just subordinate and leading up to this main theme is as desperate and bitter a story of a contest between two people as you ever knew–a man and his wife–the one with an inbred, and also an instinctive, terror and hatred of property; the other with a growing mounting lust for ownership that finally is tinged with mania–a struggle that ends in decay, death, desolation.

This is all I've time for now. I wish I could tell you more of this magnificent old town, held in a cup of green steep hills, climbing one of them, made on one plan from one material–the finest place really I've ever seen.

Write me, American Express Co., London. God bless you all.

–*The Letters of Thomas Wolfe,* pp. 111–112

Margaret Roberts, circa 1927–1928 (Ted Mitchell Collection)

As he was working on his novel in fall 1926 Wolfe often wrote to Bernstein. As these excerpts reveal, Bernstein was particularly important to Wolfe as the imagined reader of his work.

In an 11 September letter from Chelsea, London, Wolfe reported he was making good progress.

I have been writing from four to six hours a day: and I have spent the rest of the time thinking about it–and about you. The regularity of my life has helped enormously. It has been quite warm–but I do from 2000–2500 words a day–almost a book [in] a month, you see, but mine will be much longer.

. . . .

With the vanity of young men I wanted to be a great man[,] a fine artist. This last year, particularly these past few weeks[,] it has changed. I'm not exactly done for, but for the first time I'm willing to eat humble pie. I know now that I can never be anything more than one of the millions of unknown obscure people who populate the globe–and somehow I don't care.

I get tremendously excited over my book–at times in an unnatural drunken ecstasy, it seems to me to be working into one of the most extraordinary things ever done; but then I realise that no one will care to publish it, few to read it.

Somehow I'm not unhappy. I am, on the contrary, deeply moved by the experience–I have gained so much wisdom this last year from you. I know that I shall never be a great figure now–but I [have] hopes of turning out a tolerably decent person, and I know that obscurity does not keep many people from having merry lives.

This book finishes it–it is a record of my secret life–somehow I want to get it done–it is a definitive act–and give it to you.

–*My Other Loneliness,* pp. 65–66

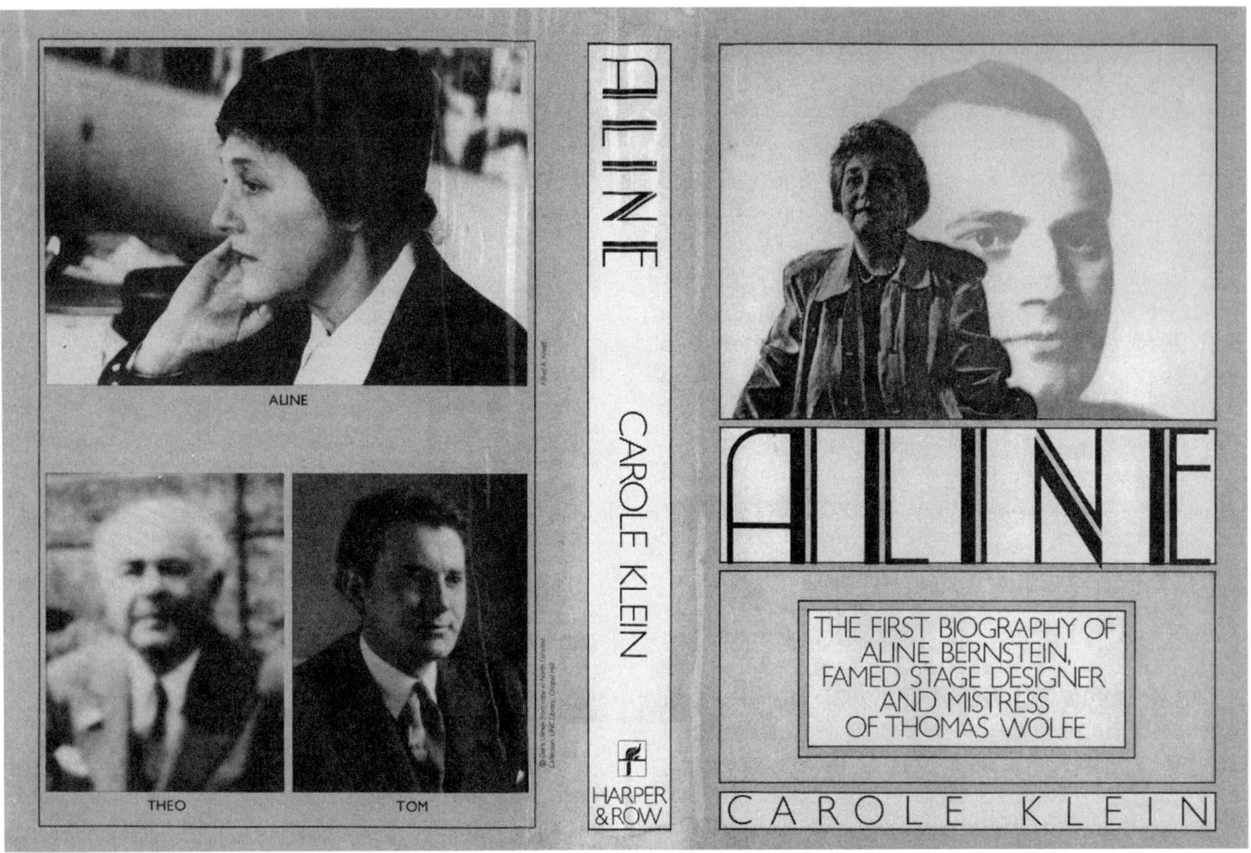

Dust jacket for the biography published in 1979

In a 2 October letter from London, Wolfe claims to be content to write for an audience of only two or three.

I have felt the agony of defeat more than most people: I suppose I am the sort the world likes to down, because they can see how it hurts. It has been hard for me ever to see myself playing second fiddle[.] But in my lucid moments, which are growing surprisingly numerous, I see now that I have always been beaten, that I have never won anything[.] Entirely without rancour or vanity, I believe, I have been beaten most often by smaller people. Everyone has gone ahead of me–for two or three years now I have accepted the empty specter of praise from a few friends who have adequately demonstrated that love is blind.

Do you know it has all become supportable. Don't think that I have lost spirit, or that I'm in a despairing mood. On the contrary. I have never felt greater strength. Thank God, I'm not a Christian, and I have no cheek-turning meekness in me. Something else has happened: I have seen a depth in me that shall never get to the end of, and a mystery that no one can touch. I'm not a man of genius, or an artist, or even a man of talent, but since that's out and freely confessed, what else have they to say about me? Having admitted this, let me also say that to call me a wonderful and extraordinary person is wild and hackneyed rubbish: I'm a miracle. And there's no one capable of getting within a mile of me.

Do you know, my dear, that in writing this book, the last thing I shall ever write, I feel for the first time as if I'm throwing my strength not at the empty air but at some object. I am deliberately writing the book for two or three people,–first and chiefest, for you. There is not the remote shadow of a chance that it will ever get published–if I cared to write salable stuff I would: I know most of the tricks, but something takes possession of me when I write, and I wear my entrails upon the page. I can't help it: I am writing, like any sensible person, for some audience–but unhappily my audience has never existed[.]

But, somehow, I am rather happy about the book. I am fashioning it somewhat as one of the men of Plantin's time might have fashioned his, or as Burton the Anatomy. I know that, at the most, it's one for two or three people. But it is evolving as a huge rich pageant, with a blending shift and interweave in the pattern. It ought to make good reading for those two or three.

–*My Other Loneliness,* pp. 87–88

P.S. If you write again, or want your letters returned, write me care of Aline Bernstein – 333 West 77th St. – New York City (I'm in good standing, however, at Harvard Club)

HARVARD CLUB
27 WEST 44TH STREET

that hell of chaos, greed, and cheap ugliness — and then I found you, when else I should have died, you were mother of my spirit who fed me with light. Do you think that I have forgotten? Do you think I ever will? You are entombed in my flesh, you are in the pulses of my blood, the thought of you makes a

Page from Wolfe's 30 May 1927 letter to Margaret Roberts (William B. Wisdom Collection, Houghton Library, Harvard University)

Wolfe returned to New York and Bernstein's Eighth Street studio in December 1926. For six months he worked on the manuscript he now called "O Lost."

In a 30 May 1927 letter to Margaret Roberts, Wolfe revealed his feelings about his former teacher as well as about his existence as a child in his mother's boardinghouse. These emotions color Look Homeward, Angel.

. . . You say that no one *outside* my family loves me more than Margaret Roberts. Let me rather say the exact truth:–that no one *inside* my family loves me as much, and only one other person, I think, in all the world loves me as much. My book is full of ugliness and terrible pain–and I think moments of a great and soaring beauty. In it (will you forgive me?) I have told the story of one of the most beautiful people I have ever known as it touched on my own life. I am calling that person Margaret Leonard. I was without a home–a vagabond since I was seven–with two roofs and no home. I moved inward on that house of death and tumult from room to little room, as the boarders came with their dollar a day, and their constant rocking on the porch. My overloaded heart was bursting with its packed weight of loneliness and terror; I was strangling, without speech, without articulation, in my own secretions–groping like a blind sea-thing with no eyes and a thousand feelers toward light, toward life, toward beauty and order, out of that hell of chaos, greed, and cheap ugliness–and then I found you, when else I should have died, you mother of my spirit who fed me with light. Do you think that I have forgotten? Do you think I ever will? You are entombed in my flesh, you are in the pulses of my blood, the thought of you makes a great music in me–and before I come to death, I shall use the last thrust of my talent–whatever it is–to put your beauty into words.

–*The Letters of Thomas Wolfe,* pp. 122–123

I am weary of the old forms–the old language–It has come to me quite simply these last three days that we must mine deeper–find language again in its primitive sinews–like the young man, Conrad–Joyce gets it at times in *Ulysses*–it is quite simple, but terrific. Build the book brick by brick.

–*The Notebooks of Thomas Wolfe,* p. 98

After his third trip to Europe, in the summer of 1927, Wolfe returned to teaching at Washington Square College. In this letter to his mother, he describes his living situation and his work.

Harvard Club
27 West 44th Street
Sunday night
Oct 9, 1927

Dear Mama:–I got Ben's watch a day or two ago. Thanks very much for the gift. It was probably the one thing I needed most. I confess it gave me a weird feeling to have his watch in my hand: I have not been able to use it yet, but I shall begin tomorrow. I wound it, and it seems to keep good time.

I am busier than I have ever been in my life. In addition to my teaching, I work four or five hours every afternoon dictating my book to a young man who is typing it for me–he is one of my former students, very intelligent, and a good typist. In addition, I have moved out of my filthy garret into a new apartment: it is a magnificent place in an old New York house owned by a wealthy old bachelor who is himself an artist. I have the entire floor–two enormous rooms, a big kitchenette, and a bath. I have a garden behind, and a quiet old New York street–one of the few remaining–in front. It is in one of the old parts of town, 8 minutes from the university.

The owner demanded a rent that would have taken almost my whole salary: it was cheap even at that price (as New York prices go), but I told him I had only an instructor's pay and couldn't afford it. He wanted me to come in: he liked me, I believe, and he doesn't like business people He cut off several hundred dollars. I now get the place for about $135 a month, half of which is paid by Mrs Bernstein–about $65 apiece, you see, or no more than I paid two years ago at the Albert. In addition, we can sublet in the summer; if any place in New York can be rented this can, and I could without difficulty get $100 or $125 for it in Summer. Thus, we get this fine place for $50 or $55 apiece. Mrs B. is going to use the big front room as a studio, and room where she can meet her business associates in the theatre. She has had to find a place–she has more work this year than ever before, and my garret was too dirty to bring people to.

I shall be tremendously busy until Christmas, but I feel like working. If Fred comes up, I have plenty of room to keep him.

Write when you can.

Love to all
Tom

–*The Letters of Thomas Wolfe to His Mother,* p. 124

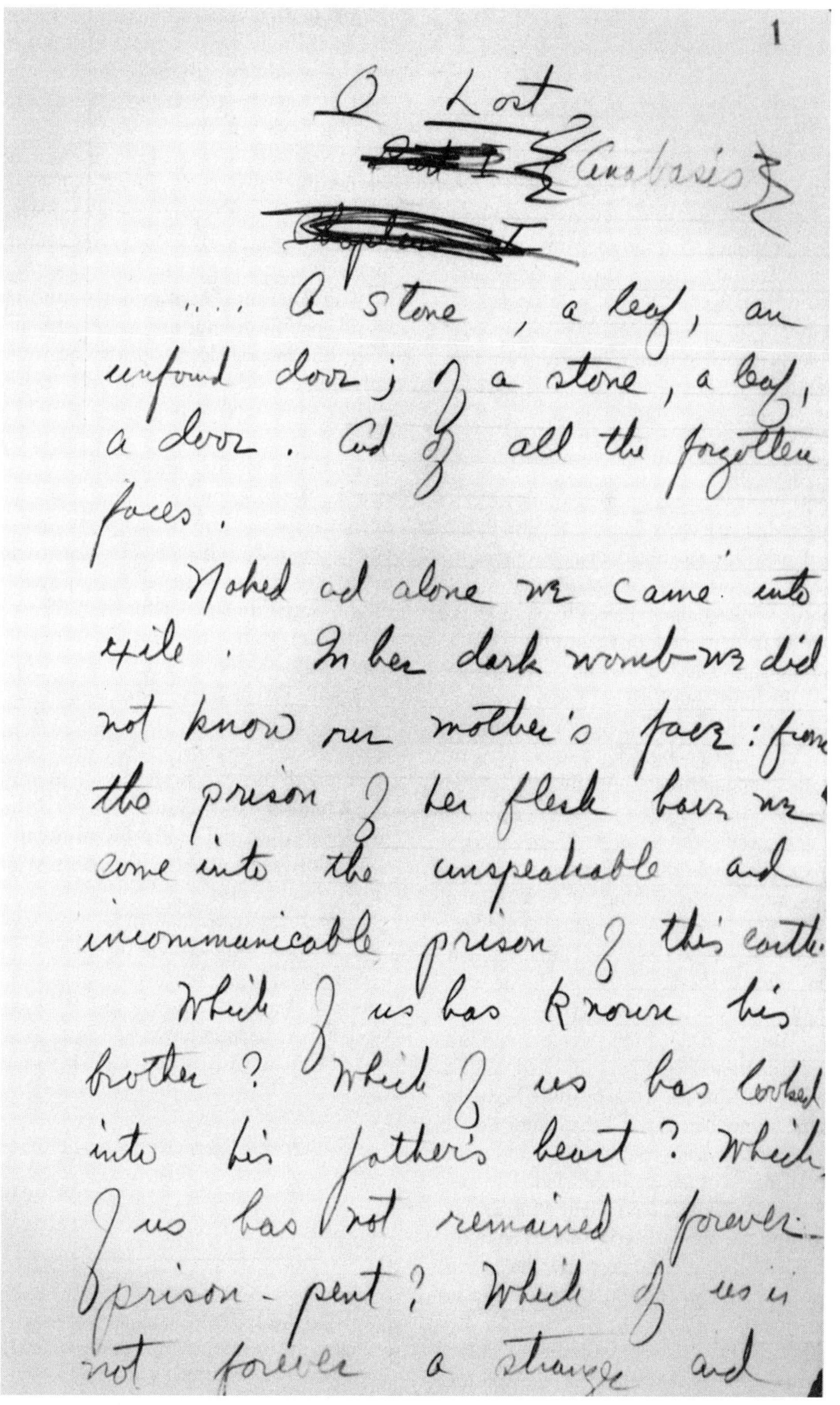

1

O Lost

~~Part I~~ {Anabasis}

~~Chapter I~~

... A stone, a leaf, an unfound door; of a stone, a leaf, a door. And of all the forgotten faces.

Naked and alone we came into exile. In her dark womb we did not know our mother's face: from the prison of her flesh have we come into the unspeakable and incommunicable prison of this earth.

Which of us has known his brother? Which of us has looked into his father's heart? Which of us has not remained forever prison-pent? Which of us is not forever a stranger and

The opening from the first ledger for "O Lost." Abe Smith, one of Wolfe's former students, typed the manuscript (William B. Wisdom Collection, Houghton Library, Harvard University).

Wolfe finished the manuscript "O Lost" on 31 March 1928. He wrote his mother the same day.

Harvard Club
27 West 44th Street
Saturday, March 31 1928

Dear Mama: I finished the book on which I have been working for the last twenty months a few days ago, and I sent a copy to a publisher for reading Monday afternoon. What their decision will be I do not know and will not for another four weeks. It is a huge book, but not too long, I hope, for publication. My friends are very hopeful about it–more so than I, because I am too tired to be hopeful or desperate, or any thing else at present. I have six weeks more of teaching at N. Y. U.–it seems to me to be six years, but I will do my work thoroughly and finish up.

Whether this book succeeds or not, I think we can both have this hope–I have always finished any job that I have begun. It seems to me most of the failure comes to people who give up half way. In spite of the fact that I know nothing of the book's ultimate fate, I have a feeling of victory: I have done a tremendous piece of work–it took up over a year and a half of my life, and almost drove me crazy at the finish, but I *did* it. I know now that if I had given up, I should have done great damage to myself–I should have had an ugly fight to wage with myself at some other time in my life. At any rate, I have at last learned how to work–and that's a big thing.

Now, mama, I need a rest desperately–but there's nothing doing for a short time. The Easter holiday comes next week–but for me it means nothing. At N. Y. U. the students are given only three days–Thurs, Fri, and Sat. Since my classes for the week are over Thurs. night it means I have only one extra day. If I came home, this means I would have to leave after 9:30 Wed night and be back before 6:30 Monday night. I am therefore coming home in May–examinations begin May 14–I should be throught by May 25. If I have a week or more between exams. I may come home then. If not, I shall come down after everything is over. I shall probably go away again this summer. My plans, as usual, are undecided. The university people want me back and have offered me a raise in salary–a small one, all they can give. But everything depends on the book: if any one takes it, I shall drop everything like a shot, and write another one I have in mind.

If not, I think the time may have come for me to get out of teaching any way. No one can ever tell me again that teaching is "easy" work: it takes the marrow out of your bones if you try to do it well. Since I have never intended to be a teacher, and since it represents a compromise whereby I may live while I write, I think I may try to compromise hereafter in a more profitable direction–advertising, for example. In other words, if I'm going to wear myself out, I see no reason why I shouldn't try to make some money out of it. Do you? I'll have more time to write hereafter. I've heard nothing from you in a long time. Please let me know about yourself at once. How is your health? How is the family? How is business? Tell Fred I am writing him. The Boston episode didn't bother me at all–I mean Hilda's gossip. Both Hilda and Elaine waste themselves in idle gabble. If they can't tell a true story, they invent one. That's one of the troubles of the world–people get nothing done because they spend all their time in foolish gossip. I've begun to find that the only thing to do is to stick to your job, grit your teeth, and let them talk. When I was a child I daydreamed about having five or ten million dollars and spending it on steam yachts, automobiles, great estates, and swank. Now I know that happiness is not to be got at in that way: the only way I know is to find the thing you want to do with all your heart, and to work like hell doing it. I may never be happy even so, but if I did nothing I'd be ready for the keepers in six months.

I am going into dry dock repairs for the first time in almost two years. I have been to the dentist, and think I shall see some one about my eyes. One of them is bothering me, but I think a few days' rest will fix it. As a matter of fact, I think nothing much is wrong with me, except my feeble mind: my brains feel like a plate of cold scrambled eggs. I thought the dentist would find me ready for grinding, yanking, and shiny false teeth, but he found only a broken filling and a small cavity.

So I may have a few more months of life in me yet.

Tell me if the wonderful mountain Springtime has begun yet. It began here, but changed its mind a day or two ago–we have had rain and cold since. But, thank God, it can't be long now.

Write when you can. Give my love to everyone.

Your Son
Tom.

–*The Letters of Thomas Wolfe to His Mother,* pp. 128–130

> But I had to write of things which were a part of me, out of my own experience, things which I knew. I don't believe that a worthy book can be produced by anyone who attempts merely to reach up into the thin air and pluck from it a story which has no background of life.
>
> – *Thomas Wolfe Interviewed,* p. 7

Wolfe (far right) at Foxhollow, the Dows family estate at Rhinebeck, on the Hudson River. Pictured with him (left to right) are Elsie Benkard; his friend Olin Dows; and Dows's mother, Margaret, and sister, Alice. Wolfe often visited the estate in the 1920s to escape the city (James C. Cleary).

After completing "O Lost," Wolfe planned to write a more conventional, commercial book, a love story about a wealthy young painter and an Austrian girl, which he called "The River People." This contrived plot did not hold his interest, although he continued working sporadically on it for most of 1928. Wolfe's friend Olin Dows was the model for Joel Pierce, the young protagonist. Passages involving the wealthy "Pierce" family, based on Dows's family, and their estate on the Hudson were salvaged for use in Of Time and the River. *Wolfe made this outline for his aborted novel in one of his pocket notebooks, sometime between fall 1927 and September 1928.*

THE RIVER PEOPLE

Persons–Grosbeak.
His sister–Ducks.
John comes through Vienna on way to India.
Next-to-Last Chapter–Lili's death at hands of John.
Last Chapter–Party of friends.

THE RIVER PEOPLE

Chap. I–Harvard
Chap. II–New York–Hotel–Summer
Chap. III–The River People–The Hudson
Chap. IV–Europe
Chap. V–New York–Autumn–The River
Chap. VI–The Winter–The Garret
Chap. VII–The Spring–The Lodge–The House
Chap. VIII–The Picnic and Lawn Party–*John* (a cousin)
Chap. IX–Fourth of July at Astor's
Chap. IX–Vienna again–They live together there
Chap. X–Winter–New York–He is now away from them completely–living with her
Chap. XI–New York again
Chap. XII–The River–Reunion–The girl–Cousin John–Mother–Pups
Chap. XIII.

–*The Notebooks of Thomas Wolfe,* pp. 136–137

Placing "O Lost"

After several attempts to market the book herself, Aline Bernstein submitted the manuscript to literary agent Madeleine Boyd. After reading a third of the novel, Boyd jumped to her feet, shouting, "A genius! I have discovered a genius!" The following Wolfe letter of late March 1928 was submitted to several publishers with the manuscript.

NOTE FOR THE PUBLISHER'S READER

This book, by my estimate, is from 250,000 to 280,000 words long. A book of this length from an unknown writer no doubt is rashly experimental, and shows his ignorance of the mechanics of publishing. This is true: this is my first book.

But I believe it would be unfair to assume that because this is a very long book it is too long a book. A revision would, I think, shorten it somewhat. But I do not believe any amount of revision would make it a short book. It could be shortened by scenes, by pages, by thousands of words. But it could not be shorted by half, or a third, or a quarter.

There are some pages here which were compelled by a need for fullness of expression, and which had importance when the book was written not because they made part of its essential substance, but because, by setting them forth, the mind was released for its basic work of creation. These pages have done their work of catharsis, and may now be excised. But their excision would not make a short book.

It does not seem to me that the book is overwritten. Whatever comes out of it must come out block by block and not sentence by sentence. Generally, I do not believe the writing to be wordy, prolix, or redundant. And separate scenes are told with as much brevity and economy as possible. But the book covers the life of a large family intensively for a period of twenty years, and in rapid summary for fifty years. And the book tries to describe not only the visible outer lives of all these people, but even more their buried lives.

The book may be lacking in plot but it is not lacking in plan. The plan is rigid and densely woven. There are two movements–one outward and one downward. The outward movement describes the effort of a child, a boy, and a youth for release, freedom, and loneliness in new lands. The movement of experience is duplicated by a series of widening concentric circles, three of which are represented by the three parts of the book. The downward movement is represented by a constant excavation into the buried life of a group of people, and describes the cyclic curve of a family's life-genesis, union, decay, and dissolution.

To me, who was joined so passionately with the people in this book, it seemed that they were the greatest people I had ever known and the texture of their lives the richest and strangest; and discounting the distortion of judgment that my nearness to them would cause, I think they would seem extraordinary to anyone. If I could get my magnificent people on paper as they were, if I could get down something of their strangeness and richness in my book, I believed that no one would object to my 250,000 words; or, that if my pages swarmed with this rich life, few would damn an inept manner and accuse me of not knowing the technique for making a book, as practiced by Balzac, or Flaubert, or Hardy, or Gide. If I have failed to get any of this opulence into my book, the fault lies not in my people–who could make an epic–but in me.

Madeleine Boyd (right) and Kathleen Hoagland, who with her husband, Clayton, became friends with Wolfe in the 1930s, at the Thomas Wolfe Biography Club, New York University, January 1958 (The Aldo P. Magi Collection, University of North Carolina at Chapel Hill)

But that is what I wanted to do and tried to do. This book was written in simpleness and nakedness of soul. When I began to write the book twenty months ago I got back something of a child's innocency and wonder. You may question this later when you come to the dirty words. But the dirty words can come out quickly–if the book has any chance of publication, they will come out without conscience or compunction. For the rest, I wrote it innocently and passionately. It has in it much that to me is painful and ugly, but, without sentimentality or dishonesty, it seems to me, because I am a romantic, that pain has an inevitable fruition in beauty. And the book has in it sin and terror and darkness–ugly dry lusts, cruelty, a strong sexual hunger of a child–the dark, the evil, the forbidden. But I believe it has many other things as well, and I wrote it with strong joy, without counting the costs, for I was sure at the time that the whole of my intention–which was to come simply and unsparingly to naked life, and to tell all of my story without affection or lewdness–would be apparent. At that time I believed it was possible to write of all things, so long as it was honestly done. So far as I know there is not a nasty scene in the book,–but there are the dirty words, and always a casual and unimpeded vision of everything.

When I wrote the book I seized with delight everything that would give it color and richness. All the variety and madness of my people–the leper taint, the cruel waste, the dark flowering evil of life I wrote about with as much exultancy as health, sanity, joy.

It is, of course, obvious that the book is "autobiographical." But, in a literal sense, it is probably no more autobiographical than Gulliver's Travels. There is scarcely a scene that has its base in literal fact. The book is a fiction–it is loaded with invention: story, fantasy, vision. But it is a fiction that is, I believe, more true than fact–a fiction that grew out of a life completely digested in my spirit, a fiction which telescopes, condenses, and objectifies all the random or incompleted gestures of life–which tries to comprehend people, in short, not by telling what people did, but what they should have done. The most literal and autobiographical part of the book, therefore, is its picture of the buried life. The most exact thing in it is its fantasy–its picture of a child's soul.

I have never called this book a novel. To me it is a book such as all men may have in them. It is a book made out of my life, and it represents my vision of life to my twentieth year.

What merit it has I do not know. It sometimes seems to me that it presents a strange and deep picture of American life–one that I have never seen elsewhere; and that I may have some hope of publication. I do not know; I am very close to it. I want to find out about it, and to be told by someone else about it.

I am assured that this book will have a good reading by an intelligent person in a publishing house. I have written all this, not to propitiate you, for I have no peddling instinct, but entreat you, if you spend the many hours necessary for a careful reading, to spend a little more time in giving me an opinion. If it is not a good book, why? If parts are good and parts bad, what are they? If it is not publishable, could it be made so? Out of the great welter of manuscripts that you must read, does this one seem distinguished by any excellence, interest, superior merit?

I need a little honest help. If you are interested enough to finish the book, won't you give it to me?

–*To Loot My Life Clean,* pp. 1–3

Wolfe took a fourth trip abroad at the end of June 1928. He traveled in France, Belgium, and Germany. On 30 September 1928 he was injured in Munich during a drunken brawl with German revelers at the Oktoberfest. Wolfe was hospitalized until 4 October, spending his twenty-eighth birthday as a patient. His nose was broken, and he suffered several head wounds. In his 5 October 1928 letter to Aline Bernstein, he describes the brawl.

To continue. I went back to the hospital today to have my head dressed and bound. My wounds have healed splendidly–there is only one at the back of my head that needs a dressing. I shall go only one more time–on Monday–after that the doctors are done with me, and the rest is up to my new growth of hair, and the good will of my nose. I have bought a little black cap that fits snug over my head–it is the thing the students wear after they have had their duels, and it makes people stare and whisper, and waiters ask me very respectfully if I've had a sword fight. When I tell them it's nothing more gentlemanly than a brawl at the Oktoberfest they are visibly disappointed.

. . . .

I was quite drunk from the beer. I started down one of the aisles towards a side entrance. There I met several men–and perhaps a woman, although I did not see her until later. They were standing up by their table in the aisle, singing perhaps one of their beer songs before going away. They spoke to me–I was too drunk to understand what they said, but I am sure it was friendly enough. What happened from now on I will describe as clearly as I can remember, although there are lapses and gaps in my remembrance. One of them, it seems to me, grasped me by the arm–I moved away, he held on, and although I was not angry, but rather in an excess of exuberance, I knocked him over a table. Then I rushed out of the place exultantly, feeling like a child who has thrown a stone through a window. Unhappily I could not run fast–I had drunk too much and was wearing my coat. Outside it was raining hard; I found myself in an enclosure behind some of the fair buildings–I had come out of a side entrance. I heard shouts and cries

An Oktoberfest beer hall. In The Web and the Rock *Wolfe writes of a "thousand beery faces . . . in that vast and murky hall . . . the image of savage faces in the old dark forest of barbaric time" (The North Carolina Collection, University of North Carolina Library at Chapel Hill).*

behind me, and turning, I saw several men running down upon me. One of them was carrying one of the fold-up chairs of the beer hall–it is made of iron and wood. I saw that he intended to hit me with this, and I remember that this angered me. I stopped and turned and in that horrible slippery mudhole I had a bloody fight with these people. I remember the thing now with horror as a kind of hell of slippery mud, and blood, and darkness, with the rain falling upon us several maniacs who were trying to kill. At that time I was too wild, too insane to be afraid, but I seemed to be drowning in mud–it was really the blood that came pouring from my head into my eyes–and there was *always, always* alive in me one bright living spark of sanity and consciousness. This place in my brain and my heart kept crying out for you–it kept crying out *Aline, Aline;* not for your help and guidance, but because it seemed to me I was lost; and I thought with pity and horror of all the sea between us–first of the actual Atlantic between us (drowning in mud and blood I seemed to hear the sound of each separate wave that lengthened out from Europe to America)–and then of a greater sea of fate and chance which had separated us–here I saw myself drowning in hell a bloody snarling beast, and you, all glorious, at the other end of the universe, unable to redeem me.

I was drowning in oceans of mud, choking, smothering. I felt the heavy bodies on top of me, snarling, grunting, smashing at my face and body. I rose up under them as if coming out of some horrible quicksand–Then my feet slipped again in the mud, and I went down again into the bottomless mud. I felt the mud beneath me, but what was really blinding and choking me was the torrent of blood that streamed from gashes in my head. I did not know I bled.

Somehow–I do not know how it came about–I was on my feet again, and moving towards the dark forms that swept in towards me. When I was beneath them in the mud, it seemed as if all the roaming mob of that hall had piled upon me, but there were probably not more than three. From this time on I remember fighting with only two men, and later there was a woman who clawed my face. The smaller figure–the smaller man–rushed towards me, and I struck it with my fist. It went diving away into the mud, and this fellow I remember no more until I saw him later in the police station. Then as I turned toward the larger figure I saw the heavy fist swing towards me. It was a great, clumsy, lumbering blow that a boy might have avoided, but I was too drunk either to avoid blows or to notice them. I saw it coming; it struck me full on the side of the nose; I was turned half around by it, and felt the numb scrunch of broken cartilage. Then I struck at this figure and missed it–it must have been six feet away–struck again and knocked it into the mud. It rose, we struggled together in the slime, I was choking in blood and cared for nothing now but to end it finally–to kill this other thing or be killed. So with all my strength I threw it to the earth: I could not see, but I fastened my fingers and hand in its eyes and face–it was choking me, but presently it stopped. I was going to hold until I felt no life there in the mud below me. The woman was now on my back, screaming, beating me over the head, gouging at my face and eyes. She was screaming out "Leave my man alone!" ("Lassen Mir den Mann stehen"–as I remember). Some people came and pulled me from him–the man and woman screamed and jabbered at me, but I could not make out what they said, except her cry of "Leave my man alone," which I remember touched me deeply because I saw you standing there in her, as indeed I sometimes see you in all women. These people went away–where or how I don't know–but I saw them later in the police station, so I judge they had gone there. And now–very foolishly perhaps–I went searching around in the mud for my hat–my old rag of a hat which had been lost, and which I was determined to find before leaving. Some German people gathered around me yelling and gesticulating and one man kept crying "Ein Arzt! Ein Arzt!" ("A Doctor! A Doctor!") I felt my head all wet, but thought it was the rain, until I put my hand there and brought it away all bloody. At this moment, three or four policemen rushed up, seized me, and hustled me off to the station. First they took me to the police surgeons–I was taken into a room with a white hard light. The woman was lying on a table with wheels below it. The light fell upon her face–her eyes were closed. I think this is the most horrible moment of my life–how far away I felt from you then I can never put into words. I thought she was dead, and that I would never be able to remember how it happened. The surgeons made me sit down in a chair while they dressed my head wounds. Then one of them looked at my nose, and said it was broken, and that I must go the next day to a doctor. When I got up and looked around the woman and the wheeled table was gone–I am writing this Saturday (six days later); if she were dead surely by this time I would know.

–*My Other Lonliness,* pp. 223–227

Wolfe's fictionalization of the aftermath of the brawl in Munich appeared in Chapter 50 of The Web and the Rock. *In the passage Wolfe was the nickname Monk for his alter ego George Webber.*

In his hospital room in Munich, Monk sat on the edge of his bed. Facing him, on the wall, was a mirror above the dresser, and he stared into it.

"Man's image in a broken looking glass." What of his broken image in a looking glass unbroken?

Out of the dark pool of the looking glass, the Thing hinged forward at the waist, the trunk foreshortened, the thick neck sunken in the hulking shoulders, the barrel contours of the chest, the big paw clasped around the knee. So was he made, so fashioned.

And what nature had invented, human effort had improved. In the dark pool of the mirror the Thing was more grotesque and simian than it had ever been. Denuded of its shock of hair, the rakishly tonsured skull between the big wings of its ears came close upon the corrugated shortness of the forehead into the bushy ridges of the brow; below this, the small, battered features, the short pug nose, up-tilted, flattened towards the right (it had been broken at the center on the other side), the long upper lip, thick mouth, the general look of the startled, quick attentiveness–it was a good job. Not since childhood had he looked so much the part the boys had made for him–the "Monk."

He looked at it now, and it at him, with a quizzical, detached objectiveness, not as a child looks in a mirror, at the silent eloquence of his pooled self, unspeaking, saying "I," but outside of it, and opposite, regardant, thinking, "Well, by God, *you* are a pretty sight!"–and meaning, not *Himself,* but *It.*

–*The Web and the Rock,* p. 689

When I write, I must write honestly. Too many have tried to imitate the gentility of the English, when we in America are different, without the lengthy background which makes their writing fit the setting, and therefore makes it real. We are pioneers, builders, and vigorous ones, too. To write of such with too much gentility is dishonest, unsatisfying. If we are to get anywhere surely we must paint life as it is, full and deep. Not all of it is sugared, sinless. If that were true, perhaps we would be less attractive, less worthy of being written about.

–*Thomas Wolfe Interviewed,* p. 7

Wolfe and Scribners

Wolfe's fortunes changed after he was released from the hospital. He received a letter from Charles Scribner's Sons editor Maxwell E. Perkins expressing interest in "O Lost." The 22 October 1928 letter had been sent to Munich and forwarded to Wolfe in Vienna.

Dear Mr. Wolfe:

Mrs. Ernest Boyd left with us some weeks ago, the manuscript of your novel, "O Lost." I do not know whether it would be possible to work out a plan by which it might be worked into a form publishable by us, but I do know that setting the practical aspects of the matter aside, it is a very remarkable thing, and that no editor could read it without being excited by it, and filled with admiration by many passages in it, and sections of it.

Your letter that came with it, shows that you realize what difficulties it presents, so that I need not enlarge upon this side of the question. What we should like to know is whether you will be in New York in a fairly near future, when we can see you and discuss the manuscript. We should certainly look forward to such an interview with very great interest.

Ever truly yours,
[Maxwell Perkins]

–*To Loot My Life Clean,* p. 3

Maxwell E. Perkins, Wolfe's editor at Charles Scribner's Sons

Wolfe soon replied to Perkins's letter.

Vienna, Saturday Nov 17, 1928

Dear Mr. Perkins: Your letter of October 22 which was addressed to Munich, was sent on to me here. I have been in Budapest for several weeks and came here last night. I got your letter at Cook's this morning.

Mrs Ernest Boyd wrote me a few weeks ago that she was coming abroad, and said that you had my book. I wrote her to Paris but have not heard from her yet.

I can't tell you how good your letter has made me feel. Your words of praise have filled me with hope, and are worth more than their weight in diamonds to me. Sometimes, I suppose, praise does more harm than good, but this time it was badly needed, whether deserved or not–I came abroad over four months ago determined to put the other book out of my mind, and to get to work on a new one. Instead, I have filled one note book after another, my head is swarming with ideas–but I have written nothing that looks like a book yet. In Munich I did write thirty or forty thousand words; then I got my head and my nose broken, and began to have things happen thick and fast with a great many people, including the police. I have learned to read German fairly well, and have learned something of their multitudinous books. But I had indigestion from seeing and trying to take in too much, and I was depressed at my failure to settle down to work. Now I feel better. I have decided to come back to New York in December, and I shall come to see you very soon after my arrival.

I have not looked at my book since I gave a copy to Mrs. Boyd–at the time I realized the justice of all people said–particularly the impossibility of printing it in its present form and length. But at that time I was "written out" on it–I could not go back and revise. Now I believe I can come back to it with a much fresher and more critical feeling.–I have no right to expect others to do for me what I should do for myself, but, although I am able to criticize wordiness and over-abundance in others, I am not able practically to criticize it in myself. The business of selection, and of revision is simply hell for me–my efforts to cut out 50000 words may sometimes result in my adding 75000.

As for the obscene passages and the dirty words, I know perfectly well that no publisher could print them. Yet, I swear to you, it all seemed to me very easy and practical when I wrote them.–But already I have begun to write a long letter to you, when all I should do is to thank you for your letter and say when I am coming back. Then the other things can come out when I see you.

But your letter has given me new hope for the book–I have honestly always felt that there are parts of it of which I need not be ashamed, and which might justify some more abiding form. I want you to know that you have no very stiff necked person to deal with as regards the book–I shall probably agree with most of the criticisms, although I hope that my own eagerness and hopefulness will not lead me into a weak acquiescence to everything.

I want the direct criticism and advice of an older and more critical person. I wonder if at Scribners I can find Someone who is interested enough to talk over the whole huge Monster with me–part by part. Most people will say "it's too long," "its got to be cut," "parts have to come out," and so on–but obviously this is no great help to the poor wretch who has done the deed, and who knows all this, without always knowing how he's going to remedy it.

I am sorry that Mrs Boyd sent you the letter that I wrote for the Reader. She said it was a very foolish letter, but added cheerfully that I would learn as I grow older. I wish I had so much faith. I told her to tear the letter out of the binding; but if it indicated to you that I did realize some of the difficulties, perhaps it was of some use. And I realize the difficulties more than ever now.

I am looking forward to meeting you, and I am still youthful enough to hope that something may come of it. It will be a strange thing indeed to me if at last I shall manage to make a connection with such a firm as Scribner's which, in my profound ignorance of all publishing matters, I had always thought vaguely was a solid and somewhat conservative house. But it may be that I am a conservative and at bottom very correct person. If this is true, I assure you I will have no very great heartache over it, although once it might have caused me trouble. At any rate, I believe I am through with firing off pistols just for the fun of seeing people jump–my new book has gone along for 40000 words without improprieties of language–and I have not tried for this result.

Please forgive my use of the pencil–in Vienna papers and pen and ink, as well as many other things that abound in our own fortunate country, are doled out bit by bit under guard. I hope you are able to make out my scrawl which is more than many people do–and that you will not forget about me before I come back.

Cordially Yours

Thomas Wolfe

My address in New York is The Harvard Club–I get my mail there. Here in Vienna, at Thomas Cook's, but as I'm going to Italy in a week, I shall probably have no more mail before I get home

–*To Loot My Life Clean,* pp. 3–5

Wolfe's notebook entry of 29 December 1928 shows his thoughts before his landing in New York City.

Saturday Night–

Today has been the stormiest weather we have yet had–afraid it has slowed the ship down considerably. Sea has been marvellous–sky sunshiney–terrific gale blowing–mountainous waves exploding in clouds of smoke–emerald green wake–The ship's stern rolls and lifts, and plunges upward into air like toy rocket–the huge waves come under the hull, and she bumps over them in a distressing way–I am enormously bored with these Italians–I feel horror and disgust and meanness at their sullen dark uncleanliness.

But most of all with the fat priest and his unending complaint, his unending eating, his unending tales of dieting.

The young sporty Italo-Americans play cards for a nickel or 3 cents and curse each other. The cur-snarl "What th' hell you want to know for what I got?" etc.

Of what I shall find in New York; of what life I shall lead there nothing yet. That must wait.

–*The Notebooks of Thomas Wolfe,* p. 297

Maxwell Perkins recalled his first meeting with Thomas Wolfe on 2 January 1929 in an essay published posthumously in The Harvard Library Bulletin *(Autumn 1947): "Wolfe arrived in New York and stood in the doorway of my boxstall of an office leaning against the door jamb. When I looked up and saw his wild hair and bright countenance–although he was so altogether different physically–I thought of Shelley. He was fair, but his hair was wild, and his face was bright and his head disproportionately small." At this meeting, Perkins did not commit Scribners to publication until details could be agreed upon, and he had made revision suggestions for Wolfe to consider.*

Wolfe made the following notes in preparation for his second meeting with Perkins.

Notes:

I propose to correct and revise the mss. 100 pages at a time, and if possible to deliver 100 pages every week.

Proposal for Condensation

First, to cut out every page every word that is not essential to the meaning or emphasis of the writing–If I can find even 10 words on every page this will be 10,000 or more in entire mss.

Then, to cut out the introductory part, and write a new beginning.

To shorten the child-in-the-cradle scenes.

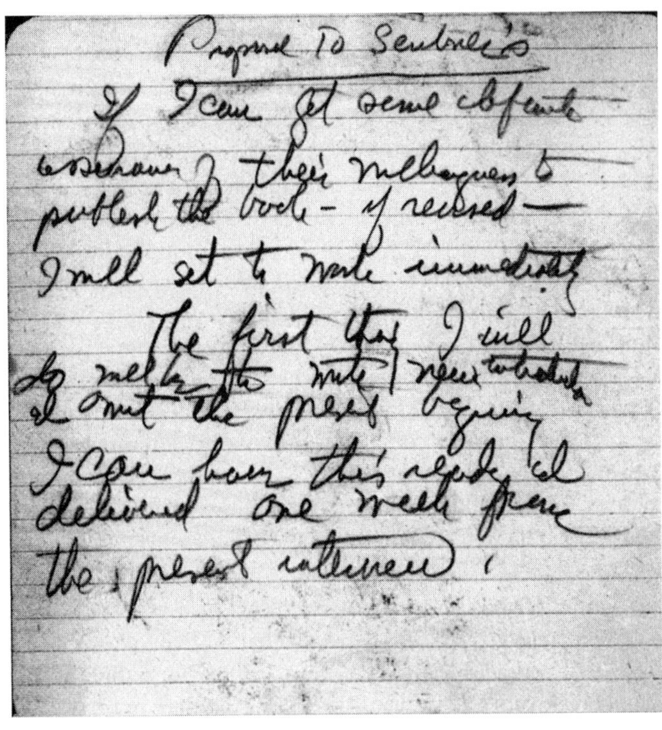

Proposal To Scribner's
If I can get some definite assurance of their willingness to publish the book – if revised – I will set to work immediately. The first thing I will do is make the cuts I need [illegible] I omit the present beginning. I can have this ready [illegible] delivered one week from the present interview.

Page from Wolfe's notebook following his first meeting with Perkins (William B. Wisdom Collection, Houghton Library, Harvard University)

To shorten St. Louis scene save for Grover's death.

To correct all unnecessary coarseness in language, and to cut out unnecessary pages and passages scattered through the book.

To revise Newport News scenes, and to omit scene with woman on the boat.

To shorten State University part as much as possible–and further, in the university scenes to keep Eugene's relations with his family uppermost.

Questions:

–What about several pages that list all the smells and odors?

–What about child's fantasies?

–What about the seduction scene with the waitress in Charleston?

–What about paper-boy scenes, and especially that one with negress?

Scribner's suggests unity of scene so far as possible.

What about Julia's various trips to Hot Springs, Florida, New Orleans, and so on?

–*The Notebooks of Thomas Wolfe,* pp. 301–302

On 7 January Wolfe and Perkins met a second time, and Perkins agreed to publish "O Lost." In his 9 January 1929 letter to Perkins, Wolfe accepted the proposed terms.

Dear Mr Perkins: I got your letter this morning and I have just come from a talk with Mrs. Madeleine Boyd, my literary agent.

I am very happy to accept the terms you offer me for the publication of my book, *O Lost.* Mrs Boyd is also entirely satisfied.

I am already at work on the changes and revisions proposed in the book, and I shall deliver to you the new beginning some time next week.

Although this should be only a business letter I must tell you that I look forward with joy and hope to my connection with Scribner's. To-day–the day of your letter–is a very grand day in my life. I think of my relation to Scribner's thus far with affection and loyalty, and I hope this marks the beginning of a long association that they will not have cause to regret. I have a tremendous lot to learn, but I believe I shall go ahead with it; and I know that there is far better work in me than I have yet done.

–*To Loot My Life Clean,* p. 8

Wolfe kept the contract for "O Lost," signed 9 January, in his inner breast-coat pocket with the advance for $450 pinned to it (a 10 percent commission had already been paid to Madeleine Boyd). In his 12 January 1929 letter to Margaret Roberts, he described his excitement following the acceptance of his first novel.

This is a horribly long letter. I'm as limp as a rag. I pity the people who have to read it and I pity the poor devil who wrote it.

Harvard Club
New York
Saturday, January 12, 1929

Dear Mrs. Roberts:

Everything you write has power to touch and move me and excite me. My heart beats faster when I see your writing on a piece of paper, and I read what you write me over and over again, exultant and happy over every word of praise you heap upon me. Nothing you have ever written me has so stirred me as your letter which I got today. I have mounted from one happiness to another during this past week since I came back from Europe, and the knowledge that you are now so generously sharing with me my joy and hope just about sends the thermometer up to the boiling point. For several days now I have felt like that man in one of Leacock's novels who "sprang upon his horse and rode madly off in all directions." I have literally been like that–at times I have not known what to do with myself. I would sit in the club here stupidly, staring at the publishers' glorious letter of acceptance; I would rush out and walk eighty blocks up Fifth Avenue through all the brisk elegant crowd of late afternoon. I am gradually beginning to feel ground again, and it is occurring to me that the only thing to do is to get to work again.

I have the contract in my inner breast pocket, ready to be signed, and a check for $450 pinned to it, $50 having already been paid to my literary agent, Mrs. Ernest Boyd, as her 10 per cent share. There is literally no reason why I should walk around New York with these documents on my person, but in a busy crowd I will sometimes take them out, gaze tenderly at them, and kiss them passionately. Scribners have already signed the contract. I am to sign it Monday, but, with their customary fairness, they have advised me to show it to a lawyer before I sign it. I am therefore going with Mrs. Boyd on Monday to see Mr. Melville Cane, a lawyer, a poet, a member of Harcourt, Brace and Co., and the finest attorney on theatrical and publishing contracts in America. I have met him once, he read part of my book, and he has since been my friend and well-wisher. He told the person who sent me to him sometime ago that I represented what he had wanted to be in his own life, that I was one of the most remarkable people he had ever met. And when he was told yesterday that I had sold my book he was delighted.

I am filled at the moment with so much tenderness towards the whole world that my agent, Mrs. Boyd, is worried–she is a Frenchwoman, hard and practical, and she does not want me to get too soft and trusting in my business relations. I wrote Scribners a letter of acceptance in which I could not hold myself in. I spoke of my joy and hope, and my affection and loyalty towards the publishers who had treated me so well, and my hope that this would mark the beginning of a long and happy association which they would have no cause to regret. In reply I got a charming letter in which they told me I would never have to complain of the interest and respect they have for my work. Mrs. Boyd herself was almost as happy as I was–although she is agent for almost every important French author in America, and publishing and acceptances are the usual thing for her–she said the thing was a great triumph for her as well, as Scribners consider me "a find" and are giving her credit for it.

It is all very funny and moving. Seven months ago when she got the book and read parts of it, she got interested–it was too long (she said), but there were fine things in it, she thought someone might be interested, and so on. Now I am a "genius"–she is already sorry for poor fellows like Dreiser and Anderson; she told the publishers that "this boy has everything they have in addition to education, background, (etc, etc,). Of course, poor fellows," she said, "it's not their fault–they never had the opportunity"–and so on and so on. Also, she pictures the other publishers as tearing their hair, gnashing their teeth, and wailing because they are not publishing the book. She gave it to one or two to read–they all said it had fine things in it, but was too long, they must think about it, etc.–and meanwhile (says she) Scribners got it. She said she was talking to one of them (Jonathan Cape, his name is) a week ago. He said at once: "Where is your genius, and when can I see him?" She told him Scribners had it and (groaning with grief, no doubt) he begged her to let him have first chance at the next one. We must salt all this down–her Gallic impetuosity, I mean–and I've got to come to earth and begin work.

I've had to tell several people, and everyone is almost as glad as I am. The University people are throwing a job at my head. I can stop in June if I want, they say. This is absurd. Of what earthly use would I be to them for only a half year–but they will give me more money, I think, than last year, fewer hours, (eight or ten) and almost no paper work. Now that this thing has happened, I feel kinder toward teaching than ever. Of course, my $450 will not last forever, and even if the book goes well I must wait until six months after its publication (so reads a *regular* clause in my contract) for my first statement, and every four months thereafter. The University people are genuinely friends and well wishers–the dean, a wealthy and fine young man (of

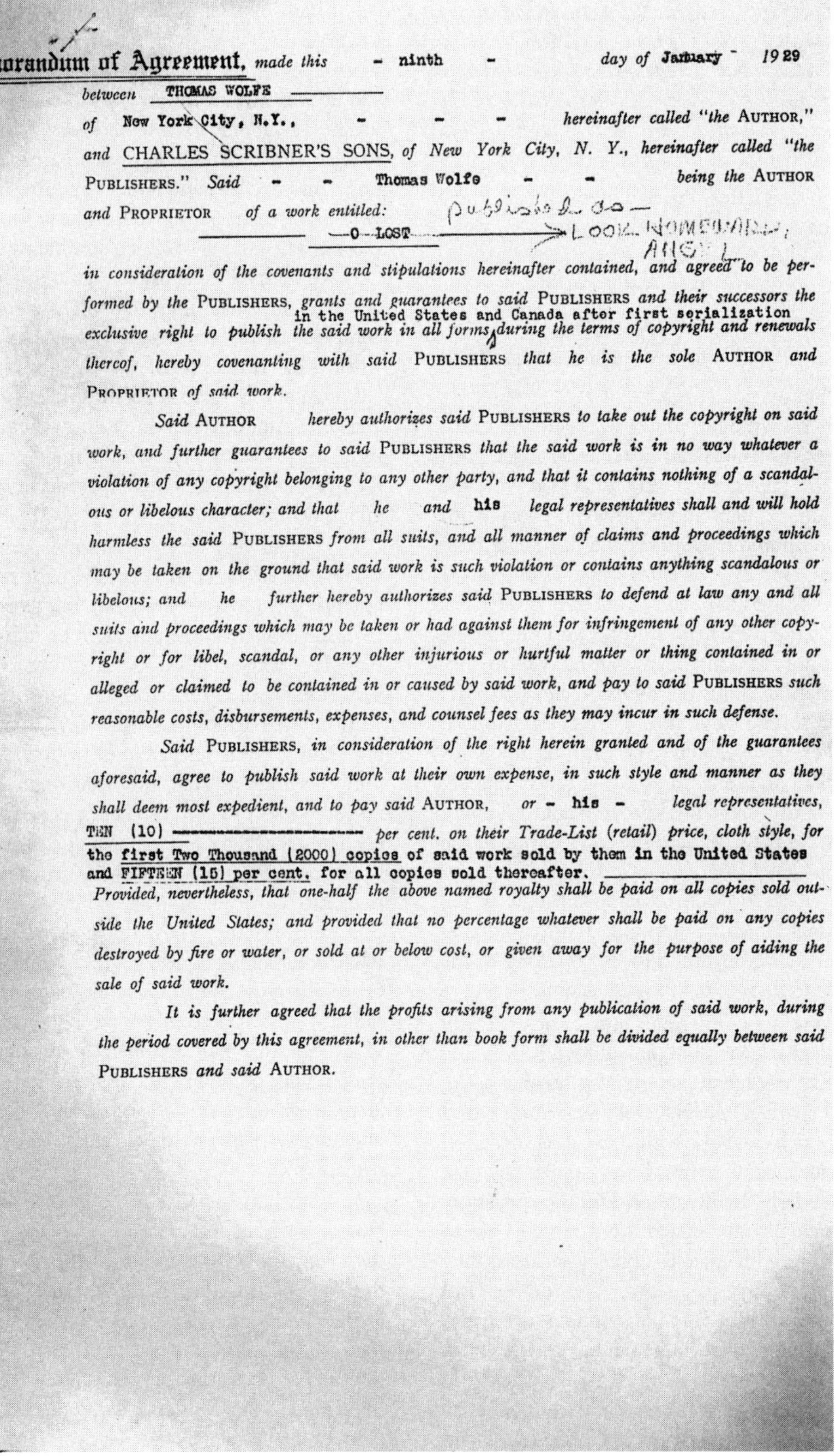

[...]orandum of Agreement, *made this* - ninth - *day of* January - 1929 *between* THOMAS WOLFE *of* New York City, N.Y., - - - *hereinafter called "the* AUTHOR," *and* CHARLES SCRIBNER'S SONS, *of New York City, N. Y., hereinafter called "the* PUBLISHERS." *Said* - - Thomas Wolfe - - *being the* AUTHOR *and* PROPRIETOR *of a work entitled:* published as — LOOK HOMEWARD, ANGEL

—O LOST—

in consideration of the covenants and stipulations hereinafter contained, and agreed to be performed by the PUBLISHERS, *grants and guarantees to said* PUBLISHERS *and their successors the exclusive right to publish the said work in all forms* in the United States and Canada after first serialization *during the terms of copyright and renewals thereof, hereby covenanting with said* PUBLISHERS *that* he *is the sole* AUTHOR *and* PROPRIETOR *of said work.*

Said AUTHOR *hereby authorizes said* PUBLISHERS *to take out the copyright on said work, and further guarantees to said* PUBLISHERS *that the said work is in no way whatever a violation of any copyright belonging to any other party, and that it contains nothing of a scandalous or libelous character; and that* he *and* his *legal representatives shall and will hold harmless the said* PUBLISHERS *from all suits, and all manner of claims and proceedings which may be taken on the ground that said work is such violation or contains anything scandalous or libelous; and* he *further hereby authorizes said* PUBLISHERS *to defend at law any and all suits and proceedings which may be taken or had against them for infringement of any other copyright or for libel, scandal, or any other injurious or hurtful matter or thing contained in or alleged or claimed to be contained in or caused by said work, and pay to said* PUBLISHERS *such reasonable costs, disbursements, expenses, and counsel fees as they may incur in such defense.*

Said PUBLISHERS, *in consideration of the right herein granted and of the guarantees aforesaid, agree to publish said work at their own expense, in such style and manner as they shall deem most expedient, and to pay said* AUTHOR, *or* - his - *legal representatives,* TEN (10) ———— *per cent. on their Trade-List (retail) price, cloth style, for* the first Two Thousand (2000) copies of said work sold by them in the United States and FIFTEEN (15) per cent. for all copies sold thereafter.

Provided, nevertheless, that one-half the above named royalty shall be paid on all copies sold outside the United States; and provided that no percentage whatever shall be paid on any copies destroyed by fire or water, or sold at or below cost, or given away for the purpose of aiding the sale of said work.

It is further agreed that the profits arising from any publication of said work, during the period covered by this agreement, in other than book form shall be divided equally between said PUBLISHERS *and said* AUTHOR.

Contract for "O Lost" (Princeton University Library)

Expenses incurred for alterations in type or plates, exceeding twenty per cent. of the cost of composition and electrotyping said work, are to be charged to the AUTHOR'S *account.*

The first statement shall not be rendered until six months after date of publication; and thereafter statements shall be rendered semi-annually, on the AUTHOR'S *application therefor, in the months of February and August; settlements to be made in cash, four months after date of statement.*

If, on the expiration of five *years from date of publication, or at any time thereafter, the demand for said work should not, in the opinion of said* PUBLISHERS, *be sufficient to render its publication profitable, then, upon written notice by said* PUBLISHERS *to said* AUTHOR, *this contract shall cease and determine; and thereupon said* AUTHOR *shall have the right, at* his *option, to take from said* PUBLISHERS, *at cost, whatever copies of said work they may then have on hand; or, failing to take said copies at cost, then said* PUBLISHERS *shall have the right to dispose of the copies on hand as they may see fit, free from any percentage or royalty, and to cancel this contract.*

Provided, also, that if, at any time during the continuance of this agreement, said work shall become unsalable in the ordinary channels of trade, said PUBLISHERS *shall have the right to dispose of any copies on hand paying to said* AUTHOR - fifteen (15) - *per cent. of the net amount received therefor, in lieu of the percentage hereinbefore prescribed.*

Said Publishers shall pay to said Author the Sum of FIVE HUNDRED ($500.) DOLLARS (the receipt of which is hereby acknowledged) as an advance payment on the royalty account, said amount to be reimbursed to said Publishers from the first monies accruing under said royalties.

All monies due under this contract shall be paid to Mrs. Ernest Boyd, 131 East 19th Street, New York City, as representative of said author, and her receipt shall be a valid discharge for all said monies.

In consideration of the mutuality of this contract, the aforesaid parties agree to all its provisions, and in testimony thereof affix their signatures and seals.

[Witn]ess to signature of
Thomas Wolfe

Madeline Boyd

Thomas Wolfe

[Witn]ess to signature of
Charles Scribner's Sons

W. D. Watson

Charles Scribner's Sons
by Charles Scribner
Chairman

L. S.

thirty-eight or forty) would give me a job at any time–but I think this rather increases my value to them: it is a big swarming place, fond of advertising.

The people at Scribners want me to set to work on revision at once, but they told me they thought I would have to find work later. No one knows how many copies the book will sell, of course, and besides, I must wait eight or ten months after publication for my first money (if there is any, but perish *that* thought.) Mrs. Boyd says the contract is fair, regular, and generous–giving an advance of $500 on a first book is unusual–of course that $500 *comes out* later from my first royalties. The contract offers me 10% of the *retail* price of the book up to the first 2,000 copies: after that 15%. As the book is a very long one, it will have to sell, I think, for $2.50 or $3.00. You can estimate from this what it is possible to make–but for the Lord's sake, don't. This is a fascinating weakness I have succumbed to, and everything is too uncertain. There are also clauses covering foreign translation and publication, and publication is any other than book form. That means serial and movies, I suppose, but *that* won't happen to me on *this* book–but if it does, the publisher and author split the profits.

Mrs. Ernest Boyd is also recognized as my agent and business representative and all checks are payable to her. This may make my thrifty friends squirm–she also gets 10% of all my profits (I hope, naturally, her share is at least $100,000)–but it's the best arrangement. How hard she worked to bring this about I don't know. Nevertheless she did it and I'll pay the 10% cheerfully–that's the regular agents' rate. Also, I think it is just as well that I am managed by a practical person who knows a little business. Although it is a business matter and I ought not to get sentimental, I can't help having a warm spot in my heart for the old girl who brought it about. I might have done it by myself sooner or later, but she certainly helped enormously at the present.

Finally, I want to start and continue my life by being decent and loyal to those people who have stood by me–whether for business or personal reasons. If we muddy and cheapen the quality of our actual everyday life, the taint, I believe, is bound to show, sooner or later, in what we create. Mrs. Boyd is so happy that Scribners took it. She said I should be very proud of that; she said they were the most careful and exacting publishers in America–others publish fifty or a hundred novels a year, but Scribners only ten or twelve, although they bring out many other books. They are also trying to get the younger writers–they now have Ring Lardner, Scott Fitzgerald, and Ernest Hemingway (to say nothing of Wolfe). They were reading sections of my book, they told me, to Lardner and Hemingway a week before I got home–I'm afraid somewhat coarse and vulgar sections.

Finally, I must tell you that the ten days since I got home on the Italian boat have been the most glorious I have ever known. They are like all the fantasies I had as a child of recognition and success–only more wonderful. That is why my vision of life is becoming stranger and more beautiful than I thought possible a few years ago–it is the fantasy, the miracle that really happens. For *me* at any rate. My life, with its beginnings, has been a strange and miraculous thing. I was a boy from the mountains; I came from a strange wild family; I went beyond the mountains and knew the state; I went beyond the state and knew the nation, and its greatest university, only a magic name to my childhood; I went to the greatest city and met strange and beautiful people, good, bad, and ugly ones; I went beyond the seas alone and walked down the million streets of life. When I was hungry [and] penniless, anemic countesses, widows . . . –all manner of strange folk–came to my aid. In a thousand places the miracle has happened to me. Because I was penniless and took one ship instead of another, I met the great and beautiful friend who has stood by me through all the torture, struggle, and madness of my nature for over three years, and who has been here to share my happiness these past ten days. That another person, to whom success and greater success is constant and habitual, should get such happiness and joy from my own modest beginning is only another of the miracles of life.

Ten days ago I came home penniless, exhausted by my terrible and wonderful adventures in Europe, by all I had seen and learned, and with only the hated teaching–now become strangely pleasant–or the advertising, before me. The day after New Year's–truly a *New* Year for me–it began: the publisher's demand over the telephone that I come immediately to his office; that first long conference, as I sat there wild, excited, and trembling as it finally dawned on me that someone was at last definitely interested; the instructions to go away and think over what had been said two or three days; the second conference, when I was told definitely they had decided to take it; the formal letter of acceptance, with the terms of the contract, and finally the contract itself, and the sight of the blessed check. Is not this too a miracle?–to have happened to a penniless unhappy fellow in ten days? Are a child's dreams better than this? Mrs. Boyd, trying to hold me down a bit, said that the time would soon come when all this would bore me, when even notices and press clippings would mean so little to me that I would not glance at them. So, she says, does her husband, a well-known critic and writer, feel and act. But isn't it glorious that this should have happened to me when I was still young and rapturous enough to be thrilled by it? It may never come again, but I've had the magic–what Euripides calls "The apple tree, the singing, and the gold."

. . . .

In this same letter to Roberts, Wolfe gave his impressions not only of Maxwell Perkins but also John Hall Wheelock, who was primarily responsible for seeing Wolfe's books through the production process.

Mr. Perkins is not at all "Perkinsy"–name sounds Midwestern, but he is a Harvard man, probably New England family, early forties, but looks younger, very elegant and gentle in dress and manner. He saw I was nervous and excited, spoke to me quietly, told me to take my coat off and sit down. He began by asking certain general questions about the book and people (these weren't important–he was simply feeling his way around, sizing me up, I suppose). Then he mentioned a certain short scene in the book, and in my eagerness and excitement I burst out, "I know you can't print that! I'll take it out at once, Mr. Perkins." "Take it out?" he said. "It's one of the greatest short stories I have ever read." He said he had been reading it to Hemingway week before. Then he asked me if I could write a short introduction for it to explain the people–he was sure Scribner's Magazine would take it; if they didn't someone else would. I said I would. I was at once elated and depressed–I thought now that this little bit was all they wanted of it.

Then he began cautiously on the book. Of course, he said, he didn't know about its present form–somewhat incoherent and very long. When I saw now that he was really interested, I burst out wildly saying that I would throw out this, that, and the other–at every point he stopped me quickly saying, "No, no–you must let that stay word for word–that scene's simply magnificent." It became apparent at once that these people were willing to go far further than I had dared hope–that, in fact, they were afraid I would injure the book by doing too much to it. I saw now that Perkins had a great batch of notes in his hand and that on the desk was a great stack of handwritten paper–a complete summary of my whole enormous book. I was so moved and touched to think that someone at length had thought enough of my work to sweat over it in this way that I almost wept. When I spoke to him of this, he smiled and said everyone in the place had read it. Then he went over the book scene by scene–I found he was more familiar with the scenes and the names of characters than I was–I had not looked at the thing in over six months. For the first time in my life I was getting criticism I could really use. The scenes he wanted cut or changed were invariably the least essential and the least interesting; all the scenes that I had thought too coarse, vulgar, profane, or obscene for publication he forbade me to touch save for a word or two. There was one as rough as anything in Elizabethan drama–when I spoke of this he said it was a masterpiece, and that he had been reading it to Hemingway. He told me I must change a few words. He said the book was new and original, and because of its form could have no formal and orthodox unity, but that what unity it did have came from the strange wild people–the family–it wrote about, as seen through the eyes of a strange wild boy. These people, with relatives, friends, townspeople, he said were "magnificent"–as real as any people he had ever read of. He wanted me to keep these people and the boy at all times foremost–other business, such as courses at state university, etc., to be shortened and subordinated. Said finally if I was hard up he thought Scribners would advance money.

John Hall Wheelock

By this time I was wild with excitement–this really seemed something at last–in spite of his caution and restrained manner, I saw now that Perkins really was excited about my book, and had said more tremendous things about it. He saw how wild I was–I told him I had to go out and think–he told me to take two or three days–but before I left he went out and brought in another member of the firm, John Hall Wheelock, who spoke gently and quietly–he is a poet–and said my book was one of the most interesting he had read for years. I then went out and tried to pull myself together. A few days later, the second meeting–I brought notes along as to how I proposed to set to work, and so on. I agreed to deliver one hundred pages of corrected manuscript, if possible, every week. He listened, and then when I asked him if I could say something definite to a dear friend, smiled and said he thought so; that their minds were practically made up; that I should get to work immediately; and that I should have a letter from him in a few days. As I went prancing out I met Mr. Wheelock, who took me by the hand and said: "I hope you have a good place to work in–you have a big job ahead." I knew then that it was all magnificently true. I rushed out drunk with glory. In two days came the formal letter (I wired home then), and yesterday Mrs. Boyd got the check and contract which I am now carrying in my pocket. God knows this letter has been long enough–but I can't tell you half or a tenth of it, or of what they said.

Mr. Perkins said cautiously he did not know how the book would sell–he said it was something unknown and original to the readers, that he thought it would be a sensation with the critics, but that the rest is a gamble. But Mrs. Boyd says that to print such a gigantic manuscript from a young unknown person is so unusual that Scribners would not do it unless they thought they had a good chance of getting their money back. . . . I should love it, of course, if the book were a howling success, but my idea of happiness would be to retire to my apartment and gloat . . . and to let no more than a dozen people witness my gloating. But I think if I ever see man or woman in subway, elevated, or taxicab reading it, I will track that person home to see who he is or what he does, even if it leads me to Yonkers. And Mr. Perkins and Mr. Wheelock warned me not to go too much with "that Algonquin Crowd"–the Hotel Algonquin here is where most of the celebrities waste their time and admire one another's cleverness. This also makes me laugh. I am several million miles away from these mighty people, and at the present time want to get no closer. All the Theatre Guild people, whom I know through my dear friend, have called her up and sent congratulations.

But now is the time for sanity. My debauch of happiness is over. I have made promises: I must get to work. I am only one of the thousands of people who write books every year. No one knows how this one will turn out. You must therefore say nothing to the Asheville people about it yet. In course of time, I suppose, Scribners will announce it in their advertisements. As for the Civic Cup business, I am afraid that's out of the question. For one thing, no one knows anything about my book at home–whether it's good, bad, or indifferent. If anything is said about it, it must be later, after its publication. For another thing–and this troubles me now that my joy is wearing down–this book dredges up from the inwards of people pain, terror, cruelty, lust, ugliness, as well, I think, as beauty, tenderness, mercy. There are places in it which make me writhe when I read them; there are others that seem to me to be fine and moving. I wrote this book in a white heat, simply and passionately, with no idea of being either ugly, obscene, tender, cruel, beautiful, or anything else–only of

The Scribner Building, 597 Fifth Avenue

saying what I had to say because I had to. The only morality I had was in me; the only master I had was in me and stronger than me. I went into myself more mercilessly than into anyone else–but I am afraid there is much in this book which will wound and anger people deeply, particularly those at home. Yet terrible as parts are, there is little bitterness in it. Scribners told me people would cry out against this, because people are unable to realize that that spirit which is sensitive to beauty is also sensitive to pain and ugliness. Yet all of this goes into the making of the book, and because of this Scribners have believed in it and are publishing it. I will soften all I can but I cannot take out all the sting–without lying to myself and destroying the book. For this reason we must wait and see. If the people of Asheville some day want to heap coals of fire on my head by giving me a cup, perhaps I shall fill it with my tears of penitence–but I doubt that this will come for a long time. The people of Asheville, I fear, may not understand me after this book and may speak of me only with a curse–but some day, if I write other books, they will. And my God! What books I feel within me and what despair, since my hand and strength cannot keep up with all my heart has felt, my brain dreamed and thought!

–*The Letters of Thomas Wolfe,* pp. 162–166, 168–171

In a passage included in You Can't Go Home Again, *Wolfe fictionalized his first visit to Charles Scribner's Sons. Wolfe's persona is the protagonist George Webber and the publishing house is named James Rodney & Co.*

And now he moved slowly, the line of his mouth set grimmer than before, and his head was carried stiffly forward from the shoulders as if he were trying to hold himself to the course he had decided upon by focusing on some distant object straight before him. But all the while, as he went along before the entrance and the show windows filled with books which flanked it on both sides, he peered sharply out of the corner of his eye like a spy who had to find out what was going on inside the building without letting the passers-by observe his interest. He walked to the end of the block and turned about and then came back, and again as he passed in front of the publishing house he kept his face fixed straight ahead and looked stealthily out of the corner of his eye. For fifteen or twenty minutes he repeated this strange maneuver, and each time as he approached the door he would hesitate and half turn as if about to enter, and then abruptly go on as before.

Finally, as he came abreast of the entrance for perhaps the fiftieth time, he quickened his stride and seized the door knob–but at once, as though it had given him an electric shock, he snatched his hand away and backed off, and stood on the curb looking up at the house of James Rodney & Co. For several minutes more he stood there, shifting uneasily on his feet and watching all the upper windows as for a sign. Then, suddenly, his jaw muscles tightened, he stuck out his under lip in desperate resolve, and he bolted across the sidewalk, hurled himself against the door, and disappeared inside.

An hour later, if the policeman was still on duty at the corner, he was no doubt as puzzled and mystified as before by the young man's behavior as he emerged from the building. He came out slowly, walking mechanically, a dazed look on his face, and in one of his hands which dangled loosely at his sides, he held a crumpled slip of yellow paper. He emerged from the office of James Rodney & Co. like a man walking in a trance. With the slow and thoughtless movements of an automaton, he turned his steps uptown, and, still with the rapt and dazed look upon his face, he headed north and disappeared into the crowd.

It was late afternoon and the shadows were slanting swiftly eastward when George Webber came to his senses somewhere in the wilds of the upper Bronx. How he got there he never knew. All he could remember was that suddenly he felt hungry and stopped and looked about him and realized where he was. His dazed look gave way to one of amazement and incredulity, and his mouth began to stretch in a broad grin. In his hand he still held the rectangular slip of crisp yellow paper, and slowly he smoothed out the wrinkles and examined it carefully.

It was a check for five hundred dollars. His book had been accepted, and this was an advance against his royalties.

–*You Can't Go Home Again,* pp. 18–19

Photograph of Wolfe, spring 1929, commissioned by Scribners (photograph by Doris Ulmann; William B. Wisdom Collection, Houghton Library, Harvard University)

Editing "O Lost"

During the spring of 1929, Wolfe worked closely with Perkins editing "O Lost." The original manuscript was 1,114 pages with 330,000 words. The net reduction was about 60,000 words with a total of 147 cuts. In a letter to his sister Mabel, Wolfe discusses the progress of the editing.

[27 West 15th Street]
[New York]
May, 1929.

Dear Mabel:

Thanks for your letter which I got to-day. I don't suppose I have written much lately–I have very little sense of time when I am working. I am working every day with the editor of Scribners, Mr. Perkins, on the revision of my book. We are cutting out big chunks, and my heart bleeds to see it go, but it's die dog or eat

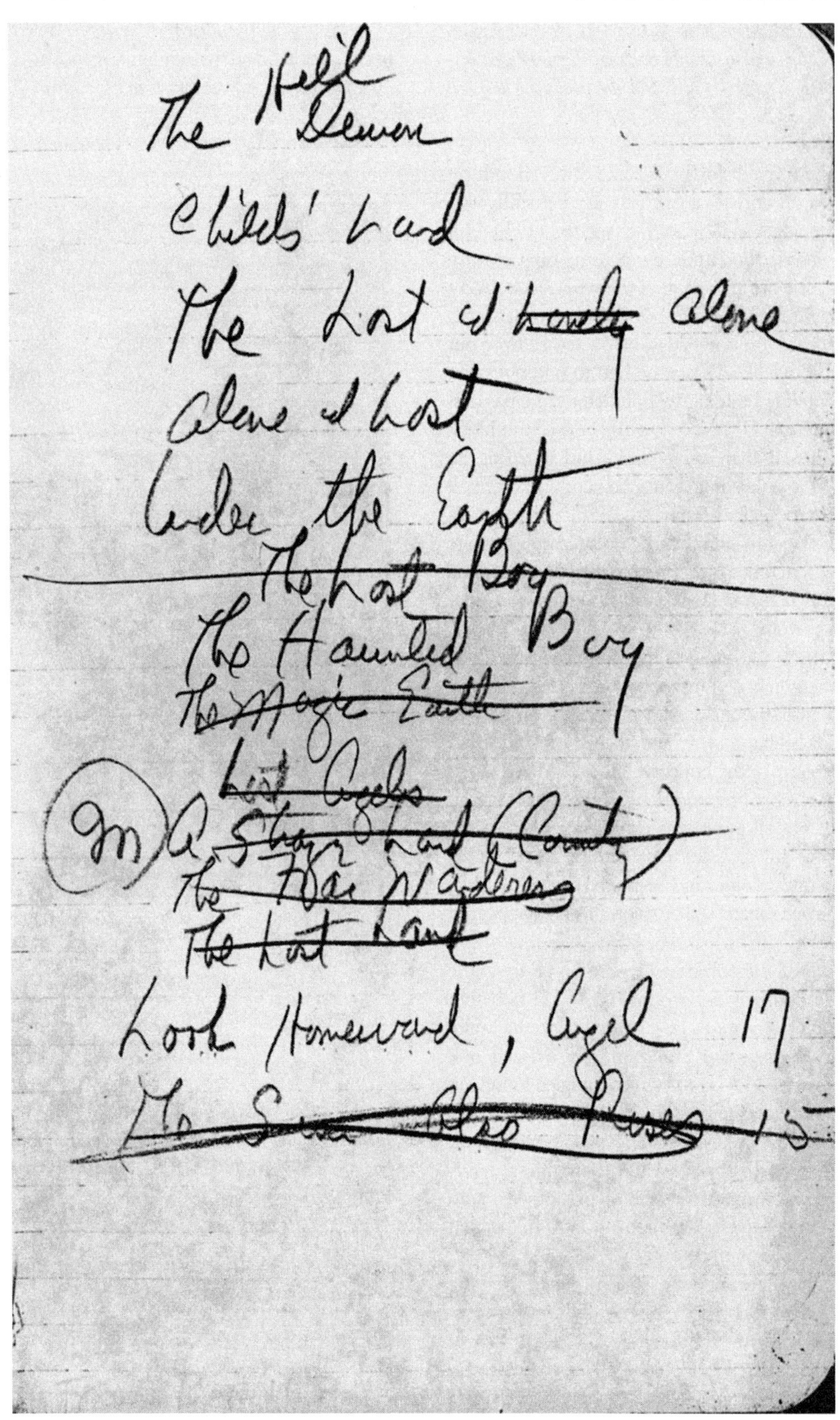
Child's Land
The Lost and alone
Alone and Lost
Under the Earth
The Lost Boy
The Haunted Boy
The Magic Earth
Lost Angels
A Strange Land (Country)
The Lost Land
Look Homeward, Angel 17

List of titles including, "Look Homeward, Angel," that Wolfe wrote in April for the editorial staff of Scribners, who wanted a better title for the book than "O Lost." Wolfe had earlier jotted down dozens of titles, including "The Buried Life," "The Childhood of Mr. Faust," and "The Lost Boy" (William B. Wisdom Collection, Houghton Library, Harvard University).

Where did the slaves sleep?

*

She had promised to take him to Baltimore where Gant had lived for several years, but she became frightened because of the cold weather, and their mounting expenses.

They had rooms in a little gas-lit lodging house on B. Street, and they ate in small lunchrooms along Pennsylvania avenue. Eliza visited the Swains, old Woodson street neighbors. Mr. Swain was one of the assistant secretaries of state. He had a precise Wilsonian face and polished manners. But he was a Republican. He had been a school teacher. He had two strapping sons who drank and fought a great deal, and were always in trouble. They caused their father much pain.

Page from the typescript for "O Lost" showing change made to Wolfe's mother's name. The complete carbon-copy typescript survives, but the printer's setting copy is lost. (William B. Wisdom Collection, Houghton Library, Harvard University).

the hatchet. Although we both hate to take so much out, we will have a shorter book and one easier to read when we finish. So, although we are losing some good stuff, we are gaining unity. This man Perkins is a fine fellow and perhaps the best publishing editor in America. I have great confidence in him and I usually yield to his judgment. The whole Scribner outfit think the book a remarkable thing–and Perkins told me the other day when I was in the dumps that they would all be very much surprised if the book wasn't a success. When I said that I hoped they would take another chance on me, he told me not to worry–that they expected to do my next book and the one after that, and so on indefinitely. That means a great deal to me. It means at any rate, that I no longer have to hunt for a publisher.

I've already seen the title page and a few specimen sheets of the type. They call this the "dummy." Of course, I'm excited about it. I can't say enough for the way Scribners have acted. They are fine people. They sent me to one of the most expensive photographers in town a few weeks ago, a woman who "does" the writers. What it cost I can't say, but she charges $150–$200 a dozen, I understand, and she kept me half a day. What in heaven's name they're going to do with them all I don't know–they say it's for advertising. They are going to begin advertising, I believe, this month or next, and they have asked me to write something about myself. Of course, that's always an agreeable job, isn't it? When the story and the book are coming out, I don't know, but everyone has become very busy this last month–I now have to go up to see the editor every day. I think the story will be held back until just before the book is published. Scribners are good salesmen, good business people, good advertisers. They are doing a grand job for me, and they believe in me.

–*The Letters of Thomas Wolfe,* pp. 177–178

As the novel was being proofread and printed, Wolfe worked mainly with John Hall Wheelock. The following excerpts provide a good example of their working relationship.

In his 17 July 1929 letter, Wheelock informed Wolfe that his story "An Angel on the Porch," an episode from the novel, was being published in Scribner's Magazine. *He then went on to discuss the text.*

Please note that I have deleted, on galley 80, several sections which it seems best to omit. You and Mr. Perkins had agreed to omit these sections, when you went over the manuscript, but in some way the printer set them up. I think nothing is lost by their omission. In the same way I have deleted one or two phrases in other places.

Is there any danger of confusion through the use of the names "Sheba," "Horty" and "Miss Amy"?

I have looked up and verified all your quotations, so you need not worry about these.

I wish I had time and space to tell you how my enthusiasm grows with the proofreading. I must content myself with the less gracious act of pointing out what seems to me a defect. If you do not agree with me, kindly disregard my criticism. It seems to me that the section beginning in the middle of galley 87 and running to Chapter 25, is too long. This is the section dealing with the conversation between George Graves and Eugene, and is full of literary allusions, very skilfully interwoven with the story. It is one of the best parts of the book but it loses by being too much prolonged. You don't want the reader to get, for a moment, the impression that the author is conscious of his own skill and virtuosity; and I am afraid this will be the feeling aroused if this section runs on as long as it now does. Won't you consider this, and if you agree indicate such parts as you wish omitted?

–*To Loot My Life Clean,* p. 11

Wolfe was impressed by Wheelock's thoroughness. In his 19 July letter, Wolfe wrote, "I cannot tell you how moved I was by your letter–by its length, its patience and care; it is a symbol of my entire relation with you and Mr. Perkins–I could not a year ago have thought it possible that such good luck was in store for me–a connection with such men, and such a house, and editing and criticism as painstaking and intelligent as I have had."

Wolfe soon responded to the specific criticisms in Wheelock's 17 July letter.

Monday, July 22

Dear Mr Wheelock: I am sending you galleys 79–90–it was for this section (79–100 that the mss., you say, has been lost. Will you please urge the printer again to try to recover it?–there are several places here that cause me difficulty. Naturally, without the mss. I cannot remember word for word the original, but it seems to me that there are omissions in several places that are not covered by the cuts Mr Perkins and I made. The most important of these is as the beginning of the boys-going-from-school Scene which you say should be cut still more. Mr Perkins and I took out a big chunk, but there is now a confusing jump that nullifies the meaning of several speeches (you have pointed out one of these) I have tried to patch it up as well as I could.

The name Sheba should always be used for ~~Horty~~, and the name Amy for ~~Emma~~–you mentioned this in your first letter and I have tried to correct wherever I found the old names.

I do not remember what Mr Perkins and I did on galley 80–where you have made a cut It does not seem to me that what happens here is more likely to give offense than many other things that remain–as an alternative I have cut out parts of it, and I submit the result to your decision. If it still seems best to cut it all, please do so. (Cut)

Will you look over the titles of the German books on Galley 85 and correct mistakes in grammar–i.e. is it Der or Die Zerbrochene Krug? etc.

–As I read over the proofs again, I become more worried–There is a reference, for example, by one of the boys in the coming-from-school scene to Mrs Van Deck, the wife of a lung specialist–but the whole section describing her as she leaves a store has been omitted. I cannot recall making this cut with Mr P. As to further cuts in this scene I will do what I can–but it seems to me that conversation between the two boys, which you say is too long, has been cut down to very little–what you do have is the undertakers scene, the W. J. Bryan scene, the Old Man Avery Scene, the Village Idiot Scene, the Old Colonel Pettingrew Scene, the Men Discussing the War Scene–all of which it seems to me are good.–But I'll do what I can–In view of the gaps I have discovered I think I shall send you by this mail only 79–90–I shall send the rest on as soon as I can do something to fill up the holes–I do hope people will not look on this section as a mere stunt–I really don't know what to do about cutting it–it is not a stunt, a great deal of the town is presented in short order. I'm going to send you galleys to 90 without further delay–I want you to go over the going-from-school scene and if you see cuts make them. I shall cut where I can in the last part of the scene

–*To Loot My Life Clean,* pp. 17–18

An Angel on the Porch

BY THOMAS WOLFE

The first work of a new writer about whom much will be heard this fall.

LATE on an afternoon in young summer Queen Elizabeth came quickly up into the square past Gant's marble-shop. Surrounded by the stones, the slabs, the cold carved lambs of death, the stonecutter leaned upon the rail and talked with Jannadeau, the faithful burly Swiss who, fenced in a little rented place among Gant's marbles, was probing with delicate monocled intentness into the entrails of a watch.

"There goes the Queen," said Gant, stopping for a moment their debate.

"A smart woman. A pippin as sure as you're born," he added, with relish.

He bowed gallantly with a sweeping flourish of his great-boned frame of six feet five. "Good evening, madam."

She replied with a bright smile of friendliness which may have had in it the flicker of old memory, including Jannadeau with a cheerful impersonal nod. For just a moment more she paused, turning her candid stare upon smooth granite slabs of death, carved lambs and cherubim within the shop, and finally on an angel poised upon cold phthisic feet, with a smile of soft stone idiocy, stationed beside the door upon Gant's little porch. Then, with her brisk, firm tread, she passed the shop, untroubled by the jeweller's heavy stare of wounded virtue, as he glowered up from his dirty littered desk, following her vanishing form with a guttural mutter of distaste.

They resumed their debate:

"And you may mark my words," proceeded Gant, wetting his big thumb, as if he had never been interrupted, and continuing his attack upon the Democratic party, and all the bad weather, fire, famine, and pestilence that attended its administration, "if they get in again we'll have soup-kitchens, the banks will go to the wall, and your guts will grease your backbone before another winter's over."

The Swiss thrust out a dirty hand toward the library he consulted in all disputed areas—a greasy edition of "The World Almanac," three years old—saying triumphantly, after a moment of dirty thumbing, in strange wrenched accent: "Ah—just as I thought: the muni-*cip*-al taxation of Milwaukee under De-*moc*-ratic administration in 1905 was two dollars and twenty-five cents the hundred, the lowest it had been in years. I cannot ima-*gine* why the total revenue is not given."

Judiciously reasonable, statistically argumentative, the Swiss argued with animation against his Titan, picking his nose with blunt black fingers, his broad yellow face breaking into flaccid creases, as he laughed gutturally at Gant's unreason, and at the rolling periods of his rhetoric.

Thus they talked in the shadow of the big angel that stood just beyond the door upon Gant's porch, leering down upon their debate with a smile of idiot benevolence. Thus they talked, while Elizabeth passed by, in the cool damp of Gant's

205

First page of the story, modified from Chapter 19 of Look Homeward, Angel, *that appeared in the August 1929 issue of* Scribner's Magazine

1
EAGLE TERRACE— s w from
junc of Spruce and Eagle
14 Sneed Kate Mad
18 Queen Elizabeth Mad
22 Cooper Emma Mad
24 Cook Mollie Mad
27 Cook Roxie Mad

Asheville directory listing madams, including Queen Elizabeth

Wolfe's Fears of the Asheville Reaction

Long before the publication of Look Homeward, Angel *on 18 October 1929, Wolfe anticipated the adverse reaction the novel would generate in Asheville. Preparing for the occasion in the spring 1929, he wrote several versions of a letter to the editor of* The Asheville Citizen. *He did not send any of these letters.*

To THE EDITOR OF THE ASHEVILLE *CITIZEN*

Thank you very much for your friendly and courteous invitation to contribute an article to your columns answering critics of my book, "O, Lost." I must decline to do so for several reasons, the most important of which are as follows: at the beginning of my career as a novelist I have determined, so far as possible, to let my books speak for me. The artist is neither a debater nor a propagandist–certainly I have no skill as either–any defense of his works should be undertaken not by himself but by critics who are competent for such work. If the Asheville critics of my work infer from this that I am anxious to avoid controversy, they are certainly right. But if, as I gather from several letters in your columns, they believe that my book is a "bitter attack" against the town, the state, the South, they are certainly wrong. One does not attack life any more than he curses the wind; shakes his fist at the storm; spits angrily at the ocean.

That there is bitterness in my book as well as pain and ugliness, I can not deny. But I believe there is beauty in it as well, and I leave its defense to those of my readers who found it there.

As to the implied criticisms of my personal life, I again have nothing to say. I honestly do not care very much what these people think. None of them knows me, a few have seen me and talked to me: their efforts to try and intrude into a life they can never know are ugly and revolting. But they are not surprising. One who has lived in New York a few years, hears too much of the sewage of a million mean lives–people who, unable to touch the sacred garments of the celebrities, feast on the familiarity of smut, contrive spurious nastiness, transfer the glittering vices they have themselves desired and have not had courage for, to the figures they honor with their venom and malice.

If the indignant Methodist ladies and gentlemen suspect me of fleshy carnalities, let them suspect no more. I am enthusiastically guilty. I have eaten and drunk with sensual ecstasy in ten countries. I have performed the male function with the assistance of several attractive females, a few of whom were devout members of the Methodist Church. [breaks off here]

–*The Letters of Thomas Wolfe,* pp. 176–177

Immediately after the appearance of "An Angel on the Porch," which described W. O. Gant's dealings with Queen Elizabeth, the madam of an Altamont house of prostitution, Margaret Roberts wrote Wolfe, fearing the rest of the novel would reveal more of his town's secrets. Wolfe could not allay his former mentor's fears.

Harvard Club
New York
Sunday, August 11, 1929

Dear Mrs. Roberts:

I have been away in Maine and Canada on a vacation and I came back to New York only two or three days ago. . . . I found your letter here when I came back. As usual, everything you say touches and moves me deeply. I wish my work deserved half of the good things you say about it: I hope that some day it will. The knowledge that you have always believed in me is one of the grandest possessions of my life. I hope it may be some slight return for your affection and faith to know that I have always believed in you; first, as a child, with an utterly implicit faith and hope, and later, as a man, with a no less steadfast trust. Life does not offer many friendships of which one can say this. I know how few there are, and yet my own life has been full of love and loyalty for whoever understood or valued it.

In your letter you say that many facts in my life you never knew about when I was a child–that much about me

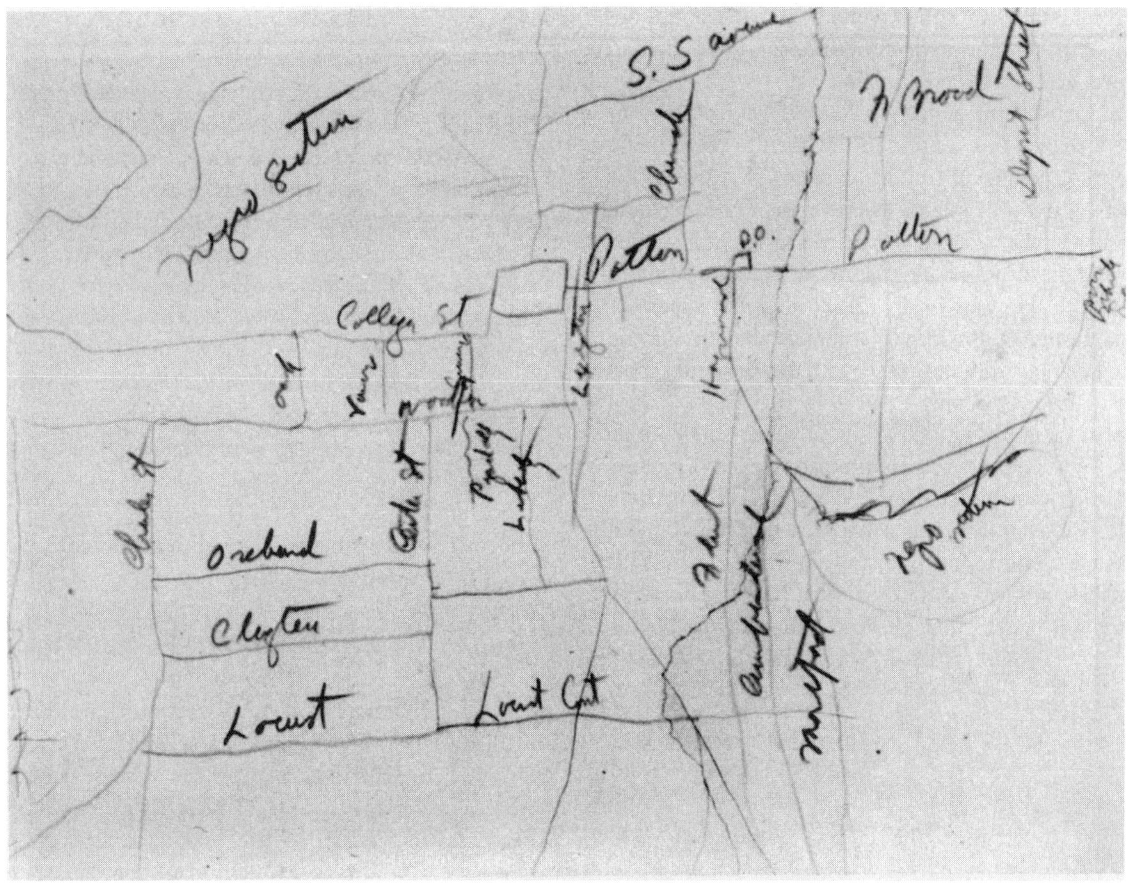

Wolfe's map of Asheville, included in the manuscript for "O Lost" (William B. Wisdom Collection, Houghton Library, Harvard University)

you did not understand until later. This does not come from lack of understanding: it comes because you are one of the high people of the earth, with as little of the earth in you as anyone I have ever known–your understanding is for the flame, the spirit, the glory–and in this faith you are profoundly right. It is a grand quality to see only with that vision which sees the highest and rarest. All that you did not see caused me great unrest of spirit as a child when I thought of you, and perhaps more now.

I hope you may be wrong in thinking what I have written may distress members of my family, or anyone else. Certainly, I would do anything to avoid causing anyone pain–except to destroy the fundamental substance of my book. I am afraid, however, that if anyone is distressed by what seemed to me a very simple and unoffending story, their feeling when the book comes out will be much stronger. And the thought of that distresses *me* more than I can tell you. Nothing, however, may now be done about this. Everything that could reasonably be done to soften impressions that might needlessly wound any reader has been done by my publishers and me. Now, the only apology I have to make for my book is that it is not better–and by "better" I mean that it does not represent by any means the best that is in me. But I hope I shall feel this way about my work for many years to come, although there is much in this first book about which I hope I shall continue to feel affection and pride.

A thousand words leap to my tongue–words of explanation, persuasion, and faith–but they had better rest unsaid. Silence is best. More and more I know that the grievous and complex web of human relationship may not be solved by words. However our motives or our acts may be judged or misjudged, our works must speak for us, and we can ultimately only trust to the belief of other men that we are of good will. I can not explain the creative act here. That has been done much better than I could hope to do it, by other people. I can only assure you that my book is a work of fiction, and that no person, act, or event has been deliberately and consciously described. The creative spirit hates pain more, perhaps, than it does anything else on earth, and it is not likely it should try to inflict on other people what it loathes itself. Certainly the artist is not a traducer or libeler of mankind–his main concern when he creates is to give his creation life, form, beauty. This dominates him, and it is doubtful if he thinks very much of the effect his work will have on given persons, although he may think of its effect on a general public. But I think you know that fiction is not spun out of the air; it is made from the solid stuff of human experience–any other way is unthinkable.

Dr. Johnson said a man would turn over half a library to make a single book; so may a novelist turn over half a town to make a single figure in his novel. This is not the only method but it illustrates, I believe, the whole method. The world a writer creates is his own world–but it is molded out of the fabric of life, what he has known and felt–in short, out of himself. How in God's name can it be otherwise? This is all I can say–I think you will understand it. Having said this, I can but add that at the last ditch, the writer must say this: "I have tried only to do a good piece of work. I have not wished nor intended to hurt anyone. Now I can go no farther. I will not destroy nor mutilate my work, it represents what is best and deepest in me, and I shall stand by it and defend it even if the whole world would turn against me." That, it seems to me, is the only answer he can make. Perhaps there are two sides to this question but this, at any rate, is my side, and the one I believe with all my heart.

– *The Letters of Thomas Wolfe,* pp. 197–198

Wolfe on the front lawn of his mother's boardinghouse, September 1929, during a short visit he made to Asheville before the publication of his novel. Although the citizens were full of interest about his forthcoming book, Wolfe did not enter into much discussion about it with anyone (The Thomas Wolfe Collection, Pack Memorial Public Library, Asheville, North Carolina).

Wolfe's Altamont

Look Homeward, Angel *was published on 18 October 1929. The novel was widely praised, except in Asheville, where the negative reaction diminished Wolfe's enjoyment of its success. The Altamont of* Look Homeward, Angel *was so transparently Asheville that local readers could identify every person and location. Such was the storm of hometown resentment toward the book that Wolfe did not return to Asheville for nearly seven years. Despite talk about lawsuits, no one in Asheville pressed a case.*

In the following essay, Floyd C. Watkins, a professor specializing in Southern literature at Emory University, identifies the originals for characters and describes how Wolfe altered his sources for the purposes of fiction.

Thomas Wolfe's Characters: Portraits from Life

Floyd C. Watkins

Thomas Wolfe's Characters: Portraits from Life

(Norman: University of Oklahoma Press, 1957), pp. 7–11

Identification of names is certainly not definition of the creative powers of a writer, but in the works of Wolfe such delving turns up facts with several significances. His artful naming of his characters was one of the traits that led to such a furious reception of *Look Homeward, Angel,* and his method of changing names is an indication of the amount of autobiography in his work.

Many places are given names entirely different in sound from the real names but very similar in meaning, and the comparisons are interesting etymologically. Raleigh, North Carolina, for example, retains the name of an Elizabethan courtier and becomes *Sydney,* just as Old Fort, a town near Asheville, is in Wolfe's works *Old Stockade.* Chapel Hill is *Pulpit Hill,* and Spruce Street, the address of Mrs. Wolfe's boardinghouse, the Old Kentucky Home, becomes *Spring Street,* the address of Eliza Gant's *Dixieland.* Government Street Wolfe calls *Federal Street. Altamont,* the name for Asheville, connotes altitude and mountains, but appropriate as the name is, it is imaginary only as a name for Asheville, because there is a small town called Altamont in western North Carolina.

The nationality of names and of the characters in the novels is in almost every instance unchanged: Jeannerett becomes *Jannadeau;* Sternberg, *Greenberg;* Guischard, *Deshaye;* Finkelstein, *Stein;* Lipinski, *Rosalsky.*

Because of their vast estates and mansion near Asheville, the Vanderbilts have played significant roles in the life of the town and in Wolfe's novels. When he wrote about them, he associated the name of their sire,

The Jackson Building, erected in 1924 on the property once occupied by W. O. Wolfe's monument shop. Julia Wolfe, who paid $1,000 for the lot in 1883, sold it in 1920 for $25,000.

old "Commodore" Vanderbilt, the railroad baron of the post–Civil War period, Jay Gould. Vanderbilt thus became *Goulderbilt.*

The connotation of grain as well as the *t-o-n* is preserved in the change from Wheaton to *Barton.* When Clara Paul became *Laura James,* as Mrs. Wolfe notes in *The Marble Man's Wife,* a similar ending for the first name was retained, and the last name was changed to that of a different disciple of Christ.

In many names one syllable is changed while another remains the same: Woodfin Street, where Wolfe was born, becomes *Woodson Street* in the novels. Biltmore, the Vanderbilt estate, is called *Biltburn;* Redwood, *Redmond;* Brigman, *Tugman.* The *Tarkington* family in *Look Homeward, Angel* were really Perkinsons; Israel became, obviously and logically, *Isaacs.* The ficticious *Montgomery Avenue* is in reality Asheville's Montford Avenue.

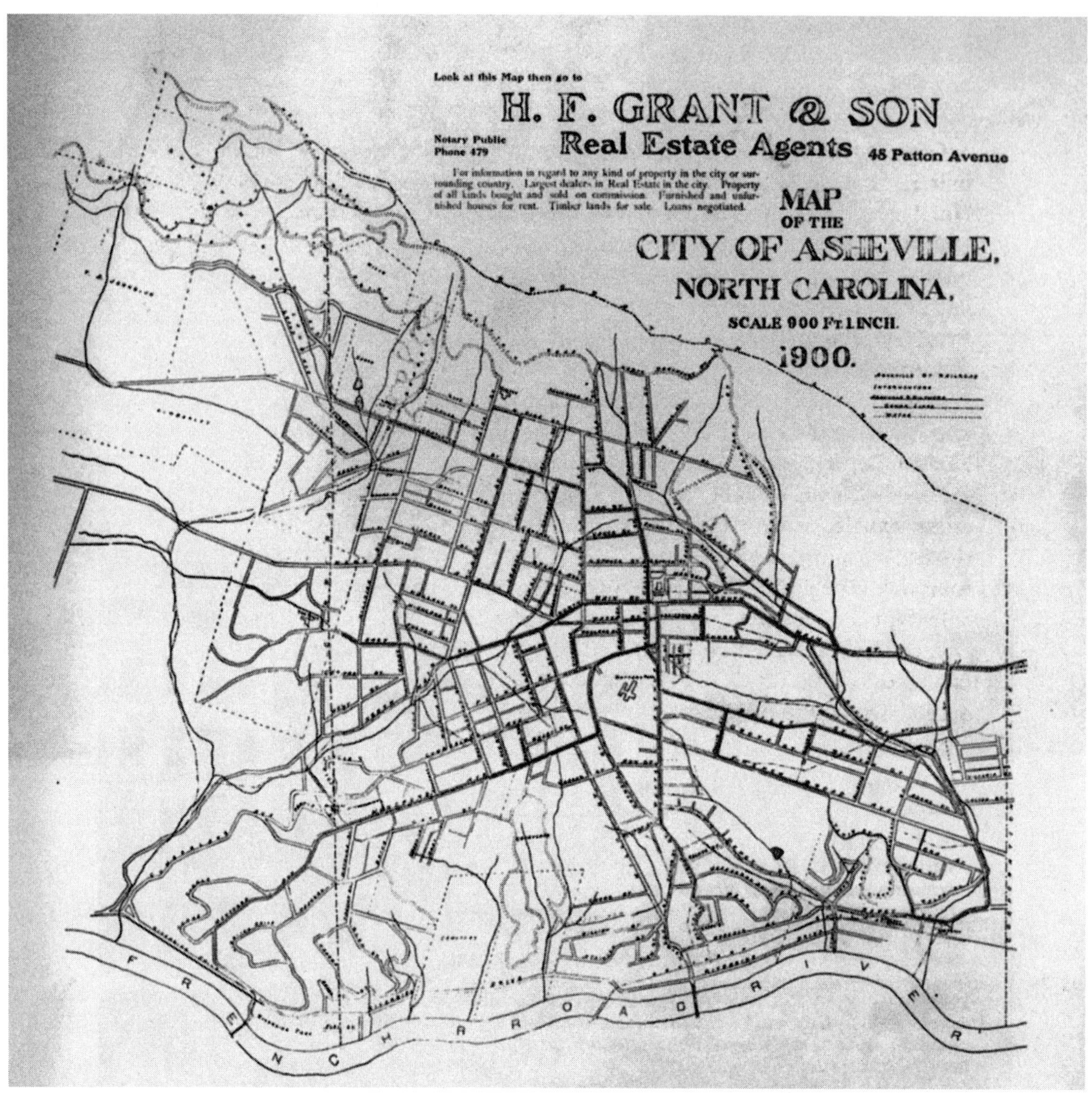

Asheville in the year of Wolfe's birth, with an enlarged view of the center of town

Fact and Fiction in *Look Homeward, Angel*
Streets

Fact	Fiction	Fact	Fiction
Eagle Terrace	Eagle Crescent	Clingman Avenue	Clingman Street
Woodfin Street	Woodson Street	Valley Street	Valley Street
French Broad Avenue	Pisgah Avenue	Southside Avenue	South End Avenue
Patton Avenue	Hatton Avenue	Haywood Street	Liberty Street
College Street	Academy Street	Sunset Terrace	Sunset Crescent
Oak Street	Ivy Street		
lower Woodfin Street	Pigtail Alley		
Spruce Street	Spring Street		
Montford Avenue	Montgomery Avenue		

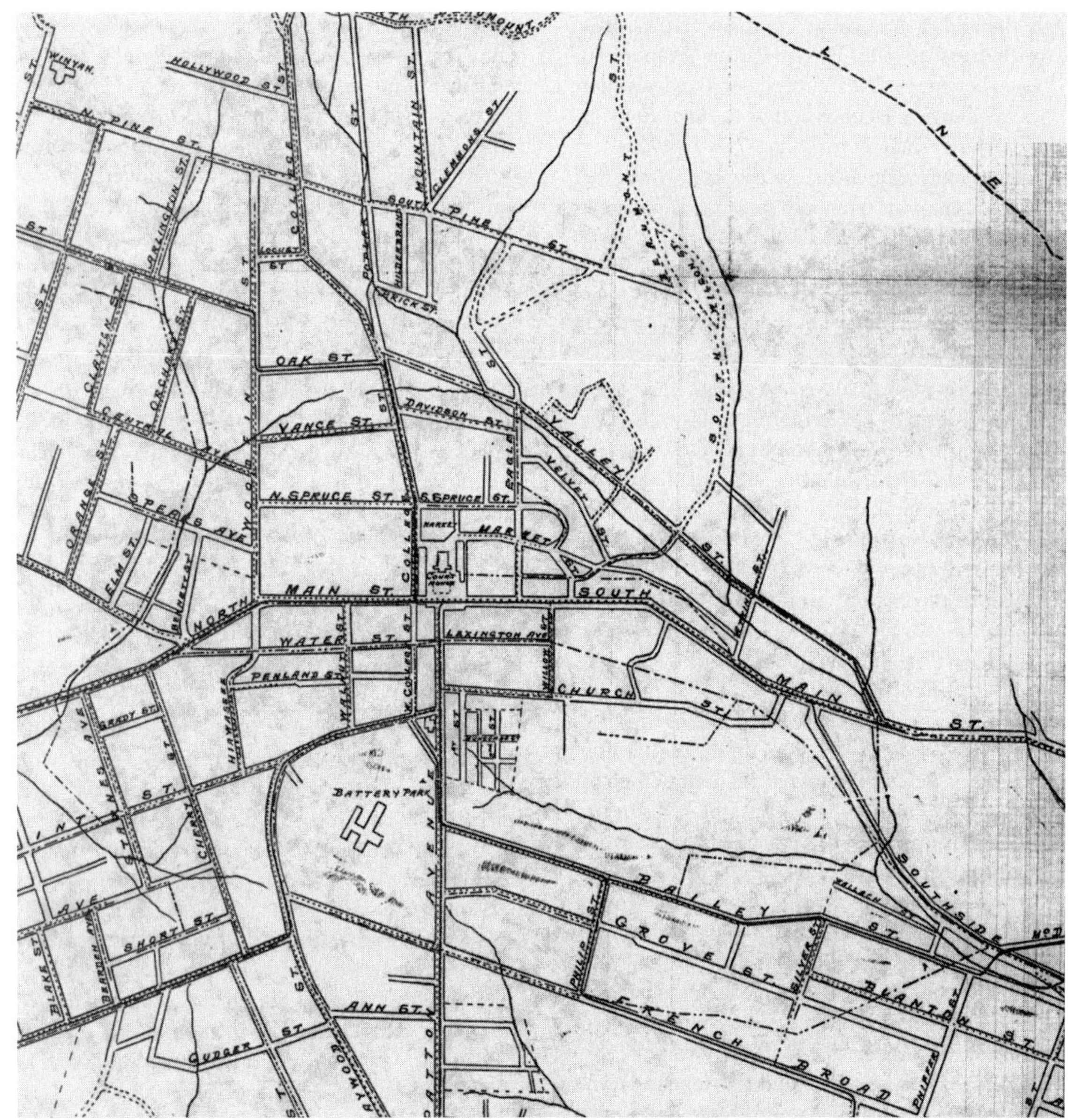

Fact and Fiction in *Look Homeward, Angel*
Places

Fact	Fiction
Frank Loughran's saloon at 43 South Main Street	Loughran's
Negro district on Eagle Street, Eagle Terrace, South Market Street and Valley Street	Niggertown
Old Kentucky Home at 48 Spruce Street	Dixieland
Orange Street School	Plum Street School
Young Men's Institute on Valley Street	Y. M. I.
Dr. Edwin P. Gruner's Sanitarium on Haywood Street	Dr. Frank Engel's Sanitarium and Turkish Bath
Saint Genevieve-of-the-Pines on Victoria Road	Convent School of Saint Catherine's on Saint Clement's Road
Majestic Theater on College Street	Orpheum Theatre
Noland-Brown Funeral Home at 16 Church Street	Rogers-Malone Undertaking Establishment
The Manor Inn on Charlotte Street	Manor House

Only the initials are changed in many names: Bus Woody is changed to *Gus Moody;* Patton Avenue, to *Hatton Avenue;* Jarrett, to *Garrett.* Wolfe enjoyed playing with names in changing Reuben Rawls to *Ralph Rolls,* in reversing Charles French Toms to get *Tom French.*

Sometimes only one name is changed while the other, although it may be extremely unusual, is retained. Changes of this sort are numerous: Pearl Shope to *Pearl Hines;* Charlie Mascari to *Pete Mascari;* Cassius or "Cash" Gudger to *Saul Gudger;* Rufus Woodcock to *Gilbert Woodcock;* Charles L. Sluder to *Fagg Sluder;* Julius Martin to *Julius Arthur;* James Barnard to *Dick Barnard;* Louis Graves to *George Graves;* Daniel Hodges to *Malcolm Hodges.*

The saloonkeeper O'Donnel, Wolfe calls *Tim O'Donnel,* but later in the same book he is given a different last name, *Tim O'Doyle.* Another such inconsistency is the spelling of the name of the groceryman as *Bradley* and *Bradly.* Jeweller Arthur M. Field is once called *Shields* and again *Arthur N. Wright.*

Why Wolfe throughout his fiction used names so near to the real ones is a speculation that Asheville has often considered. That he was aware of how he followed life and how he changed it seems to be proved by his usual care in giving entirely fictitious names to those involved in great scandals. His methods of naming characters perhaps helped him avoid the extra labor of keeping hundreds of strange names straight in his head. Perhaps, on the other hand, he wished his home-town friends to know the sources of his art. Did he realize how the use of a real name or one similar to it would increase the pleasure–or the anger? His consistency indicates that surely he must have enjoyed skirting the abyss and making fiction as close to life as possible.

Even the tourist casually driving through Asheville for the first time is able to identify some of the people and places of the novels. Old residents are still able to point out a remarkable number of things that Wolfe wrote about. Careful examination of old city directories, newspapers, telephone books–reinforced by conversations with local citizens and the identifications given in articles and stories–results in nearly complete equation of fiction and fact.

There are many more than 300 characters and places mentioned by name or described in *Look Homeward, Angel,* and probably there is not an entirely fictitious person, place, or incident in the whole novel. I have been able to identify with some accuracy about 250 places and people; and in almost every instance where the problem is difficult, there is evidence that Wolfe had in mind a real character or a place. Those migrant boarders and tourists who came to the Old Kentucky Home, rocked on the porch for a spell, and then moved on are seldom identifiable. Wolfe remembered them, but the townspeople do not; and the minor exploits of boarders rarely are recorded by the papers. The Negroes also have been forgotten. Wolfe recalled the sordid and strange details of their segregated lives, but their names in most instances are now lost. Fiction is here probably based on fact that cannot be proved. Some of Eugene's friends at the University of North Carolina have been hard to equate with those of Wolfe, but here again the research is difficult and the practice well established. On the other hand, when the character is of a type that is well known in a small town, there is hardly ever any difficulty.

When identification cannot be established for a family, a check in the city directories still reveals that Wolfe almost invariably used surnames that were prevalent in contemporary Asheville, and usually the social, economic, and racial status is unchanged in the fiction. Although there is no Tom Flack in the directories, for example, there are several Negroes with that family name.

The methods the townspeople use to identify the characters of the novels are critical comments on Wolfe's mode of creation. The temptation of the researcher is to think that everyone in Asheville was an abnormality and a strange caricature of mankind. But people, events, and places are now seen out of focus, with the books serving as a device that works all the wonders of a combination prism-camera-telescope-microscope. Wolfe remembered well, but frequently his memory adhered to the physical abnormality, the occupation, the odd personal habit, the peculiar mannerism, or the whispered story. "Wolfe makes his characters stand out–even those who have minor roles," wrote a local journalist in the *Asheville Citizen* [23 March 1932]. "He has a knack of selecting those peculiarities in characteristics which are easily forgotten by others, but which tend to bring out certain vital phases of the real person."[7] One of his uncles, for example, commented that he did not realize how often he pared his nails until his nephew described it so frequently in his book. Clarence Sumner, still a reporter for the *Citizen* and once a classmate of Wolfe at the University of North Carolina, states that "Wolfe never fictionalized except to combine, emotionalize, caricature." Thus, he created his characters, exploiting all the eccentricities of his family and of those others whom he knew well, using other townspeople for background and unimportant roles. The good-humored, deformed, and somewhat idiotic Willie Goff, the seller of pencils, is a good example. In fiction his name, personality, and deformities are described as truthfully by Wolfe as they are by the *Citizen's* reporter in a reminiscent article on local characters [*Look Homeward, Angel,* 342; *Asheville Citizen,* August 22, 1948].

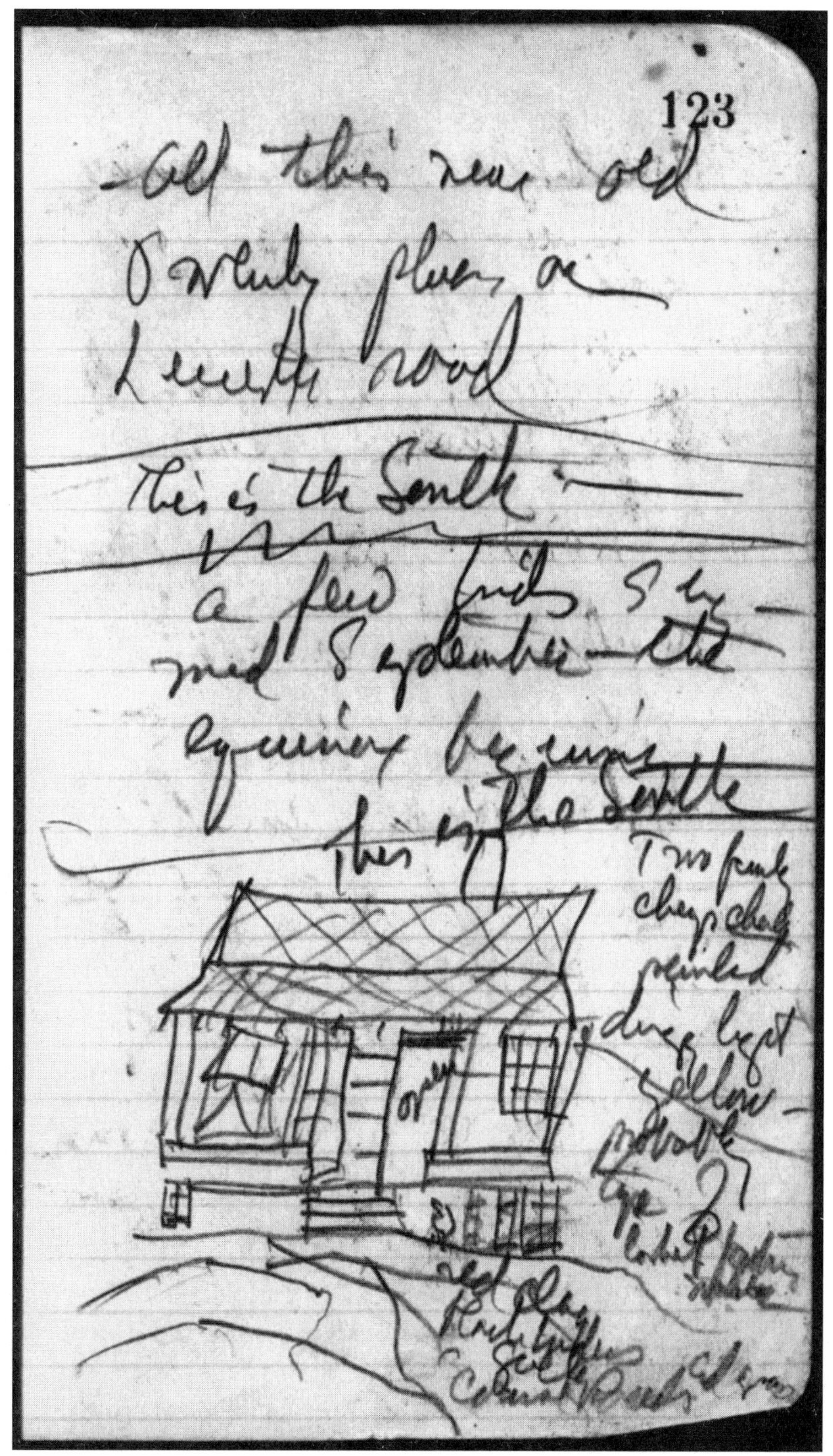

This page and the following page from Wolfe's journal written on the train going north from Asheville in September 1929 (William B. Wisdom Collection, Houghton Library, Harvard University)

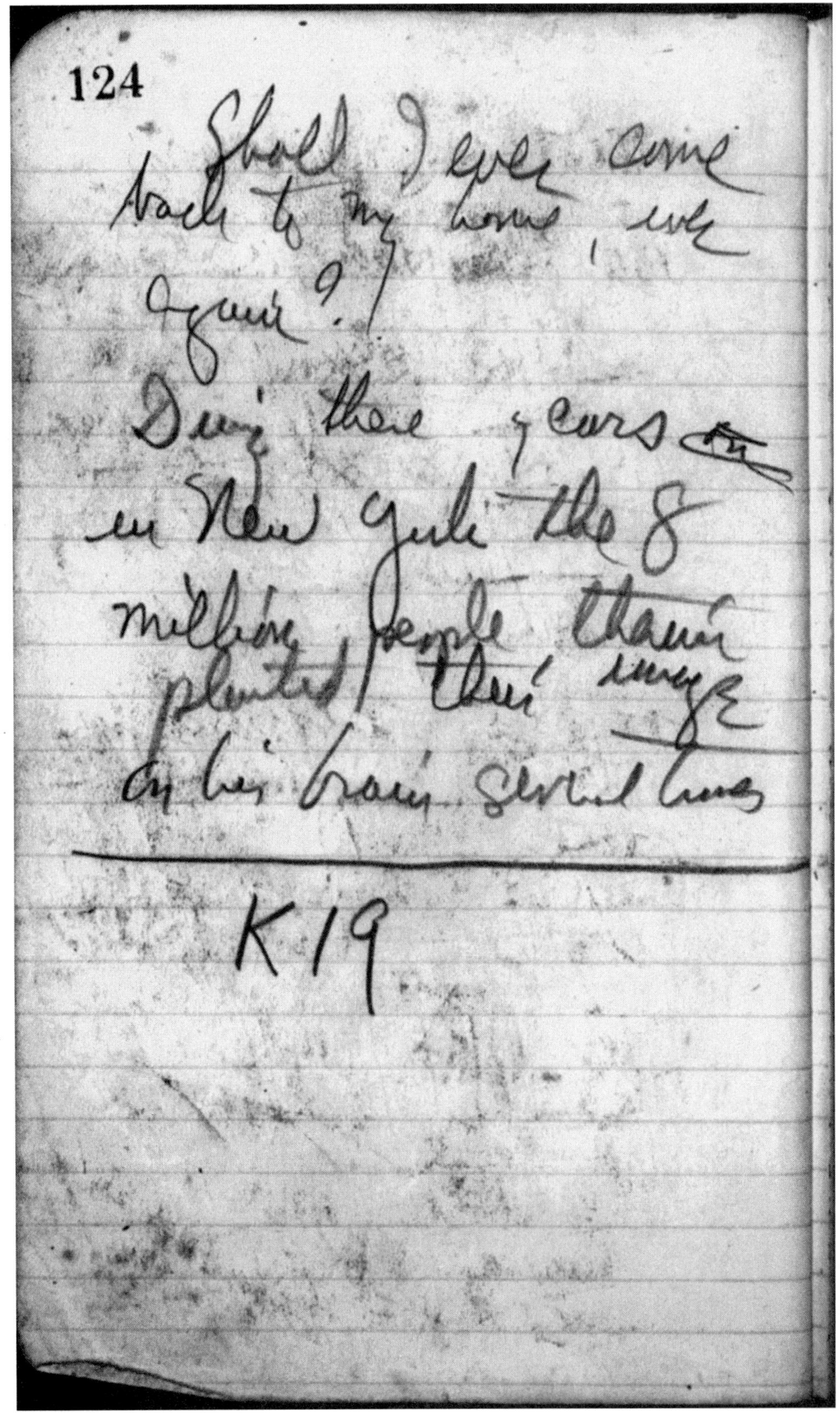
124

Shall I ever come back to my home, ever again?

During these years in New York the 8 million people that have planted their image on his brain several times

K19

At the top of the page Wolfe wrote, "Shall I ever come back to my home, ever again?" At the bottom of the page "K 19" is the number of the Pullman car on the Asheville–New York run–later a title for a novel Wolfe began and abandoned (William B. Wisdom Collection, Houghton Library, Harvard University).

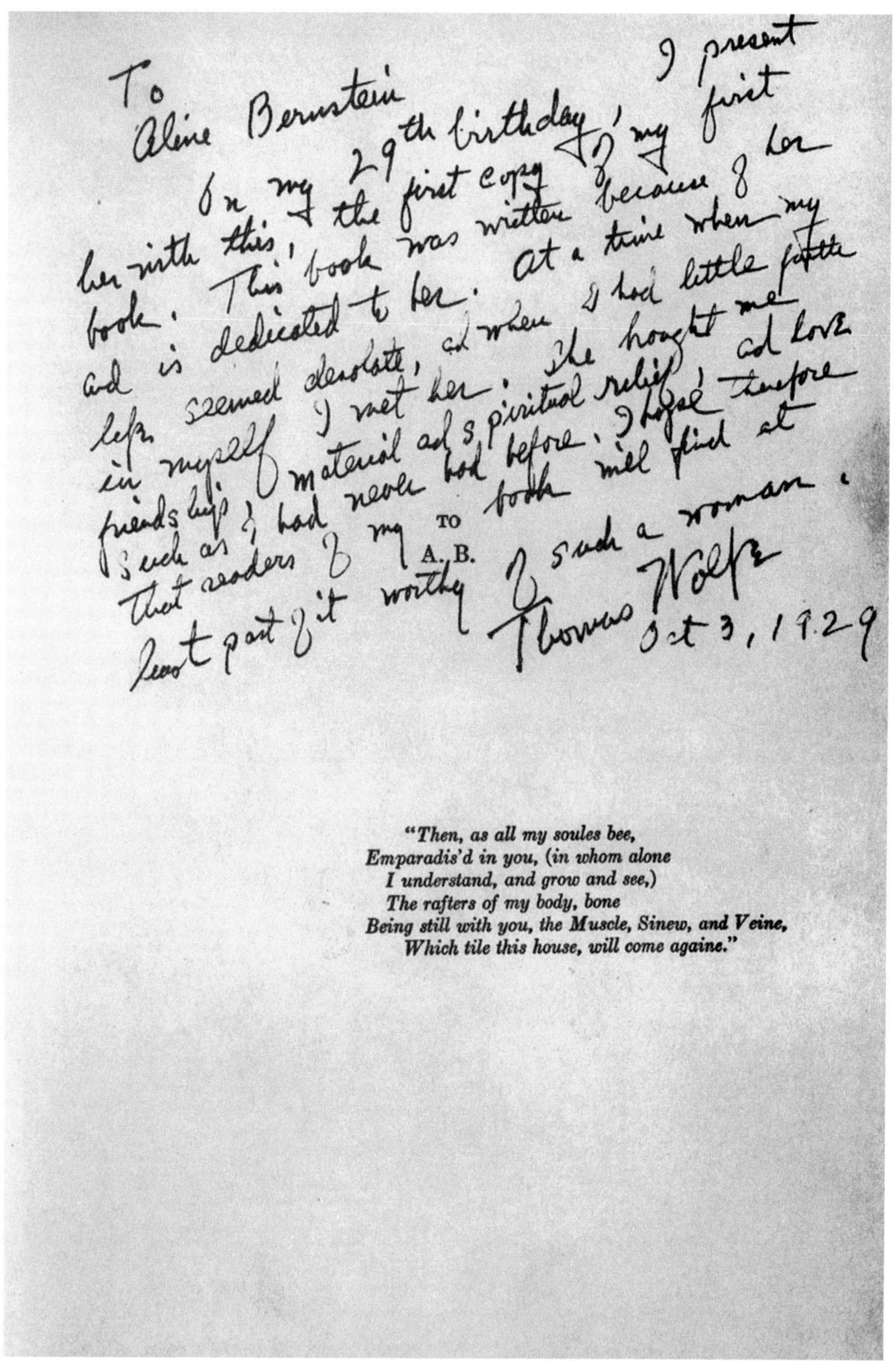

To
Aline Bernstein
On my 29th birthday, I present her with this, the first copy of my first book. This book was written because of her and is dedicated to her. At a time when my life seemed desolate, and when I had little faith in myself I met her. She brought me friendship, material and spiritual relief, and love such as I had never had before. I hope therefore that readers of my book will find at least part of it worthy of such a woman.
Thomas Wolfe
Oct 3, 1929

TO
A. B.

"Then, as all my soules bee,
Emparadis'd in you, (in whom alone
I understand, and grow and see,)
The rafters of my body, bone
Being still with you, the Muscle, Sinew, and Veine,
Which tile this house, will come againe."

The dedication copy of Look Homeward, Angel; *Wolfe used only Aline Bernstein's initials because the couple did not want to embarrass her family (William B. Wisdom Collection, Houghton Library, Harvard University).*

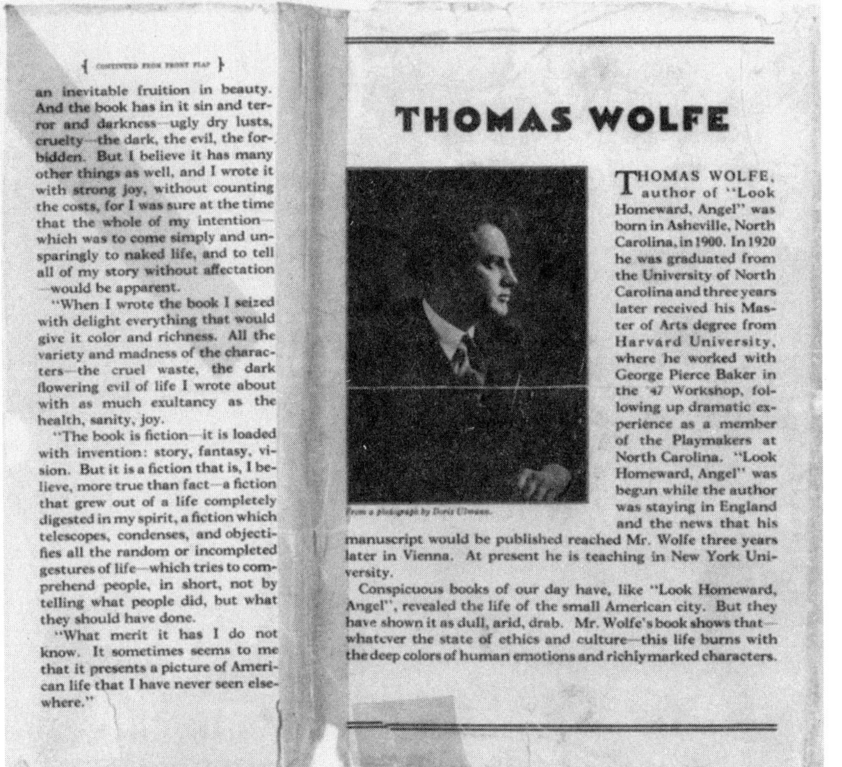

Dust jacket for Wolfe's first novel, published 18 October 1929. The book caused an uproar in Asheville. "The most famous battle of Asheville was not a military engagement," Wolfe's friend, George W. McCoy, editor of the Asheville Citizen, *wrote. "It was a verbal battle over a book–a dispute between the resentful forces of the community and the author, a native son."*

Asheville and North Carolina React

From the beginning Look Homeward, Angel *was treated as autobiography and reportage, not fiction, by the Asheville press.*

Amazing New Novel is Realistic Story of Asheville People

Walter S. Adams
The Asheville Times, 20 October 1929

An amazing new novel is just off the press which is of great and unique interest to Asheville. This community in fact, is going to be astounded by it. Some few well known residents may be shocked into chills. Others will probably be severely annoyed. Many others will snicker and laugh.

The reason is that the book is written about Asheville and Asheville people in the plainest of plain language. It is the autobiography of an Asheville boy. The story of the first twenty years of his life is bared with a frankness and detail rarely ever seen in print. The author paints himself and his home circle, as well as neighbors, friends and acquaintances with bold, daring lines, sparing nothing and shielding nothing.

Thomas Wolfe son of Mrs. Julia E. Wolfe, of 48 Spruce street, wrote the book, the title of which is "Look Homeward, Angel." The novel is just off the press of Scribners. The scene of the work is laid in Asheville with only momentary shifts to Chapel Hill and other cities. The major part of the action takes place in Asheville while virtually all the characters are residents of this city.

Young Wolfe now 29 years old and a teacher in New York University, covers the first twenty years of his life in this novel. It is the utter frank story of himself, his home, neighbors and people about town. It is quite apparent from the book that the author was not happy. His life here, as he boldly sketches it, was crowded with pain, bitterness and ugliness.

While the characters in the book are undoubtedly painted true to life, according to the author's idea of it, the names are changed and juggled around. However, any resident of Asheville who knew this city and its people during the period 1900 to 1920, will not have the slightest trouble in filling in the names of the real persons whom Wolfe made characters in his book. Asheville in this novel goes by the name of Altamount.

The sub-title of the novel terms it "A Story of the Buried Life." The character and quality of this unusual book is indicated with considerable clearness by an excerpt from a letter by the author which accompanied the manuscript when it was submitted to the publishers:

"The book covers the life of a large family (the Gants of Altamount) for a period of twenty years. It tries to describe not only the visible outer lives of all these people, but even more their buried lives.

"This book was written in simpleness and nakedness of soul. When I began to write the book I got back something of a child's innocency and wonder. It has in it much that to me is painful and ugly, but without sentimentality or dishonesty it seems to me that pain has an inevitable fruition in beauty. And the book has in it sin and terror and darkness–ugly dry lusts, cruelty–the dark, the evil, the forbidden. But I believe it has many other things as well and I wrote it with strong joy, without counting the costs, for I was sure at the time that the whole of my intention–which was to come simply and unsparingly to naked life, and to tell all of my story without affectation–would be apparent.

"What merit the book has, I do not know. It sometimes seems to me that it presents a picture of American life that I have never seen elsewhere."

Has Real Literary Merit

To the outlander, "Look Homeward, Angel" is an outstanding novel possessed of unquestioned literary merit. The portraiture is vivid, the style is incisive, the narrative flows with a freedom that sweeps along the most resisting reader.

In the preface, Wolfe raises the question whether the work is really autobiographical and then hastens to beg the question with clever twists of phrases. The net result is that the reader is left to make his own decision and the verdict of the Asheville readers will be unmistakably decisive. The intrinsic proof is overwhelming that Wolfe is relating the story of his own life and of those other lives which interlaced with his own.

This young man who is called Eugene Gant (in reality, Thomas Wolfe, the author) is of a highly sensitive nature. He suffers much from misunderstanding at home, at school and in his relations with other boys. This misunderstanding which seems to be his unvarying lot gives to his life all the aspects of a tragedy which culminates in the death of his brother.

Scandal Dragged Forth

Most of the Asheville people who appear in the novel wear their most unpleasant guises. If there attaches to them any scandal which has enjoyed only a subterranean circulation, it is dragged forth into the light. If they have any weakness which more tolerant friends are considerate enough to overlook, these defects are faithfully described. In describing them, the author must often convey the impression to the

TO THE READER

This is a first book, and in it the author has written of experience which is now far and lost, but which was once part of the fabric of his life. If any reader, therefore, should say that the book is "autobiographical" the writer has no answer for him: it seems to him that all serious work in fiction is autobiographical—that, for instance, a more autobiographical work than "Gulliver's Travels" cannot easily be imagined.

This note, however, is addressed principally to those persons whom the writer may have known in the period covered by these pages. To these persons, he would say what he believes they understand already: that this book was written in innocence and nakedness of spirit, and that the writer's main concern was to give fulness, life, and intensity to the actions and people in the book he was creating. Now that it is to be published, he would insist that this book is a fiction, and that he meditated no man's portrait here.

But we are the sum of all the moments of our lives—all that is ours is in them: we cannot escape or conceal it. If the writer has used the clay of life to make his book, he has only used what all men must, what none can keep from using. Fiction is not fact, but fiction is fact selected and understood, fiction is fact arranged and charged with purpose. Dr. Johnson remarked that a man would turn over half a library to make a single book: in the same way, a novelist may turn over half the people in a town to make a single figure in his novel. This is not the whole method but the writer believes it illustrates the whole method in a book that is written from a middle distance and is without rancour or bitter intention.

Disclaimer for Look Homeward, Angel, *which Wolfe wrote at the suggestion of Scribners to protect himself and the publisher from lawsuits. Although Wolfe insisted that he meditated "no man's portrait here," the resemblance between living persons and fictional characters was rarely accidental.*

unknowing that these weaknesses were the distinguishing characteristics of the persons.

The novel will be acclaimed to literary critics as a work of real distinction. But the suspicion is strong that Asheville people will read it not because of the literary worth but rather in spite of any artistic merit which it may possess. They will read it because it is the story told with bitterness and without compassion of many Asheville people.

The author of "Look Homeward, Angel," which is his first book, was born in Asheville in 1900. In 1920 he was graduated from the University of North Carolina and three years later received his Master of Arts degree from Harvard University, where he worked with George Pierce Baker in the '47 Workshop following up dramatic experience as a member of the Playmakers at North Carolina.

After leaving Harvard, Wolfe traveled and taught. He adopted the plan of teaching a year and traveling a year. He had traveled extensively in Europe. At New York University he teaches English literature and composition.

In his review in the Raleigh News and Observer *Jonathan Daniels, a friend of Wolfe at the University of North Carolina who had acted with him in* The Third Night, *called the novel a "curse."*

Wolfe's First Is Novel of Revolt

Jonathan Daniels

The News and Observer (Raleigh, N.C.), 20 October 1929

Former Asheville Writer Turns in Fury Upon N.C. And The South

More than a novel, Thomas Wolfe's first book, "Look Homeward, Angel," is the record of the revolt of a young spirit. Tom Wolfe, once of Asheville, has gone the way of rebels and in a sense this first novel of his is the reign of terror of his talent. Against the Victorian morality and the Bourbon aristocracy of the South, he has turned in all his fury and the result is not a book that will please the South in general and North Carolina in particular. Here is a young man, hurt by something that he loved, turning in his sensitive fury and spittin on that thing. In "Look Homeward, Angel," North Carolina, and the South are spat upon.

In this novel which is admittedly autobiographical in some part, the author Wolfe says of his hero who is easily identifiable with Wolfe:

"His feeling for the South was not so much historic as it was of the core and dark romanticism. . . . And this desire of his was unquestionably enhanced by all he had read and visioned, by the romantic halo that his school history cast over the section, by the fantastic distortion of that period where people were said to live in "mansions,' and slavery was a benevolent institution, conducted to a constant banjo-strumming, the strewn largesses of the colonial and the shuffle-dance of his happy dependents, where all women were pure, gentle, and beautiful, all men chivalrous and brave, and the Rebel horde a company of swagger, death-mocking cavaliers. Years later, when he could no longer think of the barren spiritual wilderness, the hostile and murderous entrenchment against all new life–when their cheap mythology, their legend of the charm of their manner, the aristocratic culture of their lives, the quaint sweetness of their drawl, made him writhe–when he could think of no return to their life and its swarming superstition without weariness and horror, so great was his fear of the legend, his fear of their antagonism, that he still pretended the most fantastic devotion to them, excusing his Northern residence on grounds of necessity rather than desire. Finally, it occurred to him that these people had given him nothing, that neither their love nor their hatred could injure him, that he owed them nothing, and he determined that he would say so, and repay their insolence with a curse. And he did."

"Look Homeward, Angel" is that curse. And in just so far as the curse has entered into the creation, his work has been injured but it is a novel fine enough to show that once Mr. Wolfe has got this little score paid off to his own country he should be able to move on in greater serenity of spirit.

And there may be injustice in calling this book that curse. It is not impossible that he merely chose for artistic reasons the device of writing about North Carolina and North Carolina people through the Gant family, of Altamont (Asheville). Seeing any section through the Gant family would be like looking upon that section through the barred windows of a madhouse. In such a case the hysteria of the madhouse is apt to color the whole country outside. So it is here.

It is a book written in a poetic realism, the poetry of dissolution and decay, of life rotting from the womb, of death full of lush fecondity. The book is sensuous rather than cerebral. It picture a life without dignity–cruel and ugly and touched only by a half-mad beauty. It moves slowly but at almost hysterical tension through twenty years of the life of the lower middle class Gant family, a life stirred only by the raw lusts for food and drink and sex and property. And this picture of the Gants is a cruel picture, drawn not in sympathy but in bitterness. Only one character in

TOM WOLFE PAINTS PICTURE RELENTLESS FOR TRUTHFULNESS WITH HOMEFOLKS CHARACTERS

Charlotte Observer March 30, 1930

Some Think He Ought to Be Spanked for His Impertinence in So Vividly Portraying Them, at Times With an Uncomplimentary Brush—Others Willing to Forgive the Sting of Ridicule Because of the Greatness of the Book He Has Written.

BY MAY JOHNSTON AVERY.

IN THE late fall of 1929 the city of Asheville awoke one morning to find herself the mother of a literary genius, whose book, "Look Homeward, Angel," in 10 days was in its second edition and going fine in New York—and Asheville, too, from the selling end.

EVERYBODY INTERESTED

Previously to this event on these crisp November mornings, group of men on their way to business stopped to pass the time of day by saying, "Well, what do you think of the financial situation this morning?" The stock market had risen and fallen and crashed, and no one knew just who was ruined.

But suddenly one morning, with the abruptness of the stock crash, these groups became larger and more numerous, and finance was pushed aside for the greeting of: "Well, have you read it?" Did you recognize so and so?" and some would laugh, while others whispered, "Isn't it awful! I don't see how he could do it!"

Every one knew they referred to Tom Wolfe's "Look Homeward, Angel."

EVERYBODY READ BOOK.

It was all Asheville talked of, thought of, and commented on until every one had read it, from the news boys to the ministers.

Everyone began remembering to the days when Tom Wolfe was a boy and played with their sons—or themselves. But somehow, in late years Asheville, being busy growing herself, building world-famous inns and skscrapers—one on the very spot where the Angel stood—had not noticed a curly-haired boy with discerning eyes running in and out among them.

The boy, after losing his first teeth and his baby ways, was busy about his own affairs, beginning his adventure of life in his own back yard, calling up doodle bugs under the luxuriant grape arbors and venturing upward in his world of fancy into the cherry trees, and when quite bold wandering beyond into the tall whistling pines.

GENIUS IN MAKING.

Baby days slipped away and in their place came the real games of life, marbles, kites, selling papers, going to school and then out from prep school to the state university and on to Harvard! A year or so in Europe, and Thomas Wolfe of Asheville, found himself English professor of the State University of New York.

No press agent announced his literary ability in those student days, and he was not interviewed when he dropped off the train as he returned home from time to time. So Asheville was not conscious of his astute watchfulness, nor aware that a genius was in the making. Then suddenly and unannounced this man sent forth his thundering message to the world, peopled with Asheville men and women. The author himself unknowingly expresses the feeling of his home folk while quoting on the first page of his book:

"At one time the earth was probably a white-hot sphere like the sun."

For a period of time his own people were blistered under the heat of his brilliant and often cruel local shots—some because they suddenly found themselves a part of this vivid novel, others smarted because they had not impressed themselves sufficiently upon this eery boy's imagination. Every one somehow hoped—and feared—they would find themselves within the pages.

FIRST REACTION.

The first reaction to the book in Asheville was one of indignation over Mr. Wolfe's daring, his too oftentimes ugliness of expression, and his apparent disloyalty. At bank directors' meetings staid men of finance would say: "The boy should be spanked for his impertinence." Cards and club programs were halted as women expressed themselves as being "too shocked for words." Others who had not read it trembled, fearing some slight indiscretion of the past might come to light.

Asheville tip-toed around with the book in its hand, and in the dead of night read or failed to read of themselves, as seen through the eyes of an imaginative and discerning boy, 15 years ago. Only the people who were a part of the old Asheville, who knew none, or only a few, of the characters could read the book for the book's sake alone. The bared truths of the story were to them a part of a great piece of fiction, so living and breathing that at times they gasped for breath.

The book was accepted 50 miles away from Asheville in the same spirit as it was 10,000 miles away, and except for all the unnecessary ugliness, the genius of the man, and the agony of the flesh that was poured into it, was not missed. One can fancy the author wrote some of the chapters caring not for food, nor for sleep, nor for anything until all the loneliness of his young life had been spilled upon the pages.

SERMON IN PROSE.

And then in four months Asheville had another reaction. They read the book again, for children and friends were writing from all parts of the country, "How great it is," "What a sermon it preaches!" Men of letters, like Walpole, told them through the press, from a literary standpoint, it would live when all the prize winning books have long been forgotten.

The old home town has taken a second look at their young literary giant, and beholds him towering skyward as he, meteorlike, shot himself into the world of literature. Now the personalities are one by one slowly moving to the back of the stage, realizing their individuality is only a common trait of human nature, and, as Mr. Wolfe himself said, "It is true of people of London or of Ihaho, as of people in Asheville"—his Asheville.

CRITICISM CEASES.

Society has worn itself out with the discussion, has ceased criticism. The dirty finger prints in the story are becoming dim; the cruel cuts, that only youth can deal so exquisitely, are healing; the wretched bitterness has softened; and though there are some who will never be able to see beyond the disloyalty, others who smarted under a single sentence are taking the books as a whole and thinking of the mighty effort of Tom Wolfe.

They turn backward to the boy who lived among them, wondering if they too were not a bit responsible that his youthful imagination saw so much that was ugly in life and that his mind was seared by lack of human understanding. They realize he is saying from first to last that men are strangers, that they are lonely and forsaken, that they live and die alone. Read over again his foreword and a kindred touch brings a deeper understanding. He has felt even as you and I.

"Which of us has known his brother? Which of us has looked into his father's heart? Which of us has not remained forever prison-pent? which of us is not forever a stranger and alone?"

THINKS BOOK GREAT.

It was thus Asheville indignation suddenly became tempered with a justice it felt it had not received. The reaction possibly first turned on the words of a splendid kinsman of Mr. Wolfe's whom the author unjustly caricatured who lately remarked: "Well, I don't care what Tom said about me. I'm proud he is in my family." An even nearer kinsman has remarked: "I was told Tom had not become famous, but infamous, and he surely has painted me a weakling, but I think it's the greatest book I ever read." Some now smile and say, "Why, I didn't know I was always paring my nails," nor that "I was forever winking," said another; "Do I purse my lips?" asked a third. "My how the boy watched us!" And they at last found humor through his searching eyes.

Thomas Wolfe came to his home early last fall when the book was on the press, to see everybody. Some say he could not see enough of his fr[illegible] them of the book. [illegible] the book. Maybe po[illegible] to tell them where [illegible] and with whom it was [illegible] a certain sensitivenes[illegible] lips and he could n[illegible] truth.

He may have had some [illegible] fear that a few weeks later, w[illegible] the advance copies had been s[illegible] home, he would not be under[illegible]stood. He would be exiled. His friends would no longer know the person he had become. Just so. But all great achievement is bought with a price, and Asheville now looks proudly at Tom Wolfe, writer, not from his lost land but from his home land.

And they will follow him as "he turns his eyes upon the distant soaring ranges."

Charlotte Observer, *30 March 1930*

Wolfe wrote to his mother on 26 April 1930 about the reaction to his novel.

I do not think the history of the Gant family is over: it seems to me that there is much more to be said, and I propose someday to return to that theme–I hope naturally that added wisdom, maturity, and richness of experience will enable me to handle my theme as it deserves to be handled. Very few critics who have ever written about the book have failed to mention the extraordinary quality of the people in it. I belong to a different generation from that of certain older people who were perhaps shocked by some things in my book, but I really do not think my own generation is worse than theirs: I think in many respects it is much more honest. Every writer who is honest, I think, feels the tragedy of destiny and of much of living, but I hope that I shall never be bitter, in what I write, against people. I think some people at home made that mistake about my first book–they thought the author was bitter about people, but he was not: he may have been bitter about the toil, waste, and tragedy of living.

–*The Letters of Thomas Wolfe to His Mother,* pp. 160–161

the whole book, the perpetually doomed Benfi, is drawn with tenderness and feeling.

In photographic detail the Gants are presented through 626 pages of quarrelling life. W. O. Gant, the father, is a wanderer, tombstone-maker, a selfish and self-pitying, bombastic drunkard. The mother, Eliza Pentland Gant, is a stingy, petty woman, avaricious member of the acquisitive mountain Pentlands. There are the children: Daisy, who is an unimportant figure of a girl; Helen, like her father but wiser and kinder; Steve, who is a hopeless degenerate; Luke, the buffoon; Grove, who dies in childhood; Ben, the doomed one, a night worker hungry for beauty and dignity; and Eugene, the hero, a strange figure of sensitiveness, aspiration and inferiority. And beside them are innumerable minor characters, prostitutes, white and black: loose women, Negroes and dope-fiends, drunken doctors, tuberculars, newsboys and teachers.

The book moves slowly with a somewhat too difficult point of view. There is hardly any growth in character but only growing details and passing time. The novel, with its central scene set in Asheville, moves in the South from Maryland to New Orleans and west to St. Louis. There are Negroes in it and cavaliers and all the other figures of Southern legend but the sense of reality is not in them. They are all figments of the Gant madness.

It is a book which shines too steadily with the brilliance of lurid details of blood and sex and cruelty. There is beauty in it but it is not a beautiful book. Mr. Wolfe writes with a splendid vividness but there is a heavy quality of sameness in so much stark color. The whole book seems somehow the work of a man who is staring rather than seeing.

In many places Mr. Wolfe has taken no pains adequately to disguise the autobiographical material set down as fiction. His very disguises seem made to point at the true facts. Asheville people will undoubtedly recognize factual material which escapes other readers and no one who attended the University of North Carolina contemporaneously with Wolfe can miss the almost pure reporting which he presents in the story of his life there.

North Carolinians, even if shocked, will find this book by a young North Carolinian, under thirty, interesting. Wolfe is well known in the State, particularly by University men. He was born in Asheville in 1900 and made that his home until he graduated in 1920, when he, like Eugene Gant, in his novel, sought escape through Harvard University. He is now living in New York.

While I am not exactly a disciple of the modern school, my book is part realism and part fantasy. I have tried to make it real. Some say it is an answer to Sinclair Lewis's *Main Street.* I did not write with any such intentions. As I say in the foreword, *Look Homeward, Angel* explains life in a provincial city as I saw it.

–*Thomas Wolfe Interviewed,* p. 3–4

Asheville's Angel

Attempts to identify Wolfe's angel date back to May 1930, when the Asheville Times *dispatched a reporter and a photographer to Riverside Cemetery in Asheville. For years, few people in Asheville questioned the identification of the angel made in the newspaper. Wolfe, however, was outraged by the article. In* The Story of a Novel *(1936) he described how "one of the newspapers sent one of its reporters and a photographer to the cemetery where a photograph was taken of a large and imposing looking angel and printed in the paper with a statement to the effect that the angel was the now famous angel which had stood upon the stonecutter's porch for so many years and had given title to my book. The unfortunate part of this proceeding was that I had never seen or heard of this angel before, and that this angel was, in fact, over the grave of a well-known Methodist lady what had died a few years before."*

Statue Made Famous In "Look Homeward Angel" Stands Vigil Over Grave.
Asheville Times, 4 May 1930

On A Wooded hillside far back in Riverside cemetery an angel chiseled of finest Carrara marble serenely stands vigil over a grave. It is the angel made famous in Thomas Wolfe's novel, "Look Homeward, Angel."

Discolored with time but otherwise unchanged, the statue which for years looked out from the porch of W.O. Wolfe's stone shop on Pack Square at the comings and goings of a growing town, now at last has grown into the peaceful surroundings for which it was intended.

For one who does not remember the dilapidated old stone shop and its angelic sentinel, which for nearly a score of years was a landmark, it is difficult to realize that this is the same carven creature who coldly received the admiring, almost affectionate, caresses of the strange, gawky stonecutter, disdained to look down on his frequent inebriate spasms and let his vile, violent tirades go unheeded.

WOLFE DENIES 'BETRAYING' ASHEVILLE

CLAIMS LOVE FOR PEOPLE IN 'LOOK HOMEWARD ANGEL'

Asheville Times May 4, 1930

Intentions To Cast Reflections Of Asheville And His Own People Denied; Will Sail Saturday For Europe.

By LEE E. COOPER
(Exclusive Dispatch to The Times)

NEW YORK, May 3.—A weary giant of a man, surprised at the success of his first book, and considerably troubled over the critical comments it inspired among his home folks, will sail from New York next Satrday for Europe "to sit on a rock and gaze at the pigs and peasants, the sky and the sea," so that he may rest.

Tom Wolfe cannot rest in New York. He has had but little time he could call his own since "Look Homeward, Angel" was published. Conferences with his publishers about his next book, chats with literary lights and book critics, invitations and letters have kept him on the go for weeks. But after a brief period of relaxation he will finish "October Fair" and perhaps fifteen or twenty other novels in time, he says. Some parts of his next book and much of those which may come later, will be based on his experiences in Asheville and western North Carolina. He hopes that the people he knows back there will like his later works better than the first, and come to understand his motives and his attitude. But he doesn't expect to prostitute his writing because some people have heaped calumny and threats upon him or to weaken what has been generally acclaimed as a promising literary debut by describing life "with a coat of molasses."

Physically Tom Wolfe is a worthy product of the great hills which nurtured him. In an ordinary New York apartment he would be smothered; so he has lived one flight up in an old building on West Fifteenth Street, not far from Fifth Avenue, where one great room, half studio, half loft, with a double-height ceiling, has served as his library, bedroom and reception hall. It was even more dishevelled than his heavy crop of dark hair. Books and papers were strewn all over the place, waiting to be packed away. It was with evident pleasure that he greeted one who could talk with him of places and things in the Carolina mountains.

Explains His Attitude.

"I am happy and flattered that The Asheville Times had the enterprise and thoughtfulness to inquire as to my attitude on the things I have written about," he said. "I want the people back home to understand. I gather from what some of them have said about me since the book was published that they feel I have betrayed them, that I am an outcast and that they do not want me to come back.

"If they think I intended to cast reflections on my old home and my own people they have gone far wrong. I started 'Look Homeward, Angel' about three years ago, while I was in England, and while I was lonely for a sight of my own land. The experiences of my early years welled up within me and cried out for expression. The result was a book which represented my vision of life up to the age of twenty. I intended the town which was its setting to be a typical town and I called it Altamont, a place which some folks later identified as Asheville. I came back to New York and worked on the novel for many months in a dingy loft on Eighth Street. During all that time I don't believe I actually thought of Asheville as such for more than an hour.

Proud of His Family.

"But I had to write of things which were a part of me, out of my own experience, things which I knew. I don't believe that a worthy book can be produced by anyono who attempts merely to reach up into the thin air and pluck from it a story which has no background of life.

"To me the characters in my book were real people, fullblooded, rich and interesting; they were pioneers of the sort which has built this country, and I love them.

"I am proud of my family, and I still consider Asheville my home. New York certainly is not. I like it, but it is a giant of steel and stone far different from the open spaces where a man can plant his feet on caressing earth and breathe. Only recently I took a trip down to Pennsylvania, to the Lancaster farm lands where my father lived and which I recognized from the vivid descriptions he had given me early in my youth. Part of me belongs to that country, and another part is bound up in the hills of North Carolina.

"Must Write Honestly."

"When I write, I must write honestly. Too many have tried to imitate the gentility of the English, when we in America are different, without the lengthy background which makes their writing fit the setting, and therefore makes it real. We are pioneers, builders, and vigorous ones, too. To write of such with too much gentility is dishonest, unsatisfying. If we are to get anywhere surely we must paint life as it is, full and deep. Not all of it is sugared, sinless. If that were true, perhaps we would be less attractive, less worthy of being written about.

"The people in my novel were real people to me, and I loved them. Perhaps some sanctified ones will hold up their hands in horror, and exclaim: 'Poor devil! So that's the kind of a man he is and that's the sort of person he likes!' but I repeat I love that type—the rich,

The Asheville Times, *4 May 1930*

honest, vigorous type.

"Some writers like Sinclair Lewis have missed the meat of the small town, anyway. Although people recognized his characters, his towns were painted as drab and dull. I do not consider them so, I mean the typically American towns. Life is there in all its fullness.

"I have received hundreds of letters, some praising, some filled with advice, some with abuse," he continued, pointing to a large trunk filled with them. "Many were from Asheville. I hope the people there will get to see my point of view and will like my later books better. I am not bitter and I don't want to be considered an exile, for I want very much to go back there some day."

Tells How Book Got Name.

Tom Wolfe was happy to explain just how his first novel got its name. Few who have read the book seem to have understood the significance of the title.

"As has been the case with many books," he said, "the title finally chosen was not the original one. When I submitted the manuscript to Scribner's I had it entitled 'People Lost' to express the theme of the book and the idea that people largely are lonely, seldom get to know each other. The publishers, or rather their sales promotion department, didn't like this, on the ground that it told too much.

"I submitted about a dozen more titles which wouldn't tell too much or would be likely to arouse curiosity as to the content of the novel, as they suggested. One of these was 'Look Homeward, Angel,' taken from Milton's Lycidas, the full line reading 'Look Homeward, Angel, and Melt with Ruth.' The poem, as you doubtless know, is an elegy written in memory of a friend who was drowned. The application was intended to be general or symbolic in meaning, rather than to have a definite implication concerning some character or action in the book.

"Some persons have thought it had direct reference to the angel which stood on the porch of the marble shop in one scene in the novel, but such is not the case. I think it fits in rather nicely with the character of Ben, perhaps the central figure in the book, who always is jumping up to ejaculate 'Listen to this,' or some kindred expression as if he were conversing with some unseen spirit."

To Write More About Asheville.

Mr. Wolfe's book will be published in England this month. After a few weeks of rest he will resume work on "October Fair" on which he already has done considerable work. The Guggenheim fellowship, amounting to about $2,500, awarded to him on account of his first book, will allow him to spend several months abroad, mostly in England and Germany. The award is a most generous one, with few strings attached, although the winner usually is expected to go abroad. No accounting to the fund is required.

There will be no definite setting for "October Fair," he explained Mostly it will be a moving panorama of American life. The action in the first part, to be entitled "The Fast Express" will be laid in a fast train traveling through Virginia, and in the territory through which the train passes. The title of the book, which brings up a picture of harvest time and its bounty, will have reference to a period in the life of a woman. Some parts of the story will be based on his experiences in North Carolina. Later books will contain even more of those experiences.

Spends Much Time In Europe.

Tom Wolfe has a voracious appetite for studying life and literature. In Harvard, while studying playwriting under Prof. Baker, he wrote several plays which were deemed quite promising, at least one of which he hoped would be taken by a New York producer to make the rest easy. But after waiting for several months in Asheville for such a bid, he lost his illusions and came to New York university to teach. Every time he managed to save up a few hundred dollars he hurried away to Europe, sometimes coming back in steerage. He estimates that out of the past seven years he has spent at least three in Europe. But always he gets lonely for the "spaciousness" of America and the larger grape fruit on the street vender's cart.

He has read and taken to heart all the advice and the criticism of those who have written him letters. Some have asked him in effect why he didn't write a story about good people, a clean story about the beauty of things. He answers that life isn't like that at all, that it is neither clean nor dirty, but full, rounded and sweeping, "like a wave breaking over you."

Thus he talked for two hours, sometimes with a rush of words which left him almost breathless, again haltingly, as if groping, abashed at the inadequacy of mere words to convey the depth of his meaning or his enthusiasm for life.

"Heart of America."

He doesn't agree with those skeptics who always fear that the promise of an author's first work may not reach fruition in later writing. At least he doesn't think it will apply in his case. He says so without appearing boastful, for he believes that he has learned things since he started writing "Look Homeward, Angel" which will help him to do better.

"I am going to write a good book some day," he says.

Then he poured himself another cup of tea, and began to talk again about the people he knew back home. "Grand people," he called them, "and some day I shall go back there. Tell them that for me, will you? Tell them I mean it with all my heart when I say they are the heart of America."

But for older residents, the statue which now marks the grave of a departed Asheville woman, buried in 1914, is a familiar figure hard to dissociate with the past in spite of its changed surroundings. They remember not only the stone figure and the man who yearned in vain to copy it, but also the other characters who move as living through the pages of Tom Wolfe a book. For them there is no doubt that "W. O. Gant" is W. O. Wolfe and that scores of other characters are as real as that of Gant's. They chuckle with subtle appreciation or growl with resentment because of injured feelings at this bald, bold putting into print of things which many would prefer forgotten.

Still Looks Eastward

But W. O. Wolfe's angel still stands, looking eastward as it did from his shop porch, and the characters his son has pictured bid fair to outlive the originals.

Tom Wolfe made the winged woman of stone a significant factor in the life of his father–a symbol, an ideal, a star by which destinies are guided. Many who have read "Look Homeward Angel" think that the title was derived from the statue whose face, pointedly or by chance, gazed from the stone shop where the Jackson building now stands in the general direction of the Wolfe home. There are others, however, who see the origin of the title in an entirely different light and the author himself has explained that the marble angel had nothing to do with the title.

Friends of the old man recall that he was so fond of this piece of marble that it remained at his store shortly before Mr. Wolfe's death. It was then that the angel was bought by members of an Asheville family as a memorial for a beloved woman. Tom Wolfe says in his book that the sculpture was once sold at a very high price to an Asheville resident who admired it but his father had become so attached to it that he never delivered the stone.

Serves Purpose

Be that as it may, the angel now serves its appointed purpose. With her right hand lifting a wreath to a rustic cross, she may now be seen in a rather isolated spot in Riverside Cemetery. Follow the main drive over the hill and down toward the French Broad River, then, next to the last turn, take the road to the left. There, blending into the woodland, stands the mute figure which, perhaps, if her eyes had been seeing, might be able to tell Tom Wolfe more about his father.

A Critical Success

Outside of Asheville, critics generally recognized Wolfe's first book as a major work of American fiction.

A Novel of Provincial American Life

Margaret Wallace

New York Times Book Review, October 27, 1929

Here is a novel of the sort one is too seldom privileged to welcome. "It is a book of great drive and vigor, of profound originality, of rich and variant color. Its material is the material of every-day life, its scene is a small provincial Southern city, its characters are the ordinary persons who come and go in our daily lives. Yet the color of the book is not borrowed: it is native and essential. Mr. Wolfe has a very great gift–the ability to find in simple events and in humble, unpromising lives the whole meaning and poetry of human existence. He reveals to us facets of observation and depths of reality hitherto unsuspected, but he does so without outraging our notions of truth and order. His revelations do not startle. We come upon them, instead, with an almost electric sense of recognition.

The plot, if the book can be said to have a plot at all, is at once too simple and too elaborate to relate in synopsis. "Look Homeward, Angel" is a chronicle of a large family, the Gants of Altamont, over a period of twenty years. In particular, it is the chronicle of Eugene Gant, the youngest son, who entered the world in 1900. W. O. Gant was a stonecutter, a strong, turbulent, sentimental fellow, given to explosions of violent and lavish drunkenness, and to alternating fits of whining hypochondria. Eliza Gant, his second wife and the mother of his family, was an executive woman with a passion for pinching pennies and investing shrewdly in real estate. The Gants grew in age and prosperity with the growth of the sprawling mountain town of Altamont.

By 1900 the Gants were firmly and prosperously established in Altamont–although, under the shadow of the father's whining dread of the tax collector, they continued to live as if poverty and destitution lay just around the corner. They kept a cheap, garish boarding house called Dixieland, living their daily lives on the fringe of a world of paying guests whose necessities had to be considered first. Eugene Gant grew from childhood into an awkward and rather withdrawn adolescence, hedged about by the turbulent lives of his family and singularly lonely in the midst of them. Indeed, each of the Gants was lonely in a separate fashion. Mr. Wolfe, in searching among them for the key to their hidden lives, comes upon no unifying fact save that of isolation.

Through the book like the theme of a symphony runs the note of loneliness and of a groping, defeated search for an answer to the riddle of eternal solitude.

Naked and alone we come into exile. In her dark womb we did not know our mother's face; from the prison of her flesh have we come into the unspeakable and incommunicable prison of this earth. Which of us has known his father? Which of us has looked into his father's heart? Which of us has not remained forever prison-pent? Which of us is not forever a stranger and alone?

Eugene grew into life hating its loneliness and desolation, its lack of meaning, its weariness and stupidity, the ugliness and cruelty of its lusts. For the rawness and evil of life was early apparent to him–hanging about the depressing miscellaneous denizens of Dixieland, delivering his papers in Niggertown, growing up in the streets and alleys of Altamont. He found a poignant beauty in it, too–the simple beauty of things seen in youth, the more elusive beauty to be found in books, and later, after his years at college and the death of his brother Ben, the terrible beauty flowering from pain and ugliness. But always there remained in him that loneliness, and an obscure and passionate hunger which seemed to him a part of the giant rhythm of the earth.

"Look Homeward, Angel" is as interesting and powerful a book as has ever been made out of the drab circumstances of provincial American life. It is at once enormously sensuous, full of the joy and gusto of life, and shrinkingly sensitive, torn with revulsion and disgust. Mr. Wolfe's style is sprawling, fecund, subtly rhythmic and amazingly vital. He twists language masterfully to his own uses, heeding neither the decency of a work nor its licensed existence, so long as he secures his sought for and instantaneous effect. Assuredly, this is a book to be savored slowly and reread, and the final decision upon it, in all probability, rests with another generation than ours.

In his review, poet Kenneth Fearing noted the influence of James Joyce and Sherwood Anderson upon Wolfe.

A First Novel of Vast Scope

Kenneth Fearing

New York Evening Post, 16 November 1929

"Look Homeward, Angel" an American Saga in Southern Setting

For any variation in the few elementary patterns from which the majority of contemporary novels are cut, there is apt to be stirred in the reader, depending upon his conviction in such things, a feeling of either gratitude or annoyance. And because even a little variation is felt as extraordinary, the gratitude or annoyance will perhaps be exaggerated beyond a point merited by the performance in itself.

"Look Homeward, Angel" is such a performance, an unusual novel, almost an eccentric one. The author, Thomas Wolfe, is an amateur, partly in the sense that "the artist is always an amateur," and partly in the sense that he has written a thing innocent of structural perfection. He has attempted to give life a vast, illusive American experience, using whatever language or form he was able to devise to meet the moment's need, rather than adhering throughout to a simpler, neater, but less ambitious formula. And this is not to say that "Look Homeward, Angel" is wholly an original. The book is closely related to a familiar genre, the family saga, and in its writing shows influences that are well known, notably those of James Joyce and Sherwood Anderson.

Novelist William Styron wrote of his first reading of Look Homeward, Angel *in "The Shade of Thomas Wolfe" in the April 1968 issue of* Harper's Magazine.

[I]t would be hard to exaggerate the overwhelming effect that reading Wolfe had upon so many of us who were coming of age during or just after the second world war. I think his influence may have been especially powerful upon those who, like myself, had been reared as Wolfe had in a small Southern town or city, and who in addition had suffered a rather mediocre secondary education, with scant reading of any kind. To a boy who had read only a bad translation of *Les Misérables* and *The Call of the Wild* and *Men Against the Sea* and *The Grapes of Wrath* (which one had read at fourteen for the racy dialogue and the "sensational" episodes), the sudden exposure to a book like *Look Homeward, Angel,* with its lyrical torrent and raw, ingenuous feeling, its precise and often exquisite rendition of place and mood, its bouyant humor and the vitality of its characters and, above all, the sense of youthful ache and promise and hunger and ecstasy which so corresponded to that of its eighteen-year-old reader–to experience such a book as this, at exactly the right moment in time and space, was for many young people like being born again into a world as fresh and wondrous as that seen through the eyes of Adam. Needless to say, youth itself was largely responsible for this feverish empathy, and there will be reservations in a moment in regard to the effect of a later rereading of Wolfe; nonetheless, a man who can elicit such reactions from a reader at whatever age is a force to be reckoned with, so I feel nothing but a kind of gratitude when I consider how I succumbed to the rough unchanneled force of Wolfe as one does to the ocean waves. . . .

The story is of the Gant family, Oliver and Eliza, and of their seven children, Eugene Gant in particular. Back of them is the story of the town of Altamont, in North Carolina. And in back of Altamont, the story is of the whole South from the latter part of the nineteenth century until the present. Oliver Gant, the Wanderer, driven by savage appetites and by dreams only half-understood, settled at last in Altamont and married the stolid, property-loving, patient, half-shrewd Eliza Pentland, and there began a life-long battle between them. "Eliza came stolidly through to victory. As she marched down these enormous years of love and loss, stained with the rich dyes of pain and pride and death, and with the great wild flare of his alien and passionate life, her limbs faltered in the grip of ruin, but she came on, through sickness and emaciation, to victorious strength."

But her victorious strength, if it sustained Oliver and herself and the children, at the same time blighted them all. Eliza's blindness to everything save the need for property and money drove the children into harsh, incessant contacts with the world at early ages, and in the home the struggle between Eliza and Oliver, assuming insane proportions, dulled or humiliated or embittered all feeling of the family relationship.

Of them all, Eugene Gant is the only one of the children to escape in the end, partially at any rate, the Gantian struggle and seeming spiritual self-destruction. Here the novel becomes two novels. With the adolescence of Eugene, "Look Homeward, Angel" gradually ceases to be a family saga, and becomes slowly the semi-autobiographical story of a sensitive youth. This, too, is closely related to a familiar type, but the author is still extraordinarily lavish, in the fullness with which he portrays Eugene's life, in the scope of the background, and in his own interjections, taking the form of ironic, romantic or realistic comments that sum up the given situation, and suggest some Gantian relationship with the universe as a whole.

> "Naked and alone we came into exile. In her dark womb we did not know our mother's face; from the prison of her flesh have we come into the unspeakable and incommunicable prison of this earth. Which of us has known his brother? Which of us has looked into his father's heart? Which of us has not remained forever prison-pent? . . . O waste of loss, in the hot mazes, lost, among bright stars on this most weary unbright cinder, lost! . . ."

Such writing may come uncomfortably close becoming merely fine writing, but it is sincere, and suggests the author's ambitious attempt, sustained in the book as a whole by the far reach of the actual story.

British novelist and poet Richard Aldington compared Wolfe's Look Homeward, Angel *to William Faulkner's* Soldiers' Pay *in his review.*

AMERICAN NOVELISTS

Richard Aldington

The Sunday Referee, 6 July 1930

MR. THOMAS WOLFE'S *Look Homeward, Angel* is a very long novel–well over 600 pages–and I am told that the original manuscript was even longer. But this tumultuous autobiographical fragment is a superb display of vitality. It is a first book, and is written with a gusto and exuberance which sweep the reader away through an immense series of scenes and persons and emotions. I think it is the one good book which has come from "Ulysses," because Mr. Wolfe is the first writer (so far as I know) to learn what Mr. Joyce has to teach without imitating him. I do not mention "Ulysses" to disparage Mr. Wolfe, but to praise him, because I do not think anyone can write a large-scale and really modern novel until he has been through Joyce, until he has assimilated, mastered, and controlled all the technical revolution which Joyce has made. But whereas "Ulysses" is intellectual, minutely planned, static, and *au fond* life hating, *Look Homeward, Angel* is the product of an immense exuberance, organic in its form, kinetic, and drenched with the love of life.

There is none of the note-book and lamp about Mr. Wolfe's writing. Filled as his book is with literary allusions, they are such as come spontaneous to his pen, and the book is the very reverse of "literary." He is so full of his subject, has so much to say, has seen, felt, heard, smelled, touched, tasted so vigorously and so much, that the words pour from him in a torrent unquenchably. He is not the sort of writer who has to wrack his brains for a subject and torture out his daily five hundred words. His greatest difficulty must be to control the abundance of his memory, invention, and imagination. I rejoice over Mr. Wolfe. I think this mighty David has slain once for all the tedious Goliath of "objective" fiction down to the bottommost dog of them all. His novel is as personal as a poem and as inclusive as an encyclopedia. It contains everything, from the crudest realism to flights of poetic prose which would be flowery in a writer with less energy. There is no *chichi* about this young man, no sterile tootling on the super-highbrow flute acquired at second hand and by petty larceny from last season's Paris modes in literature; he has something to say, knows what it is, and, by the Nine Gods, he says it. For me, this young American goes at one jump straight to the top-notch in novelists.

Look Homeward, Angel is a first novel. Thomas Wolfe, the author, was born in Ashville, North Carolina, in 1900 and graduated at Harvard in 1923. He began this novel and wrote most of it during a long visit to England, staying in the county of his forefathers.

In an article written during his recent visit to America, Mr. Hugh Walpole found that "American literature in its determination to move forward at all costs has, for the moment, come to a standstill." The single exception, he found, was a novel. "*Look Homeward, Angel*," he says, "has genius. It does what I have been longing for someone to do here—it restores poetry to the American scene, and poetry that is not merely contemporary. The real richness of America, its fecundity, colour, vitality, stains deeply these pages."

Look Homeward, Angel has also stirred Mr. Frank Kendon to

(continued on rear flap)

(continued from front flap)

write, in a two-page article in *John O'London's Weekly:* "It has a fury, a present passion, a forward, questioning eagerness, and it is upon this, the poetical energy with which it is written, that I should base my claim (which American readers are supporting) that Thomas Wolfe has genius. *Look Homeward, Angel* is a very long book—220,000 words—but never once, throughout, is there any slackening of intensity, not a dull or level passage . . . His book compelled him to write it. It must have wearied him, but it could not exhaust him, and one feels that he could not rest till it was done."

LOOK HOMEWARD, ANGEL

"This is a first book and in it the author has written of experience which is now far and lost, but which was once part of the fabric of his life. If any reader, therefore, should say that the book is 'autobiographical' the writer has no answer for him: it seems to him that all serious work in fiction is autobiographical—that, for instance, a more autobiographical work than *Gulliver's Travels* cannot easily be imagined.

"This note, however, is addressed principally to those persons whom the writer may have known in the period covered by these pages. To these persons, he would say what he believes they understand already: that this book was written in innocence and nakedness of spirit, and that the writer's main concern was to give fullness, life, and intensity to the actions and people in the book he was creating. Now that it is to be published, he would insist that this book is a fiction, and that he meditated no man's portrait here.

"But we are the sum of all the moments of our lives—all that is ours is in them: we cannot escape or conceal it. If the writer has used the clay of life to make his book, he has only used what all men must, what none can keep from using. Fiction is not fact, but fiction is fact selected and understood, fiction is fact arranged and charged with purpose. Dr. Johnson remarked that a man will turn over half a library to make a single book: in the same way a novelist may turn over half the people in a town to make a single figure in his novel. This is not the whole method, but the writer believes it illustrates the whole method in a book that is written from a middle distance and is without rancour or bitter intention."—*From the Author's Foreword.*

THOMAS WOLFE

Dust jacket for the first English edition, 1930; the text was cut (courtesy of Special Collections, Thomas Cooper Library, University of South Carolina)

Look Homeward, Angel, by Thomas Wolfe, will be published in this country by Hienemann on July 14. Mr. Aldington's review is written on the American edition, which has already been published.

Look Homeward, Angel is really one of Goethe's subjective epics. It is the epic of the youth of Eugene Gant, of the Gant family, of the Southern mountain town of Altamont, and even of all the Southern States. The book has little formal structure, no fabricated plot which can be easily summarised; but because it rejects the convenient devices of professional fiction and winds itself close to human life does not mean that it lacks form. It has the complex but beautiful structure of something which has grown naturally, and the sweep and variety of its rhythms, as well as the author's intense absorption in what he is writing, keep the reader's attention perpetually alert and fascinated. And it is no mere slice of life, but rather life intensely realised, brooded over, relived in an almost fierce reverie. Mr. Wolfe has given everything he had to this book, poured out riches enough to furnish a lesser novelist for life with a great spontaneous generosity. He has not tried to "save material" for other books, but he will certainly write other books, perhaps better books, for a nature so sensitive and so abundant can never lack experience.

Certain characters stand out from the mass of human beings who throng these pages. There is the central figure, Eugene Gant, whose childhood and adolescence are lived out so painfully, but with such splendid glimpses of ecstasy and happiness, through this multitude of scenes. Every figure in the Gant family is clear and startlingly alive, even when touched with fantasy–Gant the father, wanderer and stonemason, drunkard and palaverer, but somehow fascinating his children as well as strangers with his reckless force and prodigaltry of living; Eliza Gant, the mother, hapless producer of children, verbose, avaricious, insatiable collector of dollars and building lots; then the children, Steve the waster and braggart, Luke the sentimental go-getter, Ben the born salesman with his strange aloofness and bitter resentment against the avarice of his parents, and Helen the hysterical, the cautious dipsomaniac, who alone can manage the father in his mad drunken bouts. These are the central figures of the narrative, but in and out of their lives come a swarm of other figures–Mrs. Gant's boarders, the notables of the town from W. J. Bryant to Jouhanneau jeweller and fireman, the soft-padding erotic negroes, the crowds of newsboys and men about the newspaper office, the idlers and workers of the town, the school people, the War-time labourers in the Southern dockyards, Eugene's friends–an immense and palpitating throng. Along with all this teeming life are frequent outbursts of rhetorical prose, occasionally a little turgid and immature, but moving in their spontaneity and absence of calculation. It is awful to say of a man. "That he gives promise." Mr. Wolfe's first book is an achievement. If he can surpass it in later works he has an enviable future.

Mr. William Faulkner's *Soldiers' Pay* is also a good American novel. If it did not come to me pat on top of Mr. Wolfe's book I should place it as one of the few really good new novels. I shall not attempt a comparison. Mr. Faulkner works on a smaller scale and with a less noble frenzy. His novel is a pleasingly bitter comment on the American reception of the demobilised soldiers–a reception which differed not at all from that of other countries. The opening section, describing the drunken cadets on the train, is very lively and telling. There is a fall in quality when the scene is suddenly changed but gradually Mr. Faulkner works up a very telling situation between the dying airman and two women and his father and the self-appointed cadet attendant. The portrait of the selfish and rather silly fiancée is first-rate. But there is an air of improbability about the whole business which I rather dislike. How do these people earn their livings? Why should the girl picked up on the train go along with the soldiers? Why should the old Vicar take in the girl and the cadet once they have handed over his injured son, especially since the Vicar at first thinks his son will recover? What exactly is the point of the lecherous and ignominious Jones? Why should this chance acquaintance, who early proved himself so unpleasant, be tolerated for so long in a country vicarage? There is a lack of coherence about all this which offends me. I agree with Mr. Hughes (who writes an excellent little preface) that the dance scene is good, and the writing throughout is very competent, sometimes brilliant.

The setting of this book, like Mr. Wolfe's, is in South though Mr. Faulkner's is in Georgia and Mr. Wolfe's "between North Carolina and Tennessee." I do not know if this authorises us to applaud a re-birth of energy and genius in the South after the disaster of the War of Secession and brutalising of the Recontruction period. I should like to think so. I recommend both these novels warmly as examples of the variety and energy of contemporary American writing.

The London Times Literary Supplement (TLS) *was at the time the most influential review periodical in the United Kingdom. All reviews were written anonymously.*

Look Homeword, Angel
TLS, 24 July 1930

Mr. Thomas Wolfe's novel, LOOK HOMEWARD, ANGEL (Heinemann, 10s. 6d. net), was obviously written as the result of tremendous internal pressure. It is a first novel and very long, following a boy's emergence from childhood and imprisonment in the bosom of an extraordinary family to manhood and independence. Such Odysseys of youth are not uncommon: and by this time the crudities of the American scene are so familiar that the strange squalid-extravagant life of the Gant family in the hill town of Altamont, here described in profuse detail, will hold no particular surprise; what is amazing is the pressure under which this narrative is shot forth. To use a homely American metaphor, it might be called a "gusher"; for Mr. Wolfe's words come spouting up with all the force of a subterranean flood now at last breaking through the overlying strata of repression. Such native force is rare in England now; and it is impossible to regard this unstinting output of magnificent, raw vigour without a thrill and a hope that it will be channelled to great art. The present book is not great art; but its promise and its power are so extraordinary that we dwell upon them rather than upon the details of its story.

Whether or no the family life of the Gants –the Bacchic flaming father everlastingly at odds with the tight-lipped avaricious mother nursing her secret pain in dumbness, the worthless Steve, the thwarted secretive Ben, the cheery "go-getter" Luke, and the passionately serving Helen–was Mr. Wolfe's own or no, there can be no doubt that he is Eugene, the last born, who saw the light while Gant the father was booming eloquent curses outside the bedroom door and who grew up with the taints of the Gant and Pentland blood in his body and in his soul the sensuality, the aimlessness of his mother's family and the ache for wandering, the almost demoniac power of fantasy and the sense of being a stranger in an alien world which stamped his drunken but gigantically moulded father. It is the story of a boy's escape from a thralldom to which his own nature is much as circumstances subjected him. His mother's avarice, it is true, keeps him in the low boarding house that she, though rich in real property, keeps penuriously, forces him to sell newspapers at dawn before going to school, cuts short his schooldays and sends him to the State university too soon. But it is the influence of the blood which makes him return again and again willingly to that home of strife and discomfort, bound together by its very hatreds, until its fibres are at last rent apart by the death from pneumonia of Ben–a passage of remarkable power–while Gant curses, Eliza purses her tight lips and the other wrangle hideously round the dying man. The words of Ben's last moment give a measure of Mr. Wolfe's power over words when shaken, as he is often shaken, by a spasm of emotion:–

> Suddenly, marvellously, as if his resurrection and rebirth had come upon him, Ben drew upon the air in a long and powerful respiration; his grey eyes opened. Filled with a terrible vision of all life in the one moment, he seemed to rise forward bodilessly from pillows without support–a flame, a light, a glory–joined at length in death to the dark spirit who had brooded upon each footstep of his lonely adventure on earth; and, casting the fierce sword of his glance with utter and final comprehension upon the room haunted with its grey pageantry of cheap loves and dull consciences and on all those uncertain mummers of waste and confusion fading now from the bright window of his eyes, he passed instantly, scornful and unafraid, as he had lived, into the shades of death.

This is not merely an eloquent passage, it is summary and judgment of what had been fairly set out with intense vividness before.

This intensity of apprehension, whether sensuous or imaginative, is Eugene's mark in the novel, as it is Mr. Wolfe's in the performance. We do not need the catalogues, remarkable in themselves, of the books on which Eugene fed his voracious fancy or the rich foods on which the elder Gant, in the great days, gorged his sons and daughters: Mr. Wolfe reveals himself as one who has fed upon honeydew and everything else under the sun. And his most astonishing passages, crammed though they are with the clangorous echoes of English poetry and prose, too often falling into sheer metre, come when, in contemplation of his past, he sends out a cry of lyrical agony for lost beauty. One might take to pieces the paragraph on spring that begins: "Yes, and in that month when Proserpine comes back, and Ceres' dead heart rekindles, when all the woods are a tender smoky blur, and birds no bigger than a budding leaf dart through the singing trees"; or that other beginning : "In the cruel volcano of the boy's mind, the little brier moths of his idolatry wavered in to their strange marriage and were consumed"; one might trace the echoes and point out the faults, but the Marlowesque energy and beauty of them has already made such work vain. What is going to be done with this great talent, so hard, so sensual, so unsentimental, so easily comprehending and describing every sordidness of the flesh and spirit, so proudly rising to the heights? Knowing the times and the temptations of the times, we may well watch its fresh emergence with anxiety: for if Mr. Wolfe can be wasted, there is no hope for to-day.

Wolfe in his Brooklyn apartment with his manuscript for Of Time and the River *(The Thomas Wolfe Collection, Pack Memorial Public Library, Asheville, North Carolina)*

Chapter 4

Of Time and the River and *From Death to Morning*, 1930–1935

With the critical and commercial success of Look Homeward, Angel, *Wolfe resigned his teaching post at Washington Square College in January 1930 and went abroad on a Guggenheim Fellowship. He settled in Paris in May 1930 and began work on a novel he tentatively titled "The October Fair." In this novel Wolfe wanted to present the impulses of wandering and homesickness he found so characteristic of the American people. He planned to focus on an individual's symbolic search for a father, a theme suggested by Maxwell Perkins. Wolfe struggled for more than five years to produce his second novel, which was eventually published as* Of Time and the River.

After Look Homeward, Angel, *Maxwell Perkins was eager for Wolfe to publish a new novel as soon as possible. This letter, which exists only as an unsigned carbon copy, indicates that Charles Scribner's Sons was committed to remaining Wolfe's publisher.*

Dec. 18, 1929

Dear Mr. Wolfe:

We are deeply interested in your writing, and have confidence in your future, and we wish to cooperate with you so far as possible toward the production of a new novel. We think you would be able to write it to much greater advantage if you were free from the necessity of earning money at the same time, and we should be glad to undertake to pay you, as an advance on the earnings of the next novel, forty-five hundred dollars ($4500) in installments, at the rate of two hundred and fifty dollars ($250) a month, beginning with February first.

–*To Loot My Life Clean,* p. 27

Starting a Second Novel in Europe

In March 1930 Wolfe informed Aline Bernstein that he had been awarded a Guggenheim Fellowship and was leaving alone for Europe. Bernstein felt betrayed, for she was still willing to support Wolfe while he worked on his novel. As he prepared for his fifth trip to Europe, Wolfe was determined to exercise his independence and end his relationship with her. After Wolfe arrived in Paris on 19 May, he broke off nearly all correspondence with Bernstein.

Wolfe spent several weeks moving from one hotel to another before finally settling down to work on "The October Fair." These excerpts from his early notes for the manuscript indicate Wolfe's interest in writing about his relationship with Bernstein.

Monday, May 26–

It is no good denying it–I am sick at my heart for home, for a sight of that immense and terrible land. I must live out my exile here, I must conquer or keep down the sadness in my heart, above all I must work, and perhaps the answer to it all will be there.

Perhaps it is true that we have no native earth, but when it is midnight here I keep remembering that people at home are sitting down to dinner and my flesh is one long dull ache from throat to belly.

He tried to forget her but it was no use; it would never be any use. The flower-face was there to go haunting through his brain and heart forever.

Tues. May 27–

. . . .

I-I-I-I-I hardly know just how-how-how-how-I-I-I shall begin. David and Esther were . . . I-I-I you know what I mean . . . were . . . lovers. Oh, of course, I know it sounds silly, but I mean–you know . . . lovers I-I-I mean!

Tues., May 27:

I therefore will begin:

David and Esther were lovers, and in their lives they were lovely, and in their deaths they shall not be desolate.

Wed. May 28–

. . . .

Man is a measure, *the* measure, not of all things, but of himself. He may quest far, and the scope and depth of his apprehension, the amount of his knowledge can be enormous. But he cannot know all nor see all. The only infinite, the only insatiable thing in man is hunger and desire. That is unending and everlasting, and it steeps him in his deepest hell. But it is also the greatest thing in him: it is the demon that can possess him, and that may destroy him.

Love is the only triumph over life and death and living; over hunger and desire. Love begins as madness and disease: it can end as health and beauty.

The eternal coward is with us yet, is with us always. It is necessary to affirm rather than to deny, and love is the supreme belief, the final affirmation. Nor is it wisdom to call at all times for a definition.

[*From the "October Fair" ledger*]

Thurs. night–Fri. morning, Paris:

Wed. May 29 Assumption Day. Returned from movie at Gaumont Palace and dinner and wrote this:

There was the dream where you fell and the one where you soared, and the one where you stepped through walls, and the one where you were black as night and were in the wind and went hawking through the world full of a dark and terrible glee.

Lost words! Lost faces! why did they reappear so suddenly: why did whole canvasses of forgotten memory reappear to mock at time, to haunt men with the briefness of their days, as when, on going through a door we have not entered for twenty years, we find the landlord there in the same old place: he says "Good day, sir"–and the dreadful years are blotted out, and we hear our boy's voice saying "Good day," the while our mad eyes stare into the mirror behind him and see–no more the boy's face, but the yellowed skin, the veinous vinous eyes, the blackened teeth, and the smeared crooked nose, broken in a brawl. Good day! Good day!

The lost words; the forgotten faces–no, no: not lost, and never forgotten–but ghosts that might walk forth at any hour to haunt us.

. . . .

A name that will evoke an entire past:

Theda Bara, John Bunny, the old Galax Theater on the Square.

The fact that Esther's early life belonged to all this gave it an unreality when he thought of it. There was a picture that had been painted when she was 25 and at the full height of her loveliness–she was very fashionably dressed in the picture with her hands thrust into a rich little muff, and with a funny little hat that stuck somewhat comically off her head. Below it her lovely child's-woman's face was blooming like a small dark flower: the face was lovely and innocent, full of eagerness and desire; he felt, with a bitter pang of jealousy the rich young body, seductive, small, voluptuously rounded, and wondered what powerful and brilliant men had panted after her, to which and to how many she had given herself. He stared, pierced first by this bitter pang, and then with sadness and inescapable grief. She stood looking at it with him, then said in a voice that was happy but anxious:

"I don't think I've changed much since then. Do you?"

"No," he said, roughly and indifferently. "No. You haven't changed at all."

She seemed entirely satisfied with his dull answer.

"I think so, too. I was looking at one of my pictures the other day made when I was a little girl. I'm the same as I always was."

The innocent satisfaction with which she spoke the words suddenly pierced him cruelly: he wanted to cry out loudly. And he wanted to cry out because what she said was really true–the lovely child's soul, full of its strong and eager faith, that bloomed forth darkly in the painting, was radiant also in her face: she was the child, the maiden and the woman with an indelible oneness, an everlasting youth of spirit–and her hair was getting quite grey, there were deep markings underneath her eyes.

His eyes grew hot with tears; he seized her suddenly and pressed her against him:

"You're just the same! The same! The same! You'll always be the same, my dear, my darling! Only more lovely, only more beautiful!"

She knew at once what was in his heart and what he could not utter save by a cry: the cruel haunting of time and our brief days to which there are no answers. She said: "God, if only I were that age again! Nothing in the world would keep me from you! I'd come to you and live with you whether you wanted me to or not! I'd never let you get away from me!"

He seized with a harsh joy a release in bitter words: "Big talk! You know damned well you'd never look at me if you were twenty-five."

F. Scott Fitzgerald, whom Wolfe met in Paris in summer 1930

On May 31 in Paris on Saturday, after many letters to me, Mrs. Emily Davies Vanderbilt Thayer conspired that I be insulted at her ap't 6 Rue Montalivet.

At Rouen 11:25 Monday June 2:

For in this pulling of his teeth, he saw the victory of living over flesh, the victory of time and death–the victory of love and women. He had lost four teeth since meeting her: at times he cursed her and said she had taken them from him–had drawn marrow from his spine, the core of his bones, his bowels, his loins.

Immortal love, forever living and forever young.

October is the richest of the seasons; there is the harvest in, the granaries are full. October is the richest of the seasons: all of the blood and meat of living is plumped full.

The breast hangs over like a sheaf of golden grain.

And in America the chinquapins are falling. The corn sticks out in hard and yellow rows upon dried ears, fit for a winter's barn and the big yellowed teeth of crunching horses, and the leaves are turning, turning up in Maine.

Rouen, June 3–Tuesday:

The soft air that entered in easy flows into his lungs heavied and drowsed him; they recalled to him 200 other reeking days in Europe–200 days upon that soft wet continent–he missed the sharp burning oxygen of America.

Around the tower of Jeanne D'Arc the light green grass of France was growing–the sight of that kept nature so old, so clergy-staked filled him with sadness and despair–he wanted the old piercing hope and agony of Spring in his native land.

Rouen, June 3–Eating at old Opera Restaurant–vast room full of creamy yellowed baroque of 1890s.

She had done for today what is being done for today–she visited her husband and his new wife declaring she was "most awfully fond" of both of them. They were modern.

. . . .

EXILE

He was alone with his sorrow–with early sorrow, unanswered and lasting, that drinks the joy and sparkle of our youth away.

But we do not "get over it" We do not forget it. We do not get used to it. We accept it, and we live with it forever.

There is nothing to be afraid of–except fear.

–*The Notebooks of Thomas Wolfe,* pp. 456–461

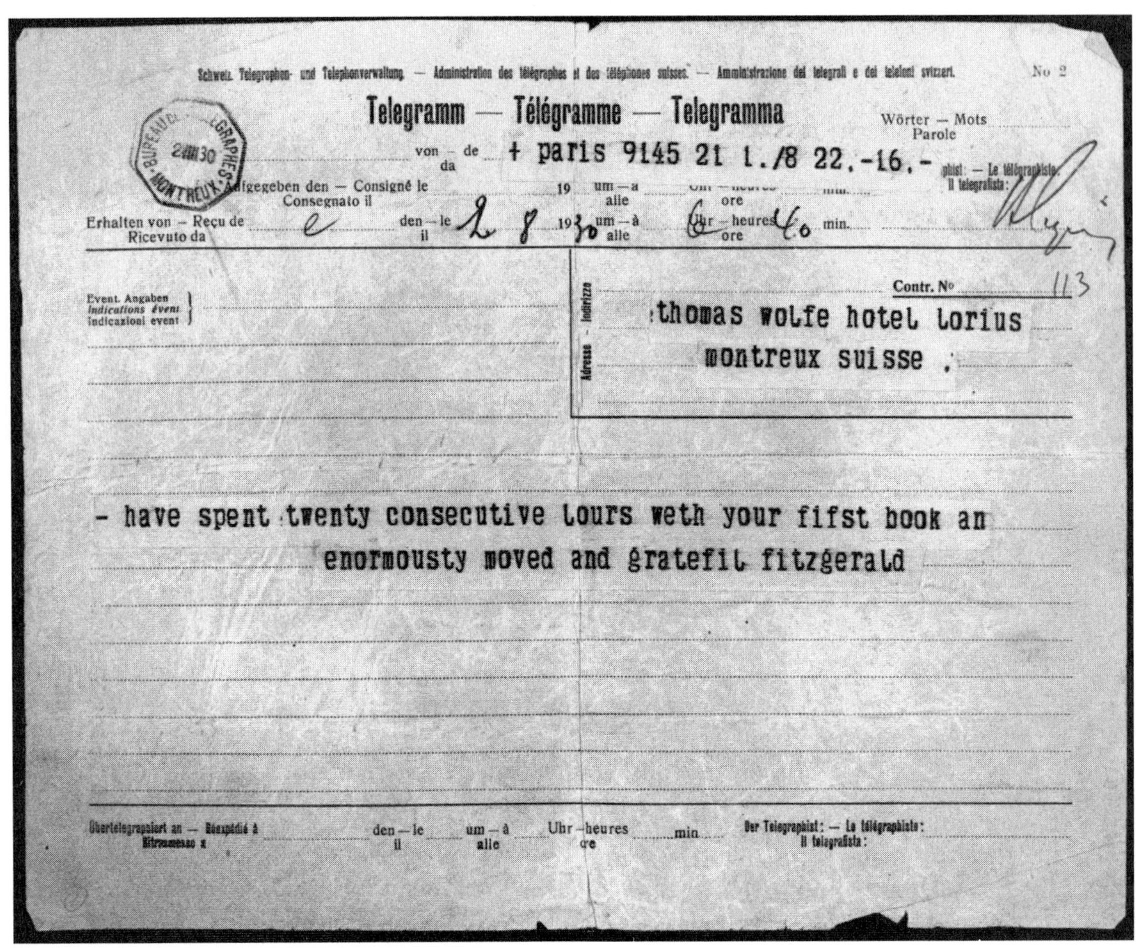

Schweiz. Telegraphen- und Telephonverwaltung — Administration des télégraphes et des téléphones suisses — Amministrazione dei telegrafi e dei telefoni svizzeri. No 2

Telegramm — Télégramme — Telegramma

Wörter – Mots – Parole

von – de – da + paris 9145 21 l./8 22.-16.-

Aufgegeben den – Consigné le – Consegnato il ... 19 ... um – à – alle ... Uhr – heures – ore ... min.

Erhalten von – Reçu de – Ricevuto da ... den – le – il 2 8 1930 um – à – alle ... Uhr – heures – ore ... min.

Event. Angaben – Indications évent. – Indicazioni event.

Contr. No 113

Adresse – Indirizzo: thomas wolfe hotel lorius montreux suisse .

- have spent twenty consecutive lours weth your fifst book an enormousty moved and gratefil fitzgerald

F. Scott Fitzgerald's congratulatory telegram to Wolfe after he read Look Homeward, Angel, *2 August 1930 (William B. Wisdom Collection, Houghton Library, Harvard University)*

In the following letter to Perkins, Wolfe describes his meeting with F. Scott Fitzgerald, who worked with Perkins. He also discusses his work on "Antaeus," the proposed prologue to the enormous saga he was writing.

July 1, 1930

Dear Mr. Perkins: I have a long letter under way to you, but I shall probably not send it until I have left Paris. The main news is that I have been at work for several weeks, and have worked every day. except last Sunday, when I met Scott Fitzgerald for the first time. He called me up at my hotel and I went out to his apartment for lunch: we spent the rest of the afternoon together talking and drinking–a good deal of both–and I finally left him at the Ritz Bar. He was getting ready to go back to Switzerland where he has been for several weeks, and had come up to close up his apartment and take his little girl back with him. He told me that Mrs Fitzgerald has been very sick–a bad nervous breakdown–and he has her in a sanitarium at Geneva. He spoke of his new book and said he was working on it: he was very friendly and generous, and I liked him, and think he has a great deal of talent, and I hope he gets that book done soon. I think we got along very well–we had quite an argument about America: I said we were a homesick people, and belonged to the earth and land we came from as much or more as any country I knew about–he said we were not, that we were not a country, that he had no feeling for the land he came from. "Nevertheless," as Galileo said, "it moves." We do, and they are all homesick or past having any feeling about anything.

I have missed America more this time than ever: maybe its because all my conviction, the tone and conviction of my new book is filled with this feeling, which once I would have been ashamed to admit. I notice that the Americans who live here live with one another for the most part, and the French exist for them as waiters, taxi drivers, etc.–yet most of them will tell you all about the French, and their minute characteristics. I have been absolutely alone for several weeks–Fitzgerald was the first American I had talked to for some time, but yesterday I was here in the bank, and in walked Jim Boyd: I was so surprised and happy I could not speak for a moment–we went out to lunch together and spent the rest of the day together. He has been quite sick with the sinus trouble, as you know. We went to see a doctor, and I waited below: this doctor made no examination and gave no verdict, but is sending him to a specialist. I hope they do something for him–he is a fine fellow, and I like him enormously. We went to a nice cafe and drank beer and talked over the American soil and what we were going to do for literature, while Mrs Boyd shopped around town: later we all drove out to the Bois and through it to a nice little restaurant out of town on the banks of the Seine–we had a good quiet dinner there and came back. I think Jim enjoyed it, and I am going to meet them again tonight. It has done me a great deal of good to see them–

. . . .

I am going to Switzerland–I have several places in mind but must go and see them–I would have gone long ago, but I did not want to move fast when I had started. I do not know how long I shall stay over here, but I shall stay until I have done the first part of my book, and can bring it back with me. It is going to be a very long book, I am afraid, but there is no way out of it: you cant write the book I want to write in 200 pages. It has four parts, its whole title is The October Fair, and the names of the four parts are 1 Antaeus; 2 The Fast Express; 3 Faust and Helen; 4 The October Fair. I am working on the part called Antaeus now which is like a symphony of many voices run through with the beginning thread of story that continues through the book. I propose to bring back to America with me the parts called Antaeus and The Fast Express (all these names are tentative and if you don't like them we'll get others. The book is a grand book if I have character and talent enough to do it as I have conceived it. The book has to do with what seem to me two of the profoundest impulses in man–Wordsworth, in one of his poems "To a Skylark," I think–calls it "heaven and home"–and I called it in the first line of my book "Of wandering forever and the earth again"–

By "the earth again"–I mean simply the everlasting earth, a home, a place for the heart to come to, and earthly mortal love, the love of a woman, who, it seems to me belongs to the earth and is a force opposed to that other great force that makes men wander, that makes them search, that makes them lonely, and that makes them both hate and love their loneliness.

You may ask what all this has to do with America–it is true it has to do with the whole universe–but it is as true of the enormous and lonely land that we inhabit as any land I know of, and more so, it seems to me.

I hope this does not seem wild and idiotic to you, I have been unable to tell you much about it here, but I will in greater detail later. I ask you to remember that in the first part–Antaeus–the part of many voices–everything moves, everything moves across the enormous earth, except the earth itself, and except for the voices of the women crying out "Don't go! Stay! Return, return!"–the woman floating down the river in flood on her housetop with her husband and family (I finished that scene the other day and I think it is a good one–the whole scene told in the woman's homely speech moves to the rhythm of the great river–yet the scene has pungent and humorous talk in it, and I think does not ring false–you understand that the river is in her brain in her thought in her speech; and at the very end, lying in her tent at night while a new house is being built where the old one was–for he refuses to go up on high ground back beyond the river where nothing moves, she hears him waken beside her–he thinks she is asleep–she knows he is listening to the river, to the whistles of the boats upon the river, that he wants to be out there upon the river, that he could go floating on forever down the river. And she hates the river, but all of its sounds are in her brain, she cannot escape it

. . . "All of my life is flowing like the river, all of my life is passing like the river, I think and dream and talk just like the river as it goes by me, by me, by me, to the sea."

Does it sound idiotic? I don't think so if you could see the whole; it is full of rich detail, sounds and talk. I will not tell you any more now,–this letter is too long and I have had no lunch. The river woman is only one thing–I'll tell you all about it later. Everything moves except the earth and the voices of the women crying out against [wandering]!

I miss seeing you and Scribners more than I can say. I hope I can do a good book for you and for myself and for the whole damn family. Please hope and pull for me and write me when you can. Excuse this long scrawl. I hope this finds you well and enjoying the summer, and also that you get a good vacation. Jim Boyd and I will think of you every time we drink a glass of beer and wish that you were here just for an hour or so to share it. I send everyone my best and warmest wishes.

Faithfully Yours,
Tom Wolfe

Don't tell any one where I am or where I'm going unless you think they have some business to find out. Tell them you don't know where I am (if anyone asks) but that mail will get to me if sent to The Guaranty Trust Co, Paris.

–*To Loot My Life Clean,* pp. 38, 40–41

Prolog to The October Fair 1

. . . . of wandering forever and the earth again. Of seed-time, bloom, and the mellow-dropping harvest, and of the big flowers, the rich flowers, the strange unknown flowers.

Where shall the weary rest? When shall the lonely of heart come home? What doors are open for the wanderer, and in what place, and in what land, and in what time? Where? Where the weary of heart can abide forever, where the weary of wandering can find peace, where the tumult, the fever, and the fret shall be forever stilled.

Who owns the earth? Did we

Page from the early draft of the prologue for "The October Fair" (William B. Wisdom Collection, Houghton Library, Harvard University)

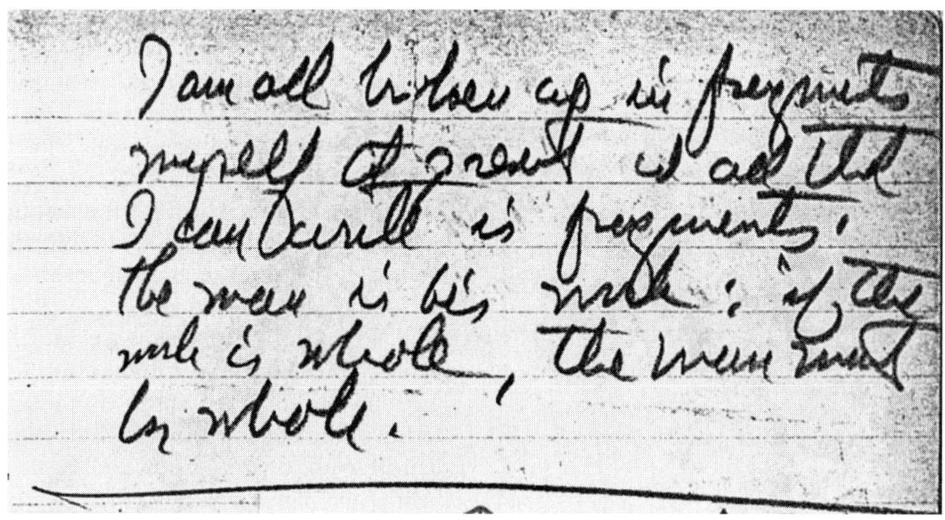
I am all broken up in fragments
myself at present and all that
I can write is fragments:
the man is his work: if the
work is whole, the man must
be whole.

Entry in Wolfe's notebook, August 1930 (William B. Wisdom Collection, Houghton Library, Harvard University)

In his notebooks Wolfe wrote poems which incorporated phrases that he took from his prose manuscript. "The October Fair," written in August 1930, shows Wolfe's concern with the themes of loneliness and wandering.

THE OCTOBER FAIR

Now October had come again,
  Had come again!
The sharp, the frosty months had come again,
  Had come again!
Cooled & a dusky glow the red sun slips.
All through the night lone star,
  Lone star!
O forested and far,
Through all the waste and lone immensity of night,
  Return! Return!

He wakes at morning in a foreign land,
  And he thinks of home.
Where are the footfalls of a million streets?
And where is the crickety stitch of mid-day now?

The adder lisps against the breast, cups fall.
Call for the robin! Call! Call! Call!
And the copperhead is crawling through the oak.

Long, long into the night I lay awake.

The dry bones and the barren earth.
The living wilderness.
The branches in the wood were dying, dying.
The fields were shorn and the sheaves were lying.

The engineer was pulling at the throttle,
He sadly smiled and opened up the bottle.

–*The Notebooks of Thomas Wolfe,* pp. 493–494

Sinclair Lewis

Sinclair Lewis praised Look Homeward, Angel, *both privately and publicly.*

October 23, 1930

Dear Thomas Wolfe: I wish there hadn't been quite so many brisk blurb-writers these past twenty years, using up every once respectable phrase of literary criticism, so that I might have some fresh phrase with which to express my profound delight in Look Homeward, Angel! There is, you needn't be told, authentic greatness in it. It and Farewell to Arms seem to me to have more spacious power in them than any books for years, American OR foreign. . . . God, your book is good!

–*The Letters of Thomas Wolfe,* pp. 270–271

* * *

In the 6 November 1930 story in The New York Times *announcing that Lewis was the first American to win the Nobel Prize, the older writer went out of his way to praise Wolfe.*

The American writer to whom he paid the highest tribute was Thomas Wolfe, a young author who has written only one novel "Look Homeward, Angel." If Mr. Wolfe keeps up the standard which he has set in this work he "may have a chance to be the greatest American writer," Mr. Lewis asserted. "In fact. I don't see why he should not be one of the greatest world writers. His first book is so deep and spacious that it deals with the whole of life."

Despite Lewis's admiration, Wolfe did not spare him in his harsh portrait of alcoholic novelist Lloyd McHarg in You Can't Go Home Again. *"You couldn't be a friend of Tom's," Lewis later stated, "any more than you could be a friend of a hurricane."*

> Some writers like Sinclair Lewis have missed the meat of the small town, anyway. Although people recognized his characters, his towns were painted as drab and dull. I do not consider them so. I mean the typically American towns. Life is there in all its fullness.
>
> –*Thomas Wolfe Interviewed,* p. 8

A few days before Christmas 1930, Wolfe began a long letter to Perkins in which he discussed his need for solitude and his plans for his novel. He did not finish or send this letter, which he wrote in London and Paris.

Dear Mr. Perkins: I suppose you have by now an enormous letter I wrote you about two weeks ago–it was filled with work and woes; I want to write you this short one to tell you my plans and intentions–

. . . .

I have told you that my new book is haunted throughout by the Idea of the river–of Time and Change. Well, so am I–and the thing that is eating at my entrails at present is when can I have this formidable work ready. You have been wonderful not saying anything about time, but I feel you would like to see something before next Fall. I dont make any promises but I'll try like hell: I am distressed at the time I spent over personal worries, excitement over the first one, and fiddling around, but its no good crying about that now–I think this came as fast as it could, now I've got it all inside me, and much of it down on paper, but I must work like hell. The thing that is good for me is almost total obscurity–I love praise and flattery for my work, but there must be no more parties, no more going out–I must live in two rooms somewhere until I hate to leave them: I want to see you and one or two other people, but I want to come back without seeing anyone in New York for several weeks except you and one or two others: don't think I'm talking through my hat, it's the only way I can do this piece of work and I must do it in this way.

Now about the place to work–this is a hell of a lot to ask you, but I don't want you to do it if you can get someone else to do it–try to help me if you can. I don't know whether it is good to live in New York now, my present obsession is that I am going within the next few years to get married and live somewhere in America in the country or in one of the smaller cities–in Baltimore, or in Virginia, or in the Pennsylvania farm country or in the West–but I have no time to go wandering all over America now (my book by the way is filled with this kind of exuberance, exultancy and joy–I know if I can make people feel it, they will eat it up: I hope to God the energy is still there, this homesickness abroad has made me feel it more than ever–I mean the richness, fabulousness, exultancy and wonderful life of America–the way you feel (I mean the young fellow, the college kid, going off on his own for the first time) when he is rushing through the night in a dark pullman berth and he sees the dark mysterious American landscape rolling by (Virginia, say) and the voluptuous good looking woman in the berth below stirring her pretty legs between the sheets, the sound of the other people snoring, and the sound of voices on the little station platforms in the night–some man and woman seeing their daughter off, then you hear her rustle down the aisle behind the nigger porter and they knock against your green curtain–it is all so strange and familiar and full of joy, it is as if some woman you loved had laid her hand on your bowels–

. . . .

[A]fter the book is written I will be afraid of nothing–but now I am afraid of anything that gets in the way: that is why I want to see you and one or two others and no one else when I come back–I should like to go with you to that 49th St speakeasy and have a few drinks of American gin and one of those immense steaks–then I should like to talk to you as we used to: these seem to me to be mighty good times, and that speakeasy was a fine place–I have remembered it and put it in my book.

Mr Perkins, no one has ever written a book about America–no one has ever put into it the things I know and the things everyone knows–it may be grandiose and pompous for me to think I can, but for God's sake let me try. Furthermore it will be a story, and I believe a damned good story–you know what you said to me over a year ago about the book that might be written about a man looking for his father and how everything could be put into it–well you were right: don't think that I gave up what I wanted to do, only I had this vast amount of material and what you said began to give

> The point of going into oblivion and exile as I have done is, of course, not to brood or wonder what they're thinking or who will write and how often when one returns–the point is solely and simply to get *a piece of work* done at the rate of *1000* or *1500* words a day. If you do that–then brood, grieve, mourn, curse God, the world, everyone, and everything all you please. *But get the work done!*
>
> –*The Notebooks of Thomas Wolfe,* p. 499

40 Verandah Place, Brooklyn. Wolfe lived in the basement apartment from March to October, 1931 (The Thomas Wolfe Collection, Pack Memorial Public Library, Asheville, North Carolina).

shape to it. I have gone through the most damnable torture not merely rewriting but in re-arranging, but now I've got it, if I can get it down on paper. The advantage of your story is not only that it is immensely and profoundly true–namely, all of us are wandering and groping through life for an image outside ourselves–for a superior and external wisdom to which we can appeal and trust–but the story also gives shape to things. Coleridge said that Ben Jonson's play The Alchemist had one of the three finest plots in the world (the other two were Oedipus and Tom Jones) and Coleridge mentions as the wonderful virtue of The Alchemist the fact that the action could be brought to a close at any point by the return of the master (the play as I remember concerns the tricks of a rascal of a servant palming himself off as the master on a world of dupes and rogues)–well, so in this story, the action could be brought to a close by the son finding his father–I have thought over the Antaeus myth a lot, and it seems to me to be a true and beautiful one; it says what I want about man's jointure to the earth whence comes his strength, but Antaeus is also faithful to the memory of his father (Poseidon) to whom he builds a temple from the skulls of those he vanquishes. Poseidon, of course, represents eternal movement and wandering and in a book where a man is looking for his father what could be more true than this?

–*To Loot My Life Clean,* pp. 268, 269, 272–273

Brooklyn

Wolfe returned to New York aboard the Europa *on 4 March 1931. That month he moved into the first of four apartments he rented in Brooklyn during the next four years. He continued to work on "October Fair" but also managed to complete shorter works for* Scribner's Magazine. *Because he was too tall to find ordinary furniture comfortable, he often wrote while standing, using the top of a refrigerator for his desk.*

In You Can't Go Home Again, *Wolfe describes his first apartment through his protagonist, George Webber.*

The tragic light of evening falls upon the huge and rusty jungle of South Brooklyn. It falls without glare or warmth upon the faces of all the men with dead eyes and flesh of tallow-grey as they lean upon their window sills at the sad, hushed end of day.

If at such a time you walk down this narrow street, between the mean and shabby houses, past the eyes of all the men who lean there quietly at their open windows in their shirt-sleeves, and turn in at the alley here and follow the two-foot strip of broken concrete pavement that skirts the alley on one side, and go to the very last shabby house down at the end, and climb up the flight of worn steps to the front entrance, and knock loudly at the door with your bare knuckles (the bell is out of order), and then wait patiently until someone comes, and ask whether Mr. George Webber lives here, you will be informed that he most certainly does, and that if you will just come in and go down this stairway to the basement and knock at the door there on your right, you will probably find him in. So you go down the stairway to the damp and gloomy basement hall, thread your way between the dusty old boxes, derelict furniture, and other lumber stored there in the passage, rap on the door that has been indicated to you, and Mr. Webber himself will open it and usher you right into his room, his home, his castle.

The place may seem to you more like a dungeon than a room that a man would voluntarily elect to live in. It is long and narrow, running parallel to the hall from front to rear, and the only natural light that enters it comes through two small windows rather high up in the wall, facing each other at the opposite ends, and these are heavily guarded with iron bars, placed there by some past owner of the house to keep the South Brooklyn thugs from breaking in.

The room is furnished adequately but not so luxuriously as to deprive it of a certain functional and Spartan simplicity. In the back half there is an iron bed with sagging springs, a broken-down dresser with a cracked mirror above it, two kitchen chairs, and a steamer trunk and some old suitcases that have seen much use. At the front end, under the yellow glow of an electric light suspended from the ceiling by a cord, there is a large desk, very much scarred and battered, with the handles missing on most of the drawers, and in front of it there is a straight-backed chair made out of some old, dark wood. In the center, ranged against the walls, where they serve to draw the two ends of the room together into aesthetic unity, stand an ancient gate-legged table so much of its dark green paint flaked off that the dainty pink complexion of its forgotten youth shows through all over, a tier of bookshelves, unpainted, and two large crates or packing cases, their thick top boards pried off to reveal great stacks of ledgers and of white and yellow manuscript within. On top of the desk, on the table, on the bookshelves, and all over the floor are scattered, like fallen leaves in autumn woods, immense masses of loose paper with writing on every sheet, and everywhere are books, piled up on their sides or leaning crazily against each other.

This dark cellar is George Webber's abode and working quarters. Here, in winter, the walls, which sink four feet below the level of the ground, sweat continuously with clammy drops of water. Here, in summer, it is he who does the sweating.

His neighbors, he will tell you, are for the most part Armenians, Italians, Spaniards, Irishmen, and Jews–in short, Americans. They live in all the shacks, tenements, and slums in all the raw, rusty streets and alleys of South Brooklyn.

And what is that you smell?

Oh, that! Well, you see, he shares impartially with his neighbors a piece of public property in the vicinity; it belongs to all of them in common, and it gives to South Brooklyn its own distinctive atmosphere. It is the old Gowanus Canal, and that aroma you speak of is nothing but the huge symphonic stink of it, cunningly compacted of unnumbered separate putrefactions. It is interesting sometimes to try to count them. There is in it not only the noisome stenches of a stagnant sewer, but also the smells of melted glue, burned rubber, and smoldering rags, the odors of a boneyard horse, long dead, the incense of putrefying offal, the fragrance of deceased, decaying cats, old tomatoes, rotten cabbage, and prehistoric eggs.

And how does he stand it?

Well, one gets used to it. One can get used to anything, just as all these other people do. They never think of the smell, they never speak of it, they'd probably miss it if they moved away.

To this place, then, George Webber has come, and here "holed in" with a kind of dogged stubbornness touched with desperation. And you will not be far wrong if you surmise that he has come here deliberately, driven by a resolution to seek out the most forlorn and isolated hiding spot that he could find.

–*You Can't Go Home Again,* pp. 399–401

Wolfe described Depression-era Brooklyn on a loose sheet of typing paper:

Jan. 1, 1932:

Yesterday was the last day of one of the unhappiest, dreariest years in the nation's history. The "depression," so-called, has a strong and oppressive physical quality. Just how one feels this I don't know, but we breathe it in the air, and we get it in a harassed and weary feeling which people have: the terrible thing in America now, however, is not the material bankruptcy but the spiritual one. Instead of revolution–which is a coherent and living act of the spirit–one feels the presence of something worse–a mindless chaos, and millions of people blundering about without a belief in anything, without hope, with apathy and cynicism. We seem to be lost. The faces of the people in the subway are sometimes horrible in their lack of sensitivity and intelligence–they ruminate mechanically at wads of gum, the skins are horrible blends of the sallow, the pustulate, the greasy: and the smell that comes from them is acrid, foul and weary. They are all going home into that immensity of mindless sprawling horror and ugliness which is known as Brooklyn.

–*The Notebooks of Thomas Wolfe,* p. 568

Asheville Tracks Wolfe

Asheville newspapers followed the turns of Wolfe's career–especially the possible subjects of his fiction–through interviewing his mother. Their readers were often given false impressions of the author's intentions and progress.

Foreign Land Is Scene Of Story Being Prepared

The Asheville Citizen, 9 August 1931

Thomas Wolfe, Asheville Author, Soon To Publish New Modern Novel
First Book, "Look Homeward, Angel," Was Sensation

The residents of Asheville, pricked by obvious references to them in "Look Homeward, Angel," Thomas Wolfe's sensational novel of 1929, may rest assured they will not appear as characters in "October Fair," Wolfe's new novel, the publication of which is expected soon.

Mrs. Julia Wolfe, of Asheville, mother of the author and one of the strongest characters in the first novel, recently visited her son in Brooklyn where he is hiding from students and admirers, and returned to the city with definite assurance that Asheville would not be on parade in the forthcoming opus.

"October Fair," Mrs. Wolfe said, is in no way connected with "Look Homeward, Angel." "October Fair," probably grew out of an incident which befell the author in Oberammergau, Bavaria, where Wolfe went to study the city and the residents which give the world every decade the famous Passion Play. To judge from the mother's conversation, "October Fair," will show a softening of the cynicism revealed in the first book.

Struck on Head

Wolfe, the mother relates, was strolling down a street in Oberammergau when a bottle struck him on the head.

Partly dazed, he continued to walk, until halted by the screams of a woman. Touching a hand to his scalp, he found blood and soon felt it stream down his face. He was taken to a hospital, where he remained without expense for several weeks. His attendants were those who had enacted the roles of the Christus, Mary Magdalene, Judas and others in the Passion Play.

The surgeon who attended him would take no fee for his services because he had a son in America, whom he wished to be taken care of in the same manner should he meet with misfortune. The unselfish treatment given Wolfe there brought sharply to his mind the thought: "Do unto others as you would have others do unto yourself."

Mrs. Wolfe said her son hoped to complete a book every three years until he reached an age too old to write.

* * *

Tom Wolfe Completes His Second Novel And Has Started On Third

The Asheville Citizen, 15 March 1932

Thomas Wolfe, author of "Look Homeward, Angel," has almost completed his second novel and has started preliminary work on a third, it was learned here yesterday from his mother, Mrs. Julia E. Wolfe, of 48 Spruce Street. Mrs. Wolfe recently returned from a visit with her son in Brooklyn, N. Y.

Actual writing of "October Fair" which is the title to be given the second book, has been completed, Mrs. Wolfe believes. Final coordination of the writing will soon be finished and Mrs. Wolfe thinks that her son will have the work ready for printers early this summer. It is expected that the book will be on sale early next fall.

Mr. Wolfe has been busy with his work, recently since he is especially anxious to have his second novel in the hands of printers soon. He has given much thought to his third novel and has already written some for it, Mrs. Wolfe said.

The plot for "October Fair," is not known by Mrs. Wolfe, she said. At one time she thought it might have connection with an incident which occurred on one of his travels several years ago–while walking on a street in Oberammergau. Now she says she does not have a hint of the tale. "His birthday is in October–October 3–and maybe that has a connection with the title of "October Fair"–though I don't know for that's the first time I ever thought of it," she said.

"A Portrait of Bascom Hawke," the first published story of Tom Wolfe since "Look Homeward, Angel," will appear in the April number of Scribner's magazine. Mrs. Wolfe believes this story will feature Mr. Wolfe's impressions of the pecularities and habits of a friend a man who once lived in Asheville. This man, she believes, was poverty stricken in youth, and though he became wealthy later, could not throw off certain characteristics of the earlier life. She said he is highly intellectual.

Mrs. Wolfe said that another short story written by her son has been accepted for publication, though she has no particulars as to the date or the publishers.

"Look Homeward, Angel," which has been rated as a remarkably literary attainment, will be published in the Swedish and German languages, Mrs. Wolfe said. Contracts have been signed by the author with large publishing houses in these two countries for publication of the novel.

. . . .

The Asheville author is expected to visit his mother here next summer. This will be his first visit here since publication of "Look Homeward, Angel."

MEMORANDUM OF AGREEMENT, made in duplicate this 12th day of July, 1933 between THOMAS WOLFE of New York City, N.Y., hereinafter called "the AUTHOR", and CHARLES SCRIBNER'S SONS, of New York City, N.Y., hereinafter called "the PUBLISHERS". Said Thomas Wolfe being the Author and Proprietor of a work entitled:

OF TIME AND THE RIVER

in consideration of the covenants and stipulations hereinafter contained, and agreed to be performed by the Publishers, grants and guarantees to said Publishers and their successors the exclusive right to publish the said work in the United States and Canada in all forms during the terms of copyright and renewals thereof, hereby covenanting with said Publishers that he is the sole Author and Proprietor of said work.

Said Author hereby authorizes said Publishers to take out the copyright on said work, and further guarantees to said Publishers that the said work is in no way whatever a violation of any copyright belonging to any other party, and that it contains nothing of a scandalous or libelous character; and that he and his legal representatives shall and will hold harmless the said Publishers from all suits, and all manner of claims and proceedings which may be taken on the ground that said work is such violation or contains anything scandalous or libelous; and he further hereby authorizes said Publishers to defend at law any and all suits and proceedings which may be taken or had against them for infringement of any other copyright or for libel, scandal, or any other injurious or hurtful matter or thing contained in or alleged or claimed to be contained in or caused by

Wolfe's contract for Of Time and the River, *which stipulated that Wolfe would endeavor to complete the novel by 1 January 1934 (Princeton University Library)*

said work, and pay to said Publishers such reasonable costs, disbursements, expenses, and counsel fees as they may incur in such defense.

Said Publishers, in consideration of the right herein granted and of the guarantees aforesaid, agree to publish said work at their own expense, in such style and manner as they shall deem most expedient, and to pay said Author, or his legal representatives, FIFTEEN (15) per cent. on their Trade-List (retail) price, cloth style, for all copies of said work sold by them in the United States. Provided, nevertheless, that one-half the above named royalty shall be paid on all copies sold outside the United States; and provided that no percentage whatever shall be paid on any copies destroyed by fire or water, or sold at or below cost, or given away for the purpose of aiding the sale of said work.

This agreement shall apply only to the publication of said Author's work by said Publishers in book form and shall have no application whatsoever to any other form of publication, it being expressly understood and agreed that,notwithstanding copyright in the name of said Publishers, the Author reserves all other rights to publication including, but without limitation thereto, moving picture, talking picture, television, radio and all dramatic rights.

Expenses incurred for alterations in type or plates, exceeding twenty per cent. of the cost of composition and electrotyping said work, are to be charged to the Author's account.

3.

The first statement shall not be rendered until six months after date of publication; and thereafter statements shall be rendered semi-annually, on the Author's application therefor, in the months of February and August; settlements to be made in cash, four months after date of statement.

If, on the expiration of five years from date of publication, or at any time thereafter, the demand for said work should not, in the opinion of said Publishers, be sufficient to render its publication profitable, then, upon written notice by said Publishers to said Author, this contract shall cease and determine; and thereupon said Author shall have the right, at his option, to take from said Publishers, at cost, whatever copies of said work they may then have on hand; or, failing to take said copies at cost, then said Publishers shall have the right to dispose of the copies on hand as they may see fit, free from any percentage or royalty, and to cancel this contract.

Provided, also, that if, at any time during the continuance of this agreement, said work shall become unsalable in the ordinary channels of trade, said Publishers shall have the right to dispose of any copies on hand paying to said Author Fifteen (15) per cent. of the net amount received therefor, in lieu of the percentage hereinbefore prescribed.

Said Publishers have heretofore advanced to said Author the sum of One thousand and fifty dollars ($1,050.) and said Author hereby acknowledges receipt of same, and said Publishers hereby agree to pay to said Author a further sum of One thousand dollars ($1,000.), making an aggregate payment of Two thousand and fifty dollars

4.

($2,050.), the same to be deemed an advance on royalty account, said aggregate sum of Two Thousand and Fifty Dollars ($2,050.) to be reimbursed to said Publishers from the first monies accruing under said royalties. The Publishers represent that it is desirable that said work be published in the Spring of 1934 and said Author will undertake to deliver to said Publishers a copy of the manuscript complete ready for press by January 1,1934, or not later than February 1st 1934, in order to make possible publication of said work in the Spring of 1934.

In consideration of the mutuality of this contract, the aforesaid parties agree to all its provisions, and in testimony thereof affix their signatures and seals.

Witbess to signature of
Charles Scribner's Sons

Witness to signature of
Thomas Wolfe

Working with Elizabeth Nowell

Having spent his advances for "Of Time and the River," Wolfe was quickly running out of money. In November 1933, at Maxwell Perkins's suggestion, he gave several pieces from his manuscript to Elizabeth Nowell at the literary agency of Maxim Lieber. Her job was to edit Wolfe's material for sale to periodicals other than Scribner's Magazine. *As their relationship developed, Nowell became an important force in Wolfe's literary development, helping him to focus his work. Her sales of Wolfe's work boosted his morale and financed him through the Depression. She managed to perform her work without alienating Wolfe. After his death she edited his letters and wrote the first full-length biography of Wolfe.*

Elizabeth Nowell in 1943, Wolfe's literary agent who became one of his closest friends and confidantes (Clara Stites)

Nowell and Wolfe: the Working Relationship

James D. Boyer

Thomas Wolfe Review (5 Spring 1981): 18–22

Contrary to the popular notion, Thomas Wolfe wrote a significant number of short stories, thirty-eight of which were published in magazines during his lifetime. This formidable body of material has been largely ignored by critics. The reasons for the neglect are too complex for examination here, but ample evidence is available for anyone who wishes to pursue it that Wolfe developed impressive skills in writing short fiction–consider that in one year he published "The Child by Tiger," "I Have a Thing to Tell You," and "The Lost Boy." To a large degree, Wolfe's development in this form was fostered by Elizabeth Nowell, who served as his magazine agent from 1933 until his death, no small achievement in light of Wolfe's problems in maintaining relationships. She was able to give him advice, usually without offending or threatening, so that over the years he came to respect her judgment about stories. Unfortunately, Nowell never wrote an account of the work she and Wolfe shared, but from some of her letters, preserved in the Wisdom Collection on Wolfe at Harvard, we can get some sense of the value of that relationship to Wolfe.

There is, for example an interesting exchange on Wolfe's "Boomtown," the first story Nowell sold. Having consulted a number of magazine editors on the story, she suggests in one letter that the stuttering brother Lee detracts too much from the theme and should be reduced or at least made not to stutter. Wolfe, obviously a bit piqued, writes back, "Of course there's no use arguing with editors who know what they want or think they do, and I don't know anything I can do to free them from their quaint superstitions concerning characters who stammer, etc. . . ." Then, in an amusingly self-righteous tone, he speaks of his inability to "do honest work by carving, shaping, trimming, and finally by changing" the stammering Lee was, of course, not fundamental to "Boomtown," and despite his protests and some further charges leveled at Nowell herself, Wolfe did eventually agree to eliminate Lee's stammering, and Nowell did sell the improved version of the story to the *American Mercury.*

In another letter dated December 15, 1933, Nowell has some advice on "In the Park." It is good, she thinks and in vogue, but "I may as well burst into the old refrain now as later. As it stands it is a narration or a reminiscence and not what our friends the editors call a story." She follows with an extended critique of the story, including some suggestions for plot changes: "I wish you would leave out the part about going to the convent which . . . is a digression and doesn't help despite its indisputable charm. I think it would help if the girl and her father went to White's and met the priests there and the conversation between them took place actually on that night instead of being vaguely remembered as having once occurred." Both of these suggestions were good, and Wolfe took her advice on them.

But Nowell also gave bad advice at times, which Wolfe had sense enough to ignore. Still of "In the Park," she says, "It seems to us [Nowell and Max

Leiber] that the automobile fades away much too much in the excitement about the dawn . . . Perhaps having the car break down and be towed home is too banal, but couldn't it just break down and leave them sitting . . .?" But Wolfe's story wasn't really about the coming of the automobile era; it was about a little girl and her father and a moment of wonder shared, and he had ended the story with that feeling, as dawn came and the bird calls began. Wolfe made no change in that ending, and he was right.

By 1935, now head of her own agency, Nowell began going through the unused portions of Wolfe's manuscripts looking for sections that might work as stories. Some of these had been cut from *Of Time and the River.* A high-spirited Wolfe letter to Nowell in April 1935 comments on Nowell's work: "Have had little news from U.S.A. . . . But heard indirectly . . . that Tom's agent has sold four stories. Darling, I am torn between joy and trepidation. The news, if true, is swell, but I don't know where the hell you *found* the four stories . . ." Nowell's note on that letter, published in the volume of Wolfe's letters, which she edited, explains where: "All four of these stories . . . had been among the portions of manuscript cut from *Of Time and the River* which Wolfe had given to Miss Nowell when he was moving out of Brooklyn, and which she had not been able to cut and edit until after he had sailed."

By this time, as the note implies, Nowell is cutting words, sentences, even scenes to shorten the pieces for magazine publications. In a May 1936 letter she says of his "Arnold Pentland," "I had to cut the daughter out of it to get it down to *Esquire* length (about 4000) and Arnold comes out pretty likeable and pathetic all around." In fact, the typescript shows other passages deleted from the story. One long sentence of exposition–"And Arnold was gone . . . , a figure lost in the manswarm jungle of the world, fleeing down the tunnel of the kaleidescopic days, to find death, sanctuary and escape in a sorrowful, strange way . . ."–is unnecessary because the idea is clearly illustrated in the action of the story, the narrator speculates on the possibility that Arnold, under "the persuasion of an old Irish woman," his landlady, finally found, by "commiting his life to the faith of the Holy Roman Catholic and apostolic church," the peace that "his tortured soul and overladen heart demanded." But that resolution does nothing for the story, and the passage is cut from the published story, leaving Arnold an isolate fleeing into the city, a more characteristic twentieth-century figure.

But always Nowell is careful not to take too much liberty. In the same letter cited above, she says, "Perkins let me copy out 'Only the Dead Know Brooklyn' and I think the new *Mercury* may take it. But I'm not going to meddle with anything else from the *October Fair* because it's mostly so personal and I know you wouldn't want me to go rushing ahead without your full authorization." Still in the same letter she confesses an amusing slip. Anticipating some new stories from him, she says that she will "cut them down," changes that to "type them out," and comments, "That crossed-out place said 'cut them down,' just taking it for granted! And I apologize."

It would be misleading to place too much emphasis on Nowell's role in shaping stories. Most of her effort in 1934–35 was directed toward selecting episodes from the unused manuscripts and patiently cutting out words and phrases to bring them down to an acceptable length for the magazine to which she was submitting them. By doing this, and by sending them from one magazine to another, she gradually built a market for Wolfe's work. For the 1937 stories, she sometimes located historical facts that he needed, like details on a New York fire that became part of "The Party at Jack's," and she did work on the final versions of those stories with him. But perhaps her most important contribution was her encouragement and belief in him late in his career at a time when troubles with Scribner's were seriously interfering with his work.

Only one serious misunderstanding appears in the sketchy record of their relationship, and it was apparently the result of Wolfe's excessive suspicions of people when he was going through a period of depression. He had called her in the night, questioning her charges for her work and accusing her of "leeching" him. In Nowell's letter dated April 21, 1936, she explains her charges and reminds him of the many hours spend on cutting *The Story of a Novel*–so that it could be published. Apparently she convinced him that she was right, and the question never comes up again in existing letters.

Though the record is far from complete, these available letters and manuscripts indicate that Nowell helped Wolfe to learn to compress material, to develop a clearer sense of plot and characterization, and to take real interest in story writing. In 1935 Wolfe says of *From Death to Morning* "I feel as if there is as good writing as I've done in some of the stories–it represents important work to me." And in 1936 and 1937, after the break with Perkins and Scribner's, he gave still more time and attention to the writing of stories. In a letter to his brother Fred in June 1936 he speaks of one five- or six-week period during which "I have been working every day and often at night with Miss Nowell . . ." It is out of this period that some of his finest stories come. And his sense of how to construct a story develops so far that Nowell is able to say of "The Pary at Jack's," the last piece they worked on together, "You've got a darn near perfect critical sense for rounding things out."

Delivering the Manuscript

Wolfe submitted the last batch of his rough draft of his novel on 14 December 1933. He then wrote to Perkins the next day.

Dear Max:

I was pretty tired last night when I delivered that last batch of manuscript to you and could not say very much to you about it. There is not much to say except that today I feel conscious of a good many errors, both of omission and commission and wish I had had more time to arrange and sort out the material, but think it is just as well that I have given it to you even in its present shape.

I don't envy you the job before you. I know what a tough thing it is going to be to tackle, but I do think that even in the form in which the material has been given to you, you ought to be able to make some kind of estimate of its value or lack of value and tell me about it. If you do feel on the whole I can now go ahead and complete it, I think I can go much faster than you realize. Moreover, when all the scenes have been completed and the narrative changed to a third person point of view, I think there will be a much greater sense of unity than now seems possible in spite of the mutilated, hacked-up form in which you have the manuscript, and I do feel decidedly hopeful, and hope your verdict will be for me to go ahead and complete the first draft as soon as I can, and in spite of all the rhythms, chants–what you call my dithyrambs–which are all through the manuscript, I think you will find when I get through that there is plenty of narrative–or should I say when you get through–because I must shame-facedly confess that I need your help now more than I ever did.

You have often said that if I ever gave you something that you could get your hands on and weigh in its entirety from beginning to end, you could pitch in and help me to get out of the woods. Well, now here is your chance. I think a very desperate piece of work is ahead for both of us, but if you think it is worth doing and tell me to go ahead, I think there is literally nothing that I cannot accomplish. But you must be honest and straightforward in your criticism when you talk about it, even though what you say may be hard for me to accept after all this work, because that is the only fair way and the only good way in the end.

I want to get back to work on it as soon as I can and will probably go on anyway writing in the missing scenes and getting a complete manuscript as soon as I can. I wanted to write you this mainly to tell you that I am in a state of great trepidation and great hope also. Buried in that great pile of manuscript is some of the best writing I have ever done. Let's see to it that it does not go to waste.

Yours always, Tom Wolfe

–*To Loot My Life Clean,* pp. 115–116

Wolfe at 5 Montague Terrace, where Of Time and the River *was completed (The Thomas Wolfe Collection, Pack Memorial Public Library, Asheville, North Carolina)*

"Boom Town"

This letter from Wolfe to Nowell concerning the story "Boom Town," which was published in the May 1934 issue of The American Mercury *and selected for* The O. Henry Memorial Award: Prize Stories of 1934, *provides a good example of their working relationship.*

February 2, 1934

Dear Miss Nowell:

Thanks for your letter and for the revised copy of "Boom Town." I have not been able to read your revision carefully yet, but I shall read it over the week-end.

I am sorry you have had to work so hard on this and have had no better luck placing it. Of course there's no use arguing with Editors who know what they want or think they do, and I don't know of anything I can do to free them from their quaint superstitions concerning characters who stammer, etc. This was surprising news to me, and now I can no longer pretend even to guess at these prejudices or know what the next will be.

Frankly, I don't see that we can do very much more with this story, and it would seem to me to be the wiser course to let it drop. I have been very hard up and badly in need of money, but as much as I need and want it, it has never yet occurred to me that I could do honest work by carving, shaping, trimming, and finally by changing the entire structure and quality of a fundamental character. I think if I knew how to do it and understood more about the mysteries of magazine publishing, I would be tempted to go ahead and try to do it in order to get a little needed money, but I don't know how to do it, and I know nothing of these mysteries. It seems to me that it would be foolish for me to try to do something I do not understand.

One thing in your letter does surprise me, and that is that you now agree with the Editor's complaint that the character of "Lee" comes as too much of a shock in the story, that he overshadows the boom theme and takes away from the emphasis. My understanding at the beginning was that both you and Mr. Lieber liked the character of "Lee," felt definitely that he had a place in the story, and even thought that the character should be more fully developed and given a more important place which, as you remember, is exactly what we did in the revision.

I know you understand, Miss Nowell, that I am not quarreling with you about this, and that I do appreciate the pains you and Lieber have taken with this story. I am genuinely sorry not only for my sake but for yours that we are not likely now to get anything out of the work we've put into it. Moreover, I also believe that as a result of your comments and suggestions, I was able to make the piece more effective and interesting than it was in the beginning; and, of course, in the end that will always be a gain. But I do think that after we have talked and argued together about a piece we ought to come to some fairly definite agreement or conclusion about it, and that we can't go jumping around like a Jack-in-the-box changing our minds and opinions every time we come up against a new Editor.

I am very grateful to you for all the extra work you've gone to on your own hook in making this new revision and shortening the piece and cutting out "Lee's" stammering; but it seems fairly evident to me now that the piece is not commercially saleable, and I doubt that we are going to have any success with it. But I will read your copy over carefully Sunday, and either call or write you about it next week.

Now about the Esquire proposition. I think something can be done about this, and if you can get $175 that will be swell. I have been talking to Mr. Perkins about it, and he has suggested two or three short pieces which are either in the manuscript of the book or have been cut out of it. One is a piece about two boys going down to see a big circus come into town, unload, and put up the tents in the early morning. I think I will send you this piece today or tomorrow. It is out of the book and in its present form is only seven typed pages long, or about 2100 words. The thing needs an introduction which I will try to write today, but otherwise it is complete enough, although, again, I am afraid it is not what most people consider a story.

I also have what Max calls one of my "dithyrambs." He and Dashiell are very kind about it, and Dashiell even suggested it might be used for the magazine, but I sold them another story the other day, which makes three they have taken recently, so I don't know whether they would care to use it. The thing is about the names of America–the names of rivers, the tramps, the railroads, the states, the Indian Tribes, etc. The only story element in it is that it begins with four episodes in dialogue of different people abroad who are thinking of home. Perkins thinks this piece goes beyond the 3,000 word limit, but I believe it could be brought within that limit without much trouble. It is to start the seventh section of my book.

I also have a piece called "The Bums at Sunset" which we cut out of the book the other day, and which is about some hoboes waiting beside the track to pick up the train, but I don't know if this is any good or could be used.

There are a great number of these pieces, and I think you might very probably find something among them that you could use, but I have lost confidence in my own powers of selection, and apparently have little idea which part of my writing is going to please people and what they're going to like. The piece about the names of America I wrote two or three years ago, and I'm almost positive I showed it to Mr. Perkins, but he says now he never saw it before and that it is one of the best things I ever wrote. In the same way he says that a section of 20,000 words or so which was cut out of one of the stories that the magazine published last summer is a fine story and some of the best writing I ever did, and that he never saw it before. So I revised it and fixed it up at his suggestion and I suppose they have taken it.

All I can do now and what I am doing in addition to revising and re-writing the book is to get all of these things typed so that he can read them. If I had time I'd ask you to go over my manuscript with me, but I haven't got the time because I am meeting Mr. Perkins every day now to work on the book, and all the rest of the time I spend in writing and in getting the manuscript typed. But I'll send the circus piece to you and you can see if there is any chance of doing anything with the Esquire people about it, and if you don't think there is, I'll send you something else.

–*Beyond Love and Loyalty,* pp. 6–8

* * *

In this article in The Asheville Citizen, *a reporter quotes extensively from "Boom Town" so that readers could determine if they recognized themselves or their neighbors.*

Tom Wolfe's New Story Describes Asheville In Real Estate Boom Days

The Asheville Citizen, 26 April 1934

Thomas Wolfe, that youthful Asheville author who startled this mountain city in 1929 with his "Look Homeward, Angel" again has painted a vivid picture of this city, of the boom days and the people of those days.

Young Wolfe uses the same naked, biting style that was evident in his former work, and it is not a pretty picture that he has painted. Older residents here may be able to recognize a few, if not all, the characters in this story–the story of a visit home during the heighth of the frenzied real estate activity.

The title of the story is "Boom Town" and it is printed in the May American Mercury as a piece of fiction.

The story concerns one John. Upon the moment of his arrival he is met at the station by relatives.

"'Well, now, sonny boy,'" the story quotes John's mother as saying, "'come on, now! I've got a good breakfast waiting for you when you get home!'

"'How's Helen, mama,' John broke in, somewhat disturbed by the failure of his sister to meet him.

"'Hah? What say? Helen?' she said quickly, in a sharp, surprised kind of tone. 'Oh, she's all right. And yes, now! She called up before we left this morning and said to give you her love and tell you she'd be over later. Said she wanted to come along to meet you but had to stay at home because Roy McIntyre had 'phoned her he had a prospect for that place of theirs on Weaver street and wanted to bring him over right away to look at it. Of course, she and Hugh are anxious to sell, want to move out there and build on one of those lots they own on Grovewood Terrace. Say they'll take eight thousand for the house–two thousand down, but I told her to take cash. I told her not to listen to Roy McIntyre if he tries to trade in on the deal any of those lots he's got up there on the hill in Ridgewood.'"

After describing further conversation, Wolfe turns to John's mother again.

"'I think mama,'" he quotes John's brother, described as Lee, "'I think that if we could–' and at this moment his tormented eyes suddenly met, stopped, rested for a moment on the astounded, bewildered look his brother gave him. For a moment they looked at each other with earnest, asking looks–then suddenly the bursting of wild glee upon his brother's face.

"'Haw-w,' Lee yelled, 'haw-w,' prodding his brother in the ribs, 'haw-w!' he cried. 'You'll see–oh, you'll see, all right!' he gloated. 'Frankly, I have to laugh when I think about it. Frankly I do!' he said earnestly. Then looking at the astonished face before him, he burst out into the devastating roar again. 'Haw-w! Whah-whah-h! You'll see,' he said mysteriously and mockingly. 'Oh, you'll get it now,' he cried. 'Nineteen hours a day, from daybreak to three o'clock in the morning–no holts barred!' he chortled. 'They'll be waiting for us when we get there,' he said. 'They're all lined up there on the front porch in a reception committee to greet you and to cut your throat, every damn mountain grill of a real estate man in town Old Horse Face Hines, the undertaker; Skunk-eye Rufe Mears, the demon promoter and old squeeze-your-heart's-blood Gibbs, the widder and orphan man from Arkansas;–and they're drawin lots right now to see which one gets your shirt and which one takes the pants and B. V. Dd's Haw-w! Whah-whah-h!' he poked his younger brother in the ribs.

"'They'll get nothing out of me,' John said angrily, 'for I haven't got it to begin with.'

. . . .

Speaking of the people of the city–which he termed Altamont, the name he used for the city in "Look Homeward Angel"–Wolfe said: "They were stricken and lost, starved squirrels chasing furiously the treadmill of a revolving cage, and they saw it, and they knew it.

"A wave of ruinous and destructive energy had welled up in them–they had squandered fabulous sums in meaningless streets and bridges, they had torn down the ancient public buildings, courthouses and city hall, and erected new ones, fifteen stories tall and large enough to fill the needs of a city of a million people; they had levelled hills and bored through mountains, building magnificent tunnels paved with double roadways and glittering with shining tiles–tunnels which leaped out on the other side into Arcadian wilderness. * * *

"Already the town had passed from their possession, they no longer owned it, it was mortgaged under a debt of fifty million dollars, owned by bonding companies in the north. * * *"

Some of the characters used by Wolfe in this new story are the same used in "Look Homeward Angel" and he also speaks of "West Altamont," as he did in his well-known book, Wolfe has lived in New York since he began writing.

Wolfe's description of the help provided by Maxwell Perkins, the model for Foxhall Edwards, during Wolfe's Brooklyn years was used in Chapter 28 of You Can't Go Home Again, *titled "The Fox."*

During all these desperate years in Brooklyn, when George lived and worked along, he had only one real friend, and this was his editor, Foxhall Edwards. They spent many hours together, wonderful hours of endless talk, so free and full that it combed the universe and bound the two of them together in bonds of closest friendship. It was a friendship founded on many common tastes and interests, on mutual liking and admiration of each for what the other was, and on an attitude of respect which allowed unhampered expression of opinion even on those rare subjects which aroused differences of views and of belief. It was, therefore, the kind of friendship that can exist only between two men. It had in it no element of that possessiveness which always threatens a woman's relations with a man, no element of that physical and emotional involvement which, while it serves nature's end of bringing a man and woman together, also tends to thwart their own dearest wish to remain so by throwing over their companionship a constricting cloak of duty and obligation, of right and vest interest.

The older man was not merely friend but father to the younger, Webber, the hot-blooded Southerner, with his large capacity for sentiment and affection, had lost his own father many years before and now had found a substitute in Edwards. And Edwards, the reserved New Englander, with his deep sense of family and inheritance, had always wanted a son but had had five daughters, and as time went on he made of George a kind of foster son. Thus each, without quite knowing that he did it, performed an act of spiritual adoption.

So it was to Foxhall Edwards that George now turned whenever his loneliness became unbearable. When his inner turmoil, confusion, and self-doubts overwhelmed him, as they often did, and his life went dead and stale and empty till it sometimes seemed that all the barren desolation of the Brooklyn streets had soaked into his very blood and marrow–then he would seek out Edwards. And he never went to him in vain. Edwards, busy though he always was, would drop whatever he was doing and would take George out to lunch or dinner, and in his quiet, casual, oblique, and understanding way would talk to him and draw him out until he found out what it was that troubled him. And always in the end, because of Edwards' faith in him, George would be healed and find himself miraculously restored to self-belief.

–*You Can't Go Home Again,* pp. 437–438

Editing *Of Time and the River*

Wolfe described his feelings as the editing of his novel progressed in a letter to author Percy Mackaye, who had written to Wolfe to praise "The Train and the City," a story published in the May 1933 issue of Scribner's Magazine.

5 Montague Terrace
Brooklyn, New York
July 1, 1934

Dear Mr. Mackaye:

Please excuse me for not having answered your letter sooner. I failed to get in touch with you when you were in New York at The Players' Club, because for several months I have been working all day at home on a manuscript and then meeting Mr. Perkins at Scribner's every night to revise and edit it. In this way time gets away from you and one loses count of the days, and I am afraid you had come and gone before I knew it. . . .

In just another month or two I expect to be finished with an enormous manuscript which has occupied most of my waking, and a good part of my sleeping time for more than four years. It is itself just one of four books, but three of them are already practically complete in manuscript; and this first one, after untold agonies of cutting, re-writing and reweaving, is about ready for the printer. I can't tell you how long these four years seemed to me. They don't seem measurable in terms of years or days or months. They seem to stretch back over eons through fathomless depths of memory, and they also have gone by like a dream.

I have never felt or known this great dream of time in which we live as I have felt and known it during these last four years. It has been a dream of constant wakefulness, of unceasing struggle, of naked reality. I don't think I have ever lived with such energy and with such perception of the world around me as during these four years of desperate labor. Yet the time has got by me like a dream. It is almost unbelievable now that I am really approaching the end of another piece of work. There were times in which it seemed that I was caught in an enormous web from which I can never extricate myself. I lived for nothing but the work I was doing, and I thought of the work I had yet to do. But I was too tired to work. I could not rest or get any peace or repose for thought of the work which was yet to come, and the work even invaded my sleep so that night was turned into an unending processional of blazing and incredible visions, and I would sleep and yet know that I was sleeping, and dream and know that I was dreaming. There were times when I felt sunk, lost forever, buried at some horrible sea-depth of time and memory from which I can never escape.

2 Gal 188—8932—Wolfe's Of Time—11-12-25-Granjon

Their feet trod pathways in the hot and fragrant grasses, where they trod, a million little singing things leaped up to life, and hot dry stalks brushed crudely at their knees: the earth beneath their feet gave back a firm and unsmooth evenness, a lump resiliency.

Once in a field before them they saw a tree dense-leaved and burnished by hot light: the sun shone on its leaves with a naked and un-green opacity, and Joel, looking towards it, whispered thoughtfully:

". . . Hm . . . It's nice that—I mean the way the light falls on it— It would be hard to paint: I'd like to come out here and try it."

And the other assented, not, however, without a certain nameless desolation in his heart that broad and naked lights, the white and glacial opacity of brutal day aroused in him,—and wanting more the wooded grove, the green-gold magic of a wooded grass, the woodland dark and thrum and tingled mystery, and the sheer sheeting silence of the hidden water.

It was a swelling, casual, nobly lavish earth, forever haunted by a drowsy spell of time, and the unfathomed mystery of an glues enchantment, and the huge dream-sorcery of the mysterious and immortal river.

It was what he had always known it to be in his visions as a child, of the Hudson Rivers, and he came to it with a sense of wonder and of glorious discovery, but without surprise, as one who for the first time comes into his father's country, finding it the same as he had always known it would be, and knowing always that it would be there.

And finally the whole design of that great earth, with the casual and powerful surveys of its great fields, its dense still woods of moveless silence ringing with the music of the birds, its far-off hills receding into time as hauntng as a dream, and the central sorcery of its shining river —that enchanted thread which ran through all, from which all swept away, and towards which all inclined—was unutterably the language of all he had ever thought or felt or known of America: the great plantation of the earth abundant to the sustenance of mighty men, and enriching all its glamorous women with the full provender of its huge compacted sweetness, an America that was so casual and rich and limitless and free, and so haunted by dark time and magic, so aching in its joy with all the bitter briefness of our days, so young, so old, so everlasting, and so triumphantly the place of man's good earth, his ripe fulfillment and the most fortunate, good and happy life that any man alive had ever known.

It changed, it passed, it swept around him in all its limitless surge and sweep and fold and passionate variety, and it was more strange in all its haunting loveliness than magic or a dream, and yet more near than morning, and more actual than noon.

It was a hot day: the two young men walked along with their coats flung back across their shoulders: towards five o'clock as they were coming home again, and coming down into the wooded hollow where Mr. Joel lived, Joel turned, and with a slight flush of embarrassment on his gaunt face, said:

"Look—do you mind wearing your coat when we go by Grandfather's house—you can take it off again when we get out of sight."

He said nothing, but silently did as his friend requested, and thus correctly garmented they passed the old man's great white house and crossed the little wooden bridge and stared up again out of the hollow, taking a foot-path through the woods that would lead them out into the road near Miss Telfair's house: she had invited them at tea.

And curiously, inexplicably, of all that they had said and talked about together on that walk, these two things were later all he could remember:—his friend's eyes narrowed with professional appraisal as he looked at the hot opacity of the sun-burnished tree and said, "—hm . . . It's nice, that—the light is interesting—I'd like to do it;" and the embarrassed but almost stubbornly definite way in which Joel had asked him to put on his coat as he went past "Grandfather's place." He did not know why, but that simple request aroused in him a feeling of quick and hot resentment, a desire to say,

"Good God! What kind of idol-worship is this, anyway? Surely that old man has been made of the same earth as all the rest of us—surely he's not so grand and rare and fine that he can't stand the sight of two young men in shirt-sleeves going by his house! . . . Surely there is some-

Corrections on galleys for Of Time and the River *(William B. Wisdom Collection, Houghton Library, Harvard University)*

I don't suppose many young men attempt a work of such proportions as the one which has occupied my time these last four years; and I don't know whether I could have faced it had I known what lay before me. The sheer physical labor has been enormous. I can't use the typewriter, and have to write every word with my hand, and during these last four years, as I estimate it, I have written about two million words. The manuscript is piled up in crates and boxes and fills them to overflowing. It inundates my room.

But now I feel like a prisoner who has been given his release and comes out of a dungeon and sees the light of day for the first time in years. Perhaps I ought not to tell you this long and tedious story of my work, but you are yourself a writing man and I know you understand the intolerable amount of anguish that goes into the work of writing and you will be able to forgive an escaped prisoner who babbles drunkenly about his release.

During these four years I have had the unfailing faith, the unshaken belief and friendship of one man, and as long as any man has that, I believe he always has a chance of coming through; but if I had not had it, it is hard for me to know what I could have done. Mr. Perkins has stuck to me all this time. He has never once faltered in his belief that everything would yet turn out well–even when I had almost given up hope myself. He has stood for all the rage and desperation and the crazy fits, and, with firm and gentle fortitude, has kept after me all the time–until now, at length, it seems to be my impossible good fortune to have come through. I have never heard of another writer who had such luck. No success that this book could possibly have could ever begin to repay that man for the prodigies of patience, labor, editing and care he has lavished on it. And now I can only hope that there will be something in the book that will in some measure justify it.

I have not known such happiness in many years as I have known these last few weeks when, for the first time, it became apparent that I would have the whole thing in hand and that we were coming to the end. Perkins never lost faith that this would be so, but there was a black and bitter period when all he had to go on was faith, because I was unable to show him the whole design, and when I had the whole thing in me but for the most part still unwritten. I would bring him fifty and eighty and a hundred thousand words at a time–sometimes even as much as two hundred thousand–and although these sections would sometimes be as long as a long book, they would still be only sections and parts of

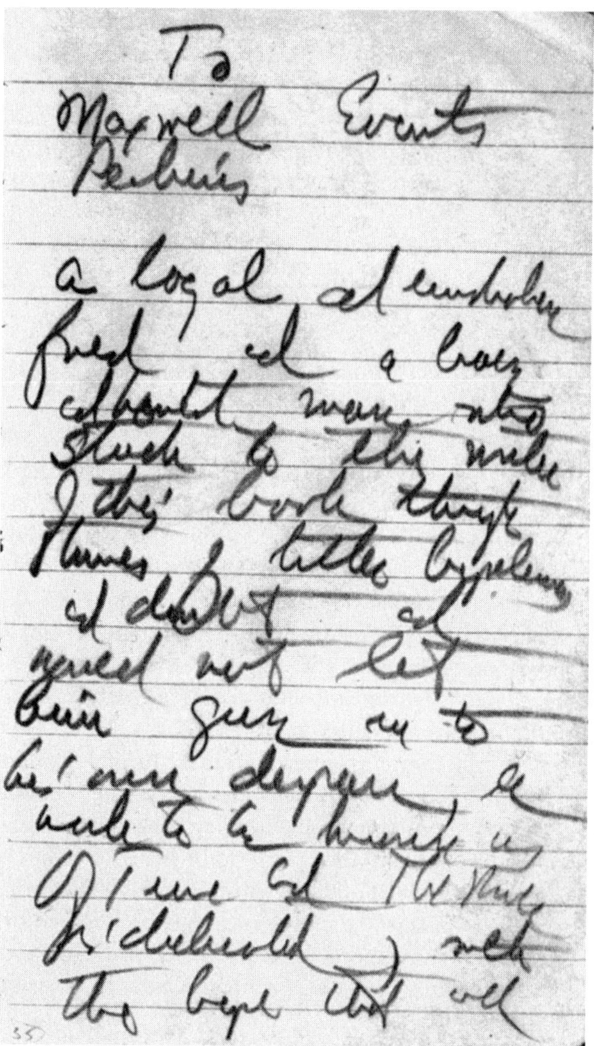
To
Maxwell Evarts
Perkins

First page from a draft of Wolfe's dedication for Of Time and the River *(William B. Wisdom Collection, Houghton Library, Harvard University)*

a whole, and there would follow a period of exhaustion when I could not write for days or even weeks and when I would wonder if I really had the thing inside me and would some day get it out of me or was only a deluded madman being devoured by his own obsession. I know you can understand now why I feel happy no matter what happens to this book or what they say about it. I know now, and Perkins knows that I was not a madman, but that I had the whole design in me all the time and had stuck to it. Therefore, I feel like a man who has swum upward from some horrible sea-depth where he thought he was lost and buried forever and come back into the friendly and glorious light of day again.

–*The Letters of Thomas Wolfe,* pp. 412–415

In September 1934, without Wolfe's knowledge, Perkins sent the last half of the novel to the printers while Wolfe was at the Chicago World's Fair. Wolfe was so dismayed with Perkins's decision that he left the proofs largely uncorrected. In this article, which appeared two weeks before he left on his sixth trip to Europe, Wolfe reflects on living with the novel for four years.

Thomas Wolfe Cuts 2d Book to 450,000 Words
Sanderson Vanderbilt
New York Herald Tribune, 18 February 1935

Author of 'Look Homeward, Angel' Weary Pruning
'Of Time and the River'
Expects to Do 5 Million
Finds It Hard to Write in America, So He's Leaving

With a good two inches of blue shirt separating the bottom of his rumpled vest from the top of his unpressed pants, Thomas Wolfe, thirty-four-year-old novelist whose "Look Homeward, Angel," made him a white hope of America's leading critics four years ago, barged into his apartment at 5 Montague Terrace, Brooklyn, yesterday afternoon.

The literary gentleman who is six feet five inches tall, stalked about the place bemoaning that he was not only a good hour late for an interview, but that his next novel, "Of Time and the River," to be issued on March 8, has been cut from 700,000 to a mere 450,000 words. It will be the second of a series of six novels planned by Mr. Wolfe, who expects to write 5,000,000 words and then sorrowfully see them pruned down to a scant 2,000,000.

Mr. Wolfe had promised to meet a reporter at 2 o'clock, but the thought of an interview so terrified him that he fled to a restaurant for luncheon. The result was that it was not until 3 that he felt sufficiently fortified to face a camera and questioner. Scrawled in the handwriting with which he turns out his bales of manuscripts was a note stuck in his letter box. It read:

"Have gone out to lunch but will be back in a few minutes. If you get no answer when you ring my bell ring superintendent's bell and she will take you up to my place. Make yourself at home until I get back.

"T. WOLFE."

Progress Shut Out Harbor

Mr. Wolfe's "place" turned out to be on the fourth floor of a five-story brownstone house on Brooklyn Heights–one which formerly commanded a view of the harbor, but which now has become simply dismal, what with larger apartments that have been built between it and the water. In the creaky old building the author has two rooms for which he pays $45 a month and considers it a bargain.

Advertisement for Wolfe's second novel

An icebox stood in the bathroom, but it evidently was not used, for Mr. Wolfe had placed a bottle of milk, half a dozen eggs, and some sliced bacon out on the window sill. There was a bridge lamp in the corner, but it lacked both shade and bulbs. A telephone on the mantle proved simply an ornament and near by rested an unpaid $17.18 bill for its services.

The bed in the adjoining room had been hastily made and beside it was an old green alarm clock that operates only when flat on its face.

In the room's lone bookshelf were such volumes as Tolstoy's "Anna Karenina," several of the de la Roche "Jaina" series, "Cakes and Ale," by Maugham; a Manhatten telephone directory, "Ulysses," by James Joyce; yellow paper-backed French novels and several copies of "Look Homeward, Angel."

A clay jug was filled with stubs of pencils with which Mr. Wolfe writes. On the table lay a first edition of "Of Time and the River" which he had corrected and which showed that typists and linotype men have their troubles in deciphering the author's jerky script.

"Elemental," for example, had been printed instead of "eternal." Mr. Wolfe had had to change "numerous" to "murmurous"; "moist" had been corrected to read "most," and the compositor had read "sweet" where Mr. Wolfe had written "secret."

Downstairs a taxicab door slammed and presently Mr. Wolfe burst into the room, penitent for his tardiness and dusting cigarette ashes off his trousers. "Gosh," he exclaimed, "I'm sorry I kept you waiting. Yes, sorry I kept you waiting." Then he settled down to discuss his writing.

There will be six novels in all, he said, and in them he will attempt to trace the development of 150 years in America. "Look Homeward, Angel" deals with the years from 1884 to 1920; "Of Time and the River" with 1920 to 1925; "The October Fair" will cover from 1925 to 1928, and "The Hills Beyond Pentland" from 1838 to 1926. Mr. Wolfe still has to write "The Death of the Enemy," which will carry the theme from 1928 to 1933, and "Pacific End" from 1791 to 1884.

Looking for a Father

"I hope the whole thing will be kind of like a plant," said Mr. Wolfe, stretching his bulk out in a rickety chair and clutching at his sparse black hair. "Now don't make that sound kind of fancy. Sort of like a plant that's had a lot of roots in it. I guess the general plan back of these books is the story of a man's looking for his father. Everybody in the world–not only men but women–is looking for a father. Looking for some person of superior strength. Some person outside of themselves to whom they can attach their belief."

Over and over again Mr. Wolfe, who was born in Asheville, N. C. the son of a stone cutter, cried out vehemently that he was "born of working people." He declared: "It's hard to write things in America, and that's why it's good to do so when you succeed. We've got a new language here–we can't talk like Matthew Arnold or James Russell Lowell; he's an American, of course, but he's trying to talk like an Englishman."

Mr. Wolfe was graduated from the University of North Carolina in 1920 and then received an M. A. degree from Harvard. He wrote his "Look Homeward, Angel" in 1930 in Switzerland and then came to Brooklyn to work at night on his second novel, sleep by day, and prowl about the borough during his hours of recreation. He is a restive bachelor.

"I thought Brooklyn was a good place to come to work," he said, staring about the disordered room with piercing black eyes. "And I've worked my head off here. But I'm going away now, at the end of this month. Yes, going away on a freight boat–to Italy, to Spain, to France, and I hope I'll get to Egypt. And I'm going as a tourist. When I see a sightseeing bus, I'm going to hop it.

"I've been learning about writing like hell in the last four years. You might say I've worked like hell. I've got to write 5,000,000 words, but you fix it up if it sounds like boasting, because, damn it, I need some money and I want to sell this book."

Mr. Wolfe said that when he started on his first novel he thought he would be able to express the entire idea in some 250,000 words, but now it has stretched well into the millions. The book swelled up within him, he said, "like a raincloud." He had always wanted to be a writer but considered that aspiration "a sort of romantic dream." His mother, he chuckled, still sends him clippings of authors who have made good. She adds as a postscript to her son, "You can be a writer, too."

"I wrote of death and love." he rambled on. "I wrote of the way it is to wake up in the morning in this country, and of riding in a Pullman train with a good-looking woman opposite you, and of getting off the Fall River boat."

All of Mr. Wolfe's writing is done with a lead pencil and he gets stenographers to type his work. The side of the room was piled high with manuscripts. He writes in ledgers, notebooks and on copy paper.

"I haven't done any work at all during the last three or four months and I feel like a bum," said Mr. Wolfe, getting up and striding about the room. "When you finish a book it's the worst time in the world. You hope you get famous and make some money. But you got too close to the book while you were writing it and you forget it when you're through. You can't believe you're guilty."

Hates and Likes Brooklyn

"Sunday," he said, suddenly, peering out of the window into the twilight. "Wouldn't you know it's Sunday just to look out at that queer light. I've hated Brooklyn–cursed it more times–I've wandered at night all over this rusty jungle to which I came because I thought I'd be able to write here. But I think I'm going to have an affection for the place when I leave.

"I've seen the damndest things out here in Brooklyn. It's a great, brutal mass. Manhatten has some integrity, but this place is a great, formless, huge, enormous blot, and 3,000,000 people live here. All the underdogs in the world live here. The dishwashers, the fellers who run the subway trains, the fellers in cafeterias, the elevator operators, the scrubwomen, the fellers who work in chain grocery stores–they all live here.

"But it's a great place, too. I've seen stuff out here in great uncharted places that nobody in New York ever heard of."

---

emorandum of Agreement, *made this* twenty-sixth *day of* December 1934

between THOMAS WOLFE

of New York City, N.Y., - - - - - *hereinafter called "the* AUTHOR,"

and CHARLES SCRIBNER'S SONS, *of New York City, N. Y., hereinafter called "the* PUBLISHERS." *Said* - - Thomas Wolfe - - *being the* AUTHOR *and* PROPRIETOR *of a* ~~work entitled~~: ~~volume of stories (title to be determined later)~~ ~~to be ready for the printer by June 1,1935;~~ FROM DEATH TO MORNING -

in consideration of the covenants and stipulations hereinafter contained, and agreed to be performed by the PUBLISHERS, *grants and guarantees to said* PUBLISHERS *and their successors the exclusive right to publish the said* ~~work in all forms, during the terms~~ in the United States and Canada *of copyright and renewals thereof, hereby covenanting with said* PUBLISHERS *that* he *is the sole* AUTHOR *and* PROPRIETOR *of said work.*

Said AUTHOR *hereby authorizes said* PUBLISHERS *to take out the copyright on said work, and further guarantees to said* PUBLISHERS *that the said work is in no way whatever a violation of any copyright belonging to any other party, and that it contains nothing of a scandalous or libelous character; and that* he *and* his *legal representatives shall and will hold harmless the said* PUBLISHERS *from all suits, and all manner of claims and proceedings which may be taken on the ground that said work is such violation or contains anything scandalous or libelous; and* he *further hereby authorizes said* PUBLISHERS *to defend at law any and all suits and proceedings which may be taken or had against them for infringement of any other copyright or for libel, scandal, or any other injurious or hurtful matter or thing contained in or alleged or claimed to be contained in or caused by said work, and pay to said* PUBLISHERS *such reasonable costs, disbursements, expenses, and counsel fees as they may incur in such defense.*

Said PUBLISHERS, *in consideration of the right herein granted and of the guarantees aforesaid, agree to publish said work at their own expense, in such style and manner as they shall deem most expedient, and to pay said* AUTHOR, *or* - his - *legal representatives,* FIFTEEN (15) --------------------- *per cent. on their Trade-List (retail) price, cloth style, for* all copies of said work sold by them in the United States. - - - - - -
Provided, nevertheless, that one-half the above named royalty shall be paid on all copies sold outside the United States; and provided that no percentage whatever shall be paid on any copies destroyed by fire or water, or sold at or below cost, or given away for the purpose of aiding the sale of said work.

It is further agreed that the terms of any publication of said work, during the period covered by this agreement, in other than book form shall be subject to mutual arrangement between said PUBLISHERS *and said* AUTHOR.

Contract for Wolfe's first collection of stories, which he signed more than two months before the publication of Of Time and the River
(William B. Wisdom Collection, Houghton Library, Harvard University)

Expenses incurred for alterations in type or plates, exceeding twenty per cent. of the cost of composition and electrotyping said work, are to be charged to the AUTHOR'S *account.*

The first statement shall not be rendered until six months after date of publication; and thereafter statements shall be rendered semi-annually, on the AUTHOR'S *application therefor, in the months of February and August; settlements to be made in cash, four months after date of statement.*

If, on the expiration of five *years from date of publication, or at any time thereafter, the demand for said work should not, in the opinion of said* PUBLISHERS, *be sufficient to render its publication profitable, then, upon written notice by said* PUBLISHERS *to said* AUTHOR, *this contract shall cease and determine; and thereupon said* AUTHOR *shall have the right, at* his *option, to take from said* PUBLISHERS, *at cost, whatever copies of said work they may then have on hand; or, failing to take said copies at cost, then said* PUBLISHERS *shall have the right to dispose of the copies on hand as they may see fit, free from any percentage or royalty, and to cancel this contract.*

Provided, also, that if, at any time during the continuance of this agreement, said work shall become unsalable in the ordinary channels of trade, said PUBLISHERS *shall have the right to dispose of any copies on hand, paying to said* AUTHOR - fifteen (15) - *per cent. of the net amount received therefor, in lieu of the percentage hereinbefore prescribed.*

Said Publishers shall pay to said Author, as may be required, the sum of One Thousand Dollars ($1,000.00) as an advance payment on royalty account, said amount to be reimbursed to said Publishers from the first moneys accruing under said royalties.

This agreement applies only to publication of said work in book form and the Author reserves all other rights to publication, including, but without limitation thereto, moving picture, talking picture, television, radio and all dramatic rights.

~~Said Publishers shall have an option on the next two novels by said Author, on terms to be mutually agreed upon.~~

CS
T. W

In consideration of the mutuality of this contract, the aforesaid parties agree to all its provisions, and in testimony thereof affix their signatures and seals.

itness to signature of
Thomas Wolfe

Thomas Wolfe

Maxwell E Perkins

tness to signature of
Charles Scribner's Sons

WWaton

Charles Scribner's Sons {L. S.}
Charles Scribner
President

Dust jacket for Wolfe's 1935 novel

Publication

When Of Time and the River *was published on 8 March 1935, Wolfe had already left for Europe aboard the* Ile de France. *He considered the novel an unfinished product and did not want to face the reviews.*

Scribners presented Of Time and the River *as the second novel in a series of six books in a "Publisher's Note."*

This novel is the second in a series of which the first four have now been written and the first two published. The title of the whole work, when complete, will be the same as that of the present book, "Of Time and the River." The titles of the six books, in the order of their appearance, together with the time-plan which each follows, are:

Look Homeward, Angel (1884–1920).
Of Time and the River (1920–1925).
The October Fair (1925–1928).
The Hills Beyond Pentland (1838–1926).
The Death of the Enemy (1928–1933).
Pacific End (1791–1884).

Despite Wolfe's intention, Of Time and the River *was the only novel published in the series.*

OF TIME AND THE RIVER

A LEGEND OF MAN'S HUNGER IN HIS YOUTH

By

Thomas Wolfe

"Who knoweth the spirit of man that goeth upward, and the spirit of the beast that goeth downward to the earth?"

CHARLES SCRIBNER'S SONS
NEW YORK
1935

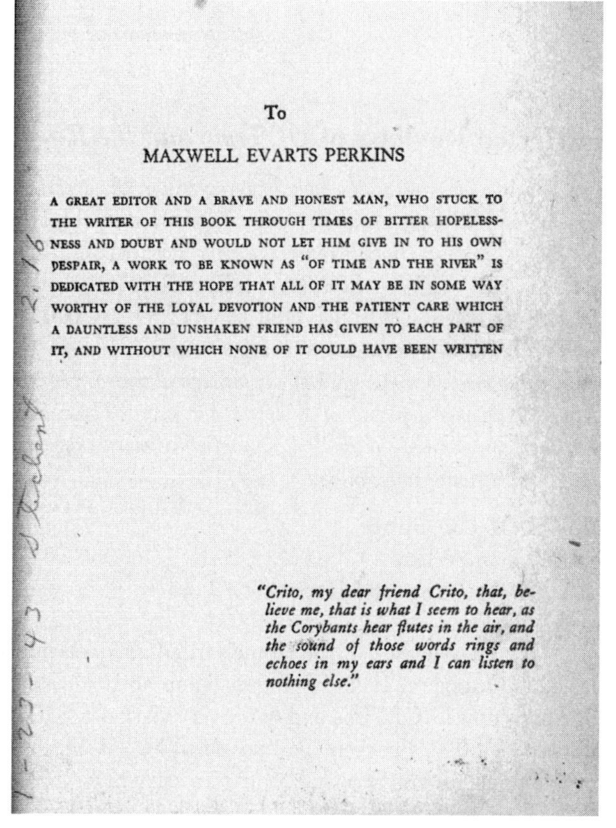

To

MAXWELL EVARTS PERKINS

A GREAT EDITOR AND A BRAVE AND HONEST MAN, WHO STUCK TO THE WRITER OF THIS BOOK THROUGH TIMES OF BITTER HOPELESSNESS AND DOUBT AND WOULD NOT LET HIM GIVE IN TO HIS OWN DESPAIR, A WORK TO BE KNOWN AS "OF TIME AND THE RIVER" IS DEDICATED WITH THE HOPE THAT ALL OF IT MAY BE IN SOME WAY WORTHY OF THE LOYAL DEVOTION AND THE PATIENT CARE WHICH A DAUNTLESS AND UNSHAKEN FRIEND HAS GIVEN TO EACH PART OF IT, AND WITHOUT WHICH NONE OF IT COULD HAVE BEEN WRITTEN

"Crito, my dear friend Crito, that, believe me, that is what I seem to hear, as the Corybants hear flutes in the air, and the sound of those words rings and echoes in my ears and I can listen to nothing else."

Title page and dedication page for Wolfe's second novel

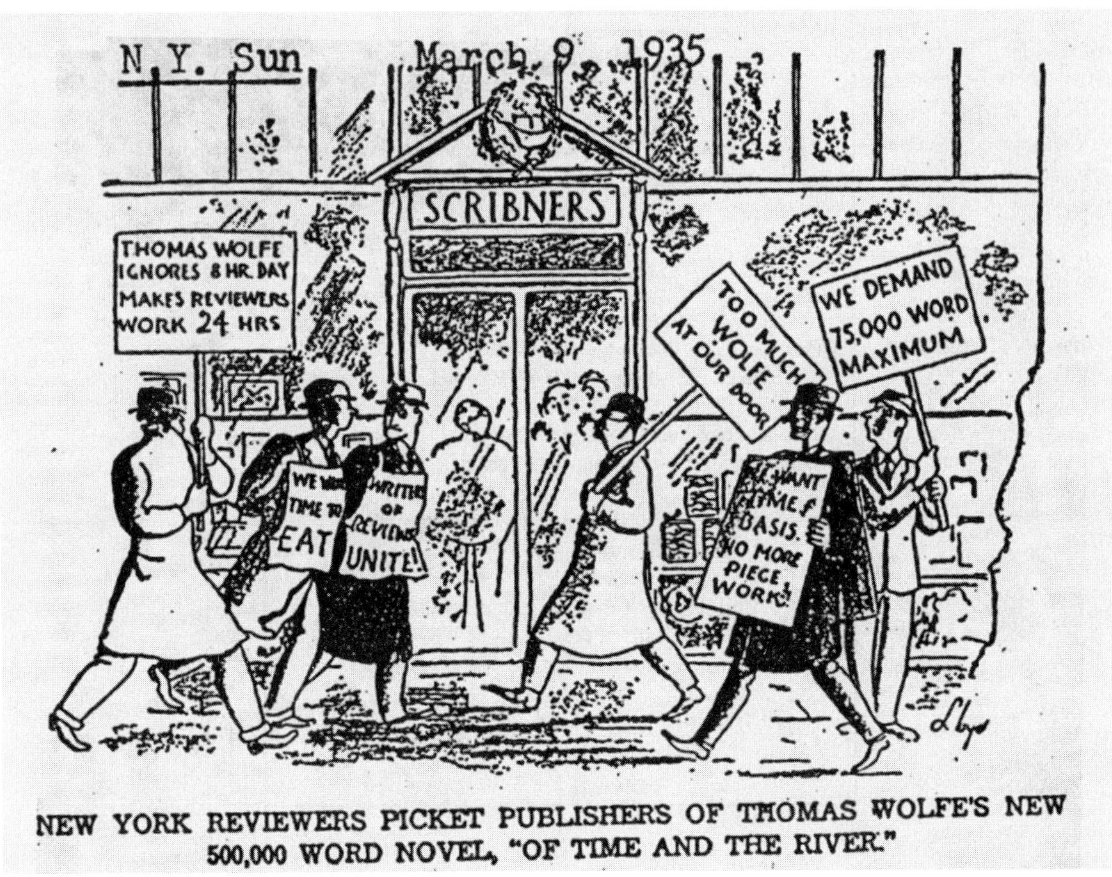

Cartoon that appeared in The Saturday Review of Literature *on 9 March 1935*

Selected Reviews of *Of Time and the River*

Wolfe was depressed about the prospects for his novel during his ocean voyage; however, when he reached Europe, he received a cablegram from Perkins reassuring him: "MAGNIFICENT REVIEWS SOMEWHAT CRITICAL IN WAYS EXPECTED FULL OF GREATEST PRAISE."

Reviewer John Chamberlain urged readers to buy Wolfe's book even though he was only halfway through it himself. He cites Aline Bernstein's depiction of Wolfe in her story "Three Blue Suits" as corroboration of the Wolfe legend of "a colossal appetite, huge energy, [and] unparalleled intensity."

Books Of The Times
John Chamberlain
The New York Times, 8 March 1935

Thomas Wolfe's "Look Homeward, Angel" was published in October of 1929. His mountainous 450,000-word, 912-page novel, "Of Time and the River" (Scribner, $3), is published today. Between the two dates Mr. Wolfe has grown to the proportions of an American legend.

The legend is that of a Gargantuan fellow with a lust to be gourmet and gourmand rolled into one. But his appetite for life, capacious as it is, is as nothing to his voracity for covering white paper with words. The Saturday Review of Literature prints a cartoon in this week's issue of an angry group of New York reviewers picketing Scribner's. They are shown carrying placards that read "Thomas Wolfe ignores 8-hour day; makes reviewers work twenty-four hours," "We want to eat," "Too much Wolfe at our door," "We demand 75,000-word maximum." But the reviewers have no real complaint; it is not every day that they have a chance to read Thomas Wolfe. The man with a legitimate grievance is Maxwell Perkins, the Scribner editor. They tell stories about Mr. Perkins wrestling with Thomas Wolfe for three days, catch-as-catch-can, over the attempted excision of a phrase. Trucks are popularly supposed to deliver Wolfe manuscripts to the Scribner door, and there is one story of the time when Mr. Wolfe took the original 900,000 words of "Look Homeward, Angel" to the country to cut the manuscript in half. He came back with 4,000 words taken out–and 40,000 new words written in the margins. Whereupon the exhausted Mr. Perkins did the requisite cutting himself. But there was little thrown away; Mr. Wolfe has, on the internal evidence of "Of Time and the River," taken the story of Father Gant as a youth watching the Confederate troops march by to

Gettysburg and worked it into the new novel as part of Old Gant's dying memories.

The Lightning Strikes

One of the most characteristic stories about Wolfe is that of the time the divine afflatus struck him as a train was pulling out of the station. He was leaving for a week-end and a rest. But just as the train got under way he suddenly thought of an appropriate ending for a story. He must, he *must,* get back to his room in Brooklyn, to his writing ledger and his pencils. After dashing down the aisle, bowling over the conductor and crashing into the news butcher, he made a dizzy, twisting leap for the ground. They picked him up–so the story goes–with a badly sprained ankle, many bruises, a torn suit and a ruined suitcase. But he finished his story to his own satisfaction while lying in bed in the hospital.

Thomas Wolfe has little in common with Nero. But the story of Nero's wishing that all mankind had only one collective neck, so that the heads of every one could be severed with one felicitous stroke, appeals to Mr. Wolfe; it expresses a lust–the lust to kill–at its highest point of intensity. Mr. Wolfe, of course, has no desire to kill, but he would like to do many other things to the point of absolute satiation. In "Of Time and the River" he tells of young Eugene Gant's reading of 20,000 volumes in some ten years' time. (A daily reviewer reads between 300 and 400 books a year, which would count up to 4,000 at the outside in ten years.) Eugene's appetite for words is part of a general appetite to see all, to experience all. "And there were other spells and rhymes," Thomas Wolfe writes of his autobiographical hero, "which would enable him to know the lives of 50,000,000 people, to visit every country in the world, to know a hundred languages, possess 10,000 lovely women, and yet have one he loved and honored above all, who would be true and beautiful and faithful to him." "In short, he would have the whole cake of the world, and eat it too–have adventures, labors, joys and triumphs that would exhaust the energies of 10,000 men, and yet have spells and charms for all of it."

Biographical Material

If one thinks all this legendary evidence of a colossal appetite, huge energy, unparalleled intensity, is wholly a matter of romantic imagination, let him turn to a story by Aline Bernstein in her "Three Blue Suits" (Equinox Cooperative Press). Miss Bernstein disguises Mr. Wolfe under the name of Eugene Lyon, but it is obviously true biography that she is writing. The story is of a writer living among a constant litter of cigarette butts, ashes, odd socks, collars, neckties, books opened and books closed, falling asleep with his pencil still in his fingers and his ledger crumpled beneath him, waking in time to be half an hour late for a luncheon appointment, unable to make up his mind which experience is preferable: walking, riding on a bus, or taking a taxi uptown, or staying at home to lunch, or going out to the cupboard for a drink of gin, or merely standing at the open window and dreaming. Every decision, to Mr. Thomas Wolfe-Gant, necessarily involves heartbreak, for to make up one's mind to do one thing means to cut off the possibility of doing something else that is dear and delightful in the same allotted space of time.

What I have read of "Of Time and the River"–and this means about one-half of it–contains God's plenty. The characters of "Look Homeward, Angel" continue their intense, garrulous, gorging, fascinating lives. Old Gant, at the point of death from a malignant carcinoma, is a most vital and uncorpse-like dying man, able to clutch life hard as he dreams of his far youth. Eugene's sister, Helen, living though she is in the daily fear that her father's passing will mean the destruction of her will and desires, is brimming with nervous energy. Eliza Pentland Gant, Eugene's mother, is still "*une des forces de la nature.*" Uncle Bascom Pentland, the Boston uncle, bursts in upon the scene with a Dickensian propensity for living in his reiterated peculiarities, one of those "flat" characters who has lived to bury any original plasticity of the organism under a mask that is always presented to the world. Professor George Pierce Baker, of the famous Harvard '47 Workshop, appears as Professor James Graves Hatcher, and Eugene, slowly, grows to maturity.

Richest Since "Arrowsmith"

But I don't want to say anything really specific about "Of Time and the River" until I have finished and digested it. It is undoubtedly the richest American fiction since "Arrowsmith" and "An American Tragedy." But it deserves more than a hurried review, dashed off after partial reading. I want to spend a week-end with it. On Tuesday of next week, then, "Of Time and the River" will be reviewed in this column. Meanwhile, readers are urged to buy it. It is not every day that a novel by Thomas Wolfe is published.

After reading Three Blue Suits, *which included Bernstein's thinly disguised account of their affair, Wolfe wrote to his former mistress on 11 December 1933:*

. . . maybe, with all this talent and cleverness with which you have been so richly endowed by nature, you can still learn something from me–the final necessity of sweat and grinding effort.

–*The Letters of Thomas Wolfe,* p. 393

Books on Our Table
Herschel Brickell,
New York Post, 8 March 1935

If you see crowds gathered in the neighborhood of bookstores today the reason will be that Thomas Wolfe's second novel, "Of Time and the River," is at last available after many postponements. It is five years since the publication of Mr. Wolfe's "Look Homeward, Angel."

If the bookstores are empty for the next couple of months the reason will be that the people who bought Mr. Wolfe's second novel are spending their time at home reading it.

For it is, as you may know by this time, a work of some 450,000 words, or 912 pages, and written in a variety of styles, none of which makes for rapid reading.

It may be as well to try to answer the most important question that can be asked about any book first, before going into the details. This is, of course, does the Wolfe novel seem worth the time it will take to read it?

My answer is an emphatic yes. I felt when I finally finished it after what seemed to me weeks in its company that I had been associating with an active volcano, a cyclone and a couple of comets; in other words, a bit dizzy, but very well aware that I had had an experience. I can still hear Mr. Wolfe's "demented winds" roaring and screaming in my ears. I can still feel the lift and surge of his rhapsodic passages on America, gloriously Whitmanesque.

"Of Time and the River" is a direct sequel to "Look Homeward, Angel," the novel which made Mr. Wolfe one of the most discussed of living writers, therefore autobiographical, and when you are with Mr. Wolfe you are in the presence of a personality that is like nothing so much as a force of nature.

You can't, if you are of ordinary stature and vitality, believe completely in his gigantic world of shadow shapes, where everything is magnified and intensified, but you will be fascinated just the same, swept along on the tides of his passions, carried away with the gargantuan appetite of a man who wishes to swallow life whole when most of us are content to chew a tiny fragment in our frightened and dyspeptic way.

There is an additional reason why "Of Time and the River" is without any question the event of the publishing season.

This is because it carries the title of a vast autobiographical novel of which "Look Homeward, Angel" was the beginning. The first four books, says the publishers' announcement, have already been written and the third, "October Fair," follows directly upon the present book in point of time.

"October Fair" will be followed by "The Hills of Pentland," which will cover the years between 1838 and 1926; "The Death of the Enemy," 1928–1933, and "Pacific End," 1791–1884.

An ambitious project in which an American of our own day relates the symbolical search for his father, which is the theme of the Wolfe books, an autobiographical novel that will reach a total of around 3,000,000 words if it is completed, thus making Marcel Proust's "Remembrance of Things Past" look like a novelette.

Mr. Wolfe writes with an inhuman, a "possessed," energy; he has produced 2,000,000 words in the five years that have elapsed since the publication of "Look Homeward, Angel," so there is no reason to doubt that "Of Time and the River" will finally stand complete upon the library shelves.

The realization that the present book, then, is merely a section of a tremendous screen upon which Mr. Wolfe expects to project the account of his wanderings in time and space makes it a reviewer's duty, I think, to talk more about what there is in the present volume than to try to write a critical essay on the place of the author in world literature.

In time the novel covers the years between 1920 and 1925; it begins with the departure of the hero, Emmet Gant, from his Altamont, Catawba–Asheville, N.C.–home for Harvard and it follows him through his months in Boston and New York and through his months of exile in Oxford and in France.

One hears that many of the figures are drawn from life, some of them, like Professor "Hatcher" of the drama department at Harvard, unmistakably so, and there will be some searching for the keys which not everybody will enjoy having found; Mr. Wolfe deals frankly with his people, no matter how close they are to him.

His novel is the saga of a lusty youth burning with a love of life and suffering from an insatiable hunger for sensations of the mind and body. Here is an example, which a

> Also lately I have been getting acquainted with some of the authors my reviewers have accused me of imitating. I'm afraid that I took my reviews too seriously, but in some instances I have reason to be glad of it. One reviewer, whose identity I have forgotten, compared me to Whitman. I had no rest until I had sought out his works, which were largely unfamiliar to me, and had digested them. He was a wonderful discovery. It seems to me that he is one of the most American of American writers. Many of his ideas now seem out of date, such as his enthusiasm for democracy, an impossible ideal to my mind, yet essentially he is the real American.
>
> –*Thomas Wolfe Interviewed,* p. 19

daily book reviewer read with an inevitable feeling of envy, Mr. Wolfe's description of Gant's reading:

> Now he would prowl the stacks of the library at night, pulling books out of a thousand shelves and reading them like a madman. . . . Within a period of ten years he read at least 20,000 volumes–deliberately the number is set low–and opened the pages and looked through many times that number. Dryden said this about Ben Jonson: "Other men read books but he read libraries"–and so now it was with this boy.

This is just a suggestion of the gusty and tempestuous quality of Mr. Wolfe's young man in search of a father, whose relation to the world is what the book is about.

But if it be necessary to await the completion of Mr. Wolfe's whole task before we can get the full effect of what he is trying to say to us about Man and the Universe, and, more especially, about us, for his book is profoundly American in spite of his occasional confusion of himself with his country and all its inhabitants, there are many things in it to be enjoyed as it stands.

Things, for example, such as pages relating to Bascom Hawke, who appeared in Scribner's Magazine some months ago, or relating to Professor Hatcher and his students, or what Gant found out about the English, or of his amusing experiences in France with a broken-down Countess, or some of the rhapsodic passages already mentioned.

A multitude, a confusion of heaped-up riches, given form of a sort, a mass of ore, some of it clean-minted, some of it not, which is rather baffling to the assayer who has to work against time as do those of us who write about books every day.

There is much more I should like to say about Mr. Wolfe's book; some things I should like to quote from it, for example. Also there is comment to be made upon the way he has woven his tapestry, in which the pattern is often worked out with great cunning. And particularly the curious depth of feeling about America and the passionate understanding of it throughout the book, a feeling that transcends sectional boundaries and embraces a continent.

I hesitate to use superlatives, particularly when I am still under the spell of a book that is as moving as "Of Time and the River," but is it out of place to suggest that perhaps there is a chance at least that Mr. Wolfe's big book will be the Great American Novel so long talked about, that his incredible vitality will enable him to do something many of us have thought would never be done?

A nice question for the future . . . In the meantime, any one who reads "Of Time and the River" is in for a rare and memorable experience. . . .

Although he claimed that Of Time and the River *was weakened by Wolfe's mixing of fact and fiction, Henry Seidel Canby declared its significance as "one of the most American books of our time."*

The River of Youth

Henry Seidel Canby,

Saturday Review of Literature, 11 (9 March 1935): 529–530

There was much laughter when years ago D. H. Lawrence in his "Studies in Classical American Literature" described an Old Indian Devil who was always plaguing the great Americans with sudden flushes of paganism, great resurgences of sex, and obstinate maladjustments between their European souls and their unfenced continent. It is not so funny now, for some devil, Indian, Marxian, or psycho-analytic, has surely been torturing the best American writers of our era. They squirm, they lash, they spit out filth and imprecations, they whine, they defy. They are not at ease in this Zion of our ancestors.

For Thomas Wolfe in his new novel, "Of Time and the River," the curse is impotence. There is for him a brooding loneliness in the American landscape which drives the man-mass into a nervous activity of hurrying on trains, motors, subways, airplanes, a restlessness which drives the sensitive writer into an agony of frustration because the towns, the cities, the countryside oppress him with unrealized and inexpressible energy. It is a country that grips the imagination and lets the heart go, a country in which humanity mixed and at the boiling point–black Negro flesh, amber Jewish flesh, dark, light, sanguine–is incited by fierce energies toward no end but movement and frustration, a country where life has sacrificed its mass for its force, and the observer can neither hold on or let go of a rush of experience that always seems to have, yet never quite achieves, a meaning.

The impotence of America is an impotence of expression. When in Wolfe's novel Gene Gant's train shrieks through the night on his first journey northward, he feels the enormous push of continental energy and can rise to it only by drunken hysteria. When in the last chapter he takes the ocean liner from France for home, he sees that vast organization of speed and change floating above his tender, and knows that it is America again, clutching at his sensitive spirit. In three hundred years the American soul has not made itself a home.

And hence the strange impulse toward autobiography which has carried so many Americans to the verge of incoherence!–Melville in "Moby Dick" wrestling with transcendental interpretations of his restless-

Publicity photograph of Wolfe, 1935 (photograph by Ossip Garber; courtesy of Clara Stites)

ness, or Whitman in the "Song of Myself" blatantly proclaiming his identity with the expansiveness of a continent. They cannot write novels, these rebel Americans, there is nothing stable to write of. They can only proclaim their egos, in defiance of the inhumanity of a continent which the energy of their race has exploited but to which they are not yet assimilated. Hence an impotence which prevents complete expression, and books which are, as the eighteenth century would have said, far more nature than art.

"Of Time and the River," time being the time of youth, the river that mysterious current of life which flows under the perplexing surface of America, is the epitome, after so many books, of the troublous and disintegrating years of the twenties when Mr. Wolfe was young. And those who wish to get in fullest and most impassioned form the spiritual record of those years, or who would see as in a news-reel the typical scenes of that period as youth saw them, will find, if they are persistent, what they want in this book, which is neither fiction nor autobiography, but both.

For although the scene of Mr. Wolfe's long expected narrative changes from North Carolina to the biting realities and warped romance of New England, from New England to the aloofness of Oxford, from Oxford to the loneliness of an American's France, yet it is a wholly American book, one of the most American books of our time. It is in the direct tradition of those earlier anguished spirits and great seekers on our soil, Thoreau, Melville, Whitman. It is in the tradition, but with a momentous difference for which the break-up of the twenties and Mr. Wolfe's own idiosyncrasies are responsible. Yet if I should wish to know what these twenties meant to an American youth still asking the questions asked by his spiritual ancestors, "Why are we here?," "What does this continent mean to us?," "What are we becoming?" I should go to this book. If I fail to give a clear account of Mr. Wolfe's thousand-page story of how a passion-driven youth tried to tear all knowledge from the Harvard library, all experience from America, all wisdom from Europe, and to pluck out, in his twenties, the secret of the loneliness and the fascination of America, forgive me, Have you ever tried to review the Encyclopedia Britannica?

Mr. Wolfe's odd thousand pages are condensed but not adequately described in the paragraphs above. He calls them fiction, and fiction they are of the kind that he put into "Look Homeward, Angel," but better organized, more poetical where poetical, more sharply realistic when realistic; and they are to be followed by a million words more or less in which the ego which is the raison d'être of them all is to conclude the story. But fiction in the strict sense they are not, nor story, nor drama, but rather spiritual autobiography in which the thousand incidents, many of them trivial, and the dozens of characters, many of them extraordinary, have as their excuse for being that a youth met them on his way. Plot there is none. Structure in the ordinary narrative sense, there is none. It is a picaresque novel with the distraught mind of a poet of the twenties as *picaro,* and the incidents adventures in seeking a spiritual home.

To be more precise, this book is a study of American dualism and it is this which gives it poignancy. Leaf through it and you will see as in a moving picture successive moments of prose and poetry. Here are the fleshy people of an intensely actual Carolina, of a literal Boston, and of a photographic France. No reporter could have done them more vividly as news, and indeed Wolfe is a great reporter. No one of them is usual, indeed for such a passionate student of humanity no man or woman could be merely usual; most of them are eccentrics, half mad from pain, or love, or greed, or vanity, or frustration; or wholly lost in what is really fantasy, like Starwick the homosexual, or the pathetic collegiate Weaver, or the gross sensualist Flood who is like some mushroom sprung from, yet alien to, the good earth. And between these flashes of intimate, literal humanity from the man-swarm, the novel leaves the literal entirely and in a poetic prose that owes much to Whitman and a little to Joyce, but has become Wolfe's own, rises into a chorus of anguish, perplexity, and delight, which chants the loneliness and the impotence and the beauty of this America, and struggles to break through to some solution which will satisfy the seeker, who is the youth Gant, the hero, and the excuse for all this profusion of words.

And linking the two worlds is the decaying but still mighty figure of the Father, the old stone cutter who was the center of "Look Homeward, Angel." Dying (and his death scene is Mr. Wolfe at his best), he still dominates the imagination of the youth, for he in his vast energy and incredible vitality is the old America where man almost became worthy of his continent; and in his cancerous decline, in his frustrated career, and in the immense confusion of his brain, he symbolizes what has happened in a twentieth century in which there seems to be no graspable relation between the prose and the poetry of a continent.

So much for the purpose of this novel. Its achievement is less. With all its richness of detail, its passion, its poetry, and its intense realism of contemporary life, there is an impotence in this book like the impotence Wolfe ascribes to his America.

In America it is an impotence of wandering men at home wherever wheels carry them yet never strong enough to grip the continent and make it serve their happiness. In this America, "so casual and rich and limitless and free," they become arid or lonely or broken, or have got the "new look" of the machine-ridden masses. With Mr. Wolfe the impotence is exactly equivalent. His imagination has provided him with a great theme and his accurate memory flashes infinite exact detail of the life of which he intends to make his book. But he cannot control the theme or reduce his substance to a medium. He will write neither poetry nor prose, but both. He will not be content with the literal autobiographic description of men and events which his journalistic sense supplies so readily but must intersperse with passages of sheer fantasy or poetical uplift. He will stick neither to fiction nor to fact. Hence the reader never enters into that created world of the real novelist which has its own laws, its own atmosphere, its own people, but goes from here to there in Mr. Wolfe's own life, seeing real people as he saw them, and often recognizing them (as with George Pierce Baker in Professor Hatcher, and many others) not as created characters but as literal transcripts from the life. So that the effect is always of being in two worlds at once, fiction and fact, until curiosity takes the place of that ready acceptance of a homogeneous life in the imagination which a fine novel invariably permits. . .

I think that this novel, like many other fiery and ambitious American books–like Melville's "Pierre," like many of Whitman's poems, like the now forgotten romantic-philosophic extravaganzas so common in the magazines of a century ago–is an artistic failure. And Mr. Wolfe's books, as wholes, will continue to be artistic failures until he finds and controls a medium in which the ego is sublimated into an imagination less involved in the immediate circumstances of his life. Yet it is an important book, and Mr. Wolfe is an important writer. He has more material, more vitality, more originality, more gusto than any two contemporary British novelists put together, even though they may be real novelists and he is not. He stands to them as Whitman stood to the wearied "Idylls of the King." And he entirely escapes the sordid, whining defeatism of so many of his American contemporaries

---

Fellow southerner Robert Penn Warren analyzed the sources of Wolfe's power in reviewing Of Time and the River. *At this time Warren had not yet published any of his novels.*

A Note on the Hamlet of Thomas Wolfe
Robert Penn Warren
American Review, 5 (May 1935): 191–208.

Thomas Wolfe owns an enormous talent; and chooses to exercise it on an enormous scale. This talent was recognized promptly enough several years ago when his first novel, *Look Homeward, Angel,* came from the press to overwhelm a high percentage of the critics. Nor was this sensational success for a first novel undeserved, even if the book was not, as Hugh Walpole suggested, as "near perfect as a novel can be." Now Mr. Wolfe's second novel, *Of Time and the River,* appears, and the enthusiasm of the reception of the first will probably be repeated; though not, I venture to predict, on a scale scarcely so magnificent. That remains to be seen; but it may not be too early to attempt a definition of the special excellence and the special limitations of the enormous talent that has produced two big books and threatens to produce others in the near future.

If Mr.Wolfe's talent is enormous, his energies are more enormous, and fortunately so. A big book is forbidding, but at the same time it carries a challenge in its very pretension. It seems to say, "This is a serious project and demands serious attention from serious minds." There is, of course, the snobbery of the three-decker. Mr. Wolfe is prolific. His publishers assure the public that he has written in the neighborhood of two million words. In his scheme of six novels, two are now published (*Look Homeward, Angel,* 1884-1920, and

Of Time and the River, 1920-1925); two more are already written (*The October Fair,* 1925-1928, and *The Hills Beyond Pentland,* 1838-1926); and two more are projected (*The Death of the Enemy,* 1928-1933, and *Pacific End,* 1791-1884). Presumably, the novels unpublished and unwritten will extend forward and backward the ramifications of the fortunes of the Gant and Pentland families.

Look Homeward, Angel and the present volume are essentially two parts of an autobiography; the pretense of fiction is so thin and slovenly that Mr.Wolfe in referring to the hero writes indifferently "Eugene Gant" or "I" and "me." There may be many modifications, omissions, and additions in character and event, but the impulse and material are fundamentally personal. The story begins in *Look Homeward, Angel* in the latter part of the nineteenth century with the arrival of Gant, the father of the hero, in Altamont, in the state of Catawba, which is Asheville, North Carolina. It continues with the marriage to Eliza Pentland, the birth of the various children, the debaucheries and repentances of old Gant, the growth of the village into a flourishing resort, the profitable real-estate speculations of Eliza, her boarding house, the education of Eugene Gant in Altamont and at the State University, the collapse of old Gant's health, and the departure of Eugene for Harvard. *Of Time and the River* resumes on the station platform as Eugene leaves for Harvard, sees him through three years there in the drama school under "Professor Thatcher," presents in full horror of detail the death of old Gant from cancer of the prostate, treats the period in New York when Eugene teaches the Jews in a college there, and takes the hero to Europe, where he reads, writes, and dissipates tremendously. He is left at the point of embarking for America. During this time he is serving his apprenticeship as a writer and trying to come to terms with his own spirit and with America. So much for the bare materials of the two books.

The root of Mr.Wolfe's talent is his ability at portraiture. The figures of Eliza Gant and old Gant, of Ben and Helen, in *Look Homeward, Angel,* are permanent properties of the reader's imagination. Mr. Wolfe has managed to convey the great central vitality of the old man, for whom fires would roar up the chimney and plants would grow, who stormed into his house in the evening laden with food, and whose quality is perpetually heroic, mythical, and symbolic. It is the same with Eliza, with her flair for business; her almost animal stupidity; her great, but sometimes aimless, energies; her almost sardonic and defensive love for her son, whom she does not understand; her avarice and her sporadic squandering of money. These two figures dominate both books; even after old Gant is dead the force of his personality, or rather the force of the symbol into which that personality has been elevated, is an active agent, and a point of reference for interpretation.

These two characters, and Ben and Helen in a lesser degree, are triumphs of poetic conception. The uncle in *Of Time and the River,* Bascom Pentland, shares some of their qualities. He exhibits the family lineaments, the family vitality, and something of the symbolic aspect of the other characters; but the method of presentation is more conventional and straightforward, and the result more static and anecdotal.

Mr. Wolfe's method in presenting these characters, and the special kind of symbolism he manages to derive from them, is subject to certain special limitations. Obviously it would not serve as a routine process for the treatment of character, at least not on the scale on which it is here rendered. The reader of a novel demands something more realistic, less lyrical; he demands an interplay of characters on another and more specific level, a method less dependent on the direct intrusion of the novelist's personal sensibility. As I have said, the figures of the Gant family are powerful and overwhelming as symbols, as an emotional focus for the novel, and as a point of reference. But the method collapses completely when applied to Starwick, a character of equal importance in Mr. Wolfe's scheme.

We amass a great fund of information concerning Francis Starwick. He was born in a town in the Middle West and early rebelled against the crudities and ugliness of his background. At Harvard he assists Professor Thatcher in the drama school and leads the life of a mannered and affected aesthete, foppish in dress, artificial in speech, oversensitive, and sometimes cruel. At Harvard, he becomes Eugene's best friend. Later he appears in Europe in company with two young women of Boston families, somewhat older then he, who are in love with him and who are willing to pay, with their reputations and their purses, for the pleasure of his conversation. With these three Eugene enters a period of debauchery in Paris. Finally he discovers that Starwick is homosexual, and in his undefinable resentment beats him into unconsciousness.

But this body of information is not all that the writer intends. F. Scott Fitzgerald and Ernest Hemingway have been able to use effectively such characters as Starwick and to extract their meaning, because as novelists they were willing to work strictly in terms of character. But in *Of Time and the River* the writer is forever straining to convince the reader of some value in Starwick that is not perceptible, that the writer himself cannot define; he tries, since he is writing an autobiography, to make Starwick a symbol, a kind of alter ego, for a certain period of his own experience. The strain is tremendous; and without conviction. The writing about Starwick, as the climax of the relationship approaches, sinks into a slush of poetical bathos. And here is the end of the long scene of parting:

> "You are my mortal enemy. Goodbye."
>
> "Goodbye, Eugene," said Starwick sadly. "But let me tell you this before I go. Whatever it was I took from you, it was something that I did not want or wish to take. And I would give it back again if I could."
>
> "Oh, fortunate and favored Starwick," the other jeered. "To be so rich–to have such gifts and not to know he has them–to be forever victorious, and to be so meek and mild."
>
> "And I will tell you this as well," Starwick continued. "Whatever anguish and suffering this mad hunger, this impossible desire, has caused you, however fortunate or favored you may think I am, I would give my whole life if I could change places with you for an hour–know for an hour an atom of your anguish and your hunger and your hope. . . . Oh, to feel so, suffer so, and live so!–however mistaken you may be! . . .To have come lusty, young, and living into this world. . . . not to have come like me, stillborn from your mother's womb–never to know the dead heart and the passionless passion–the cold brain and the cold hopelessness of hope–to be wild, mad, furious, and tormented–but to have belief, to live in anguish, but to live–and not to die." . . . He turned and opened the door. "I would give all I have and all you think I have, for just one hour of it. You call me fortunate and happy. *You* are the most fortunate and happy man I ever knew. Goodbye, Eugene."
>
> "Goodbye, Frank. Goodbye, my enemy."
>
> "And goodbye, my friend," said Starwick. He went out, and the door closed behind him.

The dialogue, the very rhythms of the sentences, and the scene itself, scream the unreality.

The potency of the figures from the family and the failure with Starwick may derive from the autobiographical nature of Mr. Wolfe's work. Eliza and old Gant come from a more primary level of experience, figures of motherhood and fatherhood that gradually, as the book progresses, assume a wider significance and become at the same time a reference for the hero's personal experience.And the author, knowing them first on that level, has a way of knowing them more intimately and profoundly as people than he ever knows Starwick. Starwick is more artificial, because he is at the same time a social symbol and a symbol for a purely private confusion of which the roots are never clear.

Most of the other characters are treated directly. Mr. Wolfe has an appetite for people and occasionally a faculty of very acute perception. The portrait of Abe Jones, the Jewish student at the college in New York, and those of the people at the Coulson household in Oxford, are evidence enough of this capacity. But his method or, rather, methods of presentation are various and not unvaryingly successful. There are long stretches of stenographic dialogue that has little focus, or no focus whatsoever; for instance, the first part of the conversation of the businessmen in the Pullman in Book I, of the residents of the hotel in Book IV, of the artistic hangers-on at the Cambridge tea parties, or even of Eugene and his companions in the Paris cafés. Some of this reporting is very scrupulous, and good as reporting, but in its mass, its formlessness, and its lack of direction it is frequently dull; the momentary interest of recognition is not enough to sustain it, and it bears no precise relation to the intention of the novel. It is conversation for conversation's sake, a loquacity and documentation that testify to the author's talent but not to his intelligence as an artist. Generally this type of presentation is imitative of Sinclair Lewis's realistic dialogue, but it lacks the meticulous, cautious, and selective quality of the best of Lewis, the controlled malice; it is too random, and in an incidental sense, too heavily pointed.

Further, there are tremendous masses of description and characters. Mr. Wolfe has the habit of developing his own clichés for description of character, and of then exhibiting them at irregular intervals. It is as if he realized the bulk of the novel and the difficulty a reader might experience in recognizing a character on reappearance, and so determined to prevent this, if possible, by repetition and insistence. For instance, Starwick and Ann, one of the young women from Boston who is in love with Starwick, have a complete set of tags and labels that are affixed to them time after time during the novel. Mr. Wolfe underrates the memory of the reader; or this may be but another instance of the lack of control that impairs his work.

Only in the section dealing with the Coulson episode does Mr. Wolfe seem to have all his resources for character presentation under control. The men who room in the house, the jaunty Captain Nicholl with his blasted arm and the other two young men from the motorcar factory–these with the Coulsons themselves are very precise to the imagination, and are sketched in with an economy usually foreign to Mr. Wolfe. The Coulson girl, accepting the mysterious ruin that presides over the household, is best drawn and dominates the group. Here Mr. Wolfe has managed to convey an atmosphere and to convince the reader of the reality of his characters without any of his habitual exaggerations of method and style. This section, with slight alternations, originally appeared as a short story; it possesses what is rare enough in *Of Time and the River,* a constant focus.

I have remarked that some of Mr. Wolfe's material is not subordinated to the intention of the book. What is his intention? On what is the mass of material focused? What is to give it form? His novels are obvi-

One of several drawings of Wolfe provided to periodicals by Charles Scribner's Sons for use in composing advertisements for Wolfe's books

ously autobiographical. This means that the binding factor should be, at least in part, the personality of the narrator, or, since Mr. Wolfe adopts a disguise, of the hero, Eugene Gant. The two books are, in short, an account of the development of a sensibility; obviously something more is intended than the looseness and irresponsibility of pure memoirs or observations. The work demands comparison with such works as Joyce's *Portrait of the Artist as a Young Man* or Lawrence's *Sons and Lovers;* it may even demand comparison with proper autobiographies, such as Rousseau's *Confessions* or *The Education of Henry Adams*. But the comparison with these books is not to the advantage of Mr. Wolfe's performance. It has not the artistry of the first two, the constant and dramatic relation of incident to a developing consciousness of the world, nor has it the historical importance of the third, or the philosophical and intellectual interest of the last.

The hero of *Look Homeward, Angel,* though a child and adolescent, is essentially more interesting than the Eugene of *Of Time and the River*. He is more comprehensible, because there is a real (and necessarily conventional) pattern to his developing awareness of the world around him. Further, the life of the Gant household, and even of the community, is patterned with a certain amount of strictness in relation to Eugene: the impress of the vast vitality of old Gant, the lack of understanding on the part of the mother and the perpetual emotional drag of resentment and affection she exerts on her son, the quarrels with Steve, the confusion and pathos of the sexual experiences, the profound attachment between Ben and Eugene, and the climactic and daring scene with Ben's spirit. There is a progress toward maturity, a fairly precise psychological interest. The novel contains much pure baggage and much material that is out of tone, usually in the form of an ironic commentary that violates the point of view; but the book is more of a unit, and is, for that reason perhaps, more exciting and forceful.

In *Of Time and the River,* as Eugene in his Pullman rides at night across Virginia, going "northward, worldward, towards the secret borders of Virginia, towards the great world cities of his hope, the fable of his childhood legendry," the following passage is interpolated:

> Who has seen fury riding in the mountains? Who has known fury striding in the storm? Who has been mad with fury in his youth, given no rest or peace or certitude by fury, driven on across the earth by fury, until the great vine of his heart was broke, the sinews wrenched, the little tenement of bone, blood, marrow, brain, and feeling in which great fury raged, was twisted, wrung, depleted, worn out, and exhausted by the fury which it could not lose or put away? Who has known fury, how it came? How have we breathed the core, until we have him in us now and cannot lose him anywhere we go? It is a strange and subtle worm that will . . .

The furious Eugene is scarcely made comprehensible. The reader amasses a large body of facts about him, as about Starwick, but with something of the same result. He knows that Eugene is big; that he is a creature of enormous appetites of which he is rather proud; that he has the habit of walking much at night; that he is fascinated by the health and urbanity of his friend Joel and by the personality of Starwick; that he ceases to like Shelley after spending an afternoon in a jail cell; that he reads twenty thousand books in ten years; that he is obsessed by the idea of devouring all of life. Then, the reader knows the facts of Eugene's comings and goings, and knows the people he meets and what they say. But the Eugene susceptible of such definition is not the hero of the book, or at least does not function adequately as such. The hero is really that nameless fury that drives Eugene. The book is an effort to name that fury, and perhaps by naming it, to tame it. But the fury goes unnamed and untamed. Since the book is formless otherwise, only a proper emotional reference to such a center could give it form. Instead, at the center there is this chaos that steams and bubbles in rhetoric and apocalyptic apostrophe, sometimes grand and sometimes febrile and empty; the center is a maelstrom, perhaps artificially generated at times; and the other, tangible items are the flotsam and jetsam and dead wood spewed up, iridescent or soggy, as the case may be.

It may be objected that other works of literary art, and very great ones at that, have heroes who defy definition and who are merely centers of "fury." For instance, there is Hamlet, or Lear. But a difference may be observed. Those characters may defy the attempt at central definition, but the play hangs together in each case as a structure without such definition; that is, there has been no confusion between the sensibility that produced a play, as an object of art, and the sensibility of a hero in a play. (And the mere fact that *Hamlet* and *Lear* employ verse as a vehicle adds further to the impression of discipline, focus, and control.)

There are two other factors in the character of Eugene that may deserve mention. The hero feels a sense of destiny and direction, the sense of being "chosen" in the midst of a world of defeated, aimless, snobbish, vulgar, depleted, or suicidal people. (This is, apparently, the source of much of the interpolated irony in both books, an irony almost regularly derivative and mechanical.) In real life this conviction of a high calling may be enough to make a "hero" feel that life does have form and meaning; but the mere fact that a hero in a novel professes the high calling and is contrasted in his social contacts with an inferior breed does not, in itself, give the novel form and meaning. The transference of the matter from the actuality of life to the actuality of art cannot be accomplished so easily. Second, at the very end of the novel, Eugene, about to embark for America, sees a woman who, according to the somewhat extended lyrical epilogue, makes him "lose" self and so be "found":

> After all the blind, tormented wanderings of youth, that woman would become his heart's centre and the target of his life, the image of immortal one-ness that again collected him to one, and hurled the whole collected passion, power, and might of his one life into the blazing certitude, the immortal governance and unity, of love.

Certainly this is what we call fine writing; it may or may not be good writing. And probably, falling in love may make a man "find himself"; but this epilogue scarcely makes the novel find itself.

It is possible sometimes that a novel possessing no structure in the ordinary sense of the word, or not properly dominated by its hero's personality or fortunes, may be given a focus by the concrete incorporation of an idea, or related ideas. Now, *Of Time and the River* has such a leading idea, but an idea insufficient in its operation. The leading symbol of the father, old Gant, gradually assumes another aspect, not purely personal; he becomes, in other words, a kind of symbol of the fatherland, the source, the land of violence, drunkenness, fecundity, beauty, and vigor, on which the hero occasionally reflects during his wanderings and to which in the end he returns. But this symbol is not the total expression of the idea, which is worked out more explicitly and at length. There are long series of cinematic flashes of "phases of American life": locomotive drivers, gangsters, pioneers, little towns with the squares deserted at night, evangelists, housewives, rich and suicidal young men, whores on subways, drunk college boys. Or there are more lyrical passages, less effective in pictorial detail, such as the following:

> It was the wild, sweet, casual, savage, and incredibly lovely earth of America, and of the wilderness, and it haunted them like legends, and pierced them like a sword, and filled them with a wild and swelling prescience of joy that was like sorrow and delight.

This kind of material alternates with the more sedate or realistic progress of the chronicle, a kind of running commentary of patriotic mysticism on the more tangible events and perceptions. For Mr. Wolfe has the mysticism of the American idea that we find in Whitman, Sandburg, Masters, Crane, and Benét. He pants for the Word, the union that will clarify all the disparate and confused elements which he enumerates and many of which fill him with revulsion and disgust. He, apparently, has experienced the visionary moment he proclaims, but, like other mystics, he suffers some difficulty when he attempts to prepare it for consumption by the ordinary citizens of the Republic. He must wreak some indignity on the chastity of the vision. This indignity is speech; but he burns, perversely, to speak.

The other promulgators of the American vision have been poets.

Mr. Wolfe, in addition to being a poet in instinct, is, as well, the owner on a large scale of many of the gifts of the novelist. He attempts to bolster, or as it were, to prove, the mystical and poetic vision by fusing it with a body of everyday experience of which the novelist ordinarily treats. But there is scarcely a fusion or a correlation; rather, an oscillation. On the tangible side, the hero flees from America, where his somewhat quivering sensibilities are frequently tortured, and goes to Europe; in the end, worn out by drinking and late hours, disgusted with his friends, unacquainted with the English or the French, and suffering homesickness, he returns to America. But Mr. Wolfe, more than most novelists, is concerned with the intangible; not so much with the psychological process and interrelation as with the visionary "truth."

The other poets, at least Whitman and Crane, have a certain advantage over the poet in Mr. Wolfe. They overtly consented to be poets; Mr. Wolfe has not consented. Therefore their vision is purer, the illusion of communication (*illusion,* for it is doubtful that they have really communicated the central vision) is more readily palatable, because they never made a serious pretense of proving it autobiographically or otherwise; they were content with the hortatory moment, the fleeting symbol, and the affirmation. (Benét, of course, did attempt in *John Brown's Body* such a validation, but with a degree of success that does not demand comment here.) It may simply be that the poets were content to be lyric poets, and therefore could more readily attempt the discipline of selection and concentration; in those respects, even Whitman shows more of an instinct for form than does Mr. Wolfe. Mr. Wolfe is astonishingly diffuse, astonishingly loose in his rhetoric–qualities that, for the moment, may provoke more praise than blame. The rhetoric is sometimes grand, but probably more often tedious and tinged with hysteria. Because he is officially writing prose and not poetry, he has no caution of the clichés of phrase or rhythm, and no compunction about pilfering from other poets.

His vocabulary itself is worth comment. If the reader will inspect the few passages quoted in the course of this essay he will observe a constant quality of strain, a fancy for the violent word or phrase (but often conventionally poetic as well as violent): "Wild, sweet, casual, savage . . . ," "haunted them like legends," "no rest or peace or certitude of fury," "target of his life," "blazing certitude, the immortal governance and unity, of love." Mr. Wolfe often shows very powerfully the poetic instinct, and the praise given by a number of critics to his "sensuousness" and "gusto" is not without justification in the fact; but even more often his prose simply shows the poetic instinct unbuckled on a kind of weekend debauch. He sometimes wants it both ways: the structural irresponsibility of prose and the emotional intensity of poetry. He may overlook the fact that the intensity is rarely to be achieved without a certain rigor in selection and structure.

Further, Mr. Wolfe, we understand from blurbs and reviewers, is attempting a kind of prose epic. American literature has produced one, *Moby Dick.* There is much in common between *Moby Dick* and *Of Time and the River,* but there is one major difference. Melville had a powerful fable, a myth of human destiny, which saved his work from the centrifugal impulses of his genius, and which gave it structure and climax. Its dignity is inherent in the fable itself. No such dignity is inherent in Mr. Wolfe's scheme, if it can properly be termed a scheme. The nearest approach to it is in the character of old Gant, but that is scarcely adequate. And Mr. Wolfe has not been able to compensate for the lack of a fable by all his well-directed and misdirected attempts to endow his subject with a proper dignity, by all his rhetorical insistence, all the clarity and justice of his incidental poetic perceptions, all the hysteria or magnificent hypnosis.

Probably all of these defects, or most of them, are inherent in fiction which derives so innocently from the autobiographical impulse. In the first place, all the impurities and baggage in the novel must strike the author as of peculiar and necessary value because they were observed or actually occurred. But he is not writing a strict autobiography in which all observations or experiences, however vague, might conceivably find a justification. He is trying, and this in the second place, to erect the autobiographical material into an epical and symbolic importance, to make of it a fable, a "Legend of Man's Hunger in His Youth." This much is declared by the subtitle.

Mr. Wolfe promises to write some historical novels, and they may well be crucial in the definition of his genius, because he may be required to reorder the use of his powers. What, thus far, he has produced is fine fragments, several brilliant pieces of portraiture, and many sharp observations on men and nature; in other words, these books are really voluminous notes from which a fine novel, or several fine novels, might be written. If he never writes these novels, it may yet be that his books will retain a value as documents of some historical importance and as confused records of an unusual personality. Meanwhile, despite his admirable energies and his powerful literary endowments, his work illustrates once more the limitations, perhaps the necessary limitations, of an attempt to exploit directly and naïvely the personal experience and the self-defined personality in art.

And meanwhile it may be well to recollect that Shakespeare merely wrote *Hamlet;* he was *not* Hamlet.

The anonymous reviewer for the London Times Literary Supplement (TLS) *argued that Wolfe was "genuinely extending the boundaries of the novel."*

Of Time and the River
TLS, 22 August 1935

The least that can be said of Mr. Thomas Wolfe is to term him one of the most extraordinary phenomena in modern literature, and of his huge novel "Of Time and the River" that the reading of it must surely be an unforgettable experience. Mr. Wolfe works on a vast scale betokening no ordinary persistence and patience. "Look Homeward, Angel," his first novel, took some 600 large pages to tell a family history of three-and-a-half decades, and a boy's life to the age of twenty. In "Of Time and the River" over 900 pages–nearly half a million words–carry on the story for only five years more; and four further volumes, doubtless as ample, have yet to appear before the saga of the Gants and Pentlands is completed. He is a writer, plainly, who not only possesses patience but demands it in his reader. He cannot be read running. To open the present volume seems at first like stepping into a distorted world. The proportions, the perspective, are all wrong. Everything is so immense, so portentous, so intense, that for a while every face appears a gargoyle and the men and women Brobdingnagian giants swimming in slow-motion in a dream-realm of violence and suffocating richness. This effect is especially apparent in the first section of all, which takes some 10,000 words to bring a train into a station and get the hero aboard. The journey which follows–itself perhaps the third of most ordinary-length novels, but a mere incident here–has something of the same formidable quality; but the vision by degrees adjusts itself, and the reader finds himself at last fully at home in a country which, with all its luxuriance, is, he realizes, indeed but his own. Here, however, all the emotional overtones and undertones which ordinarily lie unexpressed upon the very borders of consciousness are duly painted in, given forceful and moving expression.

It is the realization of this achievement which drives one to conclude that Mr. Wolfe is genuinely extending the boundaries of the novel, and not, as may sometimes appear, moving entirely outside them. There were times when one felt that his true analogue in American literature was not so much Melville, to whom he has often been compared, as Whitman, and that his basic effort was apart from his story itself, the writing rather of a new "Leaves of Grass," prose-poems strung like beads upon a tread of narrative, in equal celebration of his native land. There is a truth in this, a double truth. Superbly and dramatically forceful as are many of the episodes of young Eugene Gant's three years as embryo dramatist at Harvard, his return visits to his North Carolina home, his year in New York as university tutor, and finally his trip abroad to England and France, one cannot but be aware that the story is after all but half the tale. Like every genuine artist, Mr. Wolfe has a deeper quarry. His subject, in a sense, is not Eugene Gant and his family and friends but "dark time that haunts us with the briefness of our days" and the river of life that flows unceasingly towards each human individual's extinction; he struggles perpetually to read the riddle of "the strange and bitter miracle of life, to get some meaning out of that black, senseless fusion of pain and joy and agony," and moreover to read it in a summation of the abundant, brilliant, raucous, tender, violent, vital life of modern America. Much of the book, especially in its earlier half, is to all intents and purposes a rhapsody of lyrical prose-poetic passages celebrating the moods and manners, the scenes and smells of half a continent: the great trains that rush to and fro, whistling in the night; spring in New England, summer in New York, autumn in North and South; cities and fields and woods and rivers; moonlight, dusk and dawn–and, with all these, strange moving reveries and chants of time and death and the mystery of man's being upon this earth. They really are not quotable, for their slow heavy rhythms and catalogues demand not a paragraph but a page to make their effect; a sentence or two taken at random will serve as well as any others:–

> October is the richest of the seasons: the fields are cut, the granaries are full, the bins are loaded to the brim with fatness, and from the cider press the rich brown oozings of the York Imperials run. The bee bores to the belly of the yellowed grape, the fly gets old and fat and blue, he buzzes loud, crawls slow, creeps heavily to death on sill and ceiling, the sun goes down in blood and pollen across the bronzed and mown fields of old October.

Yet, to return, Mr. Wolfe's is, with it all, a true novelist. He has a story to tell as well as a truth and beauty to reveal, and even if the synthesis is not always complete, still in the main it must be said that the story is the means, the living flesh, of the revelation.

It would certainly be absurd to deny his power of characterization, especially of elderly men and women–Eugene's dying father, his mother, his Uncle Bascom–and there is comedy as well as deep tragic feeling in these pages. "Of Time and the River" is both as a whole and in detail far too rich to be taken in at a single reading. Mr. Wolfe may have many faults–he can be both verbose and repetitive–but they must be, for those who can stay the course to the end, burnt up in the full and steady flame of his positive achievement.

Wolfe in Berlin, May 1935 (The Thomas Wolfe Collection, Pack Memorial Public Library, Asheville, North Carolina)

Berlin

After traveling in England and Holland, Wolfe arrived on 7 May 1935 in Berlin, where he was lionized as a great new American writer. He lived luxuriously in Germany, spending the royalties that he had been prohibited from taking out of the country. His German publisher, Ernst Rowohlt, arranged for newspaper interviews, magazine articles, photos, and invitations to parties. Wolfe recorded his impressions of the visit in his notebook.

Thursday-Friday night, May 16–17:

(Written in room in Hotel Am Zoo in Berlin–I have made no notations in this book of any sort for almost two weeks and this must be here annotated briefly and expanded from memory since coming in Hanover.)

Hanover, Sunday evening and night, May 5, 1935–

Arrived Hanover about 6:40–went to Kasten's Hotel–got room–rested a little–Borrowed 10 marks Hotel porter–went out on street and had drinks in open gardens Kröpcke's great café–back to hotel for dinner–so to Wiener Café for drinks and music–later for walk–so home to hotel and bed.

Hanover, Monday, May 6, 1935–

Rose late–went to Garten of Kröpcke's Café–fine, flashing, sunny day of shell-fragile blue–went to Kröpcke's Garden for drinks–many people there including some good looking women–then to Knickmeyer's for lunch–huge, oaken Germanic, Bürgerbräu place with heavy Wotans–food to match–great ships' models hanging from ceiling–young aviators, special table, and the waiters' obsequious haste to serve them–then to Dresdner bank for registered marks–where man with bulge on neck and bandages cashed–then for Grieben's Guide (did this before bank because bookseller told me where bank was)–and after leaving bookseller and bank and going back to hotel discovered that my Grieben's for Hanover had got mixed up with Breslau one and was half Breslau–I took it back to bookseller, a pleasant, blonde, middle-aged man, and pointed out the error. He looked intently for a moment, then burst into hearty laughter–"Just a moment please–I will get you another–but hah! hah! hah! hah! hah!–you must excuse me for laughing, but it is so *comical:*–Hah! Hah! Hah! Hah! Hah!–You come in and ask for a guide of Hanover, and when you open it up–Hah! Hah! Hah! Hah! Hah!–you must excuse me, but it's veyr comical–you find you have a guide for Breslau! – Just a moment, sir, I will get you another"–He took the faulty guide and went into another room where he could be heard still chuckling to himself–In a minute or so he returned with the proper guide, and giving it to me, said: "Excuse me for laughing, sir–but when I think what the expression of your face must have been–how you must have looked–When you opened the Hanover guide and found Breslau–hah! hah! hah! hah! hah!–you must excuse me, but it is very comical!"–so left him–he with a pleasant smile, a kindly auf Wiedersehen–and I with the kindly feeling these people give me–and so to study and guide and then for a walk through town according to the guide–and again the old quarter of an old German town that haunts the soul of man with Gothic magic–the incredible design and facades of old houses, warped and leaned together like old crones, and yet still wondrous.

In the Knochenhauer Strasse a sign said Herrenhausen bier–and Frederick Wolfe proprietor–so in I went to see my 197th cousin on the job, and a filthier damned hole I never saw before or since–I opened a door–and was immediately greeted by such a slough of filth and fetid odors, and stupid and corrupted faces that my heart recoiled, then braving in I went–a narrow, dark, and filthy room with a bar at one end and some tables along the wall–an old man all hair and eyes and yellowed whiskers of the kind one sometime sees in New York shambling along the streets and picking up God knows what and dropping it into the cavernous bags of their rags–well, he was sitting at one of the tables slobbing up some mess out of a plate into his whiskers–various other people, men and women, sat around with mugs of beer, and at the door, just as I entered, a toothless, drunken, and most foully besotted hag I ever saw–she reminded me of such-like hags you used to see in moving pictures of *Les Miserables* or *The Two Orphans*–except, by God, this was no moving picture–was seated there at the door with a man who wore a working man's cap–she looked up at me with a humble, toothless, leer and muttered something, all the other people stopped talking, eating and drinking, and stared at me with a look of stupid astonishment and mistrust–which was so strong and palpable in fact that I halted there in the door and stammered something about "Bier–Bier bitte–I should like a glass of beer"–turning finally to the man who was sitting with the hag–he looked at me sullenly and stupidly, wrinkling his inch of brow in painful and suspicious perplexity–and his eyes as he looked at me just got horribly sooty, all of a sudden with the most stupid, bestial glance I have ever seen–and suddenly I thought of France *and* Germany and how wars are made–"Was?" he said, harshly and stupidly, still staring at me with his sooty, sullen look–"Was?"–I muttered my little piece about bier again, and he sat there just looking at me, his eyes getting rottener all the time–"Bier," I said more loudly, "Bier"–"Ach–*bier!*"–Someone now cried with an air of sudden enlightenment, "Its bier he wants"–"Ja, Ja."–I stumbled between the tables away from soot-eye–that horrible, toothless hag who had now begun to leer and grimace at me horribly–and sat down at a table next to the bar [*breaks off*]

. . . .

Wed. Morning, 5 A.M., May 22 (?), 1935:

Written in room in Hotel Am Zoo–Have just returned from American Embassy–beautiful green purity of Tiergarten at 4 o'clock in the morning–incredibly early light here in Berlin–incredibly lovely flowers and flower-beds in Tiergarten and ponds of dark green lovely water–So picked up taxi on Tiergarten Strasse finally–the splendid, luxurious houses facing the Tiergarten with their great lawns and gardens around them–a wagon approaching with swift-trotting horse–same the whole world over–a man on bicycle, etc.–and the beauty, purity and stillness of an incredible lovely May morning–So by taxi through Hitzig Strasse passing Bill [*William E., Jr., son of the ambassador*] Dodd's parked car–Bill and Dela locked in embrace inside–across bridge across canal and down towards Gedächtnis Kirche and around it into Kurfürstendamm–the great cafés, restaurants, konditorei, etc. closed–a couple of whores standing rather forlornly in front of [*sketch*] tall, cylindrical cigarette or chocolate turret–so paid taxi 1 m + 25 pf. (tip) and so in and to bed–buying orange and apple, and telling old man not to send telephone calls up before 11 o'clock (since newspaper articles appeared day before yesterday–have had no peace)–Martha is to call me at 11 and we will go to Weimar if she does not change mind.

Last night (Tuesday) Herr Hitler's speech to Reichstag–Martha met me at Schlichter's restaurant at 3:30–we left about 5:30–went to Amexco–got there too late–went to Hotel Adlon where I got shave and had hair slicked down–then drinks with Martha–and so home just in time to hear Herr Hitler's speech over radio–he spoke 2 hours 20 minutes–radio broke down upstairs and we went downstairs to servants' quarters where all of them were sitting around drinking it in–(Remember noting solid magnificence of house–even in porter's quarters–and the green trees of yards outside fading into last light)–Then radio fixed upstairs and so went up again–Martha and I finally ate at mother's urging while Der Fuehrer talked and filled all rooms with voice–Bill came in and helped translate parts of speech–then Bill left to go to Taverne–then Mr. Dodd returned almost immediately after speech ended and his homely, dry, and pungent remarks about the way the Jap looked "the Englishman," the "Frenchman," etc., and what he said to the "Dutchman" etc. was very homely, plain, and amusing–Also what he said to "the Dutchman" on their way out–"Good speech–but not entirely historical," etc.–and Mrs. D–"Was the Englishman [*Sir Eric Phipps*] there?"–"Yes, he was there"–"How'd he seem to like it?" etc.–wonderfully plain, practical, and amusing–Then Mr. and Mrs. Dodd upstairs to bed–Martha and I talking and quarreling, and I was just leaving when Bill arrived with Dela–he asked me to come up for drink–so up again–and Martha and I friends again–and so together rest of time until I came home while ago.

Have been in Berlin two weeks last night–and this is first time I've been able to make an entry in this book since I got here–A wild, fantastic, incredible whirl of parties, teas, dinners, all night drinking bouts, newspaper interviews, radio proposals, photographers, etc.–and dozens of people chief among them Martha and the Dodds, Rowohlt, Ledig, Lisa [*Hasait*], Mrs. Harnack, Carlla, Elinora, Dela [*Behren*], the Feuers, Grunen Zweig, etc.–May never do it again but it was interesting and worth seeing, and people told me startling things–must reconstruct from memory–viz: –[*breaks off*]

Three weeks ago I had an experience that can not happen to me often now. It was my experience again to enter for the first time one of the great capital cities of the world. This time the city was–Berlin [*breaks off*]

–*The Notebooks of Thomas Wolfe,* pp. 744–748

Wolfe in summer 1935 at the University of Colorado, Boulder, where he gave a lecture that contributed to his writing The Story of a Novel *(The Thomas Wolfe Collection, Pack Memorial Public Library, Asheville, North Carolina)*

At the Writers' Conference Wolfe was interviewed for the Rocky Mountain News.

People who go to Paris or Italy to do a little writing are only trying to get away from themselves and their own laziness. The place to write is in Boulder or Greeley or Denver or Timbuctoo, or wherever you happen to live.

–*Thomas Wolfe Interviewed,* p. 34

A First Tour of the West

After returning to the United States, Wolfe toured the West in August and September 1935. He participated in the annual Writers' Conference at the University of Colorado from 22 July to 9 August 1935.

On this western trip he wrote to Perkins about a new idea for a fictional project that he at first called "The Book of the Night." Wolfe published a section as "A Prologue to America" in Vogue *(February 1938) but left the project unfinished at his death.*

The Riverside Hotel letterhead, Reno, Nevada
Reno,
Thurs, Sept 12,
1935

Dear Max: I am a little worried about something, and if you see fit, won't you take steps about it right away? It is this–at various times during the last month–at Boulder and elsewhere–I have discoursed very eloquently and persuasively about my book of the night which is beginning to interest me more and more all the time. I have told how much of my life has been lived by night, about the chemistry of darkness, the strange and magic thing it does to our lives, about America at night–the rivers, plains, mountains, rivers in the moon or darkness (last night by the way coming up here through the Sierra Nevadas there was blazing moonlight, the effect was incredibly beautiful)–and how the Americans are a night-time people, which I have found out everywhere is absolutely true–Now, I'm afraid I've talked too much–please don't think I'm fool enough to think anyone is going to, or can, "steal my ideas"–but people have been immensely and instantly absorbed when I told about my book–and have at once agreed to the utter truth of it.–I have got hold of an immense, rich, and absolutely true thing about ourselves–at once very simple, profound, and various–and I know a great and original book–unlike any other, can be written in it–and I dont want some fool to get hold of it and write some cheap and worthless thing–the idea is so beautiful and simple that some bungler could easily mutilate it.

Wolfe at Great Salt Lake, Salt Lake City, Utah, September 1935. Fern Dalby, whom Wolfe had met the month before at the Writers' Conference at Boulder, Colorado, took the photos. When Wolfe saw these photographs, he remarked, "Ah, the Colossus of Rhodes!" (The Thomas Wolfe Collection, Pack Memorial Public Library, Asheville, North Carolina)

It will be years before I do it–but it keeps gathering in me all the time–I don't know yet exactly what form it will take–or whether it can be called a "novel" or not–I don't care–but I think it will be a great tone-symphony of night–railway yards, engines, freights, dynamos, bridges, men and women, the wilderness, plains, rivers, deserts, a clopping hoof, etc.–seen not by a definite personality,–but haunted throughout by a consciousness of personality–In other words, I want to assert my divine right once and for all to be the God Almighty of a book–to be at once the spirit to move it, the spirit behind it, never to appear, to blast forever the charge of "autobiography" while being triumphantly and impersonally autobiographical–Can't you do this, if you think best, and something tells me that it may be best?:–Make an announcement to this effect–that I have for years been interested in the life of night (not nightclubs) and have been slowly acquiring an immense amount of material about it, that the book is slowly taking form, but will not be ready for years when these other books are out of the way, and that it is at present called The Book Of The Night. You might put in something about Saturday Night in America (when I get back I'll tell you about Longmont, Colorado on Saturday night–I've told you before what Saturday night does to us here in America and one part of the book has to do with this)–at any rate, Max, I've talked to other people about it, and since this is one of the most precious and valuable ideas I've ever had–do what you can to protect it for me now–Why can't we do this–you could even say that I am so interested in the book that I am now at work on it, and that it may appear before the other books of the Of Time and the River series come out–this would do no harm, would arouse interest and discussion, and might serve the purpose of throwing some of my various Mrs B's off the track for the present–

–*To Loot My Life Clean,* pp. 170–171

Wolfe was interviewed when he returned east via St. Louis and visited the house where his brother Grover had died.

Thomas Wolfe Visits City–
Says He'll Write a 'Really Great' Book
Reed Hynds
St. Louis Star Times, 20 September 1935

Author of Best-Seller Now Busy Putting on Paper Life
He Observes–'Technique Can Come Later'

Thomas Wolfe, whose novel "Of Time and the River" has been on the best-seller lists for months and has been held by many to be the most significant work of fiction to be published this year, stopped over for a day and a night here this week on his return to New York from the west.

While in St. Louis the author visited the house near Cates and Academy avenues in which he lived during the "World's Fair" here. Wolfe remembered the house very well, although he had not seen it since he was 3 years old and the name of the avenue had been changed, without his knowledge, from Fairmount to Cates.

He related that he spoke to the woman now living in the house, and in a moment of forgetfulness pointed out that his brother had died in that room "right there." Later he was so ashamed for having startled her, he said, that he did not wish to reveal the exact address.

An "Idle" Summer

Wolfe reported he had practically wasted the summer "loafing around." The only work he had done, he said, was "a piddling 100,000 or 200,000 words of notes." His last novel ran to something like 450,000 words. His remark was made with the utmost candor, and anyone who had heard him make it would have sworn he was filled with remorse over being so lazy.

It would take Wolfe himself to describe himself adequately. Six feet six inches "or maybe a little more" in height; broad at the shoulders and rotund at the waist, he is an astonishingly big fellow. To talk with him while he stands beside one is decidedly uncomfortable, he dwarfs his companion so completely.

It is not, however, his size that is most impressive about him. It is the fact that he is continually in what writers term a fine frenzy. He is so intensely alive; so curious about everything; so keenly aware, as to make those about him seem pallid and phlegmatic.

He seems uncomfortable if he is not talking when in the presence of others. Words stream from him as though he were impatient of having to use them to transmit his thought. He stutters a bit in the urgency to say a lot quickly.

Almost anyone else who talked so much would be thought a boor. Yet Wolfe never seems to be monopolizing the conversation. His simplest statement strikes the hearer as being a profound personal revelation.

Likes People and Life

Despite his dominating presence, and the deference that is paid him, he never speaks in a didactic manner. He makes no pretensions to great wisdom. He is simply without inhibitions. He likes people and he likes living: he feels a desperate need to express those likings, and it happens that his expression of them is vivid and stimulating.

While he was a guest at the home of J. Lesser Goldman, Oak Knoll, Clayton, Wolfe leaned forward on a small bench in the midst of a dozen or so persons and made all these traits manifest. In shirt-sleeves; his bulky trousers upheld by galluses which could safely be used to tie up a fair-sized yawl; his black hair roached back but resisting the process; his rather Indian-like features sharp and his face never at rest, Wolfe talked of writing.

"I know I don't know anything about writing," he said. "I'm bewildered. But I'm going to know how to write before I get through. My father was a stonecutter, and a darned good one. That was his trade. I'm going to be as good at my trade as he was at his.

"I'm not worrying about technique now. I'm of the opinion that I have a pretty prodigious talent, but I'm not concerned yet with developing a finished aesthetic. There are too many things that I want to get down on paper. I want to put down everything I've observed about life. Technique can come later.

Report Life Accurately

"It seems to me that a novelist's first business is to report life accurately. I haven't much patience with the writers who become wonderful craftsmen but never have anything to say.

"For the first time in my life I've gotten some celebrity and a bit of money. It would be silly to say I don't enjoy it. I like it so much that I'm going to work all the harder, and get more money and more celebrity.

"I'm in love with America and I think it's important to portray Americans–how they feel when a freight train goes by, and all the rest. There is such a thing as a distinctively American culture. It's a coat of many colors, but still it's a coat. It's not simply an amalgam of European traditions."

Wolfe remarked that he had become "suspicious of those birds–reporters," since his return from abroad a few months ago. "I gave them a long spiel on the future of American writing," he said, "and all they used in their short stories was a trifling little anecdote I had told them."

Berated by Women

The anecdote had to do with Wolfe's inability to ruffle–with strong drink–the composure of an English servant. Wolfe said he was rather nettled by the ensuing crop of letters, particularly from women of the middle west, applauding the servant and berating him for his "filthy" book.

"Whatever else 'Of Time and the River' is," said Wolfe, "it is certainly not filth."

The 34-year-old author said that since critics had complained that the novel was autobiographical, readers had outdone themselves remembering exactly when and where certain events in the book had actually taken place. "Episodes which were wholly imaginary," he said, "have actually gotten me into trouble through people thinking they remembered them."

"I'm aware," he added, "that the autobiographical element has been overworked in my works, and that all the really great books have been highly original. I'll write a really great, highly original book some day."

Enthusiastic About West

When he does, it is certain to be American to the core. He is enthusiastic about every section of the country. He was especially enthusiastic about the west, which he had not seen before his recent trip, that is, all of it "except–possibly–Hollywood."

Originally from North Carolina; student at Harvard; resident of Brooklyn for five years, Wolfe had found that all Americans were "real people–like North Carolinians," and all very specially American, "with the possible exception of sophisticated society in New York."

For the most part, Wolfe illustrates in his person the qualities of his prose–its soaring, leaping, untrammeled aliveness; its lushness of imagery and phrase; its prolixity and formlessness, and excitement and continual wonder. There is, however, a difference. There is no apparent flair for comedy in Wolfe the author. It was, therefore, a surprise to find him, in person, always aware of the comical aspect of things.

He told a great many anecdotes, but one may be singled out. He had been afraid to meet Dorothy Parker–"she was supposed to be so poisonous you know"–and upon meeting her he related, he told her he was frightened, having heard of her making such scathing remarks. With a naivete equal to Wolfe's own, she replied, very earnestly and very innocently: "They do say the most AWFUL things about me, Mr. Wolfe."

Reviews of *From Death To Morning*

On 24 November 1935 Charles Scribner's Sons published Wolfe's collection of short stories From Death to Morning. *Wolfe wrote to Henry T. Volkening, a friend he made during his years as a teacher at New York University, after he read Ferner Nuhn's review for* New York Herald Tribune Books.

New York City
November 13, 1935

Dear Henry:

I'm a little sad as I write you this. I've just read the first review of this book–in next Saturday's *Herald Tribune*–which pans it and sees little in it except a man six foot six creating monstrous figures in a world of five feet eight. I do not think this is true, but now I have a hunch the well-known "reaction" has set in against me, and that I will take a pounding on this book. Well, I am writing you this because I believe that as good writing as I have ever done is in this book and because my faith has always been that a good thing is indestructible and that if there is good here–as I hope and believe there is–it will somehow survive. That is a faith I want to have, and that I think we need in life, and that is why I am writing you this–not in defense against attacks I may receive but just to put this on record *in advance* with you, who are a friend of mine. So won't you put this away–what I have written–and keep it–and if someday it turns out I am right, won't you take it out and read it to me?

–*The Letters of Thomas Wolfe,* pp. 493–494

* * *

Wolfe wrote of his difficulty settling down to work in a 30 October 1935 letter to Harry Woodburn Chase, former president of the University of North Carolina and chancellor of New York University, who had sent him a poem about the New York school.

I am sorry to say that I am not working twenty-four hours a day as I feel I should be, but I hope to get started soon. I had a wonderful vacation of more than six months which took me all the way from Denmark to San Francisco, and I am back here now, ready to work and desperately eager to get at it, but somehow I find it terribly hard to break through my own inertia and get started. I wonder why people are like that. No one knows better than I that I must work, and that my life is nothing without work, and yet I do everything in the world to avoid it–that is, before I get started. . . .

–*The Letters of Thomas Wolfe,* pp. 492–493

$2.50

FROM
DEATH
TO
MORNING

These stories reveal in Mr. Wolfe qualities as a writer unsuspected by the thousands who have read his longer works. They show what perfection he can achieve within a restricted compass — especially noticeable in some of the five and six page stories here included, which for economy and precision of style are unsurpassed. Here Mr. Wolfe recreates a world as perfectly as on the vast canvas of his novels. For all its varying moods of humor or profound perception, "From Death to Morning" has a unity and a progress, as suggested in the title, which raise it far above the average story collection.

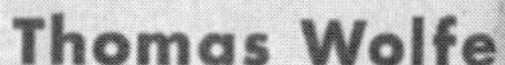

"The most prodigious book of 1935 was 'Of Time and the River' by Thomas Wolfe, who can best be characterized by being called the Walt Whitman of novelists, impassioned and magnificent" — *Carl Van Doren in The N. Y. Herald Tribune.*

"A triumphant demonstration that Thomas Wolfe has the stamina to produce a magnificent epic of American life." Peter Monro Jack in The N. Y. Times

Of Time and the River

By

Thomas Wolfe

author of "From Death to Morning" and "Look Homeward, Angel"

"The least that can be said about Thomas Wolfe is that he is one of the most extraordinary phenomena in modern literature and of his novel that the reading of it must surely be an unforgettable experience. . . Mr. Wolfe is genuinely extending the boundaries of the novel."
London Times Literary Supplement

"He has more material, more vitality, more originality, more gusto than any two contemporary British novelists put together. . . And he entirely escapes the sordid, whining defeatism of so many of his American contemporaries."
Henry Seidel Canby in The Saturday Review

"The story of the travels, sensations and ideas of Eugene Gant is told in such glowing prose that one reads for the very joy of reading. . . Thomas Wolfe is a phenomenon out of step with his generation, which is crawling on its bellies. Once one seizes and apprehends the scale on which he writes, his book becomes an adventure not to be missed."
Harry Hansen in Harper's Magazine

"We have a voice in this novel which sounds as if it were from demons, gods and seraphim — in chorus — and, strangely, a voice speaking of intimate and common things. . . A hundred stories and five years of life, richly experienced, deeply felt, minutely and lyrically recorded."
Burton Rascoe in The N. Y. Herald Tribune

CHARLES SCRIBNER'S SONS, NEW YORK

Dust jacket for Wolfe's collection of stories, which sold 5,392 copies during its first year in print

Wolfe at the Scribner office library in 1935 (photograph by Jerome Zerbe; The North Carolina Collection, University of North Carolina Library at Chapel Hill)

Wolfe's first short-story collection received disappointing reviews. Nuhn's review was one of several that disheartened the author.

Thomas Wolfe, Six-Foot-Six
Ferner Nuhn
New York Herald Tribune Books, 17 November 1935

"Some day some one will write a book about a man who was too tall–"writes Thomas Wolfe, beginning a story about a man–"who lived forever in a dimension that he did not fit, and for whom the proportions of everything–chairs, doors, rooms, clothes, shirts and socks, the berths of Pullman cars, and the bunks of trans-Atlantic steamers, together with the rations of food, drink, love, and women, which most men on this earth have found sufficient to their measure–were too small."

The story that follows, called "Gulliver," tells how the world looks from six feet six, and what six feet six has to suffer in the way of endless and unoriginal humor from a five-foot-eight world. ("How's the weather up there? . . . Ho-lee Jeez! What's de guy standin' on" Etc.) The story does not get much further than that.

But in a wider sense almost everything Thomas Wolfe writes is the story of a six-foot-six man in a five-foot-eight world. The extra exuberance, the unsatisfied longings, the oversized reactions to change, motion, scenes, events (and ships!), the outcries of loneliness, the floods of words poured forth to convey these emotions, the piling of Mississippi on top of Niagara–all this seems to proceed from the extra ten inches of body and appetite that can't be accommodated in the ordinary world.

The fourteen stories in the present volume are for the most part further experiences of an oversized organism in a standard-sized world. Few may be called short stories in any strict sense; lyrical essays, themes with variations, moods of reminiscence, they might perhaps be called.

Thus "No Door" describes the gap between exalted loneliness and ordinary modes of existence; "Death the Proud Brother" is in praise of the great leveler, with four examples of how he touches with dignity the little men he overtakes on city streets;

"The Face of the War" gives four episodes showing the sadism, hysteria, lust and crude humor of war's violation of ordinary human standards. All these and most of the other stories are oriented to the personality of the author and pitched on the plane of his heightened sensibilities.

Of particular interest, then, are the few stories which are more objective in method. One of these, "The Far and the Near," may be dismissed as a romantic "idea" for a story, and nothing more. Another, however, "In the Park," strikes a distinctive note as it pictures, about the turn of the century, a ride through Central Park in one of the first automobiles. With its well-drawn characters and sympathetic evocation of the time, it has something of the genre quality of a Currier & Ives print.

Most original in conception is a story called "The Four Lost Men." Were there actually four men named Garfield, Arthur, Harrison and Hayes? With a sort of furious affirmation, the author tries to fill in the blanks of their composite and bewhiskered legend, insisting that Garfield-Arthur-Harrison-Hayes *must* actually have lived, even if they left no evidence of the fact.

Potentially the strongest story is "The Web of Earth," a long retrospective narrative, crowded with episodes, whose underlying theme seems to contrast the homemaking stability of women with the lust, violence and wandering spirit of men. But the thread is often lost in extraneous incidents and confusing details.

The advantages of an oversized view of the world are obvious in Thomas Wolfe's work: the heightened color, mood, sweep, rush which can so easily carry lesser organisms along. But there are disadvantages, too. The bulge of an excess of emotion is as flabby in the end as the slack of an insufficient one. Readers swept off their feet have a way of picking themselves up and rejecting further rides, and this would be a pity.

There is point to the remark of the weary European traveler in "Dark in the Forest" when he said to the eager young American, "Fields, hills, mountains, riffers, cities, peoples–you vish to know zem all. Vun field, vun hill, vun riffer," the man whispered, "zat is enough." Better channeled, Thomas Wolfe's undoubted powers might carve out more solidly the shapes of the "big themes" he feels so intensely but which are too often left hollow, and the praise he has been given be protected from excessive reaction.

American Incantation

TLS, 21 March 1936

Mr. Wolfe has been widely recognized as one of the most important of younger American writers, and his work is certainly of a quality which demands attention. His two long novels, themselves only fragments of a much larger scheme, have, however, a formidability, in both size and substance, which must have deterred many readers from settling to them with the seriousness and patience which they deserve. This volume of his short stories may, therefore, be the more warmly welcomed, if with some reservations; for the bulk at least of these fourteen tales is characteristic and displays his abiding qualities not perhaps at their fullest flight–none who has read his novels would expect that–but in their barer essentiality.

Half the pieces, it might be objected, are scarcely stories at all, but more in the nature of meditations upon themes starting from relevant incidents, and despite the apparent objectivity of "The Far and the Near" and "The Bums at Sunset"–both short and clearly etched–and one or two others, it must be said that Mr. Wolfe is not a story-teller in the sense of one who dexterously invents imaginary persons and situations. His most constant subjects are the elemental human experiences and earth memories–"proud Death, and his stern brother, Loneliness, and their great sister, Sleep," man's brutality and compassion, love and betrayal, aspiration and despair. But even of these he writes most vividly as he comes closest to what is clearly his own knowledge, when he thrusts his characters wholly aside and, himself possessed by "all the brutal struggle, pain, and ugliness of life, the fury, hunger, and the wandering," strives to cry aloud the "wild intolerable longing" within himself that he "cannot utter." Cannot, of course, in the sense that total expression can never be achieved; but none can deny the power and richness of statement evoked by his tireless gusto, his desire "to eat up everything upon the breakfast table," on one side, and on the other his almost palpable sensitiveness. There is, at his best, something of incantation in his descriptive, exhortatory passages, recreating not only sights and smells but a whole emotional attitude to all that he has known and felt in teeming, seething American living and in his own being.

No one story in this collection is so characteristic as "The Four Lost Men," in which, recalling his father's words about four figures of the past, he identifies himself with them:–

Drawing of Wolfe by Georges Schreiber for Portraits and Self-Portraits, *where "Something of My Life" first appeared*

> Had they not, as we, then turned their eyes up and seen the huge starred visage of the night, the immense and lilac darkness of America in April? Had they not heard the sudden, shrill, and piping whistle of a departing engine? Had they not waited, thinking, feeling, seeing then the immense mysterious continent of night, the wild and lyric earth, so casual, sweet, and strange-familiar, in all its space and savagery and terror, its mystery and joy, its limitless sweep and rudeness, its delicate and savage fecundity? Had they not the visions of the plains, the mountains, and the rivers flowing in the darkness, the huge pattern of the everlasting earth and the all-engulfing wilderness of America?

Admittedly such writing must either succeed or fail completely. It is either magnificent or nonsense. In our view it is often the one; the depth of feeling behind saves it from ever becoming the other. To read these stories steadily through is a moving experience, though they vary widely in quality. "The Face of the War" and "The Men of Old Catawba" stand beside "The Four Lost Men" for merit, even if they, too, are scarcely stories. Three or four are definitely inferior and these unfortunately include the longest, a rather dreary episode from the Gant-Pentland saga.

Wolfe wrote the following sketch in 1935 for Portraits and Self-Portraits. *Because of space considerations, about half of Wolfe's words were excised in 1936 when the book was published. The full version of the sketch below is notable for its apologetic tone.*

Something of My Life
Thomas Wolfe
Saturday Review of Literature, 7 February 1948.

I suppose the biographical facts about birth, home-town, colleges and so on, are available to the editors of this book, so I shall not bother to give them here. Since almost all the knowledge the world has of me, concerns me as a writer, perhaps it will be better if I try to tell something of the life.

I am thirty-five years old, and although I have written more millions of words than I should like to count–how many I don't know, but perhaps as many as anyone else my age now writing–I have published not more than a tenth of them. Nevertheless, the critics say I write too much–and I don't say that they are wrong. Although I suppose the desire to be a writer has been buried in me for a long time–certainly the itch for it has been there, because I began to scribble when I was not more than fourteen years old, I never dared admit to myself that I might seriously proclaim my intentions until I was about twenty-six.

Before that, I had written a few plays and although I had hoped they might find a producer, I don't think that even then, I had sufficient confidence in my abilities to announce definitely to my family that I actually intended to be a playwright and to hope to earn my living that way. I didn't succeed, anyway. And it was not until the twenty-sixth year that I began to write a book, which occupied me for the next two or three years. During this time I was employed at the Washington Square college of the New York University as an instructor in English. I don't think that even then did I concretely and reasonably assure myself that I had found my life's direction in the work that I intended to do from that time on. I certainly did dream of finding a publisher and a public for the book, but it was really a kind of dream–a kind of intoxicating illusion which sustained me during the period of creation. I suppose I can say honestly that I wrote the book because I had to write it and after it was written and I saw the tremendous bulk of it in the cold grey light of sober actuality, I had the most serious misgivings and wondered what on earth had ever possessed me to make me spend two or three years of my life in creating such a huge leviathan or what moment of mad unreason had deluded me into thinking that I could possibly find a publisher and readers for it. My own dejected doubt was speedily confirmed by the first publisher who read the manuscript, who sent it back very speedily, with a very brief note to the effect that it was too long, too autobiographical, too amateurish and too like other books which he had published and lost money on, for him to risk a chance. This seemed to summarize and confirm my own most depressed feelings, now that the book was written and in this frame of mind I went to Europe and almost forgot about the book.

Within six months, however, another publisher had read the manuscript and accepted it. I returned to America, taught at the University and worked on the revision of the book which was published in October, 1929, a few weeks after my twenty-ninth birthday.

So far as "early struggles" are concerned, my experience has been a fortunate one. The first book I ever wrote, and a very long one, too, was accepted and published by one of the first publishers who read it, and I understand that this is an extraordinary occurrence. I have had my struggles, however, and pretty desperate ones too, but most of them, so far as writing is concerned, have been of my own making. I have to struggle all the time against indolence–perhaps it would be more accurate to say against an insatiable and constantly growing interest in the life around me, my desire to get out and explore it with an encyclopedic thoroughness, my desire to travel and make voyages and see places, things, and people I have never known. I like companionship, food and drink, going to baseball games, and having a good time. I must also struggle constantly against self-doubt–lack of confidence in what I do and the many difficulties I encounter in doing it. My knowledge of the craft and technique of my profession is still very imperfect. I believe and hope that I learn something about it and about my own capacity as a writer all the time, but I learn very slowly and at the cost of almost infinite error, waste, and confusion. I do much too much of everything; I write millions of words in the course of shaping out and defining a volume of a few hundred thousand. It seems to be an element of my creative faculty that it has to realize itself through the process of torrential production, and although I hope to be able to control and guide this force as I go on, so that I will be able to achieve my work with more and more clearness and precision and economy, without such a waste of effort, time, and material, I think that the way I work will always remain in its essence pretty much as I have tried to describe it and that it will have to come out of me in this way.

I come from a class and section of American life which regarded writing–the profession of a writer–as something very mysterious and romantic and very remote from its own life and the world of its own knowledge and experience. For this reason, as I have said, it was twenty-six years or more before I even dared to admit concretely that I might become a writer and I was almost thirty before my own admission was concretely affirmed by publication. For this reason, perhaps, and for others–which I tried to mention–a kind of tremendous inertia in me and the tendency of human kind to put off and evade for as long as possible the thing it knows it has to do, the work it cannot avoid and without which its life is nothing–and a strong sense of direction and often a very confused sense of purpose. For all these reasons my development, I think, has been a slow one. And yet it has sometimes seemed to me that in all these apparent handicaps, there may have been certain advantages, too. The belief that I may be by nature somewhat indolent and the knowledge that I may allow a ravenous curiosity for life and new experience to come between the work I ought to be doing–and the fact that as hard and grim as work itself may be, not only the intensity of effort and concentration required, but the period of spiritual imprisonment that work necessitates–the very knowledge that once a piece of work has been begun, a man's whole life must be absorbed and obsessed by it day and night until he finishes it–all of these things, together with a certain goad of conscience, have driven me to face the fact of work, to try to meet it squarely and to do it as hard as I can once I am started on it. It has been said of much that I have written thus far that it was autobiographical. I cannot answer such a very debatable and complicated word in the short space that is allotted here and I shall not attempt to. I can only say that it seems to me that every creative act is in one way or another–autobiographical.

The kind of naked directness with which the young man writing his first book is likely to make use of his material, but as I have said, much of the trouble and misunderstanding may have come from the fact that I have not yet succeeded in being autobiographical enough, instead of the fact that I was, as many people say, too autobiographical. At any rate, as I go on, my tendency I believe is to make use of the materials of living experience with an ever increasing freedom of the inventiveness and the plastic powers of the imagination.

As far as the experience of work itself is concerned, I have found that so far from isolating one from contacts with reality and a living experience with the world around one, it enhances and enriches one's perceptions enormously. In fact, it seems to me that the core of an artist's life is his work, and his deepest knowledge, his greatest power, his profoundest social feelings come through the work he does as a great current of electricity pulses and surges through a dynamo. I suppose it is true that a man at twenty is likely to have an egocentric picture of the universe, is concerned with life very largely as it reflects and acts upon his own personality. And I suppose also that this concentration on his own immediate experience and interest is likely to show itself in his earlier work. But so far as my own experience is concerned, I believe that as one grows older, he becomes a great deal more interested in the life around him in terms of itself. His interests, and the adventures and experiences of his own personality, become valuable to him more in terms of their relation to the experience of all mankind. And his social feeling, his whole understanding and sympathy with the lives of people and with the whole human experience, becomes enormously enriched and deepened as a result of this. That, I hope, has begun to happen to me. At any rate, I am working.

–*The Enigma of Thomas Wolfe,* pp. 3–7

Wolfe in the doorway of his sister Mabel's house on Kimberley Avenue, Asheville, 1937 (The Thomas Wolfe Collection, Pack Memorial Public Library, Asheville, North Carolina)

Chapter 5

The Story of a Novel and the Break with Scribners, 1936–1937

Wolfe resented what he regarded as Maxwell Perkins's premature decision to publish Of Time and the River *before the novel had been revised, and tensions between the two men increased thereafter as Perkins seemed to Wolfe to be too often discouraging. Wolfe worked on the continuation of a six-volume series announced in 1935 when* Of Time and the River *was published. He began "The Vision of Spangler's Paul" and a book about nighttime in America, "The Hound of Darkness." Much of this work was posthumously published in* The Web and the Rock, You Can't Go Home Again, *and* The Hills Beyond.

Although another major creative cycle had begun, Bernard DeVoto's essay, "Genius Is Not Enough," in The Saturday Review of Literature *altered the remaining years of Wolfe's life. DeVoto claimed that Wolfe was immature as a novelist and charged that he could not publish a novel without Perkins's help. DeVoto's criticism contributed to Wolfe's decision to leave Perkins and Scribners in order to prove he could complete his books without anyone's help.*

The Story of a Serialized Essay

The Story of a Novel, *first serialized in* The Saturday Review of Literature, *was published as a book by Scribners on 21 April 1936. Wolfe based the essay on an unused preface he had written for* Of Time and the River *and on a lecture he had given at the Colorado Writers' Conference on 6 August 1935.*

In the following excerpts Wolfe describes his coming to the realization that the book he wanted to write was much larger than any conventional novel could be and how Perkins was able to help him gain control of his material.

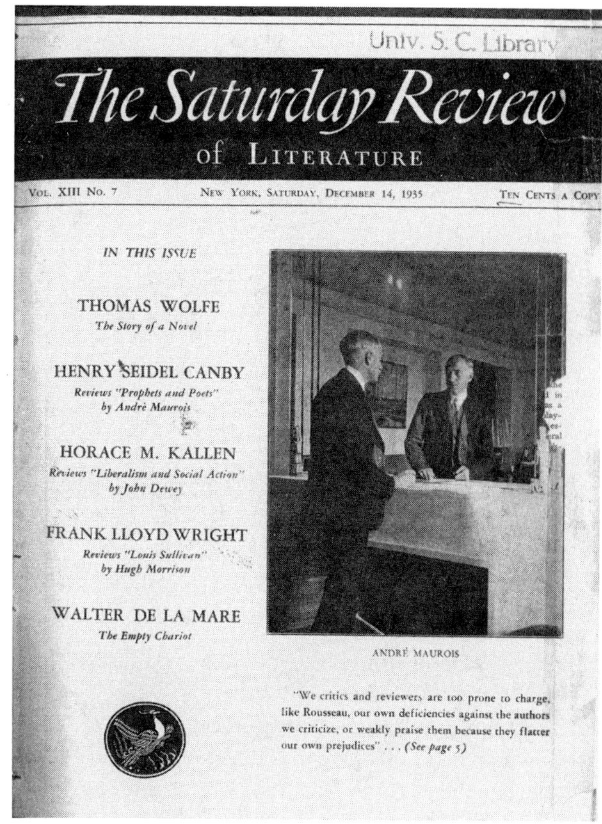

The Saturday Review of Literature

Vol. XIII No. 7 | New York, Saturday, December 14, 1935 | Ten Cents a Copy

IN THIS ISSUE

THOMAS WOLFE
The Story of a Novel

HENRY SEIDEL CANBY
Reviews "Prophets and Poets" by André Maurois

HORACE M. KALLEN
Reviews "Liberalism and Social Action" by John Dewey

FRANK LLOYD WRIGHT
Reviews "Louis Sullivan" by Hugh Morrison

WALTER DE LA MARE
The Empty Chariot

ANDRÉ MAUROIS

"We critics and reviewers are too prone to charge, like Rousseau, our own deficiencies against the authors we criticize, or weakly praise them because they flatter our own prejudices" . . . *(See page 5)*

Cover of magazine that published the first part of Wolfe's essay detailing his struggle to complete Of Time and the River. The Story of a Novel *was serialized in three issues (14, 21, and 28 December 1935).*

When I returned to America in the spring of 1931, although I had three or four hundred thousand words of material, I had nothing that could be published as a novel. Almost a year and a half had elapsed since the publication of my first book and already people had begun to ask that question which is so well meant, but which as year followed year was to become more intolerable to my ears than the most deliberate

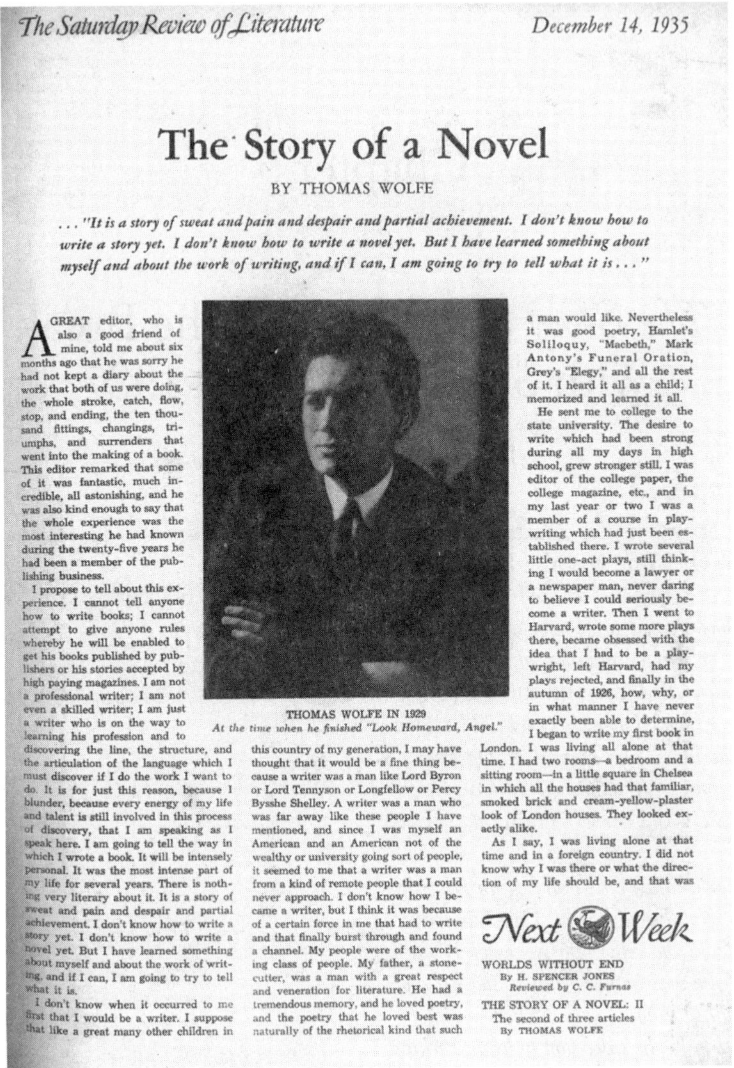

The Saturday Review of Literature December 14, 1935

The Story of a Novel

BY THOMAS WOLFE

. . . "It is a story of sweat and pain and despair and partial achievement. I don't know how to write a story yet. I don't know how to write a novel yet. But I have learned something about myself and about the work of writing, and if I can, I am going to try to tell what it is . . . "

A GREAT editor, who is also a good friend of mine, told me about six months ago that he was sorry he had not kept a diary about the work that both of us were doing, the whole stroke, catch, flow, stop, and ending, the ten thousand fittings, changings, triumphs, and surrenders that went into the making of a book. This editor remarked that some of it was fantastic, much incredible, all astonishing, and he was also kind enough to say that the whole experience was the most interesting he had known during the twenty-five years he had been a member of the publishing business.

I propose to tell about this experience. I cannot tell anyone how to write books; I cannot attempt to give anyone rules whereby he will be enabled to get his books published by publishers or his stories accepted by high paying magazines. I am not a professional writer; I am not even a skilled writer; I am just a writer who is on the way to learning his profession and to discovering the line, the structure, and the articulation of the language which I must discover if I do the work I want to do. It is for just this reason, because I blunder, because every energy of my life and talent is still involved in this process of discovery, that I am speaking as I speak here. I am going to tell the way in which I wrote a book. It will be intensely personal. It was the most intense part of my life for several years. There is nothing very literary about it. It is a story of sweat and pain and despair and partial achievement. I don't know how to write a story yet. I don't know how to write a novel yet. But I have learned something about myself and about the work of writing, and if I can, I am going to try to tell what it is.

I don't know when it occurred to me first that I would be a writer. I suppose that like a great many other children in this country of my generation, I may have thought that it would be a fine thing because a writer was a man like Lord Byron or Lord Tennyson or Longfellow or Percy Bysshe Shelley. A writer was a man who was far away like these people I have mentioned, and since I was myself an American and an American not of the wealthy or university going sort of people, it seemed to me that a writer was a man from a kind of remote people that I could never approach. I don't know how I became a writer, but I think it was because of a certain force in me that had to write and that finally burst through and found a channel. My people were of the working class of people. My father, a stonecutter, was a man with a great respect and veneration for literature. He had a tremendous memory, and he loved poetry, and the poetry that he loved best was naturally of the rhetorical kind that such a man would like. Nevertheless it was good poetry, Hamlet's Soliloquy, "Macbeth," Mark Antony's Funeral Oration, Grey's "Elegy," and all the rest of it. I heard it all as a child; I memorized and learned it all.

He sent me to college to the state university. The desire to write which had been strong during all my days in high school, grew stronger still. I was editor of the college paper, the college magazine, etc., and in my last year or two I was a member of a course in playwriting which had just been established there. I wrote several little one-act plays, still thinking I would become a lawyer or a newspaper man, never daring to believe I could seriously become a writer. Then I went to Harvard, wrote some more plays there, became obsessed with the idea that I had to be a playwright, left Harvard, had my plays rejected, and finally in the autumn of 1926, how, why, or in what manner I have never exactly been able to determine, I began to write my first book in London. I was living all alone at that time. I had two rooms—a bedroom and a sitting room—in a little square in Chelsea in which all the houses had that familiar, smoked brick and cream-yellow-plaster look of London houses. They looked exactly alike.

As I say, I was living alone at that time and in a foreign country. I did not know why I was there or what the direction of my life should be, and that was

THOMAS WOLFE IN 1929
At the time when he finished "Look Homeward, Angel."

Next Week

WORLDS WITHOUT END
By H. SPENCER JONES
Reviewed by C. C. Furnas

THE STORY OF A NOVEL: II
The second of three articles
By THOMAS WOLFE

First page of Wolfe's essay in The Saturday Review of Literature

mockery: "Have you finished your next book yet?" "When is it going to be published?"

At this time I was sure that a few months of steady work would bring the book to completion. I found a place, a little basement flat in the Assyrian quarter in South Brooklyn, and there I went about my task.

The spring passed into the summer; the summer, into autumn. I was working hard, day after day, and still nothing that had the unity and design of a single work appeared. October came and with it a second full year since the publication of my first book. And now, for the first time, I was irrevocably committed so far as the publication of my book was concerned. I began to feel the sensation of pressure, and of naked desperation, which was to become almost maddeningly intolerable in the next three years. For the first time I began to realize that my project was much larger than I thought it would be. I had still believed at the time of my return from Europe that I was writing a single book, which would be comprised within the limits of about 200,000 words. Now as scene followed scene, as character after character came into being, as my understanding of my material became more comprehensive, I discovered that it would be impossible to write the book I had planned within the limits I had thought would be sufficient.

. . . .

It was not until more than a year had passed, when I realized finally that what I had to deal with was material which covered almost 150 years in history, demanded the action of more than 2000 characters, and would in its final design include almost every racial type and social class of American life, that I realized that even the pages of a book of 200,000 words were wholly inadequate for the purpose.

just for what it's worth: I
think I may be the only young
writer of the South in my
generation who has written
about the life he knew there
with the kind of naked intensity
I have attempted to describe,
and for that reason, I believe,
I could no longer live at home.
I have read in recent years that
I am compelled to "live in exile"

Page of manuscript for The Story of a Novel *(William B. Wisdom Collection, Houghton Library, Harvard University)*

Memorandum of Agreement, *made this* fifteenth *day of* January 1936
between THOMAS WOLFE
of New York City, N.Y., - - - - *hereinafter called "the* AUTHOR,"
and CHARLES SCRIBNER'S SONS, *of New York City, N. Y., hereinafter called "the* PUBLISHERS." *Said* - - Thomas Wolfe - - - *being the* AUTHOR *and* PROPRIETOR *of a work entitled:*

THE STORY OF A NOVEL

in consideration of the covenants and stipulations hereinafter contained, and agreed to be performed by the PUBLISHERS, *grants and guarantees to said* PUBLISHERS *and their successors the exclusive right to publish the said work in all forms* in the United States and Canada *during the terms of copyright and renewals thereof, hereby covenanting with said* PUBLISHERS *that he is the sole* AUTHOR *and* PROPRIETOR *of said work.*

Said AUTHOR *hereby authorizes said* PUBLISHERS *to take out the copyright on said work, and further guarantees to said* PUBLISHERS *that the said work is in no way whatever a violation of any copyright belonging to any other party, and that it contains nothing of a scandalous or libelous character; and that he and* his *legal representatives shall and will hold harmless the said* PUBLISHERS *from all suits, and all manner of claims and proceedings which may be taken on the ground that said work is such violation or contains anything scandalous or libelous; and he further hereby authorizes said* PUBLISHERS *to defend at law any and all suits and proceedings which may be taken or had against them for infringement of any other copyright or for libel, scandal, or any other injurious or hurtful matter or thing contained in or alleged or claimed to be contained in or caused by said work, and pay to said* PUBLISHERS *such reasonable costs, disbursements, expenses, and counsel fees as they may incur in such defense.*

Said PUBLISHERS, *in consideration of the right herein granted and of the guarantees aforesaid, agree to publish said work at their own expense, in such style and manner as they shall deem most expedient, and to pay said* AUTHOR, *or* - his - *legal representatives,* TEN (10) ------------------------ *per cent. on their Trade-List (retail) price, cloth style, for* the first three thousand(3000)copies of said work sold by them, TWELVE & ONE-HALF (12½)per cent.for all copies sold thereafter up to seventy-five hundred (7500), and FIFTEEN (15) per cent. for all copies sold thereafter, - - - - - - *Provided, nevertheless, that one-half the above named royalty shall be paid on all copies sold outside the United States; and provided that no percentage whatever shall be paid on any copies destroyed by fire or water, or sold at or below cost, or given away for the purpose of aiding the sale of said work.*

It is further agreed that the terms of any publication of said work, during the period covered by this agreement, in other than book form shall be subject to mutual arrangement between said PUBLISHERS *and said* AUTHOR.

Contract for The Story of a Novel. *This agreement stipulated a reduced royalty because Scribners intended to put a low price on the thin book. (William B. Wisdom Collection, Houghton Library, Harvard University)*

Expenses incurred for alterations in type or plates, exceeding twenty per cent. of the cost of composition and electrotyping said work, are to be charged to the AUTHOR'S *account.*

The first statement shall not be rendered until six months after date of publication; and thereafter statements shall be rendered semi-annually, on the AUTHOR'S *application therefor, in the months of February and August; settlements to be made in cash, four months after date of statement.*

If, on the expiration of five *years from date of publication, or at any time thereafter, the demand for said work should not, in the opinion of said* PUBLISHERS, *be sufficient to render its publication profitable, then, upon written notice by said* PUBLISHERS *to said* AUTHOR, *this contract shall cease and determine; and thereupon said* AUTHOR *shall have the right, at* his *option, to take from said* PUBLISHERS, *at cost, whatever copies of said work they may then have on hand; or, failing to take said copies at cost, then said* PUBLISHERS *shall have the right to dispose of the copies on hand as they may see fit, free from any percentage or royalty, and to cancel this contract.*

Provided, also, that if, at any time during the continuance of this agreement, said work shall become unsalable in the ordinary channels of trade, said PUBLISHERS *shall have the right to dispose of any copies on hand, paying to said* AUTHOR - fifteen (15) - *per cent. of the net amount received therefor, in lieu of the percentage hereinbefore prescribed.*

All other rights not covered by this contract, such as moving-picture, talking-picture, television, radio and all dramatic rights, are reserved by said Author.

In consideration of the mutuality of this contract, the aforesaid parties agree to all its provisions, and in testimony thereof affix their signatures and seals.

itness to signature of
Thomas Wolfe

Maxwell E. Perkins

Thomas Wolfe

itness to signature of
Charles Scribner's Sons

R. S. Watson

Charles Scribner's Sons [L. S.]
Charles Scribner
President

How did I finally arrive at this conclusion? I think it is not too much to say that I simply wrote myself into it. During all that year, I was writing furiously, feeling now the full pressure of inexorable time, the need to finish something. I wrote like mad; I finished scene after scene, chapter after chapter. The characters began to come to life, to grow and multiply until they were numbered by the hundreds, but so huge was the extent of my design, as I now desperately realized, that I can liken these chapters only to a row of lights which one sometimes sees at night from the windows of a speeding train, strung out across the dark and lonely countryside.

I would work furiously day after day until my creative energies were utterly exhausted, and although at the end of such a period I would have written perhaps as much as 200,000 words, enough in itself to make a very long book, I would realize with a feeling of horrible despair that what I had completed was only one small section of a single book. . . .

During this time I reached that state of naked need and utter isolation which every artist has got to meet and conquer if he is to survive at all. Before this I had been sustained by that delightful illusion of success which we all have when we dream about the books we are going to write instead of actually doing them. Now I was face to face with it, and suddenly I realized that I had committed my life and my integrity so irrevocably to this struggle that I must conquer now or be destroyed. I was alone with my own work, and now I knew that I had to be alone with it, that no one could help me with it now no matter how any one might wish to help. For the first time I realized another naked fact which every artist must know, and that is that in a man's work there are contained not only the seeds of life, but the seeds of death, and that that power of creation which sustains us will also destroy us like a leprosy if we let it rot stillborn in our vitals. I had to get it out of me somehow. I saw that now. And now for the first time a terrible doubt began to creep into my mind that I might not live long enough to get it out of me, that I had created a labor so large and so impossible that the energy of a dozen lifetimes would not suffice for its accomplishment.

During this time, however, I was sustained by one piece of inestimable good fortune. I had for a friend a man of immense and patient wisdom and a gentle but unyielding fortitude. I think that if I was not destroyed at this time by the sense of hopelessness which these gigantic labors had awakened in me, it was largely because of the courage and patience of this man. I did not give in because he would not let me give in, and I think it is also true that at this particular time he had the advantage of being in the position of a skilled observer at a battle. I was myself engaged in that battle, covered by its dust and sweat and exhausted by its struggle, and I understood far less clearly than my friend the nature and the progress of the struggle in which I was engaged. At this time there was little that this man could do except observe, and in one way or another keep me at my task, and in many quiet and marvelous ways he succeeded in doing this.

I was not at the place where I must produce, and even the greatest editor can do little for a writer until he has brought from the secret darkness of his own spirit into the common light of day the completed concrete accomplishment of his imagining. My friend, the editor, has likened his own function at this painful time to that of a man who is trying to hang on to the fin of a plunging whale, but hang on he did, and it is to his tenacity that I owe my final release.

. . . .

In the middle of December of that year [1933] the editor, of whom I have spoken, and who, during all this tormented period, had kept a quiet watch upon me, called me to his home and calmly informed me that my book was finished. I could only look at him with stunned surprise, and finally I only could tell him out of the depth of my own hopelessness, that he was mistaken, that the book was not finished, that it could never be completed, that I could write no more. He answered with the same quiet finality that the book was finished whether I knew it or not, and then he told me to go to my room and spend the next week in collecting in its proper order the manuscript which had accumulated during the last two years.

I followed his instructions, still without hope and without belief. I worked for six days sitting in the middle of the floor surrounded by mountainous stacks of typed manuscript on every side. At the end of a week I had the first part of it together, and just two days before Christmas, 1933, I delivered to him the manuscript of "The October Fair," and a few days later, the manuscript of "The Hills Beyond Pentland." The manuscript of "The Fair" was, at that time, something over 1,000,000 words in length. He had seen most of it in its dismembered fragments during the three preceding years, but now, for the first time, he was seeing it in its sequential order, and once again his intuition was right; he had told me the truth when he said that I had finished the book.

It was not finished in any way that was publishable or readable. It was really not a book so much as it was the skeleton of a book, but for the first time in four years the skeleton was all there. An enormous labor of revision, weaving together, shaping, and, above all, cutting remained, but I had the book now so that nothing, not even the despair of my own spirit, could take it from me. He told me so, and suddenly I saw that he was right.

I was like a man who is drowning and who suddenly, at the last gasp of his dying effort, feels earth beneath his feet again. My spirit was borne upward by the greatest triumph it had ever known, and although my

Dust jacket for Wolfe's third book, published 21 August 1936 (courtesy of Special Collections, Thomas Cooper Library, University of South Carolina)

mind was tired, my body exhausted, from that moment on I felt equal to anything on earth.

It was evident that many problems were before us, but now we had the thing, and we welcomed the labor before us with happy confidence. In the first place there was the problem of the book's gigantic length. Even in this skeletonized form the manuscript of "The October Fair" was about twelve times the length of the average novel or twice the length of *War and Peace*. It was manifest, therefore, that it would not only be utterly impossible to publish such a manuscript in a single volume, but that even if it were published in several volumes, the tremendous length of such a manuscript would practically annihilate its chances of ever finding a public which would read it.

This problem now faced us, and the editor grappled with it immediately. As his examination of the manuscript of "The October Fair" proceeded, he found that the book did describe two complete and separate cycles. The first of these was a movement which described the period of wandering and hunger in a man's youth. The second cycle described the period of greater certitude, and was dominated by the unity of a single passion. It was obvious, therefore, that what we had in the two cyclic movements of this book was really the material of two completely different chronicles, and although the second of the two was by far the more finished, the first cycle, of course, was the one which logically we ought to complete and publish first, and we decided on this course.

We took the first part first. I immediately prepared a minutely thorough synopsis which described not only the course of the book from first to last, but which also included an analysis of those chapters which had been completed in their entirety, of those which were completed only in part, and of those which had not been written at all, and with this synopsis before us, we set to work immediately to prepare the book for press. This work occupied me throughout the whole of the year 1934. The book was completed at the beginning of 1935, and was published in March of that year under the title of *Of Time and the River*.

–*The Story of a Novel*, pp. 49–51, 53–57, and 73–78

Bernard DeVoto in a photo that appeared with his review of The Story of a Novel *in* The Saturday Review of Literature

Wolfe was bitter about Scribners handling of The Story of a Novel. *He explained his complaint regarding the royalty arrangement for the book in a 21 April 1936 letter to Perkins. Although Perkins offered to comply with Wolfe's wishes, Wolfe then decided to drop the matter.*

What I am arguing about is this,–that I agreed to accept a reduced royalty upon the basis of a dollar or dollar and a quarter book–and the reason that I agreed to accept the reduction was because it was presented to me that the cost of making the book was such that it would be difficult for the publisher to give a higher royalty and have him come out clear. Then after agreeing to this reduced royalty, upon my understanding that the book would be published at a dollar and a quarter, and having signed a contract accepting the reduced royalty, I find that the price of the book, without my knowledge, has been raised to $1.50, and is being published at that price. When I discussed that fact about a week ago, when I got my own advance copy, I told you that in view of the increase in price, I thought you ought to restore my former royalty of 15%. I still think that you ought to do so and have told you so repeatedly, and you feel you ought not to do so, and have refused to do so.

–*To Loot My Life Clean,* p. 179

Bernard DeVoto's review of The Story of a Novel, *in which he called Perkins "the critical intelligence" behind Wolfe's work, introduced new tensions into the relationship between Wolfe and his editor. Later in the year Wolfe decided to leave Perkins and "the assembly line at Scribner's" in order to prove he could write his books without anyone's help.*

Bernard DeVoto
"Genius Is Not Enough"
Saturday Review of Literature,
13 (25 April 1936): 3–4, 14–15

Some months ago *The Saturday Review* serialized Mr. Thomas Wolfe's account of the conception, gestation, and as yet uncompleted delivery of his Novel, and Scribners are now publishing the three articles as a book. It is one of the most appealing books of our time. No one who reads it can doubt Mr. Wolfe's complete dedication to his job or regard with anything but respect his attempt to describe the dark and nameless fury of the million-footed life swarming in his dark and unknown soul. So honest or so exhaustive an effort at self-analysis in the interest of esthetics has seldom been made in the history of American literature, and "The Story of a Novel" is likely to have a long life as a source-book for students of literature and for psychologists as well. But also it brings into the public domain material that has been hitherto outside the privilege of criticism. Our first essay must be to examine it in relation to Mr. Wolfe's novels, to see what continuities and determinants it may reveal, and to inquire into their bearing on the art of fiction.

Let us begin with one of many aspects of Mr. Wolfe's novels that impress the reader, the frequent recurrence of material to which one must apply the adjective placental. (The birth metaphors are imposed by Mr. Wolfe himself. In "The Story of a Novel" he finds himself big with first a thunder cloud and then a river. The symbolism of waters is obviously important to him, and the title of his latest novel is to be that of the series as a whole.) A great part of "Look Homeward, Angel" was just the routine first novel of the period, which many novelists had published and many others had suppressed, the story of a sensitive and rebellious adolescent who was headed toward the writing of novels. The rest of it was not so easily catalogued. Parts of it showed intuition, understanding, and ecstasy, and an ability to realize all three in character and scene, whose equal it would have been hard to point out anywhere in the fiction of the time. These looked like great talent, and in such passages as the lunchroom scene in the dawn that Mr. Wolfe called nacreous some fifty times, they seemed to exist on both a higher and a deeper level of realization than any of Mr. Wolfe's contemporaries had attained.

But also there were parts that looked very dubious indeed–long, whirling discharges of words, unabsorbed in the novel, unrelated to the proper business of fiction, badly if not altogether unacceptably written, raw gobs of emotion, aimless and quite meaningless jabber, claptrap, belches, grunts, and Tarzanlike screams. Their rawness, their unshaped quality, must be insisted upon; it was as if the birth of the novel had been accompanied by a lot of the material that had nourished its gestation. The material which nature and most novelists discard when its use has been served. It looked like one of two things, there was no telling which. It looked like the self-consciously literary posturing of a novelist too young and too naive to have learned his trade. Or, from another point or view, it looked like a document in psychic disintegation. And one of the most important questions in contemporary literature was: would the proportion of fiction to placenta increase or decrease in Mr. Wolfe's next book?

It decreased. If fiction of the quality of that lunchroom scene made up about one-fifth of "Look Homeward, Angel," it constituted, in "Of Time and the River," hardly more than a tenth. The placental material had enormously grown and, what was even more ominous, it now had a rationalization. It was as unshaped as before, but it had now been retroactively associated with the dark and nameless heaving of the voiceless and unknown womb of Time, and with the unknown and voiceless fury of the dark and lonely and lost America. There were still passages where Mr. Wolfe was a novelist not only better than most of his contemporaries but altogether out of their class. But they were pushed farther apart and even diluted when they occurred by this dark substances which may have been nameless but was certainly far from voiceless.

Certain other aspects of the new book seemed revealing. For one thing, there was a shocking contempt of the medium. Some passages were not completely translated from the "I" in which they had apparently been written to the "he" of Eugene Gant. Other passages alluded to incidents which had probably appeared in an earlier draft but could not be found in the final one. Others contradictorily reported scenes which had already appeared, and at least once a passage that had seen service already was re-enlisted for a second hitch in a quite different context, apparently with no recollection that it had been used before.

Again, a state of mind that had been appropriate to the puberty of Eugene seemed inappropriate as the boy grew older, and might therefore be significant. I mean the giantism of the characters. Eugene himself, in "Of Time and the River," was clearly a borderline manic-depressive: he exhibited the classic cycle in his alternation between "fury" and "despair," and the classic accompaniment of obsessional neurosis in the compulsions he was under to read all the books in the world, see all the people in Boston, observe all the lives of the man-swarm, and list all the names and places in America. That was simple enough, but practically every other character in the book also suffered from fury and compulsions; and, what was more suggestive, they were all twenty feet tall, spoke with the voice of trumpets and the thunder, ate like Pantagruel, wept like Niobe, laughed like Falstaff, and bellowed like the bulls of Bashan. The significant thing was that we were seeing them all through Eugene's eyes. To a child all adults are giants: their voices are thunderous, their actions are portentous and grotesquely magnified, and all their exhibited emotions are seismic. It looked as if part of Eugene's condition was an infantile regression.

This appearance was reinforced by what seemed to be another stigma of infantilism: that all the experiences in "Of Time and the River" were on the same level and had the same value. When Mr. Gant died (of enough cancer to have exterminated an army corps), the reader accepted the accompanying frenzy as proper to the death of a man's father–which is one of the most important events in anyone's life. But when the same frenzy accompanied nearly everything else in the book–a ride on a railroad train, a literary tea-fight, a midnight lunch in the kitchen, a quarrel between friends, a walk at night, the rejection of a play, an automobile trip, a seduction that misfired, the discovery of Eugene's true love–one could only decide that something was dreadfully wrong. If the death of one's father comes out emotionally even with a ham-on-rye, then the art of fiction is cockeyed.

Well, "The Story of a Novel" puts an end to speculation and supplies some unexpected but very welcome light. To think of these matters as contempt of the medium, regression, and infantilism is to be too complex and subtle. The truth shows up in two much simpler facts: that Mr. Wolfe is still astonishingly immature, and that he has mastered neither the psychic material out of which a novel is made nor the technique of writing fiction. He does not seem aware of the first fact, but he acknowledges the second with a frankness and an understanding that are the finest promise to date for his future books. How far either defect is reparable it is idle to speculate. But at least Mr. Wolfe realizes that he is, as yet, by no means a complete novelist.

The most flagrant evidence of his incompleteness is the fact that, so far, one indispensable part of the artist has existed not in Mr. Wolfe but in Maxwell Perkins. Such organizing faculty and such critical intelligence as have been applied to the book have come not from inside the artist, not from the artist's feeling for form and esthetic integrity, but from the office of Charles Scribner's Sons. For five years the artist pours out words "like burning lava from a volcano"–with little or no idea what their purpose is, which book they belong in, what the relation of part to part is, what is organic and what irrelevant, or what emphasis or coloration in the completed work of art is being served by the job at hand. Then Mr. Perkins decides these questions–from without, and by a process to which rumor applies the word "assembly." But works of art cannot be assembled like a carburetor–they must be grown like a plant, or in Mr. Wolfe's favorite simile, like an embryo. The artist writes a hundred thousand words about a train: Mr. Perkins decides that the train is worth only five thousand words. But such a decision as this is properly not within Mr. Perkins's power; it must be made by the highly conscious self-criticism of the artist in relation to the pulse of the book itself. Worse still, the artist goes on writing till Mr. Perkins tells him that the novel is finished. But the end of a novel is, properly, dictated by the internal pressure, osmosis, metabolism–what you will–of the novel itself, of which only the novelist can have a first-hand knowledge. There comes a point where the necessities of the book are satisfied, where its organic processes have reached completion. It is hard to see how awareness of that point can manifest itself at an editor's desk–and harder still to trust the integrity of a work of art in which not the artist but the publisher has determined where the true ends and the false begins.

All this is made more ominous by Mr. Wolfe's almost incredibly youthful attitude toward revision. No novel is written till it is revised–the process is organic, it is one of the processes of art. It is, furthermore, the process above all others that requires objectivity, a feeling for form, a knowledge of what the necessities of the book are, a determination that those necessities shall outweigh and dominate everything else. It is, if not the highest functioning of the artistic intelligence, at least a fundamental and culminating one. But the process appears to Mr. Wolfe not one which will free his book from falsity, irrelevance, and its private incumbrances [*sic*], not one which will justify and so exalt the artist–but one that makes his spirit quiver "at the bloody execution" and his soul "recoil from the carnage of so many lovely things." But superfluous and mistaken things are lovely to only a very young writer, and the excision of them is bloody carnage only if the artist has not learned to subdue his ego in favor of his book. And the same juvenility makes him prowl "the streets of Paris like a maddened animal" because–for God's sake!–the reviewers may not like the job.

The placental passages are now explained. They consist of psychic material which the novelist has proved unable to shape into fiction. The failure may be due either to immature understanding or to insufficient technical skill; probably both causes operate here and cannot be separated. The principle is very simple. When Mr. Wolfe gives us his doctors, undertakers, and newspapermen talking in a lunchroom at dawn, he does his job–magnificently. There they are, and the reader revels in the dynamic presentation of human beings, and in something else as well that should have the greatest possible significance for Mr. Wolfe. For while the doctors and undertakers are chaffing one another, the reader gets that feeling of the glamour and mystery of American life which Mr. Wolfe elsewhere unsuccessfully labors to evoke in thousands of rhapsodic words. The novelist makes his point in the lives of his characters, not in tidal surges of rhetoric.

Is America lost, lonely, nameless, and unknown? Maybe, and maybe not. But if it is the condition of the novelist's medium requires him to make it lost and lonely in the lives of his characters, not in blank verse, bombast, and apocalyptic delirium. You cannot represent America by hurling adjectives at it. Do "the rats of death and age and dark oblivion feed forever at the roots of sleep?" It sounds like a high school valedictory, but if in fact they do then the novelist is constrained to show them feeding so by means of what his characters do and say and feel in relation to one another, and not by chasing the ghosts of Whitman and Ezekiel through fifty pages of disembodied emotion. Such emotion is certainly the material that fiction works with, but until it is embodied in character and scene it is not fiction–it is only logorrhea. A poem should not mean but be, Mr. MacLeish tells us, and poetry is always proving that fundamental. In a homelier aphorism Mr. Cohan has expressed the same imperative of the drama: "Don't tell 'em, show 'em." In the art of fiction the *thing* is not only an imperative, it is a primary condition. A novel *is*–it cannot be asserted, ranted, or even detonated. A novelist represents life. When he does anything else, no matter how beautiful or furious or ecstatic the way in which he does it, he is not writing fiction. Mr. Wolfe can write fiction–has written some of the finest fiction of our day. But a great part of what he writes is not fiction at all: it is only material with which the novelist has struggled but which has defeated him. The most important question in American fiction today, probably, is whether he can win that encounter in his next book. It may be that "The October Fair" and "The Hills Beyond Pentland" will show him winning it, but one remembers the dilution from "Look Homeward, Angel" to "Of Time and the River" and is apprehensive. If he does win it, he must do so inside himself; Mr. Perkins and the assembly line at Scribners can do nothing to help him.

That struggle has another aspect. A novelist utilizes the mechanism of fantasy for the creation of a novel, and there are three kinds of fantasy with which he works. One of them is unconscious fantasy, about which Dr. Kubie was writing in these columns something over a year ago. A novelist is wholly subject to its emphases and can do nothing whatever about them–though when Mr. Wolfe says that the center of all living is reconciliation with one's father he comes close to revealing its pattern in him. There remain two kinds of fantasy which every novelist employs–but which every one employs in a different ratio. Call them identification and projection, call them automatic and directed, call them proliferating and objectified–the names do not matter. The novelist surrenders himself to the first kind, but dominates and directs the second kind. In the first kind he says "I am Napoleon" and examines himself to see how he feels. In the second kind, he wonders how Napoleon feels, and instead of identifying himself with him, he tries to discover Napoleon's necessities. If he is excessively endowed with the first kind of fantasy, he is likely to be a genius. But if he learns to utilize the second kind in the manifold interrelationships of a novel he is certain to be an artist. Whatever Mr. Wolfe's future in the wider and looser interest of Literature, his future in the far more rigorous interest of fiction just about comes down to the question of whether he can increase his facility at the second kind of fantasy. People would stop idiotically calling him autobiographical, if he gave us less identification and more understanding. And we could do with a lot less genius, if we got a little more artist.

For the truth is that Mr. Wolfe is presented to us, and to himself, as a genius. There is no more dissent from that judgment in his thinking about himself than in Scribner's publicity. And, what is more, a genius of the good old-fashioned, romantic kind–possessed by a demon, driven by the gales of his own fury, helpless before the lava-flood of his own passion, selected and set apart for greatness, his lips touched by a live coal, consequently unable to exercise any control over what he does and in fact likely to be damaged or diminished by any effort at control. Chaos is everything, if you have enough of it in you to make a world. Yes, but what if you don't make a world–what if you just make a noise? There was chaos in Stephen Dedalus's soul, but he thought of that soul not as sufficient in itself but merely as a smithy wherein he might forge his novel. And listen to Mr. Thomas Mann:

> When I think of the masterpiece of the twentieth century, I have an idea of something that differs essentially and, in my opinion, with profit from the Wagnerian masterpiece–something exceptionally logical, clear, and well developed in form, something at once austere and serene, with no less intensity of will than his, but of cooler, nobler, even healthier spirituality, something that seeks its greatness not in the colossal, the baroque, and its beauty not in intoxication.

Something, in other words, with inescapable form, something which exists as the imposition of order on chaos, something that *is*, not is merely asserted.

One can only respect Mr. Wolfe for his determination to realize himself on the highest level and to be satisfied with nothing short of greatness. But, however useful genius may be in the writing of novels, it is not enough in itself–it never has been enough, in any art, and it never will be. At the very least it must be supported by an ability to impart shape to material, simple competence in the use of tools. Until Mr. Wolfe develops more craftsmanship, he will not be the important novelist he is now widely accepted as being. In order to be a great novelist he must also mature his emotions till he can see more profoundly into character than he now does, and he must learn to put a corset on his prose. Once more: his own smithy is the only possible place for these developments–they cannot occur in the office of any editor whom he will ever know.

Initially Wolfe kept his reaction to DeVoto's critical attack in check, as in his letter to Julian Meade, who had protested against DeVoto's review to both Wolfe and to Henry Seidel Canby, editor of The Saturday Review of Literature. *Meade wrote "Thomas Wolfe on the Use of Fact in Fiction," which was published in* The New York Herald Tribune Books *on 14 April 1935.*

865 First Avenue
New York, N.Y.
May 4, 1936

Dear Meade:

Thanks for your letter. It was very generous of you to feel the way you did about the *Saturday Review* piece and to register such a vigorous protest. I was over at the Canbys' for dinner last night and of course, made no reference to the article but finally Mr. Canby himself brought it up. I think your letter had made quite an impression. He didn't mention your name but said he had got a pretty vigorous letter a few days ago denouncing the article and asking why a man's book should be reviewed by his enemies and so on. So I figured it was your letter he was talking about. I told him that personally I had no hard feelings and that although I read every scrap that was written about me in the way of a review or criticism, provided I saw it, and still took the whole thing very much to heart, it didn't bother me quite as much as it once did. I added that

I had my living to earn, and that the only way I have of earning it is through what I write, and that if a reviewer says I am no good, it's just too bad for me and perhaps occasionally for him, but that nevertheless, I was going to keep right on writing. This was all I said, and then got off the subject.

I think really my only objection to the *Saturday Review* piece was that it didn't review the book. It seems to me that it was hardly a review at all, but rather a kind of general denunciation of all my deficiencies as a writer, some of which, of course, I am prepared to admit and have done so already. I don't think a writer has any right to dictate to the editors of a literary review who shall review his book or what form the review should take, but I do think he has a right to expect a *review* of his book, whether hostile or favorable, rather than a mass assault on every other book he has ever done. And as I understand the remarks of our *Saturday Review* friend, he said at the beginning that the book he was reviewing was a good book. I think he called it one of the most appealing books of our generation–ahem, ahem, here he cleared his throat, low growls began to rumble from his diaphragm, smoke began to issue from his nostrils and he surged forward to the attack–an attack which by the way, an author has no chance of defending himself against unless he resorts to what seems to me the very unwise and ineffectual practice of writing a letter in reply, which of course gives the other fellow a chance to write a letter in reply to this, and so on, I suppose, ad infinitum, save that the man who has been attacked in this way and who answers in this way, is always in the undefended position, controls none of the means of publication and must yield to the attacker the privilege of delivering the final volley. Is it worth it?

And in this case at least, it seems to me that it doesn't matter enough. I do think this, and I suppose this is the most sensible way of looking at these matters in the end: I think you will find, if you have not found out already, that one of the pleasantest occupations of a great many people in this world is to shoot down a whole regiment of wooden soldiers, and then return triumphant from the wars, saying, "we have met the enemy and they are ours." This kind of warrior does exist. It is very comforting of course, to create a straw figure of your enemy and then shoot it full of holes, but it is not a very substantial victory and in the long run means nothing.

–*The Letters of Thomas Wolfe,* pp. 509–510

"The Vision of Spangler's Paul"

In spring 1936 Wolfe began assembling notes for "The Vision of Spangler's Paul," a novel about an author, Paul Spangler, who had achieved success with his controversial first novel, "Home to Our Mountains." Wolfe's plan to write about the people and workings of James Rodney and Company, a publishing house clearly modeled after Charles Scribner's Sons, alarmed Maxwell Perkins, who feared that his colleagues would by hurt by Wolfe's revelations. Parts of this abandoned novel were incorporated into The Web and the Rock *and* You Can't Go Home Again.

Wolfe's notes for the novel, in which Mrs. Feitlebaum is the alias for Aline Bernstein, suggests the autobiographical basis of his material.

MR. SPANGLER YEAR BY YEAR

1904:–Back from St. Louis with mother–Lyerly's porch, the sputtering corner lights, the Vance St. corner.

1905:–

1906:–Orange St. School: the fall of Revell's house, Mr. Revell borne by on shutter, a sheet, blood–Hosley and Moule's Book Store–Mr. Owenby.

1907–

1914: The Hogwart Heights Military Academy.

1920–25–Cousin Ellen, Cousin Bert; Beefsteak Charlie's (late at night); the School for Useful Cultures.

1925–1929–Mrs. Feitlebaum.

1929–31: First Glory–(Day at Rodney's)

1931–35 Brooklyn: The Whittakers; "This is Ha-a-riet"; Steve's Coffee Pot; Still Vex'd Bermoothes; Wind from the West.

1935–36: Fame (1½ years)–(Girl in Hanover; Berlin, the Ambassador's Daughter; The Magic Rock (Wartburg) Copenhagen; Return to Glory (4th July); the Great West; Fame Exploding in the City (Oct.-June–1936).

–*The Notebooks of Thomas Wolfe,* p. 805

Wolfe wrote on 10 June 1936 to Heinz Ledig, an editor at his German publisher, Rowohlt Verlag, to discuss his royalties and plans for future publication:

I do think that, in fairness to myself, as time goes on I ought to try to be a little more business-like. I am not a money-making kind of man; I have no idea how to make a deliberate popular appeal to the writing public; I am really trying to get something out of myself as well as I can and, as time goes on, I hope to do better work, work of which I can be proud and I can feel represents the best and finest use of my talent. Feeling this way, it is not very likely that I will ever become a huge popular success.

–*The Letters of Thomas Wolfe,* p. 525

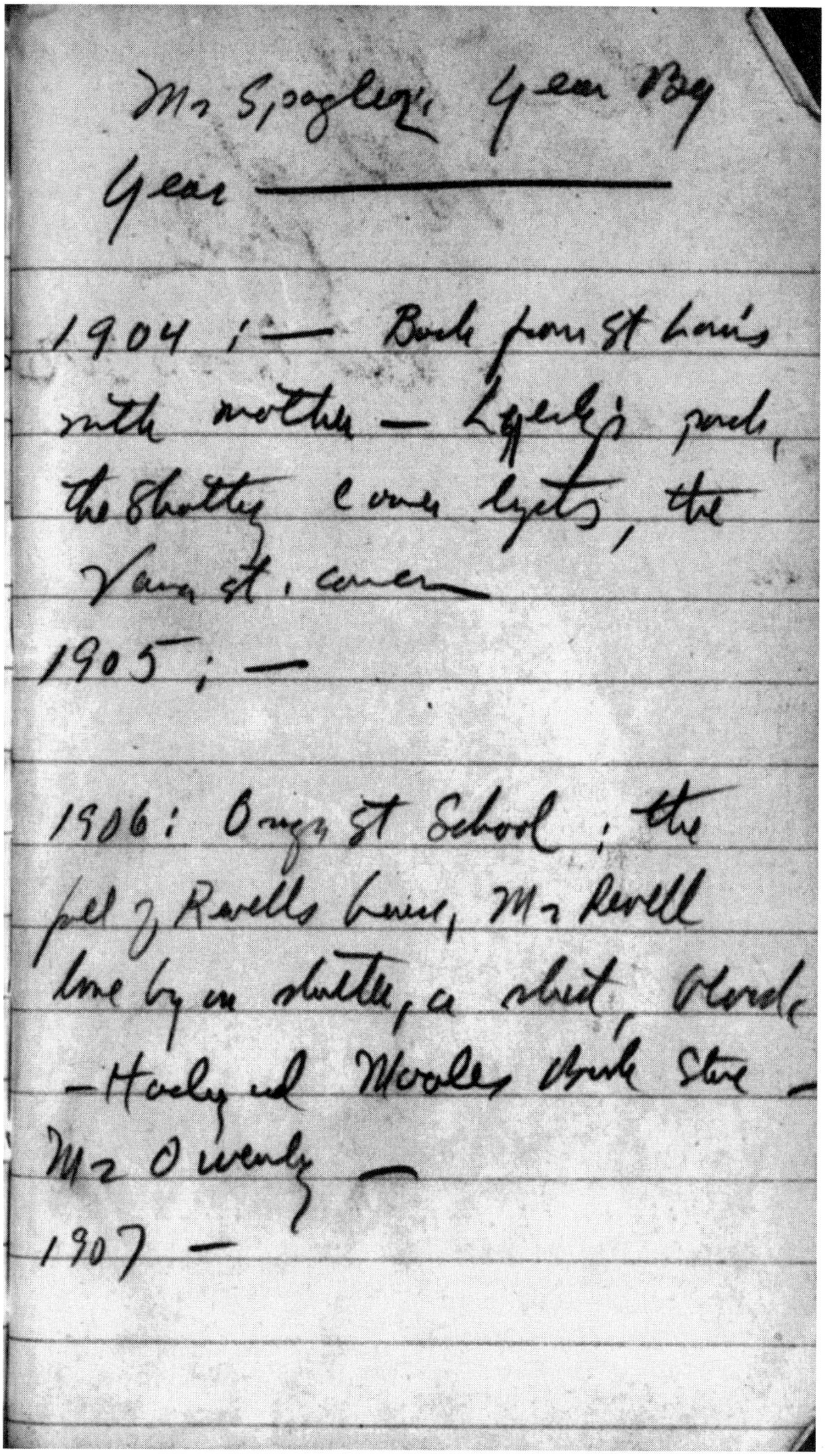

A page from Wolfe's notes for "The Vision of Spangler's Paul" (William B. Wisdom Collection, Houghton Library, Harvard University)

Wolfe with unidentified women at the 2,400-meter summit of Galtenberg in the Austrian Tirol, summer 1936 (The Thomas Wolfe Collection, Pack Memorial Public Library, Asheville, North Carolina)

Berlin, Summer 1936

Perkins's misgivings about "The Vision of Spangler's Paul" deepened Wolfe's concern about his relationship with his publisher, for to Wolfe it seemed as though Perkins was intruding on his right as an artist to deal with his material as he saw fit. When Wolfe learned that he had royalties accrued from the German translation of Of Time and the River *that could only be spent in Germany, he decided to return to Berlin. On 23 July 1936 he boarded the* Europa *for his seventh and last trip to Europe.*

Although during the previous year in Berlin Wolfe had been too busy enjoying his fame to acknowledge the problems of Adolf Hitler's regime, he could no longer ignore the increasingly oppressive atmosphere that surrounded the Olympic Games in 1936, which he attended.

Shortly before the Olympics began, Wolfe fell in love and had a brief, tempestuous affair with Thea Voelcker, who had drawn a caricature of Wolfe that had offended him. The affair ended after quarrels during a trip in the Austrian Tirol. Else von Kohler in You Can't Go Home Again *is based on Voelcker.*

On 8 September Wolfe left Berlin by train for Paris. At the border, crossing into Belgium at Aachen, he witnessed the arrest of a fellow passenger, a nondescript Jewish clerk. The bullying of the clerk by the Nazis inspired Wolfe's novella, "I Have a Thing To Tell You," which was enlarged and incorporated into You Can't Go Home Again.

And now the officers were coming out of the compartment. The curtained door opened again, and the fellow with the sprouting mustaches emerged, carrying the little man's valise. He clambered down clumsily onto the platform and set the valise on the floor between his feet. He looked around. It seemed to George and the others that he glared at them. They just stood still and hardly dared to breathe. They thought they were in for it, and expected now to see all of their own baggage come out.

But in a moment the other three officials came through the door of the compartment with the little man between them. They stepped down to the platform and marched him along, white as a sheet, grease standing out in beads all over his face, protesting volubly in a voice that had a kind of anguished lilt in it. He came right by the others as they stood there. The man's money sweated in George's hand, and he did not know what to do. He made a movement with his arm and started to speak to him. At the same time he was hoping desperately that the man would not speak. George tried to look away from him, but could not. The little man came toward them, protesting with every breath that the whole thing could be explained, that it was an absurd mistake. For just the flick of an instant as he passed the others he stopped talking, glanced at them, white-faced, still smiling his horrible little forced smile

At the Olympic Games

And all through the day, from morning on, Berlin became a mighty Ear, attuned, attentive, focused, on the Stadium. From one end of the city to the other, the air became a single voice. The green trees along the Kurfürstendamm began to talk: out of the viewless air, concealed and buried in ten thousand trees, a voice to four million people from the Stadium–and for the first time in his life, a Yankee ear had the strange adventure of hearing the familiar terms of track and field translated in the tongue that Goethe used. He would be informed now that the Vorlauf would be run–and now the Zwischenlauf–at length the Endlauf–and the winner: Owens–Oo-Ess-Ah.

–*The Notebooks of Thomas Wolfe,* pp. 912–913

Jesse Owens

Olympic Stadium, Berlin 1936

> For the first time in my life, I came upon something, I began to feel and experience the full horror of something that I had never known before–something that made all the swift violence and passion of America, the gangster compacts, the swift killing, all the confusion, harshness, and corruption that infect portions of our own life seem innocent by comparison. And this was the picture of a great people who were spiritually sick, psychically wounded: who had been poisoned by the contagion of an ever-present fear, the pressure of a constant and infamous compulsion, who had been silenced into a sweltering and malignant secrecy, until spiritually they were literally drowning in their own secretions, dying from the distillations of their own self poison, for which now there was no medicine or release.
>
> –*The Notebooks of Thomas Wolfe,* p. 907

of terror; for just a moment his eyes rested on them, and then, without a sign of recognition, without betraying them, without giving any indication that he knew them, he went on by.

George heard the woman at his side sigh faintly and felt her body slump against him. They all felt weak, drained of their last energies. Then they walked slowly across the platform and got into the train.

The evil tension had been snapped now. People were talking feverishly, still in low tones but with obvious released excitement. The little blonde woman leaned from the window of the corridor and spoke to the fellow with the sprouting mustaches, who was still standing there.

"You–you're not going to let him go?" she asked hesitantly, almost in a whisper. "Are–are you going to keep him here?"

He looked at her stolidly. Then a slow, intolerable smile broke across his brutal features. He nodded his head deliberately, with the finality of a gluttonous and full-fed satisfaction:

"Ja," he said. "Er bleibt." And, shaking his head ever so slightly from side to side, "Geht nicht!" he said.

They had him. Far down the platform the passengers heard the shrill, sudden fife of the Belgian engine whistle. The guard cried warning. All up and down the train the doors were slammed. Slowly the train began to move. At a creeping pace it rolled right past the little man. They had him, all right. The officers surrounded him. He stood among them, still protesting, talking with his hands now. And the men in uniform said nothing. They had no need to speak. They had him. They just stood and watched him, each with a faint suggestion of that intolerable slow smile

Drawing of Wolfe by Thea Voelcker that accompanied an interview in the Berlin Tageblatt. *Wolfe was offended by the caricature, complaining it gave him a "Schweinsgesicht," or swine's face. (The Aldo P. Magi Collection, University of North Carolina at Chapel Hill)*

upon his face. They raised their eyes and looked at the passengers as the train rolled past, and the line of travelers standing in the corridors looked back at them and caught the obscene and insolent communication in their glance and in that intolerable slow smile.

And the little man–he, too, paused once from his feverish effort to explain. As the car in which he had been riding slid by, he lifted his pasty face and terror-stricken eyes, and for a moment his lips were stilled of their anxious pleading. He looked once, directly and steadfastly, at his former companions, and they at him. And in that gaze there was all the unmeasured weight of man's mortal anguish. George and the others felt somehow naked and ashamed, and somehow guilty. (They all felt that they were saying farewell, not to a man, but to humanity; not to some pathetic stranger, some chance acquaintance of the voyage, but to mankind; not to some nameless cipher out of life, but to the fading image of a brother's face.)

The train swept out and gathered speed–and so they lost him.

–*You Can't Go Home Again,* pp. 698–699

THE BRIGHT ANGEL 50

understand perhaps just how it feels to us - but we are happy to be <u>out</u>."

Out? I too was out. And suddenly I knew just how she felt. ~~It~~ I too was out who was a stranger to her land, who never yet had been a stranger in it. ~~It~~ I too was out of that great land whose image had been engraved upon my spirit in my childhood and my youth, before I'd ever seen it. ~~It~~ I too was out from that great land which had been so much more to me than land , which had been for me so much more than place. It was a geography of heart's desire. It was a dark unfathomed domain of unknown inheritance. It was a soul's dark wonder, the haunting beauty of the magic land. It had been burning there forever, like dark Helen burning in man's blood. ~~And now it is lost~~ And now, like the dark Helen, was lost to me. I had spoke the language of its spirit before I ever came to it, I had known the language of its tongue the moment that I heard it spoken. I had spoke the accents of its speech most brokenly from the hour when I first entered it, yet never with a moment's trouble, never with a moment's strangeness, never with a moment's lack of comprehension. I had been at home in it and it in me. It seemed I had been born in it and it in me. I had known wonder in it, truth and magic in it, sorrow, loneliness and pain in it. I had known love in it, for the first time in my life. I had known fame. Therefore, it was no foreign land to me.. It was the other half of my heart's home, a haunted part of dark desire, a magic domain of fulfillment. It was a dark lost Helen I had found. It was a dark found Helen I had lost - and now I knew, as I had never known before, the priceless measure of my loss, the depthless measure of its truth, its glory, beauty - and its ruin: So, friend, queen, mistress, sorceress - dark land, dark land, old ancient earth - farewell!

I have a thing to tell you:

Something ~~has~~ spoken to me in the night, ~~wasting~~ the tapers of the waning year. Something ~~is~~ spoken in the night; ~~it~~ told me I shall die, I know not where. ~~Losing the land~~ you know ~~you go to~~ great knowing; losing the life you have, greater life; ~~thinking forsaking earth you own you go to greater earth; and~~ ~~leaving~~ friends you loved, greater loving; to find a land more kind than home, more large than earth.

Whereon the pillars of the earth are ~~founded, towards which~~ the spirits of the nations ~~go, there are~~ the conscience ~~and the soul of men are standing~~ - ~~the~~ wind is rising, ~~the~~ rivers flow.

Typescript page revised by Wolfe for "I Have a Thing to Tell You" first published in The New Republic *(William B. Wisdom Collection, Houghton Library, Harvard University)*

Mad Maude Lawsuit

Wolfe arrived back in New York in September 1936. His relations with his publisher were further complicated in November when Marjorie Doorman, Wolfe's landlady while he lived at 40 Verandah Terrace in Brooklyn, and members of her family sued the author and Charles Scribner's Sons because of the depiction of the family in "No Door," a story that had first appeared in Scribner's Magazine *in July 1933 and that had been included in* From Death to Morning.

You tell him about your landlady who is a hard-bitten ex-reporter. You tell him what a good and liberal-hearted woman she is; how rough and ready, full of life and energy, how she likes drinking and the fellowship of drinking men, and knows all the rough and seamy side of life which a newspaper reporter gets to know.

You tell how she has been with murderers before their execution, got the story from them or their mothers, climbed over sides of ships to get a story, forced herself in at funerals, followed burials to the graveyard, trampled upon every painful, decent, and sorrowful emotion of mankind–all to get that story; and still remains a decent woman, an immensely good, generous, and lusty-living person, and yet an old maid, and a puritan, somehow, to the roots of her soul.

You tell how she went mad several years before and spent two years in an asylum; you tell how moments of this madness still come back to her, and of how you went home one night several months before, to find her stretched out on your bed, only to rise and greet you as the great lover of her dreams–Doctor Eustace McNamee, a name, a person, and a love she had invented for herself. Then you tell of her fantastic family, her three sisters and her father, all touched with the same madness, but without her energy, power, and high ability; and of how she has kept the whole crowd going since her eighteenth year.

–"No Door," *From Death to Morning,* pp. 7–8

Wolfe was disturbed when at the first meeting to discuss the suit, his publisher pressed him to settle out of court, an action he considered cowardly.

Wolfe did not mail this 18 November 1936 letter written to a man who had accused him of anti-Semitism.

While I agree and sympathize with your feeling about anti-Semitism, I cannot agree that my little book, "The Story of a Novel," shows any trace of that hostile and ugly feeling which, I am sure, we both abhor. Certainly, nothing of the sort was intended in that little book and if anything in it is possible of such interpretation, I, for one, would be the first to regret it and to deprecate it.

–*The Letters of Thomas Wolfe,* p. 561

To that old master, now, to wizard Faust, old father of the ancient and swarm-haunted mind of man, to that old German land with all the measure of its truth, its glory, beauty, magic and its ruin–to that dark land, to that old ancient earth that I had loved so long–I said farewell.

I have a thing to tell you:

Something has spoken to me in the night, burning the tapers of the waning year; something has spoken in the night; and told me I shall die, I know not where. Losing the earth we know for greater knowing, losing the life we have for greater life, and leaving friends we loved for greater loving, men find a land more kind than home, more large than earth.

Whereon the pillars of this earth are founded, toward which the spirits of the nations draw, toward which the conscience of the world is tending–a wind is rising, and the rivers flow.

–"I Have a Thing to Tell You,"
The Short Novels of Thomas Wolfe, p. 278

A Grievous Severence

Wolfe's much-discussed break with Maxwell Perkins and Charles Scribner's Sons in 1937 did not result from a single event. There was a complex series of causes–including Wolfe's deep suspicion of virtually everyone and the compulsion to declare his independence from anyone who had a literary claim on him. These were the ingredients:

1. *Wolfe's growing resentment of Perkins's decision to publish* Of Time and the River *before the author regarded it as finished.*
2. *The cost of proof corrections in* Of Time and the River, *which were charged to Wolfe, although he was not responsible for them.*
3. *The dispute about the royalty rate for* The Story of a Novel. *Wolfe had agreed to a reduced royalty to accomodate a lower selling price, but the price was not lowered.*
4. *The response to* The Story of a Novel*–particularly from Bernard DeVoto–asserting that Wolfe was incapable of publishing a novel without Perkins's strong participation.*
5. *The suit by Wolfe's ex-agent Madeleine Boyd–who had admitted to peculation of his royalties–claiming commission on all of Wolfe's books, which he believed had been treated too leniently by Scribners.*
6. *The suit brought against Wolfe and Scribners by Marjorie Dorman claiming that she and her family had been libeled in "No Door" a story published in* Scribner's Magazine. *The case was settled out of court by Scribners against Wolfe's protests, and half the costs were charged to him.*

This festering compound made it inevitable that Thomas Wolfe would leave Scribners. Not even Maxwell Perkins's tact and extraordinary ability to pacify difficult authors could have prevented the painful outcome. Some of his friends claimed that the pain of Wolfe's break killed Perkins. That is an exaggeration. He knew enough about dealing with authors not to expect loyalty or gratitude.

On 12 November 1936 Wolfe wrote to Perkins requesting a letter in which Perkins stated that Wolfe had "faithfully and honorably discharged all obligations to Chas Scribners' Sons." Wolfe asserted "that, in view of all that has happened in the last year and a half, the differences of opinion and belief, the fundamental disagreements that we have discussed so openly, so frankly, and so passionately, a thousand times, and which have brought about this unmistakable and grievous severance, I think you should have written this letter I am asking you to write long before this." On 17 November Perkins responded with a personal note:

> I never knew a soul with whom I felt I was in such fundamentally complete agreement as you. What's more, + what has to do with it, I know you would not ever do an insincere thing,–or any thing you did not think was right.

The next day, along with the formal letter Wolfe requested, Perkins sent another personal letter:

Nov 18th 1936

Dear Tom:–With this is a more formal letter which I hope is what you want. This is to say that on my part there has been no "severance." I can't express certain kinds of feelings very comfortably, but you must realize what my feelings are toward you. Ever since Look Homeward Angel your work has been the foremost interest in my life,+ I have never doubted for your future on any grounds except, at times, on those of your being able to control the vast mass of material you have accumulated + have to form into books. You seem to think I have tried to control you. I only did that when you asked my help + then I did the best I could do. It all seems very confusing to me but, whatever the result I hope you don't mean it to keep us from seeing each other, of that you won't come to our house.

Max

–*To Loot My Life Clean,* p. 190

Wolfe wrote many drafts of letters to Maxwell Perkins in late November 1936 as he sought to come to terms with his decision to break with Charles Scribner's Sons. He decided not to mail the letters included below.

Dear Max: I am writing to tell you that I have at last taken the step of communicating formally to other publishers the severance of my relations with Charles Scribners Sons. It is true that no formal relation between us existed, and that both you and Charlie have told me I was free to go. But I think the relation existed in our minds, at any rate, and for me–I believe for you, as well,–it existed in the heart.

If any apprehensions concerning my letter to the publishers may exist in the minds of any of you–and I know they will not exist in yours–let me assure you at once that I spoke of my former publisher in such a way as left no doubt as to my own earnestness and sincerity, or as to my own belief in the integrity and high [capability] of your house. No one could read that letter without understanding that the necessity for this severance is a matter of deep and poignant regret to all of us. *[These last four words are at the head of otherwise blank page.]*

I am sick and tired, but I believe that I shall rise again, as I have done before:

. . . . I know that for a time now the world will say that you and I have fallen out, that the great sounding-board of rumor and malicious gossip that echoes round and round the granite walls of this little universe, the city, will frame its hundred little stories and all of them, as usual, will be false.

–I know that they will say this and that–

well, let them say.

That is honestly the way I feel now.

The editorial relation between us, which began–it seems to me–so hopefully, and for me so wonderfully, has now lost its initial substance. It has become a myth–and what is worse than that, an untrue myth–and it seems to me that both of us are victims of that myth. You know the terms of the myth well enough:–it was venomously recorded by a man named De Voto in The Saturday Review of Literature during this past summer–And the terms of the myth are these:–that I cannot write my books without your assistance, that there exists at Scribner's an "assembly line" that must fit the great dismembered portions of my manuscript together into a semblance of unity, that I am unable to perform these functions of an artist for myself. How far from the truth these suppositions are you know yourself better than any one on earth. There are few men–certainly no man I have ever known–who is more sure of purpose than myself. There are many many men, of course, who are more sure of means–but that assurance, with such men, is just a small one–with me, it is a hard and [thorny] one, because my means must be my own.

I know that you will not be uncandid enough to deny that these differences and misunderstandings have become profound and fundamental. *[Four lines on an otherwise blank page.]*

Plainly may I tell you that I think that looking like a plain man, you are not a plain man; that speaking like a simple man, you are not a simple man; that speaking in words and phrases that as time went on enchanted and assured me by their simplicity and innocent directness, so that they seemed to be the very character of your soul, I do not now believe that they were so!

In fact, I now believe you are not a plain man–you are an un-plain man I do not believe you are a simple man–you are an un-simple man

I do not believe your words

I impeach your motives and your conduct: may I tell you frankly, plainly, that I do not believe they have achieved and maintained always the quality of unconditioned innocence, faith, good will, and simple and direct integrity that you have always claimed for them

The fault, I think, is here: that having so much that belonged to humankind, you lacked–or you with-held–what makes us one

And therefore I renounce you, who have already, for so long a time, renounced me and got so safely, with no guilt or wrong, so freely rid of me.

* * *

. . . . and I am writing therefore now to tell you that I am, upon the date of these words, dissolving a relationship that does not exist, renouncing a contract that was never made, severing myself and of my own accord, a bond of loyalty, devotion, and self-sacrifice that existed solely, simply, and entirely within my own mind, and to my own past grief of doubt, my present grief of sorrow, loss, and final understanding.

With infinite regret, my dear Max, with the deepest and most genuine sorrow, with an assurance–if you will generously accept it–of my friendship for yourself

Faithfully And Sincerely
Yours -
Thomas Wolfe

* * *

I understand that you have been afraid that some day I might "write about" you. Well, you need not be afraid any longer The day has come–and I am writing about you. Your fears have been realized–I think you will find that your fears, like most fears, have been exaggerated.

* * *

This is one of the saddest and most melancholy occasions of my life. To say now that I have "thought about" this thing, or "arrived at certain conclusions" would be ludicrous. I have not thought about the thing–I have sweat blood about it; I have carried it with me like a waking nightmare in the day time, and like a sleeping torment in the night. I have not "arrived" at my conclusions; I have come to them through every anguish that the brain, heart, nerves, and soul of man can know–and I am there at last. I can't go on in this way: it is a matter of the most desperate uncertainty whether I can go on at all. For seven years I have been increasingly aware of the seepage of my talents, the diminution of my powers, the dilution of my force–and I can not go on.

* * *

I am therefore asking you to send me at once an unqualified and unequivocal statement to this effect: that I have discharged all debts and all contractual obligations to the firm of Charles Scribners Sons, and that I am no longer under any obligation to them, whether personal, financial, or contractual *[two words]* I want you to make this statement in your own language, but according to the terms I have mentioned, if you think them just!

* * *

In the name of honesty and sincerity, I can write no more than here I have written: in the name of justice and of fairness you can, and will, write no less, [*sic*]

* * *

I beg and request you to send me at once, without intervention of personal conversations or telephone call this letter that I am asking you to write.

–*To Loot My Life Clean,* pp. 281–283

Wolfe had not taken the final step of definitely severing his relationship with Charles Scribner's Sons when he went on a vacation to New Orleans. After his arrival on 1 January 1937, he was soon engulfed by fans and friends. The most important event of Wolfe's New Orleans excursion was meeting advertising man and bibliophile William B. Wisdom, a great admirer of his writing. After Wolfe's death, Wisdom purchased Wolfe's manuscripts and personal papers and donated them to Harvard University.

From New Orleans on 10 January 1937 Wolfe sent a twenty-seven page letter to Perkins, dated 15 December 1936. The excerpts from that letter reveal some of the tensions that were causing the breakup.

The very truth of the matter is that, so far from having been unsure of purpose and direction, in the last five years at any rate I have been almost too sure. My sense of purpose and direction is definite and overwhelming. I think, I feel and know what I want to do; the direction in which, if I live and if I am allowed to go on working and fulfill myself, I want to go, is with me more clear and certain than with any one that I have ever known. My difficulty has never been one of purpose or direction. Nothing is more certain than this fact, that I know what I want to do and where I want to go. Nothing is more certain than the fact that I shall finish any book I set out to write if life and health hold out. My difficulty from the outset, as you know, has never been one of direction, it has only been one of means. As I have already said and written, in language that seems to be so clear and unmistakable that no one could misunderstand it, I have been faced with the problem of discovering for myself my own language, my own pattern, my own structure, my own design, my own universe and creation. That, as I have said before, is a problem that is, I think, by no means unique, by no means special to myself. I believe it may have been the problem of every artist that ever lived. In my own case, however, I believe the difficulties of the problem may have been increased and complicated by the denseness of the fabric, the dimensions of the structure, the variety of the plan. For that reason I have, as you know, at times found myself almost hopelessly enmeshed in my own web.

In one sense, my whole effort for years might be described as an effort to fathom my own design, to explore my own channels, to discover my own ways. In these respects, in an effort to help me to discover, to better use, these means I was striving to apprehend and make my own, you gave me the most generous, the most painstaking, the most valuable help. But that kind of help might have been given to me by many other skilful people–and of course there are other skilful people in the world who could give such help,–although none that I know of who could give it so skillfully as you.

William B. Wisdom (Adelaide Wisdom Benjamin)

But what you gave me, what in my acknowledgment I tried to give expression to, was so much more than this technical assistance–an aid of spiritual sustenance, of personal faith, of high purpose, of profound and sensitive understanding, of utter loyalty and staunch support, at a time when many people had no belief at all in me, or when what little belief they had was colored by serious doubt that I would ever be able to continue or achieve my purpose. fulfill my "promise"–all of this was a help of such priceless and incalculable value, of such spiritual magnitude, that it made any other kind of help seem paltry by comparison. And for that reason mainly I have resented the contemptible insinuations of my enemies that I have to have you "to help me write my books." As you know: I don't have to have you or any other man alive to help me with my books. I do not even have to have technical help or advice, although I need it badly, and have been so immensely grateful for it. But if the worst came to the worst–and of course the worst does and will come to the worst–all this I could and will and do learn for myself, as all hard things are learned, with blood-sweat, anguish and despair.

. . . .

You say in one of your letters that you never knew a soul with whom you felt that you were in such fundamentally complete agreement as with me. May I tell you that I shall remember these words with proud happiness and with loyal gratefulness as long as I live. For I too on my own part feel that way about you. I know that somehow, in some hard, deep, vexed and troubling way in which all the truth of life is hidden and which, at the cost of so much living, so much perplexity and anguish of the spirit, we have got to try to find and fathom, what you say is true: I believe we are somehow, in this strange, hard way, in this complete and fundamental agreement with each other.

And yet, were there ever two men since time began who were as completely different as you and I? Have you ever known two other people who were, in almost every respect of temperament, thinking, feeling and acting, as far apart? It seems to me that each of us might almost represent, typify, be the personal embodiment of, two opposite poles of life. How to put it I do not know exactly, but I might say, I think, that you in your essential self are the Conservative and I, in my essential self, am the Revolutionary.

. . . .

I believe that I myself not only know the workers and am a friend of the worker's cause but that I am myself a brother to the workers, because I am myself, as every artist is, a worker, and I am myself moreover the son of a working man. I know furthermore that at the bottom there is no difference between the artist and the worker. They both come from the same family, they recognize and understand each other instantly. They speak the same language. They have always stood together.

. . . .

Just as in some hard, strange way there is between us probably this fundamentally complete agreement which you speak of, so too, in other hard, strange ways there is this complete and polar difference. It must be so with the South pole and the North pole. I believe that in the end they too must be in fundamentally complete agreement–but the whole earth lies between them. I don't know exactly how to define conservatism or the essential conservative spirit of which I speak here, but I think I might say it is a kind of fatalism of the spirit. Its fundaments, it seems to me, are based upon a kind of unhoping hope, an imperturbable acceptation, a determined resignation, which believes that fundamentally life will never change, but that on this account we must all of us do the best we can.

The result of all this, it seems to me, is that these differences between us have multiplied in complexity and difficulty. The plain truth of the matter now is that I hardly know where to turn. The whole natural impulse of creation–and with me, creation is a natural impulse, it has got to flow, it has got to realize itself through the process of torrential production–is checked and hampered at every place. In spite of this, I have finally and at last, during these past two months, broken through into the greatest imaginative conquest of my life–the only complete and whole one I have ever had. And now I dare not broach it to you, I dare not bring it to you, I dare not show it to you, for fear that this thing which I cannot trifle with, that may come a man but once in his whole life, may be killed at its inception by cold caution, by indifference, by the growing apprehensiveness and dogmatism of your own conservatism. You say that you are not aware that there is any severance between us. Will you please tell me what there is in the life around us on which we both agree? We don't agree in politics, we don't agree on economics, we are in entire disagreement on the present system of life around us, the way people live, the changes that should be made.

Your own idea, evidently, is that life is unchangeable, that the abuses I protest against, the greed, the waste, the poverty, the filth, the suffering, are inherent in humanity, and that any other system than the one we have would be just as bad as this one. In this, I find myself in profound and passionate conflict.

. . . .

You, better than any one, have had the chance to observe during the past year how this consciousness of society, of the social elements, that govern life today, have sunk into my spirit, how my convictions about all these things have grown deeper, wider, more intense at every point. On your own part, it seems to me there has been a corresponding stiffening, an increasing conservatism that is now, I fear, reached the point of dogged and unyielding inflexibility and obstinate resolve to try to maintain the status quo at any cost.

Since that is your condition, your considered judgment, I will not try to change it, or to persuade you in any way, because I know your reasons for so thinking and so feeling are honest ones. But neither must you now try to change me, or to persuade me to alter or deny convictions which are the result of no superficial or temporary influence, no Union Square–Greenwich Village cult, but the result of my own deep living, my own deep feeling, my own deep labor and my own deep thought.

Had I given full expression to these convictions in "Of Time and the River" I believe it would have been a better book. You do not think so. But I will say that these feelings, these convictions, are becoming deeper and intenser all the time, and so far from feeling that the world cannot be changed, that it cannot be made better, that the evils of life are unremediable, that all the faults and vices at which we protest will always exist, I find myself more passionately convinced than ever of the necessity of change, more passionately confirmed than ever in the faith and the belief that the life and the condition of the whole human race can be immeasurably improved. And this is something that grows stronger with me all the time.

. . . .

What I really want to say to you most earnestly now is this: there has never been a time when I've been so determined to write as I please, to say what I intend to say, to publish the books I want to publish, as I am now. I know that you have asserted time and again that you were in entire sympathy with this feeling, that, more than this, you were willing to be the eager promoter and supporter of this intention, that you were willing to publish whatever I wanted you to publish, that you were only waiting for me to give it to you. In this I think you have deceived yourself. I think you are mistaken when you say that all you have waited for was the word from me, that you would publish anything I wanted you to publish. There are many things that I have wanted you to publish which have not been published. Some of them have not been published because they were too long for magazine space, or too short for book space, or too different in their design and quality to fit under the heading of a short story, or too incomplete to be called a novel. All this is true. All this I grant. And yet, admitting all these things, without a word of criticism of you or of the technical and publishing requirements of the present time that make their publication impracticable, I will say that I think some of them should have been published. I still think that much of the best writing that a man may do is writing that does not follow under the convenient but extremely limited form of modern publication. It is not your fault. It is not Scribner's fault. It is just the way things are. But as I have been telling you, the way things are is not always the way, it seems to me that things should be.

. . . .

However, I am now going to write my own Ulysses. The first volume is now under way. The first volume will be called The Hound of Darkness, and the whole work, when completed, will be called The Vision of Spangler's Paul. Like Mr. Joyce, I am going to write as I please, and this time, no one is going to cut me unless I want them to.

. . . .

You have not always been disposed to take seriously what I say to you. I pray most earnestly that you will take this seriously. For seven years now, during this long and for me wonderful association with you, I have been increasingly aware of a certain direction which our lives were taking. Looking back, I can see now that although Look Homeward, Angel gave you pleasure and satisfaction, you were extremely alarmed even then about its publication, and entertained the hope–the sincere and honest hope directed, I know, to what you considered my own best interests–that the years would temper me to a greater conservatism, a milder intensity, a more decorous moderation. And I think where I have been most wrong, most unsure in these past seven years, has been where I yielded to this benevolent pressure. Because I think that it is just there that I have allowed myself to falter in my purpose, to be diverted from the direction toward which the whole impulsion of my life and talent is now driving me, to have failed there insofar as I have yielded to the modifications of this restraint. Restraint, discipline–yes, they were needed desperately, they are needed badly still. But let us not get the issues confused, let us not again get into the old confusion between substance and technique, purpose and manner, direction and means, the spirit and the letter. Restrain my adjectives, by all means, discipline my adverbs, moderate the technical extravagances of my incondite exuberance, but don't derail the train, don't take the Pacific Limited and switch it down the siding towards Hogwart Junction. It can't be done. I'm not going to let it happen. If you expected me to grow conservative simply because I got bald and fat and for the first time in life had a few dollars in the bank, you are going to be grievously mistaken.

. . . .

What I am trying to tell you, what I am forced to say, because it is the truth, is that I am a righteous man, and few people know it because there are few righteous people in the world.

. . . .

I do not know if you have always been aware of how I felt about these things, of what a naked, fiercely lacerated thing my spirit was, how I have writhed beneath the lies and injuries and at times, almost maddened to insanity at the treachery, the injustice and the hatred I have had to experience and endure, at what a frightful cost I have attained even the little fortitude I have attained. At times, particularly during the last year or two, the spectacle of the victim squirming beneath the lash has seemed to amuse you. I know there is no cruelty in your nature. I do suggest to you, however, that where one is secure in life, when one is vested with authority, established in position, surrounded by a little world of his own making, of his own love, he may sometimes be a little unmindful of the lives of people less fortunate than himself. There is an unhappy tendency in all of us to endure with fortitude the anguish of another man. There is also a tendency among people of active and imaginative minds and temperaments who live themselves conventional and conservative lives to indulge vicariously their interest in the adventures and experiences of other people whose lives are not so sheltered as their own. And these people, I think, often derive what seems to be a kind of quiet, philosophic amusement at the spectacle of what is so falsely known as the "human comedy." But I might suggest to such people that what affords them quiet entertainment is being paid for by another man with blood and agony, and that while we smile at the difficulties and troubles in which an impulsive and generous person gets involved, a man of genius or of talent may be done to death.

. . . .

I believe you may have allowed your apprehensions concerning who and what I might now write about at the period I had now reached in my writing to influence your judgments. I don't like to go into all this again. The thing that happened last summer, your reaction to the manuscript Miss Nowell brought to you while I was in Europe, and your own comment as expressed to her in a note which she sent to me and which said, after she had cut all the parts you objected to in the manuscript out of it, that "the only person it can now possibly hurt is Thomas Wolfe," was to me a shocking revelation. I am not of the opinion now that the manuscript in question was one of any great merit. I know that I've done much better work. But the point, as I told you after my return from Europe, the point that we discussed so frankly and so openly, was that your action, if carried to its logical conclusions and applied to everything I write from now on, struck a deadly blow at the very vitals of my whole creative life. The only possible inference that could be drawn from this matter was that from now on, if I wished to continue writing books which Charles Scribner's Sons were going to publish, I must now submit myself to the most rigid censorship, a censorship which would delete from all my writings any episode, any scene, any character, any reference that might seem to have any connection, however remote, with the house of Charles Scribner's Sons and its sisters and its cousins and its aunts. Such a conclusion, if I agreed to it, would result in the total enervation and castration of my work–a work which, as I have told you in this letter, I am now resolved must be more strong and forthright in its fidelity to purpose than ever.

. . . .

Tolstoi is a more autobiographical writer than I am, because he has succeeded better in using what he had. But make no mistake about it, both of us, and every other man who ever wrote a book, are autobiographical. You are therefore not to touch my life in this way. When you or any man tries to exert this kind of control, to modify or shape my material in an improper way because of some paltry personal, social apprehension, you do the unpardonable thing. You try to take from the artist his personal property, to steal his substance, to defraud him of his treasure–the only treasure he has, the only property and wealth which is truly, inexorably, his own.

. . . .

You told me when I discussed these things with you in October, after my return from Europe, that you agreed with me, that in the last analysis you were always with the man of talent, and that if the worst comes to the worst you could resign your executive and editorial functions. Well, don't worry, you'll never have to. In the first place, your executive and editorial functions are so special and valuable that they can not be substituted by any other person on earth. They could not be done without by the business that employs them. It would be like having a house with the lights turned out. Furthermore, no one is going to resign on my account. There are still enough people in the world who value what I do, I believe, to support me freely, heartily and cheerfully, with no sense that they are enduring martyrdom on my account. So if there is ever any situation that might indicate any future necessity for any one to resign anything on my account, that situation will never arise, simply because I won't be there to be resigned about.

. . . .

Now, at a time when I am more firmly resolved that ever before to exert my full amount, to use my full stroke, to shine my purest and intensest ray, it is distressing to see the very people who published my first efforts with complete equanimity, and with no qualms whatever about the possibility of anybody getting "hurt," begin to squirm around uncomfortably and call for calf-rope and whine that their own toes are being stepped upon, even when nothing has been said, nothing written. They have no knowledge or declaration of my own intention except that I intend in my own way to finish my own book. What are you going to do about it? You say you are not aware that there have been any difficulties, if this is not a threatened severance of the gravest nature, I should like to know what you consider difficult and what severance is? We can not continue in this irresolute, temporizing "Well now, you go ahead for the present–we'll wait and see how it all turns out–" manner. My life has been ravaged, my energy exhausted, my work confused and aborted long enough by this kind of miserable, time serving procrastination. I'm not going to endure it any longer. I'm not going to pour my sweat and blood and energy and life and talent into another book now, only to be told two or three years from now that is would be inadvisable to publish it without certain formidable deletions, or that perhaps we'd better wait a few years longer and see "how everything turns out."

We stalled around this way with October Fair, until all the intensity and passion I had put into the book was lost, until I had gone stale on it, until I was no longer interested in it–and to what purpose? Why, because you allowed your fond weakness for the female sex to get the better of your principle, because you were afraid some foolish female, who was inwardly praying for nothing better than to be a leading character in a book of mine, and who was bitterly disappointed when she not, might get her feelings hurt–or that the pocketbook of the firm might get touched by suits for libel. Well, there would have been no suits for libel. I never libelled anybody in my life. Certainly, there was no remote danger of libel in The October Fair, but because of our weakness and irresolution the news got around that we were afraid of publication for this reason. The lying rumor was spread around in the column of a filthy gossip-writer, and the result now is that we have a libel suit on our hands from a person who was never libelled, who doesn't have a leg to stand on, but who is willing to take the chance and make the effort to get something because we were not firm and resolute in the beginning.

. . . .

You yourself must now say plainly what the decision is to be, because the decision now rests with you. You can no longer have any doubt as to how I feel about these matters. I don't see how you can any longer have any doubt that difficulties of a grave and desperate nature do exist.

–*To Loot My Life Clean,* pp. 193–210

Perkins soon sent his full response to Wolfe's concerns.

Saturday, January 16, 1937
Dear Tom:

In the first place I completely subscribe to what you say a writer should do, and always have believed it. If it were not true that you, for instance, should write as you see, feel, and think, than a writer would be of no importance, and books merely things for amusement. And since I have always thought that there could be nothing so important as a book can be, and some are, I could not help but think as you do. But there are limitations of time, of space, and of human laws which cannot be treated as if they did not exist. I think that a writer should, of course, be the one to make his book what he wants it to be, and that if because of the laws of space it must be cut, he should be the one to cut it:– and especially with you, I think the labour and discipline that would come from doing that without help or interference would further the pretty terrible task of mastering the material. But my impression was that you asked my help, that you wanted it.–And it is my impression too, that changes were not forced on you (You're not very forceable, Tom, nor I very forceful) but were argued over, often for hours. But I agree with you about this too, fully, and unless you want help it will certainly not be thrust upon you. It would be better if you could fight it out alone–better for your work, in the end, certainly;–and what's more, I believe you are not in a position to publish with less regard to any conventions of bookmaking, say a certain number of pages almost, whether or not it had what a novel is regarded as an ending, or anything else that is commonly expected in a novel. I believe the writer, anyway, should always be the final judge, and I meant you to be so. I have always held to that position and have sometimes seen books hurt thereby, but at least as often helped. "The book belongs to the author."

I certainly do not care nor does this house–how revolutionary your books are. I did try to keep you from injecting radical, or Marxian beliefs into "Time and the River" because they were your beliefs in 1934 and 35, and not those of Eugene in the time of the book.–So it did not seem that they could rightly belong in the book. If they could have, then the times could not be rightly pictured, I thought. It must be so–Still, you were then and always conscious of social wrong and that is plainly in the book as you then saw it. There was the Astor story. What was told was not heard by Eugene. It was second-hand, and second-hand material–something told, not heard and seen–is inferior to first-hand. If cutting had to be done, ought that not to be cut? I know your memory is a miracle, but it seems as if you must have forgotten how we worked and argued. You were never overruled. Do you think you are clay to be moulded! I never saw anyone less malleable.–And as for publishing what you like, or being prevented from it, apart from the limitations of space, you have not been, intentionally. Are you thinking of K 19? We would have published it if you had said to do it. At the time I said to Jack: "Maybe it's the way Tom is. Maybe we should just publish him as he comes and in the end it will all be right." But if we had, and the results had been bad at the moment, would you not have blamed me? Certainly I should have bitterly blamed myself. I do not want the passage of time to make you cautious or conservative, but I do not want it to give you a full control–as it has done in the case of great writers in the past–over your great talent.–And if you can stand the struggle it will. But you must struggle too, and perhaps even more than in the writing, in the shaping and revising.–That might be the hardest thing of all to your nature. You have so much in you that the need with you is to get it uttered. Then to go back and polish and perfect seems petty, and goes against your nature, I guess.

Tom, you ought not to say some of the things you do,–that I find your sufferings amusing and don't take them seriously. I know something of them. I do try to turn your mind from them and to arouse your humor, because to spend dreadful hours brooding over them and in denunciation and abuse on account of them, seems to be only to aggravate them. It does no good. You have to suffer to write as you do, and the slings and arrows that strike you from outside madden you the more because you instinctively know that all that matters is your work and so why can't you be left to do it. I understand that. Have you seen me amused by other people's sufferings? You know that was unjust.

Then comes the question of your writing about the people here. I don't want to discuss it, because I agree that you have the same right to make use of them as of anyone else in the same way, and if there is an argument on it the whole thing may be bedevilled as was "October Fair" after Mrs. Bernstein protested.–(And by the way, wasn't it up to me to tell you of her visits? She went out saying I was her enemy. I conceded nothing to her.) But when I spoke of resigning after we published–and the moment I inadvertently said it I told Miss Nowell she must not repeat it, and she said she would not–I did not mean I would be asked or wanted to resign. That would never happen on any such ground. But it isn't the way you think, and it's up to you to write as you think you should.–Your plan as outlined seems to me a splendid one too. I hope you will get on with it now.

There remains the question of whether we are in fundamental agreement. But it is no question if you feel it is not so. I have always instinctively felt that is was so, and no one I ever knew has said more of the things that I believed than you. It was so from the moment that I began to read your first book. Nothing else, I would say, could have kept such different people together through such trials. But I believe in democracy and not in dictators; and in government by principles and not by men; and in less government if possible rather than more; and that power always means injustice and so should be as little concentrated as is compatible with the good of the majority; and that violence breeds more evils than it kills; and that it's better to sizzle in the fryingpan until you're sure your jump won't take you into the fire; and that Erasmus who begged his friend Luther not to destroy the good in the Church because of the bad in it, which he thought could be forced out with the spread of education, was right, though not heroic, and the heroic Luther wrong–and that Europe is the worse for his impetuosity today. I don't believe that things can't improve. I believe that the only thing that can prevent improvement is the ruin of violence, or of reckless finance which will end in violence.–That is why Roosevelt needs an opposition and it is the only serious defect in him. I believe that change really comes from great deep causes too complex for contemporary men, or any other perhaps, fully to understand, and that when even great men like Lenin try to make a whole society suddenly the end is almost sure to be bad, and that the right end, the natural one, will come from the efforts of innumerable people trying to do right, and to understand it, because they are a part of the natural forces that are set at work by changed conditions.–It is the effort of man to adjust himself to change and it has to be led,–but the misfortune of man is that strong will almost always beats down intelligence, and the passionate, the reasonable. I believe that such as you can help on change, but that it ought to be by your writings, not by violent acts. I believe that wealth is bad but that it should not be confiscated, but reduced by law, and in accordance with a principle, not arbitrarily and in passion;–and if it is done in passion and violence the result will be a new privileged class made up of delegates of the man or the oligarchy that has seized the power. But it may be that the great underlying changes will dictate Communism as the best society for most people.–Then we ought to have it; but if we can evolve into it gradually how much better (though I know many on both sides say that is impossible) than if we go in revolution and civil war. At least let us try the way of evolution first.–It seems to me that our Civil War and many of the great convulsions were caused by extremists on both sides, by those too hot-headed to wait for natural forces to disclose their direction, when the inevitable outcome could no longer be resisted. I do not believe the world can ever be perfect, of course,–thought it might in a sense approximate a political and economic perfection if conditions ceased from changing so that a long enough time was given to deal with known and permanent factors.–But this is getting to be too much of a philosophy of history or something, and I don't think it has anything to do with fundamental agreement. I had always felt it existed–and I don't feel, because you differ with me, however violently, on such things as I've said above, that it does not necessarily. It is more that I like and admire the same things and despise many of the same things, and the same people too, and think the same things important and unimportant,–at least this is the way it has seemed to me.

Anyhow, I don't see why you should have hesitated to write me as you did, or rather to send the letter. There was mighty little of it that I did not wholly accept and what I did not, I perfectly well understood. There were places in it that made me angry, but it was a fine letter, a fine writer's statement of his beliefs, as fine as any I ever saw, and though I have vanities enough, as many as most, it gave me great pleasure too–that which comes from hearing brave and sincere beliefs uttered with sincerity and nobility.

Always yours,
MEP

–*To Loot My Life Clean,* pp. 223–225

Visit to Chapel Hill

Following his visit to New Orleans, Wolfe continued to travel in the South. In late January he arrived in Chapel Hill, where his address to an English class became the subject of a newspaper article.

'Altamont' Of Novel Is Not Asheville, Tom Wolfe Insists
Irene Wright
The Asheville Citizen, 31 January 1937

(Tom Wolfe, Asheville author, discussed his novel "Look Homeward, Angel," in an address before Phillips Russell's creative writing class at the University of North Carolina recently. Miss Irene Wright, daughter of Mr. and Mrs. George H. Wright of Asheville, who is a senior in journalism at the university heard the address and wrote the following story about Wolfe's observation.–Editor.)

The Altamont that he wrote of in "Look Homeward Angel" was not Asheville but something that he created, Thomas Wolfe, well known Asheville author, said in speaking to Phillips Russell's creative writing class at the University of North Carolina, Chapel Hill, recently.

"Asheville got sore about 'Look Homeward Angel' and I got some bitter letters," Wolfe said. "One man accused me of sneaking around with a note book as a kid and jotting down things as I heard them. Another man congratulated me on my memory. But I still maintain that Altamont is not Asheville, but something that I created. If you are from North Carolina you have to use North Carolina clay to model a figure. Then the people of North Carolina recognize the clay and think that they recognize the figure. But I think I've figured out just why my book hit Asheville so hard. The people thought a writer was a person who came from way over there and who said 'hocus pocus' and pulled a book out of the air."

In opening his remarks before the class, Wolfe said that he did not go there to make a talk, but that he had never been accused of lacking in words. He confessed to a habit of using eight adjectives where only one would do, and expressed a hope that some day he would use only four where two are enough.

"As an introduction to one of my books I once wrote 15,000 words about a train," Wolfe said. "My publisher told me that I had a good piece about a train, but that nobody was going to read that much to get into my book. So I had to cut it down.

"When my writing comes it comes with a rush and therefore I have to do more cutting than anything else. You may write something which you consider the best piece of single work you have ever done, but if it does not belong in the book, you've got to cut it. I always wanted to say 5,000 words at once, and I wish the reader could get 5,000 words at once.

A 1937 pencil sketch of Wolfe by Douglas Gorsline, Maxwell Perkins's son-in-law (Alexander D. Wainwright Collection of Thomas Wolfe, Princeton University Library)

"When I was in London I decided to write 'Look Homeward Angel' and I began jotting down things that I wanted to put into it. I wrote like a cement mixer. I didn't know just what was coming out, although I knew what the beginning and the end would be. I worked on it at night while I was teaching in New York, and I watched the manuscript get higher and higher.

"When I had finished I took the manuscript to a publisher that a friend of mine knew. He read the book and then wrote me a note which said, 'I've read your manuscript. I published five like it last year and lost money on all of them,' I had gotten slips like that before, and I was glad that I had the book off my chest.

"I went to Europe after that and while I was there I received a note from another publisher who had seen the manuscript. This publisher said, 'I don't know if your book can be published in its present form, but I don't see how any editor can keep from getting excited about it.'

"When I returned I went to see this publisher and received $500 for the manuscript right away."

Wolfe described his southern trip in a 15 February 1937 letter to his mother.

I had a wonderful trip through the South and was everywhere received with the greatest cordiality and kindness. But I didn't get much rest, and I was pretty tired when I went down there. The people in New Orleans never seemed to go to bed at all and they overwhelmed me with well-meant and much appreciated hospitality, but I finally had to get out of town just to get rid of some of the people. I went up to Biloxi, Miss., on the Gulf coast, for a day or two, then up to Atlanta, where more friends were waiting for me, then up to Southern Pines, N.C., to visit my friend James Boyd, then to Raleigh and Chapel Hill, where I saw dozens of my old teachers and schoolmates again, then up to Warrenton, N.C., to stay with my friend Bill Polk, who is mayor of the town, then directly back to New York. It was a good trip, but I stayed away longer than I intended and had to get back here and get to work again. I had hoped to come to Asheville, had planned to come up from Atlanta, which is not far away, but when I telephoned from Atlanta I gathered there was some confusion about my coming and, since my visit did not seem to be convenient, I thought I'd better go on to see some of the people who had been expecting me.

However, if I can finish a big piece of work this spring I do plan to return later on, in the latter part of April or early in May. I have heard from friends in Asheville that they would be glad to see me and would be able to put me up, so there ought not to be any difficulty about that. My troubles with the lawyers and law suits still continue. It has been a hard two years but I begin now to see that the whole business is a highly organized racket–the idea being to get as much out of the victim as the victim will pay rather than go to the expense of going to court and suffering the additional cost of time, worry and money which a court trial involves.

–*The Letters of Thomas Wolfe to His Mother,* pp. 270–271

More and more I am convinced that to be a great writer a man must be something of an ass–I read of Tolstoi that he read no newspapers, that he went away and lived among peasants for 7 years at a time, and that for six years he read nothing except the novels of A. Dumas–Yet such a man could write great books–I almost think it is because of this that he did.

–*The Notebooks of Thomas Wolfe,* p. 215

Traveling South

In February 1937 Wolfe and Charles Scribner decided to settle the outstanding libel suit brought by Margorie Dorman and her family. In April, Wolfe decided to set out on his long-anticipated return trip to Asheville–his first since the publication of Look Homeward, Angel *in 1929. He journeyed down the Shenandoah Valley, stopping in Roanoke, Virginia, where he wrote Elizabeth Nowell on April 28.*

I am feeling a lot better except for a terrible feeling of guilt at having loafed so. I have begun to sleep again. In fact, it's about all I am doing nowadays and I am beginning to worry about that too. We can't be satisfied, can we? I feel like working again. I did over two thousand words yesterday and a thousand this morning. I am boiling over with ideas and in short, I believe everything is going to be all right in a few days.

I am going from here down to Bristol, Virginia, and from there over to Yancey County, North Carolina, where my Mother's people are from. I am dreading Asheville a little but I think I will be ready for it in a few days. After that I will be back at work again.

–*Beyond Love and Loyalty,* p. 57

One of Wolfe's reasons for making the trip to Asheville was to determine if he could help his mother untangle her financial troubles with Wachovia Bank. Julia Wolfe speculated in real estate during the 1920s, and when the stock market crashed in 1929, she found she could no longer pay her mortgages or taxes. Wachovia Bank was now suing her for the foreclosure of deeds of trust she had executed to secure payments. Along with the letter below, Wolfe enclosed a copy of a new will superseding an older will that had named Aline Bernstein as his beneficiary.

Roanoke, Virginia,
April 28th, 1937.

Mrs. Julia E. Wolfe,
48 Spruce Street,
Asheville, North Carolina.

Dear Mama:

I am on my way home and expect to arrive there in a few days. I am going to Bristol, Virginia, tomorrow and from there I shall probably go over to Burnsville and stay a few days. While there I hope to look up some of our relatives whom I have never seen, visit Grandpa's birthplace and get a little more sleep.

Don't worry about me. I am all right and feeling 100% better than when I left New York ten days ago. I was desperately tired–more than I have ever been. I have written over a half a million words since October and in addition, as you know, I have been fighting all along the line for the past year or so with crooks, parasites and lawyers. The lawyers now assure me that "we" have come out splendidly on all fronts and in fact won a glorious victory. I don't know who "we" means but as nearly as I can figure it, it means principally the lawyers. At any rate, there is not a great deal left except my power to work and my faith in human nature, which, in spite of everything, is stronger than it ever was. I am going to be all right. I am doing the best piece of work I have ever done and after a few more days of rest, I will be ready to go back and start in again.

I want to come down to see you and talk to you and find out what this Wachovia Bank business is all about. If there is anyway I can help, I want to do so.

It will be a very strange experience, I think, coming back to Asheville after all this time. It is my home town and certainly I have no feeling for it or for any one there except the kindest and best. I don't know what their feeling is but I hope it is the same. At any rate, I am coming down to see my family. I should like to see some of my friends but I am still too tired to be pawed over and asked ten thousand questions. I know you all understand how I feel.

I am enclosing with this letter a copy of a will I made the other day in New York. Don't get alarmed. I intend to go on living for a long time; but inasmuch as the will I made a few years ago no longer seemed to me to be a good one, I thought I had better make a new one now. It was drawn up by a good lawyer, who assured me that everything was taken care of and that he had made it as simple as possible and had covered everything. You can either keep it or give it back to me when I see you in Asheville; but I thought it best for you to become acquainted with its terms and provisions as concerning you and the family. Accordingly I am sending it on to you.

I am afraid as regards this will I am a little bit in the position of the man who said: "If we had some ham, we would have some ham and eggs if we had some eggs." If anything happened to me right now, I don't know just how much any one would be able to realize out of my so-called estate; but of course with a writer there is always the chance that the continued sale of his books or manuscripts or other royalties may amount to something after his death. At any rate, I put the whole thing in the hands of two of the ablest and very best people I know, Mr. Perkins, who is the first executor, and Nat Mobley, who as a classmate of mine at college and who is now vice-president of an insurance company in New York.

This is all for the present. I will call you up in a day or two and hope to see you all soon.

With love and best wishes to all,

–*The Letters of Thomas Wolfe to His Mother,* pp. 278–279

Wolfe at the courthouse in Burnsville, North Carolina

A Witness of a Shooting

Wolfe arrived in Bristol, Virginia, on Thursday, 29 April 1937. "One has to go away," he told a reporter from the Bristol News, *"before he learns how deeply he is attached to his own people and own country." He departed the following evening for Asheville, but stopped first in Yancey County, North Carolina, for a few days to look up Westall relatives.*

On Saturday, 1 May, between 10:30 and 11:00 P.M., Wolfe stepped out of the Gem City Soda Shop on Main Street in Burnsville, North Carolina and into an altercation among three men: Otis Chase, Philip Ray, and James O. Higgins. Shots were fired, and although no one was killed that night, a week later on the same spot Ray shot and killed Higgins. Wolfe was later subpoenaed to testify as a witness to the earlier altercation. Below are Wolfe's testimony in the court case in fall 1937 and his fictionalization of the incident in the story "The Return of the Prodigal," which was collected in The Hills Beyond *(1941).*

TOM WOLFE: (DIRECT EXAMINATION BY SOLICITOR)

My name is Tom Wolfe. At the present time I am living at Oteen in a cabin. My home for the last 8 or 9 years has been in New York City. I am a writer. I was in the Town of Burnsville the 1st day of May, 1937. I went to the Blue Ridge Grill on that visit. I should judge I went to the drug store, Gem City Soda Shop, between 10:30 and 11 o'clock, for a coca cola. I saw the defendants at that time.

Upon entering the drug store I saw no disturbance but a number of people in front of the Blue Ridge Grill were gathered together, I thought very quietly. I did not know the deceased, Jim Higgins, at that time, but I met him later. There was a group of young men or men standing together but they seemed to be having a very quiet discussion, and I went into the drug store and had a coca cola and in a few minutes I was coming out again and that was the first time I observed any signs of a disturbance. It seemed to me that after I went into the store the crowd had drawn away and I observed from the tone of one man's voice that some misunderstanding had broken out between them. I found out later that that was the deceased man, Mr. Higgins, that I heard.

To the best of my recollection and belief, I wouldn't want to quote the entire conversation because I don't think I remember it well enough but I do believe that I heard Mr. Higgins say, "Now, Phil, you are going too far," I did not hear Philip Ray make any statement at all. I didn't see anyone strike anyone; I think there was a kind of flurry among these men and I saw a man try to separate them and push Mr. Ray back. Then I saw Mr. Ray backing away and he had his hand upon his hip pocket and he had a weapon–a pistol. I got behind an automobile and after that some shots were fired but I did not see who fired the shots. I couldn't say definitely how many shots were fired but I would say three or four. I heard a bullet hit two tires, or at any rate you could hear the sound of air going out of the tires. I don't know that a bullet hit one of the tires on the automobile I was behind, but it was either that one or the one next to me. As I remember, Mr. Higgins said, "Go ahead, I am not afraid of you," and stood back and extended his arms somewhat like this (indicating by reaching his arms out in front), and seemed completely unafraid. I should say it was 20 or 30 seconds after this that the guns began to fire, and the last time I saw Higgins he was standing there with his hands extended up. 15 or 20 minutes later I saw Higgins in the Blue Ridge Grill and that is when I got acquainted with him. I saw Mr. Ray walk between the line of cars later. I went to the jail the following morning and saw Mr. Ray and talked with him.

–Case no. 146, Eighteenth District,
Supreme Court of North Carolina. Fall Term, 1937.
State v. Philip Ray and Otis Chase.

* * *

"Go on and shoot, goddam you! I'm not afraid of you!"

To Eugene, who has dodged back into the recessed entrance of the drug store, someone calls out sharply: "Better git behind a car there at the curb, man! You ain't got no protection in that doorway!"

Moving with the urgency of instant fear, Eugene dives across the expanse of open pavement just as the explosion of the first shot blasts the air. The bullet whistles right past his nose as he ducks behind a car. Cautiously he peers around the side to see Emmet moving slowly with a strange grin on his face, circling slowly to the shot, mocking his antagonist with the gun, his big hands spread palms outward in a gesture of invitation.

"Go on, goddam you, shoot! You bastard, I'm not scared of you!"

The second shot blows out a tire on the car Eugene has retreated to. He crouches lower–another shot–the sharp hiss of escaping air from another tire, and Emmet's whine, derisive, scornful:

"Why, go on and shoot, goddam you!"

A fourth shot–

"Go on! Go on! Goddam you, I'm not–"

A fifth–and silence.

Then Ted Reed comes walking slowly past the row of cars. Men step out from behind them and say quietly:

"What's wrong, Ted?"

Sullenly, the gun held straight downward at his thigh: "Oh, he tried to git smart with me."

Other voices now, calling to each other:

"Where'd he git 'im?"

"Right underneath the eye. He never knowed what him 'im."

–*The Hills Beyond,* p. 128

I don't think I will spend the rest of my life in New York. I find myself wanting to get out. I find that country people have more rugged character and upstanding traits. I used to be chiefly interested in books. Now I am attracted by people. The essential reality of human experience is as alive in the city as in the country.

–*Thomas Wolfe Interviewed,* p. 89

Return to Asheville

Wolfe returned to Asheville on 3 May 1937 and stayed with his mother in her boardinghouse for twelve days. During his visit he was besieged by friends and autograph seekers, all curious and eager to see the city's most famous prodigal son. The 4 May notice in the morning paper, The Asheville Citizen, *was followed by a fuller article in the afternoon paper,* The Asheville Times.

Thos. Wolfe Comes Home
For First Time Since Writing Novel
The Asheville Citizen, 4 May 1937

Thomas Wolfe came home yesterday for the first time since his book "Look Homeward Angel," made him famous more than seven years ago.

The author said he was glad to be back, that many times during his travels in Europe and his residence in New York he had been homesick for Asheville, its people and its surrounding mountains.

He said he was devoting all his efforts on a new book and added:

"If anything I have ever written has displeased anyone in Asheville, I hope that I will be able to write another book which will please them."

Mr. Wolfe is staying with his mother, Mrs. Julia Wolfe, at her home, 48 Spruce street. He said he expected to be in Asheville only three or four days. He will then go back to New York to work on his book but plans to return to this section around July 1, take a cabin somewhere in the mountains, and continue his work.

The author came home by way of Gettysburg, Pa., the native home of his father, the late W. O. Wolfe, of Asheville. He made the trip in short stages, coming to Asheville yesterday from Burnsville where he spent several days.

"It was an exciting trip," he said. "I was coming home. I was renewing my connection with my own neck of the woods."

Wolfe made no apology for his book "Look Homeward Angel," which, when it first appeared in 1929, aroused considerable feeling in Asheville because it contained characters which most persons said were residents of the city.

He did say, however, that he was sorry if he had displeased anyone and blamed his youth for drawing perhaps too much on the only raw material with which he had to work.

"When a young writer writes," he explained, "he takes the most direct means, and often he turns too directly to the raw material he has before him. When he grows older, he learns to transform this raw material."

* * *

Wolfe and his mother on the porch of her boardinghouse, Old Kentucky Home, in May 1937 (photograph by Elliot Lyman Fisher; The Thomas Wolfe Collection, Pack Memorial Public Library, Asheville, North Carolina)

Thomas Wolfe Welcomed By Friends Here
The Asheville Times, 4 May 1937

Man Who Wrote 'Look Homeward Angel'
Happy To Be Back Home.

Thomas Wolfe, whose last visit to Asheville seven-and-a-half years ago saw him a young university professor with a bulky manuscript his chief claim to literary fame, came back to his home town a famous author and was acclaimed by a multitude of friends and autograph seekers.

The manuscript, "Look Homeward Angel," was published shortly afterwards and Mr. Wolfe advanced to the front rank of modern American writers.

"It's grand to be back," Mr. Wolfe told newspapermen this morning. "I feel good every time I see something familiar," he said, recalling that the buildings on the north side of Pack square are much the same as the days he was a boy growing up here.

"I feel perfectly at home," he continued. "You can't change the mountains," he added as an afterthought.

Phone Rings Constantly

All morning the telephone rang at the home of Mr. Wolfe's mother, Mrs. Julia E. Wolfe, of 48 Spruce street, as friends and well wishers called to welcome the author home. Many called in person, as at one time there were as many as six persons waiting to see Mr. Wolfe.

Mr. Wolfe came to Asheville yesterday afternoon from Burnsville, in Yancey county, where he spent a few days enroute here.

Early this morning, he arose and walked to the home of his sister here, Mrs. R. H. Wheaton, of 201 Charlotte street, where he later received newspapermen over a cup of coffee at the breakfast table.

Wants Place to Work

Mr. Wolfe said he was looking for a small place in the mountains to which he could return this summer probably the end of June, and work. "I don't want anything touristy," he explained, "but just a small place." "I am getting fed up with all the noise and roar of New York, although living in New York is a grand experience."

Mr. Wolfe, six feet and five-and-a-half inches tall and weighing 240 pounds, dominated the breakfast table. As he talked over his coffee and cigarette, three members of the American Business club came in to ask him to address the meeting of the club today.

One of the three–James S. Howell–was an old friend of Mr. Wolfe's. "I can't make a talk," Mr. Wolfe told Mr. Howell. "You know the Wolfes were always tongue-tied." Finally, Mr. Wolfe agreed to make a short talk.

Returning to his mother's home on Spruce street, the author found other friends waiting in the sun parlor of the home, where his diplomas from the University of North Carolina and Harvard university hung on the wall. In a bookcase were copies of "Look Homeward, Angel," "Of Time and the River" and others of his writings.

Visits Familiar Spots

Arriving by bus yesterday from Burnsville, Mr. Wolfe took a taxi from the bus terminal to his mother's home. "Aren't you one of the Wolfe boys?" the author said the taxi driver asked. Receiving an affirmative answer, the driver continued, "I thought you talked like one of the Wolfe boys." Then he asked, "What became of your brother who sold Saturday Evening Posts?"

Yesterday and early this morning, the author walked over many sections of the city, visiting old and familiar places. He stopped by the old Wolfe residence on Woodfin street and followed the paper route he once carried out Charlotte street for The Asheville Citizen.

Until he leaves for New York the latter part of this week, Mr. Wolfe said he plans to visit around the city and drive out into the country. "I hope I don't have to make any more speeches," he said, "but I do want to see everybody."

Asked for comment on the awarding of the Pulitzer prize last night to Margaret Mitchell for her "Gone With the Wind," Mr. Wolfe said he was glad to hear of Miss Mitchell's good fortune. He said he bought a copy of the book in Roanoke, Va., on his trip to this section, and planned to read it.

Now Reads Little

Formerly, Mr. Wolfe said he read everything, but now reads very few current books. On this trip he brought along copies of the Bible, Shakespeare, the World Almanac, "David Copperfield," "Don Quixote" and an old school textbook on French literature.

He finds relaxation in reading the almanac. "After a hard day's grind on imaginative work, there is something relaxing about cold hard figures," he explained. "Too, I am interested in baseball and I like sometimes to find out what Babe Ruth hit in 1927. I have a curious interest in figures and a passion for travel, so I like to know how many people there are in a town, its industries and such as I travel."

Has Plenty Of Material

Mr. Wolfe, in answer to a question, said he was not afraid of running out of material for his books. He has completed rough drafts of two novels to go in the "Of Time and River" series. The series is to consist of six books and the two have had "October Fair" and "The Hills Beyond Pentland" tentatively selected as their titles. Another probably will be known as "Hounds of Darkness."

Mr. Wolfe's first book, "Look Homeward Angel," when it first appeared in 1929, aroused considerable feeling in Asheville because it contained characters which many persons said were residents of this city. The author made no apology for his book. He did say, however, that he was sorry if he had displeased anyone.

"If anything I have ever written has displeased anyone in Asheville, I hope that I shall be able to write another book which will please them," he said.

Before leaving Asheville Wolfe rented a cabin in nearby Oteen, where he hoped for seclusion and planned to work in the summer. Just before departing for New York, Wolfe was asked by George W. McCoy, a journalist for The Asheville Citizen, *to write an article about his feelings at being home again. The prose-poem "Return" appeared in the 16 May 1937 issue of the newspaper.*

Return

I have been seven years from home, but now I have come back again. And what is there to say?

Time passes, and puts halters to debate. There is too much to say; there is so much to say that must be spoken; there is so much to say that never can be told:– we say it in the impassioned solitudes of youth, and of ten thousand nights and days of absence and return. But in the end, the answer to it all is time and silence: this answers all; and after this, there is no more to say.

So has it been with me. For there has been a time when I would wake just at the first blue-gray of dawn to feel the shoulder strap again against my arm, the canvas bag, the blocked sheet and the final shot beneath the oak tree on the lawn before the lawyer's great white house–to know my route was ended and that work was done, and that morning had come back again–so thinking, feeling, and remembering, then, that I was far away, and that I had been long from home.

Then all old things would come again–both brick and wall, and step and hedge, the way a street sloped or a tree was standing, the way a gate hung or a house was set, the very cinders of a rutted alley way–such things as these would come again, leaf, blade, and stone, and door. So much more door than any other one could ever be–like all things that belong to men–the essence of all doors that ever were because it is his own, the door that he has passed a thousand times–all things like these would come back again, the whole atomic pattern of my native earth, my town, my childhood, and my youth, with all the faces, all lives and histories of long ago–and all forgotten weathers of man's memory would come again, there in the darkness in some foreign land, would come so poignant, swift, and vivid in the whiteness of their blazing panoply that I could feel my foot upon the street again, my hand upon the rail, the strap upon my shoulder, the whole sensuous unit of my native earth, with an intensity that I had never known before. And I could taste it, feel it, smell it, live it through again, hard to the hilt of exile, as I was born perhaps to live all things and moments, hard to the hilt, and carrying on that furious and impassioned argument of youth and solitude, contending fiercely with a thousand disputants, would think: "I have a thing that I must tell them; I'll go home again, I'll meet them and I'll say my piece: I will lay bare my purposes, strip down the vision of my life until its bare soul's nakedness, tell my people what it is to try to shape and spin a living out of the entrails of man's life, and what he visions, why he does it–oh, some day I will go back and reveal my plan until no man living in the world can doubt it–I will show them utterly:–"

Photograph that accompanied "Return," The Asheville Citizen, *16 May 1937*

–And I have come back now: I have come home again, and there is nothing more that I can say.–All arguments are ended: saying nothing, all is said then; all is known: I am home.

Where are the words I thought that I must say, the arguments I thought that I should make, the debates and demonstrations that so often, in those years of absence, memory, wandering, youth, and new discovery I had so hotly made to solitude and to the ghostly audience of an absent fellowship, the thousand things that I would prove and show when I returned–where are they now?

For I have come home again–and what is there to say? I think that there is nothing–save the silence of our speech. I think that there is nothing–save the knowledge of our glance. I think that there is nothing–save the silent and unspoken conscience in us now that needs no speech but silence, because we know what we know, we have what we have, we are what we are.

So what is there to say?

"You've put on weight since I last saw you."

"Yes, but you are just the same."

"Have you seen Bob yet? He's been looking for you."

"No; but he came by the house last night, but I wasn't there. I'm seeing him today."

"Sam Red was asking about you. . . . Here's Jim now."

" . . . Come on, boys! Here he is! We've got him now! He's on the spot! Let's pin him down and make him own up! . . . Wasn't that Whit Nelson you had in mind when you told about the night he bought up all the gold fish down a Wood's? . . . What's that he wrote, Ed, about the time you slept all night in Reagan's hearse and woke up scared to death next morning when you found out where you were?"

"Why, Lord, he got the facts right, but the figures were all wrong! I slept all night in Reagan's hearse, all right, but you and Jim were with me, too–and you were worse scared when you woke up in the morning than I was! That's all I objected to; he should have put that in!"

" . . . And what was that you said, Paul, when he told of how you used to take the grass widow from Paducah down to Riverside on Thursday night and buy her popcorn? . . . Come on, now . . . you can't back out on us: you know you said it–tell him what you said."

"Why, hell, I only said she wasn't forty-four, the way HE said, but forty-eight, and that instead of two gold teeth the way HE had it, she had three. And two of them were on the side, with a great big bright one in the middle–not one above and one below the way HE told about it. And it wasn't popcorn that I bought 'her,' but a bag of peanuts. I just wanted him to get it straight, that's all!"

"Come on, now! Own up! You had us all in mind! We've got you on the spot . . . Confess! . . . Look at his face! He don't know what to say!"

"Hell, son, there's nothing that you have to say. We all understand. There were some folks around here when that book of yours first came out who thought you'd written up the town and put them in the book; and some who were mad about it for a while. But that's all forgotten now. So much has happened since those days, that anything you said was mild. You stayed away too long. We're glad that you've come home."

And there is nothing more to say.

". . . You'll find things changed, though. It's not the place you used to know. . . . I guess you'll find it changed a lot. . . . Your father's marble shop was on this corner. . . . Do you remember the old wooden steps? . . . The draymen sitting on the steps? . . . the tombstones and the angel on the porch? . . . Your father standing there a thousand times . . . the old fire department and the city hall . . . the city market and the calaboose . . . the fountain and the street cars coming in upon the quarter hour? We've put buses in since the time you went away. . . . Have you been through the tunnel yet? . . . It's all changed so much you wouldn't know the place."

Change? There is no change. These surfaces have altered and these shapes are new. . . . There is a wrinkle by the eye we did not have before; a furrow in the cheek; a kind of worn humor in the grin about the lip, a look plain, steady, naked, touched with care that twenty did not know–our hue is rougher and our groove more deep–time passes, WE have grown older, much water and some blood has gone beneath the bridge since then: I think we know each other better–but, oh, brothers, friends, and comrades of this mortal dust–we have not changed!

For here again, again, I turn into the street, finding again the place where corners meet, looking again to see if time is there. And all of it is as it has always been: again, again, I turn, and find again the things that I have always known: the cool sweet magic of starred mountain night, the huge attentiveness of dark, the slope, the street, the trees, the living silence of the houses waiting, and the fact that April has come back again. . . . And again, again, in the old house I feel beneath my tread the creak of the old stair, the worn rail, the whitewashed walls, the feel of darkness and the house asleep, and think, "I was a child here; here the stairs and here was darkness; this was I, and here is Time."

These things will never change. Some things will never change: the groove is deeper, but the leaf, the bud, the wheel, the blade, and April will come back again.

The wheel will turn, the immortal wheel of life will turn, but it will never change. Here from this little universe of time and place, from this small core and adyt of my being where once, hill-born and bound, a child, I lay at night, and heard the whistles wailing to the west, the thunder of great wheels along the river's edge, and wrought my vision from these hills of the great undiscovered earth and my America–here, now, forevermore, shaped here in this small world, and in the proud and flaming spirit of a boy, new children have come after us, as we: as we, the boy's face in the morning yet, and mountain night, and starlight, darkness, and the month of April, and the boy's straight eye: again, again, the thudding press, the aching shoulder, and the canvas bag; the lean arm and the rifled throw again, that whacked the blocked and folded sheet against the shacks of Niggertown.

. . . These things, or such as these, will come again; so, too, the high heart and the proud and flaming vision of a child–to do the best that may be in him, shaped from this earth, as we, and patterned by this scheme, to wreak with all his might with humbleness and pride, to strike here from his native rock, I pray, the waters of our thirst, to get here from his native earth, his vision of this earth and this America, to hear again, as we, the wheel, the whistle, and the trolley bell; so, too, as we, to go out from these hills and find and shape the great America of our discovery; so, too, as we, who write these words, to know again the everlasting legend of man's youth–flight, quest, and wandering–exile and return.

–*The Complete Stories of Thomas Wolfe,* pp. 296–299

Wolfe's great-uncle John Baird Westall, the source for the story "Chickamauga," which was published in The Hills Beyond *(The Thomas Wolfe Collection, Pack Memorial Public Library, Asheville, North Carolina)*

"Chickamauga"

In a 13 July 1937 letter to Hamilton Basso, Wolfe recalled that he "worked like fury for eight weeks" after he returned to New York in May, writing six stories. The letter explains that "the ways of commercial editors are very strange and hard to fathom." He was especially puzzled that The Saturday Evening Post, *after accepting "The Child by Tiger," had rejected a story Wolfe considered superior.*

I wrote a story called "Chickamauga" and if I do say so, it is one of the best stories I ever wrote. I got the idea for it from an old, old man, my great-uncle, John Westall, who lives over in Yancey County and who is ninety-five years old. When I saw him this spring, he began to tell me about the Civil War and about the battle of Chickamauga, which was, he said, the bloodiest, most savage battle he was ever in. He told about it all so wonderfully and in such pungent and poetic language, such as so many of the old country people around here use, that I couldn't wait to get back to New York to begin on it. My idea was simply to tell the story of a great battle in the language of a common soldier–the kind of country mountain boy who did so much of the fighting in the war. The *Post* heard that I was writing it and they liked the story they had bought so much and were apparently so eager to get some more stories from me, that they telegraphed Miss Nowell even before I had finished and asked that they be allowed to see it before anyone else. Well, we sent it off to them and Miss Nowell and I thought it was a cinch. The story was so good, really much better than the one they had taken, and it simply crackled with action from the first line and besides that, it was so real, so true–it was all told in the old man's language and when you read it, it was just as if he was there talking to you. What do you suppose happened? In a week's time the story came back with a regretful note from *The Post* to the effect that although they appreciated its "literary merit"–I wonder by the way what the Hell people mean by "literary merit." Is there any other kind of merit where a piece of writing is concerned? I have never been able to see that there was, although so many people seem to think there is . . . that there really are two kinds of books, books that are good in a "literary sort of way," and "good" books, but of course . . . it is all nonsense–at any rate, *The Post* rejected "Chickamauga," apparently with the idea that it was good "in a literary sort of way," but that it did not have enough of the "story element." Nowell and I were absolutely flabbergasted. What in the name of God do these people mean by "story element"? And what is a story anyway? All this piece had was the whole Civil War, the life of a common soldier and his account of one of the bloodiest battles that was ever fought. If it had had any more of the "story element" it would have exploded into electricity.

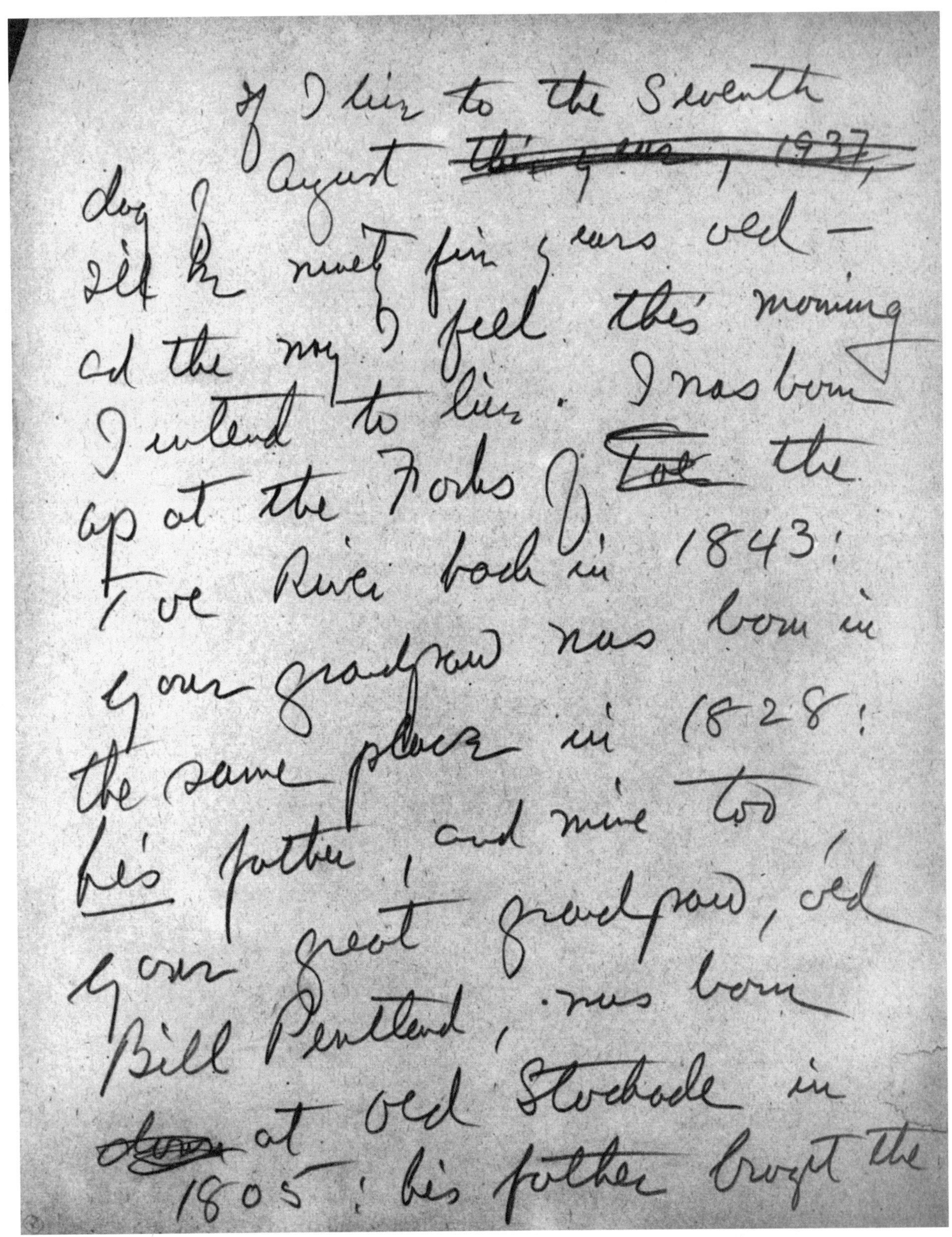
If I live to the Seventh
day of August
I'll be ninety five years old —
and the way I feel this morning
I intend to live. I was born
up at the Forks of the
Toe River back in 1843;
your grandpaw was born in
the same place in 1828;
his father, and mine too,
your great grandpaw, old
Bill Pentland, was born
at old Stockade in
1805; his father brought the

First page of the manuscript for "Chickamauga" (William B. Wisdom Collection, Houghton Library, Harvard University)

The cabin Wolfe rented in Oteen from his boyhood friend, Max Whitson. Wolfe used the tree house at the right as a workroom (The Thomas Wolfe Collection, Pack Memorial Public Library, Asheville, North Carolina).

Oteen, Summer 1937

Before he left New York, Wolfe wrote to his brother Fred W. Wolfe about his fears concerning his summer at the Oteen cabin.

865 First Avenue
New York, N.Y.
June 26, 1937

Dear Fred:

I have wanted to answer your letter before this, but I have been driving as hard as I could go ever since I got back here five or six weeks ago in an effort to get as much work done as possible before I leave here. I am trying to wind it up to-day and to-morrow. I have been working every day, and often at night also with Miss Nowell, my agent. She is coming here again tomorrow, Sunday, for another go at it and I hope then to finish up the work I have been doing. . . .

According to my present plans I hope to leave here for Asheville some time next week, possibly around Tuesday or Wednesday. I am dog-tired, just about played out, and dreading the big job of packing, getting ready, that is before me. My main concern is, of course, my manuscript. There is an immense amount of it, millions of words, and although it might not be of any use to anyone else, it is, so far as I am concerned, the most valuable thing I have got. My life is in it–years and years of work and sweating blood–and the material of about three unpublished books. I am going to bring it with me to North Carolina, but I have not fully decided yet just what means of transportation I shall use. I hate to take the chance of letting it go out of my sight. I suppose the Railway Express is safe enough. What I should prefer to do would be to take it right with me in the train, but unfortunately there is so much of it that nothing less than a good-sized packing-case would hold it. In addition, I have to buy some clothes and supplies and take along my bedding and towels. Mama has written me that she will need all that she has this summer so, as you can see, I have quite a problem in moving upon my hands.

I got a letter from Max Whitson this morning in which he informs me that he has put the cabin in good shape, waxed the floors, fixed up the road that leads to the place, and has put in some new furniture, and that everything is now comfortable and ready. If this is so, I think I ought to find it a good place to live and work, if too many people don't start coming out and paying me casual and unexpected visits.

People, of course, don't seem to be able to get this into their heads. Most people don't realize that writing is not only hard work, but that a writer, when he works, works several times as hard as the average business man. Moreover, when a writer is working he ought not to be interrupted, and few people are able to understand how big a difference that makes. A great many people apparently think that they can drop in on a man while he is writing and spend an hour or two in conversation–that it does not matter very much–that he can make it all up later. Well, this is not the way it goes: he ought not to be interrupted: if he is, it sometimes throws him completely off the track and he cannot make it up.

My experience has been that most business and professional people do not work very hard, not nearly as hard as they think they do. This is particularly true of a town like Asheville. I have always noticed in Asheville, even in my childhood, how much time nearly everyone has to waste. Lawyers and bankers and business people are always coming in and out of the drug store, fooling around and talking to one another: apparently they have time to burn. I noticed this again when I was home in May: a lot of the boys I know who are now lawyers would invite me up to their offices in the Jackson Building and we would spend an entire afternoon talking, and no one would come in. The point I am trying to make here is that, as much as I should like to, I have not got time to burn this way. I have got my living to earn: I have got an immense amount of work to do, and I sincerely and earnestly want to see my friends and members of my family this summer, but I do hope they will have understanding and consideration enough to see the problem I am faced with and to allow me privacy and peace to get my work accomplished.

I am appealing to you to help me in my purpose in any way you can. I know that Mama does not wholly understand how hard I have to work and how desperately serious I am when I say I have to work and must be given time and quiet in which to do it. I don't think that Mama has ever fully understood that writing is not only hard work, but harder work than she has any idea of. From what she said to me once or twice, I gathered that she may not even understand that it is work at all but rather a kind of lucky trick which the person lucky enough to possess can use when and where he chooses in his off moments and at absolutely no expense of time and trouble. Well, it is not a lucky trick. It is a desperate, back-breaking, nerve-wracking and brain-fatiguing labor. And, in addition to this, it is often a very thankless and heart-breaking labor because a man may give years of his youth and best effort to a piece of work and then get nothing for it except abuse. Of course, I am making no criticism of Mama whatever: her point of view is a familiar one among people who have had no experience with such work and who get a very romantic idea about it, but I am sure that I can explain it to you and that you will understand what I say and will help me in any way you can to get the peace and quiet that I so much want and need.

I don't think anybody quite understood when I was home just how tired I am and how much I need now a period of quiet and seclusion. But I do need it very badly, and that is the reason that I have taken the little cabin out near Asheville in the hope and belief that I can get it there. If I fail to get it there, it is going to be a bitter disappointment, but I really have high hopes that it will turn out well. I think my friends in New York all understand how much I need it now, and are earnestly hoping I shall get it this summer. Of course, you have not seen a great deal of me since the publication of "Look Homeward, Angel," almost eight years ago. But there has really been almost no rest or relaxation for me since then. First of all, as you know, there was the great stir and rumpus in Asheville about "The Angel," all of the talk and feeling of perturbation, and I got a full share of that. Then I was faced with the problem and task of getting another book done, of meeting the challenge of the critics, who praise you one month and revile you the next, and who keep pressing all the time to get another book out of you. I had very little money, and after the royalties on "Look Homeward, Angel" were exhausted I had to depend for my living on an occasional story or on money that Scribners advanced to me. Thus I was under the constant strain of knowing that I was in debt to my publisher and that I ought to try to do something to pay that off.

The book that I was writing developed into a project of such tremendous size that it turned out to be four or five books instead of one, and five years or more went by before I was able to get the first of these books completed and published. During most of this time I lived in Brooklyn and worked like a dog. In addition, there were personal troubles which I believe are all settled now, but which took from me a heavy toll in time, worry and anxiety. When "Of Time and the River" was published a little more than two years ago, I thought that my troubles were over. But it seems now as if they were just beginning. I went abroad to rest. I was as close to utter physical and nervous exhaustion as I had ever been in my life. There was a time there when I was seriously afraid that I might not be able to pull myself back again, but I managed to. And then, as you know, the storm broke. I returned to America feeling sure that now, at last, I had a secure position, a very modest income, the independence and, for the first time in my life, the peace and comfort that would enable me to continue my work hereafter in tranquility. I found instead that I had been thrown into a whirlpool. I was set upon by every kind of parasite, every kind of harpy, every kind of vulture, every kind of female egotist that had a string to pull, or that thought they could get something out of me–whether money, manuscript, royalties, percentages, or simply a sop to their vanity. Since I was–and this is the truth–a more or less unsuspecting and believing person who responds very quickly to people and to apparent overtures of friendship and good will, I was taken for quite a ride.

I am not kicking or complaining about this at all. On the whole, I came through it all right. I think I shall always be glad I had the experience and that it taught me something. But I am merely telling you that, instead of the peace and security I thought I should now get, I found myself in the lions' den, and I have fought it out with the animals for over two years now. On the whole, I do not think I have done badly. They have taken me for quite a promenade: . . . I have learned a good many very hard and bitter and disagreeable facts about life and about some of the adventures and people one could meet in it, but I have not lost my faith either in life or in people, I am more grateful than I have ever been for my true friends and for the many fine people I have known, and I have kept on working. So, with all humility and deference, I think I will come out all right.

However–and this is the point of the whole matter, the reason I am writing you this letter, the reason I am explaining all these things to you, knowing that I can depend on your help and understanding–the point, I say, is: I am now damn tired–and I want to get a rest. I am not merely saying I am tired, I am not just pretending I am tired–I am, actually, honestly and genuinely–nervously, physically and mentally. I believe a few weeks out there in the cabin will fix me up again. I am eager–more eager than I have ever been–to work, and I believe I will get a lot of work done out there. But I do know how I feel now; I do know what has happened to me and what I have been through these last seven or eight years; and I do know exactly what I want to do now–which is to get out to my cabin, to get some rest and relaxation, and to work–and I can only earnestly pray that all my friends and members of my family will understand this extremely normal, sensible desire, and help me every way they can. And that is why I am writing you this letter–because I know I can appeal to you and that you will understand exactly my problem when I put it before you–and that I can depend on you, tactfully and diplomatically, without hurting anyone's feelings, to get other people to understand it too.

Of course, I had a good time when I was home in May. It was wonderful to be home again after so long an absence, and it was fine to see all of you and to resume contacts with so many people that I had known. It was for me a wonderful home-coming: I am glad I got to see so many people and to talk to them, but I was pretty well fagged out when I left. My desire now, I think, is a pretty sensible one. I do not want to go out in the country and become an utter hermit; I hope that all these people who were so nice to me in May will not have forgotten they know me by the time I come back; I hope to see many of them this summer and that they will visit me at the cabin. But I also hope that they show some discretion and won't overwhelm me, and that I get a chance to rest up and to do some work. I think all of this is perfectly plain and sensible and that any intelligent person would see my point immediately and agree with me.

This is all for the present. I am sorry that the letter is so long, but I thought it would be a good idea if I wrote you and told you something of my present problems and difficulties before I come down. Of course, I should like to come to Spartanburg and meet your friends, but just at the present time, feeling as tired as I do, it seems to me it would be a better plan if I got out in the country and rested up a week or two before meeting anyone you know. At any rate, I will let you know when I arrive. Meanwhile, with all good wishes to you until I see you.

–*The Letters of Thomas Wolfe,* pp. 619–620

Leaving New York on 1 July and arriving at the Biltmore station outside of Asheville the next day, Wolfe went directly to the Oteen cabin. Wolfe was treated as a celebrity in North Carolina, especially by the Asheville newspapers. This article announcing Wolfe's return to the area was the first of many reports of his activities that summer.

Tom Wolfe To Spend The Summer Writing At Cabin Near Here

The Asheville Citizen, 4 July 1937

Thomas Wolfe, the author, has taken a mountain cabin a short distance east of Asheville where he will spend the summer writing.

Mr. Wolfe, a native of Asheville, arrived here Friday from New York, it was learned yesterday. He left the train at the Biltmore station and proceeded directly to the cabin. He came to Asheville yesterday for supplies.

His mother, Mrs. Julia E. Wolfe, said he expected to rest a few days and then "get down to hard work for several weeks." He will be host at a family dinner at the cabin this evening in celebration of the Fourth of July. Those attending will be his mother; his sister, Mrs. Ralph Wheaton, of Asheville; Mr. Wheaton; and Miss Henrietta Westall, a niece of the author's mother.

Mr. Wolfe, author of "Look Homeward, Angel," "Of Time and the River," and other works, visited Asheville early in May. It was his first visit since he became distinguished for his writing several years ago. At that time he expressed pleasure over his visit and announced his intention to come back during the summer, to rent a cabin and spend the summer at work.

He has hired a negro man to cook and do the housework. The cabin sits on a wooded knoll a few miles from the city. It includes a spacious living room in which Mr. Wolfe probably will do his writing.

Wolfe At Work In Mountain Cabin

Asheville Citizen July 11, 1937

The Citizen-Times photographer paid Author Thomas Wolfe a visit at his mountain cabin yesterday afternoon, and found him working on his new book. With shirt sleeves rolled up, tie discarded and collar open, Mr. Wolfe was writing in longhand on a book which he intends to be "a chronicle to the modern Gulliver." He took a mountain cabin near Asheville a week ago to spend the remainder of the summer working on the book. Mr. Wolfe said he expects to begin work later on the follow-up to his "Of Time and the River" series.

The Asheville Citizen, *11 July 1937*

In his 13 July letter to Hamilton Basso, Wolfe described how to get to his cabin and his feelings about being there.

I am about 6 miles from Asheville and if you come through town the best way to get here is through the tunnel. When you get to the Recreation Park you take the road to the right that leads up around the lake at the Park. This is a gravel road but not a bad one. The entrance to my place is about two-thirds of a mile from the place where you turn off at the Recreation Park. You can recognize the place by two large wooden gates which have lanterns on top of them. If I know you are coming, the gates will be open and the lanterns lit. I am on top of the hill at the end of this road: it is a cabin completely hidden from sight by tremendous trees. It is really a good place and I hope to do a lot of work here. So far I have done little except sleep–after New York it has been a blessed relief to be out here. About the only human sound I hear out here is the wail of the train whistle going by the foot of my hill in the azalea bottoms and occasionally very faint music from the Merry-Go-Around at the Recreation Park. Of course I love the trains and I don't mind the Park a bit.

–*The Letters of Thomas Wolfe,* p. 624

Wolfe accomplished little in his Oteen cabin except the third draft of "The Party at Jack's." This novella was about a fire that disrupted a party at Aline Bernstein's apartment at 270 Park Avenue, at which artist Alexander Calder entertained the guests with a circus of mechanical animals and dolls. "The Party at Jack's" rendered Wolfe's growing sense of social injustice by contrasting the harsh realities of the working class with the luxury of the privileged class.

In the latter half of July Wolfe received a letter he took to be critical of his work from F. Scott Fitzgerald. Wolfe's response is an impassioned defense of his approach to writing.

9 July 1937

Dear Tom: I think I could make out a good case for your necessity to cultivate an alter ego, a more conscious artist in you. Hasn't it occurred to you that such qualities as pleasantness or grief, exuberance or cynicism can become a plague in others? That often people who live at a high pitch often don't get their way emotionally at the important moment because it doesn't stand out in relief?

Now the more that the stronger man's inner tendencies are defined, the more he can be sure they will show, the more necessity to rarify them, to use them sparingly. The novel of selected incidents has this to be said that the greater writer like Flaubert has consciously left out the stuff that Bill or Joe, (in his case Zola) will come along and say presently. He will say only the things that he alone sees. So Bovary becomes eternal while Zola already rocks with age. Repression itself has a value, as with a poet who struggles for a nessessary ryme achieves accidently a new word association that would not have come by any mental or even flow-of-consciousness process. The Nightengale is full of that.

To a talent like mine of narrow scope there is not that problem. I must put everything in to have enough + even then I often havn't got enough.

That in brief is my case against you, if it can be called that when I admire you so much and think your talent is unmatchable in this or any other country

Ever your friend,
Scott Fitzgerald

–*F. Scott Fitzgerald A Life in Letters,* p. 332

Wolfe wrote to Fitzgerald in care of Scribners–"the old address we both know so well"–from Oteen on 26 July 1937.

The unexpected loquaciousness of your letter struck me all of a heap. I was surprised to hear from you but I don't know that I can truthfully say I was delighted. Your bouquet arrived smelling sweetly of roses but cunningly concealing several large-sized brickbats.

. . . .

I have read your letter several times and I've got to admit it doesn't seem to mean much. I don't know what you are driving at or understand what you hope or expect me to do about it. Now this may be pig-headed but it isn't sore. I may be wrong but all I can get out of it is that you think I'd be a good writer if I were an altogether different writer from the writer that I am.

This may be true but I don't see what I'm going to do about it, and I don't think you can show me. And I don't see what Flaubert and Zola have to do with it, or what I have to do with them. I wonder if you really think they have anything to do with it, or if it is just something you heard in college or read in a book somewhere. This either-or kind of criticism seems to me to be so meaningless. It looks so knowing and imposing but there is nothing in it. Why does it follow that if a man writes a book that is not like "Madame Bovary" it is inevitably like Zola? I may be dumb but I can't see this. You say that "Madame Bovary" becomes eternal while Zola already rocks with age. Well this may be true–but if it is true isn't it true because "Madame Bovary" may be a great book and those that Zola wrote may not be great ones? Wouldn't it also be true to say that "Don Quixote," or "Pickwick" or "Tristram Shandy" "becomes eternal" while already Mr. Galsworthy "rocks with age"? I think it is true to say this and it doesn't leave much of your argument, does it? For your argument is based simply upon one *way,* upon one *method* instead of another. And have you ever noticed how often it turns out that what a man is really doing is simply rationalizing his own way of doing something, the way he has to do it, the way given him by his talent and his nature, into the only inevitable and right way of doing everything–a sort of classic and eternal art form handed down by Apollo from Olympus without which and beyond which there is nothing? Now you have your way of doing something and I have mine; there are a lot of ways, but you are honestly mistaken in thinking that there is a "way."

I suppose I would agree with you in what you say about "the novel of selected incidents" so far as it means anything. I say so far as it means anything because every novel, of course, is a novel of selected incidents. There are no novels of unselected incidents. You couldn't write about the inside of a telephone booth without selecting. You could fill a novel of a thousand pages with a description of a single room and yet your incidents would be selected. And I have mentioned "Don Quixote" and Pickwick and "The Brothers Karamazov" and "Tristram Shandy" to you in contrast to "The Silver Spoon" or "The White Monkey" as examples of books that have become "immortal" and that *boil* and *pour.* Just remember that although "Madame Bovary" in your opinion may be a great book, "Tristram Shandy" *is* indubitably a great book, and that it is great for quite different reasons. It is great because it *boils* and *pours*–for the *unselected* quality of its selection. You say that the great writer like Flaubert has consciously left out the stuff that Bill or Joe will come along presently and put in. Well, don't forget, Scott,

Jack's 71

looked somewhat bewildered. The new arrivals, who had not been invited were, for the most part, young peoples and obviously they belonged to Mr. Piggy Logan's "social set". The young women had that subtle yet unmistakable appearance of having gone to Miss Spence's School for Girls and the young men, by the same token, seemed to have gone to Yale and Harvard and one was also sure that some of them were members of the Racquet Club and were now connected with a firm of "investment brokers" and in downtown New York. In addition, there was with them a large well-kept somewhat decayed looking lady of advanced middle age and a gentleman past sixty, faultlessly attired in evening dress, as were all the others, and with a cropped moustache and artificial teeth, who looked remarkably like some of the characters portrayed by Mr. Henry James. These people streamed in noisily and vociferously, headed by an elegant young gentleman in a white tie and tails whose name, curiously, was Hen Walters, and who was evidently a bosom friend of Mr. Logan. Mrs. Jack looked somewhat overwhelmed, but was dutifully murmuring greetings and welcome when all the new people swarmed right past her

Typescript page revised by Wolfe for "The Party at Jack's" (William B. Wisdom Collection, Houghton Library, Harvard University)

that a great writer is not only a leaver-outer but also a putter-inner, and that Shakespeare and Cervantes and Dostoievsky were great putter-inners–greater putter-inners, in fact, than taker-outers–and will be remembered for what they put in–remembered, I venture to say, as long as Monsieur Flaubert will be remembered for what he left out.

–*The Letters of Thomas Wolfe,* pp. 642–643

At the cabin Wolfe was plagued by the interruptions he had feared, as he makes clear in a 29 July 1937 letter to Hamilton Basso.

I intend to keep at work, and so far as I know, except for the hordes of thirsty tourists who just happen in casually to look at the elephant, I have no definite engagements. . . . Except for casual intrusions–people driving up to demand if I've seen anything of a stray cocker spaniel, gentlemen appearing through the woods with a four-pound steak saying their name is McCracken and I met them on the train four weeks ago and they always bring their own provisions with them, and the local Police Court judge and the leading hot-dog merchant, and friends of my shooting scrape in Yancey County with bevies of wild females–all of which has and is continuing to happen–I have practically no company at all out here. At any rate it's all been very interesting and instructing and in spite of Hell and hilarity I am pushing on with my work. You come on over anyway: I can't promise you long twenty-four hour periods of restful seclusion while we meditate upon the problems of life and art, but you may have an instructive and amusing time, and of course I'd love to see you and talk it over with you.

. . . .

I've just taken time out to have pictures of myself, the cabin and all three of us made by a beautiful lady and her escort, Judge Phil Cocke, who weights 340 on the hoof and is one of Asheville's famous and eminent characters. I like the Judge and the Judge curiously seems to like me; certainly I've never had as devoted and accurate a reader–he hasn't forgotten a comma or a semicolon, he annotates my book with the names of the "real" characters, and I have heard that he was especially touched and delighted because he thinks I referred to him and a very celebrated lady in Asheville who bore the name of Queen Elizabeth and who at one time was the Empress of the Red Light District. Of course, I admit nothing, I just look coy and innocent–but if that's the way they want to have it, I suppose no one can stop them.

–*The Letters of Thomas Wolfe,* pp. 645–646, 647

In a 4 August 1937 letter to author Anne W. Armstrong, who had written Wolfe to offer him the use of a cabin in Bristol, Tennessee, Wolfe clearly had Fitzgerald on his mind.

It really seems that such talent as I have has to realize itself through a process of torrential production–that is, by pouring out in a Niagara flood, millions and millions of words. After that, of course, comes the ghastly and heart-breaking labor of cutting it down, shaping and re-weaving it. It's all very well for these fellows who write forty and fifty thousand word books to talk to you about Flaubert and classical brevity: you can try honestly to mend your ways, to learn through experience and work to correct some of your most excessive faults–but what's the use of talking to a man about Flaubert if his talent–such modest talent as he has–is really more like Dickens or Rabelais? Anyway, all I can do is to learn what I can and to do my work, I pray, the best I can.

–*The Letters of Thomas Wolfe,* p. 649

Wolfe with Judge Philip Cocke and an unidentified woman outside the Oteen cabin, 29 July 1937 (William B. Wisdom Collection, Houghton Library, Harvard University)

Wolfe left Asheville on 2 September 1937. For the newspapers he was almost wholly positive about his summer experience. The day following Wolfe's departure, The Asheville Citizen *reported that he had completed "The Party at Jack's."*

Wolfe Leaves After Summer Visit Here; Finishes New Story
The Asheville Citizen, 3 September 1937

Thomas Wolfe, the author, departed Asheville yesterday after spending the summer in a cabin near the city.

Under his arm he carried an 80,000-word manuscript he has written since coming here in June. It is entitled "The Party at Jack's" and is a story about the lives of 20 or 30 people in an apartment house in New York. This story gives a cross-section of everyday life in the big city, Wolfe explained.

A native of Asheville, Wolfe came here last May for the first time since "Look Homeward, Angel" and "Of Time and The River" made him famous. He stayed a few days, and made plans to return later. When he came back in June he leased a cabin near Oteen–the cabin of Max Whitson–and started to work on the new book. He also planned to spend a summer of peace and quiet.

But it hasn't been all peace or quiet for Wolfe. Friends and others have sought him out for talks, autographs, and so on. Proud of the home town boy who made good in the literary world, Asheville people have literally flocked to the cabin to call on the author.

In spite of the fact that he was unable to do as much work as he planned, the author has "loved it all" and considers this summer "back at home" the greatest experience in his eventful life, he confided to a Citizen reporter yesterday afternoon.

"To be back among my own people has been one of the most thrilling and most memorable experiences I have ever known," he stated. "I wouldn't have missed it for anything. I have wanted for a long time to get back home. I had been away so long that it was beginning to haunt me. This summer has satisfied something in me that has wanted fulfillment for years.

"I am really grateful from the bottom of my heart for the kind reception of this summer."

Wolfe headed for Tennessee yesterday afternoon for a visit with friends. Then he will go to see his publishers at New York concerning the story he wrote while staying at the cabin near Asheville.

He said he hoped to turn out soon another large work such as "Look Homeward, Angel" and "Of Time and The River," but was undecided whether he would remain at New York to do the work.

Judging from his pleasure over his summer stay here, friends surmised that he may come back to the mountain section to pursue his literary career.

"The Child by Tiger," a short story written by Wolfe several months ago, will appear in the September 11 issue of The Saturday Evening Post. The story was suggested by an incident that occurred here more than 30 years ago when a negro ran amok and terrorized a section of the city for a night, Wolfe said.

In a 29 July 1937 letter to Elizabeth Nowell, Wolfe wrote of his work on the story "The Party at Jack's."

I am going on with "The Party at Jack's," but it is turning out to be a terrifically complicated and difficult job. But it is a very interesting one and if I work and weave and rework long and hard enough I may have something very good. The market is a different matter: my plan when I get through is to have a complete section of the social order, a kind of dense, closely interwoven tapestry made up of the lives and thoughts and destinies of thirty or forty people, and all embodied in the structure of the story. It is an elaborate design; it has to be: it is, I suppose, somewhat Proustian but this also has to be and the interesting thing about it is the really great amount of action. This action is submerged and perhaps not at first apparent, but if the reader will stick with me, if I can carry him along with me, it will be apparent by the time he finishes the story.

–*The Letters of Thomas Wolfe,* pp. 647–648

Although newspapers reported that Wolfe was planning to return to live in North Carolina, he never returned to his native state. The following article was published one year before Wolfe died.

Thomas Wolfe, 37 Today, Plans Early Return To Native Mountains To Live
Gertrude S. Carraway
The Charlotte Observer, 3 October 1937

North Carolina's Famous Novelist
Is Coming Home.

Asheville Young Man, Maturing As Artist,
Is Gaining Calmer Outlook Upon Life

Appropriate for the occasion of his thirty-seventh birthday anniversary today is the news that Thomas Wolfe, one of the most brilliant and prominent young novelists in

Tom Wolfe's Story Recalls Murderous Rampage Of Negro

Asheville Citizen September 10, 1937

Thomas Wolfe's story, "The Child By Tiger," which appeared in this week's issue of The Saturday Evening Post, led scores of Asheville persons to recall yesterday the wild, murderous rampage of Will Harris, negro, who killed five persons in one day here almost 31 years ago.

Wolfe's story is based on the story of Harris and his death at Fletcher at the hands of a posse, composed of prominent residents of the city and police officers.

In the story, Wolfe held fairly closely to the actual facts of the case. He diverged, however, in some instances. The magazine story had seven killed, whereas the actual number was five, two police officers and three negroes.

The story portrayed the negro as the servant of an Asheville family, but old residents recall that he had recently come to the city, probably from Charlotte.

Harris, old residents recalled, killed a negro on Eagle Terrace who came home while Harris was with his wife. Two policemen answered a call to the section. He shot one of them, Capt. John Page, through the arm and killed Patrolman Charles Blackstock. Capt. Page is still living. He operates a hotel in Asheville.

The negro then walked up Eagle street, shooting evidently at every moving object. He killed a negro on the street and another negro, Tom Neil, who was sitting in the door of his shop. A dog jumped up. With deadly accuracy, Harris killed him too.

A prominent resident of the city stuck his head out of a hotel window to learn what the noise was about. One of Harris' bullets hit just below the window, spattering him with brick dust.

Harris walked up South Main street (now Biltmore avenue) and reached Pack Square. Policeman Bill Bailey had just left headquarters (then on East Pack Square) and had gone to head the negro off.

He saw Harris and fired at him with a .32 calibre revolver. Harris sank to a knee, took aim and fired. Bailey took shelter behind a telephone pole near the site of the Plaza theater and fired again. Then Harris fired his second shot. It went squarely through the pole, through Bailey's mouth, killing him instantly, and landed in a molasses bottle in the window of Allison and Jarrett's grocery store.

The negro then went down Biltmore avenue, walking through the snow, and disappeared. He was killed two days later by the posse after he had fired his last shot.

Wolfe, in his story, has him kill two members of the posse, but none was actually hurt.

As the Asheville author says in the story, the negro's riddled body was brought back to Asheville and hung from an undertaker's window on South Main street, so that all might see it.

The shootings occurred on November 13, 1906.

Silas G. Bernard was chief of police then and was a member of the posse. Chief of Detectives Fred. Jones was also a member, although he did not join the police force until two weeks later. Only member of the police force then who is still in active service is Inspector W. R. Messer.

Wolfe devotes considerable space to the fact that the negro was an army man and a crack shot. Older residents recalled that he had been in the service in Texas.

Article in the 10 September 1937 issue of The Asheville Citizen *in which "The Child by Tiger," published in* The Saturday Evening Post, *is compared to the November 1906 shootings that occurred in Asheville*

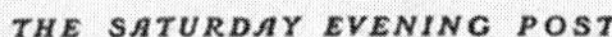

10 THE SATURDAY EVENING POST September 11, 1937

THE CHILD BY TIGER

By THOMAS WOLFE

ILLUSTRATED BY F. R. GRUGER

There Would be Times When He Would Almost Moan When He Talked to Us, a Kind of Chant

Tiger, tiger, burning bright
In the forests of the night,
What immortal hand or eye
Could frame thy fearful symmetry?

ONE day after school, twenty-five years ago, several of us were playing with a football in the yard at Randy Shepperton's. Randy was calling signals and handling the ball. Nebraska Crane was kicking it. Augustus Potterham was too clumsy to run or kick or pass, so we put him at center, where all he'd have to do would be to pass the ball back to Randy when he got the signal.

It was late in October and there was a smell of smoke, of leaves, of burning in the air. Nebraska had just kicked to us.

It was a good kick, too—a high, soaring punt that spiraled out above my head, behind me. I ran back and tried to get it, but it was far and away "over the goal line"—that is to say, out in the street. It hit the street and bounded back and forth with that peculiarly erratic bounce a football has.

The ball rolled away from me down toward the corner. I was running out to get it when Dick Prosser, Shepperton's new Negro man, came along, gathered it up neatly in his great black paw and tossed it to me. He turned in then, and came on down the alleyway, greeting us as he did. He called all of us "Mister" except Randy, and Randy was always "Cap'n"—"Cap'n Shepperton." This formal address—"Mr." Crane, "Mr." Potterham, "Mr." Spangler, "Cap'n" Shepperton—pleased us immensely, gave us a feeling of mature importance and authority.

"Cap'n Shepperton" was splendid! It had a delightful military association, particularly when Dick Prosser said it. Dick had served a long enlistment in the United States Army. He had been a member of a regiment of crack Negro troops upon the Texas border, and the stamp of the military man was evident in everything he did. It was a joy, for example, just to watch him split up kindling. He did it with a power, a kind of military order, that was astounding. Every stick he cut seemed to be exactly the same length and shape as every other one. He had all of them neatly stacked against the walls of the Shepperton basement with such regimented faultlessness that it almost seemed a pity to disturb their symmetry for the use for which they were intended.

It was the same with everything else he did. His little whitewashed basement room was as spotless as a barracks room. The bare board floor was always cleanly swept, a plain bare table and a plain straight chair were stationed exactly in

First page of the only story Wolfe sold to the mass-circulation Saturday Evening Post

America, has decided to move back permanently to his native Western North Carolina.

For two months this summer he resided in a small cabin near Oteen, and found such inspiration for his work among his beloved Blue Ridge, with such a cordial welcome from the citizens of that section, that he has made up his mind definitely to settle down again in the Old North State.

This was the first season he had returned to North Carolina in eight years, since publication of his first novel, "Look Homeward, Angel" in October 1929, when he was 29 years old. The book drew an immediate storm of protests from his native Asheville, which was depicted in the volume as the provincial "Altamont."

Some letters sent to him even threatened to murder him if he should ever dare return home. Other anonymous missives heaped insults and abuse on him. He was denounced from Asheville pulpits, in clubs and on streets. The happiness that Wolfe had experienced from the success of his first book elsewhere was thus ruined by its bitter reception in his home town.

IS HERO NOW.

But now that "Tom" has attained fame abroad, he is being welcomed back to Western Carolina with open arms. The old anger has evidently been forgotten in the new pride with which "The Land of the Sky" is now claiming the author as its native son.

It is quite apparent that he is immensely pleased at the warm reception and constant attention given him. Years ago he wanted to "escape" from his homeland and he drafted a course of solitude and travel. But now, after the "fury, hunger and all of the wandering in a young man's life," he is delighted to feel at home again.

"To find one's self, the Bible tells us, one must lose himself," he said earnestly at Asheville recently in one of his rare interviews calling his recent decision a great turning point in his entire life. "And to find one's country, one must leave it. I love to travel, and for years I wandered through Europe and America. Then I became terribly homesick. I missed the magic of our mountains here. And I love the people of my State. Now that I'm back here, I intend to remain."

TO LEAVE NEW YORK.

Accordingly, he expects to close his New York apartment for good and take up a permanent residence in western Carolina–somewhere he can continue his work. Meanwhile, he is visiting literary friends for a few weeks in Tennessee and Virginia.

Two years ago he wrote "The life of the artist at any epoch of man's history has not been an easy one. And here in America it may be the hardest life that man has ever known. Here must we who have no more than what we have, who know no more than what we know, are no more than what we are, find our America. Here, at this present hour and moment of my life, I seek for mine."

Now he is finding his America and himself in his own native region. As he said of Eugene Gant, in his autobiographical fiction, so he might have referred directly to himself: "He was hillborn. His sick heart lifted in our haunting eternity of the hills . . . Whatever we can do or say must be forever hillbound."

So he hopes from now on to accomplish better results in his literary efforts. He wants to make his literary style more coherent, poetic, spiritual. Though he knows his limitations, he has a calmer assurance as to his capacities "with less confusion, waste and useless torment."

His first novel, "Look Homeward, Angel," with the sub-caption, "A Story of the Buried Life," was described by him as "a story of sweat and pain and despair and partial achievement." Printed over five years later, his second book, "Of Tim and the River," sub-captioned "A Legend of Man's Hunger in His Youth," was begun in a "whirling vortex and creative chaos." Meanwhile he had written almost two million words. Today he has more definite objectives and more self-confidence for his future writings. In the past few weeks his stories have appeared in three national magazines.

MORE CONTENTED NOW.

He is finding the long-sought peace and contentment that he believes will be conducive to better writing. Near the government hospital at Oteen where ex-service men regain physical health and vigor, he has taken a new lease on life and labor, with a new mental outlook and spiritual regeneration. Fundamentally spiritual-minded, he is beginning to understand that he is at heart deeply religious and has a special mission in the world.

Eugene Gant "at seventeen as a sophomore, triumphantly denied God." The other day, however, Thomas Wolfe declared seriously, in viewing himself as a poet and artist:

"Every artist has a religion. William Butler Yeats said that man is nothing until his life is united to an image. Why do I want to work and write? I believe there is something in one's self that should come out bigger than self. If a person has a talent, it is wrong not to develop and improve it for the benefit of mankind. The soul of an artist must express divine love and ideal beauty in corporeal form. Love is a divine motive power for real religion."

Hence, after "brutal struggles, pain and ugliness of life," Wolfe is acquiring a new philosophy in the quiet of his hills. As he explains it, "Out of man's coarse earth the finer flowers of his spirit sometimes grow." His new creed has no denominational basis. To him religion does not mean theory or dogma, but constitutes a vital part of everyday life.

WRITES FROM LIFE.

Although he is still convinced that authors must use their own experiences to create anything of substantial value, he now admits that like other young writers he may have confused "the limits between actuality and reality" and may have adapted data from life "too naked and direct for the purpose of a work of art" in designing his first novel.

He insisted that the book was "a fiction" and that he "meditated no man's portrait" but he confesses that he portrayed various incidents and characters directly from memory with such "naked intensity of spirit" that though it was "not true to fact, it was true in the general experience of the town I came from and I hope, of course, to the general experience of all men living."

During his college days at the University of North Carolina he asserted that literary materials should be drawn from real life. In proof of this is the foreword to his first one-act play, "The Return of Buck Gavin," in which he acted as a member of the original Carolina Playmakers class: "It is a fallacy of the young writer to picture the dramatic as unusual and remote . . . It is happening daily in our lives . . . True drama is characterized by a certain all-inclusive portraiture which, I take it, may be called reality."

Having learned lessons from his first novel, however, and happy that his fellow citizens are overlooking his early indiscretions along this line, Mr. Wolfe said recently in Asheville that the new book on which he is now working for publication will contain "less identification and more generalization."

DESCRIBES BOOK.

It will be a "historical but modern" novel, about "an innocent man." Starting out from his home in North Carolina, again to be called "Catawba," the hero will "go places," somewhat similar in style to Gulliver's Travels. The narrative will be fictional in tone and spiritual in purpose, and the author promises that it will be more "humorous" than any of his previous brain children. All of which also goes to show that Tom Wolfe is "growing up."

In Asheville he admitted that he had changed more in the past eight years than had North Carolina. Of course, he found new buildings, new highways, new streets in his town and State; but on the whole there were no real changes here, unless there is a deeper sense of values brought about by the depression. He praised this feature. "We don't want any more booms," he declared. He hopes that the depression will have the further effect of bringing about a spiritual renaissance.

As he spoke with his characteristic rush of words, the same old vitality and zest were evident in his rich, throaty voice; his piercing, dark eyes; and his magnetic, dynamic personality. Still an enormous, overgrown youth, he towers six feet in height and weighs 245 pounds. His long, black, curly hair is still unruly. In his strong, shapely hands his tan felt hat was crumpled a hundred ways with his same old nervous intensity. But his former "fury and despair" seem replaced by a new inner repose and optimism.

LIKES WALKING.

One of the main reasons why he is glad to be moving back to North Carolina is his love of walking. He likes to hike along mountain trails. "You can't take such swift walks and get such fresh air on city pavements" he asserts.

During his youth he read voraciously, in his desire to cram all knowledge in his brain. Now he has so little time left over from his writing that he does not read so much. He seldom goes to movies, but does like the news reel theaters. Baseball is his favorite outdoor sport.

Every day at Oteen he tried to work from 11 o'clock in the morning to six o'clock at night, stopping only to eat a sandwich for lunch. "It's really hard work to write," he declared. "But it is easy to find subjects. When people ask me as they often do where I get my materials, I reply, 'Just look around you.'"

A main recreation he used to get in New York was going to the large railroad stations and watching throngs of people surging through the buildings. People form one of his chief studies, pleasures, and inspirations. In North Carolina he hopes to renew all the acquaintances of his youth and make many more friends. For from now on, his native State will be his "home."

Before leaving Asheville, Wolfe had called several publishers asking them whether they would be interested in publishing his work. Robert N. Linscott of Houghton Mifflin heard that Wolfe was seeking a new publisher and expressed interest in his manuscripts. In a 16 October 1937 letter, Wolfe wrote Linscott about his break with Scribners.

I'm sorry there have been "rumours"; as you know New York is a pretty rumourous place, but I want to assure you that I don't go around in the groups where these presumably originate, and in fact have not seen a publisher in almost four months. I am telling you this because to my great and deep regret my former publishers and I have separated. It is not true that I have "left" them; I am simply without a publisher. I want you to know that this severance is not the result of a temperamental explosion on the part of an author who is now trying to make terms with someone else, and get the best terms that he can; but that it is, for me, at any rate, one of the most grievous and sorrowful experiences of my whole life; it involves deep and complicated differences which touch, it seems to me, my whole life and work–differences that are by no means recent, but that began two and a half years ago. I know there are people at my former publishers who could tell you that this is true–chiefly, the man who has stood closest to me for eight years now and who knows more about my life and the problem of my work than anyone else, Maxwell Perkins.

–*The Letters of Thomas Wolfe,* pp. 657–658

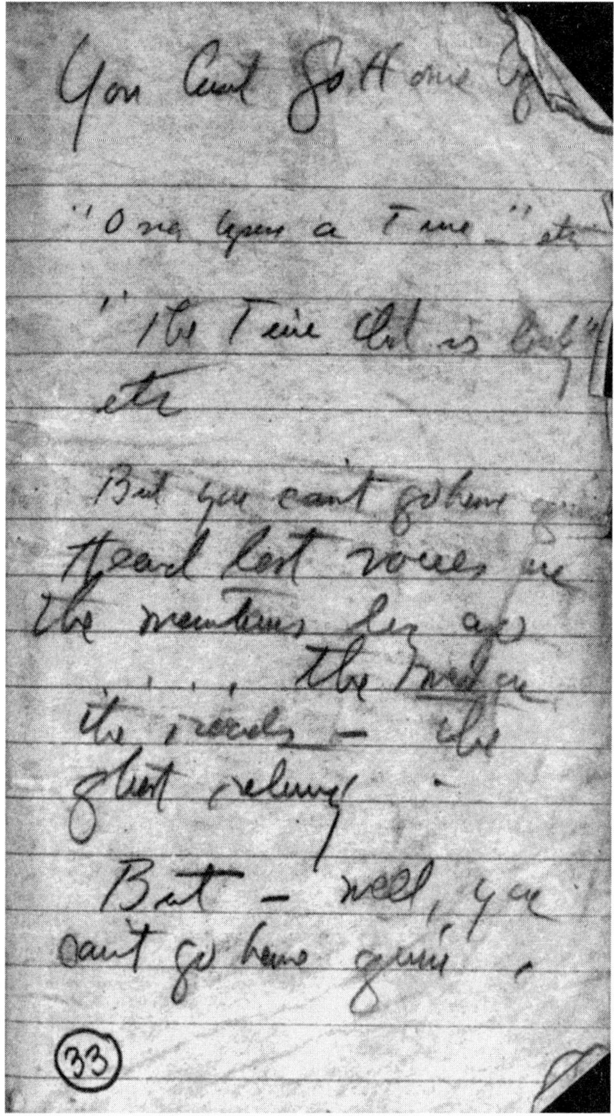

Notebook page showing Wolfe's fascination with the phrase "You can't go home again" (William B. Wisdom Collection, Houghton Library, Harvard University)

Searching for a New Publisher

For the most part, after he returned to New York, Wolfe severed nearly all contact with his family. By November, Wolfe's mother was writing Maxwell Perkins, asking for her son's address. Wolfe later explained his need for solitude in a letter of 17 November 1937 to his brother Fred: "About the summer I spent at home, my first return in seven years or more, the less said the better. I'd like to forget about it if I could. I went home a very tired man, not only with all this trouble with Scribners gnawing, but the pressure and accumulation of everything that has happened in the past two years. And when I left home I was as near to a breakdown as I have ever been." After returning to New York, Wolfe gave up his First Avenue apartment and eventually moved to the Hotel Chelsea at 222 W. 23rd Street.

On 1 December, while living at the Chelsea, Wolfe attended a dinner at the apartment of socialite Mary Emmet for the Sherwood Andersons, who were visiting New York. Also attending the party was Ella Winter, the widow of communist sympathizer Lincoln Steffens. When the party was over at dawn, Wolfe walked Winter home, all the time pouring out his grievances. As Elizabeth Nowell records in Thomas Wolfe: A Biography *(1960), Winter recalled: "He started telling me about his horror at going back to his home and what he found there, and I just said, 'But don't you know you can't go home again?' He stopped dead and then said: 'Can I have that? I mean for a title? I'm writing a piece . . . and I'd like to call it that. It says exactly what I mean." From that time on, Wolfe became obsessed with the phrase "You can't go home again."*

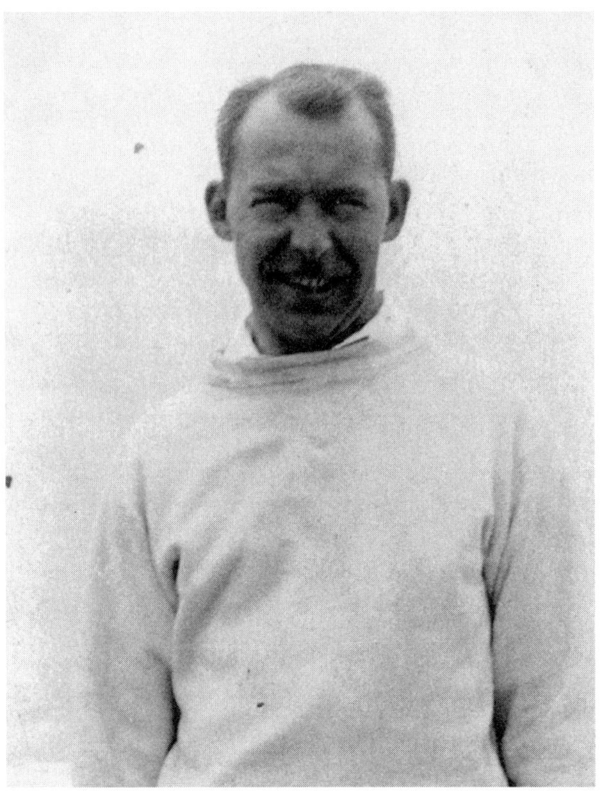

Edward C. Aswell of Harper and Brothers. Wolfe felt a strong connection with Aswell, who was from Tennessee, a Harvard graduate, and six days younger than Wolfe (Mary Aswell Doll).

In a 6 December 1937 letter to Anne W. Armstrong, Wolfe discussed his prospects with publishers.

About definite publishing connections, I have made no new one yet. I wanted to take plenty of time thinking the whole thing over, so I didn't go around soliciting people, and on the whole, I think it is just as well that I did not. At any rate, at least three publishing houses have hear that I am without a publisher, and have signified their interest. Two of them have actually gone so far as to make specific offers, mentioning terms, and the firm of Harper and Brothers has made what seems to me a very generous and fine one. At any rate, the amount of the advance they offered was so large that I was rather overwhelmed by it. And what I think is a whole lot more important than this is that they actually seem to be intensely and deeply interested in me as a man and as a writer, which, in a publishing connection, I think is a pretty important thing.

What you said in your letter about my not going back to Asheville also shoots straight to the mark, because it is exactly what I have been thinking myself, and of course at first the knowledge of it was pretty hard to face. But you are right: *You can't go home again.* I found this out this summer, of course I had to go home

Wolfe negotiated with various publishers before finally settling on Harper & Brothers. After spending Christmas with his new editor, Edward C. Aswell, and his family, he wrote about his decision in a 27 December 1937 letter to Anne W. Armstrong:

I am so glad you spoke as you did about Harper's, because I gave them my answer a week ago. I am going to be with them, and I believe somehow it is going to be one of the most fortunate and happy experiences of my life. They are giving me a great advance, if I want it. But really I was playing a personal hunch. They want me so much, they believe in me so utterly, and there is no doubt they meant everything they said. Moreover I will be associated with a young man just exactly my own age, who is second in command. I am playing this hunch, too: I think it is going to turn out to be a wonderful experience–I feel that the man is quiet, but very deep and true: and he thinks that I am the best writer there is. I know he is wrong about this, but if anyone feels that way, you are going to do your utmost to try to live up to it, aren't you?

–*The Letters of Thomas Wolfe,* pp. 694–695

to find it out, it was hard to face, but I have faced it now and I feel better. But don't be surprised some day if you see a piece, *You Can't Go Home Again.* I guess we all find this out as we go along, but it's a pretty tremendous fact and revelation in the life of any man, isn't it? But as long as I know that there are people like you, and that one meets a few of them in the course of a life time, it doesn't make things too bad. Maybe it's just there that eventually a man comes to look for home.

–*The Letters of Thomas Wolfe,* p. 686

On the last day of 1937 Wolfe signed a contract with Harpers for a novel titled "The Life and Adventures of the Bondsman Doaks." On the same day, he wrote to Edward Aswell's wife, Mary Louise Aswell, who had sent him an anti-war letter written by a captain in the Japanese Army that had been published in the December issue of The Reader's Digest *under the title "One Small Unwilling Captain."*

Hotel Chelsea
222 West 23rd Street,
New York, N.Y.

December 31, 1937.

Dear Mary Lou:

Ed has just left, and I am winding up the old year with a touch of grippe, and am not much to look at, but very hopeful.

The final grim technical details of business and contract signing have been attended to, and now I am committed utterly, in every way. It gives me a strangely empty and hollow feeling, and I know the importance of the moment, and feel more than ever the responsibility of the obligation I have assumed. But I guess it is good for a man to get that hollow empty feeling, the sense of absolute loneliness and new beginning at different times throughout his life. It's not the hollowness of death, but a living kind of hollowness: a new world is before me now; it's good to know I have your prayers.

Thanks so much for your letter and for the enclosed story about the small Japanese Captain. It was moving and beautiful, and the pity is, it's all so true. It's so wrong to hate people, isn't it? And yet I feel that there are times when we have got to hate *things.* Everywhere you look and listen nowdays there is so much hatred. I hear it on every side every day. I even hear that the Germans are organically different from other members of the human race; the Trotskyites hate the Stalinites, and tell you they are not as other men: the Stalinites reply with equal hatred.

I've been reading Huxley's book which you gave me for Christmas. He's a brilliant writer, isn't he? His mind is so clear and penetrating, and sees so many things, and yet I got the impression he was puzzled and confused, too. To be partisan about anything almost implies hatred. Apparently Huxley's ideal is a kind of non-partisan man–or rather, a man who is partisan only in his belief in life. And yet, I wonder if in this world of ours to-day we can be non-partisan. Of one thing I am sure: the artist can't live in his ivory tower any more, if he is, he is cutting himself off from all the sources of life. Tremendous pressure is brought to bear from all sides upon people like myself: we are told that we must be partisan even in the work we do. Here I think the partisans are wrong; and yet a man does feel to-day a tremendous pressure from within–a kind of pressure of the conscience. There are so many things that are damnable, and which must be fought–we all ask ourselves the question: can we be free and be effective at the same time? I think nearly all of us have a pretty strong and clear feeling in our hearts about the larger humanity we would like to achieve. But when we see such wrong and cruelty and injustice all around us we ask ourselves if we have any right to refrain from taking sides and joining parties, because taking sides and joining parties are likely to limit and distort us. I wish it were also possible for me to feel like Candide that the best thing in the end is to tend one's garden. A tremendous lot can be said for that, a tremendous lot of good, but somehow garden tending doesn't seem to be the answer either, the way things are to-day.

I wish it were possible to hate the thing that has the small Japanese Captain in its power without hating the small Japanese Captain, but you know what happens. Men start off by hating things and wind up by hating people. Well, I don't know the answers, but I'm looking for them and I think I am learning a little all the time. At any rate, there is friendship and love and faith and work. They are not just words: I have known and had them all.–Now, in a new and thrilling way, I feel that I know and have them all again. That is why I send you all my love, and all my deep and heartfelt wishes for your happiness and success this coming year.

–*The Letters of Thomas Wolfe,* pp. 698–699

Unless one can be first and best, or among the best and first, there's no point in going on writing–unless, finally, one cannot help writing.
–The Notebooks of Thomas Wolfe, p. 357

Chapter 6

Death and Posthumous Publications

With a $10,000 advance from Harper and Brothers, Wolfe launched into intensive work on "The Life and Adventures of Bondsman Doaks." He soon changed the name of his protagonist from Joe Doaks to George Webber and expanded the scope of his proposed work to incorporate material from "K 19," "The October Fair," and "The Hound of Darkness." Before leaving for a trip to speak at Purdue University in May 1938 and a vacation afterward in the Pacific Northwest, Wolfe prepared a long outline to help Edward Aswell identify parts of the enormous manuscript, which Wolfe then titled "The Web and the Rock." In early July, after completing a tour of western national parks, Wolfe contracted a respiratory infection that triggered his dormant tuberculosis. Hospitalized in Seattle and later treated at Johns Hopkins Hospital in Baltimore, Wolfe succumbed to tuberculosis meningitis on 15 September 1938, nineteen days short of his thirty-eighth birthday. He was buried in Asheville. In the next three years, Aswell assembled three posthumously published works from the material left in his charge: The Web and the Rock *(1939),* You Can't Go Home Again *(1940), and* The Hills Beyond *(1941).*

Planning a New Novel

After Wolfe signed the contract with Harper and Brothers, Edward Aswell asked him to write a statement that could be used as a press release. The original statement, which proved too long for Harpers's purposes and was excerpted, is published below.

A STATEMENT

Thomas Wolfe has signed a contract with Harper & Brothers for the publication of his next novel. The author, in a letter written to his publishers just before Christmas, says:

"This is a time of year that has some sadness in it for us all. But we can feel happy, too, in the knowledge that nothing gets lost, and that the people we have known will still be our friends, no matter where we are, and that although we can't go home again, the home of every one of us is in the future. And that is why I am looking forward to next year.

"It has been my fortunate lot always to have as publishers in this country people of the finest ability and the highest integrity. For that reason, I am glad to know that with the New Year I shall be associated with a house like yours.

"As you know, like many other young men, I began life as a lyrical writer. I am no longer a very young man–I am thirty-seven years old–and I must tell you that my vision of life has changed since I began to write about ten years ago, and that I shall never again write the kind of book that I wrote then. Like other men, I began to write with an intense and passionate concern with the designs and purposes of my own youth, and, like many other men that preoccupation has now changed to an intense and passionate concern with the designs and purposes of life.

"For two years now, since I began to work on my new book, I have felt as if I was standing on the shore of a new land. About the book that I am doing, I can only tell you that it is a kind of fable, constructed out of the materials of experience and reality, and permitting me, I hope, a more whole and thorough use of them than I have had before. The book belongs in kind with those books which have described the adventures of the average man–by this I mean the naturally innocent man, every mother's son of us–through life.

"Anyway, for better or for worse, my life, my talent, and my spirit is now committed to it utterly. Like Martin Luther, I can't do otherwise–*Ich kann nicht anders*–I have no other choice.

"Now I can only hope the end for both of us will be well.

Sincerely yours,

THOMAS WOLFE

The Notebooks of Thomas Wolfe, pp. 889–890

Wolfe conceived the central idea for "The Life and Adventures of the Bondsman Doaks" during his visit to Asheville in 1937 when he was intrigued by the ramifications of the failure of the Central Bank and Trust Company. He wrote to Margaret Roberts on 14 February 1938 to ask for her help in researching the catastrophe.

. . . Now I want you to help me if you can, and I know that I can depend on you to keep this confidential. I am also writing to my cousin, Jack Westall, with a similar request for information and help. . . . What I want is this: I am writing a long book, and I want to put everything that I have in it: and this time the book is not about a town, nor about any certain group of people, but it is about America and what happened here between 1929 and 1937. I think you will agree with me and see what I am driving at when I tell you that what happened in Asheville in that period seems pretty important and significant in the light it throws on what happened to the whole country. So, to get down to brass tacks: first of all, do you know what is the best and completest newspaper account of the events–the bank trials, the affairs of the city, etc.–which occurred between 1930 and 1932? And do you know where I can get a copy of them? I would be willing to buy them, if I could do so at a fair price: or if you know anyone who has kept such a record and would be willing to let me have it for several weeks, I would make every guarantee to preserve it and to see that it is returned to its owner safely. And if anything else occurs to you–if there are any people you think I could write or any other information that might be useful–I should be grateful if you would let me know about this too.

–*The Letters of Thomas Wolfe,* pp. 708–709

"I've got too much material. It keeps backing up on me–" he gestured around him at the tottering piles of manuscript that were everywhere about the room–"until sometimes I wonder what in the name of God I'm going to do with it all–how I'm going to find a frame for it, a pattern, a channel, a way to make it flow!" He brought his fist down sharply on his knee and there was a note of desperation in his voice. "Sometimes it actually occurs to me that a man may be able to write no more because he gets drowned in his own secretions!"

–*You Can't Go Home Again,* p. 386

Wolfe at the Chelsea Hotel, New York, in 1938 (drawing by Soss E. Melik; The Thomas Wolfe Collection, Pack Memorial Public Library, Asheville, North Carolina)

Although he was not a political writer, Wolfe's view of the artist's relation to the world had evolved as a result of his observations of the effects of the Great Depression and the rise of Nazi Germany. When humorist Donald Ogden Stewart, writing 1 February 1938 on behalf of the League of American Writers, asked Wolfe to state his position on Francisco Franco and Fascism, the author began a long reply. His letter, though neither finished nor sent, indicates Wolfe's increasing interest in social issues, evident in his developing plans for his later works. Aswell incorporated parts of this letter into You Can't Go Home Again.

In his reply Wolfe reflected that at the beginning of his career he would "certainly have disagreed positively with anyone who suggested that the artist's life and work were in any way connected with the political and economic movements of his time."

Now that I no longer feel this way, I would not apologize for having felt so, nor sneer at the work I did, or at the work of other young men at that time who felt and thought as I did. It seems to me natural and almost inevitable that a young man should begin life as a lyrical writer, that his first picture of life, as reflected in his first work, should be a very personal one, and that he should see life and the world largely in terms of its impingements on his own personality, in terms of his personal conflicts or agreements with the structure of things as they are. As for the way we felt, or thought we felt, about art and love and beauty in those days, and how they were not only sufficient to all things, but that all things else were alien and remote to them, that too, perhaps, is a natural and inevitable way for young men to feel. And it certainly was a product of the training, the culture, and the aesthetic ideas of that time.

But I have found out something else, for myself at least, in the past few years. And it is this: you can't go home again–back to your childhood, back to the father you have lost, back to the solacements of time and memory–yes, even back to art and beauty and to love. For me, at any rate, it is now manifest that they are not enough. And I do not think that this be treason, but if it be, then–.

I began to find out about it six or seven years ago, when I was living and working on a book in Brooklyn, and I have been finding out about it ever since. I do not know when it first began, perhaps such things as these have no actual moment of beginning, but I do know that one day I got a letter from a person who was speaking about love and art and beauty. It was a good letter, but after I had read it I looked out the window and across the street I saw a man. He was digging with his hand into a garbage can for food: I have a good memory for places and for time and this was half-way through December 1932. And I know that since then I have never felt the same way about love or art or beauty or thought they were enough.

–*The Notebooks of Thomas Wolfe,* pp. 903–904

On 14 February 1938, Wolfe began a letter to Aswell in which he summarized his plans for his manuscript. The letter was not finished and never sent to Aswell; instead, Wolfe turned it into a more objective declaration, which Aswell did not see until after Wolfe's death. While the statement shows Wolfe to be still uncertain about his title and the name of his protagonist, he is firm about his theme–"one man's discovery of life and of the world."

A STATEMENT OF PURPOSE

First of all, so far as the author can now make out–and the reason for any dubiety that may be apparent here is not due to any doubt on the author's part, or any lack of conviction, as to purpose or direction, but rather to the enormous masses of material with which he is working, and the tides and planes and forces which shift and vary constantly, while still holding the same general direction–here is the latest stage of definition as clearly as it can be put, and what the author thinks the book is about:

The book is about one man's discovery of life and of the world, and in this sense it is a book of apprenticeship. The author first thought of the book as a kind of American Gulliver's Travels. He used this comparison deliberately, but he also likened the book to those books that had to do with the adventures of "the innocent man" through life–he mentioned, in addition to Gulliver, such books as Don Quixote, Pickwick, Candide, The Idiot, and Wilhelm Meister. He used these names not as examples of literary models which he intended to follow, but merely as indications of the direction he was taking. Now he thinks that the illustration that comes closer to the kind of book he wants to do is Wilhelm Meister's Apprenticeship rather than Gulliver. And the reason for this is that he now believes, as the definition of the book grows clearer, the illustration he made about "Gulliver" might mislead in that as the very name Gulliver implies, it might indicate to one that he was contemplating a book about a man who was "gulled," who was expecting one thing from life and found another, etc.

This element is certainly in the book, but it does not define as directly as it should the author's position and direction at this time about the book. The book will have satire in it, swingeing and scalding satire, it is hoped, but it is not essentially a satiric book. It is a book about discovery–about discovery not in a sudden and explosive sense as when "some new plant breaks upon his ken"–but of discovery as through a process of finding out, and of finding out as a man has to find out, through error and through trial, through fantasy and illusion, through falsehood and his own damn foolishness, through being mistaken and wrong and an idiot and egotistical and aspiring and hopeful and believing and confused, and pretty much what every damned one of us is and goes through and finds out about and becomes.

And, in order that there may be no doubt as to what this process of discovery involves, the whole book might almost be called "You Can't Go Home Again"–which means back home to one's family, back home to one's childhood, back home to the father one has lost, back home to romantic love, to a young man's dreams of glory and of fame, back home to exile, to escape to "Europe" and some foreign land, back home to lyricism, singing just for singing's sake, back home to aestheticism, to one's youthful ideas of the "artist," and all the all-sufficiency of "art and beauty and love," back home to the ivory tower, back home to places in the country, the cottage in Bermuda, away from all the strife and conflict of the world, back home to the father one is looking for–to someone who can help one, save one, ease the burden for one, back home to the old forms and systems of things that once seemed everlasting,

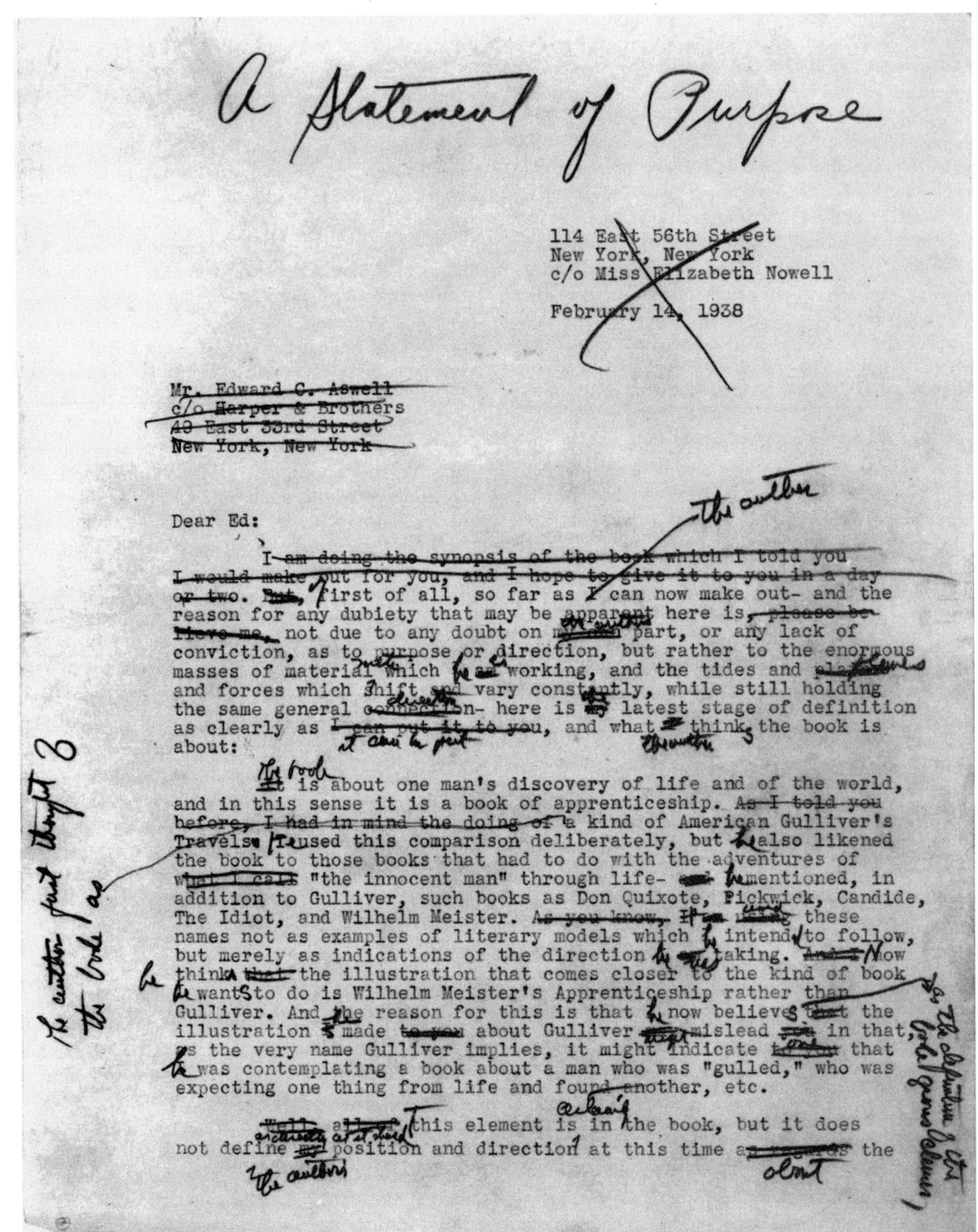

A Statement of Purpose

114 East 56th Street
New York, New York
c/o Miss Elizabeth Nowell

February 14, 1938

~~Mr. Edward C. Aswell~~
~~c/o Harper & Brothers~~
~~49 East 33rd Street~~
~~New York, New York~~

Dear Ed:

I ~~am doing the synopsis of the book which I told you I would make out for you, and I hope to give it to you in a day or two. But,~~ first of all, so far as I can now make out- and the reason for any dubiety that may be ~~apparent~~ here is~~, please believe me,~~ not due to any doubt on ~~my own~~ part, or any lack of conviction, as to ~~purpose~~ or direction, but rather to the enormous masses of material which ~~I am~~ working, and the tides and ~~plans~~ and forces which shift ~~and~~ vary constantly, while still holding the same general ~~connection~~- here is ~~my~~ latest stage of definition as clearly as ~~I can put it to you~~, and what ~~I~~ think the book is about:

~~It~~ is about one man's discovery of life and of the world, and in this sense it is a book of apprenticeship. ~~As I told you before, I had in mind the doing of~~ a kind of American Gulliver's Travels. ~~I~~ used this comparison deliberately, but ~~I~~ also likened the book to those books that had to do with the adventures of ~~what I call~~ "the innocent man" through life- ~~and I~~ mentioned, in addition to Gulliver, such books as Don Quixote, Pickwick, Candide, The Idiot, and Wilhelm Meister. ~~As you know, I'm using~~ these names not as examples of literary models which ~~I~~ intend to follow, but merely as indications of the direction ~~I was~~ taking. ~~And I~~ Now think ~~that~~ the illustration that comes closer to the kind of book ~~I~~ want to do is Wilhelm Meister's Apprenticeship rather than Gulliver. And ~~the~~ reason for this is that ~~I~~ now believe ~~that~~ the illustration ~~I~~ made ~~to you~~ about Gulliver ~~might~~ mislead ~~you~~ in that, as the very name Gulliver implies, it might indicate ~~to you~~ that ~~I~~ was contemplating a book about a man who was "gulled," who was expecting one thing from life and found ~~another~~, etc.

~~Well, all of~~ this element is in the book, but it does not define ~~my~~ position and direction at this time ~~as regards~~ the

Letter Wolfe wrote to Aswell that he revised, using "the author" and "the editor" instead of "I" and "you," and enlarged into "A Statement of Purpose" for his ongoing work on his novel (William B. Wisdom Collection, Houghton Library, Harvard University)

but that are changing all the time–back home to the escapes of Time and Memory. Each of these discoveries, sad and hard as they are to make and accept, are described in the book almost in the order in which they are named here. But the conclusion is not sad: this is a hopeful book–the conclusion is that although you can't go home again, the home of every one of us is in the future, there is no other way.

This description of the purpose of the book ought to be kept in mind and read pretty carefully, and thought about a lot, because the author is depending on his editor now for so much: he wants him to be thoroughly convinced at the outset that the author knows what he is doing and where he is going, and that although there are many, many doubts in his mind, there is no doubt; and although there are many, many confusions, there is no confusion. To get right down to cases now, even, as it has to be here, in the most broad and general way, here is what the author has in mind:

He intends to use his own experience absolutely–to pour it in, to squeeze it, to get everything out of it that it is worth. He intends for this to be the most objective book that he has ever written, and he also intends by the same token, for it to be the most autobiographical. He has constructed a fable, invented a story and a legend; out of his experience he has derived some new characters who are now compacted not so much from specific recollection as from the whole amalgam and consonance of seeing, feeling, thinking, living, and knowing many people. There are two important ones, for example, named Alsop and Joyner–who, each in his own way are pretty much what the name of each signifies–but each, the author hopes, are as convincing and living people as he has ever created. He now thinks he may be wrong in calling the central figure, the protagonist, Joe Doaks, but Alsop and Joyner can probably stand as they are–that is, both are real names, both are fairly familiar and common names: the objective to Joe Doaks, of course, is that it may carry with it too much a connotation of newspaper cartooning, slap-stick, the fellow in the bleachers, and so on. The way the author feels now, it should be more of a Wilhelm Meister kind of name–an *American* Wilhelm Meister kind of name.

. . . .

One of Wolfe's chief concerns is how to make use of previously written material, especially the writing he did on "The October Fair."

To get still further to cases: as the editor will remember, when he first talked with the author about what he had to do, the author spoke of the book which he had called "The October Fair" and told something of the conflict in his mind between this book, and the other book which he had been describing here. He told, for example, of the time several years ago when all his heart and life and energy were absorbed by the October Fair and how, at that time, he thought this was the book he had to do and had framed it in a sequence to follow "Look Homeward, Angel" and "Of Time and the River." The author explained how he had written and striven on this book for two or three years, how "Of Time and the River" finally grew out of it and preceded it, and of how finally he had gone cold on the October Fair: that is, it was no longer the burning, all-absorbing thing he had to do.

But he described also the feeling of incompletion and discontent in his mind because of this book which had been projected and never published–the feeling that it had in it some of the best and truest work he had ever done, and the feeling that this work ought to receive the consummation and release of print. He still feels that way, except–and that is what he is trying to explain about his whole position here as concerns his book–his vision has changed: he no longer wishes to write a whole book about a woman and a man in love, and about youth and the city, because it now seems to him that these things, while important, are subordinate to the whole plan of the book he has in mind. In other words, being young and in love and in the city now seem to the author to be only a part of the whole experience of apprenticeship and discovery of which he is talking. They are also a part of the knowledge that you can't go home again.

That plan, as he now sees it in his mind, as he is shaping it in the enormous masses of manuscript which he has already written, and as he is trying to clarify it in the synopsis, is as follows:

The protagonist–the central character, the Wilhelm Meister kind of figure–really the most autobiographical character the author has ever written about because he wants to put everything he has or knows into him–is important now because the author hopes he will be, or illustrate, in his own experience every one of us–not merely the sensitive young fellow in conflict with his town, his family, the little world around him–not merely the sensitive young fellow in love, and so concerned with his little universe of love that he thinks it is the whole universe–but all of these things and much more insofar as they illustrate essential elements of any man's progress and discovery of life and as they illustrate the world itself, not in terms of personal and self-centered conflict with the world, but in terms of ever-increasing discovery of life and the world, with a consequent diminution of the more personal and self-centered vision of the world which a young man has.

In other words, the author has thought of the book as a series of concentric circles–that is, one drops the pebbles in the pool–the Wilhelm Meister pebble, or whatever we shall ultimately call him–but instead of pebble and pool simply in personal terms of pebble and pool, one gets a widening ever-enlarging picture of the whole thing–the pebble becomes important, if important at all, only in terms of this general and constant pattern of which it is the temporary and accidental stimulus: in other words, any other pebble would produce the same effect–the important thing is to tell about the thing itself, the thing that happens–the pebble, if you like, is only a means to this end.

. . . .

Wolfe stresses that his protagonist will not be an autobiographical persona.

THE PROTAGONIST

The author feels that the figure of the protagonist may be, technically and in other ways, the most important and decisive element in this book. As he has told the editor, this book marks not only a turning away from the books he has written in the past, but a genuine spiritual and artistic change. In other words, he feels that he is done with lyrical and identifiable personal autobiography; he is also seeking, and hopes now to obtain, through free creation, a release of his inventive power which the more shackling limitations of identifiable autobiography do not permit.

In other words, the value of the Eugene Gant type of character is his personal and romantic uniqueness, causing conflict with the world around him: in this sense, the Eugene Gant type of character becomes a kind of romantic self-justification, and the greatest weakness of the Eugene Gant type of character lies in this fact.

Therefore, it is first of all vitally important to the success of this book that there be no trace of Eugene Gant-i-ness in the character of the protagonist; and since there is no longer a trace of Eugene Gant-i-ness in the mind and spirit of the creator, the problem should be a technical one rather than a spiritual or emotional one. In other words, this is a book about discovery, and not about self-justification: it hopes to describe the pattern that the life of Everyman must, in general, take, in its process of discovery: and although the protagonist should be, in his own right, an interesting person, his significance lies not in his personal uniqueness and differences, but in his personal identity to the life of every man. The book is a book of discovery, hence union, with life; not a book of personal revolt, hence separation, from life: the protagonist becomes significant not as the tragic victim of circumstances, the romantic hero in conflict and revolt against his environment, but as a kind of polar instrument round which the events of life are grouped, by means of which they are touched, explained, and apprehended, by means of which they are seen and ordered.

Autobiographically, therefore, he should bear perhaps about the same relation to the life of the author, as Wilhelm Meister bears to the life of Goethe, or as Copperfield bears to the life of Dickens: as to the story itself–the legend–it should bear about the same relation to the life of the author as the story of Wilhelm Meister bears to Goethe's life; even perhaps as Don Quixote bears to the life of Cervantes–although this book is perhaps more in the vain of satiric legendry than the book the author has in mind.

But the book certainly should have in it, from first to last, a strong element of the satiric exaggeration of Don Quixote, not only because it belongs to the nature of the legend–"the innocent man" discovering life–but because satiric exaggeration also belongs to the nature of life–and particularly American life. No man, for example, who wants to write a book about America on a grand scale can hardly escape feeling again and again the emotion of the man when he first saw a giraffe: "I don't believe it!"

So, the book certainly must have this element, and it seems to the author the figure of the protagonist must have it too. He must have it because the very process of discovery, of finding out, will be intensified and helped by it.

. . . .

He is somewhat above the middle height, say five feet nine or ten, but he gives the impression of being somewhat shorter than that, because of the way he has been shaped and molded, and the way in which he carries himself. He walks with a slight stoop, and his head, which is carried somewhat forward, with a thrusting movement, is set down solidly upon a short neck between shoulders which, in comparison with the lower part of his figure, and his thighs and legs, are extremely large and heavy. He is barrel-chested, and perhaps the most extraordinary feature of his makeup, which accounts for the nickname he has had since childhood–the boys, of course, call him "Monk"–are the arms and hands: the arms are unusually long, and the hands, as well as the feet are very big with long spatulate fingers which curve naturally and deeply in like paws.

The effect of this inordinate length of arms and hands, which dangle almost to the knees, together with the stooped and heavy shoulders, and the out-thrust head, is to give the whole figure a somewhat prowling and half-crouching posture.

Finally, the features, the face, are small, compact, and somewhat pug-nosed, the eyes set very deep in beneath heavy brows, the \forehead is rather low, and the hair begins not far above the brows. The total effect of this, particularly when he is listening or talking to someone, the body prowling downward, the head thrust forward and turned upward with a kind of packed attentiveness, made the Simian analogy inevitable in his childhood; therefore the name of "Monk" has stuck.

In addition to this, it has never occurred to him, apparently, to get his figure clothed in garments suited to his real proportions: he apparently has walked into a store somewhere and picked up and worn out the first thing he could get on–in this way, a way of which he is not wholly conscious, the element of the grotesque is exaggerated.

The truth of the matter is, he is not really grotesque at all: that is to say, his dimensions, while unusual and a little startling at first sight, are in no sense of the word abnormal. He is not in any way a freak of nature, although some people might think so: he is simply a creature with big hands and feet, extremely long arms, a trunk somewhat too large and heavy, the legs, and features perhaps somewhat too small and compact for the big shoulders that support them.

Since he has added to this rather awkward but not distorted figure, certain unconscious tricks and mannerisms of his own, such as his habit of carrying his head thrust forward, and peering upward when he is listening or talking, it is not surprising if the impression he first makes should sometimes arouse laughter and surprise. Certainly he knows of this, and he has sometimes furiously and bitterly resented it; but he has never inquired sufficiently or objectively enough into the reasons for it.

The truth of the matter is that although he has a very intense and apprehensive eye for the appearance of things, he does not have an intense and apprehensive eye for his own appearance: in fact, the absorption of his interest and attention in the world around him is so passionate and eager that it rarely occurs to him what kind of figure and appearance he is himself making.

In other words, he does not realize the kind of effect he has on people and when as sometimes happens, it is rudely and brutally forced upon his attention, it throws him into a state of furious anger. He is young: and he has not learned the wisdom and tolerant understanding of experience and maturity: in short, he does not see that these things are accidental and of no great consequence–that personal beauty is probably no very great virtue in a man anyway; and that this envelope of flesh and blood in which a spirit happens to be sheathed, has been a very loyal and enduring, even though an ugly, friend.

. . . .

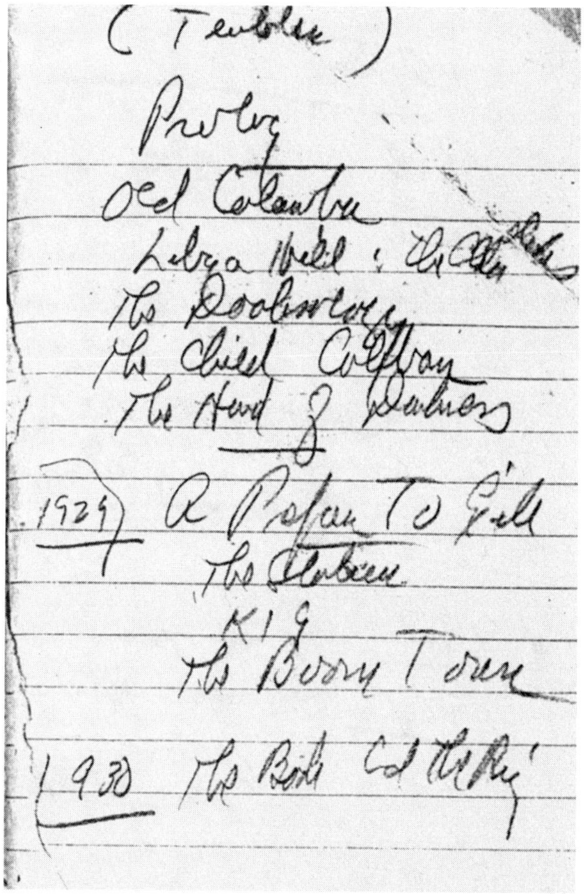

Entry from the notebook in which Wolfe outlines the work that was published as The Web and the Rock *(William B. Wisdom Collection, Houghton Library, Harvard University)*

Wolfe changes the name of his fictional Asheville from Altamont, used in his previous works, to Libya Hill.

THE STORY

The Story Begins With a Prologue
Prologue

The prologue as the author now sees it is to be called The Hound of Darkness–and states the setting. The setting is America. This is followed with Old Catawba, a description of the place from which the protagonist comes.

This was followed originally by The Doaksology: a satiric genealogy of the great Doaks family since the earliest times. If the name Doaks is changed, perhaps the genealogy could still be used. Then follows an account of the town of Libya Hill: how it got its name from the first Joyner who settled there, the connection of the Joyners with the family of the protagonist: a description of Libya Hill and the people there. All of this save the part about Libya Hill has been completely written. The Libya parts are incomplete.

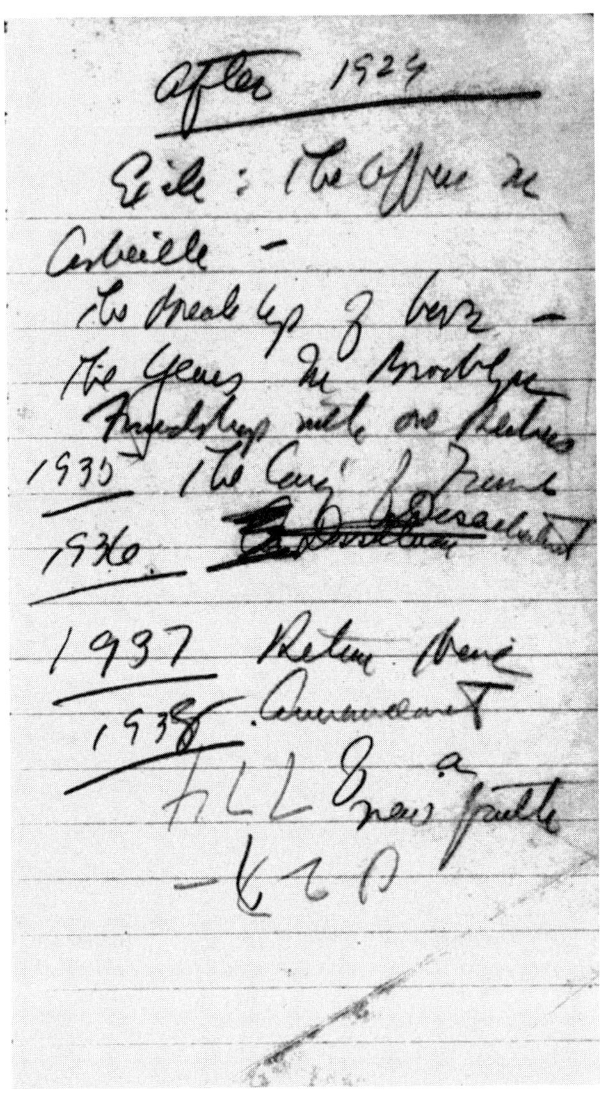

Notebook entry for Wolfe's chronology of The Web and the Rock *(William B. Wisdom Collection, Houghton Library, Harvard University)*

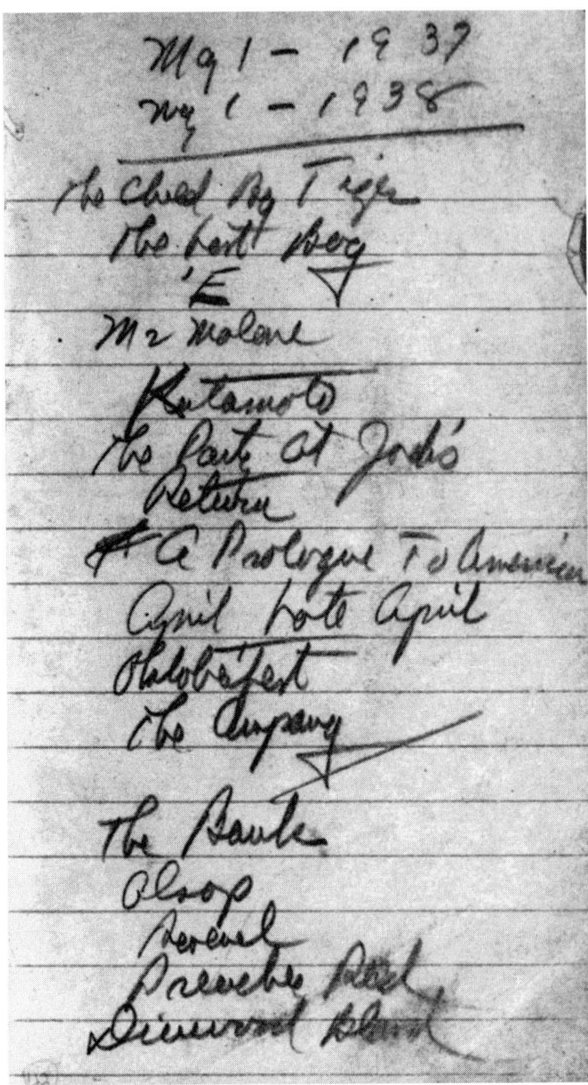

Wolfe's notes for his manuscript show that he was planning to extend his chronology to 1 May 1938 (William B. Wisdom Collection, Houghton Library, Harvard University).

THE DIRECT NARRATIVE

To Be Called
The Station or
The One and The Many or
The Pebble and The Pool

The direct narrative begins with the pebble (the protagonist) rolling home. The chapter bears the title of The Station. Perhaps a better name for it would be The Pebble and The Pool. Another, and perhaps the best of all, would be The One and The Many. For the purpose of this beginning–this setting–is to show the tremendous and nameless Allness of The Station–ten thousand men and women constantly arriving and departing, each unknown to the other, but sparked with the special fire of his own destination, the unknown town, the small hand's breadth of earth somewhere out upon the vast body of the continent–all caught together for a moment, interfused and weaving, not lives but life, caught up, subsumed beneath the great roofs of the mighty Station, the vast murmur of these voices drowsily caught up there like the murmurous and incessant sound of time and of eternity, which is and is forever, no matter what men come and go through the portals of the great Station, no matter what men live or die.

And our protagonist is introduced: he is here among them–the one and the many, the pebble and the pool.

–*The Notebooks of Thomas Wolfe,* pp. 938–945

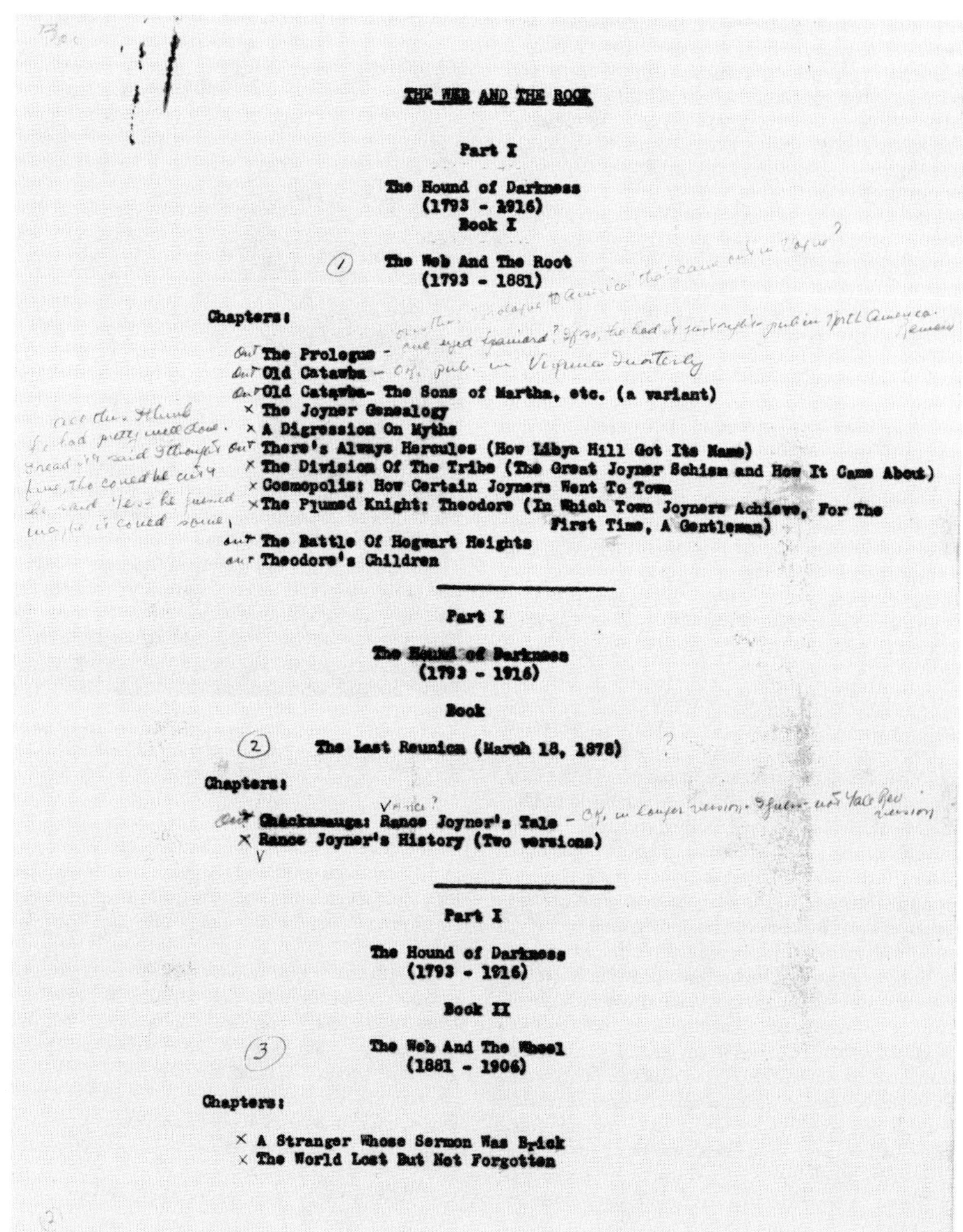

THE WEB AND THE ROCK

Part I

The Hound of Darkness
(1793 - 1916)
Book I

(1) The Web And The Root
(1793 - 1881)

Chapters:

The Prologue -
Old Catawba -
Old Catawba- The Sons of Martha, etc. (a variant)
The Joyner Genealogy
A Digression On Myths
There's Always Hercules (How Libya Hill Got Its Name)
The Division Of The Tribe (The Great Joyner Schism and How It Came About)
Cosmopolis: How Certain Joyners Went To Town
The Plumed Knight: Theodore (In Which Town Joyners Achieve, For The First Time, A Gentleman)
The Battle Of Hogwart Heights
Theodore's Children

Part I

The Hound of Darkness
(1793 - 1916)

Book

(2) The Last Reunion (March 18, 1878)

Chapters:

Chickamauga: Rance Joyner's Tale -
Rance Joyner's History (Two versions)

Part I

The Hound of Darkness
(1793 - 1916)

Book II

(3) The Web And The Wheel
(1881 - 1906)

Chapters:

A Stranger Whose Sermon Was Brick
The World Lost But Not Forgotten

First page of the outline Wolfe left with Aswell upon departing on his western trip, with notes by Edward Aswell and Elizabeth Nowell (William B. Wisdom Collection, Houghton Library, Harvard University)

Wolfe accepted an invitation to speak at the annual Literary Awards Banquet at Purdue University in West Lafayette, Indiana, on 19 May 1938. He decided to make Purdue the first stop on his second trip to the West and planned to then travel through the Northwest. On 6 May he had nearly completed the first draft of his work and wrote to Aswell with a progress report and to ask him to "put it in a place of safekeeping there at Harpers until I come back from the West."

Hotel Chelsea
222 West 23rd Street
New York, New York
May 6, 1938

Dear Ed:

. . . I have only about ten days more here before I go out to Purdue, and I hope to see you again before I go. I shall certainly call you up and talk to you.

. . . .

Although I have not begun this work yet and cannot say for sure, I have a very strong conviction that I have now reached about the same state of articulation as I had reached with "Of Time and the River" in the month of December, 1933. It was at this time that Mr. Perkins saw that manuscript in its entirety for the first time. What he saw, of course, was only a kind of enormous skeleton, but at any rate, he was able to get some kind of articulate idea of the whole. It was at that time that we went over the whole thing together, decided in general terms on the cycle of the book and on the immediate labor that remained to be done. From that point on, I moved very rapidly to completion. The whole book was written and finished within the course of the following year: although it did not appear until March, 1935, we were getting the proofs of it in November and December, 1934, within a year after we had gone over the first skeleton carefully together.

I mention all of this to you not because I think we established any kind of historic precedent that has to be invariably followed, but as indicating to you the state of things as they now stand. From the first, I have been very careful not to commit myself to any promises as to when the manuscript will be finished and ready for publication, and you have been very fair and generous in understanding this and in not asking me to make such commitments. I shall not do so now, but I can tell you that I hope with a good year of steady uninterrupted work, to complete the job. Please do not take this as a promise, but only as an expression of a reasonable hope.

The book will be a much bigger book–at least, in its first completed form–than "Of Time and the River." It will deal with a much greater sweep of time–over one hundred years, in fact. It will deal with a much greater variety of scenes, of characters, of events than "Of Time and the River," and it will present a narrative that is much more continuous and closely-woven, and that has, therefore, made a much more exacting demand upon my powers of invention and creation than anything I have done before.

Wolfe, circa 1937–1938. According to Gwen Jassinoff, Wolfe's typist in 1938, this photograph was taken at the Hotel Chelsea (courtesy of Clara Stites).

I ask you to bear this in mind, because I want you to be aware of the magnitude of the task before us. I know, and deeply appreciate, your patience and your desire to help in any way you can. It would perhaps be a good idea if you could familiarize yourself, so far as possible, with this first great batch of manuscript when I give it to you, but I am not sure about that yet until I have seen it all together myself. However, we shall see what we shall see.

My own very strong conviction at present is this: I have never been so clear in my mind before as to what I am after, and what I want to do. The analogy to "Of Time and the River" is a physical one rather than an artistic one. In other words, my very strong hunch at present is that it may be best to allow me to proceed with my work without any great assistance until I have brought it to a further state of development and completion. At the same time, it might be a good idea if the editor did get a general idea of the whole thing now.

I do not believe that I am in need of just the same kind of editorial help at this moment as Mr. Perkins so generously and unselfishly gave me in 1933, 1934. At any rate, since the whole process [is that] of trying to learn, like little Duncan, to stand erect, to toddle, and then to walk by myself, it might be better for me to go on by myself for awhile, and see what happens. It is, of course, comforting and of immense value to me to know that when I do need help it will be generously and patiently given. At any rate, I hope that is the program for the present, and that you can take care of the manuscript for me until I get back.

I really do feel it is pretty important for me to get some rest now, because such a tremendous job is before me–and for the past three years at least, what with law suits, publishing troubles, and an effort to get my work accomplished, there has been no let-up. I am due at Purdue on May 19, and where I shall go from there I shall try to keep my little secret. But I will not be gone for long and will see you early in June, at any rate. . . .

With best wishes,

–*The Letters of Thomas Wolfe,* pp. 757–759

Before Wolfe left for his trip West, he allowed Elizabeth Nowell to read through the first portion of his manuscript about the Joyners. She wrote to him on 11 May 1938.

So many reviewers have yapped so much about the "great American novel" and in connection with so many piddling writers that it sounds almost silly to use the phrase now. But again going back to the "real sense of the words," I think you're it, Toots. Because nobody else in the world could get the real flavor of those tough, salty, swell old guys like Bear and Zach and the way they talked and thought and lived so perfectly, with all the juice still there as if this was still the early rough and ready frontier America. And what's more, nobody in the world but you could bring that to life and then keep all your juice and understanding right in stride and perfect tune with the whole of changing history and come through to the swell and right-in-the-present-and-future stuff like the last parts of the book: the whole New York modern life, the literary racket, the German Nazi stuff, the ruined town and the Parson and police, and –well, the whole analysis of the world right this minute.

–*Beyond Love and Loyalty,* p. 106

Wolfe's Speech at Purdue University

Wolfe's speech, "Writing and Living," was well received. "Everything went off beautifully at Purdue," Wolfe wrote Elizabeth Nowell on 23 May 1938. "I talked and I talked, there was great applause, and everyone seemed very satisfied." In the following excerpt Wolfe makes it clear that he writes foremost to please himself.

I am going to talk shop to you, because my own experience has been that if people have anything at all interesting to say it is likely to be concerned with shop, and because anything I can say to you will have to be concerned with shop. I am coming to you from the shop–my own–where I have been at work for many months. I don't think it matters much where your shop is, as long as you can get your work done in it. For seven or eight months past mine has been in New York City, in an old hotel. I suppose there are better shops and better places to have a shop than the place where I have been; but it has served its purpose very well. In the first place, the old hotel has tremendous rooms, high ceilings, loads of floor space to walk back and forth in–something that more smartly appointed new hotels do not always have. In the second place, the old hotel is not, as hotels in New York go, an expensive one. And in the third place, although I frankly do not believe that hotels are a most desirable permanent place of residence, in New York they do have this advantage: one doesn't have to take a lease–and if one is a writer, with income insecure, and the desire occasionally to travel, that is a big advantage.

Now, I am going to tell you something more about my shop, because for me, at any rate, it is important. I have a big room where I work, and another room where I sleep: I'd like to emphasize the fact of space, because I think almost every capitalistic notion I have begins with space. I can do without a lot of things that many people not only would be uncomfortable without, but think essential. My luxury–and by an ironic paradox, in America of all places, where there is so much space, it has really come to be a luxury–is space. I like to have a big place to work in, and if I don't have it I am uncomfortable. I've tried to describe and emphasize all these apparently trifling physical things to you, because they have been so important to me. I am a writer. And no matter what you may have heard about writers, my own experience has been that a writer is first and foremost a working man. This may surprise you. It does surprise most people. For example, it has always surprised my mother, who is an admirable old woman, seventy-eight years old, who has worked all her life, as hard as any person I've ever known, and who is today as alert, vigorous, active as any person of that age you know. But my mother, like so many other people, has never been able to get it into her head that writing is work. When I was home last summer, she said to me: "Now, boy, if you can get paid for doing the kind of thing you do, you're mighty lucky–for all the rest of your people had to *work* for a living!" I keep reminding her that writing is also work–as hard work, I think, as anyone can do–I keep insisting on the fact; and my mother amiably keeps agreeing. But also she keeps forgetting–and in unguarded moments, I often get flashes of what is really going on in what the psychologists call her subconscious. And apparently, it is something like this: writing is a kind of stunt, a kind of trick which some people are born with–like being a sword-swallower or a left-handed baseball pitcher–and if one is fortunate enough to be born with this trick, or gift, he can, without much effort to himself, be paid for it. I don't believe my mother's views upon the subject are at all extraordinary: in fact, I should say they represented, unconsciously at least, the views of a majority of people everywhere. I know my mother would certainly be surprised, and possibly astonished, if I told her that I thought I was a working man–by this, I mean a man who does actual hard physical labor–in very much the same way as my father was, who was a stone-cutter; and if I told her that I looked upon the big room in which I work–with its crates of manuscript–its worktables–its floor space–in very much the same way as my father looked upon his shop in which he had his tombstones, his big trestles, his mallets and chisels, and his blocks of granite–my mother would smile, but would consider my proposition as another fantastic flight of the imagination. And yet, it seems to me, it is not fantastic. I am, or would like to be, a writer. And my own experience has been that a writer is, in every sense–particularly the physical one–a working man. And a writer, like other men who work, has a shop. And I am coming to you from the shop. And therefore, I am going to talk shop–because, it seems to me, it is likely to be the thing I can talk best, and that will be of greatest interest to you.

I wish I could tell you how to write stories in such a way that you could sell them for high prices to well-paying magazines. But the plain, bitter truth is that I can't tell you how, because I don't know how myself. I wish I could tell you how to write novels so that you could get them accepted by good publishers and enjoy a tremendous sale. But the plain and bitter truth again is that I can't tell you, because I don't know how myself. In fact, I don't think I even know for certain what a story or a novel is–a fact with which many of my critics would enthusiastically agree. I am constantly being fascinated and tempted by those glittering advertisements one sees so often in magazines today, showing a vigorous and keen-faced gentleman shooting his index finger out at you and saying: "*You* can be a writer too!"–and then going on to tell you how Chester T. Snodgrass of Bloomington took his course last year and found out about it in ten easy lessons in such a way that he *tripled* his income. Well, I'd not only like most earnestly to triple my income, but I should like most desperately to find out about it. And someday, I think, I am going to write that keen-faced gentleman with the index finger and enroll. But help of that sort, I regret to say, I cannot give you tonight, for help of that sort is not in me. A year ago, in fact, my agent called me up and in a trembling voice informed me that we had just sold a story to the *Saturday Evening Post*. The whole world reeled around us for a moment; then we became exultant. Our fortunes were made. It all looked so easy–we were on the line. The news leaked out, and friends would say to me: "I hear you've broken into the *Saturday Evening Post*," to which I would nod complacently, as if after all this was no more than was to be expected; and presently people were saying, "Well, I see you're a *Post* writer now–" at which I began to look and feel quite smug. My agent told me that the *Post* was so much interested in the story that one of its representatives had exacted from her a promise that she would not show the next story I wrote to anyone else before she had shown it to the *Post;* and we graciously consented to give them the first chance. Well, the upshot of it was, when I sat down and wrote another story, which we both gloatingly agreed was not only much better than the first story but had in it all the desirable elements that we thought a *Post* story should have–dialogue, characterization, and swift action; as for action we thought we had touched the peak, for I had the whole Battle of Chickamauga in. We debated whether we should let them have it for the same price as the first one, or whether the time had not now arrived–since I was an established *Post* writer–to demand Clarence Budington Kelland fees. We finally agreed that we would not be too severe, but would play them along diplomatically at first, and ask for only a thousand dollar raise or so. We thought it best not to hurry matters, and we agreed that it would probably be two or three weeks before we had their offer anyway. Well, we had their offer in six days–which was an offer of a flat rejection, with pained regrets that the story was not a *Post*

story, and was lacking on the side of action. It was a stern blow, but we both recovered rapidly: the agent pointed out that there was still *Redbook, Collier's, Cosmopolitan,* and so on, in the high-paying class, and that on the whole it would be better to let *Cosmopolitan* or one of the other big magazines have it anyhow, so that it would get my name around more to the great public. Well, the story came bouncing back from one big magazine after another with the regularity of a tennis ball: we decided then to try "the quality group"–*Harper's, Scribner's,* and so forth–because by this time we had decided the story was a "quality" story anyway. No matter what it was, it kept bouncing back; and after my valiant agent had tried all of them–eight months later–we landed! We sold that story! We landed in the *Yale Review*! Now the *Yale Review* is an excellent publication–an admirable one–and anyone ought to be proud to be in it. But the difference, among other things, between being in the *Saturday Evening Post* and in the *Yale Review* is fourteen hundred dollars. I could have had a trip to Europe on the *Saturday Evening Post,* but all I got out of the *Yale Review* was an overcoat. I needed an overcoat very badly, and I spent all of my *Yale Review* check on the overcoat, and I got a good one. It was an English Burberry, solid wool and very thick, and it cost one hundred dollars. And then, just when I got the overcoat, we had no winter. It didn't go below freezing the rest of the time. Anyway, I've still got the overcoat.

But you see, if you expected to get someone out here who could tell you how to write a story, and how and where to sell it to a high-paying magazine, you've come to the wrong man. You should have got that keen-faced fellow with the index finger who can tell you how. The most I can promise you is that if you ask me how to write a story that will get into the *Saturday Evening Post,* I will tell you how, and then you will wind up in the *Yale Review*. Perhaps this has its value, too; for it has occurred to me that the next time I want to sell a story to the *Saturday Evening Post,* I shall start out by writing it for the *Yale Review*.

I am thirty-seven years old, and for the past ten years, at least, I have been writing for publication. For the last nine years all my income, in one way or another, has been derived from writing. I think I can truthfully say that I have not only lived for writing, but I have also written to live. It's all I had to live on: I had no other source of income–if I was going to keep on writing, I had to live by it. I had to support myself. And yet, I can also truthfully say that, so far as I know, I have never written a word, a sentence, or a paragraph, with the immediate objective of making money out of it. Please don't think I'm being snooty. I wish to God I did know how to go about deliberately coining words and sentences and paragraphs into immediate and productive cash. I'd love it. That's why I'm so fascinated by the keen-faced gentleman of the index finger–his talk of "publics," "slants," and "writing for your market," fascinates me. But, thus far, it is all Chinese to me. I don't know how to go about it.

I can also say this truthfully. In the last few years I have rejected a number of offers that would have given me a great deal more money than I have ever had. I understand that my name as a writer is fairly well known, and one of my books, at least, two or three years ago, got pretty prominently into the bestseller list. But I counted up my total earnings, over the past ten years, since I began to write professionally, the other day, and found that they did not total forty thousand dollars. That's a lot of money–a lot more than most writers ever earn–and I certainly am not disappointed or depressed about it. But, on at least one occasion, I could have earned more than that total sum in one year's time if I had accepted employment that was offered me in Hollywood. I didn't take it. Why? I hasten to assure you that it was not because I was being noble. I have listened to writers who had a book published shudder with horror at the very mention of Hollywood–some of them have even asked me if I would even listen to an offer from Hollywood–if I could possibly submit my artistic conscience to the prostitution of allowing anything I'd written to be bought in Hollywood, made into a moving picture by Hollywood. My answer to this has always been an enthusiastic and fervent *yes.* If Hollywood wants to prostitute me by buying one of my books for the movies, I am not only willing but eager for the seducers to make their first dastardly appeal. In fact, my position in the matter is very much that of the Belgian virgin the night the Germans took the town: "When do the atrocities begin?"

But when I got an offer to go there and work, I did not take it, although it would have paid me more money than I had ever earned from writing in my whole life before; and I repeat again I have never felt noble about it. I did not go because I did not want to go. I wanted to write: I had work to do, I had writing, and still have, and I think will always have, that I wanted to get done. It meant more and it means more to me than anything else I could do. And I think that is the reason I am a writer.

–*The Autobiography of a Novelist*

14

About this time, I began to write. I was editor of the college paper- which, in my day, and under my direction, always did have at least, a certain interest since it was interesting to examine in this week's edition the ruins and relics of last month's news. But in addition to this, I wrote some stories and some poems for the magazine, of which I was also a member of the editorial staff. The War was going on then; I was too young to be in service, and I suppose my first attempts creatively may be traced to the direct and patriotic inspiration of the War. I remember one, in particular- a poem, (I believe, my first) which was aimed directly at the luckless head of Kaiser Bill. The poem was called defiantly "The Challenge", and I remember it was written directly in the style, and according to the meter, of the present crisis, by James Russell Lowell.

I remember further that it took a high tone from the very beginning: the poet, it is said, is the prophet and the bard- the awakened tongue of all his folk- and I was all of that. In the name of embattled democracy, I let the Kaiser have the works, and I remember two lines in particular that seemed to me to have a very ringing tone- "Thou hast given us the challenge- pay, dog, the cost, and go!" I remember these lines so well because they were the occasion of an editorial argument at the time: the more conservative element on the editorial staff, felt that the words, "thou dog" were too

A page from Wolfe's typescript for his Purdue speech, "Writing and Living," revised for use in The Web and the Rock *(The North Carolina Collection, University of North Carolina Library at Chapel Hill)*

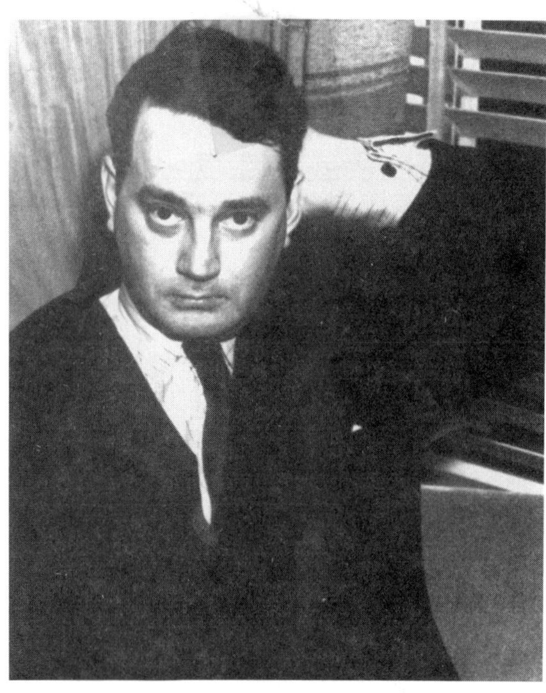

Wolfe in Denver during a newspaper interview in May 1938 (The Thomas Wolfe Collection, Pack Memorial Public Library, Asheville, North Carolina)

№ 6912 **Individual Permit** 1938

Expires Dec. 31, 1938

The individual herein named is entitled to purchase liquor in accordance with the Idaho Liquor Control Act.

Name Thomas Wolfe
(Signature of Permittee)

Address Hotel Boise

Age 38 Weight 250 Height 6 6 Color of hair Black-Brown

Issued at BOISE, IDAHO Date JUN 6 1938

IDAHO LIQUOR CONTROL COMMISSION

Subject to Forfeiture if Transferred or Altered

By Engstrome
Vendor.

PURCHASER'S PERMIT № 89687

THE UNDERSIGNED, BEING 21 YEARS OF AGE OR OLDER AND IN ALL RESPECTS OTHERWISE QUALIFIED, HEREBY APPLIES FOR A PERMIT TO PURCHASE ALCOHOLIC LIQUOR PURSUANT TO THE PROVISIONS OF THE OREGON LIQUOR CONTROL ACT.

SIGNATURE① Thomas Wolfe

NAME② Thomas Wolfe DATE③ 6 7 38

STREET ADDRESS④ CITY⑤

WEIGHT⑥ 250 HEIGHT⑦ 6 6 COMPLEXION⑧ Dark AGE⑨ 37

OREGON LIQUOR CONTROL COMMISSION
OTTO J. RUNTE, ADMINISTRATOR

IT IS A VIOLATION OF LAW, PUNISHABLE BY FINE AND IMPRISONMENT FOR ONE NOT THE PERMITTEE TO USE OR ATTEMPT TO USE THIS PERMIT.

ISSUED BY⑩ Hans
AGENT

Liquor permits Wolfe purchased on successive days in Idaho and Oregon during his western trip (Thomas Wolfe Memorial, North Carolina Department of Cultural Resources)

A Last Tour

After the Purdue speech, Wolfe spent a weekend in Chicago before boarding the Burlington Zephyr *for Denver. There he had a reunion with friends he had met in 1935 at the Writers' Conference in Boulder. After brief stopovers in Cheyenne and Boise, Wolfe arrived in Portland on 8 June 1938. He was invited by Edward Miller, Sunday editor of the Portland* Oregonian, *and Ray Conway, an executive in the Oregon State Motor Association, to be their literary passenger as they toured eleven national parks by auto. The excursion was meant to demonstrate that all of the Western national parks could be visited within an average two-week vacation. Wolfe's excitement at the prospect of the trip is clear in his letter to Nowell.*

University Club
Portland, Oregon
Wed. June 15, 1938

Dear Miss Nowell:

I'm on my way to Seattle in a few minutes after a most wonderful week here–I'll be back here Saturday but am leaving again Sunday morning on what promises to be one of the most remarkable trips of my life. It means I'll be away about two weeks longer than I intended–but it is the chance of a lifetime and after long battlings with my conscience, I have decided I'd be foolish not to take it–Here's the program: A young fellow I know on one of the local papers is starting out Sunday morning in his car on a tour of the entire West, and he has asked me to come with him–We leave here Sunday and head South for California stopping at Crater Lake on the way down–We go down the whole length of California taking in Yosemite, the Sequoias and any other nat'l. parks they have–Then we swing east across the desert into Arizona to the Grand Canyon, etc., north through Utah, Zion and Bryce Canyons, Salt Lake etc, then to Yellowstone, then north to the Canadian Border, Montana, Glacier Park, etc, then west again across Montana, Idaho, Washington–The Rainier Park–etc–in other words a complete swing around the West from the Rocky Mtns on, and every big nat'l park in the West–the cost will be very little as we are stopping at roadside cabins, etc–he's writing a series of articles to show the little fellow how inexpensively he can see the West.

The whole thing will take two weeks to the day–perhaps a day or two less for me, because I intend to leave him at Spokane, and head straight for N.Y.–I've seen wonderful things and met every kind of person–doctors, lawyers, lumberjacks, etc–and when I get through with this I'll have a whole wad of glorious material–My conscience hurts me about this extra two weeks, but I believe I'd always regret it if I passed it up–when I get through I shall really have seen America (except Texas).

–*Beyond Love and Loyalty,* pp. 115–116

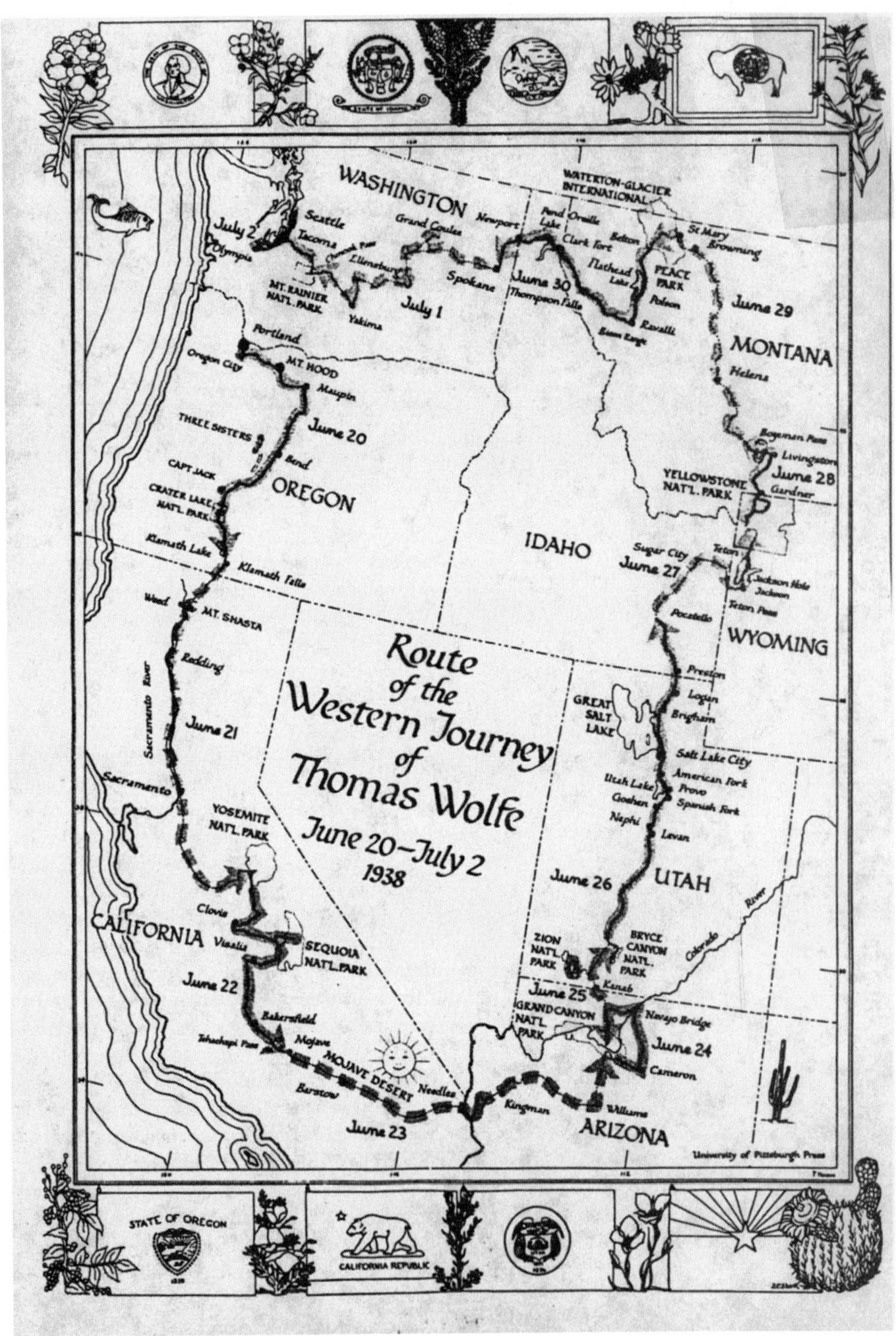

Map of Wolfe's western journey (University of Pittsburgh Press)

On the first day of their trip Wolfe and his two companions drove from Portland to Crater Lake National Park. For thirteen days and twelve nights, the three men traveled in a white Ford conspicuously displaying "Oregon State Motor Association" on its sides and trunk. Miller and Conway took turns driving, while Wolfe, who had never learned to drive, sprawled out in the backseat. Wolfe kept a record of his impressions in a large notebook, published posthumously as A Western Journal *(1951).*

Monday, June 20 (Crater Lake):

Left Portland, University Club, 8:15 sharp–Fine day, bright sunlight, no cloud in sky–Went South by East through farmlands of upper Willamette and around base of Mount Hood which was glorious in brilliant sun–Then climbed and crossed Cascades (86 miles), and came down with suddenness of knife into the dry lands of the Eastern slope–Then over high plateau and through bare hills and canyons and irrigated farmlands, here and there, Cow Valley, etc., and into Bend at 12:45–200 miles in 4-1/2 hours.

Then back at hotel and view of the 3 Sisters and Cascade range–then up to the Pilot Butte above the town–the great plain stretching infinite away–and unapproachable the great line of the Cascades with their snowcapped sentinels Hood, Adams, Jefferson, 3 Sisters, etc., and out of Bend at 3 and then through the vast and level pinelands–somewhat reminiscent of the South for 100 miles, then down through the noble pines to the vast plainlike valley of the Klamath–the virgin land of Canaan all again–the far-off ranges infinite–Oregon and the Promised Land–then through the valley floor–past Indian reservation–Capt. jack–The Medocs–the great trees open approaching vicinity of the Park–the entrance and the reservation–the forester–the houses–the great snow patches underneath the trees–then the great climb upwards–the forestry administration–up and up again–through the passes, the great plain behind and at length the incredible crater of the lake–the hotel and a certain cheerlessness in spite of cordialness–dry tongues vain-talking for a feast–the rooms, the cottages, the college boys and girls who serve and wait–the cafeteria and the souvenirs–the great crater fading coldly in incredible cold light–at length departure–and the forest rangers down below–long, long talks–too long with them about "our wonders" etc.–then by darkness the sixty or seventy miles down the great dark expanse of Klamath Lake, the decision to stay here for the night–three beers, a shave, and this–revelly at 5:30 in the morning–and so to bed!

First day: 404 miles.

Wolfe with his traveling companions, Ray Conway and Edward Miller, at Logan Pass in Glacier National Park, 29 June 1938

Tues. June 21, 1938 (Yosemite):

Dies Irae: Wakened at 5:30–dragged weary bones out, dressed, closed baggage, was ready shortly before six, and we were off again "on the dot"–at six o'clock. So out of Klamath, the lake's end, and a thread of silver river in the desert–and immediately the desert, sage brush, and bare, naked hills, great-molded, craterous, cuprous, glaciated, blasted–a demonic heath with reaches of great pine, and volcanic glaciation, cuprous, fiendish, desert, blasted–the ruins of old settlers' homesteads, ghost towns and the bleak little facades of long forgotten post-offices lit luridly by blazing morning sun, and the unending monotone, the deserted station of the incessant railway–all dominated now by the glittering snow–pale masses of Mount Shasta–the pine lands, canyons, sweeps and rises, the naked crateric hills and the volcanic lava masses and then Mount Shasta omnipresent–Mount Shasta all the time–always Mt. Shasta–and at last the town named Weed (with a divine felicity)–and breakfast at Weed at 7:45–and the morning bus from Portland and the tired people tumbling out and *in* for breakfast.

–*The Notebooks of Thomas Wolfe,* pp. 964–965

* * *

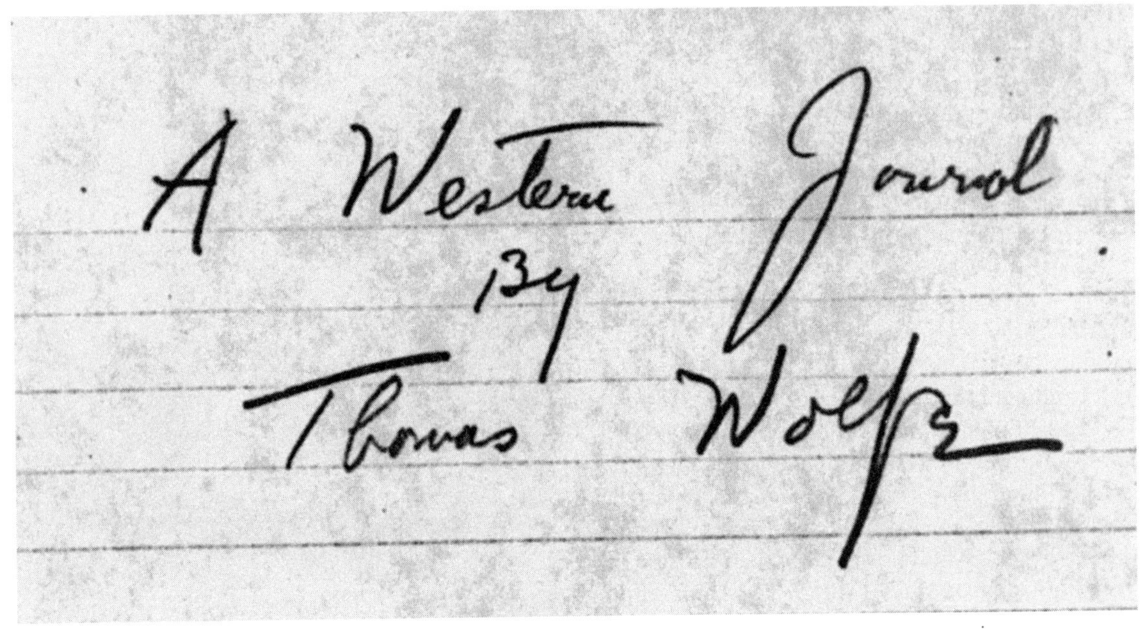

A Western Journal
By
Thomas Wolfe

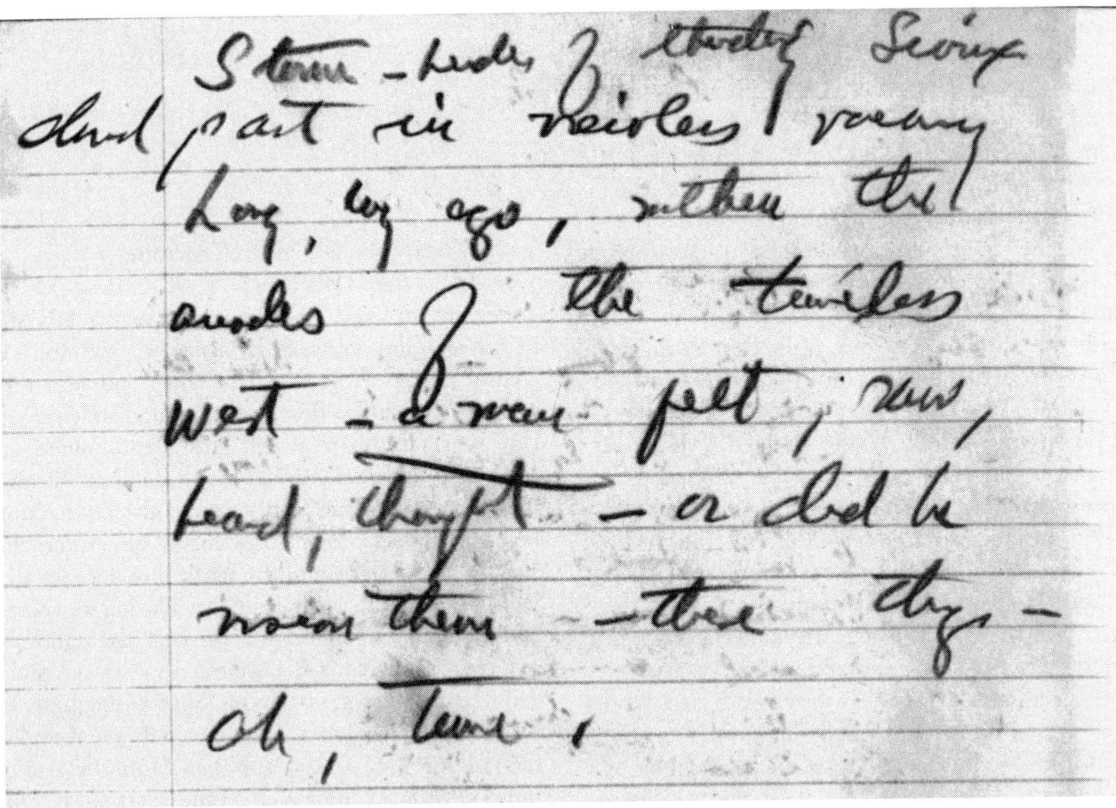

Manuscript title page and epigraph for Wolfe's A Western Journal *(William B. Wisdom Collection, Houghton Library, Harvard University)*

3

A Daily Log
of
the Great Parks Trip

First page from Wolfe's log of his two-week tour of parks that was published in A Western Journal *(William B. Wisdom Collection, Houghton Library, Harvard University)*

Wolfe during his western journey (The Thomas Wolfe Collection, Pack Memorial Public Library, Asheville, North Carolina)

In his entry for Sunday, 26 June 1938, Wolfe recorded his impressions as they passed from the Great Salt Lake region in northern Utah into Idaho.

And now the greatest beauty of the day–the swift mounting up the canyon among bald and greening knobs, a sense of grandeur, sweetness and familiarity, and suddenly, cupped in the rim of bald hills, a magic valley plain, flat as a floor and green as heaven and more fertile and more magic than the Promised Land, then down and winding down the lovely canyon and cattle, horses, and houses sheltered by the trees, and then below the most lovely and enchanted valley of them all–the great valley around Logan–a valley that makes all that has gone before fade to nothing–the very corn and fruit of Canaan–a vast sweet plain of unimaginable richness–loaded with fruit, bursting with cherry orchards, green with its thick and lush fertility and dotted everywhere with the beauty of incredible trees–clumped cottonwoods and lines and windbreaks of incredible poplars–a land of promise and promise of plenty–and then Logan, a thriving, bright town, blazing with electric light and an air of cheerfulness–the fresh bungalows and cottages and the more expensive homes–the tabernacle, and, with a curious tightening of the throat a thought of little Alladine who lived here, loved it and its canyon, and went out, like a million other kids like her, from all this Canaan loveliness to some fortune, fame and glory in the city.

And so out and on, light darkening now, and along that valley incredible, and at length across the line to Idaho, and into Preston, blazing with Idaho's electric light–and here perhaps lost the true road, for we entered now a very rough one "under construction for twenty miles"–and mounted in the darkness with a sense of strangeness and it had rained here and to the North the sky was inky rent with gigantic flashes of Western lightning–and the road perilous and slippery, too, the car sliding sideways as on balls of mercury–but we slogged through it to the good road and so on, between hogback ridges that had closed on us, through what was now, I suspect, desert country, towards Pocatello–on a splendid road–where we arrived just before eleven–registered at the Bannock hotel–out in brightly lighted streets and wakeful noctambuloes for food–a sandwich and some beer–so home–most tired–the others sleeping soundly now–perhaps somewhat too fatigued by the crowded beauty, splendor and magnificence of this day to write it down–and so to bed!

And today 467 miles! (and in our first seven days, about 2760 of our journey.)

–*The Notebooks of Thomas Wolfe,* pp. 979–980

Wolfe at Zion National Park, Utah, 1938 (The Thomas Wolfe Collection, Pack Memorial Public Library, Asheville, North Carolina)

His tour completed, Wolfe wrote to Nowell after receiving her reports of Aswell's enthusiasm for Wolfe's work as well as Aswell's congratulatory telegram. The tour, though arduous, had invigorated him.

New Washington Hotel
Seattle, Wash.
Sunday, July 3 [1938]

Dear Miss Nowell:

I got here late yesterday afternoon and found telegrams from you and Ed, and your air mail was delivered this morning: all of which relieves me and boosts me up no end. The trip was wonderful and terrific–in the last two weeks I have travelled 5,000 miles, gone the whole length of the coast from Seattle almost to the Mexican border, inland a thousand miles and northward to the Canadian border. The national parks, of course, are stupendous, but what was to me far more valuable were the towns, the things, the people I saw–the whole West and all its history unrolling at kaleidoscopic speed. I have written it all down in just this way–with great speed, because I had to do most of it at night before going to bed, usually when we had driven 400 or 500 miles and I was ready to drop with sleep–I've filled a big fat notebook with 30,000 words of it, and looking some of it over, it occurs to me that in this way I may have got the whole thing–the whole impression–its speed, variety, etc–pretty well. At any rate I've got a pretty clear record of the whole thing since I left New York six weeks or so ago, and after two or three days rest out on Puget Sounds somewhere (This is a country fit for Gods–you've never seen anything like it for scale and magnifi-

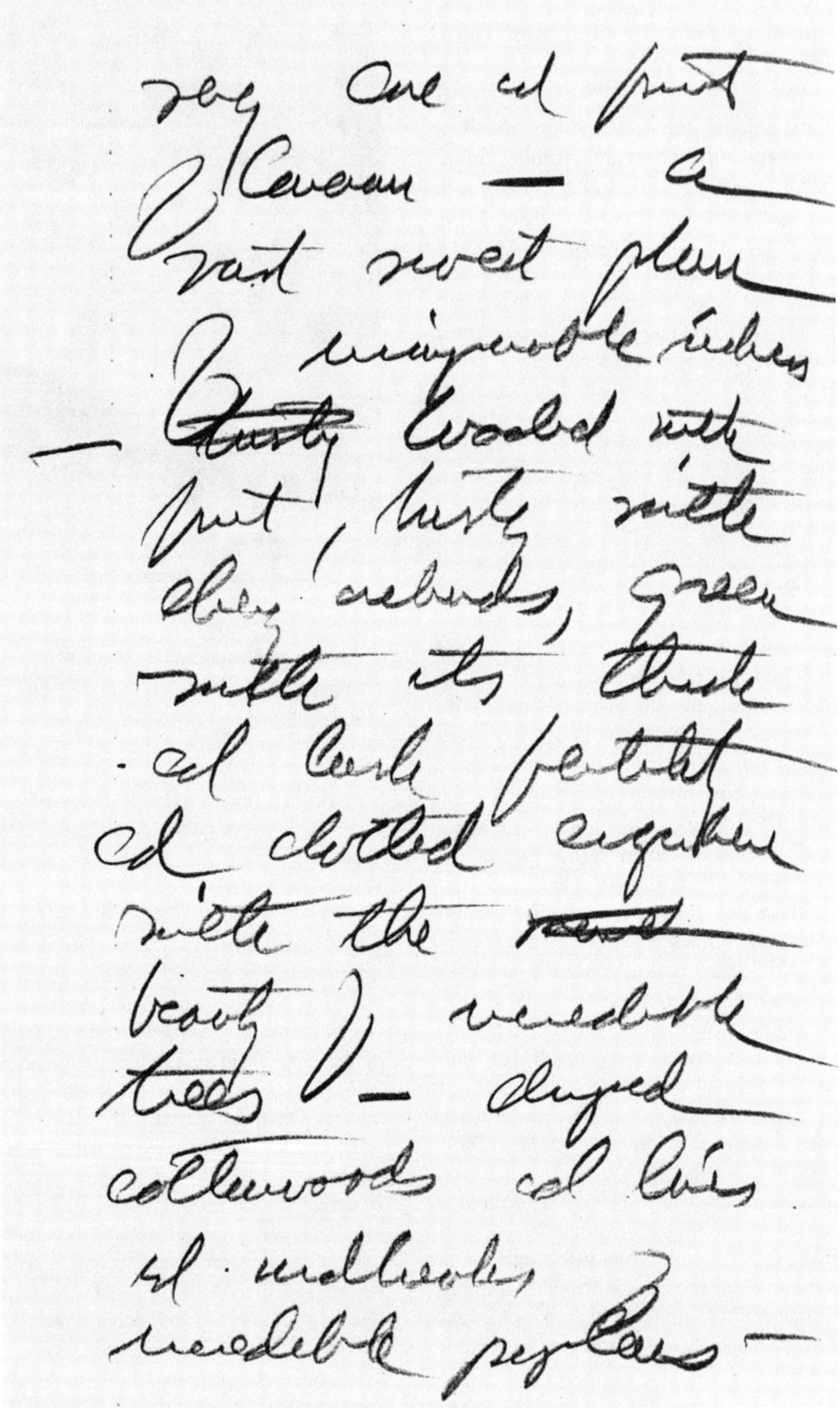

Page from the manuscript for Wolfe's A Western Journal, *which he told Elizabeth Nowell he wrote "with great speed" (William B. Wisdom Collection, Houghton Library, Harvard University)*

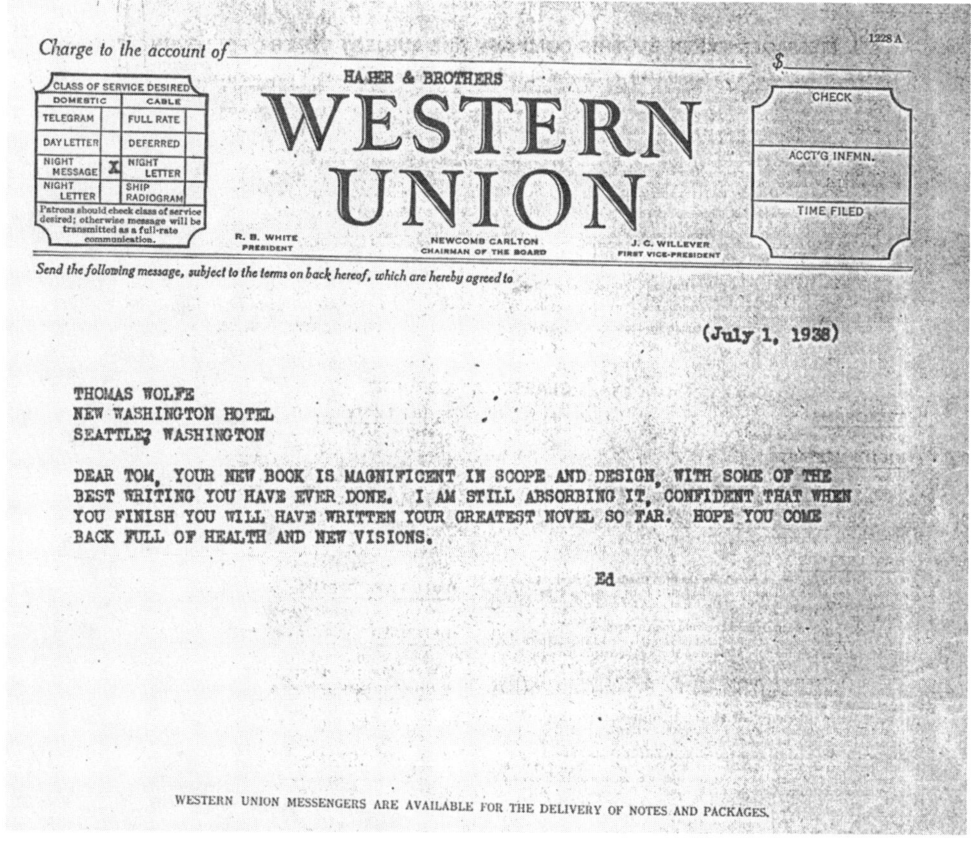
Charge to the account of
HARPER & BROTHERS

CLASS OF SERVICE DESIRED

DOMESTIC		CABLE	
TELEGRAM		FULL RATE	
DAY LETTER		DEFERRED	
NIGHT MESSAGE	X	NIGHT LETTER	
NIGHT LETTER		SHIP RADIOGRAM	

Patrons should check class of service desired; otherwise message will be transmitted as a full-rate communication.

WESTERN UNION

R. B. WHITE, PRESIDENT — NEWCOMB CARLTON, CHAIRMAN OF THE BOARD — J. C. WILLEVER, FIRST VICE-PRESIDENT

CHECK

ACCT'G INFMN.

TIME FILED

Send the following message, subject to the terms on back hereof, which are hereby agreed to

(July 1, 1938)

THOMAS WOLFE
NEW WASHINGTON HOTEL
SEATTLE, WASHINGTON

DEAR TOM, YOUR NEW BOOK IS MAGNIFICENT IN SCOPE AND DESIGN, WITH SOME OF THE BEST WRITING YOU HAVE EVER DONE. I AM STILL ABSORBING IT, CONFIDENT THAT WHEN YOU FINISH YOU WILL HAVE WRITTEN YOUR GREATEST NOVEL SO FAR. HOPE YOU COME BACK FULL OF HEALTH AND NEW VISIONS.

Ed

WESTERN UNION MESSENGERS ARE AVAILABLE FOR THE DELIVERY OF NOTES AND PACKAGES.

Telegram from Aswell Wolfe received in Seattle at the end of his journey (William B. Wisdom Collection, Houghton Library, Harvard University)

cence and abundance: the trees are as tall as the Flatiron Building and yet so much in scale that you simply cannot believe until you measure them they are as big–and you throw a hook into some ordinary looking creek and pull out a twelve pound salmon–I assure you these things are literally true–you feel there's no limit, no end to anything. The East seems small and starved and meagre by comparison, and yet I'm glad there is the East, too–we've got to have the East, there's something in the East they don't have here)–Anyway, I'd like to loaf and rest for a few days, and then get it typed, revising as much as I can but not taking too much time, and putting it down from the beginning like a spool unwinding at great speed–Perhaps it's not ready to use yet or won't be for a year or two, but I'll have it *down*–and you know what that means to me; and I thought I'd call it *A Western Journal*–Anyway, if that's O.K. by you and Ed, that's my present idea–I really feel ready to go again–I've had no rest but this movement, the sense of life and discovery, the variety has renewed and stimulated me–writing 30000 words under the circumstances of the past 2 weeks was an accomplishment and proved to me that I am getting ready again, because I *wanted* to write them–couldn't keep from it.

Anyway, use this hotel as an address for the present–if I go to Puget Sound I'll leave an address here, and anyway I'll keep you posted. Now get some rest yourself–and thanks for everything!

Yours, Wolfe

P.S. I'm thinking of buying some firecrackers and spending tomorrow in H.M. Canadian town of Victoria, B.C.

–*Beyond Love and Loyalty,* pp. 122–123

Wolfe spoke of his plan for his new work in an interview printed in the Portland Sunday Oregonian *on 3 July 1938.*

"It will be a long book–in fact, it will be published in four volumes, each one with a separate title, but working into one completed story beginning in 1793 and coming down to 1938.

"The general title of this book will be, I think, *The Web and the Rock.* Now, 'The Rock' is that thing in use that remains and never changes and 'The Web' is that thing that goes back and forth, that changes us and changes our lives–a man is what he is, he is what he came from, but still he goes and comes like the tide."

–*Thomas Wolfe Interviewed,* p. 119

Wolfe's Last Fourth of July

On 4 July 1938 Wolfe watched an Independence Day parade with James Stevens, well known in Seattle literary circles as a compiler of Paul Bunyan stories, and his wife, Theresa Stevens. After watching the parade, Wolfe and the Stevenses drove to the home of Ivar and Margaret Haglund in Alki, one of the oldest sections of Seattle.

Wolfe wrote to Margaret Roberts on 4 July.

I was ready to drop when I left New York six weeks ago, but I've seen a whole new continent, the entire West, and now I'm writing thousands of words a day again.

–*The Letters of Thomas Wolfe,* p. 775

The last photograph of Thomas Wolfe alone, 4 July 1938 (The North Carolina Collection, University of North Carolina Library at Chapel Hill)

Wolfe, center, with friends in Seattle: left to right, Margaret Haglund, James Stevens, Ivar Haglund, and Theresa Stevens (The North Carolina Collection, University of North Carolina Library at Chapel Hill)

Illness and Death

On 5 July 1938 Wolfe left Seattle for a boat trip to Victoria and Vancouver in British Columbia. He planned to be gone for only a day or two since he was eager to return to Seattle and have his "Western Journal" typed. During the trip on the coastal steamer Princess Kathleen, *he shared a pint of whiskey with a "poor shivering wretch." By the next afternoon Wolfe began experiencing chills, pain in his lungs, and a high fever. He left Vancouver by train and returned to Seattle, remaining in the New Washington Hotel for five days before seeking treatment. The respiratory infection deepened into pneumonia and activated the dormant tuberculosis in Wolfe's right lung.*

Wolfe was admitted to a private sanatorium, Firlawns, twelve miles from Seattle at Kenmore, operated by Dr. E. C. Ruge. When Wolfe seemed unable to make a complete recovery, Ruge sent him to Providence Hospital in Seattle in the first week of August so X-rays could be made of his lungs. The X-rays revealed a consolidation of the upper lobe of the right lung. When violent headaches and periods of irrationality began, the doctors suspected a brain tumor or abscess and recommended that Wolfe be taken to Johns Hopkins Hospital, where the eminent brain surgeon Walter E. Dandy could examine him.

Mabel Wolfe Wheaton, who had come to Seattle to be with her brother during his illness, took Wolfe by train to Baltimore, arriving on 10 September. Dr. Dandy performed a trephining procedure that revealed Wolfe had tuberculosis of the brain. Dr. Dandy discovered a myriad of tubercles covering Wolfe's cerebellum and decided an operation would be hopeless.

Wolfe died at 5:30 Thursday morning, 15 September 1938.

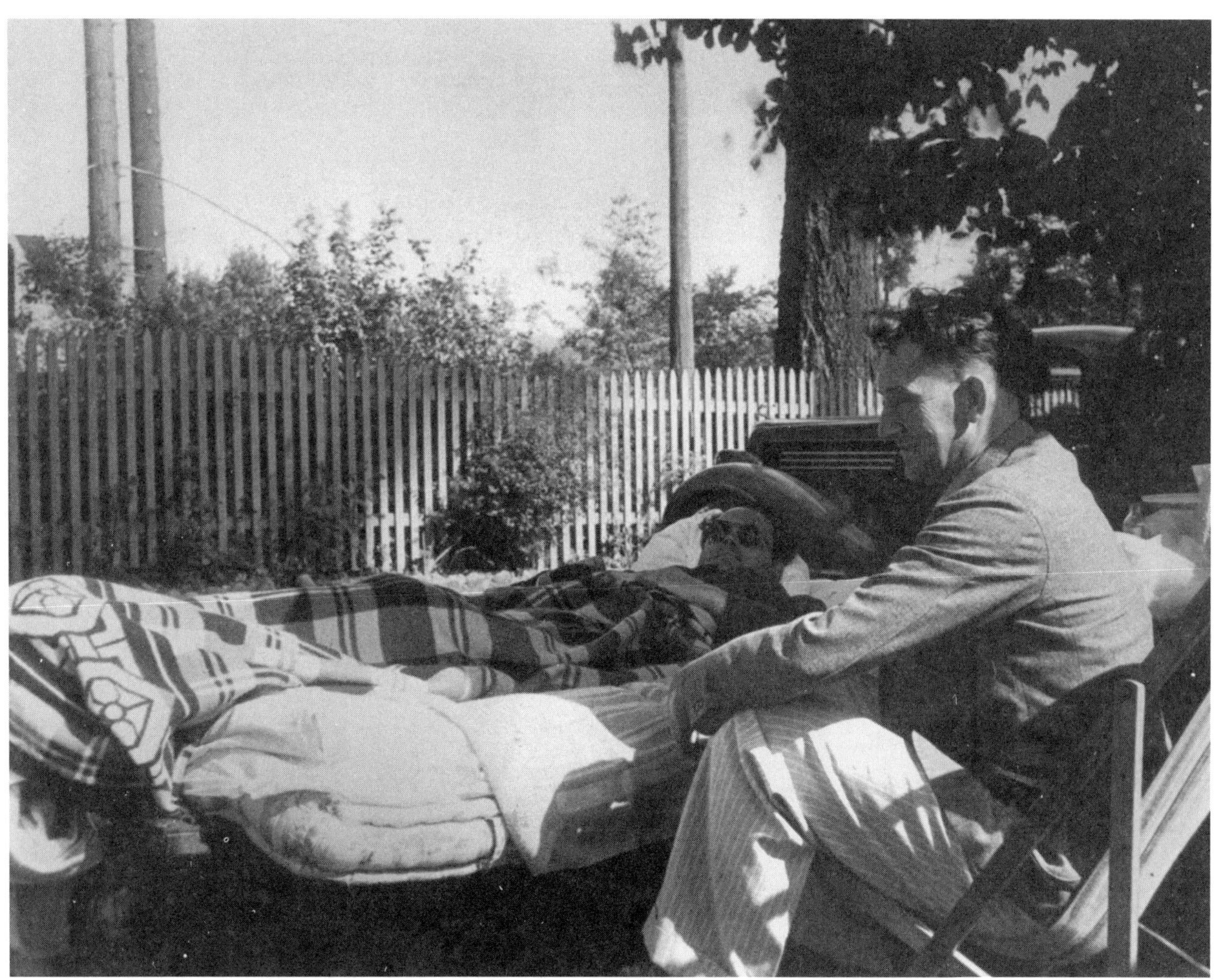

Wolfe with his brother Fred on the grounds of Firlawns Sanatorium, Seattle, circa 23 July 1938 (photograph by James Stevens; James and Theresa Stevens Collection, University of Washington Libraries, Seattle)

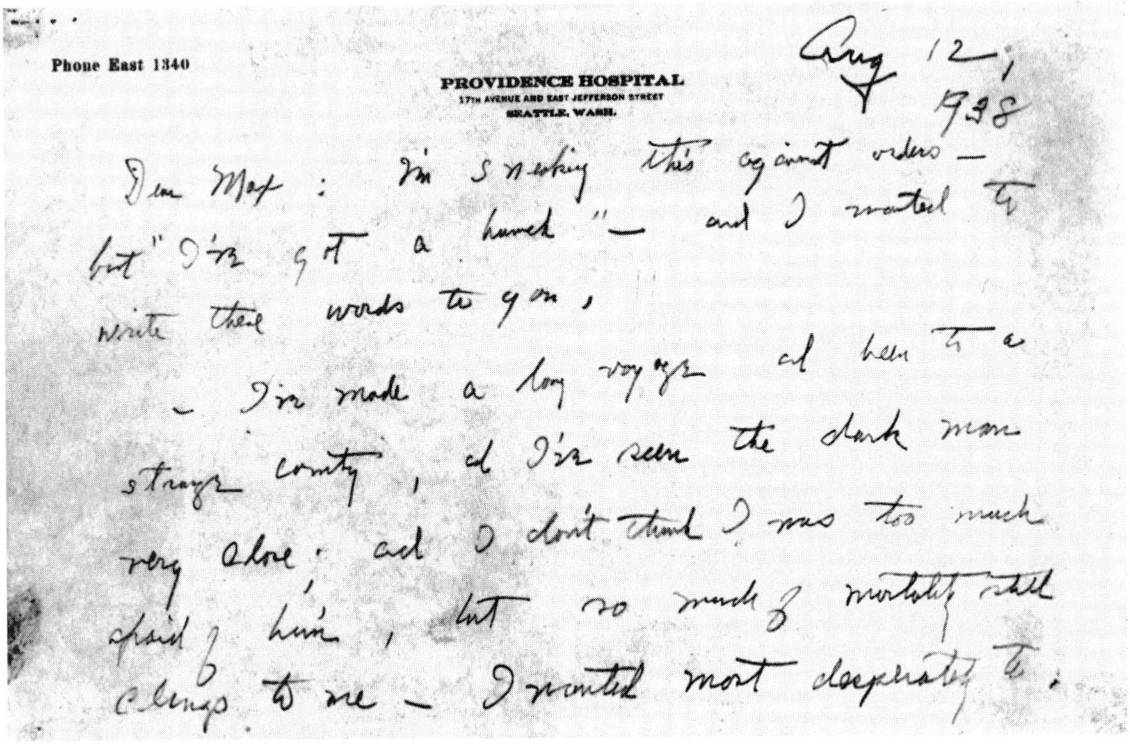

Phone East 1340

PROVIDENCE HOSPITAL
17th AVENUE AND EAST JEFFERSON STREET
SEATTLE, WASH.

Aug 12, 1938

Dear Max: I'm sneaking this against orders—but "I've got a hunch"—and I wanted to write these words to you,

—I've made a long voyage and been to a strange country, and I've seen the dark man very close; and I don't think I was too much afraid of him, but so much of mortality still clings to me—I wanted most desperately to

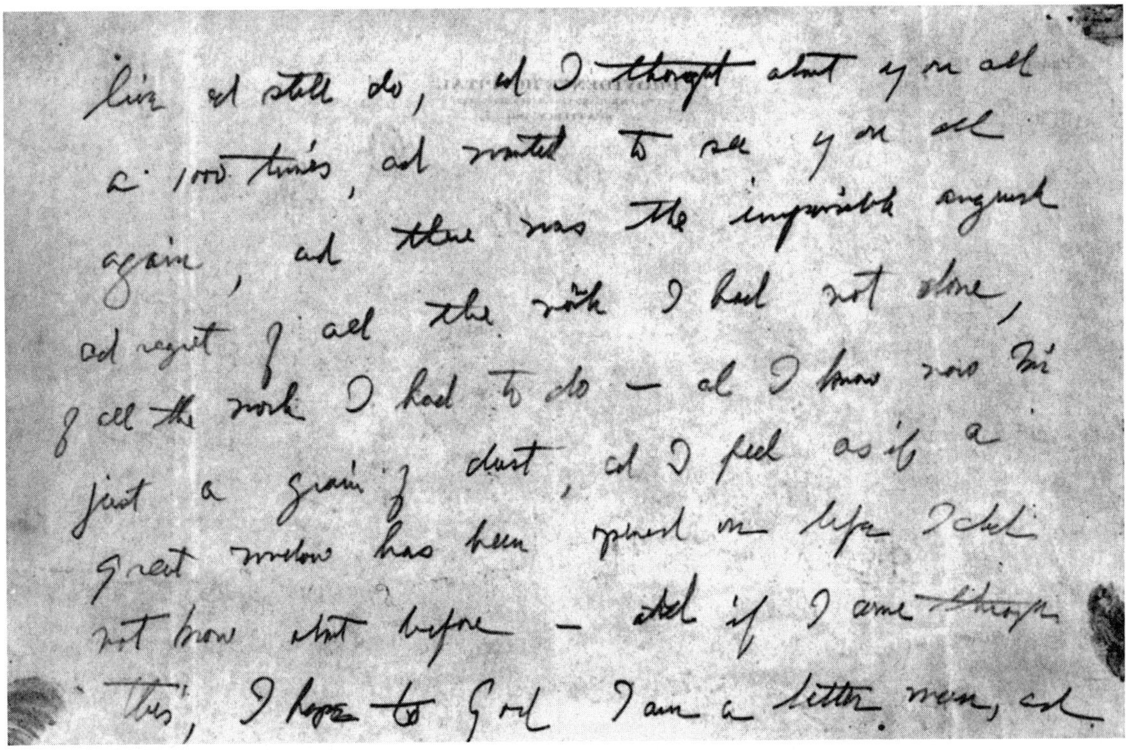

live and still do, and I ~~thought~~ thought about you all a 1000 times, and wanted to see you all again, and there was the impossible anguish and regret of all the work I had not done, of all the work I had to do—and I know now I'm just a grain of dust, and I feel as if a great window has been opened on life I did not know about before—and if I come ~~through~~ through this, I hope to God I am a better man, and

Wolfe's 12 August 1938 letter to Perkins, the last letter he wrote (William B. Wisdom Collection, Houghton Library, Harvard University)

Phone East 1340

PROVIDENCE HOSPITAL
17TH AVENUE AND EAST JEFFERSON STREET
SEATTLE, WASH.

in some strange way I can't explain
I know I am a deeper and a wiser
one – If I get on my feet and out
of here, it will be months before I head
back, but if I get on my feet, I'll
come back
– Whatever happens – I had this "hunch" and wanted

to write you and tell you, no matter what
happens or has happened, I shall always think
of you and feel about you the way it was
that 4th of July day 3 yrs. ago when you
met me at the boat, and we went out
on the cafe on the river and had a drink
and later went on top of ~~the~~ the tall building
and all the strangeness and the glory and
the power of life and of the city was below – Yours always
Tom

ASHEVILLE TIMES 7/15/38

THOMAS WOLF, NOTED NOVELIST, SERIOUSLY ILL AT SEATTLE, WASH.

Stricken last Wednesday with pneumonia, Thomas Wolfe, of Asheville, author of "Look Homeward, Angel" and "Of Time and The River," is seriously ill in Firlawn sanitarium, Seattle, Wash., Mrs. Julia Wolfe, his mother, has been notified here.

Mrs. Wolfe was notified yesterday of her son's condition. The attending physician, Dr. E. C. Buge, told Mrs. Wolfe that her son was suffering a severe attack of pneumonia, but was "past the crisis."

Mr. Wolfe, who has been on vacation in the Pacific northwest, became ill in Vancouver, B. C. Mrs. Wolfe said that her son has been working hard and has covered considerable territory in recent travels. She has heard from him in many portions of the northwest in recent weeks. He has been making a tour of national parks of the west in company with three publicity representatives of the American Automobile association.

Fred Wolfe, a brother, of Spartanburg, S. C., expects to take either a plane or train today for Seattle, Mrs. Wolfe said. If Mr. Wolfe has not continued to show improvement, as the message intimated yesterday he might, Mr. Wolfe's brother will leave by plane. His sister, Mrs. Ralph H. Wheaton, of 136 Biltmore avenue, said she will also leave Spartanburg by plane for Seattle if reports on her brother's condition are not favorable today.

Mr. Wolfe visited here several weeks last summer, visiting relatives and writing some magazine stories. He is a native of Asheville and was educated at private and public schools here, the University of North Carolina and at Harvard university. He has resided in Brooklyn for several years.

The Asheville Times, *15 July 1938*

Tom Wolfe Improving At Seattle Hospital

Ashe.-Citz.. 9-1-38

Fred Wolfe, who has been at the bedside of his brother, Thomas Wolfe, in Seattle, Wash., for the past six weeks, reported yesterday that the author and former Asheville resident was recovering slowly from an attack of pneumonia. He stopped here en route to his home at Spartanburg, S. C.

Mrs. Ralph Wheaton, a sister of the writer, will remain in Seattle for several weeks. It is possible he will return to this section this fall, members of the family here said last night.

The Asheville Citizen, *1 September 1938*

Thomas Wolfe, Ailing Novelist, En Route East

Seattle Times (Wash)

SEP 7 1938

Thomas Wolfe, noted novelist who came west last July to lecture and visit, but who spent nearly all his days here under doctors' care, was en route today to Baltimore for further medical attention.

Wolfe left Seattle last night. He will undergo treatment at Johns Hopkins Hospital. Although his physicians found he had rallied from his original ailment—pneumonia —complications developed and it was thought it would be better if the novelist were closer to his home during further treatment. He lives in Asheville, N. C.

Accompanying Wolfe on the trip east is his sister, Mrs. Ralph Wheaton of Asheville.

"Look Homeward, Angel" and "Of Time and the River" are among Wolfe's successful novels.

Seattle Times, *7 September 1938*

Thomas Wolfe Enters Johns Hopkins Hospital

Ashe.-Citz. 9-11-38

BALTIMORE, Sept. 10. (AP)—Thomas Wolfe, novelist who became ill while on the west coast, entered the Johns Hopkins hospital today.

Hospital attendants said he would be given an examination Monday.

The Asheville Citizen, *11 September 1938*

Undergoes Operation

Asheville Citizen 9-14-38

Thomas Wolfe, Asheville-born author has been operated upon at Johns Hopkins hospital, Baltimore, for an "acute cerebral infection," the Associated Press reported last night.

Hospital authorities said Wolfe is in "much better condition today (Tuesday) and is progressing satisfactorily," according to the dispatch.

Wolfe entered Johns Hopkins Saturday after a trip from Seattle, Wash. where he had been under treatment since being stricken with pneumonia July 6.

Although apparently recovered from the pneumonia attack, Wolfe had suffered severe headaches recently and an X-ray revealed the brain infection.

Mrs. Mabel Wheaton, of Asheville, Wolfe's sister, accompanied him from Seattle to Baltimore. His mother, Mrs. Julia Wolfe, of 48 Spruce street, and

The Asheville Citizen, *14 September 1938*

CONDITION OF TOM WOLFE IS 'VERY GRAVE'

Asheville Citizen 9-15-38

BALTIMORE, Sept. 14. (AP) — The condition of Thomas Wolfe, novelist, who has been operated upon twice since Saturday is "very grave", his sister, Mrs. Ralph Wheaton of Asheville, N. C. said tonight.

Physicians said the 37-year-old author of "Look Homeward Angel" and "Of Time and the River" was "very seriously ill" from an "acute cerebral infection." An exploratory operation was performed Saturday in preparation for another surgery Monday.

Mrs. Wheaton said Wolfe became ill during July in Vancouver, B. C. He later went to Seattle where his illness was diagnosed as pneumonia. Complications of the illness developed later and physicians advised he be brought to Johns Hopkins hospital in Baltimore where the operations were performed.

At his bedside tonight are his mother, Mrs. Julia E. Wolfe, a brother, Fred, and Mrs. Wheaton, all of Asheville.

The Asheville Citizen, *15 September 1938*

Thomas Wolfe Is Dead At 37 After Lengthy Illness

Asheville Citizen
September 16, 1938

Brilliant Author Dies In Baltimore From Cerebral Infection

FUNERAL RITES SET FOR SUNDAY

Asheville-Born Author Won Fame With 'Look Homeward, Angel'

Thomas Wolfe, the Asheville boy whose novels about his home-town folk brought him fame as a brilliant young author, died early yesterday morning in Baltimore from an acute cerebral infection. He was 37 years old.

Wolfe had been ill since last July 6 when he was stricken with a cold in Vancouver, B. C., while touring the northwest with friends. It later developed into pneumonia and complicating infections resulted in his death after two operations.

The body of the prolific young writer, accompanied by his mother, a sister and a brother, will leave Baltimore tonight and will arrive here at 9:15 a. m. tomorrow. Funeral services will be conducted Sunday afternoon at the First Presbyterian church. Other details of the funeral and burial will be announced after arrival of the body.

Taken To Johns Hopkins

Apparently recovered from the attack of pneumonia, Wolfe was removed from a Seattle, Wash., hospital to an apartment several weeks ago. On September 6 his mother, Mrs. Julia Wolfe, of 48 Spruce street, received word her son would have to undergo an operation and was informed he was being taken to Johns Hopkins hospital at Baltimore by his sister, Mrs. Mabel Wheaton, also of Asheville. She left immediately for Chicago where she met them, en route, and has been at his bedside since. Fred Wolfe, of Spartanburg, a brother, also was in Baltimore.

Wolfe entered Johns Hopkins hospital last Saturday and following the two operations he was reported Tuesday to be "progressing satisfactorily." His condition gradually became worse, however, and he succumbed at 5:30 o'clock yesterday morning.

"Look Homeward, Angel," the first of the chronicles of the Gant family—the story of Wolfe himself and the people and towns he had known—was published in 1929. It brought him acclaim as a writer and created a sensation in Asheville because of the bold and daring lines with which he painted himself, his neighbors and acquaintances.

"Of Time and the River," also a voluminous edition, followed in 1935. Both were semi-autobiographical and were as massive in proportion as the six-foot, seven-inch author who wrote them.

THOMAS WOLFE

Was Graduate Of Harvard

Wolfe published "Look Homeward, Angel," while teaching English literature at New York university. He was a graduate of the University of North Carolina, where he obtained his A. B. degree in 1920, and of Harvard university, where he finished with an M. A. degree in 1923. His early education was obtained in the Asheville public schools and at the North State School for Boys, a private institution operated here a number of years ago by J. M. Roberts.

As a pupil in his elementary school days Tom Wolfe was exceedingly apt. His enthusiasm knew no bounds. He was eager to learn and very early in his school life showed great fondness for books.

He was not only quick to learn, but also easy to teach, being tractable and willing to profit by every suggestion towards his improvement. But with all this he was so full of originality that his personality was never submerged.

He loved contests of all sorts. At the age of 11 in a spelling match, participated in by Asheville and various high schools in this section, he won the contest for his school on the word, "asafoetida." In public speaking of any kind in the schools he was always ready. Declamations and debates were his especial delights. In the debates his side was sure to win. In the Shakespeare tercentary celebration he won a medal offered by the Independent magazine for an essay on Shakespeare. He then gave the essay in declamation form and won a medal on it at the school commencement.

Was A Real Boy

From the very first his ability to write was manifest. The marks of genius showed early in his school compositions. But in spite of his unusual ability and interest in literary work he loved to play baseball, was active on the playground and [illegible] was a real boy.

Even before he entered high school his command of words was remarkable. He was very mature in his reading tastes and read voraciously. At 11 he was familiar with the most readable of Shakespeare's plays, and at 15 when he entered the University of North Carolina he was well versed in many of the great English classics. Surely in his ability to write and his appreciation of literature Tom Wolfe was a good example of the proverb, the child is father of the man.

Wolfe won a Guggenheim fellowship which enabled him to travel in Europe in 1930 and 1931. On his return he published "A Portrait of Btscom Hawke" and "The Web of Earth" in 1932. Beth if these were short novels.

There still are a million Wolfe words to be edited, his publishers, Harper and Brothers, said yesterday—the result of his winer's work in the Hotel Chelsea in New York.

This consisted of seven paper boxes of manuscript, containing probably a million words—material for several novels, if the publisher decides to use it all.

Will Publish Two Novels

It was announced at Harpers, however, that the new material will be divided into at least two novels, perhaps three. These will continue the story of the Gant family begun in "Look Homeward Angel."

The posthumous work probably will feed the controversy which had crackled about Wolfe's head since his first important publication in 1929.

One school insists the native-born Ashevillian was an authentic genius. Others feel that although Wolfe was a writer of great talent, the plethora of words in which his thoughts were wrapped obscured rather than clarified them.

The classic example of his wordiness is the description of the train journey made by the hero of his Gant saga from Asheville to Boston. The trip was described in "Of Time and the River" in more than 60,000 words, although it advanced the narrative only minutely.

It was this exacting description of events and people in his home town that made him the object of criticism following the appearance of "Look Homeward Angel."

It is believed that a consciousness of this bitterness, together with his work, kept him away from his home town where he drew inspiration and material for his first novel.

Returned Home In 1937

In May 1937 he came home for the first time following the publication of "Look Homeward Angel." Wolfe made no apology for his book at that time, but he did say he was sorry if he had displeased anyone, and blamed his youth for drawing perhaps too much on the only raw material with which he had to work.

"When a young writer writes," he explained, "he takes the most direct means, and often he turns too directly to the raw material he has before him. When he grows older he learns to transform this raw material.

"My father," he said, "was a stone cutter, but he couldn't go about his business without stone. It's the same way with writing. You have got to use what you've got to work with. You have to use what you know about.

"A writer," he said, "is thinking about the story that is within him and not about any particular town or any particular person."

Received Warm Welcome

The people of Asheville who thought they saw themselves portrayed in Wolfe's novel seven years previous to the author's return, had forgiven in 1937, and the son of a local stonecut-

The Asheville Citizen, *16 September 1938*

50276 HEALTH DEPARTMENT—CITY OF BALTIMORE E 50276

351421

CERTIFICATE OF DEATH

1. PLACE OF DEATH JOHNS HOPKINS HOSPITAL

CITY OF BALTIMORE: (No. St. Ward) 7-5

Registered No. 23

2. FULL NAME Thomas C Wolfe

(a) Residence: No. 222 W 23 St., Ward. New York City

PERSONAL AND STATISTICAL PARTICULARS

Sex: male | 4. Color or Race: White | 5. Single, Married, Widowed, or Divorced (write the word): single

DATE OF BIRTH (month, day, year): 10/3-1900

AGE: Yrs. 37 Months 11 Days 12

Trade, profession, or particular kind of work: Author

BIRTHPLACE (city or town) (State or country): Asheville N. C.

13. NAME [of father]: Wm Wolfe

14. BIRTHPLACE (city or town) (State or country): York Springs Pa.

15. MAIDEN NAME [of mother]: Julia Westall

16. BIRTHPLACE (city or town) (State or country): Asheville N. C.

INFORMANT: Records JOHNS HOPKINS HOSPITAL

BURIAL, CREMATION, OR REMOVAL: Place Asheville N.C. Date Sept 15, 38

UNDERTAKER: Wm. J. Tickner & Sons, North & Pa. Aves.

Filed 16 1938

MEDICAL CERTIFICATE OF DEATH

21. DATE OF DEATH (month, day, year): Sept-15 1938

22. I HEREBY CERTIFY, That I attended deceased from Sept 10 1938, to Sept 15 1938

I last saw him alive on Sept 15 1938

The principal cause of death and related causes of importance were as follows: Tuberculous Meningitis — Date of onset 9-15-38

Other contributory causes of importance: Pulmonary Tuberculosis 1938?

Was an operation performed? Yes Date of Sept. 12, 1938

For what disease or injury? Tuberculous Meningitis

Name of operation: Cerebellar Exploration

What test confirmed diagnosis? Biopsy Was there an autopsy? No

24. Was disease or injury in any way related to occupation of deceased? No

Signed William Gray Watson M.D.

Address Johns Hopkins Hospital

Wolfe's death certificate

Wolfe's coffin (The Thomas Wolfe Collection, Pack Memorial Public Library, Asheville, North Carolina)

Wolfe's grave in Riverside Cemetery, Asheville (The Thomas Wolfe Collection, Pack Memorial Public Library, Asheville, North Carolina)

Tributes and Assessments

Nation, 24 September 1938

THOMAS WOLFE BELONGED TO THE LUSTY school of writing. He was a huge man physically, and his literary productions were commensurate. Where other men write by tens of thousands he poured out hundreds of thousands of words. In describing one of his books in process he told a friend with gusto, "The first hundred pages are about locomotives." And his prodigious output gave rise to tall tales. It was said that his manuscripts were delivered in trucks and that Maxwell Perkins of Scribner's had told him he must cut at least a hundred thousand words out of his latest opus. He burst upon the world in 1929 with "Look Homeward, Angel," which overwhelmed the critics and caused his native town of Asheville, North Carolina, to disown him. It was an unabashed and undisguised picture of his own family and his own home town, in which ordinary human appetites and human relations were projected on an enormous scale in unrestrained and romantic rhetoric. In this book, as in many autobiographical novels, the material itself was compelling, while the passionate energy and youth of the author–he was in his middle twenties–suggested wide potentialities. In his later books, however, his writing remained undisciplined, highly emotional, and charged with a vague romanticism. In short the promise of maturity in thought and style did not materialize, and though there exists an audience which regards him as the great American novelist, time, which he apostrophized so eloquently, has already relegated his work to that category of literary production which is memorable for its energy rather than for its art.

> For life is more savage than any war: it is not for the million men who are slain in a battle that we should grieve, but for the hundred million men around us who are daily slain by living, and for whom, soon or late, the earth is waiting. I do not grieve that servicemen die in battle: I simply grieve that all men die–with all our hunger unappeased, with all purpose gone amort.
>
> –*The Notebooks of Thomas Wolfe,* p. 432

Tom Wolfe
The New Republic, 28 September 1938

He had more friends, he had fewer enemies than any other writer of our day. And there must have been thousands who had met him only once or twice, yet read the last news about him with a deep sense of personal loss. He talked well, but even more he was a creative listener, with an eagerness that flattered everybody and a bulk that made him respond like multitudes. He was so big and seemed so robust that it is amazing to hear of his death from a disease popularly connected with starveling poets. Pneumonia reopened an old scar in his lungs; the tubercular infection spread through his system, attacked the brain; and two operations at Johns Hopkins came too late to save him.

On one side of his literary self, Tom Wolfe was a dithyrambic poet, a Whitman turned inwards through reading James Joyce. He wrote prose-poetic hymns to America and the Artist in a language copied from Shakespeare–indeed, there are long passages in his first two novels that fall into iambic pentameters, like an Elizabethan tragedy. That is the side of his work most praised and most likely to perish. On the other side, he was an objective novelist with a talent for comic or tragic distortion that goes back to Dickens; that is the side which produced his great portraits, like the Gant family (excepting Eugene) and Uncle Bascom Hawke. There are some indications that this objective side of him was developing in his later work, though we can't be certain until Harpers edit and publish the million-word manuscript of the novel or group of novels he left behind him. Whatever that manuscript proves to be, Tom Wolfe is already a legend.

Thurston Macauley was a Newsweek *writer who had grown up in Asheville.*

Thomas Wolfe: A Writer's Problems
Thurston Macauley
Publishers' Weekly, 24 December 1938

The tragic and untimely death of Thomas Wolfe, not quite 38, leaves still unsolved his major problems, the age-old problems of a brilliant creative artist trying desperately to find his way in a world that can help him but little.

It is not my intention here to explore the full extent of that great loss to the literature of this country, indeed of all the world. No one can say what he might have done or how far yet he would have gone: he can be judged only by the millions of words already pub-

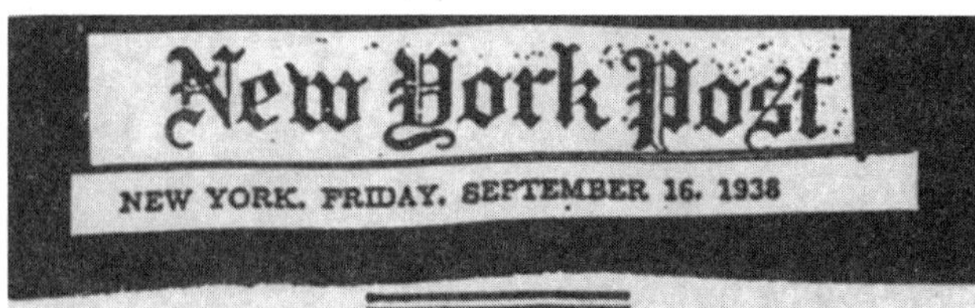

The World of Thomas Wolfe

To Thomas Wolfe the world was a place of violence, immense, desolate and dreadful, a moon-space of undulating wildness. His personal shyness was often contrasted with the energy and terror of his writing. Yet it is to the most retiring that the world seems most terrifying; Wolfe was, during all his writing life, a man who wrote as if he had just stepped out of a secret hermitage of the soul, and found a startling crescendo in such "ordinary" noises and events as the click of a nickel in a subway turnstile, a ride in a Pullman, a newsboy making change, a first encounter with sin.

The South slept under its magnolia trees until he came along with "Look Homeward, Angel." One knew what to expect in the South, cotton in the fields, the flash of Negro teeth, the colonel on the porch, elegance and sour mash whisky. But Wolfe, with his curious gift of looking upon the world, seeing its sights, hearing its noises, as if no one had ever done so before, changed the South permanently. His city of Altamont, they say, is "really" Asheville, N. C. Better to say that Asheville is really Altamont, but that no one knew it until Wolfe discovered it and laid it bare—a place of alarums and uproars, of sudden deadly flights of hostility, of terror underlying the forms of ordinary life, of all of conscience and filth flaring out in the brief description of, say, a newsboy and a prostitute.

There were so many impressions crowding in on him and each weighed so heavy that though he could convey a sense of their magnitude, and did so superbly, he never succeeded in reducing them to order. He tried. He searched for a kind of instinctive father-wisdom, but he never found it. In "Of Time and the River" his roaring world seemed to have got the better of him and he appeared lost. His death cuts him down with his development just begun; he was permitted little more than a statement of his gifts. One of the most eloquent and amazing Americans is lost, our one Gargantua after Whitman.

Editorial, New York Post, *16 September 1938*

lished and yet to be published that he left behind. But the lessons to be drawn from his experience are ones that should be studied with care by everyone having anything to do with writing.

Wolfe's first novel sold some 10,000 copies in one season and renewed its life later in a Modern Library edition. His second, the mammoth 912-page "Of Time and the River," published in 1935, sold 45,000 in about the same period, although the book was higher priced and boom times had given way to depression. In spite of the hugh bulk of his work and whatever certain critics reiterated about his lack of form and discipline, at least people in increasing numbers were reading him.

When the 350,000-word 'script of "Look Homeward, Angel" was kicking around from publisher to publisher, one reader reported it "an autobiographical novel with lashes of talent." Wolfe's "discoverer," of course, was Maxwell Perkins of Scribner's who was unquestionably the greatest individual influence in his writing life. The debt was fully acknowledged in that generous dedication to "Of Time and the River" and again in "The Story of a Novel," Wolfe's candid literary confessions and credo. (Like Somerset Maugham's "The Summing Up," it is a "must" book for all concerned with the making of books.) Perkins it was who helped to direct the mighty torrent that raged with such fury within him and poured out, as Wolfe put it, "life burning lava from a volcano," into publishable form.

Although Perkins is Wolfe's literary executor, lately, since Wolfe changed publishers, another editor, Edward C. Aswell of Harper's, is now wrestling with the mass of writing Wolfe turned over to him last spring before he went west and caught his fatal illness. No decision has yet been made about the posthumous Wolfe book or books, although Aswell says that some part of those million words will be published next year. The title is not chosen, either: Wolfe left six possible ones.

What is known is that Wolfe's last writing, on which he had worked for over three years, was in a new direction away from the ambitious program he previously set himself. "Look Homeward, Angel" and "Of Time and the River" were to have been only a part of a great sextology covering 150 years of American life, as a publisher's note in the latter book announced.

The new work Wolfe spoke of as a "legend" that would be a digest of the sum total of his experience, but as far as possible in one book instead of six. Eugene Gant, Wolfe's autobiographical protagonist in the first two novels, is no longer the central character. Wolfe further described the work to his publishers: "It seems to be a kind of American 'Gulliver's Travels'; in its essence it's one of those books about the adventures of the average man–by which I mean the naturally innocent man, every mother's son to us, through the world."

Few books in recent years could have been awaited more eagerly by public and book world alike than is Wolfe's posthumous work. Certainly its publication will be an event of first importance in contemporary literature. And just as Wolfe's reading public increased with his second novel, so will it assuredly be larger still for his posthumous work. Already his death has had an appreciable effect on sales of his books.

It might not be out of place to suggest that another excellent and moving Wolfe book, already in shape of the press and public, may be found in the short novel published in *The New Republic* last year in three installments: "I Have a Thing to Tell You." An indictment of Nazi Germany, it is not only of extremely timely interest but contains some of the best as well as the most straightforward and direct writing Wolfe ever produced. And it cost him a lot to write it, too, because he had won for himself in Germany a reputation as great if not greater than in his own land and furthermore he had always felt a deep love for Germany, its culture and its people.

From the experience of his first novel–banned from libraries in his home town (Asheville) and even denounced from its pulpits–he had already known what it was to have an irate body of people turn against him. An instance of the things that enraged them: old Gant, the lusty stonecutter (drawn from his father), sold a marble angel for the grave of a notorious townswoman. Although it was pure fiction, people "recognized" the character as they did others in the book. The local paper even sent a photographer to the cemetery: "He took a picture of the first damned angel he came to," Wolfe said, "and it was over the grave of a perfectly good Methodist lady!" Naturally the Methodist lady's family registered an indignant protest.

One of the problems that confronted Wolfe, as it does all writers, is this: how far can you go in setting down the life about you as you see it? Wolfe answered it very well for himself in his preface to the Modern Library edition of "Look Homeward, Angel": ". . . it seems to him that all serious work in fiction is autobiographical . . . If the writer has used the clay of life to make his book, he has only used what all men must, what none can keep from using. Fiction is not fact, but fiction is fact selected and understood, fiction is fact arranged and charged with purpose." Somerset Maugham also advances similar arguments for using the "clay of life" in writing.

Wolfe's short life was almost all struggle, not so much the usual one for economic independence, but other sorts: first with his family and school fellows to whom he was different (as he was) and "queer"; years futilely spent trying to write plays before finding in the novel his proper medium of expression; then that long and incessant struggle which went on to the very last of controlling the flood-tide of his work.

Another was the struggle of a six and a half foot Gulliver to live in a world of five foot eight Lilliputians. He wrote tellingly of this in "Gulliver" in the "From Death to Morning" collection of his shorter pieces; he was "for ever a stranger, and alone." That sense of loneliness, of always being lost, is one of the most poignant constantly recurring notes in his books. Whether out of choice or necessity, Wolfe led for the most part a solitary life, writing furiously always, from the time he taught English at Washington Square College until a Guggenheim fellowship and then half of a *Scribner's Magazine* short novel prize for his "Portrait of Bascom Hawke" (later incorporated in "Of Time and the River") enabled him to give himself up entirely to his writing. (It was only in later years that the "slick" magazines became sufficiently interested in him to buy his stories.)

Realizing that Wolfe was an exception to most contemporary writers, who generally lead lives as normal as any business men, nevertheless in the case of so great a talent–genius, even–the tragedy of his too early death seems one that might, perhaps, have been avoided. And yet who could cope with a writer like Wolfe–who, indeed, but the man himself? But should a man write with such fire and fury that he burns himself out before reaching 38? Or, if it were possible some way to hold that fury in check, would the writing, wrought so powerfully out of life, suffer in consequence? These are questions that are difficult to answer but they should be asked all the same and, for the sake of others, an attempt made to answer them. I am sure both Perkins and Aswell did their utmost of Wolfe, and the kind and sympathetic Elizabeth Nowell, his agent, did too.

The immediate cause of Wolfe's death was pneumonia, which opened an old healed-up tuberculosis scar in his lungs. Wolfe had had that dread disease at some point past without being aware of it, perhaps thinking it only a bad cold at the time. But the pneumonia revived it and it entered the blood stream, being carried to his brain.

In this connection, a New York *Herald Tribune* editorial after his death said: "It is inevitable that there should be speculation as to what possible effect the brain ailment which caused his death had upon his way of life, his mannerisms and his methods of work. He was, in truth, a tortured soul." Aswell answered this but for those who may have missed his reply I would like to quote what Dr. Walter E. Dandy, the distinguished brain surgeon who performed the two operations upon Wolfe, wrote Aswell: "His (Wolfe's) intracranial condition, of course, had nothing whatever to do with his mentality; this was a very acute condition, the onset of which in the brain was only of a month's duration."

It can never be known just when Wolfe had had tuberculosis, whether as a child–even then he lived quite irregularly–in Asheville (where many suffering from it go for treatment), as a too eager student trying to devour all the world's knowledge in a single gulp, or as a writer looking frantically in the "bitter briefness of his day": " . . . a terrible doubt began to creep into my mind that I might not live long enough to get it out of me."

Wolfe's chief difficulty was in finding himself. When he said with that extreme modesty that is so characteristic of him that he was not a professional or even a skilled writer and that he didn't yet know how to write a story or a novel, he was simply stating the facts. He had to learn by the trial and error method. And even his methods were as unique as he was himself. He never planned a book like other writers by outlining it in advance: he afterwards fitted together in sequential order what he had written so copiously. But that does not mean that everything he wrote was not important, charged as it was with the significance that he gave to life in the strange crucible of his richly creative mind. Unfinished and cut short though it may be, few would say–even his severest critics–that his work will not live.

Poet-critic John Peale Bishop's 1938 assessment of Wolfe's achievements and unfulfilled promise expresses reservations about Wolfe's ability to find "a structure of form which would have been capable of giving shape and meaning to his emotional experience."

The Sorrows of Thomas Wolfe

John Peale Bishop

Kenyon Review, 1 (Winter 1939): 7–17

Thomas Wolfe is dead. And that big work which he was prepared to write, which was to have gone to six long volumes and covered in the course of its narrative the years between 1781 and 1933, with a cast of characters whose numbers would have run into the hundreds, will never be finished. The title which he had chosen for it, *Of Time and the River,* had already been allowed to appear on the second volume. There its application is not altogether clear; how appropriate it would have been to the work as a whole we can only conjecture. No work of such magnitude has been projected by another of his generation in America; Wolfe's imagination, it appears, could conceive on no smaller scale. He was, he confesses, devoted to chance; he had no constant control over his faculties; but his fecundity was nothing less than prodigious. He had, moreover, a tenacity which must, but for his dying, have carried him through to the end.

Dying, he left behind him a mass of manuscript; how much of it can be published there is now no knowing. Wolfe was the most wasteful of writers.

His aim was to set down America as far as it can belong to the experience of one man. Wolfe came early on what was for him the one available truth about this continent–that it was contained in himself. There was no America which could not be made out–mountains, rivers, trains, cities, people–in the memory of an American. If the contours were misty, then they must be made clear. It was in flight from a certain experience of America, as unhappy as it had been apparently sterile, it was in Paris, in an alien land, that Wolfe first understood with hate and with love the horror and the wonder of his native country. He had crossed the seas from West to East only to come upon the North Carolina hills where he had been born. "I had found out," he says, "during those years that the way to discover one's own country was to leave it; that the way to find America was to find it in one's own heart, one's memory, and one's spirit, and in a foreign land. I think I may say that I discovered America during those years abroad out of my very need of her."

This is not an uncommon experience, but what made it rewarding in Wolfe's case was that his memory was anything but common. He could–and it is the source of what is most authentic in his talents–displace the present so completely by the past that its sights and sounds all but destroyed surrounding circumstance. He then lost the sense of time. For Wolfe, sitting at a table on a terrace in Paris, contained within himself not only the America he had known; he also held, within his body, both his parents. They were there, not only in his memory, but more portentously in the make-up of his mind. They loomed so enormous to him that their shadows fell across the Atlantic, their shade was on the café table under which he stretched his long American legs.

"The quality of my memory," he said in his little book, *The Story of a Novel,* "is characterized, I believe, in a more than ordinary degree by the intensity of its sense impressions, its power to evoke and bring back the odors, sounds, colors, shapes and feel of things with concrete vividness." That is true. But readers of Wolfe will remember that the mother of Eugene Gant was afflicted with what is known as total recall. Her interminable narratives were the despair of her family. Wolfe could no more than Eliza Gant suppress any detail, no matter how irrelevant; indeed, it was impossible for him to feel that any detail was irrelevant to his purpose. The readers of *Look Homeward, Angel* will also remember that Eugene's father had a gift, unrivaled among his associates, of vigorous utterance. Nobody, they said, can tie a knot in the tail of the English language like old W. O. But the elder Gant's speech, for all that it can on occasion sputter into fiery intensity, more often than not runs off into a homespun rhetoric. It sounds strong, but it has very little connection with any outer reality and is meaningless, except in so far as it serves to convey his rage and frustration. We cannot avoid supposing that Wolfe drew these two characters after his own parents. At the time he began writing *Look Homeward, Angel* he stood far enough apart from them to use the endlessness of Eliza's unheard discourses, the exaggerated violence of old Gant's objurgations, for comic effect. He makes father and mother into something at once larger and less than human. But in his own case, he could not, at least so long as he was at his writing, restrain either the course of his recollections or their outcome in words. He wrote as a man possessed. Whatever was in his memory must be set down–not merely because he was Eliza's son, but because the secret end of all his writing was expiation–and it must be set down in words to which he constantly seems to be attaching more meaning than they can properly own. It was as though he were aware that his novel would have no meaning that could not be found in the words. The meaning of a novel should be in its structure. But in Wolfe's novel, as far as it has gone, it is impossible to discover any structure at all.

2.

It is impossible to say what Wolfe's position in American letters would have been had he lived to bring his work to completion. At the moment he stands very high in the estimation both of the critics and of common reader. From the time of *Look Homeward, Angel,* he was regarded, and rightly, as a young man of incomparable promise. *Of Time and the River* seemed to many to have borne out that promise and, since its faults were taken as due merely to an excess of fecundity, it was met with praise as though it were the consummation of all Wolfe's talents. Yet the faults are fundamental. The force of Wolfe's talents is indubitable; yet he did not find for that novel, nor do I believe he could ever have found, a structure of form which would have been capable of giving shape and meaning to his emotional experience. He was not without intelligence; but he could not trust his intelligence, since for him to do so would have been to succumb to conscience. And it was conscience, with its convictions of guilt, that he was continually trying to elude.

His position as an artist is very like that of Hart Crane. Crane was born in 1899, Wolfe in 1900, so that they were almost of an age. Both had what we must call genius; both conceived that genius had been given them that they might celebrate, the one in poetry, the other in prose, the greatness of their country. But Wolfe no more than Crane was able to give any other coherence to his work than that which comes from the personal quality of his writing. And he found, as Crane did before him, that the America he longed to celebrate did not exist. He could record, and none better, its sights, its sounds and its odors, as they can be caught in a moment of time; he could try, as the poet of *The Bridge* did, to absorb that moment and endow it with the permanence of a myth. But he could not create a continuous America. He could not, for all that he was prepared to cover one hundred and fifty of its years, conceive its history. He can record what comes to his sensibility, but he cannot give us the continuity of experience. Everything for Wolfe is in the moment; he can so try to impress us with the immensity of the moment that it will take on some sort of transcendental meaning. But what that meaning is, escapes him, as it does us. And once it has passed from his mind, he can do nothing but recall another moment, which as it descends into his memory seems always about to deliver itself, by a miracle, of some tremendous import.

Both Crane and Wolfe belonged to a world that is indeed living from moment to moment. And it is because they voice its breakdown in the consciousness of continuity that they have significance for it.

Of the two, Wolfe, I should say, was the more aware of his plight. He was, he tells us, while writing *Of Time and the River,* tormented by a dream in which the sense of guilt was associated with the forgetting of time. "I was unable to sleep, unable to subdue the tumult of these creative energies, and, as a result of this condition, for three years I prowled the streets, explored the swarming web of the million-footed city and came to know it as I had never done before. . . . Moreover, in this endless quest and prowling of the night through the great web and jungle of the city, I saw, lived, felt and experienced the full weight of that horrible human calamity. [The Time was that of the bottom of the depression, when Wolfe was living in Brooklyn.] And from it all has come as a final deposit, a burning memory, a certain evidence of the fortitude of man, his ability to suffer and somehow survive. And it is for this reason now that I think I shall always remember this black period with a kind of joy that I could not at that time have believed possible, for it was during this time that I lived my life through to a first completion, and through the suffering and labor of my own life came to share those qualities in the lives of the people around me."

This passage is one of extreme interest, not only for what it tells us of Wolfe at this time, but for the promise it contains of an emotional maturity. For as far as Wolfe had carried the history of Eugene Gant, he was dealing with a young man whose isolation from his fellow men was almost complete. Eugene, and we must suppose the young Wolfe, was incarcerated in his own sensibility. Locked in his cell, he awaits the coming of every moment, as though it would bring the turning of a releasing key. He waits like Ugolino, when he woke uncertain because of his dream and heard not the opening, but the closing of the lock. There is no release. And the place of Wolfe's confinement, no less than that of Ugolino, deserves to be called Famine.

It can be said of Wolfe, as Allen Tate has said of Hart Crane, that he was playing a game in which any move was possible, because none was compulsory. There is no idea which would serve as discipline to the event. For what Wolfe tells us was the idea that furiously pursued him during the composition of *Of Time and the River,* the search for a father, can scarcely be said to appear in the novel, or else it is so incidentally that it seems to no purpose. It does not certainly, as the same search on the part of Stephen Dedalus does in *Ulysses,* prepare a point toward which the whole narrative moves. There was nothing indeed in Wolfe's upbringing to make discipline acceptable to him. He acts always as though his own capacity for feeling, for anguished hope and continual frustration, was what made him superior, as no doubt, along with his romantic propensity for expression, it was. But he was wrong in assuming that those who accept any form of discipline are therefore lacking in vigor. He apparently did not understand that there are those who might say with Yeats, "I could recover if I shrieked my heart's agony," and yet like him are dumb "from human dignity". And his failure to understand was due to no fault of the intelligence, but to a lack of love. The Gant family always strikes us, with its howls of rage, its loud Hah-hahs of hate and derision, as something less than human. And Eugene is a Gant. While in his case we are ready to admit that genius is a law unto itself, we have every right to demand that it discover its own law.

Again like Crane, Wolfe failed to see that at the present time so extreme a manifestation of individualism could not but be morbid. Both came too late into a world too mechanic; they lacked a wilderness and constantly tried to create one as wild as their hearts. It was all very well for them, since both were in the way of being poets, to start out to proclaim the grandeur of America. Such a task seemed superb. But both were led at last, on proud romantic feet, to Brooklyn. And what they found there they abhorred.

They represent, each in his way, a culmination of the romantic spirit in America. There was in both a tremendous desire to impose the will on experience. Wolfe had no uncommon will. And Crane's was strong enough to lead him deliberately to death by drowning. For Wolfe the rewards of experience were always such that he was turned back upon himself. Isolated in his sensations, there was no way out. He continually sought for a door, and there was really none, or only one, the door of death.

3.

The intellectual labor of the artist is properly confined to the perception of relations. The conscience of the craftsman must see that these relations are so presented that in spite of all complications they are ultimately clear. It is one of the conditions of art that they cannot be abstractly stated, but must be presented to the senses.

What we have at the center of all Wolfe's writing is a single character, and it was certainly the aim of that writing to present this character in all his manifold contacts with the world of our time. Eugene has, we are told, the craving of a Faust to know all experience, to be able to record all the races and all the social classes which may be said to exist in America. Actually Eugene's experience is not confined to America.

But when we actually came to consider Eugene closely, we see that, once he is beyond the overwhelming presence of his family, his contacts with other people are all casual. The perfect experience for Eugene is to see someone in the throes of an emotion which he can imagine, but in which he has no responsible part. From one train, he sees people passing in another train, which is moving at a faster speed than his own.

"And they looked at one another for a moment, they passed and vanished and were gone forever, yet it seemed to him that he had known these people, that he knew them far better than the people in his own train, and that, having met them for an instant under immense and timeless skies, as they were hurled across the continent to a thousand destinations, they had met, passed, vanished, yet would remember this forever. And he thought the people in the two trains felt this, also: slowly they passed each other now, and their mouths smiled and their eyes grew friendly, but he thought there was some sorrow and regret in what they felt. For having lived together as strangers in the immense and swarming city, they had now met upon the everlasting earth, hurled past each other for a moment between two points of time upon the shining rails; never to meet, to speak, to know each other any more, and the briefness of their days, the destiny of man, was in that instant greeting and farewell."

He sees from a train a boy trying to decide to go after a girl; wandering the streets of New York, he sees death come to four men; through one of his students at the university, he comes in contact with an old Jewess wailing a son dead for a year. Each of these moments is completely done; most of them, indeed, overwrought. From the country seen from a train he derives "a wild and solemn joy–the sense of nameless hope, impossible desire, and man's tragic brevity." He reacts to most circumstances, it must seem to us, excessively. But to men and women he does not really answer. The old Jewess's grief fills him "with horror, anger, a sense of cruelty, disgust, and pity." The passion aroused returns to himself. And it is precisely because his passions cannot attain their object, and in one person know peace, that he turns in rage and desire toward the millions. There is in Eugene every emotion you wish but one; there is no love.

The most striking passages in Wolfe's novels always represent these moments of comprehension. For a moment, but a moment only, there is a sudden release of compassion, when some aspect of suffering and bewildered humanity is seized, when the other's emotion is in a timeless completion known. Then the moment passes, and compassion fails. For Eugene Gant, the only satisfactory relationship with another human creature is one which can have no continuity. For the boy at the street corner, seen in the indecision of youthful lust, he has only understanding and pity; the train from which he looks moves on and nothing more is required of Eugene. But if he should approach that same boy on the street, if he should come close enough to overhear him, he would hear only the defilement of language, words which would awaken in him only hate and disgust. He would himself become lonely, strange and cruel. For emotions such as these, unless they can be used with the responsibility of the artist, must remain a torment to the man.

The only human relationship which endures is that of the child to his family. And that is inescapable; once having been, it cannot cease to be. His father is still his father, though dying; and his brother Ben, though dead, remains his brother. He loves and he hates and knows why no more than the poet he quotes. What he does know is that love has been forbidden him.

The only contemporary literary influence on Wolfe which was at all strong is that of Joyce. I shall consider it here only to note that while we know that Joyce could only have created Stephen Dedalus out of the conflicts of his own youth, we never think of Stephen simply as the young Joyce, any more than we think of Hamlet as Shakespeare. He is a creation. But in Wolfe's novels it is impossible to feel that the central figure has any existence apart from the author. He is called Eugene Gant, but that does not deceive any one for a moment; he is, beyond all doubt, Thomas Wolfe. There is, however, one important distinction to be made between them, and one which we should not allow ourselves to forget: Eugene Gant is always younger, by at least ten years, than Thomas Wolfe.

Wolfe described *Of Time and the River* as being devoted to "the period of wandering and hunger in a man's youth." And in it we are meant to take Eugene as every young man. The following volume would, Wolfe said, declare "a period of greater certitude, which would be dominated by a single passion." That, however, still remains to be seen. So far, Eugene has shown no capacity as a lover, except in casual contact with whores. When for a moment he convinces himself that he is in love with Ann, who is a nice, simple conventional girl from Boston, he can only shriek at her and call her a bitch and a whore, which she certainly is not. The one contact which lasts for any time–leaving aside the blood ties which bind him to the Pentlands, his mother's people, and the Gants,–is that with Starwick. Starwick is the only friend he makes in his two years at Harvard, and in Paris, some years later, he still regards his friendship with Starwick as the most valuable he has ever known.

It ends when he discovers that Starwick is a homosexual. And it has usually been assumed that the violence and bitterness with which it ends are due to disillusionment; the sudden turn in Eugene's affections for the young man may well be taken as a natural reaction to his learning, first that Ann is in love with Starwick, and only a little later how hopelessly deep is Starwick's infatuation with the young tough he has picked up, by apparent chance, one night in a Paris bar. But that is, I think, to take too simple a view of the affair. There is more to it than that. What we have been told about Starwick from his first appearance in the book is that, despite a certain affection and oddity of manner, he is, as Eugene is not, a person capable of loving and being loved. What is suddenly revealed in Paris is that for him, too, love is a thing the world has forbidden. In Starwick's face Eugene sees his own fate. Just as in his brother Ben's complaint at his neglect, he had looked back through another's sight at his own neglected childhood and in his brother's death foremourned his own, so now, when he beats Starwick's head against the wall, he is but raging against his own frustration and despair.

In his father's yard, among the tombstones, stood for years a marble angel. Old Gant curses it, all hope he thinks lost that he will ever get his money back for it. It stands a magnificent remainder of the time when as a boy, with winged ambition, he had wanted to be not merely a stone cutter but a sculptor. Then, unexpectedly, a customer comes for it. The one symbol of the divine in the workshop is sold to adorn the grave of a prostitute; what the boy might have been the man lets go for such a purpose. It cannot be said that Thomas Wolfe ever sold his angel. But the faults of the artist are all of them traceable to the failures of the man. He achieved probably the utmost intensity of which coherent writing is capable; he proved that an art founded solely on the individual, however strong his will, however vivid his sensations, cannot be sound, or whole, or even passionate, in a world such as ours, in which "the integrity of the individual consciousness has been broken down." How far it has broken down, I do not believe he ever knew, yet all that he did is made of its fragments.

> There was a great man named Thomas Wolfe and he wrote a book called *You Can't Go Home Again.* And that is true . . . you can't go home again because home has ceased to exist except in the mothballs of memory.
>
> –John Steinbeck,
> *Travels with Charlie,* pp. 179–183

Reviews of *The Web and the Rock*

Thomas Wolfe's Superb Farewell
May Cameron,
New York Post, 22 June 1939, p. 19

If ever a novel was thoroughly and mercilessly autobiographical, it is Thomas Wofle's "The Web and the Rock," published today. Indeed, it is more than autobiographical; for it not only tells of the author's own life, with swagger and shame, with satire, naivete, braggadocio, wisdom, and sometimes almost immeasurable power, but it is also prophetically autobiographical (if such is possible) in that again and again it reveals intimations of its author's own doom and death.

Once, for example, we hear Wolfe's hero, George Webber, meditating upon his ancestry:

> And he belonged to that fatal, mad, devouring world from whose prison there was no escape. He belonged to it, even as three hundred of his blood and bone had belonged to it, and must unweave it from his brain, distill it from his blood, unspin it from his entrails, and escape with a demonic and exultant joy into his father's new world, new lands and mornings and the shining city–or drown like a mad dog, die!

Again, speaking in his own role as author, Wolfe tells us: "One reads that giants die early, and things which are too great in nature for the measure of the world destroy themselves."

That was George Webber's story, as it was Tom Wolfe's; in both there was too much blood, too much appetite, too much life, too much curiosity, and too much courage in sniffing at the world, tasting it, trying to gulp it whole, trying to pick it up bodily and shake it to listen to the pieces inside–and too much uncompromising devotion to the self-imposed, impossible task of splitting it apart with bare fists in order to gaze upon its inner heart. And too much doubt whether, if one succeeded in cleaving inward to the core, he would find anything but draff and husks.

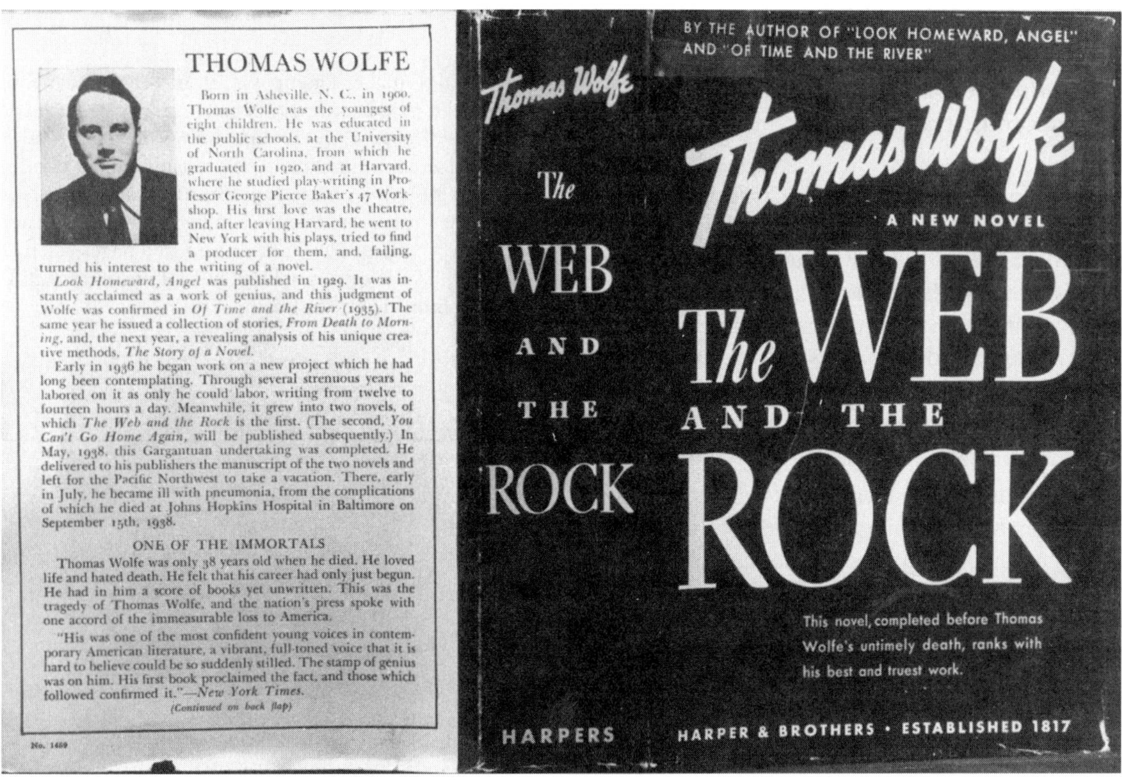

Dust jacket for the first Wolfe novel edited by Edward C. Aswell (1939)

Indeed, it seems to me that Tom Wolfe was a man whose limitless curiosity and tremendous vitality compelled him to profess exuberant belief in life; equipped as he was, no other course of thought seemed possible to him; yet, through it all, doubt gnawed at him.

He wanted to be God, and he couldn't. It is interesting to speculate what would have become of him if he had soothed his questioning, as some other contemporary writers have done, by hitching his wagon to the immediate earth, by becoming an active partisan of Loyalist Spain or organized labor or Communism or what-not–all of which, when all's said and done, may only provide shelters of escape just as an ivory tower did–and does.

The first to be published of Wolfe's two final novels, "The Web and the Rock" tells the story of a young man who was born in the South, who received a good deal of his education there, who came to New York and taught in a New York university, who traveled abroad, and who became a writer. This pattern should be fairly familiar to those who have read Wolfe's other novels.

Yet, so vast is the reservoir of his memory that–as far as I know–there is no duplication of incident in the new work, distilled with its predecessors out of millions of words. And the current hero, George Webber, attains a certain identity of his own although his parent-blood is always that which coursed with such hard passage through Wolfe's arteries.

Future scholars, grubbing for Ph.D.'s through a great man's remains, will find academic, mild joy in tracing characters through "Look Homeward, Angel," "Of Time and the River," and the new novel. Suffice it for a daily reviewer to say that "The Web and the Rock" abounds with veined and muscled people, as real and pungent as sweat; with anecdote and incident humorous, melancholy, and tragic, and with passages of prose as fine as any written in English in three hundred years.

Wolfe was crammed to the throat with the Elizabethans, great and small. And in that great age, both great and small wrote sheer drivel as well as monumental stuff. Something of the same might be said of Wolfe. He wrote page upon page that the rankest beginner would blush to put on paper, but he wrote page upon page that perhaps no writer in English since the seventeenth century has equaled or can hope to equal.

I suspect that the major interest in "The Web and The Rock" is to be found in its latter half, which tells of George Webber's love affair with Esther, a Jewish woman of wealth and charm who worked like a fury at her job of stage-designing–and of keeping Webber happy, or at least quiescent.

This whole episode is tender and gay, often broadly humorous, amorous, lecherous, ribald, and truly sweet.

One suspects that Webber was, for the first time in his life, truly happy with Esther; that if he had allowed himself the luxury, he could have continued to be so; and that if Webber had gone on living with Esther, the whole course of his life might have been changed. But there was a deep, unaccountable, uncontrollable stream of anti-Semitism in George Webber. That, and other things, drove the pair apart.

Wolfe himself was always hungry. Even when he had the means to command the world's finest chefs, he remained an unsated trencherman. So, in "The Web and The Rock," as in the other novels, there are pages of fine eating.

But he puts a reverse twist on this when he has Esther ruminate upon the horrible food that some future mistress, or wife, will give poor Webber: "Picked-up codfish with a gob of that horrible, white, gooey, Christian sauce. . . . I've got the most delicious menu fixed up. . . . I read all about it in Molly Messmore's food hints in *The Daily Curse*. . . . Monday, darling, we're going to have imported Hungarian catfish with henhouse noodles, and Tuesday, pet, we are going to have roast Long Island suckers with gastric juice, and Wednesday, love, we are going to have stewed milkfed bloaters a la Gorgonzola with stinkweed salad, and Thursday, sweet, we are going to have creamed cod with chitling gravy. . . ."

There is more humor in this, I think, than in Wolfe's other books, although some of it, in Webber's college years, leans pretty heavily on Sinclair Lewis' treatment of the YMCA-secretary type in "Arrowsmith." But there is an abundance of Wolfe's own somber laughter, and Webber's satire of an evangelist's speech is a masterpiece.

Just as Wolfe could not fit himself to the world, nor his books to publishers' dimensions, a reviewer can scarcely hope to give adequate treatment to "The Web and The Rock"–that is, not in a newspaper column, or a page either, for that matter. Run, do not walk, to your nearest bookstore.

Webber somewhere, in effect, tells Esther: There will never be another like me again. Let that be Tom Wolfe's epitaph, and his books his monument.

> Could I make tongue say more than tongue could utter! Could I make brain grasp more than brain could think! Could I weave into immortal denseness some small brede of words, pluck out of sunken depths the roots of living, some hundred thousand magic words that were as great as all my hunger, and hurl the sum of all my living out upon three hundred pages–then death could take my life, for I had lived it ere he took it: I had slain hunger, beaten death!
>
> –*The Web and the Rock,* epigraph

The "Author's Note" that Edward Aswell created from Wolfe's "A Statement of Purpose," written with no clear intention of publication, provided the focus for many reviewers.

The Web and the Rock
Clifton Fadiman
The New Yorker, 24 June 1939

> This novel, then, marks not only a turning away from the books I have written in the past, but a genuine spiritual and artistic change. It is the most objective novel that I have written. . . . I have sought, through free creation, a release of my inventive power.

So wrote Thomas Wolfe in the Author's Note to *The Web and the Rock* four months before his tragic death at Johns Hopkins Hospital on September 15, 1938. How keenly one wishes the novel itself confirmed his brave words! But the gray truth is that *The Web and the Rock,* except for some hundred-odd scattered and magnificent pages, marks no particular advance, either in power or objectivity, over *Of Time and the River.* The central character, though he is called George Webber, is still the Eugene Gant of the previous books. One may at last freely and sadly say both George Webber and Eugene Gant are Thomas Wolfe. George Webber is, again, the young writer who wishes to experience everything and is driven to frenzy because he cannot. All the motifs we are used to from the other books repeat themselves here: the attraction-repulsion exerted on the provincial by New York, the voyage-and-return pattern that marked *Of Time and the River,* the sonorous but vague celebration of America, the insistence on man's "aloneness" and on the "strangeness" of "time." You even feel that certain characters are only seemingly new and have their roots in the other books. The style, too, remains unchanged–distended, straining for impossible effects, often capable of high (but never the highest) beauty, often reminiscent of old-time movie-caption prose. No, *The Web and the Rock* does not,

AUTHOR'S NOTE

This novel is about one man's discovery of life and of the world—discovery not in a sudden and explosive sense as when "a new planet swims into his ken," but discovery through a process of finding out, and finding out as a man has to find out, through error and through trial, through fantasy and illusion, through falsehood and his own foolishness, through being mistaken and wrong and an idiot and egotistical and aspiring and hopeful and believing and confused, and pretty much what every one of us is, and goes through, and finds out about, and becomes.

I hope that the protagonist will illustrate in his own experience every one of us—not merely the sensitive young fellow in conflict with his town, his family, the little world around him; not merely the sensitive young fellow in love, and so concerned with his little universe of love that he thinks it is the whole universe—but all of these things and much more. These things, while important, are subordinate to the plan of the book; being young and in love and in the city are only a part of the whole adventure of apprenticeship and discovery.

This novel, then, marks not only a turning away from the books I have written in the past, but a genuine spiritual and artistic change. It is the most objective novel that I have written. I have invented characters who are compacted from the whole amalgam and consonance of seeing, feeling, thinking, living, and knowing many people. I have sought, through free creation, a release of my inventive power.

Finally, the novel has in it, from first to last, a strong element of satiric exaggeration: not only because it belongs to the nature of the story—"the innocent man" discovering life—but because satiric exaggeration also belongs to the nature of life, and particularly American life.

THOMAS WOLFE

New York, May 1938

31725

Proof for note salvaged by Aswell as a preface for The Web and the Rock

it seems to me, mark that "spiritual and artistic change" we were all looking for. It is simply more of the same Wolfe, which is to say more of the most gifted young American writer produced during the last fifteen years. It is not a self-contained novel any more than the others were. It is a cut-off length of the endless experiences of Thomas Wolfe.

We meet George Webber when he is a twelve-year-old boy in the small town of Libya Hill in Old Catawba (read North Carolina). George at twelve is George at twenty-five; his reactions to life have no relation to his age. He lies in the front yard of his uncle's home and muses, "How strange, and plain, and savage, sweet and cruel, lovely, terrible, and mysterious, and how unmistakable and familiar all things are!" It's the same old nonsense; the same unselective excitement; the same tyranny of words; it's Eugene Gant once more.

But it is not George Webber who makes the first sections of the book wonderful–for they are wonderful. It is the townsfolk he describes–seen, it is true, through a very special vision, but seen unforgettably. I should say, for example, that Nebraska Crane, the Cherokee boy, is almost as great a characterization as Huckleberry Finn. The terrible outsize Lampley family comprise the most memorable grotesques in the whole Wolfe gallery. Magnificent, too, is the whole account of Dick Prosser, the gentlemanly Negro who ran amok–a story that, to my mind, brings out more of the underlying violence of the Southern temperament than do all the novels of William Faulkner combined.

Much of this small-town material is magnificent, but not all. The further the event from George's own experience, the more moving it is; the nearer it approaches his own life and mind, the more tedious it becomes–and the harder Wolfe works to prevent it from becoming tedious. Thus, when Wolfe describes a dogfight, you see it before your own eyes, but when young George reflects on the dogfight, unreality sets in. I seem to be in a pathetic minority here, but it seems to me that the one crucial defect of the Wolfe books is that the central character, despite the hundreds of pages devoted to him, despite his endless monologues, despite all the introspection, never quite becomes believable. The most boring pages in Wolfe are the most personal ones; the most fascinating are devoted to people and scenes he remembers vividly, but which he does not incorporate within his gigantic sense of self.

If *The Web and the Rock* had stopped at page 170, it would have been a far finer book. Not that the succeeding 525 pages are without interest, but one must pick and choose among them, wade through over-written passages, repetitions, and almost incredible naïvetés of thought and feeling. The college sections–though there is some extremely funny if exaggerated satire here–are formless and inferior to those in *Look Homeward, Angel.* Also, the chapters dealing with George's early days in New York are dragged out beyond their natural length. Wolfe remembered with almost painful particularity everything that had happened to him. He committed the fallacy of assuming that the intensity of his memory would naturally awaken an equally intense reaction in the reader. He never seems to have asked himself the simple question: Is this detail worthy of being remembered? He could write fervently about anything, but he never knew what things one ought to be fervent about.

The second half of the book deals almost entirely with a love affair and with George Webber's introduction to the "smart" life of New York. The lady is a successful stage designer, a half-Jewess, very sensitive and lovely, rather older than George, a member of the fashionable world. Her culture is in direct opposition to George's which is primitive, provincial, puritanical. Partly because of this opposition, partly because George "tears up everything he gets his hands on," the affair is bound to end badly, and it does. Not, however, before you have waded through about 400 pages of highly conversational raptures and quarrels. I guess I may as well confess that most of this seemed to me a crashing bore. I'm not sure why. I think it's simply that there's just too much of everything–too much recrimination, too much ecstasy, too many scenes, too many reconciliations. Enough is enough.

The book ends, rather oddly, with a European-travel section, sufficiently interesting in itself but somehow tacked on, superfluous.

What is one to say of this enormous, puzzling, overwhelming, disappointing talent? Wolfe has been called genius by so many shrewd and calm judges that the temptation is strong to join the procession. At times he wrote like one inspired; there is no doubt of it. No one in his generation had his command of language, his passion, his memory, his energy, his sensitivity. Yet his books, I believe, are not great works of art. They do not add up to anything. They do not, in the end, satisfy you. They paint no single vision of life, not even the vision of multiplicity. Wolfe had a primitive, impetuous nature that rejected thought in favor of a set of titanic prejudices. Because he could bring no order into his life, he could bring no order into his prose. And so he was forced to celebrate disorder–to try to forge an epic out of sheer fury. He belongs, in Santayana's phrase, with those who create a literature of barbarism. Such a literature, depending upon the motor values of energy rather than the moral values of truth, may fascinate and overwhelm us for a time, but will it endure? Ossian seemed terrific stuff in his day, but who reads Ossian now? In all the great and almost great novels, even in such dionysian works as *Moby Dick,* there is an intellectual substratum, and this intellectual substratum acts as a quiet preservative against the ravages of time. Rhetoric, however great and however sincere–for Wolfe's rhetoric was sincere–has not the final power to endure.

All the virtues and all the defects of the provincial are in Wolfe. He had that great innocence of the provincial, the innocence the metropolitan would dearly love to own. He had the energy of the provincial, his boldness, his contempt for pseudo-intellectual conventions. He had the poetry of earth. But, on the other hand, he had the provincial's furious disregard for rationality and order. He had a naïve contempt for people and ideas and traditions he could not understand. If a thing was alien, he either drew away from it in desperate horror or engulfed it in desperate passion. He overestimated New York, and he underestimated it. His aggressiveness, his desire to conquer the city, lent him a certain passion, but at the same time it disoriented and disordered his faculties, making his reactions seem at times like those of a bad-tempered child with a superb flow of language.

It is impossible to say what would have happened to him had he lived, but it is certainly possible to say that this book shows no growth, save an increase in confusion. Perhaps the unpublished novel still remaining–to be called *You Can't Go Home Again*–may bear witness to that "spiritual and artistic change" that Wolfe so earnestly hoped had taken place in him.

In reviewing The Web and the Rock *Malcolm Cowley claimed that Wolfe was incapable of writing about anyone except himself. Cowley also charged that* The Web and the Rock *was poorly edited.*

Thomas Wolfe's Legacy
Malcolm Cowley
New Republic, 19 July 1939

When Thomas Wolfe died last year at the age of thirty-eight, he left no completed but still unpublished novel behind him. What he did leave was an enormous puzzle in the shape of a manuscript containing more than a million words, the length of a dozen ordinary novels.

Embedded in the manuscript were chapters or incidents from at least five of the novels that Wolfe had planned to write, and probably from several others as well. One of these books, dealing with his great unhappy love affair, was present in an almost complete draft, with many revisions. A second book concerned his relations with a publisher and a third described his trip across the country; these also were nearly finished. The remaining books were more fragmentary, though together they told a fairly connected story–Wolfe's own story, the subject of almost everything he had ever written. He sometimes thought of throwing all the books together into a single novel that would have been longer when completed than "Remembrance of Things Past"; he had made some of the revisions that would have been necessary. Still, as a result of his changing plans–or rather of his utter inability to follow a consistent plan–the manuscript was as wildly confused as his life had been.

This was the problem he bequeathed to his publishers and his literary executor. After much hesitation they solved it in a fashion that I think was mistaken. They decided to publish almost the whole manuscript, divided into two very long novels. It is the first of these, "The Web and the Rock," that has just appeared.

Judged as a piece of editing, it is able and conscientious. Judged as a new book by Thomas Wolfe, it is decidedly less successful. That is a fact one would hardly suspect from reading most of the reviews it has so far received. The critics have apparently been swayed by their warm personal regard for the author, which everybody shared, and by their hope that his astounding promise would somehow be fulfilled in spite of death. But the truth ought to be told, even in a review that reads like a letter of condolence. And the truth is that "The Web and the Rock" is by far the weakest of Wolfe's novels–is indeed so weak that there is a justified question whether most of it should have been published at all.

One of its obvious faults is that it breaks apart into two uneven sections. The first of these tells how Monk Webber grew up in the little city of Libya Hill in the state of Old Catawba–that is, in Buncombe County, North Carolina, where Wolfe himself was born and reared. He spends four years at Pine Rock College–that is, Wolfe's own University of North Carolina–then comes to New York in search of fame and a mistress. I understand that part of this section was written shortly before Wolfe died. Other parts of it are what he was able to salvage from the unpublished first draft of "Look Homeward, Angel" and from an abandoned novel about his mother's kinsfolk that he intended to call "The Hills Beyond Pentland." The episodes from these various sources are loosely tied together. Some of them have a powerful organic life that is lacking in the section as a whole.

The second section, beginning on page 295, is much more unified. It tells how the hero, coming home from Europe–but how did he get there?–falls in love with a Jewish theatrical designer named Esther Jack, a candid and charming woman much older than himself. He is mothered by her for three years, grows plump on her delectable cooking, meets and dislikes her literary friends, finishes a book that she inspired him to write, fails to get it published, then quarrels with her unjustly and–the word is not too strong–insanely for page after page and chapter after chapter. Most of this section seems to consist of a novel that Wolfe had written in 1936, though at least one of the original episodes has disappeared, leaving a gap in the story, and new material must have been added in 1938. It is connected with the first section only by the name of the hero. One could hardly say that it is connected by his personality, since Monk Webber has changed almost beyond recognition.

In the title of the book as published, the Rock is Manhattan Island. The Web is the subtle and unnatural world of the Jewish intelligentsia, in which the hero threatens to get involved through his love for Esther. Finally he escapes to Munich, where he starts a drunken brawl, gets a broken head that he fully earned, and finds spiritual rebirth in a hospital.

The novel as a whole contains many fine passages–for example, the stories of Baxter Lampley, the butcher's son; of Jim Randolph, the football hero who never got over it; of Dick Prosser, the pious Negro who ran amok. The chapter on Seumas Malone, the Irish critic, is a fairly effective piece of satire, especially to those who recognize Seumas Malone. The character of Esther Jack is one of the most careful and sympathetic full-length portraits that Wolfe has drawn; it is a tribute to his honesty as a novelist that he makes one sympathize with Esther instead of the hero in all their quarrels. But the book is everywhere marred by bathos, bombast, painful repetitions, middle-class prejudice and naive but offensive anti-Semitism. Whole chapters, like those on the hero's daydreams ("Alone") and on Horace Liveright's publishing house ("The Philanthropists") are so gawkily written that it is a physical discomfort to read them.

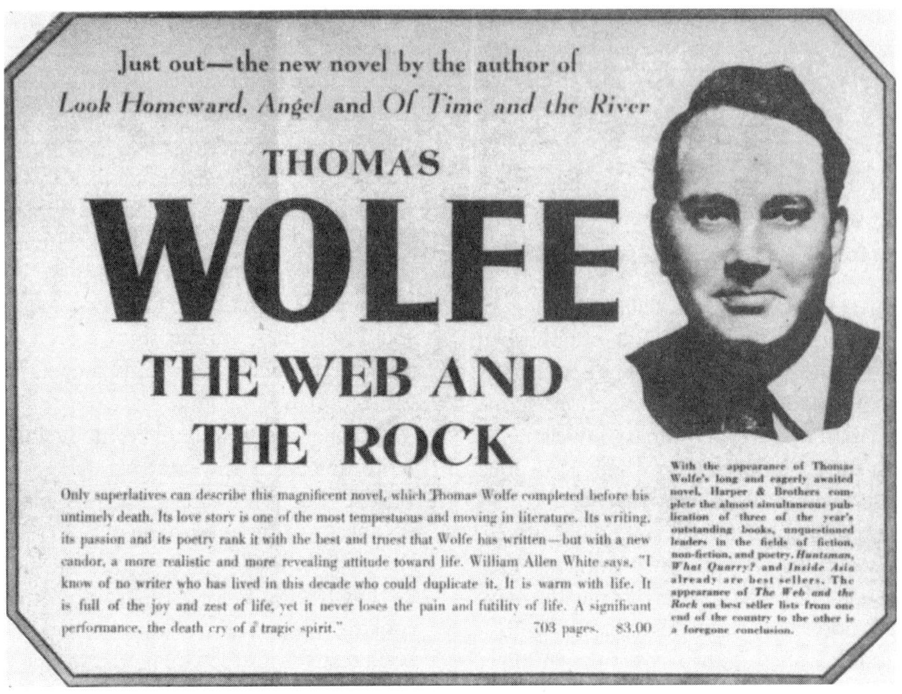

Advertisement for Wolfe's first posthumously published novel

Wolfe's novels have always presented this mixture of the nearly sublime and the silly. In this new book, however, the best passages are less nearly sublime than the best in "Look Homeward, Angel" and "Of Time and the River." The worst are sillier than anything he published during his lifetime; indeed, they are almost without a parallel in serious literature.

Here are a few examples of bad writing, chosen not at all as the most flagrant but merely as the shortest:

> Some fifteen or more years ago (as men measure, by those diurnal instruments which their ingenuity has created, the immeasurable universe of time), at the end of a fine, warm, hot, fair, fresh, fragrant, lazy, furnacelike day of sweltering heat across the body, bones, sinews, tissues, juices, rivers, mountains, plains, streams, lakes, coastal regions and compacted corporosity of the American continent, a train might have been observed by one of the lone watchers of the Jersey Flats approaching that enfabled rock, that ship of life, that swarming, million-footed, tower-masted and sky-soaring citadel that bears the magic name of the Island of Manhattan, at terrific speed.

> . . . the heights of Jersey City, raised proudly against the desolation of these lonely marshes as a token of man's fortitude, a symbol of his power, a sign of his indomitable spirit that flames forever like a great torch in the wilderness, that lifts against the darkness and the desolation of blind nature the story of its progress–the heights of Jersey, lighted for an eternal feast.

> So all were gone at last, one by one, each swept out into the mighty flood tide of the city's life, there to prove, to test, to find, to lose himself, as each man must–alone.

> But, of such was youth. And he was young.

> The sight of her face, earnestly bent and focused in its work of love, her sure and subtle movements and her full, lovely figure–all that was at once both delicate and abundant in her, together with the maddening fragrance of glorious food, evoked an emotion of wild tenderness and hunger in him which was unutterable.

In most of these passages the fault is an undisciplined and undirected energy that leads him to write about a train ride across the Jersey marshes as if it were the charge of the Lost Brigade, and about Jersey City as if it were Periclean Athens. The last passage presents a different and more illuminating problem. It would be easy to defend if Wolfe really meant it to be funny, for in that case the worst charge against it would be that he used exactly the same language for burlesque humor that he used for his serious writing and therefore left the reader uncertain of the effect he was trying to achieve. But the context seems to show that Wolfe was as serious here as elsewhere; that in fact he regarded his wild tenderness and his hunger for glorious food as being of equal value; both were "unutterable" and therefore holy. In certain African tribes, even the fingernail parings of the king-god are sacred; and Wolfe had almost the same attitude toward his own least and tritest emotions. A train ride across the Jersey marshes really was the charge of the Lost Brigade, because Wolfe was taking it.

By now it ought to be obvious that the source of his weakness, and of his abounding energy as well, was his inordinate preoccupation with himself. He was not conceited in any familiar sense of the word; indeed he was realistic and humble about his own failings. On the other hand, he regarded his life as something more than that of an ordinary mortal; it was a sacrament, a miracle, a legend of man's eternal aspirations. All his thoughts and deeds were bathed in a supernatural light that was also reflected on the people around him. When he wrote about these people, he usually wrote well–unless he hated them–and sometimes he wrote superbly. He had a thirst for knowledge about their lives, a warm sympathy, a gift for seeing, "beneath their bright, unnatural masks, something that was naked and lonely." But when he wrote about himself, as he usually did, he lost all sense of proportion.

This was a fact he realized in his later years, and he intended his new book to be "a genuine spiritual and artistic change . . . the most objective novel I have written." But the attempt was doomed to failure by his whole personality. He liked to keep people at a distance and wrote about them most confidently when he was looking at them from a train window. When a character became too interesting and threatened to distract attention from the autobiographical hero, Wolfe dropped him instantly. It was the same impulse, I think, that made him quarrel with some of his oldest friends when they threatened to become an essential part of his life. Instinctively he was driven back on himself, driven back to writing books about himself, until his apparently endless resources were in fact nearly exhausted.

Though his editors have worked with care and even piety, I am not sure that in publishing the present version of "The Web and the Rock" they have done their best for his posthumous career. They have accepted the author's valuation of himself and his mania for bigness, whereas he was actually at his best in episodes and novellas. They have been tolerant of his faults, remembering how he used to howl with pain and exasperation when one of his weaker passages was omitted. This time they have included whole chapters that should have been decently forgotten. Had they been more ruthless toward the manuscript, they would have been a great deal kinder toward its author and its readers.

Reviews of *You Can't Go Home Again*

Aswell's silent editing of Wolfe's second posthumously published novel, You Can't Go Home Again, *triggered an unresolved critical debate over his practices. The novel, set in New York and Germany during the Great Depression and the rise of Nazism, is regarded as his most socially conscious work.*

Thomas Wolfe's Torrent of Recollection

Stephen Vincent Benét

Saturday Review of Literature, 22 (21 September 1940): 5.

This posthumous novel continues and concludes the story of George Webber–the story of Thomas Wolfe–the story of seeking and finding that is at the back of all the work which Wolfe was allowed to do. They were always saying–the well-informed and the critical–that, if he could stand off from himself, be more objective, tame, and order the extravagances of his power–well, well, then he might become the really great novelist, the conscious artist, all that sort of thing.

It was good advice for nine writers out of ten, but his power was not that sort of power. In this book, as in its predecessor, "The Web and the Rock," it is shown that he came to know himself, his strength and his weaknesses, much more clearly and objectively than was supposed. But that knowledge did not make any difference. He had to write as he wrote. He had to draw upon the giant web, the torrent of recollection, the all-feeling explorativeness,

Edward Aswell transferred and revised the ending of "I Have Something to Tell You" to create the conclusion for You Can't Go Home Again, *thus conveying the false impression that Wolfe had specifically anticipated his death. Maxwell Perkins was the model for Foxhall Edwards.*

Dear Fox, old friend, thus we have come to the end of the road that we were to go together. My tale is finished–and so farewell.

But before I go I have one thing more to tell you.

Something has spoken to me in the night, burning the tapers of the waning year; something has spoken in the night, and told me I shall die, I know not where. Saying:

"To lose the earth you know, for greater knowing; to lose the life you have, for a greater life; to leave the friends you loved, for greater loving; to find a land more kind than home, more large than earth–

"–Whereon the pillars of the earth are founded, toward which the conscience of the world is tending–a wind is rising, and the rivers flow."

–*You Can't Go Home Again,* p. 743

for everything in American earth, draw upon it and pour it forth again with shouts and cries, a river of sights, sounds, smells, tastes, feelings, memories, a river deafening the ears and stunning the eyes but not to be forgotten while Mississippi ran. "The forgotten moments and unnumbered hours came back to me with all the enormous cargo of my memory, together with lost voices in the mountains long ago, the voices of the kinsmen dead and never seen, and the houses they had built and died in, and the rutted roads they trod upon and every unrecorded moment."

That is how the work was done. He lacked taste at times, he was often verbose and rhetorical. He was fond of certain rubber stamps of dialect and never got over them. He was so prodigal of talent that he could and did write a thousand passages as good as the one I have quoted above. He was so little self-critical that, when his ear and his genius deserted him momentarily, he could write such appalling English as "Aristocrats of ancient lineage who had always held to a tradition of stiff-necked exclusiveness could be seen chatting familiarly with the plebeian parvenus of the new rich." He committed the errors of a giant–a small man can write bad prose but it takes a Dickens to assassinate Little Nell. And, when all is said and done, he will stand with Melville.

"You Can't Go Home Again" is the story of a man's pilgrimage, with its successive returns that meet with defeat, its successive reachings out for something that, even when grasped, eludes the hand. George Webber returns to Esther Jack and for a time they resume their old relation. But love is not enough–the two lives are too disparate–and the relation ends. He returns to Libya Hill and the deep roots of his childhood–and finds it in the frenzy of the boom, a city of lost men. He returns to the Germany he loved–and must say farewell to it–it is being delivered over to something old and evil. His first book brings him a brief celebrity and the hatred of his own people of Libya Hill–his second book brings him fame–and he sees through Lloyd McHarg the huge, restless disillusion that comes with fame. You can't go home again–not even to the tried friend, Foxhall Edwards. So stated, the book sounds like a study in disillusion. And is nothing of the sort.

It is written with all Wolfe's furious energy, with his devouring zest for all sorts of different human beings, with his amazing gift for sucking the very last drop of juice out of a character or a scene. It contains some telling, and some very heavy-handed, satire on literary life in New York. It will be read for that and people will babble over the various names. And none of that part is going to matter, in time, except for Piggy Logan's circus at the Jacks's where Wolfe has caught a genuine horror and a genuine scorn. The party itself, the sudden irruption of Piggy Logan's senseless young friends and the effect of the monstrous little circus of wire dolls on those who watch it–these are beautifully done. The first that follows is both well done and badly done–very few people could have done it at all and yet it does not quite come off. A good deal of the rest of the satire is a dropping of five-hundred-pound bombs to demolish gnats. The lion-hunters described in the chapter of that name shouldn't, somehow, have mattered as much as they did to George Webber.

They don't, in the end–in the real plan and mass of the book. For, though there are extraneous chapters–though "You Can't Go Home Again" contains some of Wolfe's worst writing as well as much of his best–there is a clear, though winding path through the great forest of words and incidents and memories. There is a line, and a mature line. George Webber does grow up, not merely by fiat. There are such brilliant single incidents as that of Mr. Katamoto and that of the fantastic, believable meeting with Lloyd McHarg. But, more than that, though many things on the way were vanity, George Webber's pilgrimage was not vanity, and we do not feel that it was. The book ends neither in doubt nor in disillusion. It ends, in the remarkable last chapter, with a cry of faith.

> I believe that we are lost here in America but I believe we shall be found. . . . I think the life which we have fashioned in America and which has fashioned us–the forms we made, the cells that grew, the honeycomb that was created–was self-destructive in

> There came to him an image of man's whole life upon the earth. It seemed to him that all man's life was like a tiny spurt of flame that blazed out briefly in an illimitable and terrifying darkness, and that all man's grandeur, tragic dignity, his heroic glory, came from the brevity and smallness of this flame. He knew his life was little and would be extinguished, and that only darkness was immense and everlasting. And he knew that he would die with defiance on his lips, and that the shout of his denial would ring with the last pulsing of his heart into the maw of all-engulfing night.
>
> –*You Can't Go Home Again,* epigraph

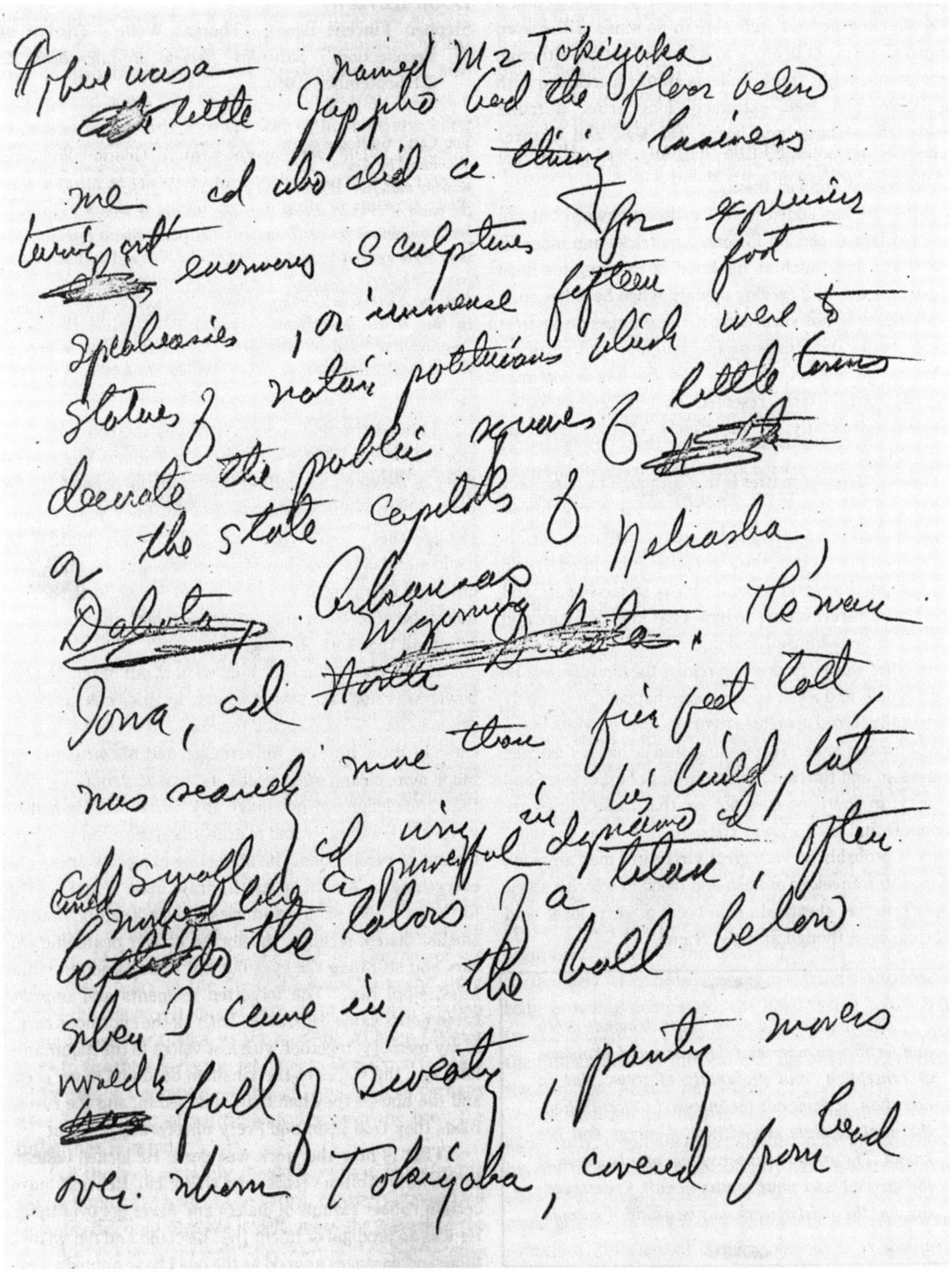

Page from the manuscript that was published as You Can't Go Home Again *(William B. Wisdom Collection, Houghton Library, Harvard University)*

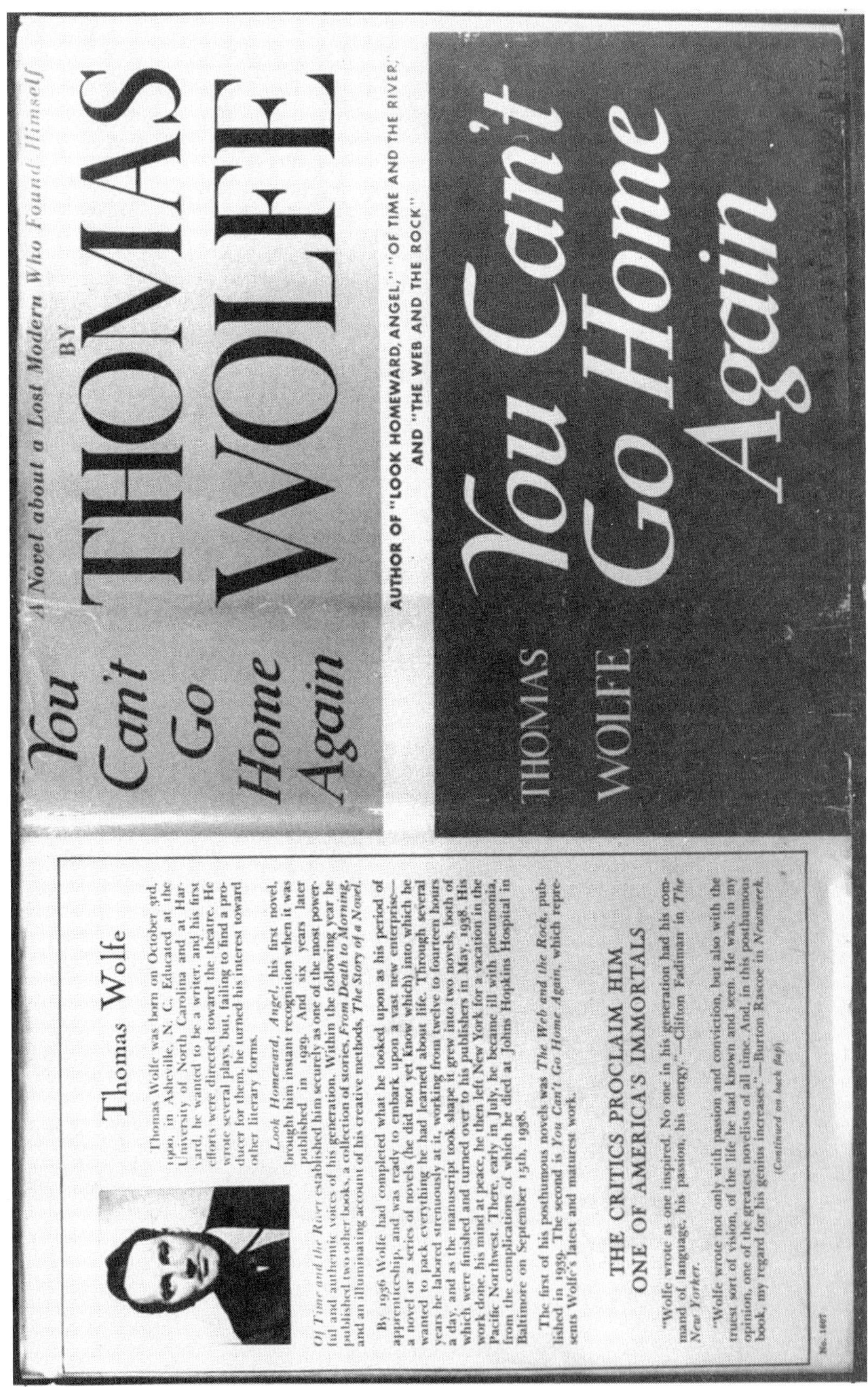

Dust jacket for Wolfe's second posthumously published novel (1940)

> its nature, and must be destroyed. I think these forms are dying and must die just as I know that America and the people in it are deathless, undiscovered, and immortal, and must live.
>
> I think the true discovery of America is before us. I think the true fulfillment of our spirit, of our people, of our mighty and immortal land is yet to come. I think the true discovery of our own democracy is still before us. And I think that all these things are certain as the morning, as inevitable as noon. . . .

The prose mounts to its moving end, with its strange premonition of death.

> To lose the earth you know, for greater knowing; to lose the life you have, for greater life; to leave the friends you loved, for greater loving, to find a land more kind than home, more large than earth–

These are great words, greatly spoken. To our loss, they come from the dead; but they speak to the living, and now. Out of passionate belief and faith they speak, and will keep on speaking, through the years, though the great tree is down and the wide and turbulent river sunk back into the ground.

Novelist Hamilton Basso was Wolfe's trusted friend. This review of You Can't Go Home Again *is based on his knowledge of Wolfe's plan.*

Thomas Wolfe: A Summing Up

Hamilton Basso

New Republic, 103 (23 September 1940): 422–423

This is the last novel that will carry Thomas Wolfe's name on its title page. The first thing to be said is that his publishers do no great service to his reputation by presenting it as a finished product of his mature talent. "By 1936," they tell us, "Wolfe had completed what he looked upon as his period of apprenticeship, and was ready to embark upon a vast new enterprise–a novel or a series of novels (he did not yet know which) into which he wanted to pack everything he had learned about life. Through several years he labored strenuously at it, and as the manuscript took shape it grew into two novels, both of which were finished and turned over to his publishers in May, 1938." This statement is not altogether correct. It is best to let Wolfe himself tell what happened–what he hoped to do and how he hoped to do it. In July, 1937, he wrote to me:

I brought most of the manuscript of the last five or six years down with me; millions of words of it, and I hope to write several hundred thousand more this summer. Eventually I hope it will begin to take shape, like another monster of the deep, and I will have another tremendous book. I believe I learn a little something about writing all the time; but I am not so sure that I will be worried so much this time by apprehensions over size and length. The very nature of a book like this is that everything can go into it. To tell such a story is to try to loot the whole treasury of human experience. . . . So I have come back here to "set a spell and think things over"–freer, I hope, from the degrading egotisms all men know in youth; here to strike out, I hope to God, a living word. To do out of the substance of my own life, my single spirit, a better and truer work than I have ever done.

The three years from 1935 to 1938 were a period during which we saw much of each other–in New York and in the mountains of North Carolina. Occasionally he would give me a batch of manuscript to read. I know, then, that in the "millions of words" Wolfe talks about, substantial portions of this novel, and the one that preceded it, were included. Most of the section called "The Locusts Have No King," for instance, stands–as far as memory can judge–just as it stood in 1936. Another section, "I Have a Thing to Tell you," was pared to the bone and published in these pages about the same time. And the part of the book revolving about the famous novelist Lloyd McHarg–or a sizable portion of it–was also in manuscript before 1937. It is not accurate, consequently, to say that Wolfe's last two books marked a "new enterprise" or that they were finished before he died. As for the critics, those who found no "advancement" in "the Web and the Rock" will likewise probably find no advancement here. But let them hold their horses! Let them remember that this book not only contains the last writing Wolfe did–the section called "The House That Jack Built," for example, which was written in the spring and summer of 1937, just about a year before he died–but also many pages that were written as early as 1934. This is one time when no generalizations are permissible.

Wolfe disliked the critics as much as any creative writer. The charge that he wrote autobiographical novels particularly annoyed him. This is worth mentioning only because the critics were partially responsible for the rebirth of Eugene Gant as George Webber: and this in an interesting way.

Wolfe's anger with the critics frequently took the form of torrential outbursts in which he argued that all good fiction is basically autobiographical. It also kept cropping up in his letters. In one of them, partially devoted to a statement of his belief that most writers were surveyors rather than explorers, he wrote:

If he had never written another line, this novel would bring him world fame

By Thomas Wolfe

The story of a lost modern who found himself, by one of the great writers of his time. The hero is George Webber, a gifted novelist whose first book has catapulted him to fame. It has turned the hands of his family and friends against him but has opened up a whole new world of society. It is the world of the frenzied boom of 1929 and the years after that. And what George Webber finds in this world is the subject of *You Can't Go Home Again.*

Entirely completed before his death, this is certainly Wolfe's most mature and most thoughtful work. Yet it has all the abounding energy, the sharp sense of environment, the special gift for creating living characters which made him one of our great writers. By the author of *Look Homeward, Angel,* and *Of Time and the River.* 285,000 words. $3.00

Advertisements for the second Wolfe novel published by Harper

In another way as well, our love of neat definitions in convenient forms, our fear of essential exploration, may be the natural response of people who have to house themselves, wall themselves, give their lives some precise and formal definition. . . . Anyway, all of these things have seemed to me to be worth thinking of, and I know that we still have to fight to do our work the way we want to do it–not only against the accepted varieties of surveyordom, that is book publishers, most of the critics, popular magazines, etc.–but against even deadlier and more barren forms; deadlier because they set up as friends of exploration when they are really betrayers and enemies; I mean little magazinedom, hound and horners, young precious boys, esthetic Marxians and all the rest of it.

Nevertheless, the charges leveled at him–"autobiographical novels," "lack of objectivity" etc.,–were still a source of annoyance. The neat definitions buzzed in his mind like mosquitoes. Then, about this time, he changed publishers–taking along with him several crates of manuscript; "millions of words." A large part of this manuscript, as has been said, went into these last two novels–but the hero of the manuscript was the same hero as that of "Look Homeward, Angel" and "Of Time and the River." His name was Eugene Gant.

When he changed publishers, Wolfe found himself faced with this major problem: How to use his unpublished parts of Eugene Gant's life in a new novel or group of novels. The hero's name, of course, had to be changed. The demands of publishing called for that. More than a mere rechristening, however, was required. The life of George Webber had to be brought to the point where his early years would flow naturally into the later years of Eugene Gant. And, in writing about Webber, Wolfe believed that he could prove that he could create a non-autobiographical character–and also prove that it was within his power to write "objectively."

The whole unhappy effort was doomed from the start. If only for credibility's sake, the new hero had to be a man exactly like Eugene Gant. How else could the books have any pattern: any meaning whatsoever? This, then, is why the early pages of "The Web and the Rock" read like a loose rewriting of "Look Homeward, Angel." How could it be otherwise? Webber had to be grafted on to Gant. A trunk had to be provided for the branches and foliage already at hand. Wolfe unquestionably believed what he wrote in the preface to "The Web and the Rock"–that it was the most objective novel he had ever written. It was. But only to the extent that he was obliged to re-examine and rework some of his basic material. Gant became Webber but Gant remained. And Gant, of course, was Thomas Wolfe.

With the publication of this novel it is possible to discern the general outlines of the job Wolfe set for himself. His plan was to write a vast cycle of novels through which the life of Eugene Gant was to run as a kind of bloodstream. They were to go back to the Civil War (somewhere among his unpublished manuscripts there must be a long short story called "Chickamauga") and would project into the future as far as Eugene Gant, in the person of Thomas Wolfe, managed to live. Speculation as to how far he would have been able to carry out this plan, and how successfully, is purposeless. It would be equally purposeless for me to try to weigh this particular book. Even if I had not already disqualified myself, I would be reluctant to say more than I used to say after reading one of his manuscripts. "When it's fine it's fine. You know what you're after better than anyone else." I still feel the same way–that he was after something, that it was something most important to be after, and that, considering the number of times he gets hold of it, the flaws in his writing do not particularly matter. I soon learned that he would never be a terse writer because he was not the least bit interested in becoming one. So what of it? It also became obvious that he would never bring the tremendous engine of his creative ability under full control and that he would be forever loose and sprawling and sometimes windy enough to blow your hat off. So what of that? The fact remains that when he gets hold, when he digs through to what he is after, he is magnificent in a way few American writers ever have been–making his detractors seem puny and feeble by comparison. This book is full of such magnificence.

The last word I had from Wolfe was a postcard mailed from Yellowstone Park about two months before he died. It was a picture of Old Faithful and on the back he had scrawled in pencil: "Portrait of the author at the two million-word point." It seems to me that that geyser is a pretty good picture of him. It looks vaguely like the way he used to look walking down First Avenue about two o'clock on a blowy morning and, like it, he gushed boiling and furious from his American earth. The landscape is lonelier without him.

In a 29 November 1940 letter to his daughter, F. Scott Fitzgerald commented on You Can't Go Home Again.

I started Tom Wolfe's book on your recommendation. It seems better than Time and the River. He has a fine inclusive mind, can write like a streak, has a great deal of emotion, thoug a lot of it is maudlin and inaccurate, but his awful secret transpires at every crevice–he did not have anything particular to say! The stuff about the GREAT VITAL HEART OF AMERICA is just simply corny. . . . However, the book doesn't commit the cardinal sin: it doesn't fail to live.

–*F. Scott Fitzgerald: A Life in Letters,* p. 472

Review of *The Hills Beyond*

Wolfe's third posthumously published work includes short stories, sketches, and a fragment of an incomplete novel, "The Hills Beyond," from which the volume takes its title. Wolfe claimed that in The Hills Beyond *he would try to tell through the hundreds of members of one family the whole story of America. He completed ten chapters of the novel.*

Thomas Wolfe's Last Book

J. Donald Adams

New York Times Book Review, 26 October 1941, p. 1.

Three years have passed since Thomas Wolfe's death, and this is the third book which has been culled from the mountain of manuscript he left behind him. It is also, we are told, to be the last, although material remains for as many more. In the judgment of the editor with whom he last worked, Edward Aswell, and of his literary executor, Maxwell Perkins, who was also his first literary midwife, there is no reason good enough to justify publication of that remainder. Much of it is early work which Wolfe would wish to revise if he were still living; some of it material which he worked over in another form; some of it purely experimental. These facts are set forth in the interesting note which Mr. Aswell appends to the present volume, and in which more light is cast on Wolfe's methods and aims as a writer.

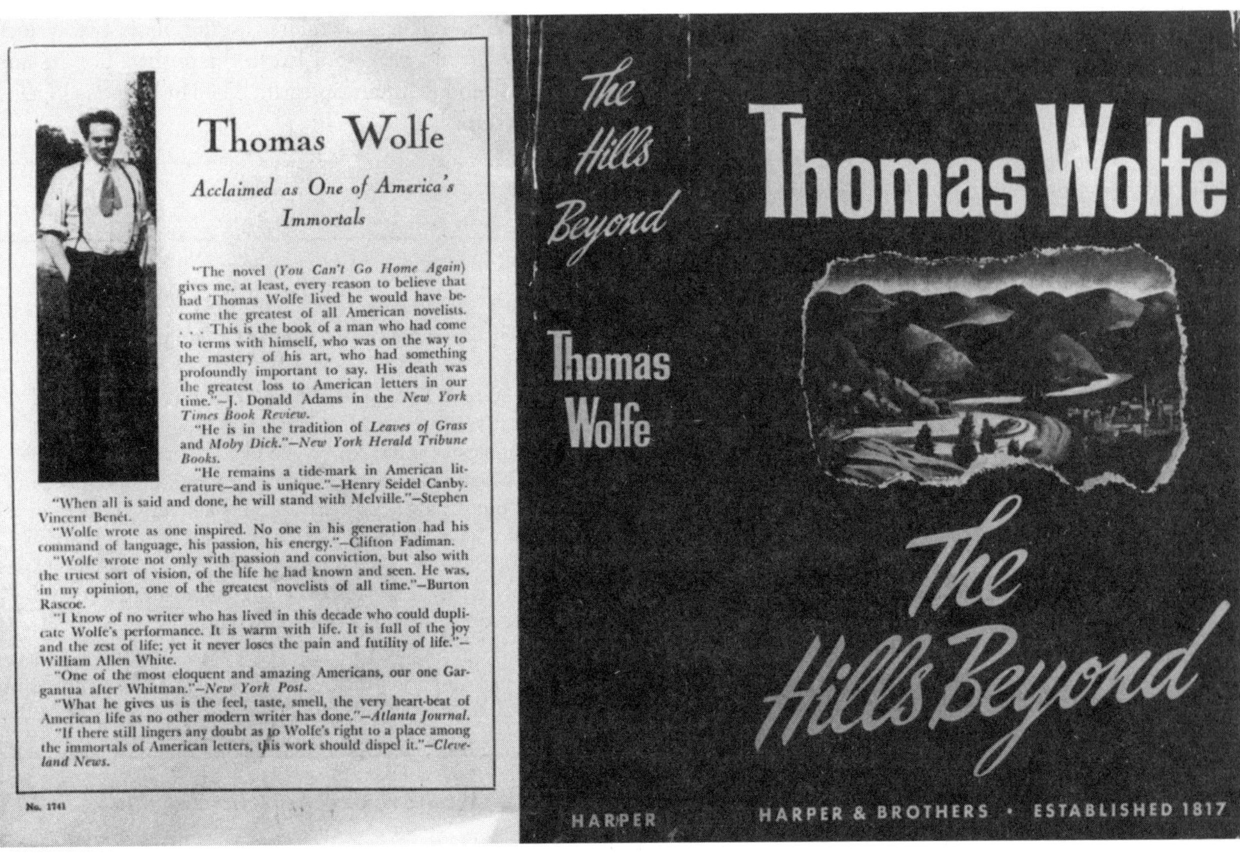

Dust jacket for the collection edited by Aswell

"The Hills Beyond" amply justifies its publication as the last work we are to have from the man who was the most promising American writer of his generation. It contains some of his best, and certainly his most mature, work. The unfinished novel from which the book takes its title would, I think, have surpassed in creative power those other four on which his reputation must rest. Besides this, "The Hills Beyond" includes one of the finest of Wolfe's shorter pieces, "The Lost Boy," and an exceedingly well done tale of the Civil War which he had from the lips of a great-uncle ("Chickamauga"). There is also a pair of pieces, one imaginary, the other factual, on the theme of his return to Asheville seven years after the publication of "Look Homeward, Angel." These, too, are excellent, each in its kind. Of the remaining miscellaneous items, the best is a brief but suggestive and revealing essay on the theme of loneliness.

The unfinished novel, Mr. Aswell informs us, was the work with which Wolfe was chiefly occupied during the year before his death. It is, therefore, in view of the unusual manner in which Wolfe's work was published (each book being a sort of mosaic of old and new material) of exceptional interest. "The Hills Beyond" was set down by a man who felt that he was through, in his own words, "with lyrical and identifiable personal autobiography." Except for one chapter, which had magazine publication in 1936, it was thought he had reached this point in "The Web and the Rock," the first of the posthumous books. I do not believe that he had. But sections of the next book, "You Can't Go Home Again," were more objective than anything previous, and with "The Hills Beyond" the goal he had set himself was definitely in sight.

In this book—how great a pity that he did not live to finish it!—he aimed to tell the story of his forebears. He found that most of what he knew that was actual about them he had already used in earlier books, and most of the people who appear in "The Hills Beyond" are not patterned after real members of the "Gant" and "Pentland" families. But they are, or would have become, full-bodied creations. Old William ("Bear") Joyner, who came into the mountains with a Revolutionary land grant in one hand and a rifle in the other, was hewn from the family tree, but the sons and grandsons who carry on the story were not. Zachariah, that fine figure of a homespun politician; Rufus, the acquisitive; Theodore, the histrionic professional Confederate warrior; Robert, the upright judge–these and others are creatures of Wolfe's making, and they are well done.

But that is not what, to my mind, is most important about this last book of Thomas Wolfe. Who would cast out from his writing those vital portraits of his own father and mother, or the tender and searing memory of his older brother which is captured in "The Lost Boy"? Whether they were real or imagined, Wolfe could make his people live. We require that of any novelist worth his salt. But Tom Wolfe had more than that to give. There was that marvelous sensory equipment of his, that vibrant sensitivity, evident from the first. He had the power of evocation as only the best writers have–the magic touch that gives wings to a reader's thought. A page of his best prose is worth a shelf full of laborious fact-finding in the name of fiction. These were qualities that came out of his emotional wealth; his mind, for nearly all his life, did not keep pace with them. But Wolfe was growing–growing fast, when death overtook him. The integration that he needed was under way. He was finding himself in relation to life, in relation to his world.

The indications of this growth in "The Hills Beyond" are plentiful. One of them is the increasing number of passages in which he does not simply feel, but thinks. There is stuff for reflection in what he writes about the American attitude toward lawyers and the law–so different from that of any other people on earth.

We made the lawyers our medicine men, and the law itself, as practiced by ambitious men, was made a means to an end–the end being that of business itself–personal advantage and private profit before all else, in politics or elsewhere. The social function of the law became obscured.

Read what he writes of the role of the county court house in our rural communities and its meaning in the whole fabric of American life:

> The county court house was, in short, America–the wilderness America, the sprawling, huge chaotic, criminal America. . . . It was America with all its almost hopeless hopes, its almost faithless faiths–America with the huge blight on her of her own error, the broken promise of her lost dream and her unachieved desire; and it was America as well with her unspoken prophecies, her unfound language, her unuttered song . . .

I think that if Thomas Wolfe had lived he would have gotten more of what has made us the people we are into his fiction than any novelist we have had, for his understanding of his country and his people was approaching the depth of his love for them. It was a love no less intense than Whitman's. It flames at the core of all he wrote.

He died at 37. And he was, I am now convinced, only on the threshold of the achievement for which he was fitted. There is talk, here and there, of a Wolfe "cult." That is foolish talk. There was, too, one remembers, a Whitman cult. Thomas Wolfe was born for greatness, and he reached no small measure of it before he left us. Much time may pass before we see his like again.

Thomas Wolfe, 1937 (photo by Carl Van Vechten; Carl Van Vechten Collection, Beinecke Library, Yale University)

Chapter 7

The Reputation of Thomas Wolfe

The critical reputation and readership of Thomas Wolfe diminished after the posthumous publication of the three volumes edited by Edward Aswell for Harper, despite the activities of the Thomas Wolfe Society and the scholarly publications of C. Hugh Holman, Paschal Reeves, Aldo Magi, John Idol, and Richard S. Kennedy.

Elizabeth Nowell's edition of Wolfe's letters and her biography stimulated interest in Wolfe, as did subsequent biographies by Andrew Turnbull and David Herbert Donald. The appeal of the many biographical studies of Wolfe indicates that interest in the writer's life became a substitution for reading his work.

Wolfe went out of fashion and in the 1980s was regarded as a one-book author. At one point The Web and the Rock *was out of print. The neglect or underappreciation of Wolfe's work resulted in large part from professorial hostility toward him: he has not been widely taught, and therefore students have had to discover his books on their own. But other writers continued to praise him during the eclipse. William Faulkner placed him at the head of his list of the best American novelists on the basis that Wolfe attempted to do more than the others. Kurt Vonnegut, Ray Bradbury, James Dickey, and Pat Conroy are among the contemporary writers who have declared their admiration for Wolfe's genius.*

Much of the posthumous interest in Wolfe had to do with the distorted Wolfe/Perkins relationship and the debates about the roles of Perkins and Aswell in the editing of Wolfe's prose into published form. The myth of Wolfe as the undisciplined genius who produced torrents of formless, unpublishable prose perseveres to the detriment of his stature.

> Wolfe tried to do the greatest of the impossible . . . to reduce all human experience to literature.
>
> —William Faulkner

Maxwell Perkins's remembrance of Wolfe was published in a special issue of his alma mater's magazine devoted to the author.

Scribner's and Thomas Wolfe
Maxwell Perkins
Carolina Magazine, 48 (October 1938): 15–17

When I knew that Tom Wolfe had died, as I knew he must after the day of his operation at Johns Hopkins—and before that it had seemed inconceivable that one so vibrant with life could die young—a line kept recurring in my mind as a kind of consolation: "He hates him that would upon the rack of this tough world stretch him out longer." For he was on the rack almost always, and almost always would have been—and for one reason. He was wrestling as no artist in Europe would have to do, with the material of literature—a great country not yet revealed to its own people. It was not as with English artists who revealed England to Englishmen through generations, each one accepting what was true from his predecessors, in a gradual accretion, through centuries. Tom knew to the uttermost meaning the literatures of other lands and that they were not the literature of America. He knew that the light and color of America were different; that the smells and sounds, its peoples, and all the structure and dimensions of our continent were unlike anything before. It was with this that he was struggling, and it was that struggle alone that, in a large sense, governed all he did. How long his books may last as such, no one can say, but the trail he has blazed is now open forever. American artists will follow, and widen it to express the things Americans only unconsciously know, to reveal America and Americans to Americans. That was at the heart of Tom's fierce life.

It was a gigantic task, and Tom was a giant in energy and in power of feeling as well as in physique. His too great dimensions seemed to represent the difficulties that almost drove him mad: he could not fit a

Cover for 1997 book that includes Maxwell Perkins's responses to would-be biographer John Skally Terry's questions about Thomas Wolfe

book to the conventional length, nor produce one in the usual space of time. He was not proportioned to these requirements, but neither was his subject, the vast, sprawling, lonely, unruly land.

It is said his books are formless, but I do not think he lacked a sense of form. Is it wanting, for instance, in "The Web of Earth"? In a large way he knew where he was going, and given twenty years and many volumes, I often thought, he might have fully achieved a proper form. But as he had to fit his body to the doorways, vehicles, and furniture of smaller men, so he had to fit his expression to the conventional requirements of a space and time that were as surely too small for his nature as they were for his subject.

Four years after the publication of "Look Homeward, Angel" about Christmas time in 1933, he brought me the huge manuscript, two feet high, of "Of Time and the River." And he was desperate. Time, his old enemy, the vastness and toughness of his material, the frequent and not always sympathetic inquiries of people about his progress toward another book, and financial pressure too–all were closing in on him. I thought, "this book has to be done," and we set to work. I, who thought Tom a man of genius, and loved him too, and could not bear to see him fail, was almost as desperate as he, so much there was to do. But the truth is that if I did him a real service–and in this I did–it was in keeping him from losing his belief in himself by believing in him. What he most needed was comradeship and understanding in a long crisis, and those things I could give him then.

After I had read the manuscript and marked it up, we began a year of nights of work. The book was far from finished. It was in great fragments, and they were not in order. Large parts were missing. It was all disproportioned. Tom, who knew all this, would come in at eight or so, and I would point these things out, part by part. But I could tell Tom nothing, if it were right, that he did not easily see, and perhaps had already seen. But his whole natural impulse was outward, not inward–to express, not compress, or organize–and even though he realized that something had to be cut, as extrinsic, or otherwise superfluous, he could not easily bear to have it done. So every night we worked and argued in my boxstall of an office over Fifth Avenue, often accomplishing nothing, and strewed the floor with cigarettes and papers. The night-watchman and the scrubwoman forgave us, because there was that in Tom that established a fellowship with all good sound people. And there was his humor too, always, except in the mortal struggle with his material.

Once I argued for a big deletion, late on a hot night, and then sat in silence. I knew he must agree to it for the reasons were strong. Tom tossed his head about, and swayed in his chair, and his eyes roved over the office. I went on reading in the manuscript for not less than fifteen minutes, but I was aware of Tom's movements–aware at last that he was looking fixedly at one corner of the office. In that corner hung a winter hat and overcoat, and down from under the hat, along the coat hung a sinister rattlesnake skin with seven rattles–a present from Marjorie Rawlings. I looked at Tom. He was eyeing that group of objects, and the rattlesnake stood out. He waved his hand at them: "Aha," said Tom, "the portrait of an editor." We worked no more that night. After the laughter we went to the Chatham Garden which Tom loved–and where the waiters all knew him as a brother–and talked and argued for an hour under the summer stars.

II

Such cutting was one thing, but there were the gaps, and Tom filled some of them in there and then, writing in his huge, heavy scrawl, on the corner of my

Fifty thousand copies of the abridged Armed Services Edition were distributed gratis to American service personnel during World War II (Bruccoli Collection, Thomas Cooper Library, University of South Carolina).

desk. When we came to the point where Eugene's father died, I said that it must be written about, but that since Eugene was away at Harvard, Tom need only tell of the shock of the news, and of Eugene's return for the funeral–a matter of perhaps five thousand words. And Tom agreed.

The next night he came in with some thousands of words about the life of the doctor who attended Gant. I said, "This is good, Tom, but what has it to do with the book? You are telling the story of Eugene, of what *he* saw and experienced. We can't waste time with all this that is outside it." Tom fully accepted this, but still, the next night, he brought in a long passage about Eugene's sister Helen, and her thoughts while shopping in Altamont, and then at night in bed when she heard the whistle of the train. I said, "How in God's name will you get this book done this way, Tom? You have wasted two days already, and instead of reducing the length and doing what is essential, you are increasing it and adding what doesn't belong here."

Tom was penitent. He did not argue back as he almost had done. He promised he would write only what was needed,–and yet the next night he brought in thousands of words about Gant's illness, all outside of what I thought was wanted. But it was too good to let go. I said so. It was wrong, but it was right, and Tom went on, and the death of Gant is one of the finest things he ever wrote. Thank God I had sense enough to see it that early, even though it seemed to me to violate the principle of form. But I do not think I could have stopped Tom anyhow. He had agreed that I was right, but underneath he knew what he was doing and had to do it.

III

All this perhaps sounds grim and desperate–and it should, for that it often was–but it gives no picture of Tom. It presents him as he was in the heat of struggle. After "Look Homeward, Angel" was published he was happy, and after the great success of "Of Time and the River," when he came home from Europe, and before he began the next long battle that ended last May when he set out on the tour of the Northwest that ended in his fatal illness, he was happy too. In that last interval he lived on First Avenue off Forty-ninth Street, and we had a house two blocks away, on Forty-ninth. Then we had many happy times before the struggle with his new book grew too fierce. The block between us and First Avenue was almost slum like. Boys played some exciting adaptation of baseball, and then of football, in the street, and the sidewalks were crowded with children. They all knew Tom. When he went by in his long, slow, country stride, looking at everything, they would call out, "Hello Mr. Wolfe." And the police all knew him too. Once my wife said, "A flower-pot has disappeared from one of our window boxes. I can't understand how it happened." The window box was too high for anyone to reach, you would think, and who would want a geranium? Long afterward, one night Tom said: "I meant to tell you, I took one of your geraniums. I was coming in but the house was dark so I just took a flower pot, and a cop saw me and said, 'What are you doing?' I said, 'I'm taking it home to water it.' He just laughed." This was New York. Was the cop afraid of Tom and his great size? No, he knew him, and understood him: that human quality in Tom had made him friends with everyone around, and they knew he was one of them.

Tom was always one of them, the regular people, and he liked them most. His talk was beyond any I ever heard when he was not in the torment of his work. He would tell you of the river Cam in Cambridge, England, and the mist over it so that you knew the magic Tennyson felt; or of the tulip fields in Holland; or the paintings he liked in the galleries of Europe so that if you knew them you saw them again and afresh; or of that ruined monastery, Fountain Abbey near York, in its old forest–and you knew it as it was when it was all alive. He could have talked to anyone about anything he had touched at all; but what he wanted, or thought he did, was to be one of the regular people. He was lonely. He inspired fellow feeling, but it could not embrace him enough. He wanted the simple, hearty life of Gant in his best times, the wife and children, and coming home for lunch, and the fire roaring up the chimney. (No door!)

He could not be like other people. He was not built on their scale. Everyone important to him in his life seemed to know that. His was not the conventional story of neglected, unrecognized genius at all. His school teachers, the Robertses in Asheville, knew, apparently, when he was a child, that he was different from the others, and so did all his family, there in the mountains, and they enabled him to go to college–I think Americans can be proud of that. Only the inescapable slings and arrows of life betrayed him, the petty obligations and duties, and the lawsuits. They maddened him because they kept him from his work. All that infuriated him in its injustice. The one important thing in the universe to him was his work, and this was so simply because it was so. It was not due to ambition in the cheap sense, and it was not what is generally meant by egotism. He was under the compulsion of genius, and all the accidents of life that got in the way of its expression seemed to Tom to be outrages and insults. He knew in his mind that man was born to trouble–that everyone was beset with anxieties and thwarted by obstacles–but that this work which he was bound to do should be interfered with by trivialities, was maddening. And so was the struggle with the work itself.

IV

From this came the dualism in Tom that made him the one man I ever knew of whom extreme opposites were true. He was proud as Lucifer and yet utterly humble. He was full of kindness and the most gentle consideration, and yet ruthless. He was totally without a sense of humor, many said, but there never was a more humorous man. And how could this be? Because there was the man Tom and this dreadful *and* beautiful obligation in him. He was not proud of anything he had ever done–not of much he had written–but the consciousness of this great thing in him that he had to do made him so. He was ruthless, as in writing about real people not because he did not realize as Tom, the pain he might give but because this obligation in him made him feel that the pain was relatively trifling and brief, and was caused by conventional standards, and that what he was about was beyond all that. He was without humor often in his writing about Eugene–though a magnificent humor pervades his writings otherwise–because Eugene, being Tom, was engaged in the same deadly serious business, was obsessed with the mortal struggle to master material.

And Tom was always harassed by time. He had always "thoughts that he must cease to be before his pen had gleaned his teeming brain." It was this that made him strive to read all the books in the Harvard library in a year or so, and sent him on his wild odysseys of Europe and the South and the Pacific Coast, and New England, and then the Northwest. And this largely it was that gave him his love of quantity, for its own sake as it seemed. He didn't have time enough, and somehow seemed to know it. One early morning when 49th Street was silent and empty, Nancy Hale who lived there heard a deep and distant chant. It grew louder, and she went to the window. A great, loose figure of a man in a black slouch hat and a swaying raincoat was swinging along in Tom's slow stride and he was chanting over and over: "I wrote ten thousand words today. I wrote ten thousand words today." Old Time was riding him, but that day Tom had won.

When I first saw Tom with his wild black hair and bright countenance as he stood in my doorway hesitating to enter–in those days Tom had more respect for editors–I thought of Shelley (who was so different in most ways) because of that brightness of his face and the relative smallness of his head and the unruly hair. Just before his illness took its fatal turn he scribbled me a letter in pencil, though he should not have done it. The last of it suggests how things sometimes seemed and looked to Tom. He recalls a good happy time we had on the day he returned from Europe several years ago, a hot Fourth of July when just before sunset we "went on top, of the tall building, and all the strangeness and the glory and the power of life, and the city was below."

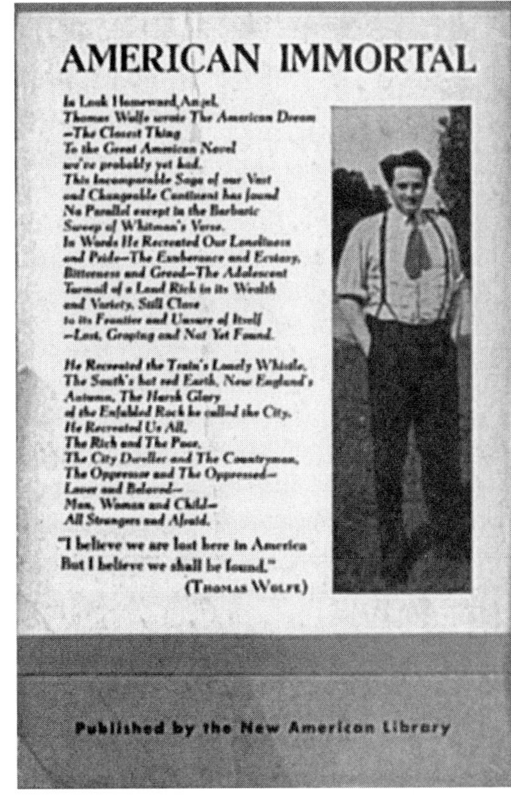

The front cover of a Wolfe story collection (1944) and the back and front covers of an abridged version of his first novel (1948)

At the time of his death Perkins was preparing an essay to mark the donation of William B. Wisdom's Wolfe collection to Harvard.

Thomas Wolfe
Maxwell Perkins
Harvard Library Bulletin, 1 (Autumn 1947): 269–279

I think that there is not in any one place so nearly complete a collection of an author's writings and records as that of Thomas Wolfe's now in the Harvard Library. When he died on that sad day in September 1938, when war was impending, or soon after that, I learned that I was his executor and that he had actually left little–as he would have thought, and as it seemed then–besides his manuscripts. It was my obligation to dispose of them to the advantage of his beneficiaries and his memory, and though the times were bad, and Wolfe had not then been recognized as what he now is, I could have sold them commercially, piecemeal, through dealers, for more money than they ever brought. I was determined that this literary estate should remain a unit, available to writers and students, and I tried to sell it as such; but at that time, with war clouds gathering and soon bursting, I could find no adequate buyer.

Then Aline Bernstein, to whom Wolfe had given the manuscript of *Look Homeward, Angel,* sold it by auction for the relief of her people in misfortune, on the understanding that it would be given to Harvard. Not long after that William B. Wisdom, who had recognized Wolfe as a writer of genius on the publication of the *Angel,* and whose faith in him had never wavered, offered to purchase all of his manuscripts and records. He had already accumulated a notable collection of Wolfiana. His correspondence showed me that he thought as I did–that the point of supreme importance was that these records and writings should not be scattered to the four winds, that they be kept intact. And so the whole great packing case of material–letters, bills, documents, notebooks and manuscripts–went to him on the stipulation, which I never need have asked for, that he would will it all to one institution. Since *Look Homeward, Angel* was already in Harvard, since Tom Wolfe had loved the reading room of the Library where, as he so often told me, he devoured his hundreds of books and spent most of his Harvard years, Mr. Wisdom made a gift of all this to Harvard. And there it now is.

Though I had worked as an editor with Thomas Wolfe on two huge manuscripts, *Look Homeward, Angel* and *Of Time and the River,* I was astonished on that Spring evening of 1935 when Tom, about to sail for England, brought to our house on East 49th Street,

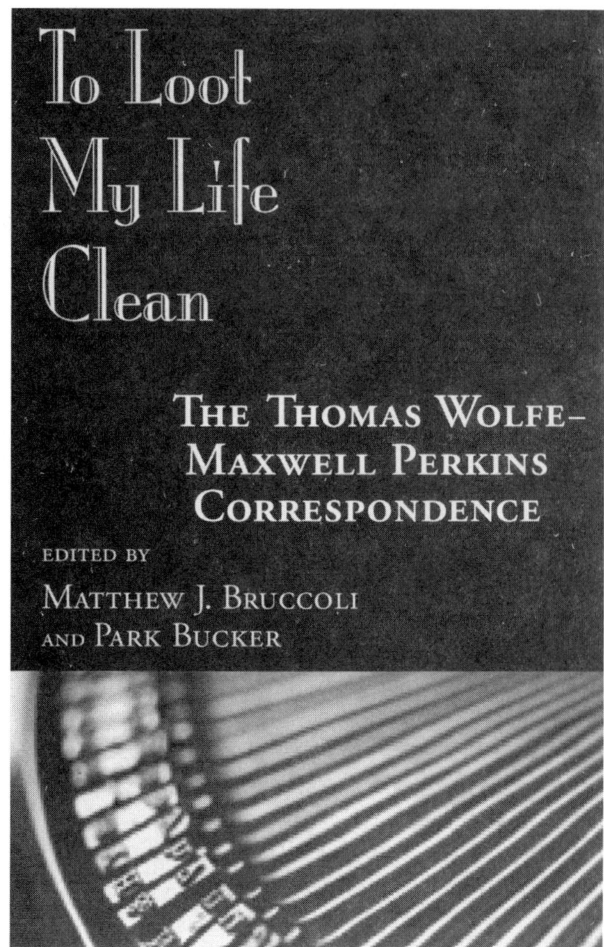

Dust jacket for the comprehensive collection of the correspondence between Wolfe and his editor published by the University of South Carolina Press in 2000

because Scribner's was closed, the huge packing case containing all his literary material. Tom and I and the taxi man carried it in and set it down. Then Tom said to the man, 'What is your name?' He said, 'Lucky.' 'Lucky!' said Tom–I think it was perhaps an Americanization of some Italian name–and grasped his hand. It seemed a good omen. We three had done something together. We were together for that moment. We all shook hands. But for days, that huge packing case blocked our hall, until I got it removed to Scribner's.

The first time I heard of Thomas Wolfe I had a sense of foreboding. I who love the man say this. Every good thing that comes is accompanied by trouble. It was in 1928 when Madeleine Boyd, a literary agent, came in. She talked of several manuscripts which did not much interest me, but frequently interrupted herself to tell of a wonderful novel about an American boy. I several times said to her, 'Why don't you bring it in here, Madeleine?' and she seemed to evade the question. But finally she said, 'I will bring it, if you promise to read every word of it.' I did promise, but she told me other things that made me realize that Wolfe was a turbulent spirit, and that we were in for turbulence. When the manuscript came, I was fascinated by the first scene where Eugene's father, Oliver W. Gant, with his brother, two little boys, stood by a roadside in Pennsylvania and saw a division of Lee's Army on the march to Gettysburg.

But then there came some ninety-odd pages about Oliver Gant's life in Newport News, and Baltimore, and elsewhere. All this was what Wolfe had heard, and had no actual association with which to reconcile it, and it was inferior to the first episode, and in fact to all the rest of the book. I was turned off to other work and gave the manuscript to Wallace Meyer, thinking, 'Here is another promising novel that probably will come to nothing.' Then Meyer showed me that wonderful night scene in the cafe where Ben was with the Doctors, and Horse Hines, the undertaker, came in. I dropped everything and began to read again, and all of us were reading the book simultaneously, you might say, including John Hall Wheelock, and there never was the slightest disagreement among us as to its importance.

After some correspondence between me and Wolfe, and between him and Madeleine Boyd, from which we learned how at the October Fair in Germany he had been almost beaten to death–when I realized again that we had a Moby Dick to deal with–Wolfe arrived in New York and stood in the doorway of my boxstall of an office leaning against the door jamb. When I looked up and saw his wild hair and bright countenance–although he was so altogether different physically–I thought of Shelley. *He* was fair, but his hair was wild, and his face was bright and his head disproportionately small.

We then began to work upon the book and the first thing we did, to give it unity, was to cut out that wonderful scene it began with and the ninety-odd pages that followed, because it seemed to me, and he agreed, that the whole tale should be unfolded through the memories and senses of the boy, Eugene, who was born in Asheville. We both thought that the story was compassed by that child's realization; that it was life and the world as he came to realize them. When he had tried to go back into the life of his father before he arrived in Asheville, without the inherent memory of events, the reality and the poignance were diminished–but for years it was on my conscience that I had persuaded Tom to cut out that first scene of the two little boys on the roadside with Gettysburg impending.

And then what happened? In *Of Time and the River* he brought the scene back to greater effect when old Gant was dying on the gallery of the hospital in Baltimore and in memory recalled his olden days. After that occurred I felt much less anxiety in suggesting cuts: I began then to realize that nothing Wolfe wrote was ever lost, that omissions from one book were restored in a later one. An extreme example of this is the fact that the whole second half of *The Web and the Rock* was originally intended to be the concluding episode in *Of Time and the River*. But most, and perhaps almost all, of those early incidents of Gant's life were worked into *The Web and the Rock* and *You Can't Go Home Again*.

I had realized, for Tom had prefaced his manuscript with a statement to that effect, that *Look Homeward, Angel* was autobiographical, but I had come to think of it as being so in the sense that *David Copperfield* is, or *War and Peace,* or *Pendennis*. But when we were working together, I suddenly saw that it was often almost literally autobiographical–that these people in it were his people. I am sure my face took on a look of alarm, and Tom saw it and he said, 'But Mr. Perkins, you don't understand. I think these people are *great* people and that they should be told about.' He was right. He had written a great book, and it had to be taken substantially as it was. And in truth, the extent of cutting in that book has somehow come to be greatly exaggerated. Really, it was more a matter of reorganization. For instance, Tom had that wonderful episode when Gant came back from his far-wandering and rode in early morning on the trolley car through the town and heard about who had died and who had been born and saw all the scenes that were so familiar to Tom or Eugene, as the old trolley rumbled along. This was immediately followed by an episode of a similar kind where Eugene, with his friends, walked home from school through the town of Asheville. That was presented in a Joycean way, but it was the same sort of thing–some one going through the town and through his perceptions revealing it to the reader. By putting these episodes next to each other the effect of each was diminished, and I think we gave both much greater value by separating them. We did a great deal of detailed cutting, but it was such things as that I speak of that constituted perhaps the greater part of the work.

Of Time and the River was a much greater struggle for Tom. Eventually, I think it was on Thanksgiving Day 1933, he brought me in desperation about two feet

> Reading about that crazy boy and his crazy family and his drunken father and his miserly mother is so like myself and my own family that I discovered I'd been a writer all along without really having realized it.
>
> –James Jones

Cover of the slipcase for two-volume edition of Wolfe's notebooks (1970)

of typescript. The first scene in this was the platform of the railroad station in Asheville when Eugene was about to set out for Harvard, and his family had come to see him off. It must have run to about 30,000 words and I cut it to perhaps 10,000 and showed it to Tom. He approved it. When you are waiting for a train to come in, there is suspense. Something is going to happen. You must, it seemed to me, maintain that sense of suspense and you can't to the extent of 30,000 words. There never was any cutting that Tom did not agree to. He knew that cutting was necessary. His whole impulse was to utter what he felt and he had no time to revise and compress.

So then we began a year of nights of work, including Sundays, and every cut, and change, and interpolation, was argued about and about. The principle that I was working on was that this book, too, got its unity and its form through the senses of Eugene, and I remember how, if I had had my way, we should, by sticking to that principle, have lost one of the most wonderful episodes Wolfe ever wrote–the death of Gant. One night we agreed that certain transitions should be written in, but instead of doing them Wolfe brought on the next night some five thousand words about Eugene's sister in Asheville when her father was ill, and a doctor there and a nurse. I said, 'Tom, this is all outside the story, and you know it. Eugene was not there, he was in Cambridge; all of this was outside his perception and knowledge at the time.' Tom agreed with me, but the next night, he brought me another five thousand words or so which got up into the death of Gant. And then I realized I was wrong, even if right in theory. What he was doing was too good to let any rule of form impede him.

It is said that Tolstoy never willingly parted with the manuscript of *War and Peace*. One could imagine him working on it all through his life. Certainly Thomas Wolfe never willingly parted from the proofs of *Of Time and the River*. He sat brooding over them for weeks in the Scribner library and not reading. John Wheelock read them and we sent them to the printer and told Tom it had been done. I could believe that otherwise he might have clung to them to the end.

He dedicated that book to me in most extravagant terms. I never saw the dedication until the book was published and though I was most grateful for it, I had forebodings when I heard of his intention. I think it was that dedication that threw him off his stride and broke his magnificent scheme. It gave shallow people the impression that Wolfe could not function as a writer without collaboration, and one critic even used some such phrases as, 'Wolfe and Perkins–Perkins and Wolfe, what way is that to write a novel.' Nobody with the slightest comprehension of the nature of a writer could accept such an assumption. No writer could possibly tolerate the assumption, which perhaps Tom almost himself did, that he was dependent as a writer upon anyone else. He had to prove to himself and to the world that this was not so.

And that was the fundamental reason that he turned to another publisher. If he had not–but by the time he did it was plain that he had to tell, in the medium of fiction and through the transmutation of his amazing imagination, the story of his own life–he never would have broken his own great plan by distorting Eugene Gant into George Webber. That was a horrible mistake. I think Edward Aswell, of Harper & Brothers, agrees with me in this, but when the manuscript that came to form *The Web and the Rock* and *You Can't Go Home Again* got to him to work on, and in some degree to me, as Wolfe's executor, Tom was dead, and things had to be taken as they were.

The trouble began after the publication of *Of Time and the River,* which the reviewers enormously praised–but many of them asserted that Wolfe could only write about himself, that he could not see the world or anything objectively, with detachment–that he was always autobiographical. Wolfe was extremely sensitive to criticism, for all his tremendous faith in his genius as an obligation put upon him to fulfill. One day when I lived on East 49th Street near Second Avenue, and he on First Avenue, just off the corner of 49th, I met him as I was going home. He said he wanted to talk to me, as we did talk every evening about that time, and we went into the Waldorf. He referred to the criticisms against him, and said that he wanted to write a completely objective, unautobiographical book, and that it would show how strangely different everything is from what a person expects it to be. One might say that he was thinking of the theme that has run through so many great books, such as *Pickwick Papers* and *Don Quixote,* where a man, young or old, goes hopefully out into the world slap into the face of outrageous reality. He was going to put on the title page what was said by Prince Andrei, in *War and Peace,* after his first battle, when the praise fell upon those who had done nothing and blame almost fell upon one who had done everything. Prince Andrei, who saved the battery commander who most of all had held back the French from the blame that Little Tushin would have accepted, walked out with him into the night. Then as Tushin left, Tolstoy said, 'Prince Andrei looked up at the stars and sighed; everything was so different from what he thought it was going to be.'

Tom was in a desperate state. It was not only what the critics said that made him wish to write objectively, but that he knew that what he had written had given great pain even to those he loved the most. The conclusion of our talk was that if he could write such an objective book on this theme within a year, say, to the extent of perhaps a hundred thousand words, it might be well to do it. It was this that turned him to George Webber, but once he began on that he really and irresistibly resumed the one story he was destined to write, which was that of himself, or Eugene Gant.

And so, the first half of *The Web and the Rock,* of which there is only a typescript, is a re-telling in different terms of *Look Homeward, Angel.* Wolfe was diverted from his natural purpose–and even had he lived, what could have been done? Some of his finest writing is that first half of *The Web and the Rock.* Could anybody have just tossed it out?

But if Tom had held to his scheme and completed the whole story of his life as transmuted into fiction through his imagination, I think the accusation that he had no sense of form could not have stood. He wrote one long story, 'The Web of Earth,' which had perfect form, for all its intricacy. I remember saying to him, 'Not one word of this should be changed.' One might say that as his own physical dimensions were huge so was his conception of a book. He had one book to write about a vast, sprawling, turbulent land–America–as perceived by Eugene Gant. Even when he was in Europe, it was of America he thought. If he had not been diverted and had lived to complete it, I think it would have had the form that was suited to the subject.

His detractors say he could only write about himself, but all that he wrote of was transformed by his imagination. For instance, in *You Can't Go Home Again* he shows the character Foxhall Edwards at breakfast. Edwards's young daughter enters 'as swiftly and silently as a ray of light.' She is very shy and in a hurry to get to school. She tells of a theme she has written on Walt Whitman and what the teacher said of Whitman. When Edwards urges her not to hurry and makes various observations, she says, 'Oh, Daddy, you're so funny!' What Tom did was to make one unforgettable little character out of three daughters of Foxhall Edwards.

He got the ray of light many years ago when he was with me in my house in New Canaan, Connecticut, and one daughter, at the age of about eight or ten, came in and met this gigantic stranger. After she was introduced she fluttered all about the room in her embarrassment, but radiant, like a sunbeam. Then Tom was present when another daughter, in Radcliffe, consulted me about a paper she was writing on Whitman, but he put this back into her school days. The third, of which he composed a single character, was the youngest, who often did say, partly perhaps, because she was not at ease when Tom was there, 'Oh, Daddy, you're so silly.' That is how Tom worked. He created something new and something meaningful through a transmutation of what he saw, heard, and realized.

I think no one could understand Thomas Wolfe who had not seen or properly imagined the place in which he was born and grew up. Asheville, North Carolina, is encircled by mountains. The trains wind in and out through labyrinths of passes. A boy of Wolfe's imagination imprisoned there could think that what was beyond was all wonderful–different from what it was where there was not for him enough of anything. Whatever happened, Wolfe would have been what he was. I remember on the day of his death saying to his

> There are no writers today of the stature of Hemingway or Faulkner or Thomas Wolfe. I grew up with these writers. They lived like mountains for us: they were summits and had much more influence. Although there weren't as many people reading them as there are reading all of us today, their books were events when they came out and changed our minds.
>
> –Norman Mailer

sister Mabel that I thought it amazing in an American family that one of the sons who wanted to be a writer should have been given the support that was given Tom, and that they all deserved great credit for that. She said it didn't matter, that nothing could have prevented Tom from doing what he did.

That is true, but I think that those mountainous walls which his imagination vaulted gave him the vision of an America with which his books are fundamentally concerned. He often spoke of the artist in America–how the whole color and character of the country was completely new–never interpreted; how in England, for instance, the writer inherited a long accretion of accepted expression from which he could start. But Tom would say–and he had seen the world–'who has ever made you know the color of an American box car?' Wolfe was in those mountains–he tells of the train whistles at night–the trains were winding their way out into the great world where it seemed to the boy there was everything desirable, and vast, and wonderful.

It was partly that which made him want to see everything, and read everything, and experience everything, and say everything. There was a night when he lived on First Avenue that Nancy Hale, who lived on East 49th Street near Third Avenue, heard a kind of chant, which grew louder. She got up and looked out of the window at two or three in the morning and there was the great figure of Thomas Wolfe, advancing in his long countryman's stride, with his swaying black raincoat, and what he was chanting was, 'I wrote ten thousand words today–I wrote ten thousand words today.'

Tom must have lived in eight or nine different parts of New York and Brooklyn for a year or more. He knew in the end every aspect of the city–he walked the streets endlessly–but he was not a city man. The city fascinated him but he did not really belong in it and was never satisfied to live in it. He was always thinking of America as a whole and planning trips to some part that he had not yet seen, and in the end taking them. His various quarters in town always looked as if he had just moved in, to camp for awhile. This was partly because he really had no interest in possessions of any kind, but it was also because he was in his very nature a Far Wanderer, bent upon seeing all places, and his rooms were just necessities into which he never settled. Even when he was there his mind was not. He needed a continent to range over, actually and in imagination. And his place was all America. It was with America he was most deeply concerned and I believe he opened it up as no other writer ever did for the people of his time and for the writers and artists and poets of tomorrow. Surely he had a thing to tell us.

> Who was the greatest writer? Wolfe! Thomas Wolfe. After me, of course.
>
> –Jack Kerouac

Maxwell Perkins died in 1947. The obituary in The New York Times *on 18 June documents the permanent linkage between Wolfe and Perkins, emphasizing the extent of the editor's participation in Wolfe's creative process.*

M. E. PERKINS, 62,
SCRIBNER'S EDITOR

Official of Book Firm for 33 Years Is Dead–
'Discovered' Wolfe and Hemingway

STAMFORD, Con June 17 (AP)–Maxwell Evarts Perkins of New Canaan, Conn., who aided many now-famous authors in their early struggles for recognition, died today in the Stamford Hospital after a brief illness at the age of 62.

As editor of Charles Scribner's Sons, New York publishing house, Mr. Perkins was credited with discovering or assisting in their early writing careers such authors as Ernest Hemingway, Erskine Caldwell, Thomas Wolfe, Ring Lardner, John P. Marquand and Scott Fitzgerald.

He began his career with the publishing firm in 1911. Besides serving as editor he was a vice president and director.

He leaves a widow, the former Louise Saunders, whom he married in 1910, and five daughters, Mrs. John C. Frothingham of New Canaan, Mrs. Douglas Gorsline of New Jersey, Mrs. Robert G. King of Reliance, Ohio, and the Misses Nancy G. and Jane M. of New Canaan.

Dean of Book Editors

Mr. Perkins was generally conceded to be the dean of editors in the book publishing world. It was a reputation earned on two admixed levels–the strict area of the literature of an era and the commercial. On the one hand, his shrewd discernment of the worth of new writers and his advice to them developed unknowns to greatness; on the other, his telling judgment on manuscripts produced scores of best sellers.

A writer who a few years ago was seeking to assess the mark made by Mr. Perkins as an editor on contemporary American literature observed that the Scribner editor had probably had more books dedicated to him than any other man in his time. In the book publishing trade and in the writing field there could be no finer tribute.

A Scribner editor for thirty-three years, director of its editorial department for many years and since 1932 a vice president of the publishing house, Mr. Perkins was interested in the young writer of modern outlook and distinctive American flavor.

Probably the best-known association in modern times of an author and an editor was his friendship with the late Thomas Wolfe. Wolfe's huge, sprawling manuscripts, which had flown out of him as if from a volcano, were virtually unprintable as they came to Mr. Perkins' desk in untidy bundles. In long, wearing sessions author and editor would attempt to reduce the mass to organization–Perkins, cool, level-headed, patient; Wolfe, aggressive, stubborn and standing firm about every line he'd written.

Wolfe Depicted Him in Novel

In the compromise came Wolfe's series of crowded novels–"Look Homeward, Angel," "You Can't Go Home Again" and others. In "You Can't Go Home Again," Wolfe depicted Mr. Perkins as an editor called Foxhall Edwards.

More succinctly, Wolfe paid his debt to his editor in the dedication to "Of Time and the River," describing Mr. Perkins as "a great editor and a brave and honest man, who stuck to the writer of this book through times of bitter hopelessness and doubt * * * "

Scribner's at the time was known as one of the old-guard publishing houses. Its list included such stalwarts as Edith Wharton, Henry van Dyke, Gertrude Atherton and John Galsworthy. The elders of the conservative firm looked with considerable dismay on Mr. Perkins' attempts to sponsor the writing of young Americans. That he succeeded is publishing history. Malcolm Cowley, the literary critic, once remarked that Mr. Perkins was the prime mover in making Scribner's take "a sudden leap from the age of innocence into the middle of the lost generation."

The editor added a string of newer writers to the trade list. One was Ring Lardner, whom the older members of the firm thought of as a slangy sports writer. Mr. Perkins contended Lardner was writing a large slice of the literature of the day. Stark Young became a Scribner author, as did James Boyd, S. S. Van Dine, Conrad Aiken, Christine Weston and Arthur Train.

His Method With Authors

In working with authors Mr. Perkins, who was by nature and backgroud gentle and courtly, never badgered or cajoled, but instead attempted to give proportion to what was already in the author. "The source of a book must be the author," he once remarked. "You can only help the author to produce what he has in his compass."

Such encouragement and guidance came in conversations in Mr. Perkins' tiny office facing Fifth Avenue–in which he was wont to wear his hat at all hours–or in understanding letters to authors in the agonies of creation.

Mr. Perkins' grandfather, William Maxwell Evarts, was a Senator from New York and served as Secretary of State under President Rutherford B. Hayes. Born in New York in 1884, son of a lawyer, he attended St. Paul's School and was graduated from Harvard in 1907.

Until 1910 he was a reporter on THE NEW YORK TIMES where associates remember a habit that continued throughout his lifetime–that of "doodling" portraits of Napoleon Bonaparte.

Dust jacket for the 1961 book in which Wolfe's sister Mabel provides her memory of the Wolfe family

Publications of the Thomas Wolfe Society

Struthers Burt (1882–1954), a Scribners author and close friend of Perkins, charged in 1951 that Wolfe's "betrayal" killed Perkins.

Catalyst for Genius
Maxwell Perkins: 1884–1947
Struthers Burt
Saturday Review of Literature (9 June 1951): 6, 38, 39

There is no doubt that Thomas Wolfe was touched with genius. But genius is not so rare as all that. There are other men and women touched with genius who are also aware of discipline and form and the right of those around them to live. Unfortunately, genius is seldom recognized as such unless it is loud, disturbing, and cataclysmic. In my opinion the collaborator of "Look Homeward, Angel" and "Of Time and the River," Maxwell Evarts Perkins, was a greater genius than the author.

Now I will say something that has never before been said publicly. But it is time it was said in the interest of truth and literary history and in order to set the record straight. There is not the slightest question in the minds of the few who knew Maxwell Perkins intimately that the Tom Wolfe episode killed him. Exactly from the date of Tom's betrayal he began to die. (His death occurred four years ago, June 17, 1947.)

I am not too much impressed by uncontrolled genius. I was when I was young, but I am no longer young. I am not sure that in the sum total the game is worth the candle. Uncontrolled genius has a dreadful, devouring, proliferating quality; cancerous. The world has had a lot of it. It seems to me that what we are in need of now is character, which after all is genius and also for any kind of genius the point of best departure. In the last two decades the world has witnessed too much uncontrolled genius. . . .

. . . No editor in history has so dramatically changed the entire course of American and even British writing as Maxwell Evarts Perkins. With Sherwood Anderson and Ernest Hemingway he changed the language and technique of writing; with Thomas Wolfe and others stream-of-consciousness became a method of national description and analysis.

Knowing him so well, I have often wondered about this. I have tried to define to myself the secret of Max's immense influence, for in all my experience I have never met an editor more deliberately non-obtrusive, less interfering. Because of the Thomas Wolfe episode, which has been emphasized out of all proportion, there has grown up in certain quarters a tradition that was hegemonical and given to chaperonage. This is completely false. Even when you asked for his advice, sometimes with anger or irritation, half the time he would merely smile, close his lips obstinately, and then tell you to go about your work. In the few instances where he broke this rule, as in the case of Wolfe, it was because he had been begged to do so and without his collaboration there would have been no author and no book. He played Pygmalion with reluctance and when he did, like most Pygmalions, he lived to regret it.

I was very close to the Wolfe incident. I first met Tom on the eve of the publication of "Look Homeward, Angel," and it was much like meeting a chorus of archangels in full jubilation. I was with Jim Boyd, who knew Tom already, and my wife; two writers who could not have been more unlike Tom both in their fine, acute, defining personalities and in their work. The meeting place was a Russian restaurant somewhere down on Second Avenue, and around half-past ten Tom came in, making his way like a behemoth between the tables. He was exhausted with joy and fulfilment, and I remember that to my amazement he ate three club sandwiches–huge, skyscraper, topheavy things–in rapid succession, remarking that he had dined at seven and "was hungry." He was very sweet. There was no getting away from Tom's unearthy sweetness and naïveté. Also, for three hours nothing was mentioned but Tom Wolfe and "Look Homeward, Angel." It is an experience to watch an elemental force eat club sandwiches with mayonnaise.

I was in New York several years later when Tom was living in Brooklyn because "it was the only place in the United States where you could be hidden and lonely." "Of Time and the River" was in process of gestation. I would meet Tom and Max around eleven o'clock at the Chatham Walk of the Hotel Chatham in Manhattan. I will not forget the languid air and the languid smells in which the street lights and the lamps of the café floated like round electric fish in the depths of a tropic ocean. Tom would come striding in like a giant who has dined well on human flesh but always a little cross and pettish with the childish crossness of a giant. Behind him would be Max, white and utterly exhausted. Max was of average height, but he looked small on those hot June nights and sparse like a drypoint etching. Every night for weeks Max and Tom had been working over in Brooklyn. Max would persuade Tom to leave five thousand words out of a new chapter. Tom would consent. Between them they would delete. The next day Tom would turn up with ten thousand new words.

Tom would leave Chatham Walk at midnight and go back to Brooklyn and write until morning. Sometimes he could not wait until Scribner's opened its doors but would cross back to New York in the dawn and sit waiting on Scribner's steps.

No better simile occurs to me to describe Max Perkins's influence than the ancient, unformulated, theory of tutorial instruction as exemplified by the great universities of Oxford and Cambridge. You are assigned a tutor. He is assumed to be a learned and pleasant man and usually is. Once a week you meet him, as a rule at teatime. He does not exhort you, he does not command you, he does not bottlefeed you. You are supposed to do your own work and to discover how work is done; in other words, you do original research. If you are lazy or a malingerer or ignorant you bore him. After a while if you have any pride at all you are ashamed to bore him and spoil a pleasant and profitable hour. And so you learn the methods and the rewards and joys of knowledge. . . .

. . . Max had a curiously humble opinion concerning the relative unimportance of editors. He was constantly begging authors not to overvalue what he said, not to rely upon him, to stick to their own ideas. This theme runs through his letters and was paramount in his conversation.

I vehemently disagree. I can imagine a great literature without a great public but I cannot conceive of a great literature without great editing. An author in actuality is a pitiful, woebegone creature. An author has no great store of firm convictions; if he had he wouldn't be an author but a banker or something else that requires only unilateral thinking. An author is an aeolian harp whose strings need constant retuning. And he cannot do it himself because he lacks self-criticism. His legs of self-esteem are wobbly. What conceit he has, and sometimes it appears to be atrocious, is shot full of holes and constantly gnawed by the rats of midnight self-depreciation. He is easily upset and all too ready for damnation. When you have poor or mean or venal editing, as you have so much of at present, you haven't authors; you have clever trapeze artists or trained anthropoids lazily content with a plentitude of bananas. It is so easy for the talented to use their gifts cheaply when deprived of pride in their work.

By all he did and accomplished Max Perkins contradicted his own theory and emphasized the need and power and subtle radiations of greatness.

Dust jackets for 1939 and 1945 volumes that excerpt poetical passages from Wolfe's writings (courtesy of Special Collections, Thomas Cooper Library, University of South Carolina)

Critic Malcolm Cowley's essay on Wolfe includes a discussion of his poetic style.

Thomas Wolfe
Malcolm Cowley
Atlantic Monthly, 200 (November 1957): 202–212

Poetry of a traditional sort can be written faster than prose, and Wolfe kept falling into traditional poetry. His books, especially *Of Time and the River,* are full of lines in Elizabethan blank verse:

> Were not their howls far broken by the wind?

> huge limbs that stiffly creak in the remote demented howlings of the burly wind,

> and something creaking in the wind at night.

Page after page falls into an iambic pattern, usually a mixture of pentameters and hexameters. Other passages–in fact there is a whole book of them called *A Stone, A Leaf, A Door,* selected from Wolfe's writing by John S. Barnes–are a rather simple kind of cadenced verse:

> Naked and alone we came into exile.
> In her dark womb
> We did not know our mother's face.

Often there are internal rhymes and half-rhymes: "October is the season for *returning:* the bowels of youth are *yearning* with lost love. Their mouths are *dry* and better with *desire:* their hearts are *torn* with the *thorns* of spring." Again there are phrases almost meaningless in themselves, but used as musical themes that are stated and restated with variations, sometimes through a whole novel. "A stone, a leaf, a door" is one of the phrases; others are "O lost" and "naked and alone," in *Look Homeward, Angel,* and "of wandering forever and the earth again," repeated perhaps a hundred times in *Of Time and the River.* All these patterns or devices–are those into which the language naturally falls when one is trying to speak or write it passionately and torrentially. They are not the marks of good prose–on the contrary–and yet in Wolfe's case, as in that of a few other natural writers, they are the means of achieving some admirable effects, including an epic movement with its surge and thunder. They also help Wolfe to strike and maintain a *tone,* one that gives his work a unity lacking in its structure, a declamatory tone that he needs for his effort to dignify a new race of heroes and demigods, to suffuse a new countryside with legend, and to bring new subjects into the charmed circle of those considered worthy to be treated in epic poems.

Cyril Connolly (1903–1974) was an influential English critic. His high opinion of Wolfe is noteworthy in view of the circumstance that Wolfe's reputation in England is not strong.

Thomas Wolfe
Cyril Connolly
Previous Convictions
(London: Hamilton, 1963), pp. 308–312

If the greatest art partakes of the condition of music, then the greatest critic is a musical critic, and his greatness is in his freedom, and his freedom is freedom from autobiography. No one can write his autobiography in music, and if he does we can pretend it is something else; but in literature there is no getting away.

I could inflict on you every word, thought, idea, feeling about myself and the people I have met in the last five years and call it a novel and you would have to read it. This tyrannical egotism, which is really neurosis, can hire the uniform of genius and borrow Joyce's cock-eyed crown. 'Oh boy, you are fine. There is no atom in you that is not fine. A glory and a chrism of bright genius rest upon you. God bless you: the world is yours.'

'I have at last discovered my own America, I believe I have found my language. I think I know my way. And I shall wreak out my vision of this life, this way, this world, and this America, to the top of my bent and to the height of my ability but with an unswerving devotion, integrity and purity of purpose that shall not be menaced, altered or weakened by anyone.'

Admittedly Thomas Wolfe is writing to his publisher, and they are gluttons for verbal beefcake, but the language is strangely like Hitler's. Why bring in America always? And who are these enemies who wish to menace, alter or weaken him? Right first time. The critics.

Not the critics one values, the constructive who praise but the sterile, the dead–the Hemingways, Fadimans, etc., who find fault. Expatriates! Waste-landers! 'Their idea of helping you is to kick you in the face.' 'A writer is an open target for anyone in the world who wants to throw a rotten egg.' 'I have been shy and silent before these liars and fools far too long. I have eaten crow and swallowed my pride for ten years before the waste-landers, the lost generations, the biter-bitters, the futility people, and all other cheap literary fakes–but now I will hold my tongue no longer: I know what I know and I have learned it with blood and sweat. . . .' And so they are all put into the gaschamber of Thomas Wolfe's novels.

KETTI FRINGS

LOOK HOMEWARD, ANGEL

A PLAY

Based on the Novel by THOMAS WOLFE

WITH AN INTRODUCTION BY EDWARD C. ASWELL

Charles Scribner's Sons, New York

Title page and photograph of set designed by Jo Mielziner for Ketti Frings's 1958 play, which won the Pulitzer Prize

I should like to say more about these novels for they belong to my youth and I remember them coming out as one remembers the sullen explosions from a quarry on some long-distant summer noontide as we sat tippling on the lawn: 'It must be twelve o'clock. They're blasting again.'

This time I have really tried to read one and I can say with all my heart: this man is not a novelist; he is an obsessional neurotic with a gift for words who should write only about himself and who cannot create other people. He is the Benjamin Robert Haydon of American literature beside whom Dreiser is a dainty Benvenuto Cellini. He is hypnotised by the growth of his own personality and by the search for a spiritual father, a hormone who will accelerate the manic urge still further.

To be looking for a father is a wonderful excuse for dropping people, and Wolfe took advantage of this to the full. Although the climax in his short life seems to have been the 'break with Scribners' or the shedding of the faithful pilot, Maxwell Perkins, my own experience as a much-dropped, deposed, dethroned, decapitated father figure, a wandering Wotan, is that the father invariably does the dropping first in so far as he senses the mist of total obscurity or the hideous alpine glow of success that is gathering round his prodigy and I think that Maxwell Perkins must have failed to conceal his apprehension, both as a publisher and a friend, about the ponderous, paranoid, turgid flow of the Wolfe novels as the lonely giant, at grips with his enormous task of holding back absolutely nothing, emerged from solitude, every few minutes, to complain about some utterly unimportant word or criticism or well-meant piece of advice. 'I don't think he *consciously* wants me to fail or come to grief,' wrote Wolfe, 'but it's almost as if *unconsciously,* by some kind of *wishful* desire, he wants me to come to grief, as a kind of sop to his pride and his unyielding conviction that he is right in everything.'

Intimate, impressive and exemplary as was his relationship with Perkins, it was thereby doomed, while the tie with Frere of Heinemanns, cooler because there was no compulsion here to justify and explain himself, less love and so less resentment, is an admirable testimony to the unassuming loyalty and understanding which he received from the older man. With Frere he could discuss beer and chophouses, with Perkins he *must* discuss his soul. Frere he called more than a publisher, a friend; Perkins was more than a friend, a father, so that it is typical that after the bitter quarrel the last deeply-moving deathbed letter should have been to him when he looked back on their meeting on a roofgarden after the success of his book– 'and all the strangeness and the glory and the power of life and of the city was below.'

The king of father-chasers and prince of autobiographers was Joyce, and this similiarity of purpose (fulfilment of genius through finding of father) united Wolfe to the great exile, with fatal detriment to his style. These echoes are apparent throughout *Look Homeward, Angel,* which mews with self-pity and Celtic twilight:

> He saw a brief, forgotten gesture, her white broad forehead, a ghost of old grief in her eyes. Ben Gant–their strange lost voices. Their sad laughter. They swam toward him through green walls of fantasy. They caught and twisted at his heart. The green ghost-glimmer of their faces coiled away. Lost. Lost.
>
> 'Let's go for a smoke,' said Max Isaacs.

The high spirits, clowning and parodying, the scenes of broken-down family life are Joycean too. I have said I do not think Wolfe was a genius, nor am I sure he was a novelist; but in these *Selected Letters* he stands out as a fascinating writer. In his letters he could permit his egotism full rein. He made copies of his best letters or else did not send them or else got them back; he gloried in the fluent medium.

As he was a large and violent young man things were constantly happening to him. There was a terrible beating-up in Munich, an encounter with Joyce on the battlefield of Waterloo. The editor of the letters does not seem aware that the account of the 'musey-room' at Waterloo forms one of the key passages of *Finnegans Wake,* and that Wolfe (chagrined at not being recognised) was present at one of the most fortunate fertilisations of modern literature.

Inexcusable I find the omission, in the edition prepared for this country, of Wolfe's most interesting letter (unsent naturally), in which he describes at great length a devastating encounter with Scott Fitzgerald at the Ritz in Paris in 1930. Here this huge, ramshackle, shy, deep, good, suspicious and resentful young man, who looks like a genius and has nothing but talent, meets the older but not very fatherly little dandy, drunk and at the height of his success, who tries to launch Wolfe on Franco-American society. 'Every writer,' Fitzgerald tells him, 'is a social climber.' Wolfe rebuts the charge splendidly, but it is, all the same, in the little man from Princeton for all his snobbery and air of talent that the genius resides. Their subsequent Zola-Flaubert arguments are all coloured by this episode.

Suppose Wolfe had lived (for his death was inadvertent): at his present age (fifty-seven) he would have been an enormous figure in American literature. His driving energy, his egotism, the basic strength and rightness of his values both as an artist and a man would have seared away the blindness and the rhetoric; he would have come to terms with his persecution mania for he could never have dried up or become a spent ranter.

His prose would have been worthy of the poetical force beneath it, his absurd rocketry about great America, decadent Europe and so on been chastened by failures–the bull blundering about after critics' capes would have learnt wisdom. He would have been the Whitman of the Beat Generation, of course–and of many others–instead of the Thinking Bull. 'Why is it that we are burnt out to an empty shell by the time we are forty. . . . Is it because we take a young man of talent–a young man proud of spirit, and a thirst for glory, and full with the urge to make his life prevail–praise him up to the skies at first, and then press in upon him from all sides with cynics' eyes and scornful faces, asking him if he can *ever do it again* or is done for, finished?'

. . . I enjoyed *Look Homeward, Angel* when I read it at the age of twenty-two or so. I read the novels in the order they were written, and lost enthusiasm before I reached the end of *You Can't Go Home Again.* I have not dipped into any of the books since, nor have I found myself wishing that Wolfe had lived longer so that I might have more of his work to read. I outgrew him, perhaps. This is a lazily borrowed opinion. Almost everybody I talk to about Wolfe says in one way or another that he wrote masterpieces for eighteen-year-olds, but that he was soon outgrown.

I met a Swedish critic at a party recently, though, who woke me up some with this opinion: "If Wolfe had lived through the war and its aftermath, he might have been your Tolstoy." I found myself believing that there might be something to this. He really might have given up enormous books about all levels of humanity, and scorned the crippling advice that Maxwell Perkins gave him, to the effect that his theme should always be a young man's search for a worthy father.

It is my opinion, incidentally, that civilizations are built mainly on masterpieces that stun eighteen-year-olds.

–Kurt Vonnegut,
Letter to The Thomas Wolfe Review, *Fall 1979*

Novelist William Styron observed, "Wolfe wrote many a bad sentence but never a dull one." He concludes that Wolfe earned "a flawed but undeniable greatness" for his ability to render "the clear glimpses he had at certain moments of man as a strange, suffering animal alone beneath the blazing and indifferent stars."

The Shade of Thomas Wolfe

William Styron
Harper's Magazine, 236 (April 1968): 96, 98, 100–101, 104

. . . Rereading Wolfe is like visiting again a cherished landscape or town of bygone years where one is simultaneously moved that much could remain so appealingly the same and wonderstruck that one could ever have thought that such-and-such a corner or this or that view had any charm at all. It is not really that Wolfe is dated (I mean the fact of being dated as having to do with basically insincere postures and attitudes: already a lot of Hemingway is dated in a way Wolfe could never be); it is rather that when we now begin to realize how unpulled-together Wolfe's work really is–that same shapelessness that mattered so little to us when we were younger–and how this shapelessness causes or at least allows for a lack of inner dramatic tension without which no writer, not even Proust, can engage our mature attention for long, we see that he is simply telling us, often rather badly, things we no longer care about knowing or need to know. So much that once seemed grand and authoritative now comes off as merely obtrusive, strenuously willed, and superfluous. Which of course makes it all the more disturbing that in the midst of this chaotically verbose and sprawling world there stand out here and there truly remarkable edifices of imaginative cohesion.

. . . .

It is when we run into *Of Time and the River* and its elephantine successors, *The Web and the Rock* and *You Can't Go Home Again,* that the real trouble begins. One of the crucial struggles that any writer of significance has had to endure is his involvement in the search for a meaningful theme, and Wolfe was no exception. The evidence is that Wolfe, though superbly gifted at imaginative projection, was practically incapable of extended dramatic invention, his creative process being akin to the setting into motion of some marvelous mnemonic tape recorder deep within his cerebrum, from which he unspooled reel after reel of the murmurous, living past. Such a technique served him beautifully in *Look Homeward, Angel,* unified as it was in time and space and from both of which it derived its dramatic tension; but in the later works as Tom-Eugene-George moved into other environments–the ambience of Harvard and New York and, later, of Europe–the theme which at first had been so fresh and compelling lost its wings and the narrator became a solipsistic groundling. Certainly the last three books are still well worth reading; there is still the powerful, inexorable rush of language, a Niagara of words astonishing simply by virtue of its primal energy; many of the great set pieces hold up with their original force: old Gant's death, the *Oktoberfest* sequence in Munich, the apartment-house fire in New York, the portraits of Eugene's Uncle Bascom, Foxhall Edwards, the drunken Dr. McGuire–there are many more. These scenes and characterizations would alone guarantee Wolfe a kind of permanence, even if one must sift through a lot of detritus to find them. But there is so much now that palls and irritates. That furrow-browed, earnest sense of discovery in which the reader participates willingly in *Look Homeward, Angel* loses a great deal of its vivacity when the same protagonist has begun to pass into adulthood.

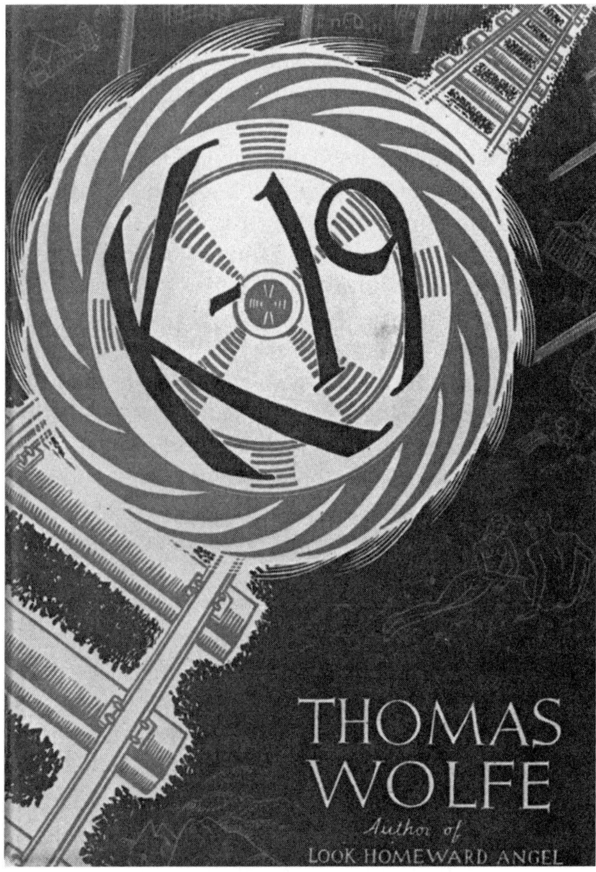

Front cover for the 1983 edition of the book that C. Hugh Holman argues should have been published in 1932

C. Hugh Holman (1914–1981), professor of English at the University of North Carolina at Chapel Hill, was an influential Wolfe scholar. He became convinced that Wolfe's natural form was the novella, but that Perkins deflected Wolfe from developing his work in this genre by pressuring him to write long novels.

The Dwarf on Wolfe's Shoulder

C. H. Holman

Southern Review (April 1977): 240–242

Holman argues that the underlying reason for Wolfe's break with Perkins was the author's resentment over what he regarded as Perkins's premature decision to call a halt to Wolfe's efforts to perfect Of Time and the River.

. . . That Wolfe was unhappy with the result of this editorial collaboration he made painfully clear in his correspondence about the book. In a letter to Perkins in March, 1935, after seeing his first copy of the book, he wrote: ". . . as I told you many times. I did not care whether the final length of the book was 300, 500, or a 1000 pages, so long as I had realized completely and finally my full intention–and that was not realized. I still sweat with anguish–with a sense of irremediable loss–at the thought of what another six months would have done to that book." Perkins had known well before publication that Wolfe did not approve of what had been done to the book. In January 1935, when he learned that the book was being dedicated to him, he wrote: ". . . you cannot, and should not, try to change your conviction that I have deformed your book, or at least prevented it from coming to perfection. It is therefore impossible for you sincerely to dedicate it to me, and it ought not to be done . . . what I have done has destroyed *your* belief in it [*Of Time and the River*] and you must not act inconsistently with that fact." The many factors that entered into this discontent were exacerbated by a series of events and libel suits which occurred between the publication of *Of Time and the River* and Wolfe's final break with Scribner's in the late fall of 1937 when he signed a contract with Edward Aswell for the future publication of his work by Harper and Brothers. Among the reasons Wolfe stated for the break were Perkins' unwillingness to allow him to express fully what he believed to be his Marxist sentiments, Perkins' unwillingness to allow him to publish in the order that he chose, and, in general, Perkins' control of the nature and shape of his work. But behind it all there lingers the sense of frustration and angry bitterness expressed in Wolfe's long, long letter in the spring of 1935, when he read his first copy of *Of Time and the River* and declared that he could have made it a better book if he had had the chance to do so. Thus ended an editor-author relationship but without ending the strong personal feeling of deep affection and friendship between the two men, a feeling which resulted in Wolfe's last written words being a letter to Perkins and in Perkins's being appointed literary executor for the Wolfe estate.

. . . .

Holman claims that Perkins did not fully realize the power he had to influence Wolfe's artistic decisions.

At no point in Wolfe's career did he have the full courage of his artistic convictions, and certainly not when he had to pit what he took to be his ignorance against Perkins' knowledge and grace. He did his work with a kind of romantic self-expression, and the test which he applied to it was its seeming rightness to him. The ability to analyze deeply the intricate interrelationships of his work seems not to have been a part of his aesthetic or artistic equipment. Yet he had, too, an awareness of the special genius which was his.

. . . .

Andrew Turnbull reports that Maxwell Perkins once told his wife that "he would like to be a little dwarf on the shoulders of a great general, advising him what to do and what not to do without anyone's noticing." As the most famous and successful literary editor of his generation, Maxwell Perkins in a sense achieved that role. Hemingway, who seems to have recognized this quality in his editor, remarked after the deaths of Wolfe and Fitzgerald, "You realize you're through, don't you? All your generals are dead." And indeed these three–Hemingway, Fitzgerald, and Wolfe–were generals, the shape of whose careers Maxwell Perkins saw himself as significantly shaping. These writers had enormous talent, and Perkins built his career and a revitalized position for Charles Scribner's Sons out of what he was able to do with this potential.

. . . .

Yet almost certainly Maxwell Perkins did not understand Thomas Wolfe, however well he knew and however much he loved him. To imagine Perkins or anyone else persuading Hemingway to do anything contrary to Hemingway's own sense of artistic propriety is almost ridiculous. Perkins once said, "Nobody ever edited Hemingway, beyond excising a line or two," and much the same was true of Fitzgerald. There seems every reason to believe that Perkins made a few distinctions in regard to this quality in his "three generals." The suggestions he made to Wolfe for deletions, changes, or modifications in Wolfe's manuscripts initially resulted in explosions that were almost violent, but almost always Wolfe returned in a day or two and made the changes that Perkins had proposed. That this represented Wolfe's basic lack of confidence in his own artistic judgment rather than his having given careful consideration to the matter and coming to agree with Perkins' judgment seems never to have occurred to Perkins. The result was that Perkins continued through the crucial years of Wolfe's career to sit as the dwarf on this general's shoulder, directing the deployment of one of the massive talents which America has produced, almost certainly without realizing the full extent to which that deployment represented a distortion.

. . . .

The issue here is very plainly one of the difference between form and material. After *Look Homeward, Angel* Wolfe seemingly was able to deal with emotions in elaborate prose poems and remembered incidents in self-contained dramatic short stories and short novels, and to depend ultimately upon some controlling frame for the places where they would finally fall in his total work. This does not mean that they needed to be fitted into some such controlling frame before they were published, and it is upon the rock of that fact that the charting of the course which Perkins made for Wolfe finally came seriously aground. In 1932 Wolfe wished to publish a fragment of the total work under the title *K-19,* an account of a long train ride to Altamont. It was to have been his second book, and Perkins and Scribner's agreed with him that it would be published in this form. It was actually put into production and announced, and salesmen's dummies of *K-19* were prepared and used by Scribner's salesmen: one such dummy still exists in the Thomas Wolfe Collection in the Pack Memorial Library in Asheville, North Carolina. Then Perkins decided that *K-19*–not a great work, it must be admitted–should not be the one with which Wolfe would follow the great critical success of *Look Homeward, Angel,* although that novel was not a tremendous success in the marketplace, selling only 12,000 copies during its first year. When Wolfe was making the fatal break with Perkins in 1937, this matter came very forcefully to Perkins' mind, and in his letter in response to Wolfe's twenty-eight-page diatribe, he said: "And as for publishing what you like, or being prevented from it, apart from the limitations of space, you have not been, intentionally. Are you thinking of *'K-19'*? We would have published it if you had said to do it. At the time, I said to Jack [Wheelock]: 'Maybe it's the way Tom is. Maybe we should just publish him as he comes and in the end it will be all right.'" Perkins once planned to issue the short novel *No Door* in book form in 1933, but later decided against it. The next work which Wolfe wished to publish was a collection of his short works which would have included *A Portrait of Bascom Hawke, The Web of Earth,* and one other short novel. This work, too, was originally agreed to by Perkins and then withdrawn. Had this volume been published, it would have been, like *K-19* and *No Door* in 1933, and *Bascom Hawke* and *The Web of Earth* in 1934, probably Pentland material in *Of Time and the River* impossible, but it would have presented to the public a different Wolfe, one working in brief and reasonably self-contained units of the sort which he had regularly published.

Imagine that Wolfe's career after 1929 had included *K-19* in 1932, *No Door* in 1933, and *Bascom Hawke* and *The Web of Earth* in 1934 probably the projected Hudson River people book in 1935, and then *The Good Child,* dealing with Esther Jack's life, in 1936. These would have been relatively short books, more self-controlled and objective than *Of Time and the River,* and they would have reflected the way in which Wolfe normally thought and wrote. Had this happened, the expectations which were gallingly present and pressing in upon him with spiritually destructive force in *The Story of a Novel* would not have been there. The image of the vastly prolific writer who lacks a sense of form or control would hardly have appeared, and the shape of his career would have been radically different. It would have been that of a man whose work is of a piece but which appears in various parts at different times, with no necessary chronology to the order of its presentation nor consistency in the generic form in which it appears.

But Perkins, not Wolfe, made the decision and Perkins' decision was quite different. It was that Wolfe must follow *Look Homeward, Angel* with a large book in which the materials find somehow some vast controlling organization; that they must not be about David Hawke or John Hawke or Joe Doaks but about Eugene Gant; that, although most of the parts had been written in the first person, they must be converted to third person in order to be consistent with *Look Homeward, Angel;* and that some vast structure or controlling overarching organization must be found. Wolfe's letters during this period are a record of his endless and agonizing struggle to find such an organization, whether it be in mythology, in history, or in something else, and *Of Time and the River* is truly a cooperative effort in which the editor gives much of the large shape and the author gives the parts. The attack of Bernard DeVoto is cruel primarily because it is painfully accurate. The difficulty, however, in DeVoto's attack is that he is attacking the wrong person. He is attacking Wolfe rather than Perkins, though it must be acknowledged that ultimately a basic part of talent is the ability, willingness, and toughmindedness necessary to use it.

There can be no question of Perkins' view of Wolfe. He loved him as a man, misunderstood him as a person, found him strange, eccentric, and rather frightening, and admired his talent just this side of idolatry. He said after Wolfe's death, "He was wrestling as no artist in Europe would have to wrestle with the material of literature–a great country not yet revealed to its people. . . . It was this struggle that in the large sense governed all that he did." The estimate is remarkably accurate, but Perkins seemed not to have understood that that struggle which governed all Wolfe did, did not have to determine how he did it. And it was for the best intentions in the world that Perkins, sitting as a dwarf on the shoulder of his giant, directed his struggle into the paths which he thought best and did not let that struggle take its own necessary shape.

Dust jacket for a novel Wolfe wrote in the mid 1930s, published by the University of North Carolina Press in 1991

The provincial boy from the North Carolina mountains was in this particular conflict no match for the urbane New York editor who sat on his shoulder and directed his finest talents to a vast battlefield not properly shaped for them. The results seems to me to be almost tragic, but it is a tragedy created by Wolfe's lack of artistic self-confidence.

The debate over Wolfe's structural ability and the role of his editor was reopened when John Halberstadt's "The Making of Thomas Wolfe's Posthumous Novels" in the Yale Review *attracted attention by charging that Aswell's work on* The Web and the Rock *and especially* You Can't Go Home Again *had exceeded the proper responsibilities of an editor to become unacknowledged collaborations. Although Aswell's participation in the publishing process had been widely known, the extent of his involvement had not been recognized as having been as extensive as claimed by Halberstadt. His alleged discovery was reported in* The New York Review of Books *and* Village Voice.

Richard S. Kennedy, who had studied the composition and publication of The Web and the Rock *and* You Can't Go Home Again *in* The Window of Memory: The Literary Career of Thomas Wolfe *(1962), replied that Halberstadt's charges were false or distorted. Kennedy's "The Wolfegate Affair" in* Harvard Magazine *(1981) resulted in published exchanges between Halberstadt and Kennedy.*

The Making of Thomas Wolfe's Posthumous Novels
John Halberstadt
Yale Review, 70 (Autumn 1980): 70–94

. . . Aswell's immediate difficulty was the circumvention of Wolfe's contract prohibiting "changes, additions, and alterations." He turned for advice to Maxwell Perkins, who had become the estate's literary executor, and together they devised a remarkable solution.

They discovered another clause in the contract which could be construed to contradict the "no changes" clause: "The AUTHOR agrees to deliver to the publisher on or before the first day of January 1939 a complete copy of said work in its final form of which the minimum length shall be 100,000 words and the maximum length 750,000 words." Aswell and Perkins reasoned that since Wolfe's manuscript contained at least a million words (by my estimate, it is closer to one and a quarter million words), and since Harper and Brothers had agreed to publish no more than 750,000 words, Aswell could legitimately "omit as many as 250,000 words," as Perkins put it. However, Perkins insisted with amusing strictness, Aswell did not have the right to perform any "detailed editing" because the contract expressly forbade "changes." Thus Perkins and Aswell read the contract as prohibiting minor changes but permitting wholesale cuts.

. . . .

In the end, then, Aswell created new chapters by collaging useful passages–and even passing phrases–from several chapters; he changed the order of Wolfe's original chapters; he cut material at will; and he wrote wholly new material to weave the various pieces into a single narrative. He had the printer set all this into galleys, but he was a little anxious, he wrote Perkins in the spring of 1939, about letting reviewers inspect them:

> Because of the changes we had to make in the names of certain characters, as well as other changes designed to minimize the danger of libel, we have been very careful about distributing the uncorrected galley proofs to critics and others who have wanted to see them. In fact, we have allowed none of the uncorrected proofs to go out to anyone except the Book-of-the-Month-Club. It will obviously be desirable not to have reviewers know about these changes, because some of them, no doubt, would jump to the conclusion that, if we could change certain things, we could also change others, and that we probably did, and this might lead to some speculation as to how much of the work was really Tom's and how much was the work of some alien hand. All of this, of course, is pretty far-fetched. . . .

Aswell published *The Web and the Rock* in June of 1939 with no acknowledgment of his own contributions to it.

He then returned to his desk, a veteran, in order to create the second posthumous novel, *You Can't Go Home Again,* which appeared in 1940. Again he cut

In the Shadow of the Giant: Thomas Wolfe

Correspondence of Edward C. Aswell and Elizabeth Nowell, 1949-1958

Edited by Mary Aswell Doll and Clara Stites

*

Dust jacket for a 1988 book of letters between Wolfe's last editor and his agent

chapters (about twenty in this case), collaged others, scrambled the sequence, wrote original connective passages. But this time Aswell used his collage technique to create new characters as well. For example, he created "Tim Wagner" by combining the character of Tim Weaver, a millionaire turned town sot, whom he had discovered in an early portion of Wolfe's manuscript, with the character of Rufus Mears, a cocaine addict turned real estate oracle, whom he found in a later portion of the manuscript. Aswell's "Tim Wagner," of course, is a town sot turned real estate oracle.

He created "Randy Shepperton" in the same fashion. The name came from a boyhood acquaintance of the hero in *The Web and the Rock*. Wolfe had not, however, written a word about Randy as an adult. Aswell invented the character himself by combining two young salesmen, an older literary executor, and perhaps still other characters.

Aswell felt he had only one book left, which he titled *The Hills Beyond*. He produced it by making an anthology of an unfinished group of chapters he had cut from the introduction of the manuscript and publishing them as a short novel, to which he attached sketches cut from various portions of the manuscript.

At the end of *The Hills Beyond,* which came out in 1941, Aswell appended a lengthy essay called "A Note on Thomas Wolfe" in which he skillfully left the impression that Wolfe had given him a manuscript so coherent that one could cut "reams" from it–"Whole chunks and reams . . . came out," Aswell admitted–and what remained would still fit together like a "jigsaw puzzle." Perhaps recalling the construction that he and Perkins had given Wolfe's contract, he added that "small cutting" of the manuscript was "often impossible."

He admitted writing "a few paragraphs" of the posthumous novels himself, but these paragraphs were all "printed in italics." This admission, which was so deeply buried in his postscript that even careful readers could miss its significance, proved to be deceptive: not only had Aswell written these italicized connective passages, some of them running two or three pages in length, but hundreds of other passages in the manuscript as well are marked with his writing or rewriting.

. . . .

It would set the record straight if an essay describing the general contents of Wolfe's original manuscript were prepared as a preface to an anthology of its sketches and short novels–for the fact remains that many of Wolfe's writings have never been published at all. They are lost in the poundage of those million and a quarter words. Only when such a detailed account of the manuscript is available–or, indeed, when the manuscript itself is published as part of his "working papers" –will readers and critics be able to distinguish the voice of Wolfe from the voice of Edward Aswell, the vision of Wolfe from the editorial administration of Aswell. The *words* of Wolfe's three posthumous works–most of them, anyway–were written by Wolfe. But the *books* were made by Aswell. He was the dominant contributor to the books that bore Wolfe's name; Wolfe himself was mainly a supplier of raw materials. Although Aswell may have felt he was rescuing three accessible novels from Wolfe's manuscript, he might have been wiser to publish them, as Elizabeth Nowell once wished, as a great "notebook." Certainly the service would have been every bit as great if Aswell had acknowledged exactly what his contributions to the final products had been (although the income to Harper and Brothers, we may presume, would have been substantially less). That leaves us with two questions.

The first one I raised a moment ago. How is the critic supposed to know who Thomas Wolfe really was if the words and intentions and visions attributed to him are really the work of his editors? To what extent is the Thomas Wolfe we know a creation of Edward Aswell? And that, of course, brings us to a crucial ethical question. Grant that many authors have benefitted from and even depended upon the ruthless editing of a friend or publisher. Ezra Pound's trimming of Eliot's *Waste Land* comes to mind, as, of course, does Maxwell Perkins's work with Thomas Wolfe. But these are collaborations between active editors and living authors, and if the terms of the collaboration are sometimes stretched, as Wolfe thought was the case with Perkins, at least the author is there to declare whether the resultant work will bear his or her name. In the case of posthumous editing, of course, this basic condition does not exist. Aswell's editing not only violated the spirit (if not the letter) of Wolfe's contract with Harper and Brothers, but also fundamentally changed the character of Wolfe's work. Does an editor or publisher have the right to make such posthumous changes–even if they genuinely improve the manuscript–and then represent them to the public as the work of the original author? I think the answer to that question is no: an editor's responsibility to a dead author, to that author's reading public, and to generations of critics and scholars to follow is to declare as precisely as possible what editorial liberties have been taken.

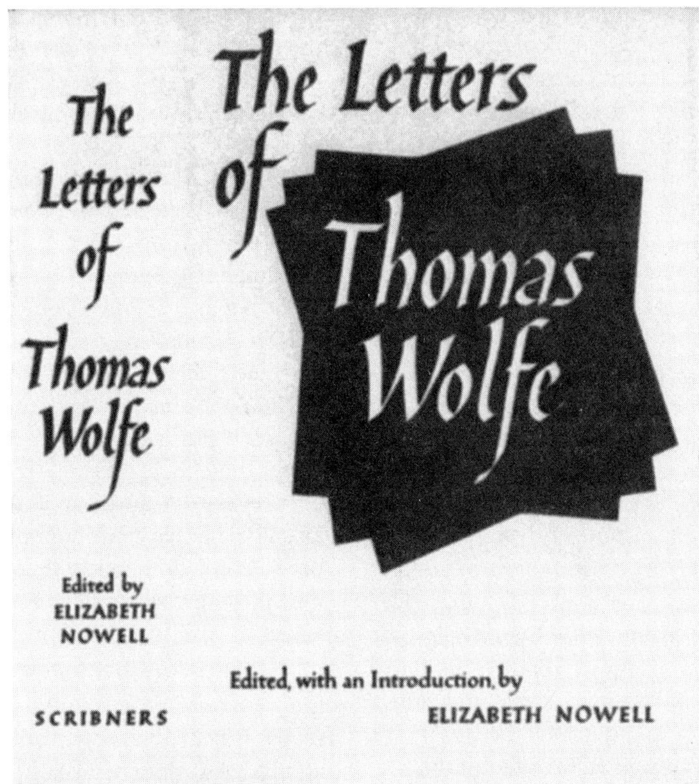

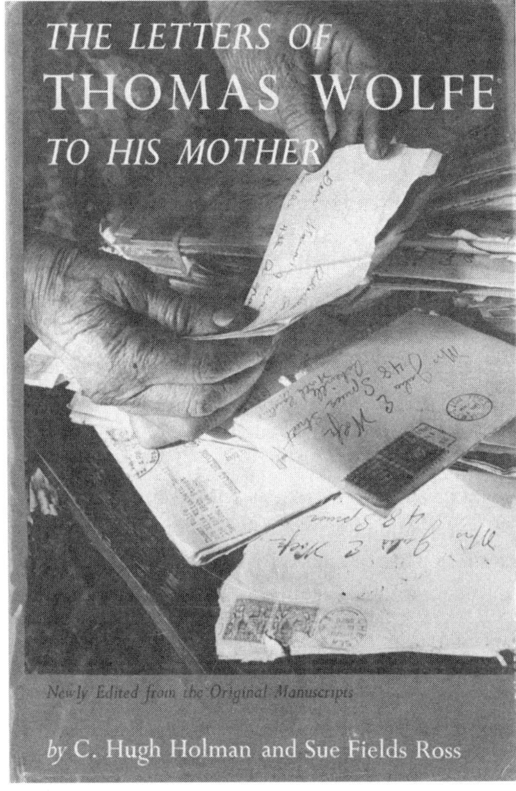

Editions of Wolfe's letters (top, 1956; bottom, 1968 and 1983)

Dust jacket for the 1987 collection published by Scribners

Wolfe places us where we all, critics included, secretly wish to be; beyond criticism at the center of our lives, called there by words beyond the narrowness of academic judgement. Our lives and all their million particulars and possibilities are around us at every second. All we need to do is to feel what we actually feel, and go with it where it takes us, to the lowest depths of despair and hopelessness or to the heights of whatever heights there are. The risk is great, but as another writer, D. H. Lawrence, said, "I will show you how not to be a dead man in life." Wolfe stands us in good stead here, in these stories as elsewhere, which tell us in bewildering and heartening plenty to open up entirely to our own experience, to possess it, to go the whole way into it and with it, to keep nothing back, to be cast on the flood.

–James Dickey, Foreword,
The Complete Stories of Thomas Wolfe

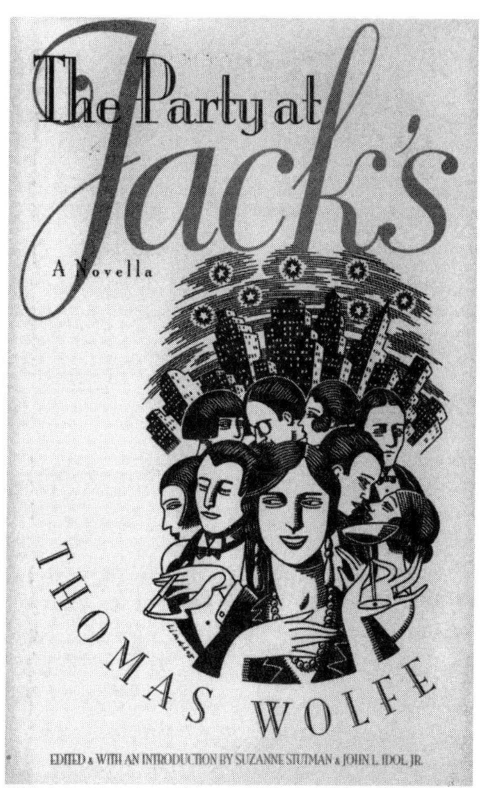

Dust jackets for editions of Wolfe's works published by The University of North Carolina Press in 1992 and 1995, respectively

Last Poem
Brooklyn (1934)

Oh, will you ever return to me,
my wild first force, will you return
When the old madness comes to
blacken in me and to burn
Slow in my brain like a slow fire
in a blackened brazier - dull
like a smear of blood,
Humid and hot and evil, slow-sweltering
up in a flood!
Oh, will you not come back again - will
you not come back, my fierce song?
Jubilant and exultant, triumphing over
the huge wrong
Of that slow fire of madness that feeds
on me - the slow mad blood
Think with its hate and evil, sweltering
up in its flood!
Oh! will you not purge it from me -
my wild lost flame?
Come and restore me, save me from the
intolerable shame
Of that huge eye that eats into my
naked body constantly
And that has no name
Gazing upon me from the immense and
cruel bareness of a sky
That leaves no mercy of concealment
That gives no promise of revealment
And that drives us on forever with its
lidless eye
Across the huge and houseless level of
a planetary vacancy.

Oh, wild song and fury, fire and flame,
Lost magic of my youth, return, defend
me from this shame!
And oh! You golden vengeance of bright
song
Not cure, but answer to earth's wrong,
Give me, I beseech you, but one touch
of grace,
One atom of your magic, as to one
Who bent before your face
From his first youth, and loved you,
knew you,
Knelt in a little place before you -Oh,
immortal state
Of poetry! - Speak for one who loved
you dearly -
And who spoke too late!
And you, wild words of that wild
tongue that had no voice,
Wild cries of that wild heart that
had no tongue
Be to me aiding now with however
rude a choice
However harsh or by what anguish
wrung,
Come to me, cries that one swept from
me like a song
And songs that were torn from me like
like a cry,
Oh you music of pain and joy and
exultancy strong
You were mad, o furious and intolerable-
so was I.

Typescript with manuscript words in Perkins's hand (Princeton University Library)

Maxwell Perkins had kept his angry and abusive letters from Thomas Wolfe hidden in his desk. When Charles Scribner III (actually the fifth Charles Scribner) inherited Perkins's desk in 1983, he found an unsigned typescript clipped to a photograph of Wolfe. He could not type, but the poem has been definitely identified as by Wolfe.

Crying Wolfe

Charles Scribner III

Princeton University Library Chronicle (Spring 1984): 225, 226–227

The desk had belonged to the legendary Scribners editor, Maxwell Perkins. Before that, it had belonged to my (great-great) Uncle Arthur, youngest of the three Charles Scribner's Sons. I had "inherited" it the first day I started work (largely because the senior editor with the best claim to it complained that she ran her stockings on it). The massive Victorian oak piece had occupied the fifth-floor office on the southwest corner of 597 Fifth Avenue ever since the company's move to the building in 1913. . . .

. . . The desk had been cleaned out several times as it passed to senior editors John Hall Wheelock and Burroughs Mitchell before I, too, had the chance to fill its drawers with a mixture of official and personal business. We believed that the original contents of the desk had found their way into the company archives (now in the Princeton University Library). But several months ago, while clearing out the desk for its first move to a new office, I became irritated that one drawer would not shut completely. Something was blocking it. I removed the drawer and reached into a half-century of dust to find two crumpled sheets of paper clipped to a photograph. Not exactly buried treasure–at least not at first sight.

. . . . . .

The accompanying sheets of paper were a typescript of a poem, titled (in a very rough hand) "Last Poem," with "Brooklyn (1934)" written below the

Proposed design for postage stamp honoring Wolfe on the centenary of his birth

title. It took no literary Sherlock Holmes to deduce its authorship. Aside from the circumstantial evidence of the desk and the photo, the impassioned voice and baroque imagery were as telltale as the frenzied handwriting.

It just happened that the very next week we were to host a party for the Thomas Wolfe Society in our editorial library, where Wolfe had spent many a night sleeping on the floor (he had wanted to read all his publisher's books). What better way to welcome the society than with Wolfe's lost and last poem?

The first public reading of the poem resulted in more than good cheer. One of the guests, Professor Richard Kennedy, the noted Wolfe scholar and biographer, immediately recognized the title from an itemized list of manuscripts that Wolfe, before his final trip west, had sent to his new editor, Edward Aswell (at Harpers). One item on the list had never been accounted for: "Last Poem." For this, there had been no corresponding manuscript–until now.

Preview of new Thomas Wolfe stamp available
Paul Clark
Asheville Citizen-Times, 19 October 1999

Postal Service puts design on Web

ASHEVILLE – You can now get a sneak preview of the new 33-cent stamp honoring Asheville's own Thomas Wolfe.

The U.S. Postal Service put on its Web site a preliminary design of the stamp honoring the author of "Look Homeward, Angel." The stamp shows a pensive Wolfe, caught in an attitude of seeming reflection. His 100th birthday would have been Oct. 3, 2000.

Wolfe, whose mother had a boarding house in downtown Asheville, is the 17th writer honored in the Postal Services' Literary Arts series. His image being on a 33-cent stamp – the stamp most people use to pay bills – will bring his likeness to more than just literary types, said Wolfe biographer, Ted Mitchell.

"I've been looking at this picture all day. I just can't take my mind off of it," Mitchell, site interpreter at the Thomas Wolfe Memorial, said. "I have to get my thesaurus and start looking up adjectives. It is absolutely beautiful and a fitting and deserving tribute to Asheville's native son."

The Postal Service has not yet decided when the stamp will be issued, but authorities have indicated the first-day cancellation may be in Asheville, possibly on Wolfe's 100th birthday, said Susan Albro, customer relations coordinator at the Brevard post office.

Several people involved in the project credit Asheville physician Claude Frazier with the idea of getting Wolfe on a stamp. The Citizen-Times was unable to contact Frazier, but project organizers said Frazier began campaigning for the stamp in the late 1970s.

The Thomas Wolfe Society, an organization formed to celebrate the author's writings, took up the work in the early 1980s.

"We were just determined to get him a stamp," said society co-founder Aldo Magi of Sandusky, Ohio. "Of all the authors in America, Thomas Wolfe was certainly the most American. He couldn't say enough about America in his books. If any American author should be represented on an American stamp, it should be Thomas Wolfe."

"Wolfe finds heroic qualities in the non-celebrities," said Bob Powell, who chaired the Society's stamp committee. "He finds heroic qualities in the people who struggle the most.

"Every one of us encounters a piece of art, music or literature at that time in our lives where it changes the structure and form of our life. And for me, Wolfe was one of those rare moments."

Ironically, stamps play a central role in "The Lost Boy," the Wolfe novella that N.C. State University English professor James Clark edited. The character whom Wolfe based on his younger brother receives postage stamps as change at a candy store at Pack Square. And he was short-changed.

"The poetical fluidity of his prose, the imaginative investment of the promise of youth and the gigantic accomplishments of his memory – all those serve to make him the most courageous and understandable of the modernists," Clark said.

The stamp was designed by Michael Deas, who designed the F. Scott Fitzgerald stamp in 1996, as well as stamps commemorating Marilyn Monroe and James Dean. Other writers the Postal Service has honored in the Literary Arts Series include Ernest Hemingway, T.S. Eliot, Edith Wharton and Dorothy Parker.

Albro expects the Wolfe stamp to be just as popular.

"There are a lot of Thomas Wolfe fans out there. They'll be using those stamps," she said.

Look Homeward, Angel was my spawning ground, my birthplace, and my cradle. While reading that fabulous book, I learned that there was a connection between literature and ecstasy. I had been waiting my whole life for Wolfe to present himself to me. My writing career began the instant I finished *Look Homeward, Angel.* Thomas Wolfe taught me that the great books change you immediately and forever.

–Pat Conroy

Cover for biography published in 1997

CAPTURING A GIANT:

Selections from The Thomas Wolfe Collection of Aldo P. Magi

Above: Thomas Wolfe as a student at UNC-Chapel Hill, 1919. From the North Carolina Collection archives.

A collector of "Wolfeana" for more than 40 years, Aldo P. Magi amassed a spectacular array of artwork, books, pamphlets, photographs, and other keepsakes pertaining to North Carolina-born author Thomas Wolfe. The exhibition features items from Magi's collection which help to interpret the life and literary career of one of America's most celebrated writers.

Exhibition Dates: May 5 - September 18, 2000

North Carolina Collection Gallery
Wilson Library, UNC-Chapel Hill

Monday - Friday 9:00am - 5:00pm
Saturday 9:00am - 1:00pm
Sunday 1:00pm - 5:00pm

Guided tours offered every **Wednesday at 2:00pm** or at any time by appointment.

Call (919) 962-1172 for more information

Advertisement for an exhibition of materials amassed by a nonacademic scholar who devoted much of his life to building a major Wolfe collection

Thomas Wolfe Centenary

The hundredth anniversary of Thomas Wolfe's birth, 3 October 2000, was marked at Asheville, by the University of North Carolina at Chapel Hill (Pulpit Hill), and by the University of South Carolina. In addition to academic activities, the University of North Carolina celebrated the gift of the Aldo Magi Collection of Thomas Wolfe: a forty-year assemblage with some five thousand books, photos, artifacts, artwork, and periodicals. On Wolfe's birthday the University of South Carolina Press published the first complete edition of O Lost, *restoring some sixty thousand words cut in 1929. The Press simultaneously published* To Loot My Life Clean, *the complete correspondence of Wolfe with Perkins and others at the House of Scribner. An annotated excerpt from* O Lost*–the boys' walk from schools through Altamont–was published for University of South Carolina students. Kitti Frings's dramatization of* Look Homeward, Angel *was produced in Asheville and at the University of South Carolina.*

The centenary observances are expected to generate a reassessment of Thomas Wolfe's work and a restoration to his proper high place in American literature.

Front and back of schedule of events celebrating Wolfe's one-hundredth birthday

SEPTEMBER

Friday, SEPTEMBER 1 - Tuesday, OCTOBER 3:
"Thomas Wolfe's Angels", a Helga Bessent Photo Exhibit, at Pack Place Exhibit Hall.

Wednesday, SEPTEMBER 6, 13, 20, & 27:
7:00-9:00pm: ***Look Homeward, Angel* Class**, at Thomas Wolfe Memorial Visitor Center. Limited registration, must have copy of *Look Homeward, Angel.*

Friday, SEPTEMBER 29 - Saturday, DECEMBER 30:
Look Homeward: Douglas Gorsline Illustrates Thomas Wolfe, exhibit of drawings for the illustrated *Look Homeward, Angel*, at Asheville Art Museum. *Fee. Please call 828-253-3227 for details.

sponsored by Asheville Art Museum

Friday, SEPTEMBER 29 - Tuesday, OCTOBER 3:
Look Homeward Angel (a play by Ketti Frings), at Asheville Community Theatre. Ticket prices: adults $15 evening/$13 matinee, students $9 (with ID). Call 828-253-4931 for tickets or more information.

Friday, SEPTEMBER 29:
**Thomas Wolfe Exhibit* at Pack Memorial Library continues.
*"*Thomas Wolfe's Angels" Exhibit* at Pack Place continues.
**Douglas Gorsline Exhibit* at Asheville Art Museum continues.

5:30-7:30pm: **Opening Reception for Douglas Gorsline Exhibit**, at The Asheville Art Museum. *Fee.

8:00pm: **Opening Night of *Look Homeward Angel***, at Asheville Community Theatre. "Afterwords" with the cast following performance, Thomas Wolfe retrospective exhibit in lobby. (Student matinee preview at 9:30am). Please call 828-253-4931 for tickets. *Fee.

Saturday, SEPTEMBER 30:
**Thomas Wolfe Exhibit* at Pack Memorial Library continues.
*"*Thomas Wolfe's Angels" Exhibit* at Pack Place continues.
**Douglas Gorsline Exhibit* at Asheville Art Museum continues.

10:00am: **Children's Tour and Scavenger Hunt** in "Thomas Wolfe's Asheville." Tour begins at Thomas Wolfe Memorial Visitor Center. Registration suggested.

2:00pm & 4:00pm: **Walking Tour of "Thomas Wolfe's Asheville."** Tour begins at Thomas Wolfe Memorial Visitor Center. Registration required.

8:00pm: ***Look Homeward Angel,*** at Asheville Community Theatre. Please call 828-253-4931 for tickets. *Fee.

OCTOBER

Thomas Wolfe Exhibit at Pack Memorial Library continues.
"*Thomas Wolfe's Angels"* Exhibit at Pack Place continues.
Douglas Gorsline Exhibit at Asheville Art Museum continues.

Sunday, OCTOBER 1: Thomas Wolfe Celebration
- **Children's "Trunk" Birthday Party** (with cake and homemade ice cream), at Thomas Wolfe Memorial Visitor Center. 2:00pm.
- ***Look Homeward Angel* matinee**, at Asheville Community Theatre. 2:30pm. Call 828-253-4931 for ticket information.
- **Historic Riverside Cemetery Walking Tour.** 3:00pm. (Bus leaves Thomas Wolfe Memorial parking lot at 2:45, round-trip bus service $5.)

Monday, OCTOBER 2:
Thomas Wolfe Day at Pack Memorial Library. Dr. Matthew J. Bruccoli, Park Bucker, and other speakers. Wolfe readings with music. Please call 828-255-5203 for schedule and details.

Tuesday, OCTOBER 3: Thomas Wolfe 100th Birthday Celebration
- **Thomas Wolfe Commemorative Stamp**, First-Day Issue. Location and time TBA.
- 9:00am-5:00pm: **Thomas Wolfe 100th Birthday Party**, at Thomas Wolfe Memorial:
  - 12:00pm: Welcoming Remarks and Time Capsule presentation by Sec. Betty Ray McCain and Dr. Jeffrey Crow.
  - 1:00-2:00pm & 4:00-5:00pm: **Musical selections** from Pfeiffer University's production of the musical *Angel.*
  - 2:00-4:00pm: **Reception and Book-signing:** *O Lost* (first publication of Wolfe's original manuscript for *Look Homeward, Angel*) and *To Loot My Life Clean* (the Correspondence of Thomas Wolfe and Maxwell Perkins); book-signing by editors Matthew J. Bruccoli and Park Bucker

sponsored by Harrah's Cherokee Casino

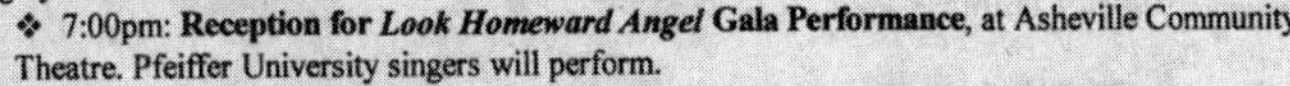

- 7:00pm: **Reception for *Look Homeward Angel* Gala Performance**, at Asheville Community Theatre. Pfeiffer University singers will perform.
- 8:00pm: **Gala Performance of *Look Homeward Angel***, at Asheville Community Theatre. Introduction by Wilma Dykeman, reading of Thomas Wolfe Centennial poem by Fred Chappell. Please call 828-253-4931 for ticket information.

sponsored by Harrah's Cherokee Casino

Dust jacket for Wolfe's first novel, edited from his manuscript and published in 2000 by the University of South Carolina Press

Books for Further Reading

Interviews:

Thomas Wolfe Interviewed, 1929–1938, edited by Aldo P. Magi and Richard Walser (Baton Rouge & London: Louisiana State University Press, 1985).

Bibliographies:

George R. Preston Jr., *Thomas Wolfe: A Bibliography* (New York: Charles S. Boesen, 1943);

Elmer D. Johnson, *Of Time and Thomas Wolfe: A Bibliography with a Character Index of His Works* (New York: Scarecrow Press, 1959);

Johnson, *Thomas Wolfe: A Checklist* (Kent, Ohio: Kent State University Press, 1970);

John S. Phillipson, *Thomas Wolfe: A Reference Guide* (Boston: G. K. Hall, 1977);

Carol Johnston, *Thomas Wolfe: A Descriptive Bibliography* (Pittsburgh: University of Pittsburgh Press, 1987);

John E. Bassett, *Thomas Wolfe: An Annotated Critical Bibliography* (Lanham, Md. & London: Scarecrow Press, 1996).

Biographies:

Agatha Boyd Adams, *Thomas Wolfe: Carolina Student, A Brief Biography* (Chapel Hill: University of North Carolina Library, 1950);

Elizabeth Nowell, *Thomas Wolfe: A Biography* (New York: Doubleday, 1960);

Andrew Turnbull, *Thomas Wolfe* (New York: Scribners, 1967);

Neal F. Austin, *A Biography of Thomas Wolfe* (Austin, Tex.: Roger Beacham, 1968);

David Herbert Donald, *Look Homeward: A Life of Thomas Wolfe* (Boston: Little, Brown, 1987).

References:

Brian F. Berger, *The Final Journey* (West Linn, Ore.: Willamette River Press, 1984);

Madeleine Boyd, *Thomas Wolfe: The Discovery of a Genius,* edited by Aldo P. Magi (N.p.: The Thomas Wolfe Society, 1981);

Ray Bradbury, *Forever and the Earth: Radio Dramatization* (Athens, Ohio: Croissant, 1984);

Richard Cooper, *Thomas Wolfe: Voice of the Mountains* (Raleigh, N.C.: Creative Productions, 1985);

Alice R. Cotton, ed. *"Always Yours, Max": Maxwell Perkins Responds to Questions About Thomas Wolfe* (N.p.: The Thomas Wolfe Society, 1997);

Mary Aswell Doll and Clara Stites, eds., *In the Shadow of the Giant: Thomas Wolfe: Correspondence of Edward C. Aswell and Elizabeth Nowell, 1949–1958* (Athens: Ohio University Press, 1958);

Elizabeth Evans, *Thomas Wolfe* (New York: Ungar, 1984);

Leslie A. Field, *Thomas Wolfe and His Editors: Establishing a True Text for the Posthumous Publications* (Norman: University of Oklahoma Press, 1987);

Field, ed. *Thomas Wolfe: Three Decades of Criticism* (New York: New York University Press, 1968);

Vardis Fisher, *Thomas Wolfe As I Knew Him* (Denver: Swallow Press, 1963);

Elaine Westall Gould, *Look Behind You, Thomas Wolfe: Ghosts of a Common Tribal Heritage* (Hicksville, N.Y.: Exposition Press, 1976);

John Chandler Griffin, *Memories of Thomas Wolfe: A Pictorial Companion to Look Homeward, Angel* (Columbia, S.C.: Summerhouse Press, 1996);

Leo Gurko, *Thomas Wolfe: Beyond the Romantic Ego* (New York: Crowell, 1975);

Margaret Mills Harper, *The Aristocracy of Art in Joyce and Wolfe* (Baton Rouge: Louisiana State University Press, 1990);

Clayton Hoagland and Kathleen Hoagland, *Thomas Wolfe Our Friend, 1933–1938,* edited by Magi and Richard Walser (Athens, Ohio: Croissant, 1979);

C. Hugh Holman, *The Loneliness at the Core: Studies in Thomas Wolfe* (Baton Rouge: Louisiana State University Press, 1975);

Holman, ed., *The World of Thomas Wolfe* (New York: Scribners, 1962);

John L. Idol Jr., *A Thomas Wolfe Companion* (Westport, Conn.: Greenwood Press, 1987);

Pamela Hansford Johnson, *Thomas Wolfe* (London: Heinemann, 1947); republished as *Hungry Gulliver: An English Critical Appraisal of Thomas Wolfe* (New York: Scribners, 1948); republished as *The Art of Thomas Wolfe* (New York: Scribners, 1963);

Carol Ingalls Johnston, *Of Time and the Artist: Thomas Wolfe, His Novels, and the Critics* (Columbia, S.C.: Camden House, 1985);

H. G. Jones, ed., *Thomas Wolfe at Eighty-seven* (Chapel Hill: North Carolina Society, 1982);

Jones, ed., *Thomas Wolfe of North Carolina* (Chapel Hill: North Carolina Society, 1982);

Richard S. Kennedy, *The Window of Memory: The Literary Career of Thomas Wolfe* (Chapel Hill: University of North Carolina Press, 1962);

Kennedy, ed., *Thomas Wolfe: A Harvard Perspective* (Athens, Ohio: Croissant, 1983);

Carole Klein, *Aline* (New York: Harper & Row, 1979);

Aldo P. Magi, *Portraits of a Novelist: Douglas Gorsline and Thomas Wolfe* (N.p.: The Thomas Wolfe Society, 1995);

Bruce R. McElderry Jr., *Thomas Wolfe* (New York: Twayne, 1964);

Ted Mitchell, *Thomas Wolfe: A Writer's Life* (Asheville, N.C.: Thomas Wolfe Memorial, 1997; revised edition, Raleigh, North Carolina Division of Archives and History, Historical Publications, 1999);

Herbert J. Muller, *Thomas Wolfe* (Norfolk: New Directions, 1947);

Hayden Norwood, *The Marble Man's Wife* (New York: Scribners, 1947);

Thomas Clark Pollock and Oscar Cargill, eds., *Thomas Wolfe at Washington Square* (New York: New York University Press, 1964);

Paschal Reeves, *Thomas Wolfe's Albatross: Race and Nationality in America* (Athens: University of Georgia Press, 1968);

Reeves, ed., *Studies in Look Homeward, Angel* (Columbus: Merril, 1970);

Reeves, ed., *Thomas Wolfe and the Glass of Time* (Athens: University of Georgia Press, 1971);

Reeves, ed., *Thomas Wolfe: The Critical Reception* (New York: D. Lewis, 1974);

Robert Reynolds, *Thomas Wolfe: Memoir of a Friendship* (Austin: University of Texas Press, 1965);

Louis D. Rubin Jr., *Thomas Wolfe: The Weather of His Youth* (Baton Rouge: Louisiana State University Press, 1955);

Rubin, ed., *Thomas Wolfe: A Collection of Critical Essays* (Englewood Cliffs, N.J.: Prentice-Hall, 1973);

Fritz Heinrich Ryssel, *Thomas Wolfe,* translated by Helen Serba (New York: Ungar, 1972);

William U. Snyder, *Thomas Wolfe: Ulysses and Narcissus* (Athens: Ohio University Press, 1971);

Richard Steele, *Thomas Wolfe: A Study in Psychoanalytic Literary Criticism* (Philadelphia: Dorrance, 1977);

Igina Tattoni, *The Unfinished Door: Innovative Trends in Thomas Wolfe's Fiction* (Rome: Bulzoni Editore, 1992);

Morton I. Teicher, ed., *Looking Homeward: A Thomas Wolfe Photo Album* (Columbia: University of Missouri Press, 1993);

Richard Walser, *Thomas Wolfe: An Introduction and Interpretation* (New York: Barnes & Noble, 1961);

Walser, *Thomas Wolfe, Undergraduate* (Durham, N.C.: Duke University Press, 1977);

Walser, ed., *The Enigma of Thomas Wolfe: Biographical and Critical Selections* (Cambridge, Mass.: Harvard University Press, 1953);

Floyd C. Watkins, *Thomas Wolfe's Characters: Portraits from Life* (Norman: University of Oklahoma Press, 1957);

Mabel Wolfe Wheaton and Legette Blythe, *Thomas Wolfe and His Family* (Garden City, N.Y.: Doubleday, 1961);

William B. Wisdom, *My Impressions of the Wolfe Family and Maxwell Perkins,* edited by Magi and David J. Wyatt (N.p.: The Thomas Wolfe Society, 1993);

Wisdom, *The Table Talk of Thomas Wolfe,* edited by John S. Phillipson (N.p.: The Thomas Wolfe Society, 1988).

Cumulative Index

Dictionary of Literary Biography, Volumes 1-229
Dictionary of Literary Biography Yearbook, 1980-1999
Dictionary of Literary Biography Documentary Series, Volumes 1-19

Cumulative Index

DLB before number: *Dictionary of Literary Biography,* Volumes 1-229
Y before number: *Dictionary of Literary Biography Yearbook,* 1980-1999
DS before number: *Dictionary of Literary Biography Documentary Series,* Volumes 1-19

A

B

D

E

F

E

H

I

J

K

L

M

O

P

Q

R

S

T

U

V

W

X

Y

Z

ISBN 0-7876-3138-8
90000
9 790787 631382